The Dynamics of

Interpersonal Behavior

# The Dynamics of Interpersonal Behavior

## Abraham Zaleznik

Professor of Organizational Behavior
Graduate School of Business Administration
Harvard University

## David Moment

Associate Professor of Organizational Behavior
Graduate School of Business Administration
Harvard University

John Wiley & Sons, Inc., New York · London · Sydney

Library of Congress Catalog Card Number: 64-23867
Printed in the United States of America

# Preface

Rᴇᴀᴅᴇʀꜱ of a new book often have more than a passing curiosity about its genesis and intellectual heritage. We should like to acknowledge and satisfy such curiosity in this brief preface.

*The Dynamics of Interpersonal Behavior,* along with the companion volume entitled *Casebook on Interpersonal Behavior in Organizations,* began when the senior author collaborated in 1957 with Professor F. J. Roethlisberger in a new course at the Harvard Business School. The course, offered as an elective, set out to help students of business administration learn more about the structure and dynamics of groups in work settings. By presenting relevant theory along with case studies and experimental problems we expected students to acquire substantial competence in the analysis of the human problems encountered in ordinary face-to-face situations in organizations.

Professor Roethlisberger turned his full-time attention to the training of doctoral students in organizational behavior so that upon the completion of the first semester of the course, the senior author took over its development. During the following seven years the course underwent considerable revision and experimentation yet maintained a consistent pursuit of its original aims. The junior author was involved in this further development of the course.

Our experience in research along with efforts of co-workers at other universities convinced us that the scientific study of human behavior provided the lead for the pursuit of competence. Until the beginning of our work, certainly at the Harvard Business School, great stress had been given to the values of learning from experience.

Elton Mayo in distinguishing *knowledge of acquaintance* from *knowledge about* suggested that intuitive understanding growing out of knowledge of acquaintance preceded systematic understanding. We found Mayo's distinction valid and exciting, but only up to a point. It soon became apparent that many advocates of *knowledge of acquaintance* as the guiding principle in the teaching of human relations had little interest in systematic inquiry. Where the search for explanatory theory has been lacking, the teaching of interpersonal and organizational behavior has tended to advocate old wisdoms to the neglect of new knowledge. We set out, therefore, to work on and develop explanatory theory as the foundation for the course in group and interpersonal relations.

The question we faced then was, "What theory"? Here an important change took place in our thinking. The senior author's research experience during the 1950's led him into rigorous testing of the frame of reference in sociology exemplified in the work of George Homans, and also in the functional schools in sociology and anthropology. We experienced the possibilities in these approaches, and their impact on our work can be appraised in referring to two publications: *Worker Satisfaction and Development*, by Abraham Zaleznik, and *The Motivation, Productivity, and Satisfaction of Workers: A Prediction Study*, by A. Zaleznik, C. R. Christensen, F. J. Roethlisberger, with the collaboration of George C. Homans.

The preceding works and their theoretical foundation placed the burden of explanation of interpersonal behavior in the technical, social, cultural, and organizational environments. This particular emphasis, common to much of current sociological theory, avoided the heart of the data we found so fascinating in field investigations of interpersonal behavior. It seemed to us that the exciting problem for study concerned the different ways in which individuals experience affectively and symbolically interpersonal relations at work. If the environments, or the external factors, cause individuals to act in patterned ways, they do so only in relation to the individual's capacity to experience these forces, to internalize them, and symbolize them within the continuities of the person's total development. The energy for interpersonal relations, as with all action, belongs to the individual. To extend the ideas a step further, evidence of a convincing nature led to the conclusion that the understanding of the environment and the manner in which it changed requires a firm grasp of the intrapsychic processes of the individual. The meaning of the technical, social, and organizational environments in which interpersonal relations unfold and the process of behavior itself can be viewed fruitfully as an extension of the individual's tendency to define symbolically the world in which he lives. The environment and its collective relations is itself a product of how man makes external that which he experiences internally.

In short, our mode of inquiry led to the works of students of George Herbert Mead and their concern with interaction and symbolization, but more importantly, to the work of Sigmund Freud and his psychoanalytic psychology. Freud's work pointed the way to-

ward relating the internal experience of the individual, both develop-
mentally and dynamically, with the interpersonal and collective phenomena of society and organizations.

The research outcomes of this changed direction of inquiry are
represented in several doctoral dissertations completed at the Harvard
Business School since 1961, and in related publications by the Division
of Research of the Business School. These efforts include the work
of the junior author, as well as Gene W. Dalton, Louis B. Barnes,
and Richard C. Hodgson.[1] In addition, two projects are currently
in process—those of J. B. Kassarjian and Gerald C. Leader—as parts
of a series of cumulative investigations into the individual's experiencing of work, people, and career choices. Our investigations have
brought us into close contact with psychologists, social psychologists,
and managers who share our concern with the process of individual
development.

To some readers of this book, it may appear that the work of
transition which we have just described has not yet been completed.
We would agree heartily with this observation. To others, it may
seem as though the book does not present many new ideas. We are
inclined to agree with this observation as well. We have not originated
theory in this book. Our job instead has been to bring together
lines of thought and inquiry, and to arrange these in a pattern consistent with our growing understanding of the problems of explanation.
This is not to say that all we have here is a collection of works of
other authors. We believe we have added something new in writing
this book, even though we have leaned heavily upon the contributions
of pioneers in the study of human behavior. Our hope is to absorb
readers into a kind of inquiry that cannot be inferred strictly from
common sense experience.

Although this book is an outgrowth of work in developing a course
of instruction at the Harvard Business School, we hope it will prove
valuable for students of the social sciences as well as men of affairs.

[1] See Moment, D., and Zaleznik, A., *Role Development and Interpersonal Competence*, Boston, Division of Research, Harvard Business School, 1963. Unpublished works include Dalton, G. W., *Identity and Career Development Among
Engineers*, 1962, and Hodgson, R. C., *Role Relations in an Executive Group*,
1963, both unpublished doctoral dissertations submitted at the Harvard Business
School. Three manuscripts in process reflecting this new direction of inquiry
are: A. Zaleznik, G. W. Dalton, and L. B. Barnes, *Orientation and Conflict in
Career*, R. C. Hodgson, D. J. Levinson, and A. Zaleznik, *The Executive Role
Constellation: An Analysis of Personality and Role Relations in Management*,
G. W. Dalton, L. B. Barnes, and A. Zaleznik, *Organizational Change and the Struc-
ture of Authority Relations: An Experimental Study*.

We take a great deal of pleasure in acknowledging the help we have received.

To Professor F. J. Roethlisberger for the early collaboration in this work.

To the various administrative officers of the Harvard Business School, George P. Baker, Stanley F. Teele, George F. F. Lombard, Russell H. Hassler, and Bertrand Fox, whose implicit support encouraged this project.

To the various participants in our research, including Professors L. B. Barnes, Gene Dalton, and Richard Hodgson, who labored within and contributed to the evolution of this book.

To Marjorie Van Leuvan, Susannah Nickels, Arlene Walter, and Jane MacDougall, who helped in the preparation of the manuscript.

To Mrs. Ruth Hetherston who helped with the final revisions including bibliographic work.

To Mr. Dalmar Fisher, who prepared the indexes, and who conceived the idea of a separate index of research sources.

Finally, to Ann Allen who supervised the final work on the manuscript.

*June 1964*                                                ABRAHAM ZALEZNIK
                                                          DAVID MOMENT

# Contents

*Part One*

*Group and
Interpersonal Processes*

*Chapter One*

# Group and Interpersonal Behavior
# in Organizations: Perspectives

THE small work group in organizations is probably the smallest of any formal social unit. Despite its size, however, it is vital to the effectiveness of the total society. There are probably few organizational problems in which its structure and dynamics can be safely excluded from consideration.

In dealing with the small work group, two concerns arise. First, the development of those skills in social analysis necessary for working with data on human behavior requires knowledge of theory, appropriate analytical methods, and ample material for practice. In this book we shall explore all three ingredients.

The second concern is more intellectual in character. We shall try to incorporate in this study the research findings and theories that hold promise for both theoretical and practical understanding of group behavior. We shall examine, for example, studies that try to show what forces determine the formation of groups in organizations; how individual and group interact and their attitudes change; and how problems of group productivity and change emerge as well as individual development and satisfaction in groups.

The study of human behavior in organizations, particularly in applied schools such as schools of business administration, is frequently criticized for its lack of intellectual perspective and depth. There seems instead to be an emphasis on the practical, a concentration on action questions. We agree with the main burden of this criticism. All men, we believe, men of affairs as well as of books, require an intellectual perspective on what they are doing. To help correct this error often encountered in applied schools, we shall review the studies that have contributed to our present understanding of small group behavior.

## WHY STUDY SMALL GROUP BEHAVIOR?

The study of small group behavior spotlights the most persistent and probably the oldest form of social organization known to man. As George Homans points out in his book *The Human Group*, society has shown its capacity to cohere at the level of the small group.[1] Civilizations, governments, and institutions come and go but the small group has remained as the persistent form of social organization. Its survival affirms that small groups satisfy important human needs which no other form of organization can supply.

Although the small group lies at the foundation of society and persists despite the rise and fall of institutions in the large social structure, it is also true that the effectiveness of large-scale organizations depends, in large measure, on the development of effective small groups. Not only must groups build their own cohesion and continually resolve their internal problems, they also must maintain a positive identification with other groups and with the larger organization. The fact that small groups satisfy important human needs assures their survival as a form of organization. But this does not assure the development of effective groups and consequently effective organizations in the larger institutions of society. It is on this point that administrators or applied social scientists face an important challenge.

Any formal organization creates, with some degree of consciousness, many small groups. The system of interlocking and overlapping group structures is the very essence of organizations such as business. Each group has a function in the effectiveness of the whole. Viewing organizations as a system of group relationships immediately poses questions of major import for continuity and effectiveness. What are the conditions beyond spontaneous tendencies for the development of group cohesion? By what processes are members selected for inclusion or exclusion from the group? How do groups influence the attitudes and actions of members? How do groups maintain relationships with "outside" groups? Why do groups at times develop internal cohesion but at the cost of antagonistic relationships with other groups and the organization as a whole?

The preceding questions suggest the practical concern for the functioning of small groups in larger organizations. Implied in these

[1] George C. Homans, *The Human Group*, p. 468.

questions is the possibility of a significant area for the development of professional competence by administrators as applied social scientists interested in organizational behavior.    Just as we cannot depend on spontaneous processes for the development of effective groups, so are we unable to depend on the usual learning from experience in society for the development of competence in group membership and leadership.    Later in this chapter, we shall examine briefly what are the constituents of competence in group relations.    For the present, let us continue our exploration of the importance of the small group by considering various points of interest in group behavior.

Riecken and Homans present a classification of interests in small group behavior which, for our purposes, provides a useful way of examining further the theoretical and practical motives for the study of group behavior.[2]    This classification consists of four sources of interest.    First, the small group is not only an instrument for performing useful work but it also provides, especially for students of organization, a most fruitful setting to gain understanding of problems in productivity.    Second, the small group can be studied as though it were a small-scale replica of organizations.    As a miniature social system, it can provide many insights into the workings of massive organizations.    Third, the small group is a center of influence.    Membership in a group has an effect on the attitudes and behavior of a person; it can influence his modes of thinking, feeling, and acting.    Fourth, the small group is a strategic center for understanding personality dynamics and interpersonal relationships.    This line of interest centers on the individual, his motives, defenses, and style of relating to others.

The succeeding paragraphs explore each of these lines of interest. They indicate the many-sided values to be gained from the study of group behavior.

## The Small Group as An Instrument for Performing Useful Work

Although some small groups, such as the pure friendship groups, exist solely for their internal gratifications, most groups have a wider purpose as well.    In factories and offices, group purpose consists of a yield of output that is frequently measurable and only

[2] Henry W. Riecken and George C. Homans, "Psychological Aspects of Social Structure," in *Handbook of Social Psychology*, G. E. Lindzey, Ed., Vol. 2, pp. 786–787.

part of the total purpose of the enterprise. In staff groups in organizations, the purpose may be as general as policy formulation or problem solving and not susceptible to precise measurement. But the purpose exists and governs much of the surface activity of the group.

An important characteristic of group purpose and of the tasks groups are supposed to perform is the requirement of some degree of co-ordination or collaboration by members. The intensity of this collaboration varies greatly. In work groups where men and women are brought together to do identical work and where there is no division of labor the collaboration requirements are minimal; they consist of maintaining a structure which permits each member to perform optimally. On the other hand, other groups have a purpose that demands the utmost in conscious collaborative effort and co-ordination of individual activities. Problem-solving groups fit this second type.

Group tasks or purpose besides requiring some degree of collaboration are not synonymous with individual goals. Group purpose is one means for an individual to attain the goals important to him. He collaborates in a group to gratify needs through performances on tasks in relationship with other persons. Presumably, the reason groups persist is because their purposes cannot readily be accomplished by individuals acting singly.

While stressing that groups have a purpose and are instruments for performing socially useful work, we should not obscure the fact that groups also proliferate purposes beyond those required. Sometimes the means in groups become ends as well. In considering problems of work in groups, therefore, we shall have to be alert to the way new purposes arise and alter the original ones.

### The Small Group as a Small-Scale Social System

One attractive feature of small group analysis is the convenience and accessibility of data. Insofar as all social systems have elements in common, the small group provides a convenient setting for understanding the processes of large-scale social systems where data are less readily available.

What do small groups and large-scale organizations have in common as social systems that makes possible the transfer of knowledge from one to the next? As we have indicated, groups typically have a common *purpose* to their members and yet it is one that transcends the goals of any individual. Groups evolve some sort of *structure* that differentiates the positions and roles of members. They evolve *rituals* and *symbols* which identify the group and demand the member's loyalty. Furthermore, groups take care of *rewarding and punishing* members; through member motivation they provide for continued participation and control within the group.

All these attributes of small groups also can be identified as attributes of the larger units in society. For example, take a business organization as a whole. It has a *purpose* that in no sense can be thought of as the goals or objectives of a single individual. Its purpose is attached to the organization as a system. A business organization also has *structure*. Its formal organization chart, for instance, attempts to represent the division of labor necessary as well as the different positions various jobs occupy in this structure. The lines of authority are another means of differentiating positions in the organizational structure and also are an attempt to represent the prevailing system of communication. The organization as a whole also tends to develop an informal structure just as small groups do.

A business organization can be analyzed in terms of the *rituals* and *symbols* that create its imagery to its members and to outsiders. It does not take an astute observer too long to identify the essential character of an organization when he pays attention to the physical surroundings, dress, mode of interacting, and atmosphere. An organization that is tightly controlled by higher levels of authority reflects this fact in the scrutiny and suspicion directed toward an outsider by the receptionist, or by the barriers toward entry reflected in the physical arrangements of buildings, offices, and furniture.

Finally, the larger business organization, as well as the small group, has in operation a system of reward and punishment that tends to control the behavior of its members. Starting with the pay a person receives for work in an organization and moving through the prestige, respect, and interest he receives from others, the member of an organization is continually involved in the processes of gratification and deprivation.

These elements that small groups have in common with all larger-scale organizations in society suggest a possible transfer of learning from the smaller to the larger social system. But this possibility should not be overdrawn. Although social systems have elements and processes in common, size alone and the difficulties in communication resulting from size introduce new elements of complexity. We do not suggest, therefore, that the study of small groups alone will tell us all we need to know about organizations. Such study will provide significant parallels and also will indicate where the transfer of knowledge is inadequate.

## The Small Group as the Center of the Influence Process

Any social system, whether a society as a whole or subdivisions within it like business organizations, the military, or churches, manages to assume a measure of continuity between past and present. Members enter and depart and make their impact upon the system, yet its over-all characteristics remain remarkably stable. Relationships between old and new members, superior and subordinate, the more responsible and the dependent are bound within traditions governing the behavior of persons in these rigorous relationships. Anthropologists document how expectancies differ from one culture to the next but they also record the means whereby continuity in customs, beliefs, and expectations remain stable within any culture during the course of time.[3] This process of transmitting the culture is referred to as the socialization process.

Socialization, or the preparation provided the young for their new and mature roles in society, begins in the family, the prototype of all small groups. The newborn enters his society in a state of complete dependency for the satisfaction of basic needs. Gradually, society imposes its controls on the individual through actions of the parents. The age at which toilet training and other rules of hygiene begins and the degree of severity with which this training is imposed are governed in large measure by the traditions of the culture. Later, as the infant matures, the routine in the family centers less on his dependency needs and the child is expected to broaden his relationships to playmates and then to teachers and peers in the classroom. The classroom represents an introduction to authority outside the family. Here again the small group, in the school setting, with its own system of rewards and punishments supported by parents, exerts its influence on the child. The motivation to achieve by adult standards tends to intensify as experiences within and outside the home broaden.

Even though the impact of society on its new members is exerted initially and most strongly through the family as a small group, the process of socialization continues throughout his lifetime in the various small groups of which he is a member. Sociologists at times

[3] Clyde Kluckhohn, *Mirror for Man*. Ruth Benedict, *Patterns of Culture*. Margaret Mead, *Coming of Age in Samoa*. Margaret Mead, *Male and Female*.

bemoan the fact that other social scientists are forever rediscovering the small group as a source of influence on the individual.[4] This so-called rediscovery represents, in the opinion of the writers, not lapses of knowledge or memory but fresh empirical evidence on how the person is continually influenced through his memberships. The range of illustrative material we shall present in subsequent chapters will demonstrate the variety of group settings in which the influence process is significant. But it would be appropriate at this point to cite a few results of empirical studies which show where and how the group affects the thoughts and feelings of the individual well beyond his formative years.

In groups of modern factory workers, for example, beliefs about authority often take expression in the form of codes which implicitly require individuals to produce at a given level.[5] This code, called restriction of output, has been reported so frequently that it can no longer be viewed as an unusual event in the industrial scene. Although it is now a cultural phenomenon, restriction of output as a practice is transmitted and reinforced in the small group at work. Through the method of reward and punishment, not different conceptually from reward and punishment in the family, new members are made sharply aware of the group's expectations. We shall have more to say about restriction of output in later chapters.

In the study of how people vote and why they vote as they do in political elections, investigators report on the strong influence of group memberships, especially as this influence is exerted by opinion leaders.[6] The particular act of voting represents a set of attitudes and beliefs about political parties, candidates, and issues that are transmitted and given impetus in groups relevant to the individual. The study of influence as a process in the formation of public opinion clearly requires analysis of group memberships and how they affect the individual.

Similarly, the bearing of group membership on the influence process is to be found in the decisions of consumers on what and when they buy.[7] The act of buying also represents an integration of thought and sentiment ranging from expectations of future economic well-being to acceptance of buying decisions by family and

[4] Robert K. Merton, *Social Theory and Social Structure*, p. 67.
[5] F. J. Roethlisberger and W. J. Dickson, *Management and the Worker*, pp. 378–384.
[6] Elihu Katz and Paul Lazarsfeld, *Personal Influence*.
[7] Robert A. Dahl, Mason Hare, and Paul F. Lazarsfeld, *Social Science Research on Business: Product and Potential*, pp. 108–110.

friends. So-called product images are communicated within groups and probably such communication is the backbone of successful advertising campaigns.

In the field of social action, the place of the small group as an influence on the individual is well established. Kurt Lewin, probably as much as any other social scientist, established the idea that change and movement toward desired social ends required the impetus of group acceptance and support.[8] The individual alone, without the support of his group, generally would be less inclined to move toward change. In a study of minority relationships, Lewin pointed out how strong support from a minority in-group made feasible the maintenance of attitudes and beliefs out of line with the majority. Without a strong group, minorities would be rapidly assimilated into the larger culture. The fact that diverse subcultures exist in the United States attests to the strength of group memberships as well as to the tolerance for variation within our culture.

As another piece of current evidence on the importance of the small group as a continuing source of influence, we can mention the problem of juvenile delinquency. Newspaper articles and commentary in reporting on acts of juvenile crime and disturbance give wide coverage to the juvenile "gang." Seldom are acts of lawlessness committed by the youngster alone. He acts under the influence of the gang whose culture expresses the alienation of the urban adolescent from his society. The gang develops a lore, with identification in its name, mode of dress, hangout, and particular kinds of activity. Authorities recognize the fact that the gang, as an outgrowth of alienation, motivates the individual member to perform delinquent acts. In an attempt to channel energy in these groups into more socially productive ends police and social agencies assign special workers to the gangs. These workers seek to gain group acceptance, following which they in turn attempt to influence the group goals and modes of behavior.[9]

Finally, we can turn to the field of mental health. In Caudill's study of a mental hospital[10] he shows how the emotional qualities of group relationships at the staff level affect the individual in his dealings with patients which in turn affects the course of the patient's therapy and recovery. The concept of the therapeutic community in the

[8] Kurt Lewin, "Studies in Group Decision," in *Group Dynamics: Research and Theory*, D. Cartwright and A. Zander, Eds., pp. 287–301.

[9] Gertrude Samuels, "Rescue for the Wayward Girls," *The New York Times Magazine*, July 23, 1961, pp. 14+.

[10] William A. Caudill, *The Psychiatric Hospital as a Small Society*.

mental hospital seeks to develop qualities in group relationship which can speed the recovery of patients.[11]

In reporting briefly on the various fields in which the group as the source of influence on the individual has become a strategic factor, we have ranged from organizations to juvenile gangs. In subsequent chapters of this book we shall examine intensively how the influence process develops within the small group experiences of one person. For our purposes now, it is sufficient to have established the idea that socialization and influence are not restricted to childhood or the formative years alone, but remain a part of individual and group experience as long as persons seek to become members of groups. The work group as a source of influence on the individual is among the more important of these collective experiences since the stakes are high for the individual in his workaday world.

## *The Small Group as the Setting for Understanding the Dynamics of Personality and Interpersonal Relationships*

If we had an opportunity to observe an individual as he moved from one small group to another in his life experience, we should probably be able to see uniformities in his behavior in relation to others. We might, for example, note that Person A is very passive in his behavior. He talks little in the group, seldom initiates discussion, and generally waits to be invited before he speaks or acts. We might observe this pattern of behavior in all his group relationships, but with some interesting variations. We might note that his passivity increases when there are authority figures around and that his passivity decreases when the group is made up of members who resemble him in such characteristics as age and occupation.

If we turned our attention to another hypothetical person and watched his behavior in his various groups, we might observe a completely different pattern as compared with our first example. Person B appears to be very aggressive in his group relationships. Not only does he talk a lot, but he initiates conversation frequently and tends to interrupt others to say what is on his mind. He appears to be competitive, especially in relations with persons similar in age and position. On the other hand, he becomes less aggressive when authority figures are present. He talks less, tends to address his remarks to the persons in authority positions, and seems to seek their approval.

[11] Maxwell Jones et al., *The Therapeutic Community: A New Treatment Method in Psychiatry.*

The terms with which we described the two hypothetical individuals are associated with dynamic aspects of personality and interpersonal relationship. The term personality refers to the inner organization of the person;[12] the term interpersonal relationships refers to the outward expression of this inner organization in the individual's relationships with other persons.

Obviously, the group is an interpersonal setting in which the dynamics of personality are manifested through behavior. Any behavior in a group, whether it ranges from withdrawal and passivity to aggression and domination, carries meaning in relation to the inner state of the person.

Earlier, we stated that the family group frequently was considered the prototype of all groups. This generalization has special relevance when we consider the group as the interaction of personalities. In work groups, for example, the formal leader easily becomes the father figure to group members. This perception may evoke the sentiments of love and fear characteristic of the early father-son relationship. The peers in the group easily become the siblings with whom the person can create alliances or engage in rivalries and competitive behavior. Certain individuals have a tendency to create the imagery of a mother figure. They assume nurturant and protective roles in groups, develop favorites, seek adulation, and acquire other behavioral characteristics sometimes associated with the mother role in our culture.

These comparisons between past family groups and present work groups may appear farfetched because they represent interpretations of latent meaning from observable data. Needless to say, the actors in a group who re-enact early life problems in present situations are not aware of this meaning. We should say also that persons who had experienced gratifying relationships in the past tend less to act on distortions of perception that confuse the past and the present. But no matter how free they are from neurotic conflicts, all persons will represent the past in their present groups to some degree.

The individual's style of behavior and characteristic defenses are expressions of personality development in which past experience is an important influence. The "intellectualizer," for example, frequently develops this mode of behavior to avoid closeness with other people and to keep removed from the expression of feelings. The completely "open" person who is all too ready to express feelings often seeks protection and support from others to avoid competitiveness and to foster dependency. The "businesslike" or task-oriented person may

[12] David C. McClelland, *Personality*, pp. 69–70.

seek to express independence and aggressiveness in group relationships possibly to avoid revealing to himself and to others the opposite tendencies in his personality.

The richness of the group setting in evoking the dynamic aspects of personality and interpersonal relationship has resulted in the use of the group as a training-learning instrument. There is increasing interest, for example, in group psychotherapy. Several patients and a therapist work together to express blocked feelings and to interpret their meaning with therapeutic results for the individual.[13]

Application of training group methods (T group) for helping individuals learn more about themselves and to gain interpersonal competence has gained considerable interest in schools and universities, as well as in management development programs held within and outside companies.[14] We shall discuss training group theory more fully in a later chapter on change. The point requiring emphasis here is that the capacity of a group to evoke behavioral dynamics makes it a significant setting for learning.

We have presented in this section a review of the main lines of interest in the study of small group behavior. First, the group is an important instrument for the accomplishment of work. Practitioners and students of organization who are especially concerned with performance and productivity will find important material in the study of group behavior. Second, the small group can be thought of as a miniature social system. The study of the small group should make possible a deeper understanding of large-scale social systems such as business organizations. Third, the small group is at the center of the influence process. Anyone interested in the formation of attitudes and decisions by the individual needs to understand the effects of group membership. Fourth, the small group is a setting for learning more about the dynamics of personality and interpersonal relationships. In this sense, the study of small group behavior, especially in those groups where one is an involved member, provides an opportunity for developing self-awareness and interpersonal competence.

In these four major points of departure there is implied a fifth: the small group as a setting for understanding and effecting change. Change can occur at several levels simultaneously. The small group can be viewed as the setting in which change in individual personality occurs. The small group itself in its structure and dynamics can be

---

[13] W. R. Bion, "Experiences in Groups: I–VI," *Human Relations*, Vol. I, Nos. 3 and 4, Vol. II, Nos. 1 and 4, Vol. III, Nos. 1 and 4. S. H. Foulkes and E. J. Anthony, *Group Psychotherapy: The Psychoanalytical Approach.*

[14] Leland P. Bradford et al., *Explorations in Human Relations Training.*

the focal point for change.   Change in larger institutional settings can occur also through intervention at the level of the small group.   For administrators, as well as social scientists interested in applied problems, intervention to achieve change is a significant aspect of their professional competence.   The study of group behavior can contribute much toward developing competence in leadership and change.

## CLASSIFICATIONS AND DEFINITIONS OF GROUPS

So far we have said little about various definitions of the term "group."   Organizations and society consist of many kinds of groups. We intend to concentrate on the small work group but need a workable definition of the group we shall study and how it compares with other types of associations.   Toward this end we need to clarify the distinctions between *primary* and *secondary* groups, and *autonomous* and *formal* groups.

### Primary and Secondary Groups[15]

Group associations can be distinguished as primary or secondary depending on their size, degree of face-to-face interaction in the group, and above all on the type of influence the group has on the individual. Primary groups are typically small enough to permit frequent interaction among members.   This term is reserved for those associations where there is considerable intimacy among group members and where the individual is influenced markedly as a result of his participation. The classic primary groups Cooley used as illustrations were family groups, play groups, and neighborhood groups.   All of us have experienced and continue to experience life in this type of intimate association.   As we have observed, the primary groups are the centers of socialization and influence on the individual and strongly affect his personality development.

Secondary groups are typically large-scale associations.   They do not necessarily provide settings for face-to-face interactions.   Their influence on the individual is based largely on the effects of identifications with values and beliefs common to members of the group. The term used frequently to designate them is *reference group*.[16] Obviously the term refers to the individual's identifications rather than actual interactions.

[15] The Terms *primary* and *secondary* groups were proposed by C. H. Cooley in *Social Organization*, pp. 23–31.

[16] Robert K. Merton, *op. cit., pp.* 225–386.

Individuals "belong" to many secondary or reference groups. Let us take a hypothetical individual who has the job of comptroller of a large company. Among his many reference groups, we can include his occupational associations; he is probably a member of the National Association of Cost Accountants. His company is also a reference group for him as may be the community in which he lives. If he is of an ethnic-religious group that maintains distinctive characteristics, then this ethnic association is also a reference group for him.

These illustrations emphasize the identifications the person has with large-scale aggregations that may in some cases never involve him in face-to-face interactions. They do, however, affect his thinking and feeling in the development of values, beliefs, and ideals.

## Autonomous and Formal Groups

Another way to distinguish types of groups is by discovering the purpose of the group and how it came to be formed. The term autonomous groups refers to those spontaneous associations that form without a predesignated purpose. Whyte's Norton Gang described in *Street Corner Society*[17] is a good example of an autonomous group. The boys came together in Cornerville through the formation of friendships. They had no conscious purpose. The main purpose, of course, was to maintain the group and provide for member satisfactions. Besides corner gangs and play groups, friendship groups in communities are good examples of autonomous groups.

Formal groups are found largely in organizations. They have a purpose which initially at least derives from their position and function in the organization. Members are selected and come together in relation to this purpose. Socio-emotional bonds do develop, of course, but these emerge from the group's work purposes. Joining the group does not at first depend on affective ties.

The small work groups in organizations are all formal. They are small enough to allow face-to-face interactions among all members. They are clearly not autonomous nor are they secondary. We cannot, however, designate formal work groups in organizations as primary in that the extent of group cohesion and influence on member behavior is a matter for empirical investigation.

Many students of group behavior unwittingly use the term "group" to refer to cohesive associations having all the characteristics of the primary group. For the purposes of this study, the small work group will be defined as a small unit of a larger organization, with a formal

[17] William Foote Whyte, *Street Corner Society*, pp. 3–51.

designation and a purpose. The group in our terms could be the "department" or "section" of an organization. Typically the work group has a formal leader who occupies a position in the formal hierarchy and whose designation comes from outside the group. The members of the group similarly are assigned from outside the group. Their selection is based on organizational and purposive criteria. Social-psychological criteria for group membership typically have little or no part in this selection.

Much of our analytical problem hinges around the relationship between the formal group structure and the actual patterns of behavior which emerge. Logically, as well as empirically, there is no necessary set of conditions in formal organizations making for group cohesion beyond the minimal level required to assure the group purpose. We shall be seeking throughout this study for the interrelationship between formal structure and actual group behavior. We shall endeavor to understand what processes result in cohesion or disintegration, or complex or minimal group development.

For our purposes, then, the small group has a formal designation in a larger organization. It has a purpose; and both the formal leader and members have been externally designated. Its degree of development as a social unit, sometimes referred to as group solidarity or group cohesion, is at once a group problem and a matter for observation and analysis. How group development affects and in turn is conditioned by the group's productivity and the members' satisfaction are also problems for analysis. This definition of group grows out of the nature of organizations and the particular problems we wish to study.

## THEORIES AND CASE STUDIES IN THE ANALYSIS
## OF GROUP BEHAVIOR

To this point, we have examined the various rationales for the study of group behavior, the types of groups in society, and the definition of the small work group for our purposes. This section introduces the materials we shall be using in this study. These materials are of two kinds: theory and case studies. It is important to understand the different kinds of theories and case studies in use and the types we shall encounter in this book and the companion volume, *Casebook on Interpersonal Behavior in Organizations*.

### Theories

The term theory has a wide number of uses which are all important but need clarification. Generally speaking, theories are the utilization of concepts that attempt to explain the order and relationships among concrete phenomena. All human beings have theories in the sense that they use ideas about the world to explain what they observe. These ideas grow out of experience. A person as a result of past experience expects certain things to happen on which he bases his behavior. He acts, observes, and notes in what respects his expectations were fulfilled and how they were violated. He reviews this experience and makes modifications in his ideas which become the basis for somewhat different expectations and behavior in new situations.

But the fact that we all use ideas in everyday living and can be said in this sense to have theories should not lead us to confuse this type of theory with the concept of theory as used in science. Theory development in science is a conscious activity. It has reasonably systematic methods for building and renovating the structure of ideas labeled as theory. In everyday life, the ideas in the minds of men vary in the degree to which each individual is conscious of them and how they govern his behavior.

In the development of any professional field such as medicine, there is a gradual movement in the direction of replacing the ideas derived from common sense experience with those derived from the conscious activity of those using scientific methods.[18] This trend is now under way in the slowly developing profession of executive administration or management. Through the process of research we shall gradually come to know more about organizations and behavior in organizational activities. We shall rely to a lesser degree on pure intuition and common sense to govern the professional development of administrators.

In the realm of science, there can be four different but interrelated levels of theory. First, there are conceptual schema; second, systems of classification; third, hypothetical-propositional statements of relationship; fourth, interpretive theories of explanation.[19]

A *conceptual scheme* represents a consciously contrived means for constructing the way an investigator will look at the phenomena he wishes to study or act upon. In the study of personality, for example, there are two main competing conceptual schema. One school of thought views personality from a phenomenological point of view;

[18] A. Zaleznik, "Science vs. 'Common Sense' in Human Relations," *Harvard Business School Bulletin*, December 1960, pp. 22–26.
[19] For an illuminating discussion of theory development as a methodological process see: Paul F. Lazarsfeld, "Problems in Methodology" in *Sociology Today*, Robert K. Merton, Leonard Broom and Leonard Cottrell, Jr., Eds., pp. 39–78; and L. J. Henderson, *Introductory Lectures* (unpublished) to his course, "Concrete Sociology," at Harvard University.

another school of thought views the human personality from a deterministic and structural-dynamic point of view.[20]    A phenomenological conceptual scheme regards the person as a total organism whose striving is toward growth and the integration of the Self. The experience of the person from this frame of reference is from the inside looking out. The real world to the person is framed by the concept of Self and the need to maintain consistency in the Self image.

A competing conceptual scheme developed by Freud and continued by his followers in the psychoanalytic movement regards the human personality as consisting of three structural areas: the id, ego, and superego. This conceptual scheme is rooted in the understanding of biological drives or instincts and in genetic development. The taming of the biological drives and the constraints of human relationships and society take place in the family. Personality development which consists of dynamic organization of the three structural parts is determined in large measure therefore in the early, formative years.

Examination of these two conceptual schema, although brief and oversimplified, helps to clarify the nature of a conceptual scheme, what it is, and what it emphatically is not. A conceptual scheme at the outset is not reality. Neither of the two ways of looking at personality is synonymous with the way persons *are* in reality. A conceptual scheme is a man-made way of thinking about reality. What reality is *really* is something known only to God; all mortals do is create ideas about reality. Another characteristic of a conceptual scheme is that it is neither true nor false.[21]    Whether man is a product of history and biology or the striving for self-integration and growth cannot be proven true or false simply because there are no direct tests of these concepts. The purpose of a conceptual scheme is to provide the initial structure for exploration. The test of a conceptual scheme, in Henderson's words, is its utility, whether it permits an investigator to do things which will later be testable for truth or falsity.

Conceptual schema are at once man's most creative product and his greatest mental hazard. Conceptual schema can be proliferated and elaborated almost without moving into the examination of phenomena in the real world. Without a conceptual scheme, there is little fruitful exploration of phenomena.[22]    But the presence of a conceptual scheme does not by itself assure the succeeding steps required in building a body of knowledge.

[20] Calvin S. Hall and Gardner Lindzey, *Theories of Personality*.
[21] L. J. Henderson, *op. cit.*
[22] James B. Conant, *On Understanding Science*, p. 37.

In our field of group and interpersonal behavior in organizations, there are also somewhat competing conceptual schema. We have the choice, for example, of viewing small groups in organizations as input-output systems for accomplishing a consciously designated purpose, as fields of forces with direction and magnitude, or as a social system in which group purpose, group development, and human motivation are interrelated in various processes.

It would be useful at this point to describe briefly the conceptual scheme we shall use in this book. At the most general level, we adopt the position that views a group as a social system. The social system can be analyzed at three somewhat different, but interrelated levels of analysis: (1) the processes in group development, (2) the dynamics of interpersonal relations, and (3) the organization as a system of constraints.

In studying group behavior from the standpoint of *processes in group development*, we shall examine in turn the various problems or crises groups face in the interactions of members over time. These crises occur within the complexity of everyday interaction and can be separated out only as convenience in analysis. The crises we shall consider are four: (1) Establishing the *identity of the group* in the minds of members as a basis for consensus in the perceptions of individuals; issues on consensus arise around the task of the group, its way of working, and the symbols for ready communication, among other developmental issues in group behavior. (2) Developing a *group structure* relevant to the purposes of the group and the bases for member participation. (3) Establishing and maintaining a system of norms for *the social control* of member behavior. (4) Managing *affect and work* in the problem solving or other means of achieving group purpose.

In analyzing *the dynamics of interpersonal relations* in groups, our unit of analysis shifts from the group to the individual. The particular emphasis is on *developmental issues* for the individual as he establishes relationships with others. We shall concern ourselves with the individual's *crises in identity* as he seeks to establish himself within a group. The problem of "who am I" is a recurrent issue for the individual who at once attempts to maintain his uniqueness while identifying with and relating to the group as a whole and as individual members. Relevant here as well is the issue of *character and personality* as evidenced in styles of interpersonal behavior.

A further issue in interpersonal dynamics is that of *role development*. Individuals tend to adopt a fairly limited number of roles as their repertoire in interpersonal relationships. Any individual's repertoire can be examined from three points of view: (1) the external situations that evoke one or another of his role sets; (2) the "here and now" predispositions related to role performance; and (3) the genetic or developmental patterns constituting his history which result in his "here and now" capacities and limitations in role performance in a group. Perhaps the most significant of all aspects of role performance is the particular way in which role taking relates to psychological defense mechanisms. The view here is that a role repertoire exists within the individual's structure of defenses. To know what roles a person takes easily and the role he tends to evoke in others is a path toward understanding his characteristic ways of dealing with anxiety.

A final issue in interpersonal relationships is the *dynamics of the various person-object structures* recurrent in group settings. Several simple structures appear frequently for all individuals: (1) the superior-subordinate structure where person is superior and object is subordinate; (2) the reverse structure where person is subordinate and object is superior; and (3) the peer structure where both person and object have equal status. Dynamically, these structures can be examined as, and frequently become for individuals, settings for "acting out" historically relevant patterns. In this sense, the superior-subordinate relationship in the group becomes a setting where the previous father-son relationships are recreated. Or, the peer relationship acts as a stimulus for invoking in the "here and now" the experienced sibling relationships of the past. The various latent person-object relationships result in a constellation of roles in a group which can be analyzed dynamically in the terms of the family as a model.

The third level of analysis in the conceptual scheme of this book takes *the group in the organizational setting* as its unit of study. The wider organization is viewed essentially as establishing the constraints that limit or channel the development of groups and the quality of interpersonal relationships. The constraints, or to use Homan's term, the "givens,"[23] acting as determinants of group behavior, stem from the formal organization, the system of technology, and the composition of the group.

So far we have discussed the characteristics of a conceptual scheme as a type of theory and have described briefly the main elements of the conceptual scheme of the book. A second type of theory different from a conceptual scheme is a *system of classification*. Classification or taxonomy is essentially a descriptive process which sets out to differentiate phenomena according to properties or groups of properties. The classification is an important tool in the hands of naturalists

[23] George C. Homans, *Social Behavior*, pp. 205–231.

and clinicians. It is important also in the social sciences insofar as a system of classification provides a point of departure for more interpretive and analytical work. The sheer description of types of groups, for example, or forms of juvenile delinquency, or types of mental illness carry us only a part of the way toward understanding. The significant step is to specify the causes underlying the "types" established in a classification scheme. In the theory presented in this book we shall have occasion to present classifications of behavior. For example, we shall present and utilize the Bales system for classifying behavioral acts in groups.[24] Or, as another example, we shall utilize classification of roles into the two types known as *task* and *maintenance* roles.[25] But nowhere in this book shall we pretend to develop a grand system of classification. Instead, we shall utilize *ad hoc* classifications where these help simplify the data under investigation.

*Hypothetical or propositional statements of relationship* provide the simplest form of explanation, one of the important utilities in theory. A proposition consists of a statement asserting how two or more variables are related. Here is an illustration, taken from studies of satisfaction, of a proposition that has substantial support in empirical findings: Satisfaction of individuals varies directly with environmental rewards and inversely with desires or needs. Restating this proposition we would find that a person who has a strong need for group acceptance would be less satisfied than a person who has less strong needs for group acceptance when the actual degree of acceptance for both individuals is equal. A proposition such as the one just cited permits the ordering of complex data and also has *predictive utility*. In addition, it provides an example of *economy;* the same proposition could explain and predict diverse types of satisfactions. Unfortunately the field of group behavior has relatively few propositions of the kind just described. But the few that exist will be utilized whenever possible in this book, especially as they relate to research findings.

A fourth level of theory to be employed in this book consists of the more general *interpretive theories of explanation* of behavior. Unlike the propositional statements that explain behavior by showing how two or more variables are associated, the interpretive theoretical statements are at once more general and, presumably, capable of leading into specific propositions. An illustration of an interpretive theory to be presented in this book is the theory of social certitude. This theory attempts to explain why conditions of ambiguity in social

[24] Robert F. Bales, *Interaction Process Analyis.*
[25] Kenneth D. Benne and Paul Sheats, "Functional Roles of Group Members," *Journal of Social Issues,* Vol. IV, No. 2, Spring 1948, pp. 41–49.

perceptions or conflicting social perceptions result in anxiety. It attempts also to interpret the behavior associated with the ambiguous situation as an attempt to eliminate the ambiguity and to reduce the attendant anxiety. Specific hypotheses and propositions in the form of statements showing the association among variables can be derived from the interpretive model.[26] Throughout this book several such interpretive theories will be presented to explain phenomena encountered in group behavior. Here again, we shall not rely on one interpretive model, but shall use several in the course of the analysis.

*Case Studies*

Case studies as instruments for investigation have a rich tradition in several disciplines, with law, medicine, psychology, sociology, and business being among the most significant. The case studies to be utilized in *Casebook on Interpersonal Behavior in Organizations* generally will present fairly extensive descriptions and interpretations of group behavior in some natural setting such as factory and office. The studies are not intended to be "projective" instruments on which students will be encouraged to displace their attitudes and concerns. As instruments for learning and investigation, the studies presented will require a mature approach in which the central interest is to learn through the unique collaboration of theory and concrete data. Needless to say, the theory presented in this book is intended to illuminate the concrete data. Hopefully the analysis of the data will suggest fruitful modifications and elaborations of the theory.

The case studies generally are taken from field situations and are diverse in the types of groups studied. The range is from executive to blue collar groups and presents an interesting cross section of work groups found in modern-day organizations. Most of the case studies appear in print for the first time. All of them were collected by field workers who had a professional interest in the study of human behavior.

## SUMMARY

The purpose of this introductory chapter has been to outline the several rationales supporting the study of small group behavior in organizations. The particular lines of analysis implied in the rationales illustrate the types of theoretical interests and empirical problems characteristic of small group analysis.

[26] A. Zaleznik, C. R. Christensen, and F. J. Roethlisberger, *The Motivation, Productivity, and Satisfaction of Workers: A Prediction Study.*

The material in this chapter also has attempted to define what we mean by the term "group" for purposes of this study. The criteria defining the small work group in this book establishes as a central question the understanding of the dynamics of group behavior under varying environmental conditions.

Finally, this chapter has illustrated types of theory to be employed in this book and the use of case studies in relation to theory.

*Chapter Two*

# Processes in Group Development:
# Group Identity

T HE effective development of any group, work or social, requires that members share an imagery of the group. At the outset, members bring to the social situation individual images of the group. Each in his thought and fantasy anticipates what the group will be like in its purpose, its methods of interacting, and the positions of its members. He even anticipates what the termination of the group life will be and which symbols will indicate that the life of the group has halted either temporarily or permanently.

These highly individual representations are determined largely by the past experience of the persons involved. Each selects from his repertoire of past group experiences analogues of the anticipated group setting as a basis for the fantasy or expectations he brings to the new group. Since no two persons share identical experience, it follows that no two persons in a group have identical images of the group. On the other hand, the degree of shared experience in a common society results in overlapping individual images of the group. In other words, no group is so unusual that common analogues from the past are unavailable. Yet no group situation is so completely related to the past that the presumption can be safely made that members will bring completely common group images to the new situation.

To the extent that members share an image of the group, they have common expectations out of which stability, order, and pattern develop. This may or may not be adequate to the reality problems of the group. But order and pattern in themselves promote the formation and the continuity of the group.

One of the initial crises in group development involves the process of achieving an identity common in the minds of group members. The identity serves as a *definition of the situation*[1] and provides a source of continuing expectations of the behavior of Self and others. It facilitates preselection of behavior patterns learned in the past, which are appropriate to the present events.

The definition of the situation seldom is verbalized or considered directly. It grows out of interaction and is subject to continuing modifications. It is true that group charters, where these exist, furnish formal mechanisms for a definition of the situation. But most groups lack a written charter and even where it exists the charter leaves much that is undefined.

Group identity also exists at more than one level of awareness in the minds of members. Frequently it can include overt definitions of the situation, and also covert or hidden definitions. Needless to say, both types of definitions may exist independently or in conflict. The existence of overt and covert definitions that are out of line may be the source of emotional problems in group behavior.

The dynamics of the group as it seeks its identity and creates a definition of the situation will be examined in four sections: (1) the definition of the situation; (2) dimensions of group identity; (3) determinants of the definition; and (4) two contrasting identities: (*a*) the hierarchical group and (*b*) the egalitarian group.

## THE DEFINITION OF THE SITUATION

The concept "definition of the situation" points to the processes through which persons select and organize perceptions of reality as a basis for action. Thomas and Znaniecki describe reality or the *situation* as the center for action in the following terms:

The situation is the set of values and attitudes with which the individual or the group has to deal in a process of activity and with regard to which this activity is planned and its results appreciated.[2]

To "values and attitudes" we should add other more tangible aspects of reality that go into making up a situation. These include the physical environment and the persons as objects in the situation.

Every concrete activity is the solution of a situation. The situation involves three kinds of data: (1) The objective conditions under which

[1] William I. Thomas and Florian Znaniecki, *The Polish Peasant in Europe and America,* 2 vols.
[2] *Ibid.,* Vol. I, p. 68.

the individual or society has to act, that is, the totality of values—economic, social, religious, intellectual, etc.—which at the given moment affect directly or indirectly the conscious state of the individual or the group. (2) The pre-existing attitudes of the individual or the group, which at the given moment have an actual influence upon his behavior. (3) The definition of the situation, that is, the more or less clear conception of the conditions and consciousness of the attitudes.[3]

The "objective conditions" referred to as one of the kinds of data that make up a situation are typically the material of interest to sociologists and anthropologists. These conditions are what make up a society or culture and exist independently of particular persons. The second type of data, the "pre-existing attitudes of the individual" are the material of primary interest to the psychologist. These data have to do with the predispositions, or the needs, values, and beliefs of the person as he enters a situation.

The definition of the situation, the third type of data, represents the state of awareness or the set of ideas around which the person organizes the two types of data referred to above. The objective conditions and the individual's predispositions are synthesized into an organized state preliminary to taking action.

And the definition of the situation is a necessary preliminary to any act of the will, for in given conditions and with a given set of attitudes an indefinite plurality of actions is possible, and one definite action can appear only if these conditions are selected, interpreted, and combined in a determined way and if a certain systematization of these attitudes is reached, so that one of them becomes predominant and subordinates the others. It happens, indeed, that a certain value imposes itself immediately and unreflectively and leads at once to action, or that an attitude as soon as it appears excludes the others and expresses itself unhesitatingly in an active process. In these cases, where most radical examples are found in reflex and instinctive actions, the definition is already given to the individual by external conditions or by his own tendencies. But usually there is a process of reflection, after which either a ready social definition is applied or a new personal definition worked out.[4]

In the early stages of its development a group expends much energy in creating a definition of the situation held in common by members. Once the definitions are held consensually the group identity has crystallized and acts as a condition governing behavior in the group.

[3] *Ibid.*, Vol. I, p. 68.
[4] *Ibid.*, Vol. I, pp. 68–69.

The definition of the situation held in common permits a degree of *routine* in the interaction of members. Behavior becomes more *predictable* in their minds and evokes a state of certainty with respect to the future. The combination of routine and predictability serves to reduce *ambiguity* and *anxiety*, thereby freeing members for attention to group work.

## Routine and Predictability in Social Interactions

A definition of the situation involves establishing the identity of the social setting in the minds of the participants. The identity evokes behavioral responses deemed appropriate to it. Once an identity is established, the participants can rely on routine, learned behavior in the past, to guide their interactional responses.

Let us take as an illustration of the place of routine in social interaction a simple two-person situation—the job interview. The two principals have identified their relative positions as "employer" and "applicant" well before the actual interaction takes place. These symbols are socially derived with wide meaning in the society at large. "Employer" looks for cues to enable him to assess the qualities of "applicant" in relation to the requirements of the job. The applicant is concerned with giving off cues to represent his qualities in terms of his understanding of the job requirements. The interactions then are well formed in the minds of the two—employer evokes cues and applicant produces cues. The process stems from this definition of the situation where both principals are committed to support the interaction in these terms, at least at the outset. Both presumably are motivated to carry out the interaction in these terms since there is a purpose in common—the selection for a job.

The actual interaction would find the employer asking questions to elicit descriptive responses from the applicant. In this verbal part of the interview the applicant would occupy the largest proportion of this interchange—he would talk and the employer would listen.

In the nonverbal part, the definition of the situation also places the participants in a structure. Employer is expected to assess the genuineness of applicant's representations of himself, paying careful attention to signs of tension thrown off by applicant. Conversely, applicant attempts to read cues with respect to the degree of interest in himself as he elicits it from his listener, the employer.

At some point in the interview, the roles are reversed. Employer begins to dominate the conversation when he describes the job, and applicant assumes the role of listener and probes with questions designed to evoke more talk on the part of employer. Similarly, positions are reversed in evaluating the nonverbal aspect both as to the genuineness of employer's statements and the degree of interest generated in the applicant.

In this illustration of behavior in a job interview, the tension is expected to be high because of the emotional involvement of the participants in the decision. But the routine established by a common definition of the situation limits the tension produced and helps in the interchange. When we speak of routine growing out of a definition of the situation, we mean that the participants have a feeling that behavior of Self and others is predictable. Expectations of behavior are stabilized in their minds and they proceed to act accordingly.

When the definition of the situation is vague, or the definition by one of the participants is disruptive, uncertainty persists and tension is evoked in the members.

Consider, for example, what occurs when an employer adopts stress interview techniques to see how the applicant responds. What the employer does, in effect, is to alter sharply the definition of the situation. Instead of the typical employer-applicant identity, he may, through his behavior, create a prosecutor-accused relationship by engaging in sharp cross-examination. Or an employer may create a therapist-patient identity and assume a permissive, nondirective stance. By varying these social identities without the collaboration of the applicant, routine is removed from the interactional process and tension is bound to mount especially in the case of the applicant.

Goffman describes vividly in *The Presentation of Self in Everyday Life* what follows when a definition of the situation fails or discrepancies in expectation are revealed:

Given the fact that the individual effectively projects a definition of the situation when he enters the presence of others, we can assume that events may occur within the interaction which contradict, discredit, or otherwise throw doubt upon this projection. When these disruptive events occur, the interaction itself may come to a confused and embarrassed halt. Some of the assumptions upon which the responses of the participants had been predicated become untenable, and the participants find themselves lodged in an interaction for which the situation has been wrongly defined and is now no longer defined. At such moments the individual whose presentation has been discredited may feel ashamed while the others present may feel hostile, and all the participants may come to feel ill at ease, nonplussed, out of countenance, embarrassed, experiencing the kind of anomie that is generated when the minute social system of face-to-face interaction breaks down.[5]

An example of this kind of breakdown in interaction described by Goffman occurs when a group of students suddenly becomes aware of the presence of a young professor who had been mistaken for a student. The identity of the group based on the definition of the situation as a social reality of peers collapses. Much effort then is expended to overcome embarrassment. Attempts at a new definition are made in which an authority relationship prevails, the interaction ends, and the participants withdraw from the event.

Complete routine and predictability in human interaction are not, of course, anticipated by participants in group activity. We are trained somewhat for the unusual even though we have fixed anticipations of how events should evolve. When unexpected behavior occurs discomfort is experienced by the participants and behavior then is directed toward reducing the discomfort. Several investigators studying the social psychology of group relationships have pointed to a general tendency for individuals to seek congruity between their expectations and social reality.[6] When a disparity exists,

[5] Erving Goffman, *The Presentation of Self in Everyday Life* (Garden City, N.Y., an Anchor Book, Doubleday, 1959), p. 12.

[6] American writers concerned with this problem include Theodore Newcomb who uses the concept of "symmetry of orientation" in attitudes among actors in an event. Festinger states, "The existence of a discrepancy in a group with respect to opinions or abilities will lead to action on the part of that group to reduce the discrepancy." Heider proposes the concept of "balance" as a motivating force in the interaction of persons. Anselm Strauss in *Mirrors and Masks* deals with symbols and folkways as the anticipatory and underlying processes to interaction. Strauss writes, for example:

The act of identifying objects, human or physical allows a person to organize his action with reference to those objects . . . .

Elaborate sequences of acts likewise occur because you must identify social situations in order to cope with them. Consider the following mundane situation: a man enters his house at the end of the afternoon, kisses his wife who has come to the door to greet him, engages in a few conventional remarks, and sits down to listen to the radio newscast while his wife continues to prepare dinner. Sociologists would say that the situation was "well-defined." Both man and wife identify the over-all situation, recognize their agreed upon division of labor, and know in general what preceded and what will follow. The myriad of cues striking their eyes and ears are perceived as conventionally named objects—living room, greetings, kiss. Many cues are not noticed, but those noticed tend to be relevant to performances within the domestic drama. Implicit also in the organization of either participant's line of action is the

or where one's expectations are out of line with the situation as it evolves, the behavior of the persons in the group attempts to re-establish the congruity.

Incongruity between expectations and the actual situation, and ambiguity—the failure to achieve over time a common definition of a situation—give rise to one very prevalent type of discomfort, anxiety. Anxiety is a generalized feeling of uncertainty and fear with an unclear cause or object of this fear. Let us examine such anxiety and the spontaneous activities that serve to reduce it.

Zaleznik, Christensen, and Roethlisberger[7] developed a theory of "social certitude" to explain the anxiety arising from incongruity in social relationships in groups. The particular incongruities they were dealing with centered around conflicting elements of status in the social attributes of group members. An ambiguous person in a social situation is one who has certain attributes of both high-status and low-status persons. An example of this out-of-lineness is the group member who has high education, is older than other members of the group, yet whose occupation or job status is low relative to other group members. This person becomes an ambiguous object in the group. Should group members act toward him in relation to his high or low status attributes? How should he himself act toward others? As an ambiguous object, he becomes at once a source of anxiety in the group and probably experiences anxiety himself.

In the face of ambiguity and its attendant anxiety, the tendency for group members is to work out an accommodation. This counterbalances the ambiguity and relieves the anxiety. Members may develop a joking relationship with the ambiguous object. Or he may

---

assumption of each that the identities of both self and other are known. The husband sees or recognizes or defines or classifies—depending upon which verb one chooses to use—his wife and himself vis-à-vis each other in this sequence of familiar acts. Who and what she is and he is, so far as this situation is concerned, are not in question. This is not to say that all matters of reciprocal identity are settled, but only that each knows which of his and her possible identities—their possible "I's" are likely to enter into this conventionally acted out situation.

Theodore M. Newcomb, "An Approach to the Study of Communicative Acts," in *Small Groups: Studies in Social Interaction*, A. Paul Hare, Edgar F. Borgatta, and Robert F. Bales, Eds., pp. 149–163. Leon Festinger, "A Theory of Social Comparison Processes," in *Small Groups*, pp. 163–187. Fritz Heider, *The Psychology of Interpersonal Relations*. Anselm L. Strauss, *Mirrors and Masks: The Search for Identity*, pp. 45–46.

[7] A. Zaleznik, C. R. Christensen, and F. J. Roethlisberger, *The Motivation, Productivity and Satisfaction of Workers*.

isolate himself from the group—that is, minimize interactions to absolute basic necessity. In other instances, he may become the group scapegoat and, if possible, withdraw from the group.

There are styles of behavior that members of a society seem to learn in coping with ambiguity. Radcliffe-Brown, in his essay on joking relationships,[8] pointed out that certain types of relationships contained strong disjunctive elements. By disjunctive, Radcliffe-Brown meant elements that would tend toward conflict or ultimate dissolution of the relationship. An example of a relationship with strong disjunctive elements is the one between a person and his brother-in-law. In primitive society organized along clan groupings, a marriage that cuts across clan lines brings together as principals members of different groups. This confrontation becomes a disjunctive element in the relationship between brothers-in-law since male peers representing different groups can, in other situations, fight and be competitive. The conjunctive element to counteract the divisive factor is, of course, the marriage. The marriage, however, defines the co-operation between husband and wife. It leaves ambiguous in primitive and modern societies the relationship with the immediate families of the principals. Radcliffe-Brown shows that a joking relationship becomes the style of interaction between the person and his brothers-in-law. The joking permits a certain amount of hostile expression, yet in socially acceptable ways which prevent the hostility from dominating the relationship.

In the case of the relationship between a person and his mother-in-law, the principal style is one of minimizing interaction, with the person required to present gifts to his mother-in-law. The disjunctive elements in the person-mother-in-law relationship are at least two: the question of whether husband or mother exercises authority over wife-daughter; and the problem of maintaining the appropriate relationship between male and female who are separated by age but not by direct kinship. Mother-in-law is neither mother, a relationship appropriate to her age, nor is she a love object, a potential relationship appropriate for their respective sexes. In the face of such disjunctive or ambiguous elements, distance or minimum interaction becomes the means for managing the ambiguity.

In the Zaleznik, Christensen, Roethlisberger study, ambiguous persons, such as older workers of lower ethnic background who had high job status, developed a relationship of distance between themselves and group members. They and others kept interaction to a minimum.

[8] Alfred R. Radcliffe-Brown, *Structure and Function in Primitive Society*, pp. 90–104.

Among ambiguous persons who were similar in age to most group members but of different ethnic background and high job status, a joking relationship prevailed. The content of the joking consisted of derogatory references to the ethnic backgrounds of the "out-of-liners." The prevailing norm that joking should be accepted and returned made visible the differences and expressed the hostility, yet kept tight limits to prevent the hostility from dominating.

Another way of identifying and explaining the anxiety resulting from ambiguity was presented by Festinger in his *Theory of Cognitive Dissonance*.[9] Dissonance occurs when events fail to meet expectations or when ideas or facts are inconsistent or out of line. Festinger presented a dramatic instance of dissonance as it occurred when events failed to meet expectations, particularly where the events were integral to a group's definition of the situation.

In a paper entitled "When Prophecy Fails," Festinger, Riecken, and Schachter[10] described and analyzed the effects of nonoccurrence of an event on a group whose identity centered on the belief that the event would actually happen. The dissonance existed in belonging to a group whose purpose was incongruent with one's rational beliefs about events, and also in the experience of belonging to a group, yet finding its central purpose unrealized.

Festinger, Riecken, and Schachter joined a group led by Mrs. Marion Keech and a Dr. Thomas Armstrong. Mrs. Keech attracted a number of people who joined her in believing that Lake City would be inundated just before dawn on December 21. Mrs. Keech's prophecy came about as a result of "messages" she had received from an outer planet. These messages predicted widespread floods. The believers, however, were to be spared and their group formed in preparation for the cataclysm and their safe removal. The evidence indicated that all participants except the three authors believed in the prophecy and their salvation. They supported one another and made dramatic preparations for the events of December 21.

Why the "believers" accepted the prophecy and joined the group is uncertain. Many complex motivations were at work. But the main point to be stressed here is that the identity of the group was formed around a prophecy not acceptable in rational terms. The study itself sought to determine how people reacted to dissonance. Midnight of December 21 arrived and the foretold departure on a

---

[9] Leon Festinger, *Theory of Cognitive Dissonance*.

[10] Leon Festinger, Henry W. Riecken, and Stanley Schachter, "When Prophecy Fails," in *Readings in Social Psychology*, Eleanor E. Macoby, Theodore M. Newcomb, and Eugene L. Hartley, eds., 3rd ed., pp. 156–163.

flying saucer to escape the floods did not take place.  Neither did the disaster take place according to Mrs. Keech's prophecy.  The group members had made elaborate preparations for the event including disposing of their possessions, yet their expectations as a group were unfulfilled.  The group and its members were in a condition of dissonance.  Members displayed considerable anxiety.  Some wept and were in a state of confusion and despair.  Let us now quote from the study.

But this atmosphere did not continue long.  At about 4:45 A.M. Mrs. Keech summoned everyone to attention, announcing that she had just received a message.  She then read aloud these momentous words: "For this day it is established that there is but one God of Earth and He is in thy midst, and from his hand thou hast written these works.  And mighty is the word of God—and by his word have ye been saved—for from the mouth of death have ye been delivered and at no time has there been such a force loosed upon the Earth.  Not since the beginning of time upon this Earth has there been such a force of good and light as now floods this room and that which has been loosed within this room now floods the entire Earth.  As thy God has spoken through the two within these walls has he manifested that which he has given thee to do."

This message was received with enthusiasm.  It was an adequate, even an elegant, explanation of the disconfirmation.  The cataclysm had been called off.  The little group, sitting all night long, had spread so much light that God had saved the world from destruction.[11]

The dissonance had been overcome through this new message and, of course, its enthusiastic acceptance was accounted for by the need of group members to re-establish the group identity and thereby restore their emotional investment in their past behavior in joining and participating in the group.

A group without identity, some common definition, and a set of expectations in the minds of members, cannot survive for long.  Once members join a group, a force toward eliminating dissonances, which cast doubt on the identity of the group, is set in motion.  That individuals sometimes delude themselves to restore an acceptable definition of the situation is explicable in view of the seemingly greater penalty of dealing with anxiety resulting from dissonance.

The condition of social certitude, or congruity between expectations and events, and the avoidance of ambiguity and anxiety are central aspects of creating a group identity.  They help explain the tendency for groups over time to develop considerable uniformity in

[11] *Ibid.*, p. 162.

the attitude of group members.   Homans in *The Human Group* states the proposition this way:

The more frequently persons interact with one another, the more alike in some respects both their activities and *sentiments* tend to become.[12] (Italics added.)

Members of groups who are attracted to the group will attempt generally to remove disparities in beliefs among their ranks.   Incongruities create anxiety, a condition not too many persons are able to sustain for any significant time period.   Much of literature, drama, the arts, and humor captures the interests of audiences simply because it plays with ambiguity and evokes the attendant anxiety in a relatively safe way.   The audience "identifies," it shares the anxiety ordinarily to be avoided and ultimately experiences the resolution.

Shakespeare's *Twelfth Night* is a good case in point.   The play, a comedy, develops around confusion in sex roles.   Characters disguise themselves as members of the opposite sex and are engaged in courtships between male and female, with each in the role of a member of the opposite sex.   This play also deals with underlying themes of homosexuality, an exceedingly ambiguous and anxiety-provoking theme, reinforcing the experiences of the comedy.

Jack Benny, the comedian, is a master at using ambiguity for humor. He presents himself as an urbane sophisticate, yet one who behaves in completely contradictory ways.   He is penny pinching and has a good deal less "savvy" than his partner Rochester who provides the contrast: Rochester, a Negro, is constantly coping with his boss's mistakes and eccentricities.

An outstanding play demonstrating a continuing acting out of situations not identified or defined is *Harvey*.[13]   Harvey is the large rabbit visible only to his companion, Elwood P. Dowd.   Interaction with Dowd is easy as long as one is willing to accept his definition that Harvey is one of the principals in the interaction.   One theme of the play is the superficiality of ordinary human affairs where men engage in shows and delusions through conventional means to avoid ambiguity. Harvey is no more nor less than a symbol of the crutch each of us leans on to sustain ordinary interaction.   "Social reality" many times is an illusion converted into an agreed on definition, while the realities remain hidden from view and are turned into illusions.

Man's need for an acceptable definition of social situations does not

[12] George C. Homans, *The Human Group*, p. 120.
[13] Mary C. Chase, *Harvey: A Play*.

negate the possibility that dysfunctional elements also exist in the process of creating acceptable group identities. We turn now to an examination of how established definitions of a situation, while eliminating ambiguity, may also develop dysfunctions in group relationships.

The definition of a situation, as we have seen, involves the connecting of experience and learned behavior from the past with persons and events in the present. Expectations are met and some sense of routine, predictability, and emotional balance exist. In a group setting the definition is a consensus in the minds of members and a common set of images of the present group.

Not all definitions of a situation, or all the processes evoked to develop a definition, have positive effects. The process of *stereotyping*, for example, provides a good illustration of negative consequences resulting from attempts to reach a definition. Stereotyping consists of classifying all new experiences, and especially persons, using symbols learned in the past. These symbols consist of significant cues for the classification. Important in this list of cues are race, ethnic background, socio-economic status, and others. Persons and situations are infinitely more complex than these simple cues will admit. Yet establishing relationships in which such cues are dominant and forcing persons into styles of behavior that they might find dissatisfying, although tolerable, prevents significant new learning.

For instance there is little question that in the traditions of the old South, with its strict practices of social segregation, interpersonal situations tended to be well defined. Persons knew what to expect from one another and proceeded to meet these expectations. But segregation is represented as a static solution to interracial relationships, especially for the Negro. With movement now toward integration, there is little question that more social situations are ambiguous; old expectations are unreliable guides to future behavior. Yet this ambiguity and tension may be the cost of evolving a different society where individual aspirations have a higher value than in earlier times. Man's need for certitude does not permit him to engage in stereotyping for long. The static society makes defining situations easy. Changing society, on the other hand, requires the ability to develop increasingly more complex and alterable group identities.

Experimentation in interpersonal relationships and learning go hand in hand. The more one invokes the past as a model for present and future behavior, the less learning takes place. One may become adept at securing one's "masks" and at maintaining a stylized form of behavior but at a cost of learning.

Erikson provides a dramatic example of how personal development at times involves disengagement from the past.[14]  George Bernard Shaw, in his autobiographical writing, told of his decision to become a writer.  Shaw was raised in a reasonably well-to-do Irish, middle-class society.  He entered business and then became alarmed, not at the possibility of failure, but at the prospect of success.  Shaw left his work and went to London for a three-year experiment in writing.  History has recorded the results of this experiment.

Erikson, in analyzing these autobiographical comments, characterizes Shaw's disengagement as a psycho-social moratorium.  The previous definitions of expectations and style of life were halted, and a new mode of behavior was established.  Erikson intimates that one may view all significant learning experiences as involving a psycho-social moratorium.  The period of life in which conscious experimentation or the search for new definitions of social reality is very high is ordinarily in adolescence and early adulthood.  It is here that formal education becomes society's main instrument for helping to make this period of experimentation fruitful.

Another instance in which a conventional definition of the situation may have negative effects is in problem solving or other creative work, either in group or individual settings.  Creative activity is characterized by originality in ideas or combinations of ideas.  Invoking past solutions to problems, or utilizing as a criterion of effective problem solving the degree to which present solutions resemble those of the past, slows down originality and the quest for new combinations.

One of the chief characteristics of creative persons is their high capacity to tolerate ambiguity without becoming overanxious.  Delaying a definition of a situation while seeking creative combinations requires a capacity to manage the anxiety attendant upon amorphous situations.  There is evidence to suggest that individuals with low tolerance for ambiguity tend to stereotype, to reflect conservative attitudes, to think in dichotomous terms, and to display rigid adherence to conventional forms.[15]  The term "authoritarian personality" encompasses all these particular characteristics.

One of the interesting possible consequences of human relations training is an increase in tolerance for ambiguity and reduction in degree of stereotyping.  A secondary effect might be to increase individual creativity in interpersonal and problem-solving settings.  Unfortunately there is little concrete evidence to indicate the extent to

[14] Erik H. Erikson, "The Problems of Ego Identity," *Identity and Anxiety*, Maurice R. Stein, Arthur J. Vidich, David Manning, Eds., pp. 37–87.
[15] T. W. Adorno et al., *The Authoritarian Personality*.

which, if at all, these objectives are accomplished, primarily because of the dearth of research on the effects of human relations training. Certainly the most interesting approaches to training involve dealing with and learning from ambiguity.[16]

## Overt and Covert Definitions of the Situation

Extremely important to understanding the problems arising in definitions of a situation is the existence of two levels of group identity. One level at which group identity evolves is overt and manifest. The other level is covert or hidden from the conscious awareness of the members. The extent to which definitions exist at both levels and, more importantly, are conflicting may explain emotional difficulties and "blocked" behavior in groups.

Shepard and Bennis[17] in discussing overt and covert images of group relationships and their effects on the behavior of members provide a hypothetical case of a mixed group of men and women in which the overt definition of the situation centers around a task to be accomplished. The covert definition pivots on flirtations between one of the pairs. This flirtation, while not acknowledged by group members, acts as a determinant of modes of behavior in the group. Presumably, accomplishment of the task is impeded as these modes of behavior divert concentration from the task to preoccupation with the flirtation. Obviously group development requires a minimum of conflict between overt and covert definitions.

This conflict has been discussed also under the rubric "hidden agenda."[18] The announced agenda of a group might be to decide on a marketing program for a company. The hidden agenda, the issue unspoken among members, might be the competition among certain members for status. The declared agenda is then used to provide content for the hidden agenda, which may tap off the bulk of energy of group members.

To show how hidden definitions of a situation impede group work, we cite the case of a task group organized to consider executive development in a company:

[16] F. J. Roethlisberger et al., *Training for Human Relations: an Interim Report.* Also, Leland P. Bradford et al., *Explorations in Human Relations Training.*

[17] Herbert A. Shepard and Warren G. Bennis, "A Theory of Training by Group Methods," *Human Relations*, Vol. 9 (1956) No. 4, pp. 403–414. Also, Warren G. Bennis and Herbert A. Shepard, "A Theory of Group Development," *Human Relations*, Vol. 9 (1956) No. 4, pp. 415–437.

[18] Leland P. Bradford, "The Case of the Hidden Agenda," *Adult Leadership*, September 1952, pp. 3–7.

The president of a large company became concerned with the possibility that his organization had failed to develop executive talent. This concern of his arose in connection with his own retirement. He organized a committee composed of assistants to vice presidents to study this problem and to report to him with recommendations. The president's forthcoming retirement was well known and there was private speculation as to who among the vice presidents would be named as his successor. This succession obviously implied that several persons among the assistant vice presidents would be promoted. The task force met several times, but their discussions were not too productive nor interesting. The group spent most of its time attempting to define what the president wanted the committee to do. The hidden agenda concerned the rivalry among the assistants as to which one of their superiors would become the president and how this would affect their advancement. The committee, coping with this hidden agenda, found itself unable to deal with the issues the organization faced in attracting and developing executive talent.

Groups concerned with learning and creative problem solving are faced constantly with the tendency for members to seek definitions of the situation apart from their relevance to immediate problem solving. Individuals face problems of avoiding rigid responses, such as stereotyping, under the compulsion to define the interpersonal situation in which they find themselves. One method for limiting the negative effects of defining situations is to understand the basis on which such definitions are made.

In the next section we turn our attention to group identity and consider the elements in the situation which provide cues for the establishment of group identity.

## DIMENSIONS OF GROUP IDENTITY

The cues utilized in the development of a group identity can be divided usefully into four categories, or dimensions: (1) the *location* of the group in time and space; (2) the *expectations* conditioned by past experience; (3) the *symbols* expressing the definition of the situation; (4) the *membership* in the group, that is, the characteristics of persons included and excluded from participation.

### Location of the Group in Time and Space

The location of a group in time and space is an important element in the establishment of group identity. A group exists in and through time in two senses.    First, *time* places the group at some point in the cycle or rhythm of a day.    Society and man's responses are governed in large measure by the routine of a day.    A man in a group during working hours moves in an atmosphere of purposiveness.    For the same man, a leisure-time group proceeds in a different atmosphere —one less concerned with purpose.    For the housewife, the daily rhythm is equally if not more significant in establishing the definition of the situation.    Here, however, the day has shorter time blocks and more frequent shifts in routine.

Elliot Jacques in *Measurement of Responsibility*[19] uses time as the important dimension in analyzing the content of work.    His argument, essentially, is that jobs vary in the time span in which the individual functions.    For a production worker on an assembly line the time span of work is measured in minutes if not seconds.    For an executive at the top levels of an organization the time is calculated, on the other hand, in units of a year and more.

A similar analysis can be applied to the time span of group life as a factor in establishing a definition of the situation.    As we have seen, the location of the group in the rhythm of the day is one relationship of time in defining the situation.    Closely related to the daily rhythm is the timespan expectancy of the group.    The family, for example, is tied closely to the movement throughout a day.    It is also a group that has a history and a long time-span expectancy.    Many work groups are limited in their past and future.    The more *transient* a group in the life of its members, the less it may command involvement in the group.    On the other hand, transient groups with important purposes may create a sense of urgency in members and a high degree of emotional commitment.

Time as a factor in the definition is important in still a third way; it identifies the group in relation to stages in the *life cycle* of members. Groups organized for adolescents will contain in their identity important functions of the passage from childhood to adulthood.    The problems of dependent-independent relations with authority figures will enter strongly into either or both the overt and covert definitions of the situation.

The problem of group identity as a function of the life cycle of members may be seen in the groups organized for elderly persons who are retired.    These groups, sometimes called "Golden Age Clubs," are important in view of the fact that our society has not had an easy time in finding a place for older persons, male or female, when their formal responsibilities have diminished.    With the old patterns among

[19] Elliot Jacques, *Measurement of Responsibility*.

the several generations no longer acceptable and workable, the groups formed by social work agencies are attempting to meet a new need. Much of the activity, however, resembles that which goes on in social groups ranging from preadolescence to early adulthood with the emphasis on leisure, hobbies, and companionship. The experimentation is in working with time—either filling it or using it. How good such definitions are in satisfying the needs of Golden Age members remains to be seen.

Location of the group in *space* provides cues in the definition of the situation along with time. The physical settings in which groups function become important in the definition. The family's space in the house and the boundaries separating it from other groups are clearly delineated. The sense of privacy of the family group is important for its proper functioning. That the boundaries among lower income groups are inadequate for the establishment of privacy acts in no small way to weaken the solidarity of the family unit.

Work groups' physical boundaries are also significant in their identity. It is not uncommon for work groups in factories, for example, to refer to themselves as "the third floor group" or in some other terms of reference to their physical location. These references also incorporate imagery based on the characteristics of the space the group occupies. The space may be highly masculine in character with heavy machinery and much pounding. Or it may be quiescent and feminine.

Corner gangs also use their physical space to mark themselves off from one another. One gang "takes over" a corner and its space becomes its private ground to be protected from invaders. This penchant for a corner secure to the group, so typical of adolescent group members, reflects a need for relative isolation.

Goffman in discussing the physical location of a group and the behavioral demands created by the areas refers to regional behavior as behavior appropriate to a certain space.[20] In certain locations, a group is in a "front region"; the performance of members is defined in terms of the expectations of outsiders. In other locations, the group is in a "back region" or "backstage"; the internal relations of members can be sustained in forms of behavior considered appropriate under these circumstances. Goffman provides an interesting example from his study of Shetland Island culture. He is concerned with problems faced by groups in a tourist hotel in controlling regions; that is, in preventing front-region persons or those who are out-group from invading the backstage of the area reserved for those who are in-group.

[20] Goffman, *op. cit.*, Chapter III.

Shetland Hotel provides another example of the problems workers face when they have insufficient control of their backstage. Within the hotel kitchen, where the guests' food was prepared and where the staff ate and spent their day, crofters' culture tended to prevail. It will be useful to suggest some of the details of this culture here.

In the kitchen, crofter employer-employee relations prevailed. Reciprocal first-naming was employed, although the scullery boy was fourteen and the male owner over thirty. The owning couple and employees ate together, participating with relative equality in mealtime small talk and gossip. When the owners held informal kitchen parties for friends and extended kin, the hotel workers participated. This pattern of intimacy and equality between management and employees was inconsistent with the appearance both elements of the staff gave when guests were present, as it was inconsistent with the guests' notions of the social distance which ought to obtain between the official with whom they corresponded when arranging for their stay, and the porters and maids who carried luggage upstairs, polished the guests' shoes each night, and emptied their chamber pots.

Similarly, in the hotel kitchen, island eating patterns were employed. Meat, when available, tended to be boiled. Fish, often eaten, tended to be boiled or salted. Potatoes, an inevitable item in the day's one big meal, were almost always boiled in their jackets and eaten in the island manner: each eater selects a potato by hand from the central bowl, then pierces it with his fork and skins it with his knife, keeping the peels in a neat pile alongside his place, to be scooped in with his knife after the meal is finished. Oilcloth was used as a cover for the table. Almost every meal was preceded by a bowl of soup, and soup bowls, instead of plates, tended to be used for the courses that came after. (Since most of the food was boiled anyway, this was a practical usage.) Forks and knives were sometimes grasped fist-like, and tea was served in cups without saucers. While the island diet in many ways seemed to be adequate, and while island table manners could be executed with great delicacy and circumspection—and often were—the whole eating complex was well understood by islanders to be not only different from the British middle-class pattern, but somehow a violation of it. Perhaps this difference in pattern was most evident on occasions when food given to guests was also eaten in the kitchen. (This was not uncommon and was not more common because the staff often preferred island food to what the guests were given.) At such times the kitchen portion of the food was prepared and served in the island manner, with little stress on individual pieces and cuts, and more stress on a common source of servings. Often the remains of a joint of meat or the broken remains of a batch of tarts would be served— the same food as appeared in the guest dining hall but in a slightly different condition, yet one not offensive by island kitchen standards. And if a pudding made from stale bread and cake did not pass the test of what was good enough for guests, it was eaten in the kitchen.

Crofter clothing and postural patterns also tended to appear in the hotel kitchen. Thus, the manager would sometimes follow local custom and leave his cap on; the scullery boys would use the coal bucket as a target for the well-aimed expulsion of mucus; and the women on the staff would rest sitting with their legs up in unladylike positions.

In addition to these differences due to culture, there were other sources of discrepancy between kitchen ways and parlor ways in the hotel: for some of the standards of hotel service that were shown or implied in the guests' regions were not fully adhered to in the kitchen. In the scullery wing of the kitchen region, mold would sometimes form on soup yet to be used. Over the kitchen stove, wet socks would be dried on the steaming kettle—a standard practice on the island. Tea, when guests had asked for it newly infused, would be brewed in a pot encrusted at the bottom with tea leaves that were weeks old. Fresh herrings would be cleaned by splitting them and then scraping out the innards with newspaper. Pats of butter, softened, misshapen and partly used during their sojourn in the dining hall, would be rerolled to look fresh, and sent out to do duty again. Rich puddings, too good for kitchen consumption, would be sampled aggressively by the finger-full before distribution to the guests. During the mealtime rush hour, once-used drinking glasses would sometimes be merely emptied and wiped instead of being rewashed, thus allowing them to be put back into circulation quickly.*

Given, then, the various ways in which activity in the kitchen contradicted the impression fostered in the guests' region of the hotel, one can appreciate why the doors leading from the kitchen to the other parts of the hotel were a constant sore spot in the organization of work. The maids wanted to keep the doors open to make it easier to carry food trays back and forth, to gather information about whether guests were ready or not for the service which was to be performed for them, and to retain as much contact as possible with the persons they had come to work to learn about. Since the maids played a servant role before the guests, they felt they did not have too much to lose by being observed in their own milieu by guests who glanced into the kitchen when passing the open doors. The managers, on the other hand, wanted to keep the door closed so that the middle-class role imputed to them by the guests would not be discredited by a disclosure of their kitchen habits. Hardly a day passed when these doors were not angrily banged shut and angrily pushed open. A kick-door of the kind modern restaurants use would have provided a

---

* These illustrations of the discrepancy between the reality and appearances of standards should not be considered extreme. Close observation of the backstage of any middle-class home in Western cities would be likely to disclose discrepancies between reality and appearance that were equally as great. And wherever there is some degree of commercialization, discrepancies no doubt are often greater.

partial solution for this staging problem. A small glass window in the doors that could act as a peephole—a stage device used by many small places of business—would also have been helpful.[21]

## Expectation

Another dimension which enters into the formulation of group identity is concerned with the expectation conditioned by past experience. Organized events in any social system act as a learning experience for individuals so that when similar events recur particular expectations are aroused. The situation is anticipated in the minds of individuals in at least two distinct senses. The *taking of roles* is expected[22] and so are the *affective or emotional states.*

Role taking means acting according to specific patterns of behavior. The acts are tied to norms or standards governing how persons *should* behave in a specified situation. These "shoulds" of behavior define a range of actions associated with a particular position in a social structure.[23] The individual, working within this range selects acts and expressively plays his role in some manner integral to his personality. Yet the expectancies associated with a role and status are inherent in the situation and are not personal. In work groups, in particular, the status or position around which role taking develops is closely related to the formal hierarchy and also to the occupations of the participants.

The particular behaviors involved in role taking are defined by the activities performed by a member of a group and the style of interaction expected from group members. Activities are rooted in the group's purpose. In the family, for example, the activities of members are related to their positions (mother, father, etc.) and also to the requirements of nurture and training, two very important purposes of the family. Style of interaction, although more closely related to personality characteristics than activity in groups, is also part of the web of expectations. How much of active-dominant as against passive-submissive behavior is expected varies with positions in the group.

Anticipated role taking is a form of fantasy in which the individual creates in his mind images of future events and portrays, in his thought processes, what he and others will do. The sources of these images are in past experiences. Although no two situations are alike, there

[21] *Ibid.,* pp. 116–119.
[22] Anselm Strauss, Ed., *The Social Psychology of George Herbert Mead,* pp. 227–228.
[23] Ralph Linton, *The Study of Man; an Introduction,* pp. 113–114.

is enough recurrence in life experiences to provide persons with a workable range of expectations.

Then there are the affective or emotional states of the individuals in group situations. Without a set of emotions appropriate to the situation, role taking would be empty and would proceed without conviction. Individuals learn to associate a particular range of emotional states with situational requirements. A problem-solving conference requires a large measure of seriousness, interest, and sustained attention. A party, on the other hand, calls for joviality, vivacity, and easiness.

Situations have the capacity to induce the appropriate state in the individual. Some of this stems from sharing a mood once the event begins. The sharing is related to the contagion of emotions. But another part of the induction occurs before the event. Anticipation of a party sets the conditions for joviality; anticipating a conference induces seriousness.

Homans in *The Human Group*[24] provides a brilliant illumination of the relationship between situations, the induction of affect in the individuals, and the discharge of affect in the interaction itself. He begins his discussion with the general problem of the relationship between the individual and the group. He presents two classical and opposing schools of thought: (1) the school of thought that views society as a network created by individuals to satisfy their needs (the social contract theory), and (2) the school of thought that views society as the entity constraining individuals to behave in prescribed ways (the social mold theory). Homan's intent is to show that both theories are valid and, moreover, that they are not opposite or mutually exclusive theories. Group behavior represents the result of forces in the individual and in the group as a social entity.

To illustrate the reconciliation of apparently opposite theories Homans brings together the opposing theories of Malinowski and Radcliffe-Brown on the relationship between anxiety and ritual in society. Malinowski, a well-known social anthropologist, noted in the primitive society he studied the presence of magical rites whenever groups undertook dangerous activity or acts whose outcome was uncertain. According to his view, the individual experienced anxiety in the face of danger. The performance of prescribed magical rites alleviated the anxiety and gave the individual more confidence in the face of uncertainty.[25] Radcliffe-Brown also noted the presence of ritual preceding dangerous and uncertain ventures. But for him the

[24] George C. Homans, *op. cit.*, pp. 316–330.
[25] Bronislaw Malinowski, *Magic, Science and Religion*, pp. 28–32.

situation induced the anxiety since individuals were expected to experience concern in given situations. The magic made this sharing of anxiety a group process and in a sense reaffirmed the implied willingness of the individuals to maintain their relationship to their society.[26]

For Homans' reconciliation of these two viewpoints, let us quote his summary:

At the end, let us summarize the theory of magic we have reached by comparing the theories of two great anthropologists. Magic is apt to be performed in situations of danger, such as sea fishing or childbirth, when people cannot be sure that results they greatly desire will in fact be gained. As the body mobilizes for action in these situations, magic takes the place of the unknown or impossible actions that would have made certain the desired results. Magic releases tension, and since people believe that the rites, like any other technique, actually help them in a practical way, magic gives them the confidence they need to carry on necessary work. Before the worry that might otherwise paralyze them has a chance to spread, magic drains it off. But the proof that anxiety is latent is the fact that, when the rites are not properly performed, anxiety reappears. And although magic is an expression of the emotions of individuals in the face of danger and uncertainty, it is also performed as a matter of obedience to social norms. Society, demanding the performance of ritual and specifying the dreadful consequences of nonperformance, creates, in part, the anxiety that magic alleviates. Magic, moreover, has a function in helping the group to survive, both by giving confidence to individuals and by solemnizing, for the group, activities of essential importance. The social contract theory, which holds that social behavior results from the characteristics of individuals, and the social mold theory, which holds that individual behavior results from the characteristics of society, are both correct, both incomplete, and complementary to one another.[27]

This reconciliation of the relationship among affect, the individual, and a social situation suggests that an emotional state in the individual is stimulated in anticipation of an event. Events in which one has experienced a particular emotional state can induce a similar set of feelings long before the actual event takes place again. It is the individual and only the individual who experiences affect. But affective states among members of a group are shared and many times are induced as a condition for participation in an interpersonal situation.

If part of the definition of the situation involves expectations of role taking and affect based on past experience, it would follow that

[26] A. R. Radcliffe-Brown, *The Andaman Islanders*, pp. 233–234.
[27] George C. Homans, *op. cit.*, p. 330.

events, particularly recurrent events, can be differentiated according to expectations. Let us take two quite different social events frequently experienced in our culture, such as an athletic competition and a religious ceremony. If we limit behavioral expectation to active or passive and confine affect induction to elation or melancholy we can readily specify important aspects of the definition of the situation. This specification is represented in the graph shown below.

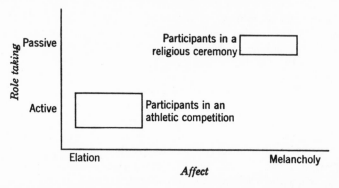

The capacity of individuals to anticipate behavior and corresponding affect from situations experienced in the past acts as a "self-fulfilling prophecy."[28] The anticipation or expectation defines the situation and where the definition has broad acceptance, the individuals proceed to act and express emotions appropriate to the definition.

In experimental studies of group behavior under laboratory conditions, much reliance is placed on anticipation as a condition for the establishment of the experimental conditions. The problem in creating laboratory conditions is simply one of taking subjects who have never interacted before and rapidly achieving the experimental conditions, say of high and low group cohesion, so that results can be measured in terms of other variables such as group and individual productivity. Participants are introduced to the experimental conditions simply by the experimenter, generally an authority figure, telling them in advance how they will feel or react to the group and its members. In inducing the conditions of high and low cohesiveness, for example, the experimenter tells the subjects they will like or dislike the group and its members or that they will have much or little in common with other group members. His success in generating anticipation is, of course, measured by how subjects report their feelings during and after the experiment.

[28] Robert K. Merton, *Social Theory and Social Structure*, pp. 125–129 and 421–436.

In one set of experiments conducted by Schachter et al.,[29] the experimenters induced the affect appropriate to "cohesiveness" by saying to the subject in advance of the experiment. "You will be a member of an extremely cohesive group and there is every reason to expect that the other members of the group will like you and you will like them" (high cohesiveness condition). A similar type of statement but opposite in content represented the induction into the condition of low cohesiveness.

At the conclusion of the experiment, subjects were asked to complete a "cohesiveness" questionnaire with the following questions:

A. How did you like your team?
B. If you were taking part in another experiment, how much would you like to work with these same girls?
C. How much do you think you would like to see your teammates?

The questions were answered on a scale of 1 to 5, the higher the number the more positive the feelings. In the table shown below, we can ignore the references to "type 1 or 2" groups and concentrate on the differences in the averages of the responses to the three questions. The table shows clearly that the subjects who were told in advance of the "congeniality" of the group and the positive feelings of members for one another in fact responded more positively in the questionnaire than those subjects who received negative induction.

*Responses to Cohesiveness Questionnaire*[30]

| Cohesiveness N | Question A "Like Team" | Question B "Work With Same Girls" | Question C "Like to See Teammates" |
|---|---|---|---|
| Hi Co (Type 1) 13 | 3.62 | 3.77 | 3.77 |
| Hi Co (Type 2) 13 | 3.85 | 4.31 | 3.69 |
| Lo Co (Type 1) 12 | 2.92 | 2.92 | 2.50 |
| Lo Co (Type 2) 12 | 3.50 | 3.25 | 2.75 |

A more general explanation of this close correspondence between affect induced and affect experienced may be made in terms of the theory of dissonance discussed earlier. If a person expects to feel a certain way in an event and actually does not, he is in a condition of dissonance. To avoid a condition of conflict between expectations and experience may strongly motivate one to feel or experience as one has anticipated. This motivation becomes a precondition for the

[29] Stanley Schachter et al., "An Experimental Study of Cohesiveness and Productivity," in *Group Dynamics,* pp. 401–411.
[30] *Ibid.,* p. 405.

definition of a situation where anticipations and expectancies play an important part in the outcome.

## Symbols and Group Identity

Objects in the environment play an important part in formulating a group identity, particularly in establishing the expectations. The importance of the symbolic value of objects lies in their capacity to become invested with emotion and meaning. Implied in this concept is the focusing on certain aspects of the past and recreating them by attaching their meaning to objects in the environment. Such objects are of two kinds: (1) physical objects and (2) persons. Physical objects capable of taking on symbolic meaning are unlimited. The surroundings, furniture, tools, and implements used by a group in its work are all subject to this attachment of emotion and meaning.

In a study of a machine shop group reported by Zaleznik in *Worker Satisfaction and Development*,[31] physical objects entered into the group identity in numerous ways. The group was composed of skilled workers called "machinists" and relatively unskilled workers called "operators." Machinists tended to be located in the front of the room where a long bench was situated. The bench was placed in the room to enable machinists to work on blueprints, layouts, and job orders. Operators worked in the back of the room where the old, general purpose equipment was placed along with sinks and sand-blasting equipment used for clean-up work. Even though the reasons for separating skilled from unskilled work in the room could be and were easily rationalized in terms of work requirements and functional utilities, the fact of this separation defined the geography of the room into zones for those of high and low status. This separation did not mean that highs and lows never crossed over. The crossovers, however, took on social significance in that high-status persons who were socially oriented crossed over more frequently than highs who preferred social distance as their mode of relating themselves to others. Similarly, lows who crossed over tended to be persons who were mobile and who aspired to improvement in their status.

Physical objects other than the room geography also became important as social symbols. The tool box, for example, served to hold the complex array of tools owned by a skilled machinist. The tool box, however, also served to identify the owner in the minds of group members as a person high in status. Operators who aspired toward becoming high-status machinists communicated the fact, in part, by buying and displaying a tool box that could be identified with them.

[31] A. Zaleznik, *Worker Satisfaction and Development*.

The clothes a person wore also had a symbolic value. High-status machinists wore a long coat; low-status operators wore a sleeveless apron. It was clearly inappropriate for a person relatively low in status to discard an apron for a coat. One younger worker tried and then gave up the coat after using it only a day.

The importance of physical objects in establishing the definition of the situation applies to all types of groups, not just those that manipulate physical objects in the course of their daily work. Blau, in his study *The Dynamics of Bureaucracy*,[32] noted how the preparation of reports were symbolic of investigators' competence. He studied a group of investigators in a law enforcement agency. Highly competent investigators dictated their reports to stenographers; less competent investigators wrote their reports out and then turned them over to a typist. Blau interprets the difference in report-writing practice according to the relative degree of confidence one has in his ability. Highly competent investigators felt confident and were therefore free to dictate reports and make the occasional mistake or to hesitate in the course of their dictation. Less competent investigators did not have the confidence to hesitate in dictation and felt embarrassed at the prospect of appearing unsure of themselves in the eyes of secretaries whose status was lower than their own. A secondary meaning of this difference in report-writing practice is related to establishing the competence and hence relative status of investigators. To be sure, competence was established in ways more fundamental than how a person prepared his reports. Yet report-writing practices came to be associated with competence established in many other ways. In this sense, the use of stenographers became symbolic of competence and status.

Persons as objects are, of course, fundamental to our study of group behavior. For the moment, however, we are concerned with how persons take on symbolic significance relevant to the definition of the situation.

For purposes of discussion, let us imagine a newly formed group which is meeting for the first time. In a matter of a few minutes, the members will have absorbed a series of cues "given off" by other members consciously and unconsciously. Moreover, cues would symbolize how persons wanted to be perceived and the kinds of positions and roles they expected to fulfill in the group.

Cues can be divided into three main classes: (1) primary attributes, (2) secondary attributes, and (3) verbal. Let us examine each class in turn.

---

[32] Peter M. Blau, *The Dynamics of Bureaucracy*, pp. 128–129.

*Primary attributes* of persons as objects in a group consist of visible status factors over which the individual has no control. The most crucial of these are age and sex.[33]   The significance of these primary attributes is in their fundamental tie to human development on the one hand and to the culture on the other hand.   Persons progress through life developing and changing in their biological, cognitive, and emotional capacities.   The behavior expected of a person relates closely to his age and sex.   Presumably the role expectations must be in harmony with the general conditions associated with his particular age and sex.   Society could not long persist, for example, if parents did not care for their young, or if the sexes did not reproduce.   There are, of course, wide ranges of permissible behavior within the age and sex differentiations.   But limits and potentialities exist and thereby act as cues governing how persons will establish relationships.

Two important normative prescriptions surrounding age and sex differences are as follows.

1. Younger persons should show deference and respect toward older persons.   (The model for the old-young relationship is to be found in that of the parent-child and teacher-student.)

2. Men should take aggressive-active roles.   Women should take submissive-passive roles.   (The model for the male-female relationship is based initially on biological differences and requirements for success-ful sexual relationships.   Although we have ample evidence of role reversals, that is, aggressive-active women and submissive-passive men, this does not negate what is a general prescription in society.)

Age and sex are not the only primary status attributes attached to a person as object.   But these serve to illustrate how visible status symbols act as forces in establishing a definition of the situation.

The *secondary attributes* act in much the same way as the primary attributes of age and sex.   Secondary attributes consist of status factors as symbols of a position and role but, unlike the primary attributes, they are not obvious.   The person must present these secondary attributes for them to serve as cues.

Secondary attributes include such status factors as education, ethnic and religious background, socio-economic class, occupation, marital status, place of birth (i.e., urban, rural), and others.   These status factors are converted into cues in the course of interaction.   Dress, posture, the way a person talks, and what he says communicate the cues which, in turn, begin to set forth how people expect to be per-ceived and how they expect to relate to others.

[33] Talcott Parsons, "Age and Sex in the Social Structure of the United States," *American Sociological Review*, October 1942, pp. 604–616.

For purposes of illustrating some of the ways the secondary attributes are communicated, let us examine part of a transcript taken from the first meeting of a training group. The members were enrolled in a human relations course in which part of the experience involved working in a "free-floating" group where the data resulting from the interaction became the subject of analysis. During the course of the first meeting the members decided that each person should introduce himself to the group. The group members were between 30 and 35 years of age and all were male.

PERSON A: Well, all right, I work for IBM and am married. Live and work close to New York City. I have been with IBM for almost ten years and I worked all the way up from manager to clerk. I started out as a clerk-typist in San Francisco, Los Angeles, and New York. I've worked in clerical, administrative, sales, and most recently in the financial area of the business so the job position shown on the sheet is not correct any more. So I had a smattering of a lot of things. I went to school in California, high school and college, and majored in psychology, if you can forgive that, and so I didn't have any business background and one of the reasons I liked the course so much was the fact that I could get some good business background other than what I acquired working for one company and possibly the reason I want to know more about you fellows is because I only have worked for one company. I don't know, maybe everybody is in the same boat. I had never worked for any other company and I'm sure that there are a lot of things that we should be doing that others are doing and I want to find out. That's about it for me.

PERSON B: Well, it sounds like we should have compared notes before we sat side by side here. I've worked with only one company. Of course, as you see my name is _____ and I am married with four children. I've worked for Scott Paper Company for the past decade following graduation from the University of Delaware where I majored in psychology (*participants laugh*) and have worked with Scott in the manufacturing capacity, quality control, and subsequently in personnel work of a line nature and then into manpower development and recruitment and college relations and am now manager of the corporate staff personnel division for the corporation. So I am here in much the same way you are to broaden my scope in this activity and understanding.

PERSON C: I also work for IBM. This has not been the only company, but it has been the company for the last nine almost ten years. I graduated in electrical engineering and went to work for the past eight and a half years in what is known as an electrical analysis laboratory which is concerned about the development and analysis of _____ reliability. From there I went to work setting up what was known as a memory technology group, that is to develop memories for systems for computers and within the recent week I had the whole job of standard tempo drills, which includes memories, occupies circuits and so on. I'm married and have six children. I had no interest in coming to Harvard Business School. As a matter of fact I was somewhat opposed to it because I was more interested in engineering and less in management. I didn't have a closed mind about coming.

PERSON D: I've been with the National City Bank for eleven years and I served in practically every portion of the bank. In the last three years I've been concentrating on research and development, computers and new machines and so forth. Basically I'm an operations man. Wife, two children and I was very happy to come to Harvard. I've been up for two years and I've been unable to get away.

PERSON E: I'm with the Bell Systems, an affiliate company of the AT & T, which happens to be an Illinois company. I've unfortunately had no college education. I spent half of my life with the Systems. I'm thirty-four and I've had seventeen years. I started at the bottom and have gone through various phases of the business installation and right on through construction work and on up into installation engineering, seven years, and two years of personnel work and I'm now currently in engineering in charge of a good size exchange outside of the city of Chicago with about 100,000–150,000 telephones and the latest cross-wire dial equipment and several hundred people. I'm married and have three children and was very glad to be able to come to Harvard to express myself and to learn what I could learn.

It is interesting in reviewing what each of the five men said about themselves to note the recurrence of emphasis on their company, their occupations, work experience, educational background including college attended, marital status, and what they, in general, hoped to get from the course. Each member in turn gave cues to establish himself with the slowly emerging identity of the group. Those who reported they majored in psychology, for example, later became important contenders for leadership in the group and presented the longest and more detailed introductions of themselves. We could go into a more detailed analysis of how persons in the group presented the cues we are calling secondary status attributes, but the examples illustrate sufficiently the importance attached to these attributes in the evolution of a group identity.

*Verbal* cues, as a third class of symbols, are to be differentiated from the secondary attributes, also communicated verbally, since cues concerning how people expect to be accepted in a group are not entirely based on status factors. Expected relationships are based also on what persons perceive as likely to occur to them as well as what they find psychologically comfortable.

Based on past experience, a person may expect to take a leadership role in a group. He communicates this expectation subtly, but nevertheless clearly, or he may expect to be rejected and treated with hostility based on his past experience and his motivation. He may wish for a dependency relationship—to have someone look after him. Or, he may wish to be a figure in the group who looks after other people. The motivations underlying the expected and desired positions in the group will be considered in a later chapter where we discuss role development and role patterns in groups. For the time being, we need only to recognize how verbal communications cue group members on the more subtle motivating aspects of interpersonal relationships. An example taken from taped recordings of a training group meeting will serve to illustrate the point.

At the first meeting, Person 1 in the group initiated the discussion following the trainer's brief introduction with this statement:

PERSON 1: I guess the most natural thing to talk about and bring up are your own problems and have somebody else solve them.

PERSON 2: Let's hear yours.

PERSON 1: (continues) Well I can do this but there are a lot of problems. *Some of them I wouldn't want to bring up.* Let me say that a typical thing we see around us all the time is people who are being lost by technology. That is, ten, fifteen years ago, they started into business and were doing very well. For some reason or other they either didn't work hard enough or just couldn't keep up. Technology kept changing so they were no longer in the stream of things. These people had been in the business for a long time. Just what do you do with them? [*Appealing to the group.*]

Symbolically, Person 1 was talking of lost people; people without a place or who are rejected. The idea that he was talking perhaps about himself in this group and or other groups was communicated by the affect-laden, "Some of [the problems] I wouldn't want to bring up."

Shortly after he completed his statement, another member symbolically displaced Person 1 by bringing up his own examples of "technological change in industry." Person 1 withdrew and when he re-entered the discussion later in the meeting, it was to attack angrily a member who came from India and was dominating the discussion with his descriptions of the plight of people in underdeveloped countries.

Later, when Person 1 introduced himself to the group, following the ritual described above, he indicated that he was an engineer, who was not particularly interested in management, an area of expressed interest of other group members. He said also that he did not want to come to the course, but that he had been sent by the management of his company.  He communicated, in other words, rejection of the group, perhaps just as he had experienced rejection earlier in the group meeting and perhaps in other experiences in his life.

## Membership and the Definition of the Situation

So far we have discussed three elements of group identity: (1) the location of the group in time and space; (2) the expectations of role taking and affect in anticipation of the group situation; (3) the symbols activated inside the group, including the importance attached to things and persons as objects.  As a final aspect of group identity, we shall consider the concept of membership in a group.

The formal memberships of work groups usually are assigned according to the requirements of the over-all organization.  Assigned membership, however, should not be confused with actual membership in a social-psychological sense.  Who is "in or out," accepted or rejected, is an integral part of the identity of the group and conditions behavior and attitudes of members.  Two examples taken from field studies of groups will illustrate the relationship between membership and group identity.

The first illustration is taken from a study of a group of workers in a factory reported by Zaleznik, Christensen, and Roethlisberger in *The Motivation, Productivity, and Satisfaction of Workers: A Prediction Study*.[34]

The group of workers reported in this study were employed in a medium-sized factory located in one of the large cities of the United States.  Their department employed about 50 persons, both men and women.  Most of the workers had lived all their lives in the city.  The city had as its dominant ethnic group a large population of Irish Catholics and the majority of workers came from this background.

In analyzing patterns of behavior in the group the researchers found that most activities and relationships tended to follow the customary ways of acting found in the culture from which these workers came.  Male and female, old and young, whether engaged in work or play, defined their activities according to the ethos of the urban Irish Catholic.

In analyzing degrees of group acceptance, the single most important criterion for predicting the well-accepted member of the group was his or her ethnic-religious background.  The Irish workers "belonged"; the non-Irish were excluded or at best tolerated.  The way

[34] Zaleznik, Christensen, and Roethlisberger, *op. cit.*

behavior and lines of membership evolved in the group was not a conscious product of the group. Instead the identity of the group in its reproduction of the Irish-Catholic community within the plant represented the acting out of forces long familiar and acceptable to the dominant members in the department. This presistence and carry-over of patterns of behavior learned in the past attests, of course, to the idea that the identity of new social situations is likely to lean heavily on the identity established in earlier social experience. In other words, the identity that groups establish in the "here and now" is *determined* by a set of forces of which the culture is but one. In the next section of this chapter we shall examine the determinants more fully.

The second example of the relationship between membership and group identity is taken from Whyte's study of the Norton Street Gang reported in *Street Corner Society*.[35] The Norton Street Gang was a group organized spontaneously as one of many autonomous groups in a slum district of a large city. Most of the group members were well into their twenties and past the age when a corner group is ordinarily an important center for the social life of a male. The impact of the depression, however, in part delayed the progress of the young members beyond adolescent patterns of the street corner gang. Membership in the group developed around prior associations with Doc and with one of his lieutenants. The crucial requirements for membership were residence in the district, Italian ethnic background, and no aspirations for mobility. Group members expected to remain part of the Cornerville slum and acted accordingly.

In contrast, another group centered in the same locale formed around Chick Morelli. Members of this gang had been raised in Cornerville, and were also of Italian ethnic background. The crucial differences between Morelli's and Doc's gangs lay in the level of aspiration of its members. Persons who belonged to Morelli's group were socially mobile. They were college students and hoped to advance socially and economically beyond the level of achievement of their parents.

The style of life, or the favored activities of the two groups, reflected the crucial differences in the definition of who was "in" or "out" of either of these two groups. Doc's boys gambled, bowled, discussed girls not as possible objects for marriage but for their immediate availability. Their more serious activities (serious defined in the terms of the wider culture) centered on local ward politics. Even here, however, political activity was important in providing

[35] William Foote Whyte, *Street Corner Society*.

opportunities for jobs, favors, and small sums of money, commodities important in the group's life.

Attempts to alter the mode of group activity and in turn possibly to change the membership were made by the settlement house workers who themselves had middle-class backgrounds and values different from the members of the Nortons.   Needless to say, their attempts met with little success.

The style of life of Chick Morelli's gang with its membership defined in terms of mobility aspirations resembled the middle-class culture.   Members had discussions, read books, and dated girls who were serious possibilities as marital partners.   The language was "refined," and characteristic of college boys.

Belonging to either the Norton gang or Chick Morelli's gang created an unconscious commitment to accept and perpetuate a mode of activity that in our terms added up to the group identity.   A change in aspiration would have required leaving the group and altering one's behavior more in conformity with the requirements of members of some other group whose identity embodied the new values and aspirations.

## DETERMINANTS OF GROUP IDENTITY

Let us now turn to three main classes of determinants of group identity: (1) the culture, (2) the group purpose, and (3) the identification with the leader.

### The Culture

In the preceding discussion of the elements in the definition of a situation, we placed much stress on the importance of behavior patterns learned in the past as the material out of which the present or "here and now" in a group emerges.   Bringing the past into the present is another way of introducing "culture" into the consideration of group identity.   Man's strongest tendency is to repeat in the present the behavior that he found relevant in similar situations in the past. This tendency to repeat is both a strength and a weakness.   Repetition reflects learning under conditions where the behavior was adaptive or rewarding.   Repetition can also reflect maladaptiveness under conditions where the behavior had proven costly or nonrewarding in the past.

The term culture is used by anthropologists to denote the study of the total life as it affects individuals in a society.   Kluckhohn states: "By 'culture' anthropology means the total way of life of a people, the social legacy the individual acquires from his group."[36]

[36] Clyde Kluckholn, *Mirror for Man.*

To this definition of culture, we should add the social legacy the individual *brings* to his group. In modern societies, unlike the primitive societies, individuals enter and leave many groups in the course of a lifetime. Culture is an abstraction referring to the inter-related behavioral modes the individual learns as a member of a particular society and that he carries with him into new societies and groups in which he interacts:

Culture is a way of thinking, feeling, believing. It is the group's knowledge stored up (in memories of men; in books and objects) for future use. We study the products of this "mental" activity: the overt behavior, the speech and gestures and activities of people, and their tangible results such as tools, houses, cornfields, and what not. It has been customary in lists of "culture traits" to include such things as watches or lawbooks. This is a convenient way of thinking about them, but in the solution of any important problem we must remember that they, in themselves, are nothing but metal, paper, and ink. What is important is that some men know how to make them, others set a value on them, are unhappy without them, direct their activities in relation to them, or disregard them.

It is only a helpful shorthand when we say, "The cultural patterns of the Zulu were resistant to Christianization." In the directly observable world of course, it was individual Zulus who resisted. Nevertheless, if we do not forget that we are speaking at a high level of abstraction, it is justifiable to speak of culture as a cause. One may compare the practice of saying "syphilis caused the extinction of the native population of the island." Was it "syphilis" or "syphilitic germs" or "human beings who were carriers of syphilis?"

. . .

Since culture is an abstraction, it is important not to confuse culture with society. A "society" refers to a group of people who interact more with each other than they do with other individuals and who cooperate with each other for the attainment of certain ends. You can see and indeed count the individuals who make up a society. A "culture" refers to the distinctive ways of life of such a group of people . . . .

A culture is learned by individuals as the result of belonging to some particular group, and it constitutes that part of learned behavior which is shared with others. It is our social legacy, as contrasted with our organic heredity. It is one of the important factors which permits us to live together in an organized society, giving us ready-made solutions to our problems, helping us to predict the behavior of others, and permitting others to know what to expect of us.[37]

The experiences of individuals in and through a culture determine member behavior in groups. At the same time, groups create new forms of behavior that over time result in cultural change. We cannot, therefore, be completely deterministic; otherwise it would be

*Ibid.*, pp. 24–25, 27.

difficult to account for change in individuals, groups, and society as a whole.

All the elements of group identity are culturally derived. The fact is, however, that no two individuals experience a culture in quite the same way. Nor are cultural experiences alike. The United States, for example, is a pluralistic society in which regional, ethnic, and socio-economic class differences permit variations in style of life and in sets of values.

In his chapter entitled "An Anthropologist Looks at the United States"[38] Kluckhohn discusses both the common as well as the diverse-elements in the American culture. Starting with the transcending themes, he lists some important elements:

(1) Faith in the rational—the belief that action guided by reason will result in a good society. This belief underlies the emphasis on education for all.

(2) A need for moralistic rationalization—"No people moralizes as much as we do. The actual pursuit of power, prestige, and pleasure for their own sakes must be disguised (if public approval is to be obtained) as action for a moral purpose or as later justified by 'good works.' Conversely, a contemplative life tends to be considered idleness."[39]

(3) An optimistic conviction that rational effort counts—"The American mother offers her love to her child on the condition of his fulfilling certain performance standards. No conversational bromides are more characteristically American than, 'Let's get going'; 'Do something'; 'Something can be done about it.' . . . The dominant American reaction is still—against the perspective of other cultures—that this is a world in which effort triumphs."[40]

(4) Romantic individualism—"Americans are not merely optimistic believers that 'work counts.' Their creed insists that anyone, anywhere in the social structure can and should make the effort! Moreover they like to think of the world as 'man-controlled.' This view about the nature of life is thus intimately linked with that conception of the individual's place in society which may be called 'romantic individualism.' . . . To this day, Americans hate 'being told what to do.' They have always distrusted strong government. The social roles most frequently jibed at in comic strips are those that interfere with the freedom of others: the dog-catcher, the truant officer, the female social climber (Mrs. Jiggs) who forces her husband and family to give up their habitual satisfactions. 'My rights' is one of the commonest phrases in the American language. This historically conditioned attitude toward authority is constantly reinforced by

[38] *Ibid.*, pp. 175–200.
[39] *Ibid.*, p. 178
[40] *Ibid.*, p. 179.

child-training patterns. The son must 'go further' than his father and revolt against the father in adolescence is expected."[41]

(5) The cult of the common man—". . . Americans are characteristically more interested in equality than in liberty. 'I'm as good as the next man' seems at first a contradiction of the American emphasis upon success and individual achievement within a competitive system. It is true that there are relatively few places at the top in a social pyramid— *at any one time*. But the American faith that 'there is always another chance' has its basis in the historical facts of social mobility and the fluidity (at least in the past) of our economic structure. 'If at first you don't succeed try, try again.' The American also feels that if he himself does not 'get a break' he has a prospect of vicarious achievement through his children."[42]

"The cult of the average man means conformity to the standards of the current majority. . . . But . . . the American is not a passive automaton submitting to cultural compulsives like European provincials. The American voluntarily and consciously seeks to be like others of his age and sex—without in any way becoming an anonymous atom in the social molecule . . .

"Because of the cult of the average man, superficial intimacy is easy in America. People of every social class can talk on common topics in a way that is not so easy in Europe where life is based more on repetition of patterns of early family routines that are differentiated by class. However, American friendships tend to be casual and transitory."[43]

(6) High valuation of change—which is ordinarily taken to mean progress—"thanks to our expanding economy and to national folk lore created by various historical accidents, the nineteenth century faith in 'progress' became entrenched in the United States as nowhere else. . . . There are, to be sure, wide disparities in American hospitality to change. We take pride in national change but are, on the whole, more hostile than contemporary Europeans to changes in our institutions (say the constitution or the free enterprise system). . . . American attitudes toward change make generational conflicts more serious. These very generational conflicts, however, make certain types of social change possible. As Mead points out, children can be more 'successful' than their parents, hence 'better.' "[44]

(7) The conscious quest for pleasure—"Americans publicly state that having a good time is an important part of life and admit to craving 'something new and exciting.' In terms of this ideology we have created Hollywood, our Forest of Arden type of college life, our National Parks, Monuments and Forests. Leaders of our entertainment industry are the

---

[41] *Ibid.*, p. 179.
[42] *Ibid.*, pp. 179–180.
[43] *Ibid.*, p. 181.
[44] *Ibid.*, p. 182.

best paid men and women in the United States.  In 1947 the American
people spent nearly twenty billion dollars for alcoholic beverages, theatre
and movie tickets, tobacco, cosmetics and jewelry.  We spend as much
for moving pictures as for churches, more for beauty shops than for
social services.  However, because of the Puritan tradition of 'work for
work's sake,' this devotion to recreation and material pleasure is often
accompanied by a sense of guilt—another instance of the bipolarity of
many features of similar culture.  The pleasure principle attains its fullest
development in American youth culture.  Youth is the hero of the
American dream.  Most especially, the young girl ready for marriage
is the cynosure of American society."[45]

These seven themes of American culture deal with the transcending
aspects of American experience.  They do not discuss, however, the
variations and alternatives based on regional and ethnic differences.
When we speak of the American culture, we are really dealing with
transcending values that bind together specific subcultures with their
own enduring patterns.  A person raised in Boston's Irish community,
or Detroit's Polish community known as Hamtramck, or in the
prosperous Yankee suburbs of Philadelphia known as the Main Line,
could expect substantial variations in the social conditioning provided
by each of these distinctive subcultures.

Florence Kluckhohn clarifies the dimensions along which subcultures
differ.[46]  The conceptual scheme she presents is based on the following premise: "There is a limited number of basic behavior problems
for which all people at all times and in all places must find some
solution."[47]  She lists five such human problems:[48]

(1) What are the *innate predispositions* of man?  (Basic human
nature.)
(2) What is the relation of *man to nature?*
(3) What is the significant *time* dimension?
(4) What is the valued *personality type?*
(5) What is the dominant modality of the *relationship of man to
other men?*

Taking these five basic human problems and considering the range of
solutions, she develops a scheme based on cultural variability for com-

[45] *Ibid.*, pp. 182–183.
[46] Florence Kluckhohn, "Dominant and Variant Value Orientations" in Clyde
Kluckhohn, Henry A. Murray and David M. Schneider, *Personality in Nature,
Society, and Culture,* pp. 342–357.
[47] *Ibid.*, p. 346.
[48] *Ibid.*, p. 346.

paring sets of values. As a culture develops its particular solutions to these five human problems, it provides a set of value in which members are conditioned and that governs their perceptions. The following table shows the range of solutions to the problems stated above.[49]

*Human Problems and Type Solutions*

| Basic Human Problems | Type Solutions | | |
|---|---|---|---|
| 1. Innate predispositions: | Evil (mutable or immutable) | Neither good nor bad (mutable or immutable) | Good (mutable or immutable) |
| 2. Man's relation to nature: | Man subjugated to nature | Man in nature | Man over nature |
| 3. Time dimension: | Past | Present | Future |
| 4. Valued personality' type: | Being | Being in becoming | Doing |
| 5. Modality of relation-ship: | Lineal | Collateral | Individualistic |

Cultures vary in their basic view of man and his motivations defining him as evil (the Puritan view), neither good nor bad, (a "psychological" view), or as good (an optimistic or idealized view). Within any category cultures can also vary in their view of the changeability of man.

A fatalistic attitude characteristic of many groups low in socioeconomic status in the United States sees man as completely determined by nature, over which he has no control. In contrast, man as a *determiner* is characteristic of the American middle class which sees man as capable of controlling nature.

Time variations also differ among cultural subgroups. Many persons in working classes are oriented toward the present and *immediate* gratifications. The modern business executive in line with the middle-class heritage of this group stresses the future.

The valued personality types in certain subgroups may stress "being," or are closely related to the present. The "doing" approach is closely related to the future—binding present desires for future gratifications. This approach is also associated with "man over nature" and the capacity to *control* events rather than being controlled by them.

Differing modalities or relationship are stressed in particular subcultures. The lineal is traditional and hierarchical, stressing age and

[49] *Ibid.*, p. 346.

differences of generation which persist over time.  Collateral relationships stress peer and group relationships.  The individualistic modality stresses the person and resembles the "inner directed" type characterized by Reisman in *The Lonely Crowd*.[50]

Florence Kluckhohn's conceptual scheme permits careful descriptions of how cultural patterns influence individuals in different ways.  In the study of group relationships, we must be alert to the effect of varying values and perceptions of events, based on cultural conditioning, on the relationships within groups.  We can take as a working hypothesis the concept that group relationships will be defined in terms of the past cultural experiences of the individuals.  The emerging group identity generally will resemble the shared patterns taken from the cultural experiences of group members.  In heterogeneous groups, the process of developing a definition of the situation becomes more difficult simply because cultural backgrounds and the resulting sets of values of members will differ.  Until there is some shared definition we would expect to find considerable conflict and reevaluation taking place in the minds of members, particularly where group members are highly motivated to remain in the group and overt withdrawal is not easy.

## Group Purpose

A second set of forces determining the identity of a group stems from the purpose of the group.  A work group, like many factory groups with a fixed purpose set externally, will develop relationships by superimposing its cultural outlooks on the purpose of the group.  For work groups whose purpose is somewhat more vague, such as committee and task groups dealing with abstract problems, the purpose of the group as it defines the status and role of members is less rigid.  Here emergent behavior is potentially more significant than past behavioral patterns.  The tendency for members to seek definitions of the situation quickly leads them, however, to use group purpose to create structures that may be psychologically comfortable, but of negative value in the work of the group.  We tend to find, therefore, a persistent tendency to detail tasks beyond the limits we consider functional, to invoke authority to define the group in terms of its task, particularly in those cases where ambiguity is intolerable to individual group members.  Although group purpose as a means for defining the situation is readily available we need to recognize the

[50] David Riesman et al., *The Lonely Crowd: A Study of the Changing American Society*.

dangers inherent in overly rapid definition and over delineation of tasks especially where group tasks demand creative solutions.

## Identification with the Leader

Later we shall deal at length with leadership and group behavior. At this point we shall limit ourselves to considering the leader as a determinant of group identity.

The classic statement of the function of the leader in the emotional life of the group has been presented by Freud in *Group Psychology and the Analysis of the Ego*.[51]  Freud viewed the leader as the source of cohesion among group members in their common identification with him.  Their emotional attachment to him becomes a common element in the psychic experience of group members and becomes the source of the tie binding members to each other.  The withdrawal of the leader figures, or the abandonment of him as an object for identification, breaks the attachment among group members and induces anxiety. Where group members succeed in identifying with their leader, their loyalties toward him, as well as their fear of him, serve to establish the definition of the situation.  All relationships are bound in his activity.  His values are adopted by group members and his behavior becomes unconsciously, at least, a model for them.

It is not uncommon to find groups being referred to by the name of their leader.  The Norton Street Gang in Whyte's *Street Corner Society* was known as Doc's gang.  Whyte showed how the group remained immobile until Doc appeared on the scene.  Although Doc did not initiate all activity for the group, his approval of action was required.

The powerful position of a leader figure is, of course, subject to abuse.  It can result in extreme dependency on the part of members as well as chaotic behavior when the leader's position is challenged or undermined.

Freud's position should not be taken to define how a leader should behave in a group or his role in its identity.  But the position of the leader does indicate the exceptionally crucial problem leadership poses in and for groups.  We shall deal with this problem at length in a later chapter.

## HIERARCHICAL AND EGALITARIAN GROUP IDENTITIES

This chapter has been concerned with the analysis of group identity as an elementary process in group development.  We have considered

---

[51] Sigmund Freud, *Group Psychology and the Analysis of the Ego*.

the elements and determinants of group identity analytically. Now we turn to a synthesis by describing two opposing ideal types of group identity: (1) the hierarchial group and (2) the egalitarian group. As ideal types, these hypothetical groups will not be found in real life as pure cases. Our position, however, is that the hierarchical and egalitarian types represent opposing trends in group identity.

The hierarchical group is built upon a system of status and ranking that tends to *differentiate* the position of members. The contributions of members are weighted unequally and the rewards distributed to members are similarly apportioned unequally. The source of the hierarchy, that is its particular determinants, need not concern us here. As long as a group supports differentiation, we find the emergence of a hierarchy.

Any hierarchical group reserves for its members different ranges of acceptable behavior. Those who rank high in the group's evaluation scheme are permitted a greater range of performance than lower-ranking members. But the existence of the hierarchy is not necessarily fixed. Mobility exists to the extent that changes in a member's activity result in changes in his rank.

Any group that depends for its existence on adaptation to its environment will tend to differentiate among members and become hierarchical. This differentiation and the resulting hierarchy apply to groups ranging from the family to the work group. Failure to differentiate and to free members to vary their contributions, one from the other, all too frequently results in maladaptation.

The limit to the hierarchical group lies in the very fact that it centers around a ranking and authority system that distinguishes members and gives them varying degrees of autonomy and control. Differentiation when carried too far—that is, where the costs of control outweigh the rewards received from group participation—results in loss of cohesion and becomes a threat to the maintenance of the group. Under these circumstances, a reversing trend takes place in the direction of the egalitarian group.

The egalitarian group follows the principles of peer relationships or fraternity. The maintenance and integration of the group are important goals and efforts to reduce differentiation are paramount in the life of the group. The model of the egalitarian group is to be found among adolescents. They are in revolt from authority and act out this revolt by creating the leaderless group where all members are equal. Attempts of members to impose their will on others are beaten down. Many times, the existence of the *idea* of egalitarianism is more important than the fact. It is difficult if not impossible to avoid differentiation. But as long as members believe and conceive of the group in terms of egalitarian ideals, deviations can be sustained. The universal code against "bossiness," "pushing people around," and "acting like you're better than others" is sustained even though to an observer there may be differences in authority and control.

Egalitarian groups stress friendliness and being helpful. They shun evaluation, especially the type that becomes visible and potentially distinguishes members.

Egalitarianism induces group integration, but may not be too fruitful for adapting to the immediate situation. Under conditions where a group, for its survival, depends on achieving a purpose in relation to its environment, the processes of differentiation begin to take hold.

The two types of groups, the hierarchical and egalitarian, represent trends or modalities in group development. During one phase in the life of a group, strong forces toward differentiation take hold in reaching certain goals. As a counterbalancing force, trends toward equality may show themselves to reintegrate the group. As we shall see later we frequently find members of a group who are catalytic or focal in one or the other of the trends. The differentiation process may be set off by a task leader, the integration process by a social leader.[52]

The emotional tone of the group shifts with its modalities. During its hierarchical or differentiating mode, aggression may dominate; during its integration mode, affection and intimacy may dominate.

It is possible and found frequently in real life that the two modes come in conflict. The formation of subgroups whose latent expressions are those of differentiation or integration enter into hostile instead of collaborative relationships. Such group conflicts are difficult to resolve, especially since many personality issues find expression in hierarchical or the egalitarian ideals. The individual who favors distance and a task orientation may oppose and disapprove of another individual for whom any condition but warmth and intimacy is intolerable.

The two types of groups and their existence as alternating modes in a single group are intended as diagnostic aids in the understanding of problems in group identity. In subsequent chapters, we shall return to the theme of hierarchy and egalitarianism in the assessment of role patterns in groups, the dynamics of leadership, and change.

[52] Robert F. Bales, *Interaction Process Analysis*.

*Chapter Three*

# Processes in Group Development: Structure

THE preceding chapter centered on the initial crisis in group development in which an appropriate definition of the situation is achieved, providing identity for the group. The identity of the group exists only in the minds of its members and cannot be observed. This does not imply that identity in the attitudes of group members is unimportant. On the contrary, its absence results in anxiety and threatens the survival of the group.

A second crisis in group process is the development of a structure. Like identity, structure is achieved through time. Somewhat similarly, it represents a crystallization of an originally unrelated membership into a whole. Unlike identity, its existence is not confined to the minds of group members. Rather, group structure represents the relatively more observable part of group interaction. It may be thought of as the discernible properties of groups to which members attach important meaning.

This chapter describes and analyzes various properties of group structure and how these may be observed and measured. Throughout the chapter, we shall emphasize measurement, applying various techniques and their underlying theories as they have emerged in relatively recent social science research. In defining group structure we shall stress two factors: (1) the existence of a pattern of stable relationships, and (2) the conditions that give rise to the pattern. In discussing the properties of group structure, we shall analyze five elements: patterns of authority and influence, communication-interaction networks, subgrouping, patterns of role taking, and patterns of interpersonal sentiment.

## DEFINITION OF GROUP STRUCTURE

As we have noted group structure refers to the properties of a group which result from the *interaction* of its members and which can be *observed* and *measured*. Structure does not depend for its definition on the states of mind of the participating members; the existence of structural characteristics in a group is a fact of the group as a whole.

Since group structure results from the interaction of members, it becomes the *representable* and *recurrent* pattern of relationships through which group activities are channeled. At the same time the structure of the group expresses the condition of the group, that is, *how* members relate to one another.

### Structure as the Pattern of Relationships

In the analysis of group behavior, the student starts with an assumption: that group relationships tend to develop, over time, into stable forms which recur in the course of interaction. This assumption can be likened to the premise, underlying all science, of the existence of an order in nature.[1]

Human events are not chaotic or subject to random fluctuation. The forces underlying human behavior operate continuously and make circumstances repeatable and reproducible. Even the changes that occur in groups result from the existence of forces within the structure. Although we are ignorant of how to conceptualize and measure these forces adequately, we assume they exist. The philosophy of determinism in science which we allude to briefly here should not be mistaken for the specious argument that if something is *determined* it cannot be changed. Man discovers how phenomena in nature *are* determined so that he may change them in desired directions.

Group structure results from forces acting on the group in a manner such that a pattern of stable relationships exists through which group activity is channeled. Any event in a group will be directed through the structure born of previous group interaction. The direction of the interaction maintains the structure and preconditions how future interaction in the group will take place. The most basic element of group life is the fact that who participates with whom in a particular sequence, and the defined consequences, is *probably* the process to be repeated in continuing interaction.

### Structure as an Expression of Condition

The condition of the group, a result of interaction, consists of the sentiments associated with the stable relationships constituting group

[1] Alfred North Whitehead, *Science and the Modern World*, p. 4.

structures. The significant sentiments include those pertaining to member *influence* on each other, to *liking* or *hostility* among members, and to the formation of subgroups within the group.

For purposes of exploration, we assume that relations among group members reach stable forms of interaction. This is determined by the forces acting on them as persons or on the group. Members have varying degress of awareness of these forces. However great the awareness, the stable patterns of interaction reflect the forces that influence the members to produce the behavior out of which structure emerges.

## STRUCTURAL PROPERTIES OF GROUPS

Let us begin our description and analysis of the structural properties of groups by following an inductive procedure. We shall take a classic example of a particular group structure and from it conceptualize about group structure in general. The example is drawn from William F. Whyte's *Street Corner Society*. Whyte presents the following diagram to summarize the relationships he observed among the members of the Norton Street Gang.[2]

[2] William Foote Whyte, *Street Corner Society*, p. 13.

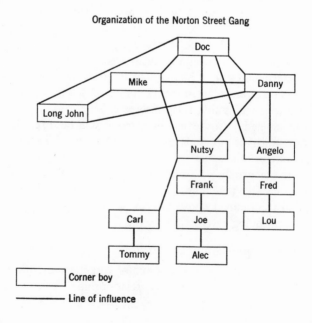

Organization of the Norton Street Gang

In examining this diagram we must remember that it represents a reality far more complex than suggested by the drawing.  In fact, the usefulness of the diagrammatic scheme stems from its simplification of reality and ordering of many facts about the group.  What, then, has Whyte attempted to represent about relationships?  Three elements of group structure are incorporated in his diagram:

1. The boxes representing members of the group are placed on a vertical scale.  This scale indicates relative *authority, power, or influence* of group members.  We can take the diagram to mean that Doc has the greatest amount of authority in the group and that Alec has the least.  The evidence for placement of members on the scale is taken from the minute interactions of members.  Whyte observed, for example, that whenever Doc suggested or approved of an activity, the group members tended to engage in the activity.  If Alec initiated an activity, which was not likely, members would not undertake it.

2. The lines connecting the boxes indicate the *channels of communication or interaction* in the group.  From observation, Whyte concluded that Doc interacted most frequently with Mike and Danny, his lieutenants, and also with Long John.  Interaction between Doc and his lieutenants would proceed from member to member as indicated by the lines linking boxes.  The diagram shows the number of steps required to complete a communication from either the top or the bottom of the hierarchy.  The diagram also shows the strategic position of lieutenants.  In contrast, Long John represented a "dead end" in the communication network since he, according to the diagram, did not continue the chain.  The representation of a communication network should not be mistaken to mean that interaction proceeded only as indicated in the diagram.  The diagram indicates only the dominant pattern.  When group members interacted in set events the actual lines of communication would be considerably more involved than a single network would seem to indicate.[3]

3. The diagram of the Norton Street Gang also suggests the pattern of *subgrouping*.  A subgroup is basically a cluster of members who interact more with one another than with other members of the group.  Whyte's diagram suggests the following subgroups: (*a*) a threesome consisting of Angelo, Fred, and Lou; (*b*) a foursome made up of

[3] Interaction takes place within events.  The events involving three or more persons within the same time space are called "set" events.  When only two persons act within a time space, the interaction is referred to as a "pair" event.  See Eliot D. Chapple and Conrad M. Arensberg, *Measuring Human Relations: An Introduction to the Study of the Interactions of Individuals*, pp. 53–55.

Nutsy, Frank, Joe, and Alec; (c) a pairing of Carl and Tommy; and
(d) the subgroup composed of the leader and his lieutenants.

Despite the fact that Whyte succeeded in describing a great deal
about the structure of the Norton Street Gang, there were at least
two additional elements of group structure not readily evident from
the preceding diagram, but nevertheless important in the analysis of
group properties: (1) *the patterns of role-taking* in group behavior,
and (2) *the patterns of sentiment,* or put more simply, the friendships
and antagonisms existing in the group. With the addition of these
two dimensions to group structure, we have a list of five that will
be discussed in turn.

## Patterns of Authority and Influence

Despite ideological leanings toward equality, groups evolve a
structure of authority based on the differences in which members'
actions are able to influence those of the others. Influence is derived
from and exercised through the behavioral and attitudinal patterns of
members. One individual influences another to the extent that he
changes the other's behavior and attitudes. When Person A behaves
in such a manner (verbally and nonverbally) that he alters the behavior
or thinking of Person B, we can say that Person A has influenced
Person B.[4]

Although it is difficult to get precise measurements of relative degrees of influence in a group, a rough index may be found in the
ratio of a person's successful influence acts compared with his influence
attempts. This ratio is expressed as follows:

$$\text{Index of Influence} = \frac{\text{Successful influence acts}}{\text{Number of influence attempts}}$$

The index recognizes that attempts at influence are probably much
more frequent than successful influence acts. Authority can be said
to exist only insofar as attempts at influence succeed.

An influence act can vary considerably in content and behavioral
style. In content, an influence act can include a direct order, a suggestion, or a request. The behavioral styles can range from highly
autocratic influence attempts to relatively permissive attempts in which
gestures, tone of voice, and expressions become meaningful. Despite
the importance of differences in style, for purposes of the analysis of
the authority structure, we should recognize the similarity between
an order and a suggestion and between a forceful and a permissive

[4] George C. Homans, *Social Behavior,* Chapter V.

way of exerting influence: in all cases, influence seeks to alter behavior or attitudes.

The structure of authority in a group represents the differences in influence among members' actions. This differential has been represented by the index described above. An important aspect of authority not indicated thus far is the tendency over time for authority to transfer itself from an act of behavior to a person. When an individual is referred to as an "authority figure" he must at one point have been successful in influence attempts. But the term authority figure further implies that the person has potential influence, and that group members expect that his future acts will influence behavior. When the authority figure does in fact act, the expectation gives his behavior such an authority that his potential influence is translated into a reality.

An essential ingredient of authority and its transfer from behavior to a person is that influence must produce reward. We shall have considerably more to say about reward presently. Here we seek only to suggest how authority transfers from behavior to a person and ultimately back again to the behavior of the so-called authority figure. The experiencing of some reward for influence or being influenced results in the expectancy that future attempts at influence will be at least as rewarding. The rewards range anywhere from helping, learning, friendship, or emotional support, to goal achievement, which result in more tangible reward. But whatever the reward, some gain must be forthcoming for influence to take place. We can say, therefore, that the amount of authority of group members varies directly with the degree to which their past successful influence acts have been rewarding to others. In a later chapter on leadership, we shall consider the sources of authority which become invested in a person. For the moment, we limit ourselves to the definition and measurement of authority as a structural property of a group.

## Communication-Interaction Network

The communication-interaction network can be considered the most significant structural property of a group. Fundamental to any description of group behavior is the statement of how interaction develops. The pattern of interaction in a group is also the most readily observable phenomenon of group life, which has led some investigators to base their entire conceptual apparatus on it.[5]

[5] Eliot D. Chapple and Leonard R. Sayles, *The Measure of Management: Designing Organizations for Human Effectiveness.*

The consideration of interaction as a structural property requires separation of three elements: (1) the element of quantification; (2) the element of direction; and (3) the element of content.

The quantitative element of interaction derives from the fact that groups operate in time and space. Members of a group share this time-space but not equally. Common-sense observations of groups at work usually show that one member participates more than another. The hierarchy of participation is closely related to the relative degree of influence or authority allocated to members. The typical relationship is summarized in the following graph.

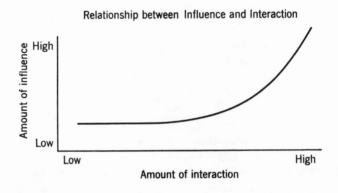

Relationship between Influence and Interaction

Members high in influence participate more than members low in influence. The high influence figures are encouraged to participate while the low influence figures are generally discouraged. The relationship between authority-influence and interaction will be clarified in this and succeeding chapters in reviewing studies showing how behavior is converted into actual influence.

The directional element in interaction is based on the process of selectivity in communication. Individuals tend to interact with members who have somewhat higher status than themselves and also with members with whom they share values. The outcome of this selectivity is a network that typifies who speaks to whom and who follows whom in the communication activity.

The element of content in interaction is based on variation in the material which persons communicate and the emotional quality of the communication. Content of interaction can be related to the task of the group and to the social and emotional aspects of group development.  A system of analyzing interaction content, developed by Bales, is based on the distinction between the task or instrumental acts and the emotional or expressive acts.  This system will be discussed in detail farther along in the chapter.  But one finding derived from Bales' work is germane at this point.  In his study of hundreds of problem-solving groups the following distribution in the content of interaction became apparent.[6]

| Conduct | Percentage of Acts |
| --- | --- |
| Instrumental-initiating acts | 50.0% |
| Instrumental-asking acts | 12.5 |
| Positive emotion acts | 25.0 |
| Negative emotion acts | 12.5 |

These percentages are approximate for a large number of problem-solving groups.  Although most groups conform to this profile, one would expect significant variations depending on the type of group, the relative cohesion of the group, and the length of time the group continues to exist.  Certainly comparative analyses of groups could be made using the content of interaction as a variable.

Let us now consider various ways of measuring interaction and how indices can be derived for purposes of description and analysis. Keeping in mind the threefold division of interaction as a quantitative variable with direction and content, we shall present and discuss several measures.

1. THE FREQUENCY OF INTERACTION

The frequency of interaction attempts to measure the rates at which individual members in a group participate.  This rate can be expressed as follows:

$$\frac{\text{Number of interactions}}{\text{Time}}$$

This ratio serves as an index of frequency.

In some cases, interaction cannot be observed over a sustained period, as where the group operates in a setting in which continuous observation is impossible.[7]  Here we sample interaction by scanning the setting at regular intervals and noting who is talking with whom

[6] Robert F. Bales, "The Equilibrium Problem in Small Groups," in *Small Groups*, Hare, Borgotta and Bales, Eds., pp. 424–456.
[7] A. Zaleznik, C. R. Christensen, and F. J. Roethlisberger, *The Motivation, Productivity and Satisfaction of Workers: A Prediction Study*, p. 21.

without regard for content.   The index of frequency for each participant may then be stated:

$$\frac{\text{Number of interactions}}{\text{Number of observations}}$$

From frequency, expressed either as a ratio of interactions to time
or as an average for a series of observations, there can be derived a
rank order for the interactions of group members.   This ranking
becomes a measure for a variable that can be related to other variables,
as we shall see.

### 2. DURATION OF INTERACTION

The measure of frequency does not indicate how long a person
occupies the time-space of the group.   Amount of participation can
serve this purpose.   A record of the total amount of time each
person participates during the observation periods helps to rank the
order of the different durations of interaction.   Closely related to the
frequency index, the index of interaction duration can be constructed
as follows:

$$\frac{\text{Total time duration of participation}}{\text{The number of participations}}$$

Individuals scoring high on this index occupy group attention longer
during each participation than those who score low.

Another way of expressing the index of duration was developed by
Moment in his study of discussion groups in problem-solving sessions.[8]
Meetings were recorded on tape.   Each meeting was arbitrarily
divided into 12-second intervals, and records were developed showing
who talked during each interval.   An index was then devised, indicating the degree to which individual members tended to interact in
short sequences, sharing the time of the group with others, as contrasted with "speechmakers" who tended to continue an interaction
over a relatively sustained time period.   This was an index of "interval
sharing."

### 3. INITIATION AND RECEIPT OF INTERACTION

The measurement of the initiation of interaction attempts to discern consistencies in group performances as to the degree to which
individual members initiate or receive interaction.   As one would
expect, the findings show that generally persons high in influence
initiate interaction more than those low in influence, and that they have

_____

[8] David Moment and Abraham Zaleznik, *Role Development and Interpersonal
Competence,* pp. 198–200.

a larger proportion of initiations to receipts. The index of initiation can be expressed by the ratio:

$$\frac{\text{Total initiations of interaction}}{\text{Total receipts}}$$

This index is valuable in the observation of work groups that operate in a sustained setting. It is less valuable in discussion-type groups since it is difficult to judge where an initiation takes place.[9]

## 4. RANGE OF INTERACTION

The term range, as a measure of interaction, refers to the number of persons in a group with whom an individual interacts. Individuals vary considerably in their tendency to develop relationships. Some members restrict their interaction to a few persons while other members tend to develop relatively widespread relationships. Usually persons high in influence have a larger range of interaction than individuals low in influence. The measure of range consists simply of the number of *different* persons with whom an individual interacts without regard for content or duration. It is especially important for the index of range to include members outside the group. It is characteristic of authority figures in groups that they interact with outsiders more frequently than do other group members. This characteristic would become evident in the range of interaction.

## 5. THE INTERACTION MATRIX

Studies of interaction patterns in groups can be extremely revealing if they include records of "who-to-whom" communications. This record is closely related to the initiation-receipt distinction, but when the data are summarized in the form of an interaction matrix, the group pattern of interaction appears. A matrix consists of a table with group members listed in similar order in both rows and columns. The resulting grid permits easy summary of the flow of communications. The rows indicate from whom interaction flows and the columns indicate to whom it flows.

Bales presents a matrix of interaction that is constructed as a composite of 18 problem-solving sessions of six-man groups. These groups met for one session each and among the records kept were the flow of interaction from person to person in the group. The interaction matrix is reproduced below.[10]

[9] George C. Homans, "The Cash Posters: A Study of a Group of Working Girls," *American Sociological Review*, Vol. 19, No. 6, December 1954, pp. 724–735.

[10] Robert F. Bales, *op. cit.*, p. 438.

*Interaction Matrix—Six-Man Group Composite*

| Rank Order of Person Originating Act | Speaking to Individuals of Each Rank: | | | | | | Total to Individual | To Group as a Whole | Total Initiated |
|---|---|---|---|---|---|---|---|---|---|
| | 1 | 2 | 3 | 4 | 5 | 6 | | | |
| 1 | | 1,238 | 961 | 545 | 445 | 317 | 3,506 | 5,661 | 9,167 |
| 2 | 1,748 | | 443 | 310 | 175 | 102 | 2,778 | 1,211 | 3,989 |
| 3 | 1,371 | 415 | | 305 | 125 | 69 | 2,285 | 742 | 3,027 |
| 4 | 952 | 310 | 282 | | 83 | 49 | 1,676 | 676 | 2,352 |
| 5 | 662 | 224 | 144 | 83 | | 28 | 1,141 | 443 | 1,584 |
| 6 | 470 | 126 | 114 | 65 | 44 | | 819 | 373 | 1,192 |
| Total Received | 5,203 | 2,313 | 1,944 | 1,308 | 872 | 565 | 12,205 | 9,106 | 21,311 |

The list of group members on the above matrix is in order of number of initiations.[11] This order, however, correlates highly with prestige, or status and influence, attributed to these members.[12] The matrix indicates that for the group as a whole, 58 per cent of the interactions are directed to individuals and 42 per cent to the group. All members except the highest ranking member direct interactions to individuals more than they do to the group as a whole. The reverse is true for the highest ranking members. This suggests that the member with the greatest influence and authority directs his interaction to the group as a way of maintaining his influence. The group members direct interaction to individuals as a way of establishing and seeking support.

In the martix the ranking by number of interactions received consistently corresponds directly to the ranking by number of interactions initiated. The direction of interaction similarly corresponds to the originating rank of the recipient. Each member tends to direct his

[11] In comparing the findings of small group researches, there will be apparent inconsistencies in some of the findings that are attributable to differences in methodology or to differences resulting from the study of natural versus experimental groups. For example, in discussing the Norton Street gang we indicated that influence proceeded from individual to individual in the form of a hierarchy. In the experimental findings we indicated that the high-influence members directed comments to the group as a whole more than other members. If we were to have available quantified interaction data on the Nortons during "set" events, or those instances where the group meets as a whole, we would expect to find Doc addressing the total group more frequently than did the other members.

[12] Robert F. Bales, *op. cit.*, p. 439.

interactions upward and the numbers of his interactions are divided among recipients in the order of their originating rank.

## Subgrouping

Subgrouping as a structural dimension is closely related to repeated interactions and is a result of them. Most groups tend over time to develop a series of subgroups consisting of two or more members. These subgroup members tend to interact more with one another than with other members of the group. The psychological basis for subgrouping lies in the inclination of group members to seek support from others who have attributes and values in common with them. Such attributes may differ from those common to the whole group or may simply represent varying degrees of the latter. Once these factors in common are identified, interaction tends to be directed to subgroup members in some internally consistent way.

The simplest procedure for identifying subgroups is to note the patterns of participation. In groups in a relatively fixed setting, records of recurrent activities and participating members will confirm the existence of subgroupings. In problem-solving or discussion groups, identification of subgroupings is more difficult. Here the directions of interactions from member to member must be followed and the patterns of support or rejection of ideas noted. Frequently decision-making points disclose subgroupings, particularly where decisions are reached by vote. Members who tend to vote alike repeatedly can be thought of as an operating subgroup.

An illustration of the procedure for identifying subgroups is taken from Zaleznik's *Worker Satisfaction and Development*. The group under study consisted of 14 workers in a machine shop. There were several recurrent activities with fairly fixed memberships. The activity matrix taken from this study illustrates how subgroups may be identified.[13]

The five recurrent activities are listed in the columns and members in the rows. An X in the cell designates a member's participation in a particular activity. The matrix arrangement is reached by trial and error, the aim being to arrange rows and columns to indicate the clusters or subgroups. The matrix indicates the existence of two main subgroups in the machine shop. These subgroups are blocked in on the matrix for purposes of emphasis. The subgroups consisting of Steve, Marc, Larry, Luke, Paul, Nick, Hal, and Bruce was organized around coffee-drinking and card-playing activities during rest periods.

[13] A. Zaleznik, *Worker Satisfaction and Development*, p. 73.

Activity Matrix

| | Card-playing subgroup | | Helping and lending tools | Conversation subgroup | |
|---|---|---|---|---|---|
| | Coffee A | Bid whist* | | Coffee B | Conversation |
| Steve | x | x | | | |
| Marc | x | x | x | | |
| Larry | x | x | x | | |
| Luke | x | x | x | | |
| Paul | x | x | x | | |
| Nick | x | x | x | | |
| Hal | | x | x | | |
| Bruce | | x | x | | |
| Ron | | | x | | |
| Jim | | | x | x | x |
| Vito | | | x | x | x |
| George | | | | x | x |
| Charlie | | | | | x |
| Axel | | | | | |
| Foreman | | | | | |

*No distinction is made between "players" and "observers."

The members of this subgroup had several values in common. They were the younger members of the shop and generally of relatively low job status. The members of the conversation subgroup—Jim, Vito, George, and Charlie—were older and had higher job status as compared with the other subgroup.

The matrix also indicates the link between the subgroups. The activity of helping and lending tools involved more members than any other activity and included members of both subgroups.

Three group members could not be identified with subgroups as such. One was Ron who participated only in the helping activity. Other data indicated he was the group's informal leader and characteristically avoided identification with either subgroup. By not identifying with a subgroup he maintained a potential for leading the total group.[14] Two other persons in the group participated in no activities. Axel was an isolate with high job status. The foreman as formal leader of the group maintained social distance and avoided participation in informal group activities.

[14] A similar finding was reached by A. Zaleznik, C. R. Christensen, and F. J. Roethlisberger in *The Motivation, Productivity and Satisfaction of Workers: A Prediction Study*, p. 163.

The ordering of activities in the form of a matrix provides a useful way of identifying subgroups. The matrix could include a record of votes taken in decision-making groups; it is not restricted to recurrent activities. Careful scrutiny of the attributes of members in the various subgroups, their values and styles of behavior, would indicate the social forces underlying the subgroup formations.

## Patterns of Role Taking

We have so far considered two related elements of group structure: (1) interaction-communication and (2) subgrouping. We turn now to the structural aspects of role taking in groups. A later chapter will deal with role taking from the standpoint of individual motivation and development. Our purpose here is to consider the pattern of role taking as a property of the group. Role taking in this sense is another way of examining the process of interaction since it represents the behavior of group members in interaction.

From the standpoint of the group, role taking represents the performances of individuals that relate to the continuing processes of the group. The concrete forms of role taking are the behavioral acts of individuals. A behavioral act can be thought of as a role in relation to some problem facing the group in the accomplishment of its purpose or in the development of social cohesion.

Over a period of time, the role taking of members tends to develop some stability. When allocated special functions members find past role taking validated. This allocation represents a division of functions among members. A workable role structure exists in a group when the roles taken and allocated fulfill needed functions at the appropriate times and when the members complement rather than compete in their role specializations.

The description and measurement of role taking always entails some conceptual framework for classifying roles and a procedure for analyzing the content of interaction in order to move from observation of concrete behavior to analysis of role taking. There are a number of bases for the analysis of role taking. We shall limit our discussion to two that have proved most meaningful in diagnostic and research work on group behavior. The first has been presented by Benne and Sheats in their paper "Functional Roles of Group Members."[15] The second is that of Bales described in *Interaction Process Analysis*.[16]

[15] Kenneth D. Benne and Paul Sheats, "Functional Roles of Group Members," *Journal of Social Issues*, Vol. IV, No. 2, Spring 1948, pp. 42–47.
[16] Robert F. Bales, *Interaction Process Analysis*, Chapter 2.

Benne and Sheats conceive of two main types of roles necessary to the continuing function of the group: (1) task roles and (2) group building and maintenance roles.

Task roles are behavioral acts related to the direct accomplishment of group purpose. They include the seeking of information, initiating, seeking and giving of opinion, evaluating, and the like, and they are generally applicable in Benne and Sheats' analysis to discussion-type or problem-solving groups. The group building and maintenance roles deal with problems of group integration and social solidarity. They cover such behaviors as encouraging, harmonizing, compromising, and gatekeeping. This final term is perhaps the least clear of all.

Gatekeeping refers to those behaviors that permits members to enter into interaction or that exclude members from interaction. Presumably a nonparticipating member of a group may signal indirectly his desire to interact. A person playing a gatekeeping role might be alert to such overtures and would guide the group action to permit the previously nonparticipating member to interact. Gatekeeping, along with other maintenance roles, seeks to drain off tensions and to reassert group cohesion by limiting and directing conflict which might provoke destructive acts.

Benne and Sheats propose a third set of behavioral acts they term "individual roles." These include such things as aggressing, blocking, seeking recognition, and dominating. Individual roles represent behaviors that are primarily concerned with the inner needs and tensions of the individual and are not addressed to group requirements. It is, of course, difficult to distinguish an individual role, as Benne and Sheats define this term, on the criterion of personal need. All behavior has some inner referent such as the needs of the individual. The point is that the behavior may be inappropriate to the situation. Furthermore, the strength of the need may be the factor distorting the individual's perceptions of the situation and may prevent him from taking more relevant roles.

Bales and his associates present a more fully developed conceptual scheme for the analysis of role taking in groups. Like Benne and Sheats, Bales distinguishes between two main types of acts: (1) the instrumental or task acts and (2) the social-emotional or expressive acts. Groups function in a cyclical fashion. During one phase of the cycle, behaviors may be heavily directed toward accomplishing a purpose—toward tasks. Effective work inevitably creates tensions, especially where the group is concerned with a joint product dependent on the co-ordination of individual contributions. As instrumental behavior persists, tensions mount and must be released. The group may then enter the integrative phase of the cycle where the release of tension and the expression of positive feelings serve to rebuild the group.

The continuing expression of cohesion tends toward the establishment of an equalitarian group culture. If this persists effective work and adaptation to the environment of the group require the performance of instrumental acts to differentiate members. If the strains are so strong that differentiation cannot occur, accomplishment of the group task is imperiled. The competing strains of tensions and positive feelings become the basis for Bales' system of measurement of role-taking in groups.

After much experimentation Bales developed a standardized, highly reliable system of measurement. The basic unit of measurement is an "act" which consists of the

. . . smallest discriminable segment of verbal or nonverbal behavior to which the observer . . . can assign a classification under conditions of continuous serial scoring . . . . Often the unit will be a single sentence expressing or conveying a complete simple thought . . . . Complex sentences always involve more than one score. Dependent clauses are separately scored . . . . As an example of the foregoing points, the following sentence would be analyzed into four units: "This problem we talked about for three hours yesterday/impresses me as very complicated/difficult/and perhaps beyond our power to solve./"

In addition to speech centered around the issue being discussed, interaction includes facial expressions, gestures, bodily attitudes, emotional signs, or nonverbal acts of various kinds, either expressive and nonvocal, or more definitely directed toward other people. These expressions and gestures can be detected by the observer, given an interpretation in terms of the categories, and recorded.[17]

Bales' system for recording performances in interaction is shown in a chart (see p. 82) indicating how categories of observation are related to his underlying conceptual scheme.[18]

The method for scoring requires the observer to note the interaction from "who-to-whom" and to interpret the acts in the interaction according to their content, following the 12 categories in the system. Bennis and Shepard in a paper entitled "Group Observation"[19] illustrate the scoring method. We reproduce below the excerpt of behavior

[17] *Ibid.*, pp. 37–38.
[18] *Ibid.*, p. 9.
[19] Warren G. Bennis and Herbert A. Shepard, "Group Observation," abridged in *The Planning of Change*, Warren G. Bennis, Kenneth D. Benne, and Robert Chin, Eds., pp. 743–756.

The System of Categories Used in Observation
and Their Major Relations

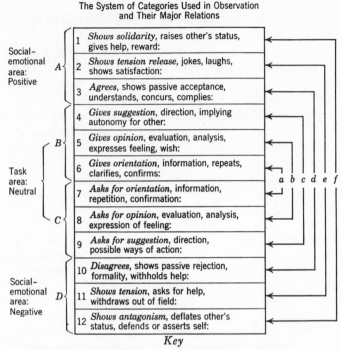

Key

a. *Problems of Communication*     A. *Positive Reactions*
b. *Problems of Evaluation*        B. *Attempted Answers*
c. *Problems of Control*           C. *Questions*
d. *Problems of Decision*          D. *Negative Reactions*
e. *Problems of Tension Reduction*
f. *Problems of Reintegration*

and the scoring information and show in the following table (see p. 84) the procedure for entering scores.

BILL(speaker 1, to group): In other words, we all want to share in leadership and that is what Gordon, for instance, thinks is the most efficient way for a group to act. (6, 1-0) In other words, it's real unanimous approval rather than an authoritarian mind. (6, 1-0) It seems to me that we have been destroying leadership that we needed in the past, that is for the last three or four meetings we have been doing that. (5, 1-0) And I wonder if that is really happening, if we are trying to accomplish this diffused leadership. (7, 1-0)

JIM(speaker 2): This diffused leadership (6, 2-1), I don't think it's a question of efficiency. (10, 2-1) I think it's a question of satisfaction. (5, 2-1) As far as efficiency, if someone says "You do this, that and the other thing," that gets things done faster and it gets more things done. (5, 2-1) But as far as people in the group feeling that they are a part of a decision . . . .  (5, 2–1)

BILL: If something doesn't last, it's not efficient; that's the only way I look at it.  (10, 1-2) In other words, unless it's a real approval . . . (6, 1-2).

JIM: In other words, efficiency . . . (6, 2-1)

BILL: . . . or participation, I don't consider it to be efficient.    (10, 1-2)

JIM: You mean efficiency doesn't mean getting things done and the quantity . . . (6, 2-1)

BILL: Yeah, (3, 1-2) well, I didn't mean that (6, 1-2) that's a good point.  (1, 1-2)

JIM: You had the idea of satisfaction.  (6, 2-1)

BILL: Right.  (3, 1-2) That's probably a better way of putting that.[20] (1, 1-2)


With this brief description of the Bales' method of scoring the content of acts in group interaction, let us return to the more theoretical aspects of role taking in groups.

Both the Benne and Sheats' and the Bales' concepts of role are based on the assumption of changing group problems in which various roles become more or less crucial.   During "task" phases role taking related to the problems of the group tasks are paramount.   During the phase of reaffirmation of group solidarity, social and emotionally expressive roles are required.   A workable structure of roles is achieved when group members can behave in ways appropriate to the immediate issues facing the group.   A preponderance of task role taking would suggest a weak role structure because of the absence of social-emotional behaviors.   The assumption is that the shift from task-instrumental to social-emotional problems is to be expected in the group process.   The absence of appropriate role taking weakens the total structure of the group.

All this raises the question of whether the role structure in a group with its task-emotional balance implies that members take on role specializations.   Role specialization means that specific group members take on their particular specialty when the group problems require it.   The center of active role taking shifts as the problem of the group shifts.

Role specialization is to be found in the structure of many families.[21]

[20] Ibid., p. 752.

[21] Talcott Parsons and Robert F. Bales, Family, Socialization, and Interaction Process Analyis, pp. 307–315.

## Scoring of Interaction[21]

| | | | | | | | | | | | | | | | | |
|---|---|---|---|---|---|---|---|---|---|---|---|---|---|---|---|---|
| 1 | Shows *solidarity*, raises other's status, gives help, reward: | | | | | | | | | | | | | | | 1–2 |
| 2 | Shows *tension release*, jokes, laughs, shows satisfaction: | | | | | | | | | | | | | | | |
| 3 | *Agrees*, shows passive acceptance, understands, concurs, complies: | | | | | | | | | | | | 1–2 | | | |
| 4 | *Gives suggestions*, direction, implying autonomy for other: | | | | | | | | | | | | | | | |
| 5 | *Gives opinion*, evaluation, analysis, expresses feeling, wish: | | | 1–0 | 2–1 | 2–1 2–1 2–1 | | | | | | | | | 1–2 | 2–1 |
| 6 | *Gives orientation*, information, repeats, clarifies, confirms: | 1–0 1–0 | | | 2–1 | | | 1–2 2–1 | 2–1 | | 1–2 | | | | |
| 7 | *Asks for orientation*, information repetition, confirmation: | | 1–0 | | | | | | | | | | | | | |
| 8 | *Asks for opinion*, evaluation analysis, express feeling: | | | | | | | | | | | | | | | |
| 9 | *Asks for suggestion*, direction possible ways of action: | | | | | | | | | | | | | | | |
| 10 | *Disagrees*, shows passive rejection, formality, withholds help: | | | | 2–1 | | 1–2 | | 1–2 | | | | | | | |
| 11 | *Shows tension*, asks for help, withdraws "out of field": | | | | | | | | | | | | | | | |
| 12 | *Shows antagonism*, deflates other's status, defends or asserts self: | | | | | | | | | | | | | | | |

84

[22] Bennis and Shepard, op. cit., p. 750.

The family, as all groups, faces instrumental and emotional problems. The structure of the family may be such that father is the task specialist for the group's adaptation to its environment (the external relations). Father may also be the social-emotional specialist vis-à-vis daughters. Mother, on the other hand, may be the task specialist with respect to the tasks internal to the group: caring for infants, preparing meals, maintaining the house. She may also take on the expressive roles, especially in relation to sons. The case of infant care would be a good example of role taking that combines both task and expressive roles. Nursing babies, for example, combines providing food and love, both important in the nurture of the young.

The family as an example of role taking can be elaborated further in the types of role taking among the siblings of various ages and in the role taking of members of the wider family—uncles, aunts, grandparents, and so forth. An illuminating discussion of role structure in kinship systems is provided by Homans in his analysis, based on the work of Raymond Firth, of the Tikopean family.[23] Here the crucial issues, as in all groups, are the allocations of roles where the relationships vary in the degree to which one person exercises authority over another. In the primitive group discussed by Homans, when a relationship between members in a group is based on authority or control (for example, the father-son relationship) its emotional quality will be one of distance, reserve, and respect. Other relationships are then required: for mother's brother and son a more equalitarian and friendly mode of behavior is permitted and, in fact, encouraged to offset the emotional quality of the father-son relationship.

A different model or role taking is that of flexible role-taking. Here the same underlying concept of cyclical movement from instrumental to social-emotional problems holds. The difference, however, is in the flexibility in role taking. Instead of individual members specializing in one role, every group member is capable of varying his role in accordance with the requirements of group process, thereby enhancing group and individual effectiveness.

There is little research evidence from which to derive definitive conclusions about the specialization and flexible models. Some experimental evidence which we shall consider later seems to indicate tendencies toward specialization.[24] Where the consensus among mem-

[23] George C. Homans, *The Human Group*, Chapter 9.
[24] Philip E. Slater, "Role Differentiation" in *Small Groups*, Hare, Borgotta and Bales, Eds., pp. 498–515.

bers in their perceptions of the performances of others is low there seems to be relatively low satisfaction compared with groups in which the consensus in perceptions of member role performance is high.[25] Other evidence would indicate that role flexibility in a given group is possible for some individuals who are able to combine task and expressive roles.[26] Looking at individual development and learning, role flexibility would seem to derive from an enriched personality, as well as contribute to it.

Studies which have analyzed different types of group activities in natural settings indicate specialization as the mode. It is not uncommon to find, for example, division of role taking between formal and informal leaders.[27] The formal leader takes over the task roles, particularly those involving evaluation. One type of informal leader takes over task roles when helping and nonevaluation are important. Another type of informal leader takes over the ceremonial aspects of group life that are concerned indirectly at least with maintaining group cohesion.

As we can see, the analysis of role taking as an element of group structure leads into many interesting and significant issues of group development and individual behavior in a group setting. We shall resume this discussion in Chapter Five (The Management of Affect and Work) and also in Part Two when we become concerned with the determinants of individual role performance in groups.

The description of role taking in group behavior depends on some method of observation of interaction content. Bales' method, besides providing an important research tool, also helps sharpen skills in group observation, a skill important in membership.

## Patterns of Interpersonal Sentiment

A fifth way of describing the structural properties of groups is the pattern of interpersonal sentiment that develops among members. The term sentiment refers generally to internal states of individual group members. A sentiment cannot be observed directly since it exists in the inner or private world of the person as a feeling toward a person, an attitude toward an event, or a value toward an idea. But these

[25] Ibid.

[26] Moment and Zaleznik, op. cit., pp. 37–45. See, also, Edgar F. Borgotta, Arthur S. Couch, and Robert F. Bales, "Some Findings Relevant to the Great Man Theory of Leadership," in Small Groups, Hare, Borgotta, and Bales, Eds., pp. 568–574.

[27] A. Zaleznik, op. cit. See also Peter M. Blau, The Dynamics of Bureaucracy, Part II.

sentiments underlie behavior—what a person says and does—which can be observed. From our observations we then make inferences about the sentiments of the individual. Sometimes an individual attempts in his behavior to describe directly his feeling; at other times his behavior leaves much to be inferred.

Despite the difficulties we experience in making accurate inferences of emotional states of individuals, sentiment plays a very important part in group processes. In Chapter Five we shall concentrate on emotional aspects of group activity. Our more limited purpose now is to consider *interpersonal sentiments*—what they are, how they are measured, and how they converge in time into a consistent pattern which becomes a significant structural component, or property, of groups.

Much of the understanding of interpersonal sentiments in groups is an outgrowth of the work of J. L. Moreno and his associate, Helen Jennings. Moreno and his colleagues studied small groups using as their main variable the patterns of positive and negative feelings of group members toward one another. They described their work as studies in "sociometry," which means the measurement of the network of attraction among group members. The principal researches of these investigators took place in a New York State correctional school for girls. The girls lived in small cottages with a housemother. Moreno set out to discover the effects on behavior of groups formed according to existing patterns of attraction between individuals. The researchers administered a simple questionnaire that asked subjects to indicate by name which of the girls they would like *to work with*, which *to live with*, and which *to spend their leisure time with*. The working, living, and leisure time choices were separate sociometric questions.

The theory underlying the sociometric test begins with the premise that one of the main processes in interpersonal relations has to do with choice—the selection and rejection of individuals as objects for relationships of particular kinds. This premise has, of course, been substantiated by the fruitfulness of sociometric analysis of group behavior. But the premise is also substantiated by commonplace observation.

The observation of groups of children reveals most clearly the importance of the choice process. As children play games, the members chosen and left out reflect the value attached to individuals for a particular activity. In sports, for example, members vie to be on the same team with the children who appear to be most competent. In selecting guests to be invited to a birthday party, the child reflects degrees of attraction to the various youngsters in his circle of friends. The choices for inclusion and exclusion in the many activities of children clearly mark the bases of attraction and rejection in interpersonal relationships.

This process seen so clearly in groups of children also applies to groups of adults in work activities. Persons actively seek out others with whom relationships are desired. They avoid ties with individuals who, for whatever reasons, appear unattractive. The basic premise of sociometry, therefore, can be accepted for the study of work groups despite the fact that choice and rejection may be expressed in subtle ways.

The main question open for exploration is how choices are formed. Do individuals, for example, make global choices or do they carefully differentiate in their selections? Moreno and Jennings' work indicates that choices differ depending on whether the issue is the selection of a *work partner* or a *leisure time partner*.[28] This distinction was elaborated in Jennings' concepts of the "socio" group and the "psyche" group. The "socio" group is the work group where accomplishment of task becomes the main criterion for interpersonal associations. Presumably members tend to work with those persons who appear relevant to the task of the group based on perceived levels of competence or skill. The "psyche" group, on the other hand, is the friendship group where the interpersonal ties are based more on associations with persons with whom one has values in common. In the friendship group, one seeks to avoid competition and to be able "to let his hair down." An individual selects particular persons with whom he is willing to abandon the masks that take some energy to maintain in work interactions.[29] The distinction implicit in the comparison of

[28] Jacob L. Moreno, *Who Shall Survive?: Foundations of Sociometry, Group Psychotherapy and Sociodrama.* See, also, Helen H. Jennings, *Leadership and Isolation: A Study of Personality in Inter-personal Relations,* p. 278.

[29] The features underlying the distinctions between "psyche" and "social" groups resemble, but are not identical with, those of "Gemeinschaft" and "Gesellschaft." These latter concepts are discussed by Loomis as follows:

Certain patterns of social relations tend to predominate in underdeveloped, nonindustrialized societies; others appear and have primacy in highly technological societies. This theme which, as Sorokin has noted, has been a major preoccupation of philosophers and scholars through the ages, was observed and explored with insightful clarity by Ferdinand Toennies [in *Community and Society—Gemeinschaft and Gesellschaft*]. In the nineteenth and early twentieth centuries, Toennies designated as Gemeinschaft the "social order which—being based upon consensus of wills—rests on harmony and is developed and enabled by folk ways, mores, and religion;" he gave the name Gesellschaft to the "order which—being based upon a union of rational wills—rests on convention and agreement, is safeguarded by political legislation, and finds its ideological justification in public opinion." In the work teams,

the work and the friendship groups is the presence or absence of evaluations of competence and competition. The work relationship implies evaluation of skills and contributions to the task, and competing for influence. The friendship relationship, although having its own evaluations, implies the absence of active evaluations of abilities as well as avoidance of competitive behaviors.

The tendency toward differentiation between work associations and friends exists even within work groups. Studies of choice in work groups show relatively low correlations between the selection of persons who are valued for task contribution and those who are valued as possible leisure time or friendship companions. The choices of persons one would like to know socially correlate reasonably well with the perceptions of individuals as "congenial" persons, but poorly with the perceptions of individuals as leaders in the group tasks. These relationships are indicated in a correlation matrix taken from a study by Moment and Zaleznik of behavior in problem-solving groups.[30]

### Degrees of Association Among Choices

|  | Leadership | Chosen High On Like to "Work With" | Like to "Know Socially" |
|---|---|---|---|
| Chosen high on { Ideas | .50 | .26 | .00 |
| Guidance | .42 | .05 | .14 |
| Congeniality | .17 | .00 | .20 |

The matrix generally confirms the direction of the findings by Bales and associates on perceptions and choices in problem-solving groups.[31]

The process of choice in group relationships is largely perceptual. Individual group members observe behavior and characteristics of other members, and in relation to their own motivations are attracted to or withdrawn from others. Perception is a complex psychological process, and we cannot undertake here an analysis of its sources and dynamics. Our main object is to indicate the dimensions along which perceptual sets are established in the sociometry of groups. The basis

families, communities, societies and other collectivities which are Gemeinschaft-like, human relations are ends in themselves; intimacy and sentiment are expected among the actors; norms are traditional . . . . In the Gesellschaft-like associations, relations and actors are used instrumentally; interaction is impersonal and affectively neutral; actors are not known in their entirety to each other; and norms are rational rather than traditional.

Charles P. Loomis, *Social Systems: Essays on Their Persistence and Change*, pp. 57, 59. Loomis' footnotes have been omitted.

[30] Moment and Zaleznik, *op. cit.*, p. 34.

[31] Philip E. Slater, *op. cit.*

of choices appears to be the individual's perceptions of others in terms of their desirability as work associates on the one hand and as friends on the other hand.

A variation of the sociometric test commonly found in research on small problem-solving groups is a post meeting reaction questionnaire (PMRQ). A sample PMRQ form is reproduced below.

## POST MEETING REACTION QUESTIONNAIRE[32]

The questions in the following questionnaire refer to the group discussion experience in which you have just participated. We would like your opinions on the participation of yourself and the other members during this meeting. Since this material is for research purposes only, and is completely confidential, please indicate your opinions as honestly as you can.

Eight of the questions refer to all of the people who took part in the discussion, including yourself. In order to help you answer the questions, we have prepared a list of the names of the participants on a card attached to this questionnaire. Following each question, there appears a series of numbered scales. If you line up the index mark on the name card with the index marks to the left of the scales, you will find that a scale will line up following each name. Each question will instruct you on how to use the scales.

We hope that you will find these questions interesting and will answer them as frankly as you can, taking about 15 minutes.

1. In many groups there are some people who, regardless of how effective their opinions are in the group, seem to have exceptionally *good ideas*. They frequently show a very good grasp of the problem and clear reasoning ability.

Will you please indicate your impression of the *quality* of the ideas that each person, including yourself, presented at the meeting by circling the appropriate number on the scales that will appear to the right of each name on the name card after you line it up with the index marks. One (1) indicates "not so good" on ideas; 8 indicates "outstanding" ideas.

|  | Not So Good Ideas | | | | | | | Outstanding Ideas |
|---|---|---|---|---|---|---|---|---|
| (Index) | 1 | 2 | 3 | 4 | 5 | 6 | 7 | 8 |
| (Mark) | 1 | 2 | 3 | 4 | 5 | 6 | 7 | 8 |

2. In many groups there are some people who seem to *guide the discussion* and keep it moving effectively. They try to keep the group on track, suggest procedures to follow, tie together the members' contributions, and act as moderators.

[32] Moment and Zaleznik, *op. cit.*, pp. 219–221.

Will you please indicate your impression of how much each person, including yourself, did in the meeting to *guide the discussion* by circling the appropriate numbers on the scales. . . .

|  | Not Much Guidance |  |  |  |  |  | Very Much Guidance |  |
|---|---|---|---|---|---|---|---|---|
| (Index) _____ | 1 | 2 | 3 | 4 | 5 | 6 | 7 | 8 |
| (Mark) | | | | | | | | |

3. In many groups there are some people who, regardless of how good their ideas are, seem to have strong *influence* on the final group decision. Their ideas and opinions seem to be accepted by the group without much question.

Will you please indicate your impression of the *amount of influence* that each person, including yourself, had in the meeting by circling the appropriate numbers on the scales. . . .

|  | Not Much Influence |  |  |  |  |  | Very Influential |  |
|---|---|---|---|---|---|---|---|---|
| (Index) _____ | 1 | 2 | 3 | 4 | 5 | 6 | 7 | 8 |
| (Mark) | | | | | | | | |

4. In many groups some people stand out clearly as *leaders*, no matter how one would choose to define leadership.

Will you please indicate your impression of the *leadership* demonstrated by each person at the meeting, including yourself, by circling the appropriate numbers on the scales. . . .

|  | Not Much Leadership |  |  |  |  |  | Outstanding Leader |  |
|---|---|---|---|---|---|---|---|---|
| (Index) _____ | 1 | 2 | 3 | 4 | 5 | 6 | 7 | 8 |
| (Mark) | | | | | | | | |

5. In many groups there are great differences in the amount of *participation* by members. Some people speak more than others.

Will you please indicate your impression of the amount that each person, including yourself, *participated* in the meeting by circling the appropriate numbers on the scales. . . .

|  | Little Participation |  |  |  |  |  | Very Much Participation |  |
|---|---|---|---|---|---|---|---|---|
| (Index) _____ | 1 | 2 | 3 | 4 | 5 | 6 | 7 | 8 |
| (Mark) | | | | | | | | |

6. In many groups there are some people who add to the *congeniality and friendliness* of the meeting. They tend to be well liked by the members because they seem to show consideration for others.

Will you please indicate your impression of the amount that each person, including yourself, added to the *congeniality* of the meeting by circling the appropriate numbers on the scales. . . .

| | Contributed Little to Congeniality | | | | | | | Contributed a Great Deal to Congeniality |
|---|---|---|---|---|---|---|---|---|

(Index) _____     1   2   3   4   5   6   7   8
(Mark)

7. In many groups there are differences in the extent to which the various members *agree or sympathize* with the views of other members. Members tend to agree with some people more than with others.

Will you please indicate the extent to which you *agreed* with each of the other people in the discussion by circling the appropriate numbers on the scales. . . .

| | Disagreed With Him | | | | | | | Agreed With Him |
|---|---|---|---|---|---|---|---|---|

(Index) _____     1   2   3   4   5   6   7   8
(Mark)

8. In many groups there are wide differences in how satisfied each member is with the *group decision* or conclusions. Some members will like it, some will not.

Please indicate how satisfied *you* are with the decision or conclusion reached in this meeting by circling the appropriate number on the following scale.

| Very Dissatisfied | | | | | | | Very Satisfied |
|---|---|---|---|---|---|---|---|

1   2   3   4   5   6   7   8

9. In many groups there are wide differences in how satisfied each member is with the way the group *operates.*

Please indicate how satisfied *you* were with the way this group operated by circling the appropriate number on the following scale.

| Very Dissatisfied | | | | | | | Very Satisfied |
|---|---|---|---|---|---|---|---|

1   2   3   4   5   6   7   8

10. There are sometimes differences between the way people act at meeting and the way they usually act outside the meeting.

Will you please indicate your impression of the extent to which each person's actions during the meeting seemed to be similar to his actions in other situations by circling the appropriate numbers on the scales. Please include yourself. . . .

|  | Very Much Different |  |  |  |  |  |  | Very Similar |  |
|---|---|---|---|---|---|---|---|---|---|

(Index)                          1   2   3   4   5   6   7   8

(Mark)

The questions ask the subjects to name desirable persons in the "work with" and "know socially" categories. They also ask subjects to identify the contributions of other members along the lines of ideas, guidance, and congeniality. The responses represent perceptions of role performances of the type discussed in the preceding sections. These perceptions are based on the attention subjects pay to behavior of others.

In work groups whose individual and group task is essentially manipulative or nonverbal, the sociometric tests can be summarized usefully in the form of a *sociogram* or *matrix* to show the structural subgroupings based on interpersonal sentiment. A sociogram consists of a diagram on which members are placed and lines drawn to designate choices and rejections. A typical sociogram is reproduced below from a study of a group of clerical workers in an accounting office.[33]

Data similar to those used in the sociogram can be presented in the form of a matrix somewhat similar to the activity matrix discussed earlier. A matrix of sociometric choices in the Cash Posters study is shown below.

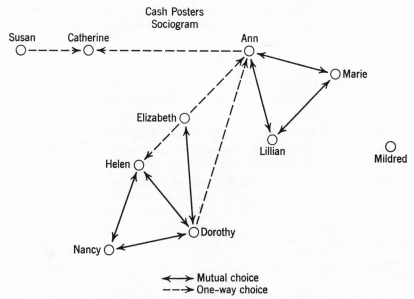

Cash Posters Sociogram

←——→ Mutual choice
- - -→ One-way choice

[33] The sociogram is adapted from George C. Homans, "The Cash Posters," *American Sociological Review*, December 1954, p. 728.

*Cash Posters*
*Matrix of Sociometric Choices*

| Chooser | Nancy | Helen | Dorothy | Eliz. | Ann | Lillian | Marie | Cath. | Susan | Mildred |
|---|---|---|---|---|---|---|---|---|---|---|
| Nancy |  | 1 | 1 |  |  |  |  |  |  |  |
| Helen | 1 |  | 1 |  |  |  |  |  |  |  |
| Dorothy | 1 | 1 |  | 1 | 1 |  |  |  |  |  |
| Elizabeth |  | 1 | 1 |  | 1 |  |  |  |  |  |
| Ann |  |  |  |  |  | 1 | 1 | 1 |  |  |
| Lillian |  |  |  |  | 1 |  | 1 |  |  |  |
| Marie |  |  |  |  | 1 | 1 |  |  |  |  |
| Catherine |  |  |  |  |  |  |  |  |  |  |
| Susan |  |  |  |  |  |  |  | 1 |  |  |
| Mildred |  |  |  |  |  |  |  |  |  |  |

The subgroupings are indicated clearly when the matrix rows and columns are arranged so that members who choose one another appear in adjacent positions. There are mathematical techniques for processing sociometric matrices of large groups. The procedure facilitates identifying subgroups. We shall not discuss the mathematical approach since it is a procedure somewhat more complex than required for our purposes. Readers interested in the matrix analysis of sociometric choice should refer to a paper, "Matrix Analysis of Group Structures," by Festinger, Schachter, and Back.[34]

## SUMMARY

This chapter has presented a discussion of five dimensions of group structure: (1) influence, (2) interaction-communication, (3) subgrouping, (4) role taking, and (5) interpersonal sentiment. Influence as a dimension of group structure refers to the differences in degree of influence exercised by group members or, in other terms, the structure of authority in the group. Influence and authority is exercised in a group through the established network of interaction and communication. The observation of group behavior demonstrates the tendency for interaction to proceed in regular channels. The centers of the communication network in groups are also those persons high in influence and authority.

[34] Leon Festinger, Stanley Schachter, and Kurt Back, "Matrix Analysis of Group Structures," in *The Language of Social Research*, Paul F. Lazarsfeld and Morris Rosenberg, Eds., pp. 358–367. See also John G. Kemeny, J. Laurie Snell, and Gerald L. Thompson, *Introduction to Finite Mathematics*, Chapter VII.

Subgrouping can be considered a separate dimension of group structure insofar as activities and attitudes in groups tend to become standardized with particular parts of the group. In another sense, however, a subgroup can be thought of as a set of group members who interact more frequently with other members of the set than they do with group members outside of the set. Subgrouping as a structural aspect of group development is therefore closely related to interaction. Subgrouping has sometimes been referred to as a clique formation.[35]

A fourth dimension of group structure is the pattern of role taking. Role performance is behavior classified in some systematic way. We followed the division of roles into two main classes: the task-instrumental acts and the emotional-expressive acts. The first class of roles is directed toward the accomplishment of group purpose; the second class is concerned mainly with group maintenance. A third class of roles called "individual" roles is considered relevant to certain personal problems of the individual and irrelevant, if not harmful, to the group development.

The fifth dimension of group structure is the pattern of interpersonal sentiment. This concerns description of the choice process through which members express for one another their liking, friendship, and attraction, on the one hand, and hostility, antagonism, and rejection, on the other. These particular choice or sociometric patterns were discussed in relation to perceptions of members' roles and contributions to group development. In those instances where the roles played by members result in their exercising authority or control over others, the sentiment expressed toward them tends to be one of respect but not warmth. The sentiments of warmth and affection tend to be directed toward those members who take expressive roles and who emphasize equality.

Throughout this chapter we have emphasized methods of measuring and describing group structure. The methodologies have resulted from researches in small group behavior. They are of value also to participants in group activity since training in group observation requires some understanding of the frames of reference underlying the observation.

[35] F. J. Roethlisberger and W. J. Dickson, *Management and the Worker*, Part IV.

*Chapter Four*

# Group Process:
# The Control of Behavior

THE most casual observation of groups indicates the existence of strong mechanisms for controlling the behavior of members. This capacity of groups to direct, limit, and influence what members do gives considerable power to the group setting and to individuals who are at the center of power in the group. The use of this power can have either positive or negative consequences for the individual and society.

Much of the socialization process and the transfer of culture to the young seeks as one important aim the training of the person to govern his behavior according to standards that have their origin in the society and the group. Managing one's instincts, for example, results from acceptance of society's standards and the anticipation of painful outcomes for violation of them. Securing the effort of individuals toward goals considered desirable by society depends in part on group pressures on individuals to adopt these objectives as personal standards. Learning new skills is also supported by group pressures. When an individual sees his support enhanced as he succeeds in mastering new skills, he is generally more highly motivated toward learning. In any organized activity, securing co-operation of members toward the goals of the organization will depend in large part on the direct and indirect operation of group standards on individuals.

This same pervasiveness of group standards can have serious negative effects on the individual and society. Rabble rousers and demagogues utilize group pressures to elicit attitudes and responses they deem desirable. Hitler was a prime example of this phenomenon. Through his personal magnetism, attractive to the German desire for a strong

96

leader figure, through the use of supernationalism, racism, and scape-goating together with allegiances to groups that supported the Nazi ideology, he was able to induce acquiescence to, if not active support of, inhumane practices.

In more recent times, the Chinese Communists have provided an example of systematic use of group pressures to win conversion to their doctrine. Schein reported these practices based on interviews with repatriated prisoners of war following the Korean War.[1] The Chinese captors used their understanding of groups as controlling agents in an attempt to break down systems of belief and attitude. They prevented the formation of spontaneous primary groups which ordinarily serve as instruments for validating and sustaining beliefs of individuals through relationships with fellow group members. By segregating those who adamantly refused to co-operate and by exerting skills in the exposition of their tenets and in the use of group pressures, the Chinese Communists were able to induce a few of this isolated group to accept communist doctrine.

Group standards and forces toward individual conformity to them are as ubiquitous as groups themselves. The strength of groups as controlling agents can operate morally or immorally, in accordance with principles respecting the individual or in denial of the individual and his uniqueness.

In this chapter, we shall analyze the process of social control in groups. We shall investigate the source of control in groups and how controls are established, maintained, and altered. The chapter is divided into three parts: (1) the definition of social control in groups, (2) the elements of social control, and (3) a summary. There can be no more relevant investigation of organizational behavior than studying social control in groups, since much group management revolves around the operation of norms and how they influence the behavior of individual members.

## THE DEFINITION OF SOCIAL CONTROL IN GROUPS

In this section, we shall attempt to do two things. First, we shall define what we mean by social control and its relationship to other aspects of group process. Second, by examining instances of effective and ineffective control, we shall illustrate *how* groups manage to control the behavior of members.

[1] Edgar H. Schein, "The Chinese Indoctrination Program for Prisoners of War: A Study of Attempted Brainwashing," in *Readings in Social Psychology*, Maccoby, Newcomb and Hartley, Eds., pp 311-334.

The term control refers to the operation of constraints that govern what men do. In society as a whole, there are various forms of institutional control. Through the legal apparatus of laws the state makes visible the practices that violate codes of conduct and the consequences that await transgressors. Organized religions establish controls in the sense that they create moral imperatives whose violation will result in generalized painful aftereffects, notably of conscience.

The laws and rules associated with the various institutions of society are agents of control. These formal codes establish standards to govern conduct in society; the institutions also establish and render visible the consequences of violation so that standards can be enforced. Although the formal agents of institutional control are apparent, they depend for their effectiveness on the operation of social control in primary groups. It is this form of control which is the center of interest in this chapter.

Here, we need to emphasize the term *social*. Control in this sense is interpersonal and grows out of the relationships men build with one another. We should also emphasize that control in *primary groups* differs from institutional control in that the standards of behavior in primary groups are invisible and lack codification. The instruments through which standards are enforced are equally invisible since few primary groups have a juridical procedure apart from the rituals implicit in group interaction. Thus, social control in primary groups is informal while in institutions it may be built upon a foundation of formal standards and mechanisms of enforcement.

Yet we should recognize that formal and informal systems of control in society are interdependent. It is especially pertinent to recognize that without control practices in small groups, institutional control could not remain effective.

As George Homans in *The Human Group* puts the case of the relationship between institutional and primary group controls:[2]

A student of social control will go hopelessly wrong if he thinks of it [social control] as always lying in the hands of policemen, district attorneys, judges, and their like. Historically, this kind of control, which we shall call external control, appears late. As societies grow in size, activities like religion, war, and law enforcement are delegated first to individual specialists and then to specialist organizations, but the original basis of control always persists. Many small societies show an admirable obedience to law without having anything like law officers. Even in our own

[2] George C. Homans, *The Human Group*, p. 284.

society, external control is concerned with relatively few, though perhaps important crimes, and in dealing with them, can be effective only when supported by controls other than formal law.  The history of law enforcement, of the Prohibition Amendment, for example, is the history of the degree to which informal controls have backed up, or failed to back up, the formal.

The informal controls to which Homans refers in the preceding quotation are the constraints on behavior exercised in the interpersonal processes of small groups.

In the present study we make a distinction beyond legalistic-formal control, on the one hand, and interpersonal-informal control, on the other.  Interest in informal controls as they operate in interpersonal relationships within primary groups would seem to direct attention to the controlling forces of the group as a whole.  That control, however, is also related to the motivations of the group members as *individuals*.  We are not suggesting that social control resides in some mystical property of a group.  The mechanisms for control are indeed elaborated in the group independent of the individual.  But these mechanisms depend for their effectiveness on the desires of individuals to gratify their needs and avoid punishment.  Thus the effectiveness of the controls also depends in part on the identifications individuals establish with groups and persons so that individual desires can be brought into play.

Since there can be no informal social control without the interpersonal relations in the primary group, and since the nature of group controls rests on psychological forces within the individual, we shall consider both group and individual attributes as they affect the process of social control.

These attributes were observed by Blau in a study of the relative effectiveness of two different types of social control in inducing productivity in work groups.[3]  Blau studied two sections of interviewers in a state employment agency which handled job placements in the textile industry.  The same rules of procedure governed both sections.  Job orders—or openings—received over the phone by individual interviewers were to be noted on a form and filed alphabetically in boxes to be available to all interviewers in a section.  Applicants for jobs were to be interviewed in order of arrival at the agency.  After each applicant had filled out an application form, the interviewer would try to place him by finding a suitable opening and referring him to the appropriate employer.

[3] Peter M. Blau, *The Dynamics of Bureaucracy*, Part I.

Besides rules of procedure, the same official circumstances applied to both sections. Interviewers were under civil service and their advancement was based on annual ratings by their supervisor. Higher administrative officers of the employment agency emphasized productivity among interviewers. Formerly measured by the number of interviews, productivity was now judged by the number of placements. To induce more fruitful interviews, the head of the department had instituted a monthly statistical report covering eight phases, or relationships, of each interviewer's activities, which he circulated among all interviewers.

The patterns of behavior differed between the sections. Section A interviewers were much more competitive with each other. They practiced "hogging" evidenced by the greater degree to which job openings were monopolized by the person who received them, and by the more frequent practice of keeping job orders on their own desks rather than filing them in the boxes. This resulted in Section A interviewers "hopping around" to other desks seeking job orders. In Section B the interviewers not only filed the order more promptly, but also told each other of all the openings they had received and even would bring a job order over to another interviewer who needed that kind of opening for a particular applicant. Section B was also more socially cohesive; four out of the five interviewers in B were always together during the rest periods, whereas none of the seven A interviewers took these rest periods together.

These performances represented differences in standards. In Section A competitive acts were expected and the highest social status was accorded the most competitive member who also made the most placements. An interviewer who took a job order from another desk and filed it in the box jeopardized his social status. In Section B co-operative acts were expected and the person who conducted painstaking interviews but made relatively few placements was considered the best interviewer by other members of the group. The B interviewer who indulged in competitive practices was excluded from the exchange of information and the rest-period gathering.

Underlying these differences in social control, Blau recognized three causes: the supervisor's approach, the historical code of the group, and job security. The supervisor of Section A had relatively little personal contact with the interviewers and was known to rely heavily on the record of placements in making appraisals. The Section B supervisor, new to the job, supervised interviewers directly and, his very first ratings, showed that he did not limit himself to the record but rated his personnel on the over-all quality of their performances.

Blau then described the development of a "professional code" in the B Section:[4]

. . . Three of its present members had joined the section upon being discharged from the Army after the last war, when large numbers of returning veterans needed occupational advice. Counseling and intensive interviewing had therefore been stressed at the time when they, together, received their training under a supervisor who was especially interested in these phases of operations. One of them described this period in the following words: ". . . At that time, the veterans came back, and there was a lot of emphasis on counseling. Nobody asked you how many placements you made, then. The emphasis was on quality, and we consulted with each other all day."
In this situation, the group developed a professional code of its own. It was considered most important to help each client find a job that interested him and to give him all the occupational advice he needed; quick interviews were unacceptable, since they could not meet these objectives. This code condemned the goal of maximizing productivity as interfering with proper service to clients. In effect, this transformed competitive practices from the state of being illegitimate means for desirable ends into illegitimate means for worthless ends.

Section A's history, in contrast, offered no opportunity for the development of a professional code. The A interviewers had received their training individually, prior to the time of emphasis on intensive interviewing of returning veterans, when the agency goal stressed a high number of interviews. Thus, Section A's code stressed production.

Lack of job security, also, made production records important for Section A. Most of its members had originally been appointed to temporary civil service positions during the war and were still subject to layoff if the staff were reduced. In Section B four of its five members held superseniority as veterans and could not be terminated except for cause. Thus, they could more easily afford to ignore the pressures toward competition among group members and induce, instead, pressures toward mutual help.

In comparing the effectiveness of the social controls of the two groups on the basis of group productivity, Blau found that Section B controls led to higher productivity as compared with Section A. Furthermore, the most competitive member of A was its most productive while in B the most competitive member was its least productive. Blau explained this paradox by the fact that anxiety over

[4] *Ibid.,* p. 58.

status interfered with productivity. In Section A an outstanding record relieved such anxiety, whereas in Section B social cohesion reduced it by making the individual's standing in the group independent of his productivity.

## THE ELEMENTS OF SOCIAL CONTROL

In the foregoing discussion, we illustrate qualitative group relationships that develop quite opposite patterns of social control. A close analysis of Blau's cases would suggest that social control results from the interdependence of four main elements: (1) norms of behavior, (2) a system of rewards and punishments, (3) a system of ranking, and (4) the predispositions of members to conform. These elements may be viewed as variables contributing to the effectiveness of control in groups. A highly developed system of norms supported by a complex system of rewards and a stable ranking structure would produce powerful group forces promoting standardized behavior. These forces combined with strong predispositions of members to conform would result in a tightly controlled social situation.[5] In this section we shall consider each of these elements as they influence the process of social control.

### Norms of Behavior

Control of behavior implies the existence of standards or norms that set expectations for group members. Homans provides a definition of a norm of behavior:[6]

A norm . . . is an idea in the minds of the members of a group, an idea that can be put in the form of a statement specifying what the members or other men should do, ought to do, are expected to do, under given circumstances . . . . A statement of the kind described is a norm only if any departure of real behavior from the norm is followed by some punishment.

[5] For the moment, we are excluding from our consideration evaluation of the consequences of social control. We refer to our earlier discussion where we pointed out that control may serve humane or inhumane causes, moral and immoral goals. In the later section on implications, we shall face squarely the problem of evaluating the effects of various kinds and degrees of social control on the individual and society. We shall consider, for example, the question of overconformity as it affects creativity, tolerance for differences and related matters. These important questions are dealt with most productively following the analysis of the social psychology of control in group behavior.

[6] George C. Homans, op. cit., p. 123.

The parts of this definition that should be emphasized are the following:

1. A norm exists as an *idea* in the minds of men. It should not be confused with *actual* behavior. What men actually do and what they are expected to do are often quite different. We should, therefore, recognize in the study of group behavior that some of the most important problems in group relationships result from variations in the behavior of members from the group norms.

2. For an idea to operate as a norm, there must be common acceptance of the expectation even on the part of the most iconoclastic of group members. How consensus is achieved in the development of group norms is, in itself, a significant question for exploration. It should be emphasized that a norm is an idea which cannot be observed directly, and that the norm need not be stated. Thus group members or an observer may first become aware of the consensus through the interactions that depart from the norm.

3. A norm is an expectation. It establishes what a member *should* do and acts as a standard against which actual behavior is *evaluated*. When deviations occur members react in a way indicating there has been a violation of an expected behavior.

4. The last part of the Homans' definition of norms of behavior stresses specific punishment following deviations from the norm. An idea cannot be considered a norm unless punishment is introduced to restore behavior in the direction of the group norms. The system of reward and punishment is an element to be considered separately.

The nature of norms of behavior can best be illustrated by citing several norms operating in a group. We shall use the norms noted by researchers in the study of The Bank Wiring Room in the Western Electric studies.[7]

1. You should not turn out too much work. If you do, you are a "ratebuster."
2. You should not turn out too little work. If you do, you are a "chiseler."
3. You should not tell a supervisor anything that will react to the detriment of an associate. If you do you are a "squealer."
4. You should not attempt to maintain social distance or act officious. If you are an inspector, for example, you should not act like one.

We should be careful, in reviewing these norms, not to confuse them with group conduct. Through observation the investigators

[7] F. J. Roethlisberger and W. J. Dickson, *Management and the Worker*, p. 522.

could see these standards operating in the control of behavior. The group members themselves would not have been able to formulate their norms as elegantly as did the researchers.

The norms related specifically to the social context of the group. The terms "ratebuster," "chiseler," and "squealer" represented social evaluations of those who violated the norms. Finally, each statement of a norm stressed the "should"—the expectation. Both investigators and group members recognized the difference between the norm as an idea and actual behavior. To quote Homans again:[8]

> One point must be made very clear: our norms are ideas. They are not behavior itself, but what people think behavior ought to be. Nothing is more childishly obvious than that the ideal and the real do not always, or do not fully coincide, but nothing is more easily forgotten, perhaps because men want to forget it.

We have stressed the fact that norms in a group are specific and grow out of social relations within the particular group. Yet no group lives unto itself, nor is any particular set of norms isolated from the larger social reality that forms the environment for a primary group. Norms of behavior are conditioned by the cultural experience of group members and grow out of standards that apply to society as a whole.

Two broad classes of ideas are rooted in the culture which act as standards for the governing of behavior: values and ideals. In Chapter Two, we explored the relationship between culture and small group behavior. The relationship between values and ideals, on the one hand, and norms, on the other, continues this line of analysis.

*Values.*    Values are ideas in the minds of men comparable to norms in that they specify how people should behave. Values also attach degrees of goodness to activities. For example, in some societies the ministry and the professions are *valued* more highly than the business or mercantile activities. Values also prescribe how people should behave in certain relationships. We are expected to behave respectfully and deferentially toward older persons.

Whereas norms of behavior in a group are quite specific and establish limits to behavior, values represent "shoulds" and "goodness," which are unlimited in degree. A person cannot, for example, have too much education, but in many groups, he is expected to avoid differentiating himself too sharply from others. A person with substantial formal

[8] George C. Homans, *op. cit.,* p. 124.

education is expected to avoid showing his erudition in a group whose members have received limited education.

Values are expressed continually in interaction both verbally and nonverbally. The most prevalent expression of values exists in the aphorisms handed down from one generation to the next and found in stories told and read to children. A few illustrations of common aphorisms will help clarify the nature of values.

### 1. VALUES REGARDING WORK AND LEISURE

"All work and no play makes Jack a dull boy." This common saying indicates the desirability of leisure, of relaxing and getting away from work. It translates itself into a norm in many student groups by the disapproval expressed toward "grinds" or the preference expressed for "the gentleman C" as a grade indicating that the individual can work leisurely. But an interesting aspect of aphorisms is the ease with which contradictions can be found. For example, "The early bird catches the worm" reflects the importance of being alert, energetic, and anticipating problems. Of course, the individual must find his way in the contradictions implied in these two sayings.

### 2. VALUES REGARDING FRIENDSHIP

"A friend in need is a friend indeed." This aphorism approves of helpfulness and generosity in human relationships. It translates itself into a norm: the expectation that group members will provide help to one another.

### 3. VALUES REGARDING THE MANAGEMENT OF TIME

A peculiarly strong value in the Anglo-Saxon culture is expressed in the following aphorisms: "Never put off until tomorrow anything you can do today" or "A stitch in time saves nine." Whether these values become translated into norms in a particular group will depend, of course, on social conditioning and other environmental influences on group members.

### 4. VALUES REGARDING MONEY

"A penny saved is a penny earned" expresses the merits of thrift and foregoing immediate gratifications for longer run rewards. A common contradiction of this value is expressed in the saying, "Live for today and let tomorrow take care of itself."

The interplay between values and norms as standards of behavior in group relationships is illustrated in a field report of a factory work group. The researchers describe the differences in the ideas and behavior deemed important by "regular" and "nonregular" group members.[9]

. . . Observation of differences in shared values highlighted the difference between "regulars" and "deviants." Let us look at some of these values and norms of behavior which members of the five regular groups expressed that were not shared by the members of deviant groups.

One such value, which members of regular groups communicated time and time again, was *generosity*. As one listened to the regulars speak, he would hear declarations such as, "He's all right. He'd lend you money if you needed it," or "It's right to give a guy a real boost; giving him a little boost is just like cheating." Specifically, with regard to collections, there were norms of generosity. PS5(F),* a regular, was given approval by other regulars because she always complied with amounts specified.

Conversely, members of the deviant groups gave to the ever-present collection box but often gave grudgingly and amounts less than were appropriate. DP4B and LM3F, for example, were held up by the regulars as examples of "tightwads." They gave only a 5-cent or a 10-cent piece when more was appropriate. Among members of the deviant groups, one would hear muttered comments about "There are too damn many collections around here," and a general lack of enthusiasm for this activity. These comments drew attack from regular group members.

*Generosity* as a value also came up in other ways. Members of regular groups spoke of spending more often than they did of saving and ownership. LM3D(F), a regular, would announce to approving G7D(F) and DB5A(F), regulars, that she had bought each of her grandchildren four Christmas presents and that she was broke until payday. Conversely, when A4U(F), a deviant, talked about her savings account, she aroused the antagonism of A4D(F), a regular. A4D(F) commented, "She's just an old money bags. For Christ's sake, all she does is to talk about going to the bank. You'd think she was money-mad. I spend my money and have a good time."

Deviants, such as L5B, who did save and who owned their own homes, came in for judgments such as, "He's hungry," "He's just a money lover," or "What kind of a guy is it who makes his wife work just to get more money?" When DP4C, a deviant, complained about having to draw money out of the bank to pay his State Income Tax, some of the male regulars chided him for being so wealthy and gave him suggestions as to how he might spread his wealth around.

*Helpfulness* was another value common to the five groups we called "regular." They strongly voiced their feelings about this and practiced it in their daily lives. On the job, the regulars stressed the necessity of

[9] A. Zaleznik, C. R. Christensen, and F. J. Roethlisberger, *The Motivation, Productivity and Satisfaction of Workers: A Prediction Study*, pp. 153–158.
    * Code to designate group member.

helping their associates learn, as A4A, a regular, put it, "the tricks of any job," or uniting to protect the individual in case management assigned blame for certain actions such as scrap loss. Helpfulness held too for outside-the-plant life. A common characteristic of most regular groups was their aid to other group members in circumstances such as illness or major work projects too large for one person to handle. As one regular put it, "You don't have to have money to help—just heart and hands."

Conversely, the deviant group members stressed their own strength and resourcefulness rather than group helpfulness. A4J(F), for example, stated, "Your best friend is a dollar bill. I'll take care of myself." When LM3F was asked to fill out 25 postcards to help another worker win a community audition contest, he refused. Such an action was clearly out of place with the dominant sentiments of the regular groups.

*Loyalty* was another "regular" value, and here too there was a difference in attitudes of regulars and deviants. Loyalty in this circumstance had specific meanings. You shouldn't want to leave the group unless an opportunity for security came along (city police, sewer department jobs, etc.). You shouldn't mix too much with the outsiders—management or other department workers. You shouldn't want to advance to a management position because this would mean "you aren't one of us." You shouldn't speak approvingly of management policies and attitudes unless they are favorable to us. You shouldn't squeal on another worker. You should speak and act as though your department was the best place to work.

Members of the deviant groups did not accept these values fully. As individuals, they talked often in terms of personal advancement so they might leave the factory. As L5B, a deviant, said, "I want to learn so I can better myself and leave here if I have to. I was a fool not to go to college and be an engineer. If I had had training, it would have been different." The "deviant" card game (whist) had outsiders playing in the game and observing the game. DP4B, a deviant, complained to the union steward about a work assignment given to a regular. This brought him severe criticism from other regulars.

At one stage of our research, management introduced a campaign to increase production. To accomplish this, teams of managers toured the factory making reports on workers who were away from their machines. The regulars responded to this with bitter criticism. The inspectors were labeled spotters and were given titles not to be found on any organization chart. Some members of the deviant groups, however, responded differently. LM3B(F), for example, commented, "Now that they are clamping down, this is a much better place to work. There should be lots more discipline around here."

Finally, a cardinal value for the regulars was *friendliness*. They expected their fellow workers to speak to them, to inquire about their health and problems, and generally to be happy and lead a carefree life. They were suspicious of members who did not meet these criteria. One of their major criticisms of certain deviant members was that they were the re-

verse of friendly; they were "serious." Being "serious" had various connotations such as being one who saved or wanted to get ahead. But it
was also a label used for workers who did not clearly indicate that they
enjoyed the friendship of their fellow workers—110% of it . . . .

Members of the regular groups tended to share strongly certain values
and abided by the resultant norms. They emphasized the importance of
group strength in their workday and social life; the need to maintain
group values such as generosity and helpfulness, and the importance of
being loyal to the group membership and their aspirations.

In varying measure the remainder of the department rejected (isolates)
or questioned (deviants) these standards. They stressed the importance
of the individual and questioned whether their present work was what they
wanted for the rest of their lives.

The dominant values and resultant norms in this work group are
particular to the upper-lower class Irish-American groups formed in
urban centers along the East Coast. Most workers of Irish descent are
regulars. The non-Irish, including rural Protestant, are nonregulars.
These different membership positions reflect identification with the
values and norms of the "regulars."

*Ideals.* Another class of imperatives different from norms and
values is the ideals of behavior. Ideals are standards that can be
considered absolute in the sense that they derive from religious
doctrine and ideology and brook no compromise. Included as ideals
of behavior are the Ten Commandments and the teachings of the
Sermon on the Mount. Inasmuch as ideals are generalized throughout societies, we find little contradiction among them, as among
values that are particular to subcultures. At the same time, ideals are
difficult to follow in actual behavior. Furthermore, the observance
of these precepts is a matter of conscience, or if you prefer, of the
superego. Violations result in feelings of guilt, whereas deviations
from norms of behavior result in concrete punishment meted out in
interpersonal relationships.

Having thus described norms of behavior and their relationship to
the wider values and ideals established in society, let us now turn to
the forces that determine the *strength of norms* or the degree to
which norms exert influence on the behavior of group members.
Relevant here are the attractiveness of the group to its members and
the length of time that members have participated in the group.
Although these two factors should be viewed separately, they may
be considered together as conditions defining *group cohesiveness.*[10]

[10] Leon Festinger, "Group Attraction and Membership," in *Group Dynamics,*
D. Cartwright and A. Zander, Eds., pp. 92–101.

## 1. ATTRACTIVENESS OF THE GROUP[11]

Norms of behavior tend to be strong when members are attracted to and identify with the group. Work groups create conditions for identification simply because membership is economically important to the individuals. We do not lightly undertake to leave jobs and abandon existing work groups. When group members, in addition, have few other group memberships the value of the group is enhanced for them. This phenomenon is seen most clearly in minority group formations. Where ethnic barriers prevent free movement among groups in a society, the restricted opportunities for membership result in strong systems of norms because the attraction to the group is high for its members.[12]

In a study of group cohesiveness in factory settings, Seashore classified groups according to the attraction they had to members. Where attraction was high, the groups tended to develop strong norms around productivity. In the high cohesive groups levels of productivity had a high degree of consistency as compared with individual productivity levels in the low cohesive groups.[13] This finding is expressed most generally in Homans' proposition: "The more frequently persons interact with one another, the more alike in some respects both their activities and their sentiments tend to become."[14] Interaction is related to a group's attractiveness to its members.

## 2. LENGTH OF TIME IN GROUP PARTICIPATION

Under conditions of continued interaction, groups members tend to develop more values in common. This is another way of saying that norms of behavior in time develop increasing group consensus and therefore exert stronger influence on member behavior.

Two studies are relevant to this discussion. Newcomb studied changes of attitude among college students who came from wealthy and conservative family backgrounds.[15] He found that as their membership in the Bennington College community, which was influenced by liberal attitudes of the faculty, proceeded from freshman to senior years, students tended to adopt increasingly the dominant tenets of the

[11] See: Leon Festinger, "Informal Social Communication" in *Group Dynamics*, D. Cartwright and A. Zanders, Eds., pp. 190–203.

[12] Kurt Lewin, *Resolving Social Conflicts*, p. 163.

[13] Stanley E. Seashore, *Group Cohesiveness in the Industrial Work Group* (Ann Arbor, Michigan, Survey Research Center, Institute for Social Research, University of Michigan, 1954).

[14] George C. Homans, *op. cit.*, p. 120.

[15] Theodore M. Newcomb, "Attitude Development as a Function of Reference Groups," in *Readings in Social Psychology*, Macoby, Newcomb and Hartley, Eds., pp. 265–275.

community. Those who maintained their conservative positions remained relatively apart from activity in the community. Their prestige in the college community was relatively low.

In a comparison of two housing units at M.I.T., Festinger and
colleagues found in one unit, called Westgate, considerable uniformity
of opinion within its housing courts, but differences between courts,
on the operation of a tenants' organization.[16] In the second unit,
called Westgate West, there seemed no exceptional degree of homo-
geneity of opinion even within its housing courts. The researchers
attributed the differences to the strength of norms operating in the
two units:[17]

Unlike the residents of Westgate who had been living there up to 15
months and had had four months actual experience with the organization,
the residents of Westgate West were all relative newcomers . . . . We
might expect, then, that in Westgate West, where the social groupings
had not had time to form cohesive units, and where the contact with the
tenants' organization was only recent, group norms would not have
developed to any considerable degree.

In other words, residents of the older community, Westgate, were
more influenced in their opinions by group norms. In the newer
community, Westgate West, opinions were arrived at independently,
less influenced by group norms, which had not yet evolved.

One of the most interesting, yet elusive, problems in group behavior
is the method by which groups communicate, and thereby reaffirm,
their norms. As we shall see in the discussion of rewards and punishments, the communication of norms occurs most frequently where
deviations occur and the group seeks to restore behavior to the norm.

Another means for communicating the norms is in the elaboration
of group myths. Group members may tell stories or describe events
in which the moral is the terrible consequences of violation of the
norms or the virtue in conforming to them. Blau provides an
interesting illustration in his study of a group of government law
enforcement agents.[18] In discussing the group norm that discouraged
reporting of attempted bribery one of the group members told the
following story:[19]

---

[16] Leon Festinger, Stanley Schachter, and Kurt Back, "The Operation of Group
Standards" in *Group Dynamics*, Cartwright and Zander, Eds., pp. 205–222.
[17] *Ibid.*, p. 211.
[18] Peter M. Blau, *The Dynamics of Bureaucracy*, Part II.
[19] *Ibid.*, p. 154.

I'll tell you of one case . . . . He did exactly what you say: He went into a bar with a guy who had promised him money. He was supposed to give it to him in the bar. Then the FBI came in, and they actually came in just like in the movies; the sirens were blasting. They happened to be late, and could only get there on time by using their sirens. And they came in with their guns, asking, "Who is offering a bribe here?" By that time the client had said, "Excuse me, I have to go to the washroom," and had left the place. You know what happened? The FBI didn't say it had made a mistake. It wrote to the [commissioner] telling him that the agent had handled the case badly. So, you get into all kinds of trouble if you turn a man in.

Whether the events as described actually occurred, or parts of the story add color, is less significant than the moral communicated in this group myth. It is best summed up in the statement, "So, you get into all kinds of trouble if you turn a man in." By telling and retelling myths involving norms, group members reinforce the acceptance of the norms as much as by punishing violations. Myths are also useful in the indoctrination of new group members.

The question of establishing and maintaining norms of behavior leads directly to the consideration of a second element in the process of social control: reward and punishment. Before turning to this analysis, we should underscore several ideas just presented.

1. Norms of behavior are informal rules governing what members are supposed to do under given circumstances. They are not actual behavior.

2. Norms are specific imperatives or "shoulds" and are limited in application. But the norms derive from experience with more widely applied values and ideals of behavior that are more general than norms, and also in the case of values, more contradictory.

3. The strength of norms in a group depends on the attractiveness of the group to its members. Where groups satisfy members' needs and induce a strong willingness to stay in the group, the norms tend to be strong. Newly formed groups will have a less well-developed system of norms than groups with a history.

## Rewards and Punishment

The capacity of a group to maintain its norms and enhance its solidarity depends on the existence of a system of rewards and punishments. When members conform to the norms and are rewarded, they presumably will be motivated to continue to conform. On the other hand, where deviations from the norms engender punishments that *succeed in restoring behavior to an approximation of the norm,* control exercised by the group is enhanced. Note the emphasis placed on punishment followed by behavior more in line with the norms. Where punishment fails, the system of norms deteriorates. And there can be no more devastating breakdown in social control than that which follows the infliction of punishments that are too severe, or the continuation of punishment when deviation no longer exists.

Analysis of the place of reward and punishment in the process of social control requires an examination of the rewards groups provide for members, and how punishment results in unpleasant consequences following deviant behavior.

The basic premise we wish to establish, reserving detailed discussion for a later chapter, is the idea that men in groups seek to gratify fundamental needs. A person is rewarded in a group when the behavior and affect of others satisfies his needs. One can get involved easily in premature concern about what needs are, particularly those whose satisfaction may depend heavily on group membership. This problem relates to the psychology of human motivation and is beyond the scope of this chapter (see Chapters Six through Eight). But without acceptance of the notion of reward and need satisfaction in group behavior, we cannot get very far in understanding how groups affect the control of behavior.

Groups reward members in many ways. They provide the means to material satisfactions through co-operative activity. They also provide many psychic rewards. The satisfactions of performing interesting activities are available in many types of groups. Members also provide psychic rewards in showing respect, affection, and support for one another. Acceptance and support in turn make it possible for members to learn new skills and in other ways to develop their competence and self-confidence. The help given and received in groups is rewarding in several ways. Helping evidences support and at the same time may be very important for learning. Groups may also provide prestige and esteem to members with resultant beneficial effects for ego development. Finally, and of great significance for the psychological well-being of members, is the reward realized in the *validation* of thoughts, ideas, and feelings. Most healthy individuals have some desire to communicate with others, to share their thoughts and feelings. To secure validation of ideas can be significantly rewarding. To take the extreme case, complete absence of validation of our perceptions can undermine our sense of reality.

With this brief, oversimplified statement of the kinds of rewards distributed in group memberships, we can surmise why men will tend to conform to group norms. Where conformity results in being rewarded in a number of ways, the likelihood of continued conformity to norms of behavior remains high.

Punishment in groups occurs when members actively deviate from the norms. Punishment can be both direct and indirect. Direct punishments occur when members ostracize others for deviant behavior, or use epithets to single out the deviant. The familiar childhood rhyme, "Sticks and stones will break my bones, but names will never hurt me," recalls the fact that names *do* hurt when it counts most, for adults as well as children. When pride and self-worth are concerned ostracism can be deeply wounding.

Blau, in his study of law enforcement officers, provides several interesting examples of punishment by ostracism. A strong norm existed against reporting bribe offers. Agents felt that reporting led only to trouble, as shown earlier, and that an agent should not let his relationship with the potential briber get to the point where bribe discussions are seriously entertained. In one of the few instances where an agent reported a bribe offer to authorities other agents ostracized him. Agents refused to talk to him and several years after the incident, he continued to be isolated in the group.[20]

In another incident, to test his understanding of the use of punishment to discourage violation of this same taboo, Blau engaged an agent in a discussion that seemingly put him in a position of questioning the norm. As soon as Blau began the questioning, the agent called a colleague to join the conversation. Blau points out that the reaffirmation of norms is usually carried out with more than one group member present to add support in influencing the skeptic or the outsider.[21]

. . . Then the two agents together involved him [the observer] in discussions of many side issues, forcing him to state opinions which they alternated in attacking. An excerpt of this cross-examination follows:
CRONER: Do you think that it's all right to take a bribe?
OBSERVER: No.
CRONER: So you think it's wrong. What do you think about somebody taking a cigar?
OBSERVER: That is something different.
CRONER: Oh, so you think it's all right for an agent to take a cigar!?
OBSERVER: I think it's all right; sometimes it might be a bad technique.
LEHMANN: Do you know that some agents won't even take a cigar?

[20] *Ibid.,* p. 149.
[21] *Ibid.,* p. 157.

CRONER: How about the boss's saying, "Mr. Blow [note aggressive distortion of the observer's name], it's nearly twelve o'clock, why don't you go to lunch with me?" Is that all right?

OBSERVER: Sometimes it is; sometimes it's probably disadvantageous to go out with him. [This as well as all previous answers of the observer were paraphrases of comments other agents had made.]

CRONER: Oh, it is?

LEHMANN: Do you know that some of the best information is gotten informally over the luncheon table? The books are closed, and he'll tell you "off the record." You know that there's no such thing as "off the record." But he'll tell you things like that over lunch that he wouldn't tell you in the office.

Interactions of this type provide an individual who has violated a taboo with a brief but concentrated experience of what it is like to be ostracized. Two agents showed the observer that his opinions conflicted with theirs and rejected him, by making aggressive remarks, for this reason. Simultaneously, they presented him, through their agreement, with a demonstration of the desirability of being accepted by others. Even the observer, not a genuine part of the group, found this disconcerting. If several colleagues treated a member of the departmental group in this way—for example, by laughing together at aggressive remarks directed against him—he was momentarily put into the worst state of anomy: being alone and feeling disoriented while witnessing the cohesiveness of others. This threat constituted a strong inducement to surrender unorthodox opinions and to cease deviant practices.

Another form of direct punishment sometimes encountered in group enforcement of norms is physical punishment. In the Bank Wiring Room of the Western Electric Company, workers would hit deviant members on the arm following some violation of a norm. These workers called this practice "binging." Besides inflicting pain on the violator it visibly called attention to deviant behavior so that group members collectively could reaffirm the norms.

Lombard described another example of physical punishment aimed at deviant group members. In his study of the behavior of salesgirls in a department store, he reported the practice of leaving storage drawers open in aisleways so that a person passing hurriedly along the aisle would strike her shin against the open drawer. This practice was aimed at group members who failed to observe norms that prohibited a clerk from "grabbing" or attempting to wait on several customers at once in order to build a large sales record.

[22] F. J. Roethlisberger and W. J. Dickson, *op. cit.*, pp. 422–423.
[23] George F. F. Lombard, *Behavior in a Selling Group.*

So far, we have examined various forms of direct punishments aimed at reducing violation of group norms. Of equal significance in maintaining levels of conformity is indirect punishment. Indirect punishment consists of withholding reward or isolating deviant members from the centers of interaction. This form of punishment is effective, particularly where the deviant has a strong emotional investment in the group and seeks reward in interaction with other members. For individuals for whom a particular group is less relevant, isolation is less punishing and instead of producing conformity may result in even greater deviant behavior.

The effectiveness of isolation where a member does identify with the group is based on early experience with this form of punishment. Many families, particularly in the middle classes, use isolation and temporary withdrawal of love as forms of punishment for violation of standards of conduct. This temporary isolation produces feelings of shame and anxiety which act to induce acceptance of the norms. Adults who have experienced isolation as a form of punishment in childhood will be aware of its effect in later group experiences. To be effective as punishment, isolation or any other form of deprivation requires true isolation. The member who is supported in his deviant behavior by another member will experience far less deprivation because interaction continues, in part at least, with someone else.

The behavior of group members in seeking to establish conformity to norms through rejection of deviants has been illustrated in a series of experimental studies conducted by Schachter.[24] The value of these studies warrants detailed examination of their results. The experiments attempted to examine the effects of group cohesion and relevance of group purpose on reactions to deviant members, conforming members, and "sliders" (members who shift from deviance toward conformity). The subjects were given a case involving a juvenile delinquent and were asked to take a position on degrees of punishment ranging from severe to relatively lenient treatment. In each experimental group all subjects but three were led to believe they were participating in a club and had no reason to suspect a contrived experiment. The three subjects in each group were briefed to assume one of the following positions: the deviant, the conformer, and the slider. By predetermining the positions most group members would take on the case, the experimenters briefed the conforming members to assert the dominant opinion in the group. The slider could take a deviant position and later move toward conformity. The deviant,

[24] Stanley Schachter, "Deviation, Rejection and Communication," in *Group Dynamics*, D. Cartwright and A. Zander, Eds., pp. 423–428.

on the other hand, could take a position quite different from most group members. He was instructed to hold to his opinion.

As we can see, the measure of conformity and deviation in these experiments relates to a popular opinion and not overt behavior. The premise underlying this experiment, and one consistent with the theory presented so far in this chapter, assumes that conformity in a group results in tendencies toward standardization of thoughts and feelings as well as behavior. Of course this standardization is not necessarily extreme and will vary in degree from group to group. But the premise of the experiment does point to the danger we have alluded to before, namely, that although forces toward conformity exist in groups, if the norms fail to permit differences among members, the group effort will yield only mediocre work and will have a bland, uncreative atmosphere. This is particularly true of problem-solving groups.

But to return to the experiment and its findings, the investigators used two post-meeting questionnaires to assess rejection or acceptance of group members. During the meeting they observed the communication patterns toward the deviant, slider, and conforming members as direct indications of how acceptance and rejection may appear in overt behavior. One questionnaire item asked members to rank others in the degree to which they preferred to be in the same group with them. According to the researchers this sociometric question was a measure of perceived *congeniality*.

The findings showed consistently that the "deviant member" was least chosen on the sociometric measure. The penalty for holding to an opinion markedly different from the rest of the group was rejection as a possible future member of the group. Significantly enough, groups of high cohesive condition rejected the deviant more strongly than the low cohesive groups. This finding is consistent with the expectation that cohesive groups tend to develop stronger norms which they enforce with rewards and punishments.

The attitudes toward the deviant, conformer, and slider indicate a group disposition to influence all toward conformity. The conforming member received a steady, but low amount of communication from the group throughout the meetings. The slider received a large amount of attention as the group endeavored to influence him to conform. As he moved toward conformity, the communication dropped off to become steady but low. The deviant usually received the highest degree of communication as group members sought to change his views. Although this might seem on first consideration to be rewarding, actually it is not. The communications directed at him emphasize his different position and burden him with considerable pressure to change. In one of the high cohesive groups there was an additional interesting aspect to the pattern of communication involving the deviant. Communications increased in the early part of the meeting, but then declined as it appeared that the deviant would not reverse his opinion. This suggests the beginning of attempts to isolate the nonconforming member.

The acceptance and rejection of group members represent the important expressions of reward and punishment. Without a system of reward and punishment, groups would be unable to exert controlling influences on behavior of members.

## Ranking in Groups

The third element in the process of social control is the influence on behavior of the stabilizing of interpersonal relationships in a group. This stabilization evolves as a group, develops its structure and ultimately achieves a series of interrelated social positions. These positions and the attitudes of group members toward them can be thought of as a system of ranking within which individuals secure their group membership.

The term rank implies the existence of a scale with evaluations of positions according to some criteria of "goodness." Positions occupied by members vary in the degree to which they are accorded prestige, respect, esteem, and other rewards. The rank of a position will reflect the extent to which members in their characteristics and behavior realize the norms and values of the group.[25] The more nearly an individual conforms to group norms, the higher his rank or social position in the group. With this statement of the relationship between conformity and ranking we face two necessities: (1) to illustrate this relationship through examination of empirical studies; and (2) to examine how the phenomenon of ranking can be considered distinct from the other elements significant in social control. Here we refer to the fact that ranking appears to be no more than the relationship between observance of group norms and the distribution of rewards and punishments. Yet the very process of developing a system of ranks in a group brings into play additional forces toward social control.

Various studies illustrate the effects of ranking on conformity to group norms. One of these, an analysis of behavior among workers

[25] George C. Homans, *op. cit.*, pp. 140–141.

in a machine shop,[26] showed the importance of two norms in their everyday relationships. The first required that high-status machinists offer help to low-status operators *when the help* was requested; and the second demanded that high-status machinists lend tools to other workers in compliance with requests. Needless to say, machinists were high-skilled workers compared with operators and received more pay. Nothing in the formal arrangements of work required machinists to give help or to lend tools. The norms were spontaneous and related, of course, to the values of helpfulness and sharing in the wider culture.

It is significant that not all machinists observed the norm. Two of the most skilled disclosed sharp contrasts: one machinist, Ron, was active in helping relationships and was seen by most other persons in the group as the major source of help; another, Axel, almost never helped or loaned tools and was seen as least receptive to the needs of less skilled and less competent persons. As we would expect, the group members accorded higher rank to Ron than to Axel. They expressed liking and esteem for Ron, rewards evidently of some importance to him, and on the contrary, expressed uncomplimentary remarks toward Axel.

So far, we can say that conformity to norms and reward varied directly. That this relationship had persisted for some time and stabilized itself into a ranking system created additional spurs to the maintenance of existing degrees of conformity and deviation. As with established positions in society, the individuals concerned took some care to maintain the system. For a high-ranking member like Ron, rank in the group became an emotional investment assuring his continued observance of group norms. Actually, we could consider the establishment of ranks as an inducement to conform to certain expectations. Or, in terms of reward, its realization through rank in the group results in the maintenance of existing levels of conformity as a basis for further reward.

Just as high rank in a group assures conformity to norms, paradoxically the lack of reward, or deprivation, in a low peripheral rank may result in continuing deviation. The lack of reward experienced by Axel did not result in his increased conformity to the helping norms. His low social rank and its deprivation perpetuated the deviation, leading him to seek other rewards than those realized in interaction among group members. He could and did seek the rewards of doing a craftsmanlike job and of earning praise from

---

[26] A. Zaleznik, *Worker Satisfaction and Development.* Another illustration is found in Peter M. Blau, *The Dynamics of Bureaucracy*, Part II.

persons outside of the group—engineers and management personnel. Lower ranking or deviant members of a group may be motivated to find alternative rewards to support their deviant behavior.

The effects of ranking on levels of conformity have been analyzed by Whyte in his study of the Norton Street Gang. Whyte's analysis centered on the mutual obligations of corner boys expressed in doing favors for one another and in loaning money. Whyte said:[27]

Not all the corner boys live up to their obligations equally well, and this factor partly accounts for the differentiation in status among them. The man with a low status may violate his obligations without much change in his position. His fellows know that he has failed to discharge certain obligations in the past, and his position reflects his past performances. On the other hand, the leader is depended upon by all the members to meet his personal obligations. He cannot fail to do so without causing confusion and endangering his position.

The relationship of status to the system of mutual obligations is most clearly revealed when one observes the use of money. During the time that I knew a corner gang called the Millers, Sam Franco, the leader, was out of work except for an occasional odd job; yet, whenever he had a little money, he spent it on Joe and Chichi, his closest friends, who were next to him in the structure of the group. When Joe or Chichi had money, which was less frequent, they reciprocated. Sam frequently paid for two members who stood close to the bottom of his group and occasionally for others. The two men who held positions immediately below Joe and Chichi were considered very well off according to Cornerville standards. Sam said that he occasionally borrowed money from them, but never more than fifty cents at a time. Such loans he repaid at the earliest possible moment. There were four other members with lower positions in the group, who nearly always had more money than Sam. He did not recall ever having borrowed from them. He said that the only time he had obtained a substantial sum from anyone around his corner was when he borrowed eleven dollars from a friend who was the *leader* of another corner gang.

The situation was the same among the Nortons. Doc did not hesitate to accept money from Danny, but he avoided taking any from the followers.

The leader spends more money on his followers than they on him. The farther down in the structure one looks, the fewer are the financial relations which tend to obligate the leader to a follower. This does not mean that the leader has more money than others or even that he necessarily spends more—though he must always be a free spender. It means that the financial relations must be explained in social terms. Un-

[27] William Foote Whyte, *Street Corner Society*, pp. 127–128.

consciously, and in some cases consciously, the leader refrains from putting himself under obligations to those with low status in the group.

Whyte emphasized the importance of ranking in sustaining adherence to norms and fulfilling obligations at existing levels. The crucial point is the inequality in conformity and fulfillment of obligations. This inequality produces the ranking system which becomes a new source of obligation for those high in rank.

The consideration of ranking leads to additional paradoxes in social control. The obligations of high rank induce continued conformity. The expectations of low rank induce continued deviation. The paradox results from the behavior of all group members and not just those low in rank. In the Norton Street Gang we have a vivid demonstration of how group members seek to prevent changes in the ranking system that would in turn lead to changes in degrees of conformity and deviation. The Nortons participated in bowling contests as a regular group activity. Whyte observed very shrewdly the high positive correlation between high rank in the group and success in bowling. Let us examine Whyte's description of the social process involved in maintaining rank.[28]

. . . Alec, Joe Dodge, and Frank Bonelli bowled several nights a week throughout the winter. Others bowled on frequent occasions, and all the bowlers appeared at the alleys at least one night a week.

A high score at candlepins requires several spares or strikes. Since a strike rarely occurs except when the first ball hits the king-pin properly within a fraction of an inch, and none of the boys had such precise aim, strikes were considered matters of luck, although a good bowler was expected to score them more often than a poor one. A bowler was judged according to his ability to get spares, to "pick" the pins that remained on the alley after his first ball.

There are many mental hazards connected with bowling. In any sport there are critical moments when a player needs the steadiest nerves if he is to "come through"; but, in those that involve team play and fairly continuous action, the player can sometimes lose himself in the heat of the contest and get by the critical points before he has a chance to "tighten up." If he is competing on a five-man team, the bowler must await a long time for his turn at the alleys, and he has plenty of time to brood over his mistakes. When a man is facing ten pins, he can throw the ball quite casually. But when only one pin remains standing, and his opponents are shouting, "He can't pick it," the pressure is on, and there is a tendency to "tighten up" and lose control.

[28] *Ibid.*, pp. 17–25.

When a bowler is confident that he can make a difficult shot, the chances are that he will make it or come exceedingly close. When he is not confident, he will miss. A bowler is confident because he has made similar shots in the past and is accustomed to making good scores. But that is not all. He is also confident because his fellows, whether for him or against him, believe that he can make the shot. If they do not believe in him, the bowler has their adverse opinions as well as his own uncertainty to fight against. When that is said, it becomes necessary to consider a man's relation to his fellows in examining his bowling record.

In the winter and spring of 1937–38 bowling was the most significant social activity for the Nortons. Saturday night's intra-clique and individual matches became the climax of the week's events. During the week the boys discussed what had happened the previous Saturday night and what would happen on the coming Saturday night. A man's performance was subject to continual evaluation and criticism. There was, therefore, a close connection between a man's bowling and his position in the group.

The team used against the Community Club had consisted of two men (Doc and Long John) who ranked high and three men (Joe Dodge, Frank Bonelli, and Tommy) who had a low standing. When bowling became a fixed group activity, the Nortons' team evolved along different lines. Danny joined the Saturday night crowd and rapidly made a place for himself. He performed very well and picked Doc as his favorite opponent. There was a good-natured rivalry between them. In individual competition Danny usually won, although his average in the group matches was no better than that of Doc's. After the Community Club match, when Doc selected a team to represent the Nortons against other corner gangs and clubs, he chose Danny, Long John, and himself, leaving two vacancies on the five-man team. At this time, Mike, who had never been a good bowler, was just beginning to bowl regularly and had not established his reputation. Significantly enough, the vacancies were not filled from the ranks of the clique. On Saturday nights the boys had been bowling with Chris Teludo, Nutsy's older cousin, and Mark Ciampa, a man who associated with them only at the bowling alleys. Both men were popular and were first-class bowlers. They were chosen by Doc, with the agreement of Danny and Long John, to bowl for the Nortons. It was only when a member of the regular team was absent that one of the followers in the clique was called in, and on such occasions he never distinguished himself.

The followers were not content with being substitutes. They claimed that they had not been given an opportunity to prove their ability. One Saturday night in February 1938, Mike organized an intraclique match. His team was made up of Chris Teludo, Doc, Long John, himself, and me. Danny was sick at the time, and I was put in to substitute for him. Frank, Alec, Joe, Lou, and Tommy made up the other team. Interest in this match was more intense than in the ordinary "choose-up" matches, but the followers bowled poorly and never had a chance.

After this one encounter the followers were recognized as the second team and never again challenged the team of Doc, Danny, Long John, Mark, and Chris. Instead, they took to individual efforts to better their positions.

On his athletic ability alone, Frank should have been an excellent bowler. His ball-playing had won him positions on semiprofessional teams and a promise—though unfulfilled—of a job on a minor-league team. And it was not lack of practice that held him back, for, along with Alec and Joe Dodge, he bowled more frequently than Doc, Danny, or Mike. During the winter of 1937–38 Frank occupied a particularly subordinate position in the group. He spent his time with Alec in the pastry shop owned by Alec's uncle, and, since he had little employment throughout the winter, he became dependent upon Alec for a large part of the expenses of his participation in group activities. Frank fell to the bottom of the group. His financial dependence preyed upon his mind. While he sometimes bowled well, he was never a serious threat to break into the first team.

Some events of June, 1937, cast additional light upon Frank's position. Mike organized a baseball team of some of the Nortons to play against a younger group of Norton Street corner boys. On the basis of his record, Frank was considered the best player on either team, yet he made a miserable showing. He said to me: "I can't seem to play ball when I'm playing with fellows I know, like that bunch. I do much better when I'm playing for the Stanley A.C. against some team in Dexter, Westland, or out of town." Accustomed to filling an inferior position, Frank was unable to star even in his favorite sport when he was competing against members of his own group.

One evening I heard Alec boasting to Long John that the way he was bowling he could take on every man on the first team and lick them all. Long John dismissed the challenge with these words: "You think you could beat us, but, under pressure, you die!"

Alec objected vehemently, yet he recognized the prevailing group opinion of his bowling. He made the highest single score of the season, and he frequently excelled during the week when he bowled with Frank, Long John, Joe Dodge, and me, but on Saturday nights, when the group was all assembled, his performance was quite different. Shortly after this conversation Alec had several chances to prove himself, but each time it was "an off night," and he failed.

Carl, Joe, Lou, and Fred were never good enough to gain any recognition. Tommy was recognized as a first-class bowler, but he did most of his bowling with a younger group.

One of the best guides to the bowling standing of the members was furnished by a match held toward the end of April 1938. Doc had an idea that we should climax the season with an individual competition among the members of the clique. He persuaded the owner of the alleys to contribute ten dollars in prize money to be divided among the three highest scorers. It was decided that only those who had bowled regularly should be eligible, and on this basis Lou, Fred, and Tommy were eliminated.

Interest in this contest ran high. The probable performances of the various bowlers were widely discussed. Doc, Danny, and Long John each listed his predictions. They were unanimous in conceding the first five places to themselves, Mark Ciampa, and Chris Teludo, although they differed in predicting the order among the first five. The next two positions were generally conceded to Mike and to me. All the ratings gave Joe Dodge last position, and Alec, Frank, and Carl were ranked close to the bottom.

The followers made no such lists, but Alec let it be known that he intended to show the boys something. Joe Dodge was annoyed to discover that he was the unanimous choice to finish last and argued that he was going to win.

When Chris Teludo did not appear for the match, the field was narrowed to ten. After the first four boxes, Alec was leading by several pins. He turned to Doc and said, "I'm out to get you boys tonight." But then he began to miss, and, as mistake followed mistake, he stopped trying. Between turns, he went out for drinks, so that he became flushed and unsteady on his feet. He threw the ball carelessly, pretending that he was not interested in the competition. His collapse was sudden and complete; in the space of a few boxes he dropped from first to last place.

The bowlers finished in the following order:

| | | | |
|---|---|---|---|
| 1. | Whyte | 6. | Joe |
| 2. | Danny | 7. | Mark |
| 3. | Doc | 8. | Carl |
| 4. | Long John | 9. | Frank |
| 5. | Mike | 10. | Alec |

There were only two upsets in the contest, according to the predictions made by Doc, Danny, and Long John: Mark bowled very poorly and I won. However, it is important to note that neither Mark nor I fitted neatly into either part of the clique. Mark associated with the boys only at the bowling alleys and had no recognized status in the group. Although I was on good terms with all the boys, I was closer to the leaders than to the followers, since Doc was my particular friend. If Mark and I are left out of consideration, the performances were almost exactly what the leaders expected and the followers feared they would be. Danny, Doc, Long John, and Mike were bunched together at the top. Joe Dodge did better than was expected of him, but even he could not break through the solid ranks of the leadership.

Several days later Doc and Long John discussed the match with me.

LONG JOHN: I only wanted to be sure that Alec or Joe Dodge didn't win. That wouldn't have been right.

DOC: That's right. We didn't want to make it tough for you, because we all liked you, and the other fellows did too. If somebody had tried to make it tough for you, we would have protected you. . . . If Joe Dodge or Alec had been out in front, it would have been different. We would have talked them out of it. We could have made plenty of noise. We would have been really vicious . . .

I asked Doc what would have happened if Alec or Joe had won.

"They wouldn't have known how to take it. That's why we were out to beat them. If they had won, there would have been a lot of noise. Plenty of arguments. We would have called it lucky—things like that. We would have tried to get them in another match and then ruin them. We would have to put them in their places."

Every corner boy expects to be heckled as he bowls, but the heckling can take various forms. While I had moved ahead as early as the end of the second string, I was subjected only to good-natured kidding. The leaders watched me with mingled surprise and amusement; in a very real sense, I was permitted to win.

Even so, my victory required certain adjustments. I was hailed jocularly as "the Champ" or even as "the Cheese Champ." Rather than accept this designation, I pressed my claim for recognition. Doc arranged to have me bowl a match against Long John. If I won, I should have the right to challenge Doc or Danny. The four of us went to the alleys together. Urged on by Doc and Danny, Long John won a decisive victory. I made no further challenges.

Alec was only temporarily crushed by his defeat. For a few days he was not seen on the corner, but then he returned and sought to re-establish himself. When the boys went bowling, he challenged Long John to an individual match and defeated him. Alec began to talk once more. Again he challenged Long John to a match, and again he defeated him. When bowling was resumed in the fall, Long John became Alec's favorite opponent, and for some time Alec nearly always came out ahead. He gloated. Long John explained: "He seems to have the Indian sign on me." And that is the way these incidents were interpreted by others—simply as a queer quirk of the game.

It is significant that, in making his challenge, Alec selected Long John instead of Doc, Danny, or Mike. It was not that Long John's bowling ability was uncertain. His average was about the same as that of Doc or Danny and better than that of Mike. As a member of the top group but not a leader in his own right, it was his social position that was vulnerable.

When Long John and Alec acted outside the group situation, it became possible for Alec to win. Long John was still considered the dependable man in a team match, and that was more important in relation to a man's standing in the group. Nevertheless, the leaders felt that Alec should not be defeating Long John and tried to reverse the situation. As Doc told me:

"Alec isn't so aggressive these days. I steamed up at the way he was going after Long John, and I blasted him. . . . Then I talked to Long John. John is an introvert. He broods over things, and sometimes he feels inferior. He can't be aggressive like Alec, and when Alec tells him how he can always beat him, Long John gets to think that Alec is the better bowler. . . . I talked to him. I made him see that he should bowl better than Alec. I persuaded him that he was really the better bowler. . . . Now you watch them the next time out. I'll bet Long John will ruin him."

The next time Long John did defeat Alec. He was not able to do it every time, but they became so evenly matched that Alec lost interest in such competition.

The records of the season 1937–38 show a very close correspondence between social position and bowling performance. This developed because bowling became the primary social activity of the group. It became the main vehicle whereby the individual could maintain, gain, or lose prestige.

Bowling scores did not fall automatically into this pattern. There were certain customary ways of behaving which exerted pressure upon the individuals. Chief among these were the manner of choosing sides and the verbal attacks the members directed against one another.

Generally, two men chose sides in order to divide the group into two five-man teams. The choosers were often, but not always, among the best bowlers. If they were evenly matched, two poor bowlers frequently did the choosing, but in all cases the process was essentially the same. Each one tried to select the best bowler among those who were still unchosen. When more than ten men were present, choice was limited to the first ten to arrive, so that even a poor bowler would be chosen if he came early. It was the order of choice which was important. Sides were chosen several times each Saturday night, and in this way a man was constantly reminded of the value placed upon his ability by his fellows and of the sort of performance expected of him.

Of course, personal preferences entered into the selection of bowlers, but if a man chose a team of poor bowlers just because they were closest friends, he pleased no one, least of all his team mates. It was the custom among the Nortons to have the losing team pay for the string bowled by the winners. As a rule, this small stake did not play an important role in the bowling, but no one liked to pay without the compensating enjoyment of a closely contested string. For this reason the selection by good bowlers or by poor bowlers coincided very closely. It became generally understood which men should be among the first chosen in order to make for an interesting match.

When Doc, Danny, Long John, or Mike bowled on opposing sides, they kidded one another good-naturedly. Good scores were expected of them, and bad scores were accounted for by bad luck or temporary lapses of form. When a follower threatened to better his position, the remarks took quite a different form. The boys shouted at him that he was lucky, that he was "bowling over his head." The effort was made to persuade him that he should not be bowling as well as he was, that a good performance was abnormal for him. This type of verbal attack was very important in keeping the members "in their places." It was used particularly by the followers so that, in effect, they were trying to keep one another down.   While Long John, one of the most frequent targets for such attacks, responded in kind, Doc, Danny, and Mike seldom used this weapon.   However, the leaders would have met a real threat on the part of Alec or Joe by such psychological pressures.

The origination of group action is another factor in the situation.   The Community Club match really inaugurated bowling as a group activity, and that match was arranged by Doc.   Group activities are originated by the men with highest standing in the group, and it is natural for a man to encourage an activity in which he excels and discourage one in which he does not excel.   However, this cannot explain Mike's performance, for he had never bowled well before Saturday night at the alleys became a fixture for the Nortons.

The standing of the men in the eyes of other groups also contributed toward maintaining social differentiation within the group.   In the season of 1938–39 Doc began keeping the scores of each man every Saturday night so that the Norton's team could be selected strictly according to the averages of the bowlers, and there could be no accusation of favoritism.   One afternoon when we were talking about bowling performances, I asked Doc and Danny what would happen if five members of the second team should make better averages than the first team bowlers.   Would they then become the first team?   Danny said:

"Suppose they did beat us, and the San Marcos would come up and want a match with us.   We'd tell them, those fellows are really the first team, but the San Marcos would say, 'We don't want to bowl them, we want to bowl you.'   We would say, 'All right, you want to bowl Doc's team?' and we would bowl them."

Doc added:

"I want you to understand, Bill, we're conducting this according to democratic principles.   It's the others who won't let us be democratic."

In Whyte's description and analysis of how social rank acted as a source of control in bowling, a competitive group activity among the corner boys, we have seen how group members resist behavior that could disturb their social ranks.   The group prevented a low-ranking member from improving his position by success in bowling. The established social rank also discouraged behavior by high-ranking members which might have reduced their prestige.   We have noted how the leader in the corner gangs always tries to keep members in debt to him and avoid being obligated to low-ranking group members.[29]   This suggests that the distribution of obligations as part of the ranking process assures conformity to norms.   The more that low-ranking members become obligated to high-ranking members the greater the likelihood that they will conform to the norms carefully

[29] *Ibid.*, 127–128.

observed by group leaders. The favors received are themselves rewarding, but once taken, the obligation to repay is strong; and one form of repayment is conformity. We shall have more to say about reciprocity and exchange of obligations later in this chapter. Meanwhile, one final example illustrates how fear of "loss of face" or loss of rank tends to induce conformity on the part of high ranking members. This example comes once again from the study of machine-shop workers.

We mentioned the helping norm that required high-ranking machinists to offer help to low-ranking operators. The other side of this norm made it embarrassing for a relatively high-ranking machinist to ask for and receive help. In the terms of the norm, a machinist should not need help, and he placed his social position in jeopardy if he could not manage on his own. This situation arose:[30]

.... Marc, a machinist, one day was machining a cylindrical piece on a lathe. Specifications called for a rather tight tolerance. Marc did not seem too sure of himself. He checked and rechecked his micrometer reading and examined and reexamined the drawing. He said to this researcher, "Watch this, I'm going to have some fun." He motioned me to come with him and he walked over to Ron. Marc said smilingly: "Say, Ron, let's see how good a reading you can make. What's the outside diameter of this piece?" Marc winked very playfully at another worker who looked up while Ron took the reading. Ron reported his reading to Marc. Marc smiled and said, "just for fun, let's see how many different readings we can get." He then took the part over to Axel and, in a similar "kidding" vein, asked him to take a reading. Axel complied and reported a reading which differed slightly from Ron's. Marc laughed and said in a loud voice, "You see what I mean? That's a different reading." Marc returned to Ron and reported Axel's reading. Ron then checked his "mike" reading, obviously somewhat disturbed. This time, Ron used a magnifying glass to be sure he was reading the micrometer properly. He reported his original reading again. Vito, who was working on the lathe just in front of Ron, took the piece and checked the measurements. He was a fraction off from Ron, but closer to Ron than to Axel. Marc made great sport of the three different readings, but significantly enough he decided that he had machined to meet the tolerance called for on the blueprint. The point is that Marc, by "playing it up," had managed to get some help, without making it seem as though he needed any.

The machinist was stuck and needed help. To protect his social position, he made a joke of it, and got what he wanted. He did not jeopardize his own position by anxiously seeking assistance.

[30] A. Zaleznik, *op. cit.*, pp. 37–38.

The stabilization of social positions in a group creates the conditions for stronger control of behavior largely through the system of obligations, norms, and rewards which help bring about the ranking. Ranking, however, stabilizes the degree of conformity present in the group. Not all members conform to the same extent; otherwise there would be less differentiation in rank than generally found in groups. As patterns of conformity and their rewards produce social ranking, the conditions for continued conformity are established.

Homans in *The Human Group* sets forth a crucial distinction in understanding the stability in degrees of conformity. He presents the idea that individuals can anticipate the consequences of departing beyond existing levels of deviation from accepted norms. The anticipation of deprivation and punishment is enough in many cases to deter deviation. This capacity to anticipate or "fantasy" behavior and its consequences is a *virtual* or hypothetical change compared with an *actual* change. To quote Homans: [31]

In everyday social life virtual changes are the more important of the two [types of change active in social control: actual and virtual], for through them intelligence takes part in control. Without intelligence— if we can conceive of human society as existing at all without intelligence— violations of social norms would be commoner and greater than they are in fact. The members of a group are obedient to its norms not only because they have actually disobeyed and·been punished in the past, but also because *they see what would happen if they did disobey.* [Italics added.]

Anticipating consequences occurs more accurately when the ranking system develops some stability.

## Predispositions of Members to Conform

We have concentrated thus far on three elements: norms of behavior, rewards and punishment, and ranking. These elements are forces acting as a group within a group. The degrees of conformity and deviation in the behavior of group members, however, result not only from the strength of the external forces acting on them in the group, but also from internal forces acting within themselves as individuals. These internal forces can be thought of as predispositions of members to conform. The term predisposition suggests the existence of tendencies within the individual which are established well in advance of

[31] George C. Homans, *op. cit.*, pp. 292–293.

membership in a work group.   They are best understood within the context of personality analysis because they stem from the individual's life history.   Again, we should like to sidestep a lengthy and detailed consideration of personality development as it relates to group behavior, reserving this topic for a series of chapters in Part Two. Nevertheless, we do injustice to our efforts to understand social control in groups if we avoid explicit attention to the relationship between predispositions to conformity and group efforts to control member behavior.

We can state fairly simply at the outset the main conclusions we hope to establish in this discussion:

1. All individuals have some tendency to conform to group norms. Even in cases of persons with severe psychotic or neurotic trends in their personality the latent predisposition to conform exists.   The basic reasons for this initial predisposition to conformity are twofold. First, the strong need for interpersonal relationships can gain little gratification without some tendency toward conformity.   In addition, the history of an individual's attempts at establishing satisfying relationships with others "trains" him in accepting some conformity as a condition of successful human relationships.   This training carries over into successive interpersonal experiences.   A second factor, related to the first, is the need for validation of perceptions and experiences. In no sense can a person withdraw himself completely from the necessity of validating what he knows and believes.   Such validation occurs in communication and implies some degree of acceptance of group control.

2. Despite the pervasive tendency toward conformity as a basis for human relationships and validation, individuals vary considerably in their predispositions to conform.   Individuals who, for example, are highly dependent will conform beyond the point of reasonableness and submit themselves to complete control from others.   Some experimental evidence which we shall cite later indicates that "overconformists" may form a larger part of our population than we care to believe.

3. Some of the conditions that determine the degree to which individuals conform or act independently are social class membership, parental emphasis on training in independence, and need deprivation or satisfaction in early childhood.

Let us examine the evidence supporting these conclusions.

The pervasive need for human relationships as a basis for conformity is revealed clearly in the literature on human development.[32]   Briefly,

[32] See, for example, Erik H. Erikson, *Childhood and Society*.

the infant is born into the world in an utterly dependent position. Nurture, both physiologically and psychologically, is the essence of the mother-child relationship during the earliest period of infancy. This relationship is the prototype of the dependency that successively results in the exercise of self-restrictions and limits on behavior. These self-restrictions provide the earliest experiences with conformity as a condition for reward or need satisfaction. We refer, of course, to toilet training as an essential experience in conformity. Since every adult once had to learn control while in a relatively helpless state of development and within an elementary reward relationship, it is not surprising that the conformist tendency exists in all human beings. Group control, let us recall, acts through a reward system that contains elements of approval and shame which can easily recreate the affect generated in early childhood.

The second aspect of the pervasive tendency toward conformity lies in the experiences of validation through human relationships. Validation refers to the way individuals assess and confirm reality. An individual's perceptions of his environment can be *validated* as he receives confirmation that they are shared by persons with whom he communicates. Not only are simple perceptions of physical reality subject to confirmation, but also the more complex beliefs and attitudes are held securely or modified depending on the extent to which they are confirmed in relationships with others.

The process of validation describes essentially the means by which groups develop norms. It is essentially a trend toward standardization in group behavior. We are suggesting that the basis for standardization is the needs of the individual for confirmation from others.

Validation of individual perceptions and the development of norms as a social process have been the subjects of a series of classic experiments conducted by Sherif.[33] The data in these experiments deal with the relationship between individual perceptions and group norms as illustrative of the need for validation.

In the experimental setting, the investigators created a situation in which "reality" was left very indefinite. Subjects entered a dark room in which it was impossible to orient themselves through spatial relationships. The subjects were shown a light and asked to indicate when the light moved and how far it moved from the point at which

[33] Muzafer Sherif, "Group Influences Upon the Formation of Norms and Attitudes," in *Readings in Social Psychology*, Macoby, Newcomb and Hartley, Eds., pp. 219–232. A more elaborate treatment of these experiments is given in Muzafer Sherif, "A Study of Some Social Factors in Perception," *Archives of Psychology*, 1935, No. 137.

it was first seen. In fact, the light was stationary. Perception of movement was a result of the "autokinetic" effect—apparent movement resulting from a lack of reference point against which to establish the position of the light.

Subjects were tested individually and in groups to determine whether, over successive trials, norms would be established that influenced judgments. Two experimental conditions were developed: first, some subjects were tested individually and then brought together and tested as a group; second, other subjects were tested as a group for a number of trials and then tested individually. The results of the experiments would show, among other findings, whether individuals originally tested singly would have widely disparate perceptions compared with their perceptions in the group situation and, conversely, whether original group influences on perception were sustained in the later individual trials. If group norms were developed and influenced judgments, then we should expect to find a greater degree of similarity of perceptions in groups as compared with individual trials. Similarly, we should expect to find a greater degree of similarity in perceptions in individual trials *following the group trials* as compared with individual trials preceding the group test conditions.

We reproduce below two sets of graphs showing the results under the two sets of circumstances.[34]

The left-hand column graphs in each set, showing the results under conditions of individual trials followed by group trials, demonstrate clearly that judgments of individuals vary considerably when they are not influenced by others. When coming together as a group, a marked tendency toward common judgments is evident. This result is attributed to the development of group norms. When individuals are tested singly following a series of tests in a group setting, as shown in the right-hand column, their responses bear a strong resemblance to the group norms previously established.

Let us now quote Sherif as he summarizes his experimental results:[35]

The experiments, then, constitute a study of the formation of a norm in a simple laboratory situation. They show in a simple way the basic psychological process involved in the establishment of social norms. They are an extension into the social field of a general psychological phenomenon that is found in perception and in many other psychological fields, namely, that our experience is organized around or modified by frames of reference participating as factors in any given stimulus situation.

[34] Muzafer Sherif, *The Psychology of Social Norms*, pp. 226-227.
[35] *Ibid.*

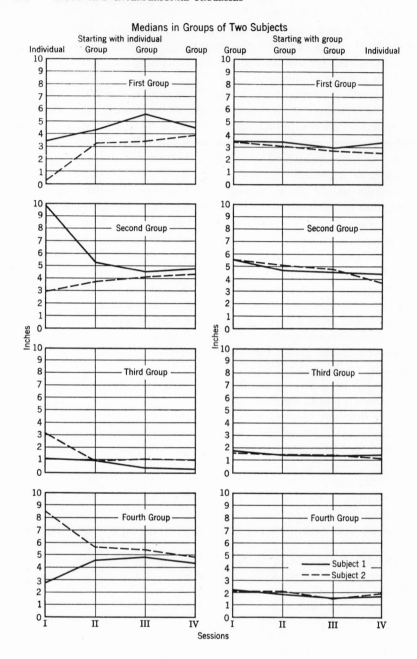

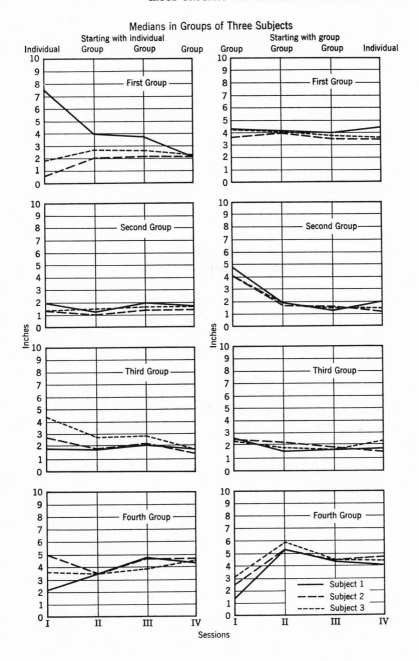

Medians in Groups of Three Subjects

On the basis of this general principle considered in relation to our experimental results, we shall venture to generalize. The psychological basis of the established social norms, such as stereotypes, fashions, conventions, customs and values, is the formation of common frames of reference as a product of the contact of individuals. Once such frames of reference are established and incorporated in the individual, they enter as important factors to determine or modify his reactions to the situation that he will face later—social, and even nonsocial at times, especially if the stimulus field is not well structured. Of course this is a very general statement. It gives us only the broad basic principle with which we can approach any specific social norm. In each instance we have to take into consideration particular factors that participate in its production.

The "common frame of reference" referred to by Sherif is related to the need for validation of perceptions as a basis for reality. This need operates as a force within the individual predisposing him to conform to the norms of groups with which he actually seeks membership.[36]

For purposes of theory, we should note that this standardization is not a conscious concern of the group members. Yet the startling degree to which similarities appear in the behavior of members suggests strong individual disposition toward conformity. The explanation suggested in discussing validation as need for organizing reality is thoroughly consistent with the researches cited.

The need for consensual validation of experience generally motivates conformity in interpersonal settings. Yet other selected and special motivational factors explain the frequent overconformity. The individual may be so strongly predisposed to conform that he underestimates personal judgments and capacity to influence others to accept his ideas.

Overconformity in group interaction provided the main interest in a series of experiments reported by Asch.[37] The term overconformity describes the emphasis of the experiments because the issue posed was how frequently individuals would acquiesce to group pressure when concession necessitated distorting perceptions of reality. In an ex-

[36] Another good illustration of standardization of behavior in groups is available in the results of the Relay Assembly Test Room Experiments reported in Roethlisberger and Dickson, *Management and the Worker,* and in T. M. Whitehead, *The Industrial Worker* (Cambridge, Massachusetts, Harvard University Press, 1938). Investigators noted that girls who sat adjacent to one another showed remarkable similarities in their output rates and also in their variations in output. This finding was especially strong in those cases when the pairs developed strong affinities. Where conflict developed, the similarity in output disappeared.

[37] Solomon E. Asch, *Social Psychology,* pp. 450–501.

periment a group of subjects was asked to state individual judgments on the lengths of lines displayed on cards. Each member was specifically asked to match one of these sample lines with a standard shown on a separate card. All of them but one were primed to give the same incorrect answer. The exception, the naive or critical subject, was forced to respond after he had heard the incorrect answers of other participants. He then faced the conflict of responding to group pressure, on the one hand, or to his own perceptions and judgments of reality, on the other.

Among 31 critical subjects tested in several trials, one-third of the total responses conformed to the incorrect answers of the "primed" majority. Forty-two per cent of the subjects erred only once or acted independently. The rest distorted their judgments to coincide with the majority opinion at least twice. A few subjects overconformed by going along with the majority on all trials. Asch also tested a control group in which the subjects gave their answers privately in writing. The results from the control group showed without doubt that the distortions did not occur in the absence of group pressure. Only 7.4 per cent of total responses were reported erroneous in the control group, compared with 33 per cent in the experimental groups, and almost the entire control group made no more than one error during its trials, compared with 42 per cent in the experimental groups.

Asch described the actions of "independents" and "nonindependents" during group discussions following the trials. The naive subjects were all under considerable pressure and felt it. The independents held to their judgments while the nonindependents distorted to go along with the majority.

There is not enough evidence from these experiments to suggest the personality difference between independents and nonindependents. Chapters Six and Seven of this book will throw some light on the factors underlying acquiescence. The main idea we have attempted to establish in this section is that individuals vary considerably in their predisposition to conform. The need for consensual validation represents one of the forces tending toward conformity in all individuals. But excessive acquiescence and overconformity are related to a special set of personality characteristics that are established in the individual well before he reaches the interpersonal settings in organizations.

## SUMMARY

In this chapter, we have presented a definition of social control in groups which stresses the forces governing behavior in interpersonal settings. With a distinction between formal and informal control established, the emphasis throughout this chapter has been placed on understanding interpersonal processes in informal social control.

The elements of social control discussed in this chapter were: (1) the norms of behavior, (2) rewards and punishments, (3) the systems of ranking, and (4) the predispositions of members to conform. The norms of behavior are the undeclared rules of conduct which grow out of the ideals and values present in the wider culture but which operate with specificity in interpersonal relationships. The specificity turns on the existence of rewards and punishments that act to maintain the system of norms. The individual's responsiveness to the rewards and punishments in groups reflects a basic predisposition to conform; this is an aspect of personality development.

In concluding this chapter we should caution the reader against assuming that norms once established are fixed for all time. Just as the values and ideals of a culture change, albeit slowly, so do the norms of behavior change. The process of modifying norms is very important in introducing changes in interpersonal relations and organizations. The issue of change will be discussed in the concluding chapters of this book and will lead us to review many of the ideas on social control presented here.

The next chapter continues the discussion of group and interpersonal processes and deals specifically with the flow of emotions, or affect, in groups and its relations to work.

*Chapter Five*

# Affect and Work in Groups

THIS is the final chapter devoted to the analysis of group processes. As a single topic, it deals with problems of affect—the emotions that arise in the course of group interaction—and problems related to the regulation of work. These are two strikingly different kinds of processes; the emotions are internal to the life of the individual, while work is a boundary process for the individual and for the group. Work is defined by the relations between a group and its environment; the purposes of the group are stated in terms of environmental interchanges. (An exception is the friendship group in which the sole purpose is to maintain and enrich the emotional life of its members.) The emotions are processes confined within the boundary of the individual person. In this chapter we shall detail the nature of the relationship between emotional processes and work in groups.

The emotional state of members and the ebb and flow of different affective qualities that make up a group atmosphere are related to the type and quality of the work performed in an interpersonal setting. Emotions are experienced in response to the changing structure and dynamics of the group. Work is accomplished as a result of the energies made available for group and individual output; but the energy sources of the emotions and of work are the same, emanating from within the individuals who participate in the group. Before relating work performance to emotional states, we shall examine the types of work performed in groups.

## TYPES OF WORK IN GROUPS

Work in interpersonal settings is distinguishable with respect to three criteria: (1) the *psychological interdependence* among members required by the task, (2) the personal *involvement* of the individuals with the task, and (3) the personal *risks* facing group members by virtue of their working together. Psychological interdependence is the condition in which the individual feels that his task contribution is related to and interdependent with the contributions of others toward a shared goal. The goal cannot be attained by any one individual independent of the others in the group. Personal involvement with the task is a condition in which the individual identifies the results of his efforts as a "product"; he psychologically "owns" and cares about that product and the processes by which he produces it. A sense of craftsmanship or artisan pride reflects personal involvement in the production of "things," but a similar sense of involvement may be experienced in the production of less tangible products. Finally, personal risk is involved in work group situations in which the individual psychologically invests his self-esteem and personal concern in a process in which he may lose as well as gain considerable rewards. Prospective losses include feelings of personal failure, frustration, and wasted time.

The first type of work consists of individual tasks performed in a group; the second, information exchange; the third, problem solving; and the fourth, learning. These four types of work involve an increasing degree of psychological interdependence among members that, in turn, becomes the basis for heightened individual involvement an intensified emotional reaction. Since these conditions increase the individual's psychological investment in the group, they are accompanied by an increase in personal risk.

## Individual Tasks in the Group Setting

There are many types of work groups whose task is defined in terms of the individual outputs of group members. In these instances, the degree to which the members are psychologically interdependent is quite limited. Many work groups in factories, for instance, a drill press department, are such groups. In a drill press department, each member is assigned to a machine or a job for which he is expected to meet specified output standards. The absence of psychological interdependence stems from the fact that the worker typically sees only *his* job and thus does not depend on anyone else in the group for completing it.

In addition, he usually has little reason, as far as his work is concerned, to experience involvement in the total purpose of his group or organization. Such lack of involvement may exist even in those work groups in which there is considerable technological interdependence, such as an assembly line.   On an assembly line, each individual performs a task on the conveyor as the work progresses from one station to the next.   Typically, the individuals performing the work see their own jobs as related to the inanimate conveyor, and not to the group of persons with whom they work.   In such cases, the psychological experience stemming from the condition of interdependence and involvement belongs to the engineers and designers who create the technological achievement, rather than the workers.[1]

The psychological condition of work resulting in feelings of impoverishment by the worker has been described as the condition of *anomie*, or rootlessness and lack of a sense of identity.[2]   Not all work groups made up of individual tasks create the condition of *anomie*.   Highly skilled jobs allow the individual to remain involved through pride in his work and the rewards of exercising competence.[3] The psychological interdependence of individuals in many highly skilled jobs may be relatively low, but their sense of personal involvement is frequently high because of the challenge of task accomplishment.   Psychological interdependence may occur as a result of shared identification with the ideals and standards of skilled work.

If personal involvement is absent because psychological interdependence or interest in the intrinsic features of the job are lacking, the group tends to alternate between apathy, related to the sense of *anomie*, and outbursts of anger.   At the same time, the group may be cohesive, engaging in nonwork social activities which are elaborations of the family and community experience of the workers' dominant social class.[4]

Many contemporary studies point out the extent to which the culture of these work-alienated groups is directed toward protecting the group against outsiders.   Researchers report the common occurrence of restriction of output and resistance to change, as well as highly elaborate social patterns within the groups—patterns built around nonwork activities such as coffee groups, card playing groups, and betting pools.   The elaboration of such social patterns within work groups often follows from the absence of conditions necessary for task-based psychological interdependence.   In these instances, the

[1] See A. Zaleznik, *Worker Satisfaction and Development*, pp. 120–123, and C. R. Walker and R. H. Guest, *The Man on the Assembly Line*.

[2] Durkheim, *Le Suicide*, and Mayo, *The Human Problems of an Industrial Civilization.*

[3] Zaleznik, *op. cit.*

[4] See A. Zaleznik, C. R. Christensen, and F. J. Roethlisberger, *The Motivation, Satisfaction, and Productivity of Workers: A Prediction Study*, pp. 169 ff.

design and organization of jobs do not facilitate identification with the task. Technically required functional interdependence among various jobs may be effectively concealed by individual job constraints. Thus, there is no sense of craftsmanship, so that there is little identification with common ideals of work and competence. Instead, identification takes place around a need to protect members from external authority figures.

This social outcome results from job designs and organizational constraints which fail to create psychological interdependence, either through a lack of technological interdependence or a lack of the bases for craftsmanship ideals in the intrinsic content of the job. The more specialized or subdivided the work is, and the shorter the completion cycle of the job, the less chance there is that the conditions necessary to psychological interdependence will be attained.

The element of psychological risk is minimized in individual task settings, since the individual invests little of himself in terms of emotional involvement. Beyond a minimal feeling of technical responsibility in response to the economic threat of loss of job, the individual has little reason to care about his group's outputs or the organization's success. Hence, poor group or organizational performance will not be experienced by the individual as a *personal* failure.

## Information Exchange in the Group Setting

The second kind of work performed in groups is primarily an information exchanging process. Many groups in industry are brought together to pool information required by the members in their jobs outside of the information exchange group. The basic assumption underlying this type of work is that each individual has some information that the others need, and that each individual's job will be facilitated by pooling information in the group meeting. During such meetings, the individuals are called upon to contribute their information to the group.

The main job in this setting is to share information and not to solve particular problems, produce new ideas, or make decisions. There is little expectation of arriving at conclusions. As a result, there tends to be little psychological identification with a group product or outcome. Members of such groups often become bored with having to listen to others talk; the over-all emotional tone of the group tends to be apathetic.

A typical example of this kind of group activity is found in organizations where work is done in shifts. Members of the night shift talk with departing members of the earlier shift to gather routine information relevant to their work operations. This occurs in hospitals, military posts, and other operations calling for around-the-clock activity.

Information exchange meetings are a valuable and necessary aspect of organizational life. The major difficulty encountered is the tendency of individuals to confuse this type of work with other kinds. Boredom and apathy, coupled with latent interpersonal competition, may lead the information exchange group to create problems and call for decisions more appropriately handled in other settings. Similarly, a problem-solving or decision-making group may find itself wandering off into information exchange activities. This may relieve tension and divert attention and energy from conflict, but information exchange could be done more effectively in another setting. A certain amount of energy waste, confusion as to group goals, and uncertainty as to the appropriate expectations of individuals result from such inadvertant shifts in type of group work.

Work defined as information exchange requires little psychological interdependence or group identification on the part of group members. The individual has little to risk. The greatest demand on the individual is that he listen and understand the content of the remarks of others and that he present information to them which is relevant to their work as individuals. The great advantage of group exchange over nonpersonal exchange, such as circulating memos, is that it allows for more immediate and economical questioning and clarification. However, requests for clarification and questions often lead the group into more aggressive and competitive forms of work, which, though relevent in other settings, may merely create confusion with regard to the content of the information which was supposed to be exchanged.

## Problem Solving in Group Settings

Problem solving produces a high level of tension and psychological interdependence among group members. In problem-solving activity, the group attempts to define issues or problems involving a variety of solutions. Besides attempting to define its problems, a potentially creative task in itself, the group approaches solutions through data-gathering and evaluation. A group decision is reached when members achieve a consensus. A solution to a group problem may range from the agreement to search for additional data, to selecting the one of several plans of action which they think will most effectively resolve their problem.

Consensus may be achieved in a variety of ways. The process may culminate in formal voting. Or it may lie in the silent consensus of the traditional Quaker meeting. Regardless of the particular process used by the group, consensus is necessary for obtaining effective results *after* the decision has been reached.

Consensus as we define it is quite different in meaning from the legalistic idea of obtaining a majority vote; it is also quite different from the idea that 100 per cent agreement has to be reached. Our meaning of consensus lies in the degree of personal commitment the members feel toward the group decision after it is reached. This means, for example, that even though some members might disagree with the decision on principle, they will accept it and personally carry out their part. Their emotional commitment to the group is measured by willingness to put the plan decided on into effect, in their own personal behavior.

In this view of consensus, the high degree of psychological interdependence and personal involvement which are concomitants to effective group problem solving are apparent. In the case of token decisions, where majority rule or the need to appease a strong superior determines the outcome, uncommitted minority members, or individuals who harbor hostility toward the leader, can easily make the decision fail by deliberately or inadvertently not doing what the decision implies they should. If they are not emotionally involved with the decision, they have little to lose by its failure. Since the quality of a decision is measured after the fact by its consequences, a lack of commitment to the group on the part of its members, a low degree of psychological interdependence, and the resulting lack of consensus may produce ineffective results.

The need for consensus commits group members to the high degree of psychological interdependence and risk that arises from attempts of group members to influence one another. The influence process is accompanied by high emotional involvement and risk because individual members' views, attitudes, and feelings toward the problem have to undergo change; in this continuing process of change, some members may gain, while others lose, a degree of respect from others as well as self-respect. The attendant emotional involvement tends to center around aggressive attempts to change another person's views and equally aggressive attempts to defend one's own. Hence, a relatively high degree of psychological risk is involved.

Not all problem-solving groups feature high personal involvement by the members; some such groups may be quite dull and apathetic. Similarly, the output of low-involvement groups may be dull and unimaginative, leading to compromising, sporadic, and confused action. The quality of the group's decision will be determined not only by the competence of its members as individuals, but also by the member's motivations and the processes which the group follows in making its decisions.

We are assuming that the problem-solving group includes the salient individuals whose actions outside the group will determine the effectiveness of its decisions. Such members would have personal stakes in the outcomes. Some groups may actually include people who will be personally unaffected by the group's decision. These might be staff consultants or outside experts whose function is to provide information upon which the committed members of the group will base their decision. Their low involvement reflects the fact that the group's decision will not cause them to do anything differently themselves. They have nothing to lose. This requirement for commitment on the part of the individuals embodies the element of risk in problem-solving groups.

The condition of psychological interdependence is most clearly understood when we compare the social-psychological requisites of the effective problem-solving group with the performance of individual tasks in the group setting. The group output in the case of individual tasks is merely the *aggregate* of the performances of the individual members. The output of a group of drill press operators may easily be measured by adding up the number of completed pieces produced by each member over a particular accounting period. Thus, if the group produces a certain number of pieces on a particular day, and one individual is absent the next, even though the other group members produce at the same rate, the total output for the day falls by the quantity of the absent individual's production. His performance has no effect on the others' output except for their response to the nonwork aspects of their purely social relationships. As far as the task itself is concerned, there is no interdependence among members, and no psychological interdependence is required. Little risk is involved in belonging to this kind of group.

The output of the problem-solving group is of an entirely different nature. The contributions of the individual members do not accumulate by simple addition to determine the group's output. The output is *more than* the aggregate of individual contributions, or in some instances less. Such a group deals with the kind of problem that actually requires group activity for its resolution.

On the other hand, the problems of some artificially contrived groups can easily be solved by any one individual acting alone. It is important to understand this difference, because many artificial problem-solving groups are set up in organizations and in educational settings for the major purpose of training. In these groups, members merely check their answers, which they arrive at alone, with others who correct or help or learn from them. If this type of group starts out with competent, well-trained members rather than inexperienced trainees, group activity adds nothing to the best of the individual solutions.

The kinds of problems and groups with which we are concerned involve specialized competences and sources of data; characteristically, they also involve maintaining balance among multiple, noncommensurate value criteria. Typical of this kind of problem would be a company's way of dealing with foreign trade opportunities involving legal problems, national interest, company-government relations, international trade interests from the point of view of the foreign nations, humanitarian interests, and dollar economics. Each of these interests implies specialized knowledge and competences as well as sometimes disparate value systems. An editorial group of a campus newspaper faces some of the same issues in its attempts to define and redefine policies and operating procedures. Even a small group of children trying to decide how they will occupy an idle afternoon faces similar problems as long as its members are committed to playing as a group.

For the problem-solving group, the problems toward which the primary work is addressed lie *outside* the group. Decisions have to do with ways in which the group will attempt to modify conditions; such decisions imply changes in members' relationships and behaviors— as a group, as representatives of an organization, and as individuals— toward their external environment. Although decision, planning, and implementation are most often associated with active modes of behavior toward the environment, they may, in fact, involve more passive behaviors such as waiting or gathering more data.

## Learning in Group Settings

Learning is the fourth type of work which takes place in groups. Learning changes group members. Change of this type may range from cognitive change, in which the individual has learned to think differently, to emotional change or relearning, in which the relationship between the person's perceptions, thoughts, and feelings are altered. Either extreme, or combination of them, may result in behavior change.   Small group discussions in educational environments are examples of learning groups, as are the training groups in human relations training programs, therapy groups in psychotherapy, and some policy and planning groups in organizations.

The therapy group stands out as the most clear-cut example of learning in a group setting.   Individual members of the therapy group define themselves as sick and in the need of help.   They enter the group to discuss their problems and gain insight into them so that they can work more effectively as individuals in their everyday environments.   A unique atmosphere is created in the therapy group. Individuals are encouraged to face their problems honestly and to confront one another with their views and reactions to the problems. The offering of reactions, views, and interpretations becomes a group task, rather than the exclusive domain of the therapist.   No group decisions are reached other than those related to internal, group procedures.   The outcome for the group is the learning and relearning experienced by the individual members.   The group learning process may confront the individual with the need to make personal decisions or choices, but these are individual choices, rather than major group agenda.

The training group, often used in human relations programs, is also designed to help individuals learn more about themselves and about interpersonal relations.   Unlike the therapy group, its members do not define themselves as sick.   Moreover, training group members differ widely in the particular kinds of help and learning they initially seek. The task of the group is to provide internal procedures and experiences that will enhance individual learning.   Again the output of the group is measured in terms of how much the individual member learns; but this outcome is dependent upon the quality of the internal processes and activities of the group.   Since the individual member's behavior plays a large part in determining the quality of the group processes, the group's attention to the behaviors of individual members is an important part of the learning process.

The policy and planning group in organizations seems at first glance to be quite different from either therapy or training groups.   However, there are a number of important similarities and common features. Although it is often difficult to distinguish between a problem-solving group and a policy and planning group, there are important differences; the time spans with which they are concerned, the degree of concreteness or abstractness of their conclusions, and the degree of practical immediacy, as against imaginative, creative, and future-oriented outlooks, serve to distinguish between them.

Policy and planning groups may come together for the purpose of dealing as creatively and imaginatively as possible with the long-range future of their organization. Their purpose is not to make decisions or to evolve specific and detailed plans with respect to a limited problem, but rather to engage in relatively abstract and imaginative thinking about the long-range problems of the organization. Such groups are, in a sense, actively engaged in writing their future history. Discussions are intended to affect the quality and procedures of work in other groups. But the policy group constrains itself to avoid working on short-range, specific problems and concentrates on long-range, relatively ambiguous issues facing the organization as a whole.

Ambiguity in the task of the group, in its internal procedures, and in its work processes, is common to the therapy group, the training group, and the policy and planning group. Ambiguity in task and group procedures creates the conditions for heightened involvement on the part of group members and a heightened sense of psychological interdependence. Under such conditions the opportunity for individual learning is strongest.

The same conditions provide the opportunity for achieving the most creative group outcomes, or the greatest failures. Intrinsic to the condition is high risk of failure, along with high potential returns, for the individual in the learning group, and for the group itself, as well as its organization, in the policy and planning group. The element of risk, that is, potential loss *or* gain in an atmosphere of ambiguity and uncertainty, leads to high personal involvement and psychological interdependence. Each member has much at stake personally; *sharing* this high investment leads to the strong feelings of psychological interdependence.

This classification of work, ranging from the individual task in the group setting through learning in groups, differentiates among the four types of work along three dimensions. The degree of *psychological interdependence* among members refers to the feeling of being closely, emotionally related through working together. The degree of *personal involvement* with the group's task is largely determined by the way in which jobs are defined and organized. Psychological interdependence and personal involvement with the task increase along with the *amount of risk* experienced by the members.

The risk for the individual is highest in the learning group. The changes and the influence attempts that accompany them sometimes aim at the core of the individual's personal identity and feelings of worth. Change is thus a risky venture. Hence, the learning group's processes are exceedingly important. It is in the group setting, under certain conditions which the group strives to attain, that the individual may find the resources to maintain certain aspects of himself while changing other aspects. The risk is that the continuity of self-identification will be lost, and that too much of the self-esteem which the individual has brought to the situation will be liquidated.

We shall limit our further discussion in this chapter to problem-solving and learning group settings. In order to pursue our major topic, the relationships between emotionality and work in groups, we must examine situations in which both elements are actually involved to a high degree. Because of the heightened personal involvement and psychological interdependence in these kinds of groups, the phenomena which we want to study and understand is available in abundance.

Four attributes of problem-solving and learning groups tend to make them different from other kinds of groups and provide the bases for the importance of emotional processes in these settings. First, the task or purpose is important; the importance is symbolized by the relatively high status afforded individuals engaged in problem solving or learning work and the relatively high status attributed to the group. A definite outcome—that is, a decision, individual learning, or both— is expected. This outcome is expected to change organizational, group, or individual activities in *important* ways. This feeling of importance is quite different from the view of individual tasks and information exchange processes as relatively routine. Routine tasks are not expected to lead to important changes in anyone's activities.

The second attribute of problem-solving and learning groups is the need for pooling, sharing, and evaluating data. Although information-exchange groups handle data, there is little need for evaluation in that setting. Furthermore, problem-solving and learning groups' data include opinions and new ideas; the unique competences of individuals are brought to bear on the spot. The data they bring in from outside are of some importance, but the processes of evaluation, modification, and creativity which go on in the group are major determinants of the quality of the outcome.

The kind of information processing which characterizes these groups is intimately tied to their third major attribute; individual members stand as unique resources in relation to one another. There is a built-in interdependence of experience, knowledge, and skills. This characteristic of the process requires individuals to have and express *specialized* expertise, emphasizing individual differences to a great degree.

The fourth attribute follows from the need for specialization. *Integration* must take place, in the form of group consensus. This consensus effects closure for the group and for its members. Without consensus, the individual does not know what he is to do differently, and his learning is not confirmed. The processes of specialization will have led to a splitting apart of knowledge, ideas, opinions, and persons. Hence, the problem is resolved only when the separate pieces of data are integrated into a consensus. The group feels its task completed only when this condition has been achieved, and the individual's learning becomes confirmed after he has tested it for validity in the group.

One effect of these attributes of problem solving and learning is that the groups tend to feature widely varied and fluctuating emotional moods over time. These emotional moods are associated with different levels of work within the group, ranging from polite and superficial work to deeply involving work where something new is taking place. As a next step in our analysis, we shall examine the differences between these various levels of work, the sequence in which they tend to occur, and the accompanying emotional moods.

## LEVELS OF WORK IN PROBLEM-SOLVING AND LEARNING GROUPS

The emotional tone of the work process in learning and problem-solving groups may range from dull and routine, at one extreme, to creative and exciting, at the other. The heightened psychological interdependence, involvement with task, and high personal risk characterizing these groups can be sensed in the emotional tone of the group at a particular time. Some groups may exhibit a consistently dull atmosphere. Others may be so constantly keyed up that they heighten involvement and drain energies. Usually, however, a particular group will fluctuate in emotional mood, sometimes being dull, other times exciting. Particular emotional moods tend to occur along with particular ways of working. Just as types of work groups may vary in over-all emotional tone, the tone of one group varies over time; since this variation may be related to changes in the way the group is working, let us examine the concept of "levels of work."[5]

Low-level work consists of bringing in and providing data oriented toward the personal needs of the members. For example, the members talk about outside personal experiences related to the problem at hand. They react to one another, giving personal opinions, agreeing,

[5] See Bennis and Shepard, "Group Observations," in Bennis, Benne, and Chin, *The Planning of Change*, p. 753.

disagreeing, and supporting. These reactions provide new data; that one member disagrees with another is data, in this sense. At this level, however, data of both kinds remain unanalyzed. No attempt is made to find out what, if anything, the data mean in relation to the group task. Beyond the aggregated expressions of individuals' personal needs, nothing new in the way of group work has transpired.

The next level of work is attained when a minimum of questioning and inquiring around the data takes place. For example, the individual's reasons for presenting some data and not others are examined. An explanation of why one person supports or disagrees with another is sought. However, the kind of explanation which satisfies the group engaged in this level of work tends to be conventional, common sense, and superficial, for example, a treasurer's comment that he has to watch the funds because that is his job. Such explanations do little to define or resolve the group's problems. They are usually defenses or justifications of individuals' views. They are designed to cut off, rather than facilitate inquiry and exploration and they have a deceptive tone of finality.

When the group begins to pursue its data in more depth, it is ascending to the third level of work. There is some consensus as to the questions the group should be addressing, and it is able to stay with a particular point or issue for some time. The members squeeze the point dry and feel that something is being learned or settled. Individuals' resources and positions are clarified. They are beginning to know where they stand as individuals and as a group, but they have not yet begun to work together. Their major source of data at this level is their own history as a group.

The observer might view this transition through the first three levels of work as getting ready. The lowest level is getting to know one another through fairly safe, routine, conventional behaviors. The group is fairly quiet, except perhaps for some nervous joking. Members do not really hear what they are saying to one another, or do they seem to care. Placing people, rather than knowing people, seems to be the strategy.

The second level of work involves a kind of warm-up or practice at pursuing issues with the understanding that no one will get hurt. Figuratively, the members are taking off their coats in preparation for action. At the third level, they are rolling up their sleeves, lining up their tools and materials. Real work is about to begin. However, nothing new has yet emerged.

Top level work creates a new product from an aggregate of individual parts. Members engage actively and openly in helping one another.

Feedback is direct; the masks and stage props are dropped, so that each member can clearly see the effects of his contributions as he makes them. Communication becomes more valid, in that members are sending the messages they want to send and the recipients are receiving the intended messages and have the opportunity to check their understanding. New insights and ideas emerge spontaneously and are tested immediately and openly. Although each member has brought his unique experiences, information, and competences to the group, the source of the newness and the originality of the ideas developed in the group is difficult to locate in any one member.

Those who have been involved in this transition process in a group will recall the emotional changes experienced as they moved through these levels of work. Initially, the mood is one of uncertainty and perhaps some mistrust, accompanied by a compulsion to play it safe. Then some tentative testing, probing, and experimenting takes place to eliminate some of the uncertainty as to why they are there and who is going to do what to whom. Attention narrows from a broad concern with everything that is going on—such as the nervous mannerisms of individuals and their physical appearance and grooming—down to who has what to offer and ultimately to involvement in the task itself. As we look for the relationship of emotional processes to work, we can easily visualize a transition from a condition where feelings of anxiety block to one where emotional energies flow unimpeded into work. Levels of work in groups are results of the ways emotional energy is utilized. These uses range from anxiety reduction to direct engagement in work.

Emotions exist in the members of a group. The nature of the individuals' emotions and the existence of groupwide emotional effects can be inferred from individuals' behaviors. The reality of this *group* emotionality may be questioned. However, we know from our own experiences that under certain conditions individuals' emotions are shared by others; they may be transmitted from person to person in a manner suggestive of a contagious disease.[6]

We shall describe the particular mechanisms by which the individual responds emotionally to social situations, to the appearance and behavior of other individuals, and to the intrinsic content of work as we proceed. Similarly, we shall discuss the processes by which the affects take on the properties of a "substance," how they are transferred among persons, modified within persons, become "painted onto" ex-

---

[6] See Caudill, *The Psychiatric Hospital as a Small Society*, pp. 8–9, 87–127, for a description of the "mood sweeps" which permeated the atmosphere of the hospital at certain times.

ternal objects, both personal and inanimate, and are built up or drained off within the person.[7]

We have tried to construct a rough outline of our topic—the management of affect and work—by describing different kinds of work in groups, the attributes of problem-solving and learning groups which most clearly relate to affective processes, and levels of work. We shall now be more specific in our analysis of work as it relates to problem solving in groups.

It is fairly easy to understand the meaning of work as it applies to an individual operating with tools on materials to convert the materials from one form to another. But group problem-solving work is more vague, complex, and difficult to visualize. The reality of the process is clearly evident in such complex group products as the Constitution of the United States, the Allies' invasion of Europe in 1944, or a finished automobile. But its importance becomes clear when we think of the failures in history which may be attributed to ineffective group problem solving.

## MODELS OF PROBLEM-SOLVING ACTIVITY IN GROUPS

Our task here is to describe in more detail the requirements for effective problem solving in groups. One approach is to list the rational thought processes and activities that members must engage in to solve the problem. In this approach, where a rational model of problem solving is the goal, the emotional aspects of the process are looked upon primarily as interferences. Rational processes are assumed to be emotionally neutral, or conflict-free. Some individual problem solving is, in fact, conflict-free. An example would be the solution of an elementary mathematical problem where the individual applies purely cognitive processes. The symbols used and the operations performed have no emotional meaning for the individual, but feelings of frustration or elation, or a sense of asthetic beauty, may accompany the phases of task completion.

However, even the most rational model of problem solving is based on some assumptions which do, in fact, involve emotional processes. At the beginning of the process, the existence of a problem is experienced as a disturbance. This disturbance is of an emotional nature, and the individual is impelled to eliminate it. Hence, the intellectual processes follow from pre-existing conditions of emotional disturbance and motivation.

[7] Although the term "affect" appears to be the root of the word "affection," the sentiments of liking which we think of as affection are only one of a variety of affects.

There are several means other than problem-solving activity by which emotional disturbances may be eliminated by the individual— notably the psychological mechanisms of defense such as denial (the problem really does not exist), projection (it is someone else's problem), or repression (the disturbance gets pushed into the unconscious while conscious attention goes elsewhere). However, once the existence of a problem is accepted psychologically, and the motivation to approach it through problem-solving activity is activated, the next steps may be viewed as involving conflict-free, rational processes.

The literature of problem solving makes frequent reference to John Dewey's six-phase model:

(1) Felt disturbance, motivation to resolve the problem,
(2) Analysis and diagnosis,
(3) Search for alternative solutions,
(4) Evaluation of alternatives for their consequences,
(5) Experimental try out of one alternative,
(6) Acceptance or rejection of that alternative, and so forth.[7a]

March and Simon list some general characteristics of human problem-solving processes:[8]

(1) No matter how complex the problem, it may be broken down into a number of simple elements.
(2) Search processes are inherent; the problems solvers search for data and alternatives.
(3) The products of the searches must be screened for utility as parts of potential solutions, or as possible solutions.
(4) The search and screening processes tend to be random; the sequence of processes may vary. Beneath this randomness there are two kinds of organization which provide structure:
   (a) Certain procedures tend to be followed—these are in general agreement with Dewey's model described above.
   (b) The nature of the problem itself dictates a structure on which the problem-solving process takes place. For example, the problems encountered by an organization reflects the organization's structure, in that the elements of the problem are defined as marketing, finance, production, and so forth. This structure of the organization, which was presumably set up to solve problems in the first place, also provides a search and screening mechanism by which specialized data (such as market descriptions, financial resources, and productive facilities) are processed.

[7a] See, for example, March and Simon, *Organizations,* pp. 178–179.
[8] *Ibid.*

(5) These processes of organization (4a and 4b above) are of an hierarchical nature, in that the phases of problem-solving re-cycle continually, starting with broad-scale definitions of the problem and ultimately narrowing down to increasingly minute definitions of
subproblems. As the focus of the process swings from broad and
general to narrow and specific, and then back again, there is a developing sense of the relative importance of issues, and the hierarchical
relationships among issues and processes.

The processes described above are similar for both group and
individual problem-solving activity. However, group problem solving has additional requirements not involved in individual problem
solving. These are testing for consensus, the allocation of roles for
implementation, and preparation for observing, recording, and re-
evaluating the results of the action. While parallel processes are
required in the case of an individual effort, there is presumably little
need for communication and the processing of independent judgments.
The group, on the other hand, requires processes by which the independent views and specializations of the members may be integrated.
These needs are independent of the emotional aspects of group life,
psychological interdependence, and personal involvement with the
task. Integration of individual efforts must take place even when
the "group" is merely a set of specialized computer components and
the "group product" is the solution of a complex mathematical problem by the computer as a whole.

The omission of problems of managing affect, or emotions, helps us
see the raw outline of what has to be done in order for a group to
engage in effective problem solving. The analogy of a computer
tells us something about a sequence of operations and feedback cycles
by the ways in which the wires are hooked up. Nothing happens in
a computer until power is modulated to the various parts of the
system, even though the wires may be hooked up properly. In
human groups, power takes the form of emotional energy.

As work centers, humans usually have more emotional energy
available than is needed to power their problem-solving activities.
Perhaps this surplus is left over from when work and dangers were
primarily physical and the psychological defenses were more closely
related to survival in the physical environment. In any case, the
relevant environment for problem solving tends to be social, rather
than physical, in the modern world; but the same primitive sources
and forms of emotional energy are aroused. The problem of managing affect in problem-solving groups is thus one of channeling surplus emotions into a variety of activities, as well as into the resolution

of personal problems that are not directly relevant to the *external* problem of the group.

Managing affect in groups is not simply preventing some emotions from emerging and allowing others to do so. Just as we can talk about the *external* realities of the group's problem, we can also deal with the *internal* realities. Group members are people, not computer components; they really do use the group setting as an arena for testing and resolving personal problems around which their emotional energies become organized. Hence, although we may identify some of the affect in groups as surplus in relation to the task, the fact that it exists creates its own set of internal problems. These must be managed in some way if the group is to channel some of its members' energies into externally directed work.

To take these internal realities into account while keeping in mind the primary external task of the group, R. F. Bales developed a social-psychological model of group problem-solving activity.[9] This model assumes two separate sets of problems in the group. One set corresponds to the contents of the rational models described above. This is called the instrumental-adaptive set of activities. It refers primarily to acting on, and adapting to, the group's external environment. The second set is called social-emotional and refers to the internal environment of the group. Thus, an action in the group may be addressed to the external task, to the internal problems inherent in humans' social interactions, or, in some instances, to both.

Bales' classification scheme, which was also used in Chapter Three, is reproduced here. Our earlier interest in this scheme centered around problems of observation and description in identifying structural attributes of groups, notably role structures. Here we are concerned with the theoretical underpinnings of the scheme that provide a social-psychological model of group problem solving.

Starting with the rational models described above, the social-psychological model includes two sides of three information-processing problems—orientation, evaluation, and control. One side consists of asking questions; the other of attempted answers to these questions. Through empirical research, Bales found that there were about eight times as many attempted answers as actual questions asked. This in itself is an intriguing finding. It suggests that much of the data presented in groups consists of answers in search of questions. It also confirms the idea held by experienced problem solvers that a most important element of the process is formulating the appropriate questions.

[9] R. F. Bales, "The Equilibrium Problem in Small Groups," in Hare, Borgatta, and Bales, *Small Groups*, pp. 424–463.

Interaction Process Analysis

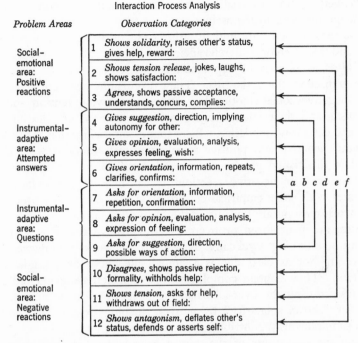

*Problem Areas*                    *Observation Categories*

Social-emotional area: Positive reactions

1  *Shows solidarity,* raises other's status, gives help, reward:

2  *Shows tension release,* jokes, laughs, shows satisfaction:

3  *Agrees,* shows passive acceptance, understands, concurs, complies:

Instrumental-adaptive area: Attempted answers

4  *Gives suggestion,* direction, implying autonomy for other:

5  *Gives opinion,* evaluation, analysis, expresses feeling, wish:

6  *Gives orientation,* information, repeats, clarifies, confirms:

Instrumental-adaptive area: Questions

7  *Asks for orientation,* information, repetition, confirmation:

8  *Asks for opinion,* evaluation, analysis, expression of feeling:

9  *Asks for suggestion,* direction, possible ways of action:

Social-emotional area: Negative reactions

10  *Disagrees,* shows passive rejection, formality, withholds help:

11  *Shows tension,* asks for help, withdraws out of field:

12  *Shows antagonism,* deflates other's status, defends or asserts self:

*a  b  c  d  e  f*

*A subclassification of system problems to which each pair of categories is most relevant:*

*a  Problems of orientation*
*b  Problems of evaluation*
*c  Problems of control*

*d  Problems of decision*
*e  Problems of tension-management*
*f  Problems of integration*

*From Robert F. Bales, Interaction Process Analysis (Cambridge: Addison-Wesley Press, 1950), p. 9.*

A fourth kind of information-processing problem, that of decision, is included in the social-emotional area, as agreement—a positive social-emotional reaction—and disagreement—a negative social-emotional reaction. In our discussion of rational models, consensus was a requisite for group problem solving. Although this may seem to be a purely task requisite, it is clearly a connecting link between task and social-emotional problems. Bales includes the activity out of which consensus emerges—that is, agreement and disagreement—as a social-emotional activity. This set of categories and the ambiguity it engenders (are agreement and disagreement task *or* social-emotional elements?), along with the opinion categories, are those around which social-emotional tension builds up in groups. Since the individual identifies with his ideas, he tends to defend himself when his ideas are challenged. Thus, to challenge the ideas of other persons tends to challenge the persons themselves.

The tension build-up, initially arising out of an ambiguity between task and social-emotional relevancies, and confusion between persons and ideas as objects of aggression and defense, can and sometimes does transcend the task area. These excursions are represented in such negative social-emotional reactions as showing tension and antagonism, and their countervailing positive reactions of releasing tension and exhibiting solidarity. Bales found empirically that the balance between negative and positive social-emotional reactions were about equal in dissatisfied groups and extended to a 5 to 1 preponderance of positive over negative reactions in satisfied groups. His model indicates with some empirical confirmation that during the process of task work tensions are built up in the form of negative reactions; these, in turn, are neutralized or overcome by positive reactions with the process continuing cyclically as the group works. However, the cycles are not as clear cut as a simple sine curve or a single wave diagram. They contain complex subcycles which are generated continuously during the over-all balancing process. For example, if one member "shows solidarity" by actively helping or praising another, he is simultaneously contributing toward group integration and antagonizing the opponents of the person he supports. Hence, each act sets off a chain reaction of reinforcing and compensating activity cycles. In any case, task *and* emotionally relevant activities take place in the process of group problem solving. These activities simultaneously create and solve internal problems, as well as deal with the major external problem.

The over-all balance of these various kinds of activities was found by Bales to be approximately as follows:[9a]

| | |
|---|---|
| Social-emotional, positive reactions | 25% |
| Instrumental-Adaptive, attempted answers | 57% |
| Instrumental-Adaptive, questions | 7% |
| Social-emotional, negative reactions | 11% |

In terms of the utilization of emotional energy, this means that more than one-third of the groups' "attention" was devoted to creating and dealing with social and emotional problems, while about two-thirds of the activity dealt directly with the task. We may speculate with confidence that this balance varies widely from group to group and during the life of any one group. The questions for group members

[9a] See R. F. Bales, "The Equilibrium Problem in Small Groups," in Hare, Borgatta, and Bales, *Small Groups*, p. 427. The figures were derived from a study of 16 five-man experimental groups working on a standard task.

and leaders posed by this formulation are: What balance between internal and external problem activities represents the best that we can do, in view of human capacities? What constitutes necessary waste? What constitutes unnecessary waste? How can we measure the utility of social-emotional activity? How can we more effectively use our inherent emotionality for the furtherance of our individual and group goals? To what degree, or under what conditions, are these personal and group goals diametrically opposed and in conflict?

To pursue these questions, or perhaps to formulate more appropriate questions, we must look more intensively at the affective processes themselves. We shall, therefore, temporarily detach ourselves from the rational requisites for problem solving in groups and concentrate exclusively upon the affective processes that take place.

## AFFECT IN GROUPS

It is important that we recognize the major differences between properties of groups and properties of individuals. Affect, emotions, or feelings are experienced by individuals. They are not experienced by groups except in a metaphorical sense. Groups do not feel; individuals do. The source of affect is within the individual.

The combined *effects* of individuals' feelings may be properly described as group attributes. Such effects include the concepts of group cohesion, that is, the relative attractiveness of the group to its members; group social structure, that is, the hierarchy of influence, the communication channels, and the subgroupings that characterize the group; and group norms, that is, the code of behavior shared by group members. Other properties of groups are dictated by their designed relationships to the environment; these include the group's purpose and its technical and status relationships to other groups. The latter properties are independent of the feelings of members. The degree to which they are internalized as shared sentiments and as the individual emotions varies from group to group, and within one group, from time to time.

The source of the individual's emotions is his drives or needs. His particular configuration of drives, needs, and psychological defense mechanisms provides him with a predisposition to respond emotionally to external stimuli in certain limited and patterned ways. His affects are aroused in response to internal tensions and his environment. This predisposition to respond affectively in certain ways to both internal and external stimuli lies within the individual's personality structure.

Some conceptual simplification is required to explain affective processes in groups. The simplifying model may be based on the entrance of a new member into an existing group or the formation of a new group. Let us assume that the affective problems and processes characterizing these events are prototypical of the more complex events and processes that may be observed in long-established groups. The seeds of such affective processes in group development are sowed in the initial encounters which provide our analytical models.

The individual's affective state is a prior condition.[10]  It exists before he enters the group.  His prior feelings bring him to the group in the first place.  In addition to such intellectual, rational, or technical reasons for his entry as formal job requirements, he brings a personal set of feelings toward authority or aggression and toward intimacy in interpersonal relations.  He has a feeling, or a set of feelings, related to being close to people physically.  His intimacy feelings are reflected in the degree of pleasure or discomfort with which he anticipates being with people.

Another relevant pre-existing affect is the individual's potential aggressiveness or passivity.  At one extreme, he may be predisposed to work *on* people, to initiate influence upon others.  At the other, he may be emotionally set to have others work on him, that is, to be influenced by them.  These predispositions relate to work as well as to interpersonal relations; even in the purely social group, where no task work occurs, there are dominantly aggressive or passive modes of interaction.  Aggression and passivity are especially relevant in the clearly nonwork settings of friendship, courtship, and love.

These are only a few group-relevant pre-existing affects; others will be discussed later in this chapter.  Here we are merely emphasizing the fact that the emotional processes which take place in groups follow from and elaborate on, the affective states brought into the group by its members.  As the group functions, particular events arouse within the members certain emotional responses which are unique to the situation, but which bear clear relationships to the members' pre-existing states.  Such emotional states may be shared by several, or all, members.  Even though individual members have unique emotional predispositions and expressive styles, certain events or problems in the group may arouse common sources of anxiety.

Thus, although affect resides solely within the individual, its combined effects may be observed and described as an affective response of the *group*.  "Mood sweeps,"[11] "contagion,"[12] and mass hysteria[13]

---

[10] See Fritz Redl, "Group Emotion and Leadership," in Hare, Borgatta, and Bales, *Small Groups,* for a more complete elaboration of these ideas, pp. 71 ff.

[11] See Caudill, *op. cit.*

[12] See Redl, *op. cit.*

[13] See S. Freud, *Group Psychology and the Analysis of the Ego.*

represent the pervading influence of a particular emotional tone. Riots, rebellions, religious revival meetings, campus "panty raids," and lynch mobs feature this characteristic. In small groups the effects are not so dramatic. But even in this setting certain extreme emotional conditions are clearly evident in outbreaks of group-wide giggling, laughing, and foot-shuffling in the active mood, and yawning, boredom, apathy, and depression in the passive mood. Something is going on; it spreads among members and "takes over" to the point where members who are not affected feel lost in the midst of a movement they do not understand.

Other emotional themes in groups are more subtle and are relatively unnoticed by members; they occur outside of the members' conscious intentions. One or several individuals may suddenly become aware that something funny is going on; they are not doing what they thought they were doing. Perhaps they have unwittingly joined an unconscious conspiracy to run away from their major problems and engage in shared fantasy. This may be exhibited in an uncontrollable rash of off-color jokes or stories around common themes such as death, the fallibility of authorities, or troubles in the world outside of the group. To understand the meanings of these emotional experiences in groups, let us examine the types of affect brought to the group by its members.

## Types of Affect

Two types of affect within individuals may be attributed to primary drives. These are, first, aggression—taking action on external objects including persons—and second, affection—attraction to or liking external objects including persons. Each of these primary types of affect varies in intensity and each has a negative as well as a positive direction. Thus, negative aggression is passivity, or being acted upon, and negative affection is hostility, disliking, or avoidance. These dimensions may be represented schematically as follows:

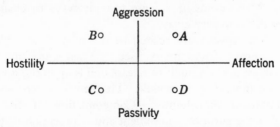

The emotional tone felt and expressed by one person toward another person or object can be described by an infinite number of combinations of aggression-passivity and affection-hostility which vary in intensity. For example, the feeling and expression may be described as aggressive-affectionate, indicated by point *A* on the above diagram. This would apply to the friendly backslap, the hug, the squeeze, "outgoing warmth," the attempt to embrace or include or engage with the other actively. An aggressive-hostile act or expression, indicated by point *B* on the diagram, would be real or symbolic hitting, punching, cutting, and otherwise attempting to destroy the other through one's own activity. Passive hostility, represented by point *C*, would be expressed by waiting for, or allowing, the other person to be destroyed by his own activity or the activity of a third party. Passive affection, point *D* on the diagram, would be expressed by waiting for or allowing the other person to demonstrate affection actively. The intensity of such feelings may vary from neutral, through weak, to strong.[14]

These primary affects are rooted in the earliest problems of the infant in adapting to his environment. Their outward manifestations, in cultural forms such as war and brotherly love, primary work activities, and passive contemplation, are functionally related to the survival and adaptation of the society. The universal sources and external applications of affect will be discussed in more detail later in the book.

To these primary affects may be added a second set which are related to the first and which are especially likely to be aroused in group situations. These are anxiety, depression, and elation. Anxiety is a free-floating fear or dread of something unknown. In contrast, fear is attached to an identifiable object. We may fear the assailant's fist, so we try to get out of its path. We may fear heights, so we avoid high places. The feeling of fear is attached to an object or person, and the means of avoidance is thus clarified. With pure anxiety, the lack of an object to "avoid" causes an accompanying feeling of helplessness. The feeling does not suggest its remedy; contemplation merely serves to compound the anxiety unless an object is found to be the cause of the feeling. Mechanisms of defense provide ways to change anxiety to fear or to drive anxiety away.

Feelings of depression are related to the manner in which the individual's aggressive drives are released. When aggression which the individual cannot allow himself to release builds up in the group setting, he may turn it inward upon himself. He then feels depressed, hollow, empty, "down in the dumps." Contemplation of the condition typically takes the form of punishment and deprecation of the self.

[14] See T. Leary, *Interpersonal Diagnosis of Personality,* pp. 62 ff.

Elation takes the form of an active turning outward, "jumping with joy." It accompanies a successful, guilt-free, consummation of an aggressive activity—the batter connects for a home run or the hard-working problem solver finds the answer. Conversely, when the batter swings and misses or when the problem solver cannot find an answer, the aggression tends to turn inward and he feels depressed. Mood sweeps of depression and elation accompany the group's feelings of frustration or success in its work. To the individual in the group, these affects accompany his experiencing of his personal failures and successes in the group setting.

Although these descriptions of the affects are overly simplified, we need not, at this point go deeper into them before we examine the process by which affect is managed in groups. We should have a feel for the variety of types of affect, the variety of objects and events to which it may be attached or from which it may be aroused, and the various forms in which it may be experienced inwardly by the individual, expressed outwardly in his behavior, and shared in a group.

## Problems of Affect Management in Groups

In our discussion of a social-psychological model for problem solving in groups, we concluded that much of the individuals' energy is involved in creating and dealing with the social-emotional problems inherent in group problem-solving activities. Our comments about affect in groups have described some of the sources and kinds of affect which pour into, and are aroused by, the group's processes.

Now let us detail more specifically the means by which groups control and utilize their members' emotional energy. These means are similar to the individual's mechanisms of defense but take on particular forms because they are shared in a group. As is the case with the individual's mechanisms of defense, group mechanisms for managing affect vary in the degree to which they allow the group and its members to perform effectively in their respective environments.

W. R. Bion has described a sequence of emotional modalities which he found in the therapy group.[15] Other trained researchers and learning group leaders have observed these same modalities occurring in other kinds of groups, including learning groups, problem-solving groups, and groups engaged in even simpler forms of group work. The idea of the modality is that at times in a group's development there seems to be covert consensus among all members around an emotional theme that is relevant to their shared individual problems. In these in-

[15] W. R. Bion, *Experiences in Groups.*

stances, no one has proposed or voted on the particular mode of emotional activity in which they engage; the members are "carried away" together, so to speak, by a particular emotional theme.

These themes tend to work in sets such as "fight" or "flight" modalities. In the fight modality, the mood is one of aggressive hostility; members argue with one another or with present or absent authority figures. They act as if there were an unknown danger in their midst which can be discovered and eliminated by fighting. When this proves unsuccessful, the members engage in flight from the danger. They psychologically move away from the unknown danger by sharing a fantasy episode, such as "wouldn't it be wonderful if . . .", the members join in free association to transport themselves to another time and place.

Fight *or* flight are paired for several reasons. One is that while the group is in this mood, it can see no *other* course than to fight with authorities or with one another, *or* to join in flight from the task or social problems which confronts it. When these modalities are dominant in the group, its activities tend to fluctuate widely from one extreme to the other. A period of interpersonal fighting is typically followed by the members' uniting in an excursion away from the group's here-and-now problems. When the flight is called off or ends, the group often resumes its fight activities.

Another basis for the set relationship between fight and flight modalities lies in the genetic development of the individual. The primitive response to an inner disturbance such as anxiety is to lash out aggressively against some external object or to run away from the situation. Neither of these responses solves the problem, in the sense that we have analyzed that process. Nonproblem-solving activity characterizes the primitive human organism as well as the infant group; in both instances the organism is characteristically *dependent* on external authorities and protectors and thrashes about helplessly and aimlessly in response to anxiety.

To illustrate the ways in which the fight, flight, and other modalities tend to occur in groups, we shall use simplified examples from personal experiences. Since the original data were technically complicated, we have deliberately oversimplified for the purposes of illustration. Some original group data, in the form of transcripts of actual group meetings, appear in published case studies and in the references cited in this chapter.[15a]

A student group was assigned the task of producing recommendations for handling a human relations problem in a case they had all

[15a] See, for example, cases in Zaleznik and Moment, *Casebook on Interpersonal Behavior in Organizations.*

read.    The instructions were handed to the members individually by the instructor.    The members, after shuffling chairs and getting seated, sat with their instruction sheets before them on the table.

STUDENT A TO GROUP: It says here (reads instruction sheets).

1. B: I don't know what he means.

2. C: (Looks at clock.)    We have 45 minutes.

3. D: I think he deliberately made the instructions vague to confuse us.

4. (Laughter, then silence.)

5. A: Anyone got any ideas?

6. (Shuffling of chairs and papers.)

7. E: Maybe we should go over the case again.

8. B: I'd rather try to figure out what they want.

9. D: I don't think he really knows.    This whole course is that way.    I feel like a damn guinea pig.

10. F: Oh, it's not that bad.    Look, it says here (quotes a sentence on instruction sheet) . . . isn't that clear enough?

11. E: Look, the guy in the case said that (discusses a detail in the case) . . . .

12. B: So what?    You can interpret that a lot of ways.

13. C: Yeh.    It is obvious that (gives a view different from E).

14. E, B, and C argue a point in the case.    Some of the others gradually join in.    The comments are individualistic, having nothing to do with preceding or following ideas but clearly indicating that each person thinks that he is right and the others are wrong.    The members eventually start to become frustrated and depressed.    At one point they all are silent.

15. A: Boy, this reminds me of the football game last Saturday.

16. Others laugh.

17. D: I didn't see it.    What was the score?

18. (Several members join in recounting the football game.    The tone becomes frivolous and somewhat elated.    Some members physically imitate the aggressive actions of hitting and jumping with wild gestulations as they talk.)


In the above proceedings, we see a group put into an ambiguous situation in which the members have real doubts as to what they should be doing.    The response to this ambiguity initially hinted at some hostility toward the authority, the instructor in this instance, who put them in the uncomfortable situation (events 3 and 9).    Rather than engage this underlying feeling directly, they became involved in fighting (events 12, 13, and 14).    This not only deflected the hostility away from the authority, it also deflected attention from the need to clarify goals and procedures.    The fighting activity made no progress toward goal clarification or work; it tended to increase, rather than decrease, the discomfort level. The tension-releasing comment (events 15 and 16) led the group to flight from their primary problems. The subject of the particular flight, football, reflected the lingering aggression and hostility theme; but the "game" aspect tended to legitimize the latent hostility, since the group's relationship to the instructor disallowed direct expressions of hostility toward him. The instructor had the power to evaluate them in the course, and thus posed a real threat.

One of the dominant problems confronting any group is that of authority. How will the group relate to external authority figures, and what interpersonal authority relations will obtain among the members? Because of an underlying concern with this problem, group members tend to engage in another modality set which is called dependency-counterdependency. In the counterdependent mood, the group actively rebels against authority figures, either the representative of external authority in the group, such as its formal leader or teacher, or absent authority figures whose presence or influence is sensed within the group. In the dependent mood, the group wants direction and affection from the authority figure. These are the only alternatives for dealing with authority available to the immature individual and group. At later stages of development, independence and interdependence became possible choices.

In our example, one individual exhibited counterdependency (events 3 and 9) which was not directly shared by other group members. In another group situation, the following transpired.

19. MEMBER 1: It's awful smoky in here. Why don't you open the window, member 2?

20. (Member 2 opens the window.)

21. MEMBER 3: (Shivers) Now it's cold. (Turns to staff members) Can't you get us a better room?

22. MEMBER 2: Yeh. We can hardly move here. And it gets too smoky.

23. MEMBER 4: (Laughs) We're wasting our time on him. He won't do anything for us.

24. (Short silence.)

25. MEMBER 5: (To staff member) Can't you get us another room?

26. STAFF MEMBER: I don't think so.

27. MEMBER 6: There he goes, noncommittal as usual.

28. MEMBER 4: (To group) Boy, you should hear the secretaries talk about the staff. They try to be so damn nice that the secretaries never know what they want them to do. You'd think a guy who teaches human relations would at least know how to tell his secretary what he wants her

to do—but they have more problems than bosses who just tell them. (While talking, member 4 nervously polished his large military academy class ring with the fingers of his other hand—a fact which others commented upon later.)

29. MEMBER 2: (Grins "knowingly") Queer, huh?

30. (Group laughter, then silence.)

31. MEMBER 7: (A girl.) I know what let's do! Why don't we meet outside on the grass. It's such a nice day. Then we'd be out of this awful room.

32. MEMBER 8: Will you bring the Cokes?   (Laughter.)

33. MEMBER 5: We could have a picnic.

34. (Several members joined in around the theme of having a picnic on the grass.)

35. MEMBER 7: (The girl.)  Should we invite him (the staff member)?

36. MEMBER 6: That's putting him on the spot.

37. MEMBER 7: (Softly to staff member) Would you really care if we went out?

38. STAFF MEMBER: That would be up to you.

39. MEMBER 4: There he goes again.

Much of the behavior in the above excerpt was a form of testing the authority figure's apparent "permissiveness," which clearly infuriated some of the group members. The unsubtle attack on his masculinity by Member 4 (event 28) who characteristically emphasized his own masculinity (the class ring was a symbol of this), and the taunting by the girl (member 7, events 31, 35, and 37) are examples of particularly loaded attacks on the staff member and human relations instructors in general. The transition from the counterdependent challenge to flight (the picnic theme) with all too clear consistency of emotional meaning is notable. The flight took place following the group's confrontation with its own accusations (events 30 and 31). They were, perhaps, afraid that the staff member might actually respond directly.

The swing from counterdependence to overdependence was apparent in a quite clear request for guidance. The group acted as if it had given up and wanted to be rescued from itself. The girl foreshadowed this mood in event 37, but the rest of the group—at least as reflected in member 4's immediate response in event 39—was still in a counterdependent mood.

In many early group situations, the fight or flight response to a disturbance is superimposed upon the dependency-counterdependency response to the authority problem. This process centers around the presence of an authority in the group—a formal leader, a teacher, or perhaps a clearly senior and authoritative member. One of the most universal of the many emotional sets brought into the group by its members is an emotional orientation toward authority and authority figures. Everyone experiences the emotionally laden authority problem; each individual is continually faced with situations in which his own autonomy and the question, "Who is the boss here?," are at stake. Hence the emotional set is within the individual members; the actual or symbolic presence of an authority figure in the group activates the emotions of the members. Since the immature group is not clear as to the cause of the shared discomfort, it will typically engage in the primitive fight-flight response. Fighting among themselves provides the members with a convenient outlet for expressing any feelings of hostility or counterdependency they may hold toward the leader without overtly challenging authority. To confront the authority issue head-on is too threatening, since the members may not know the extent of his power. Furthermore, it is very likely that the members' ambiguous feelings toward the leader contain a good deal of guilt along with hostility and affection, so that the ultimate confrontation with the authority problem can be extremely uncomfortable.

Intermember fighting also eventually makes the members feel guilty and arouses feelings of dependency on the leader to intervene and settle the conflict "as mother used to do." But if the leader is a man, the members may become even more anxiety ridden because of the emotional connotations of interacting sex roles and resentment toward their feelings of helplessness. The next step has to be flight, until the group can arrive at a way of dealing directly with its authority problems and with intimacy and affection issues.

The third set of emotional themes revolves around intimacy and affection, which are strongly related to the authority problem. The authority figure seems to be not only a source of power, punishment, and control, but also a source of protection, affection, and support. Thus, the individual's emotional response to authority contains the ambivalent elements of hostility and affection. Intimacy also has positive and negative facets. Schutz calls these directions personal (positive) and counterpersonal (negative). Personal means wanting to be close and intimate, counterpersonal means wanting to keep apart and avoid intimacy.[16]

In addition to being related to the authority issue, intimacy and affection are also, and perhaps even more strongly, part of the problem of relationships among peers. When a group joins in flight, for example, its members react to sharing the experience, aside from the

[16] W. C. Schutz, *FIRO: A Three-Dimensional Theory of Interpersonal Behavior.*

purpose of the flight. The individual's emotional attitude toward being with people is a complex mixture of his orientations toward authority and sex-role relationships. Moreover, he is reacting to group events as well as to the particular personality characteristics of the other persons. Whether he wants to get close to another or remain aloof depends on his perceptions of the authority relationship which is measured by age differences in some instances, or on whether the other is male or female, physically attractive, and likely to accept and like him.

Cultural roles are related to these processes. For example, women might be more comfortable in approaching intimacy head-on than men, primarily because men dread the homosexual connotations that may be attached to male-to-male closeness. In addition, women are expected to gossip about interpersonal relations, while cultural training tends to forbid such activity to men. Hence, not only would you expect different affective tones to be experienced by men and women in response to the group's problems, but we would also expect to find differences in their predispositions to confront the problems directly. Although our example of cultural effects deals primarily with sex roles, similar effects may be found with respect to age, occupation, and current familial statuses.

The intimacy issue in groups is demonstrated in the emotional modalities of pairing and cohesion. Pairing refers to the situation in which members pair up, in twos or cliques, to support each other. This is observable in side conversations; while some common agenda occupies the group as a whole, two members withdraw psychologically into a conversation between themselves. Or two members may engage in a person-to-person conversation "across" the group. It is emotionally and psychologically easier for some people to deal with others one at a time. When the fight-flight and dependency-counterdependency modalities have resulted in little comfort or stability for the individual, the alternatives of pairing or "grouping" may emerge.

Although initially comforting to the individual, the pairing response eventually becomes unstable for several reasons. For one thing, the pair is "being watched." In addition, the individual seeking a pair relationship must choose his partner from the group. He is bound somewhat by the physical constraints of the group meeting—chair and table arrangements, for example—and thus may not be able to get close to an appropriate partner. Furthermore, the pair faces the same issues as the group, only in smaller scale: Who is the boss? How close shall we get? The issue of appropriate sex-role relations, especially in a public setting, is another discomforting issue which faces a pair.

The instability of particular pairings may lead members to engage in behaviors which search for optimum pairings or coalitions. A "chaperone," or third person, may help dispel some of the anxieties of a particular pair. But the third person may compete with, rather than chaperone, one of the pair, and thus raise more new issues than his presence would settle.[17]

Each member experiences feelings which are to some degree shared with others as the group moves through these various emotional modalities. The sharing of feelings and experiences becomes the basis for group-wide cohesiveness. Several symptoms may indicate that the group has arrived at this stage. For example, members may discover a common joke around a shared historical event within the group. They may start to recognize their group history, to which they refer in the process of revising their agenda. They may discover that they have been through difficulties together, and recounting and interpreting this newly discovered history may draw the group together.

Although we have been describing these emotional modalities as a sequence of problems which the group must face, it is clear that bits and pieces of unsettled issues from previous moods will recur, adding subthemes to the major trends of group development. This is clearly observable when the group begins to become cohesive. The elation of discovering an identity typically leads to a flight into groupiness. The boys may make a big event of bringing coffee or the girls may bring cakes to the meeting. If these events do not take place in actuality, they may be represented in symbolic behaviors. Smokers pass their cigarettes around the room and gum-chewers and candy-eaters do likewise. In addition, rituals are followed, special languages unique to the group are used, and the group transcends the time and space limits imposed by its task in the form of outside social activities. The group goes out into the private lives of its members, and the members bring their private lives into the group. The tone and content of conversation becomes more intimate. First names are used comfortably.

However, such flight may abruptly end on the authority issue, back where the group started. The precipitating event may involve planning an outside party. Questions arise: Should the leader be invited? Is "he" one of "us"? Or members may hesitate to address the leader by his first name. Such confrontations will, of course, lead the members to re-examine one another and to become self-conscious, as a group, about what they are doing.

[17] See T. M. Mills, "Power Relations in Three-Person Groups," in Cartwright and Zander, *Group Dynamics*, pp. 428 ff.

When we return to visualizing energy flows, these various emotional modalities and the behaviors which accompany them give the impression of a horde of blind animals running into the walls of a maze, searching for limits and the way out.   Some of these limits are internal to the individuals—such as the growing guilt they feel, and share, while fighting and fleeing.   Other limits are imposed by reality; the members discover "the truth" about what the leader can and cannot do—to them and for them.   Similarly, they discover truths about themselves and their relationships—what they really can and cannot do to and for one another in the group.   Each modality involves individual and group fantasies.   The members become carried away with these fantasies, acting as if they were realities until, at some point, the differences between fantasy and reality become clearer.

The ultimate modality is work.   However, in spite of knowledge and experience of these emotional processes, and of the ideal condition of work, every group must pass through some or all of these phases in order for individuals to discover for themselves what work can mean to them.   In the mood of work, the members can clearly distinguish the main line of progression toward task achievement from other directions of activity.   This is not to say that they try to rule out pure socializing, for example.   But they do know and accept the difference between work and socializing.   In the earlier phases they had a difficult time assessing their progress and tended to confuse one kind of activity with another.   When they recognize the difference, they have built themselves a set of shared standards, a culture unique to themselves.

The terms used in the rational models of problem solving, such as searching, screening, and defining the problem, may now be seen as referring to some highly emotional processes, problems, and resolutions. Searching, screening, and defining are the outcomes of fighting and fleeing, depending on or rebelling against the leader, maneuvering for closeness or distance, and testing pair relationships against group cohesion.   New courses that appear as old ones are tried and fail; each group apparently has to discover for itself the requisites of problem-solving behavior.

Not all groups are successful in working out their problems and achieving the work modality.   They can easily become fixed upon one or a combination of modalities.   The leader or responsible group member, as much as he may be aware of the difficulty, is often powerless to help the group move because he is part of the problem.   His offers to help, if conveyed at the time when the group emotional mood is related to authority problems, may be blocked by the very mood he is trying to change.

Group progress or frustration depends on the initial emotional predispositions of the members and the mixture of these conditions found among the various members. The individual's stages of emotional development are based on the same kinds of issues which face the group. At certain stages of emotional development, the individual is particularly apt to resonate with the corresponding problems as they are encountered in the group. If, for example, the individual is currently undergoing counterdependence in his life—if his dominant emotional tone outside the group is one of criticizing, debunking, and otherwise rebelling against his salient authority figures—he will grasp this issue as it comes up in the group with a tenacity which cannot be lessened until he experiences a resolution of his *personal* problem. To resolve the problem, the other members may try to isolate him and go ahead with further stages of group development. However, if they do so, they may become so involved in authority issues and potential guilt for ostracizing him that the group experiences more complex predicaments than that posed by the original problem member.

Another solution is for the individual to learn in the group and to change in the direction of resolving the personal problem. This possibility gives problem-solving groups the potential for making great contributions to the individual's personal development. Ideally, the individual can address his problem head-on in the group with some help from other members. The group setting confronts him with the reality of his own effects upon others. If he resolves his personal problem, the group and he can move on to other problems. If he cannot learn in the situation, group progress is unlikely.

This example of the effects of an individual problem on group progress and the individual's development is based on authority relationships. Similar effects may be found with respect to the individual's predispositions toward intimacy. A single counterpersonal individual, who actively seeks to avoid intimacy and increase social distance, can hold up the development of an entire group. His relative inaccessibility to group help can be as strong as that of the counterdependent individual. But the individual may learn and continue on in his personal development while allowing or helping the group to move ahead.

The group situation initially tends to bring out adolescent emotional extremes in its members. This is especially true of relatively unstructured learning or policy-setting groups. To the extent that each member uses the group situation as an opportunity to relearn and engages in personal reality testing, the group can progress through its various problems. Conversely, the less personal learning of this nature that takes place, the greater the likelihood that group results will be conventional, mediocre, and ineffective.

Group progress usually depends on the development and relearning of its members while in the group. However, some mixtures of personalities in a group may allow it to become highly effective with little *conscious* learning or personal change taking place. To understand this possibility, let us examine one mechanism by which a group may move spontaneously from one emotional modality to another.

Just as each group problem may become strongly related to the emotional problems of the individual, so can these group problems "bounce off" an individual who has already resolved the issue personally. He can then remain relatively unaffected by the particular problem, while the other members' personal problems and conflicts are highly involved. This means that he is free to act on other problems and is a convenient object for the group to follow. Thus, some of the group affect is carried by him out of one set of issues into another. For example, the group typically experiences a good deal of guilt after punishing their leader. The members are stuck with the feeling and enter into a downward spiral of group depression. However, one member does *not* feel guilty because the authority problem is not a conflict *for him*. So he "saves" the group by introducing a new set of problems, perhaps by leading them off into flight. With him as flight leader, the other members now have someone to pin their own guilt feelings on. This, of course, is the dynamics of childhood group vandalism; everyone can conveniently blame the leader, thereby transferring their own guilt feelings to him. This carrying of the affect by the one person frees the others to deal with other problems. Thus, the individual who is not involved in the conflict can move the group from one emotional modality to another.

It is unlikely that one person will escape conflict on all of the various emotional problems confronting the group. Hence, we would expect to find different persons "leading" the group as its moods change. Recognition of this can, of course, rekindle authority problems, especially in groups where one or more members, and possibly the formal authority figure, want to be in control of the group at all times.

Although discrete "leadership" events are important in understanding the movement of the group from one emotional modality to another, the overwhelming significance of authority and dependency to group situations must lead to an examination of the emotional dynamics of leadership. Even though some very effective work groups have substituted certain shared ideas and goals for a leader or directing influence, a more common tendency is for groups and individuals to personalize their authority in a central figure. For example, God tends to be thought of as a *person* by some, while others find it possible to feel governed by religious ideas. Our discussion of the central person will deal with his use by the group as an object for dealing with its affective problems.

## The Central Person and Group Emotions

Under certain emotional conditions within a group, one person may provide behaviors that transform the emotional atmosphere. The presence of a catalyst in a chemical reaction facilitates or accelerates the process, while the catalyst itself remains unchanged. In a similar way, the presence of a central person, at a particular time in the group's emotional life, can transform the group's emotional energies. The central person need not be a formally appointed or recognized leader. More often than not, he is completely unaware of his catalytic role on the process. To understand this catalytic effect, let us examine some of the elementary processes by which the individual's emotional energies are modified by external objects, especially other people.[18]

The simplest mechanism is the process by which love and aggression drives within the individual find release in activities and feelings directed toward another person. Through the acts of love or aggression toward another person, the tensions aroused by the drives are released. When the drives are aroused within the group, it may use the central person as a *shared* object of the *common* drives of its members. Thus, the group can draw together in the act of sharing love for or feeling and expressing aggression toward the same person. A particularly attractive person of the opposite sex, or even of the same sex, can become the group's "love object," while a particularly obnoxious person can become their shared object of aggression. In either case, a *group* emotion, shared by the individuals in the group, centers on the particular person. His or her presence has apparently mobilized the particular affect in the group.

Another way in which the central person may transform the group's emotional climate is through the process of identification. Psychological identification occurs when the object person, or some limited aspect of the person, is incorporated into certain thought and feeling process centers of the individual's personality. This incorporation is,

[18] See Chapters Seven and Eight for a more detailed discussion of these processes. See also Redl, *op. cit.*

of course, a symbolic one. The external influence becomes internalized, or "part of" the individual.

Redl describes three different ways that the central person provides identification service for the group members.[19] On the basis of affection two kinds of identification can occur: The conscience, or *super ego*, of the object person can be incorporated into the conscience of the individual. To the extent that this process is shared by group members, the effect is a form of group emotion. The rules of behavior imposed by the conscience are the rules that the central person holds; the members feel impelled to behave in ways that will earn the central person's affection.

The second kind of identification based on affection takes place when the object person is symbolically incorporated into the *ego ideal* of the individual. The individual's ego ideal is that cluster of thoughts and feelings which center around his idea of what he wants to be. Thus, the individual wants to be like the object person, so that others will feel toward him as he feels toward the object. Again, this process may be shared as a group emotion.

A third kind of identification is not motivated by affection, but by fear. This is called identification with the aggressor. As in the first form of identification rising from affection, the conscience of the central person, a powerful, stern, aggressor in this case, is incorporated into the conscience of the individual. But the process is directed toward avoiding punishment rather than earning affection from the central person. Thus, the group may mobilize emotionally around identification with the aggressor's rules of behavior in order to escape the punishment implied by his stern manner.

In addition to mechanisms motivated by affection and fear, the central person may be used to support the individuals' ego processes. The ego processes are those mechanisms by which the individual attempts to cope with his internal drives (including love and aggression), his conscience (which may be a source of uncomfortable feelings of guilt), and the demands of external realities. In this sense, the ego processes "manage" the relationships between the individual's internal conditions and external demands by attempting to establish a viable balance.

One way that the central person may provide ego support to the members is by presenting them with a convenient means for satisfying their drives. In this sense, the central person is a "procurer." He may be the person who sneaks the liquor into the "dry" party, the boy who has the cigarettes, or the man who knows the girls. Besides

[19] Redl, *op. cit.*

providing a means for drive satisfaction, this central person provides an object upon which members' guilt may be displaced. The central person is "guilty" because the members would not have done the "bad" things without his "leadership." Thus, he not only provides a means for satisfying a drive, he also provides a means by which the individuals may conveniently resolve their internal conflict between the drive and the dictates of their consciences.

The other form of ego support mentioned by Redl has to do with the use of the central person as a means of resolving conflict within the individual without supplying or procuring the means for drive satisfaction. The central person *initiates* the drive-satisfying act, and the others follow. In the prototypical group situation, the members' instinctual drives impel them toward a particular behavior, but their consciences restrain them from following the drives. The ego processes are then confronted with an internal conflict; feelings of guilt and anxiety are imminent. When the central person initiates the act, the impending guilt feelings may be displaced from the individuals' conscience to the external object, the initiator; this relieves the internal conflict of the individuals who follow.

Under these circumstances, the initiator is often conflict free with respect to the issue which is latently bothering the others. His own conscience may be insensitive to that particular issue. He may "think nothing of it," while the others are deeply concerned. By allowing himself, through his initiatory act, to assume the guilt, his "thinking nothing of it" spreads infectiously through the group. To them, he is the bearer of the guilt which would reside within them if they had initiated the act, and as a result they are guilt free. The particular act which they are now free to perform involves, in most instances. an expression of aggression, such as the real or symbolic destruction of property or a more direct form of rebellion against authority. However, the same mechanism could work in the service of expressions of affection. For example, a group of "tough" executives may harbor genuine feelings of affection for their leader, and dependence on him, which their work situation will not allow them to express. The individual who is free of conflict can free the group to share in the releasing of these feelings.

These various ways in which the central person is used by the group to serve its emotions become the dominant leadership mechanisms in some group settings. "The patriarchal sovereign"[20] or paternalistic manager attempts to influence his subordinates to identify with him through affection and incorporating his rules of behavior.

[20] Redl, *op. cit.*, discusses these and other "leadership" types in more detail.

The "modeler" (called "the leader" by Redl) attempts to become the ego ideal of his subordinates so that they will imitate him. "The tyrant" attempts to establish identification with himself through fear. "The organizer" provides his subordinates with means for satisfying their drives. "The seducer" and "the hero" take initiating action on issues which immobilize the group, thus freeing them from guilt or fear. Some of these processes may continue over time, in that they become a dominant tone of the group's relationship to authority represented by the central person. In other instances, especially in the case of the gradually developing problem-solving group, several or all of the catalytic processes may occur, with different people playing the central role from time to time.

## AFFECT AND WORK: CONCLUSIONS

Our original proposition was that emotional activities and work activities arise from the same source of energy within the individual. When the individual or group "product" is primarily expressive, such as a painting or a musical composition or literary composition, the "work" aspect of the enterprise would consist of fitting feelings into the technical constraints of the particular art form. When the product is the solution to a problem, tests of utility and consequences enter the process, in addition to the needs for meeting technical constraints. This need for reality-testing and maintaining contact with changing internal and external realities characterizes the difference between problem solving, adaptive, instrumental work and purely expressive activities.

The individual's and group's involvement in emotional modalities— that is, fight or flight, dependency or counterdependency, interpersonal intimacy or distance, pairing or group cohesion, and work—provide experiences which dramatize the human dilemmas of social life. Awareness of these emotional processes can confront the individual with a choice between learning and producing something new, or compulsively repeating old resolutions. Bion has commented on the apparent "hatred of learning by experience" which characterized certain stages of his groups.[21] The most pessimistic view is that the emotional processes tend to operate against learning and work.

Regardless of feelings about the legitimacy and potential of emotionality in groups, the existence of these processes must be accepted. Although individuals may be trained for more effective rational problem solving and may highly value intellectual, rational processes,

[21] Bion, *op. cit.*, p. 86 ff.

they cannot escape the realities of their own, and others', emotional problems by ignoring them or labeling them as bad. The issue for the individual and the group is, "What, if anything, can be done to work with, rather than against, the inevitable presence of emotionality in problem-solving groups?"

Group emotions and the catalytic effects of the central person are shared or common results of the individuals' intrapsychic processes. The emotional phases through which the group moves reflect, to a great degree, the emotional development of the individual members in and out of group settings. The emotional problems blocking the group and the resolutions which facilitate group movement are parallel to individual emotionality and problem solving. However, it would not be appropriate to think of the group as a complex individual and thus to try to take action on the group, or within the group, as if it were merely a more complex person. Understanding the nature of group emotional processes does not automatically suggest means by which a responsible individual, in the role of group member or leader, can control or change the processes. Such understanding does suggest, however, some ideas with which the individual can address *himself* and which might indirectly affect the emotional processes in his groups. Nevertheless, the object of such action would be the individual himself rather than the group.

Problems of affect management in work groups raise two kinds of issues with respect to facilitative measures. One concerns the part that one member, sophisticated in his understanding of what is going on, can play in helping the group move toward dealing with its problem-solving task. The other is related to the kinds of group norms which complicate or facilitate the group's internal problem of managing affect. Both issues demand conscious attention, by the individual and the group, to processes which usually take place at unconscious or unspoken levels of awareness.

Individuals vary in the degree to which they can handle affect in groups. Paradoxically, the private emotional response by the individual to the public expression of affect in the group raises "second level" emotional problems for the group. That is, individuals' feelings about feelings can cause more serious problems than might result from straightforward engagement of the primary feelings. For example, one person may have an absolute dread of engaging in or of witnessing interpersonal aggression. Hence, the very feelings which compel him to avoid behaving aggressively, or to intervene as peacemaker, may block his own and the group's progress.

Other individuals may dread engaging in or witnessing expressions of affection. Their compulsive avoidance behavior prevents them and the group from effectively resolving intimacy issues. Both of these examples feature a marked inability for the individual to handle affect. He gets carried away by personal feelings of dread, which are most likely based on a fear of being carried away in the expression of the primary affect. By not wanting to be "carried away" with one kind of affect, he inadvertently becomes "carried away" with another.

Handling or accepting affect implies that the individual takes the full brunt of the expression without deflecting it or otherwise allowing it to get past him. If, for example, he feels aggressed upon, he takes the aggression inside himself and possibly feels hurt. He can then respond clearly and directly to the emotional meaning of the inter-action. In this way he has helped consummate the expression, rather than letting it bounce off and "float around" unattached in the group. Similarly, if the expression is one of affection, he takes it directly and feels liked. He accepts the expression and does not feel compelled to intellectualize a defensive response or otherwise keep the feeling ambiguous and unattached.

The description is, of course, a statement of an ideal seldom achieved by even the most mature and experienced individuals. People normally prefer to defend themselves intellectually rather than accept feeling hurt; they prefer to modify an interpersonal expression of affection into a conventional social nicety. The "proper thing" to do *socially* is to reciprocate, rather than accept, expressions of liking. Social relations involve exchange and trading, as we dis-cussed earlier. Interpersonal affect is a different kind of "substance"; it has to "flow" out of one person and into another for the expression to be completed. Lovers, for example, do not thank each other for loving and being loved.

To handle affect comfortably in the group, the individual not only lets it "flow" he also refrains from raising or perpetuating the second-level issue of feelings about feelings. In this sense, handling the affect helps clarify what is going on in the group, rather than further confusing an already ambiguous situation. When aggression, for example, is taken or accepted, the aggressor and the group can clearly see what is happening. These thought-feelings, when pursued for their implications, may ultimately lead the group toward being better able to separate emotional problems from problem-solving requisites. This cannot happen as long as the affect floats around hidden behind conventional social behavior or the usual intellectual defenses.

Handling aggression does not imply saintliness or "turning the other cheek." If the taker cannot accept his own feelings of hurt and address them in his response, he is quite likely to stimulate a round of ambiguous, second-level guilt feelings in the group. He is in the awkward position of being able to use the aggressor's impending guilt as an *indirect* weapon of counteraggressiveness, leading the group into emotional depression rather than freeing it for work.

A second issue underlying our discussion has to do with the group's norms governing emotional expression. To the degree that norms are subject to conscious review and modification by group members, an examination of the possibilities may suggest a course for the group to pursue. Some groups' norms rule out emotional expressivity and demand "cool rationality"; individuals are punished for expressing emotions. The norm, of course, will not prevent members from having feelings inside themselves. It just ensures that the feelings inside the individuals will emerge in disguise.

This does not mean that the effects of the contained feelings will not be evident. It means that feelings will tend to emerge behind a facade of intellectualization; the group's processes will feature rationalization, rather than rationality. This does not allow the group to learn the difference between emotional and task problems.

Another extreme kind of group norm encourages the free expression of feelings to the point of condoning and encouraging irresponsibility. By allowing anything to happen and *not* providing for an examination of the meaning of the event for the group and its task, this norm can lead to the orgiastic acting out of feelings to the point at which reality issues around the task are locked out of the group.

The optimum norm would allow free expression of feelings but would require that the expressions be treated as data and processed as is the other data related to the group task. Thus the individual may express himself, but he is forced to think twice. If he does not concern himself with how his feeling relates to what is going on in the group, he can be sure that others will do so. This does not imply prosecution or justification; it means that the group and its individual members accept responsibility for understanding and processing *all* the relevant data at their disposal. It also implies a model for responsible individual behavior.

Neither the individual's handling of affect nor group norms enforcing responsibility, however, deal directly with how to manage affect in groups. In the process of group development, each group must pass through and work out its own particular emotional and task problems; this process apparently has to be experienced by every problem-solving group. The individual's ability to deal with affect and the group's norms pertaining to the expression of feelings can facilitate the process, but cannot substitute for it.

*Part Two*

# *Interpersonal*
# *Dynamics*

## INTRODUCTION

THE first part of this book dealt with processes of group development. The unit of analysis was the group itself. The group is
characterized by a structure, by problems which transcend the problems of individual members, and by processes of control which exist
in the interaction of two or more individuals. These group properties
and performances have an existence which is relatively independent,
within limits, of changes in membership. Hence it was justifiable to
treat the group as an object of analysis.

Ultimately, however, we must leave the group as the unit of
analysis and focus upon the individual and relationships between individuals, treating the group as an influence on individual and interpersonal behavior, rather than as an entity that might explain itself.
Social processes can explain themselves only in the teleological sense
that since the group exists, its processes must be directed in some ways
toward maintaining and enhancing its existence. The explanations of
the ways in which processes contribute toward the maintenance and
enhancement of the group are functional explanations. Although
useful for accepting and understanding the existence of the group,
they do not really explain why it exists, or why its processes take the
forms that they do. For this more fundamental level of explanation
we must look at the individual, his personality structure and intrapersonal processes, and the ways that interpersonal behavior relates
to the individual's personality.

We know, of course, that even this level of explanation ultimately leads to some form of functional analysis where the existence and enhancement of the individual becomes the goal of the relevant processes. However, since we choose to stay within the limits of human behavior, our explanations will stop at the outer limit of the biological sciences. Within our limits, we hope to contribute to a useful understanding of the ways in which the individual and groups relate to each other. In the third part of the book, we shall examine relationships between groups and their organizational and cultural environment. The fourth and final part of the text will deal with problems of leadership and change.

The sequence of three chapters which make up this part starts by looking at the individual *in* the group in terms of his performances of group roles. Chapter Six will be primarily descriptive and will present initial formulations of the problems, challenges, and satisfactions that roles in groups create for the individual. Chapter Seven will explain the individual's predispositions for taking on certain roles and avoiding others in terms of his genetic development. This discussion will concentrate on the intrapsychic aspects of individual development. The final chapter in this part of the book will fuse explanations of the individual's role performances and his behaviors in interaction with others which form the basis for understanding group processes at a deeper level of analysis.

The differences between the meaning of *group* processes and *interpersonal* processes are crucial to the organization and meaning of this entire book. One purpose of dwelling on the individual in this part of the book is to clarify these differences. Briefly, and perhaps too simply, we can state that the individual's behavior in his work group is partly explained by attributes of the group, by his own social attributes, and by the relationships between these two sets of attributes. On the other hand, group attributes do not completely explain the interaction between the individual and other specific individuals in the group. Identification of the behavioral event as an interaction between two or more particular personalities requires a level of explanation that we call interpersonal dynamics. Here we are dealing with attributes of individuals which include their own social attributes but are not limited to them. In one sense, interpersonal dynamics are more *specific* than group processes, for the analysis deals with particular characteristics of particular individuals. In another sense, interpersonal dynamics provide a more *general* explanation than do group processes because explanations of social events ultimately hinge on the more general theory of individual behavior.

# Chapter Six

# Role Performances in Groups

W HEN a new group forms, one of the first concerns of all members is to know something about each other. When a new member enters an established group, the old members want to know about him. In some groups, selection processes prior to the new member's entrance give the old members some information about him. Conversely, the new member wants to get to know the established members. When the process of getting acquainted is to some extent completed, the members proceed with the group's normal mode of operation.

In this chapter, we shall attempt to follow what happens to the individual after he enters the group. Our main concern shall be to define and describe individual *role performances* in groups. Role performances are the attributes that group members "know" about each other, the ways by which they characterize each other. These attributes become a force that provides the group with a basis for stable, predictable social and interpersonal relations on the one hand, and constrains members to behave consistently with others' knowledge and expectations of them on the other hand, sometimes at the expense of learning and development.

Role performance describes the individual's interaction with other individuals, the psychological conditions within him as he interacts, and his effects on other group members before, during, and after the interaction. This combination of spatial and temporal dimensions goes beyond ordinary ways of thinking about individuals.

The spatial dimensions of role performances include conditions internal to the individual, events which take place between the individual and his social environment, and the social environment's response to the individual. These limits include those aspects of the individual's view of his identity which refer to his relations with his social environment and the individual's identity as seen by others in his social environment. Our view of role performances includes the *public* aspects of personality and individual behavior, as well as those aspects of the *private*, inner self which relate to the public performances.

The temporal dimensions of role performances are analogous to a musical theme. In attempting to describe the individual's "theme" as he moves through social time and space, we are concerned with two kinds of patterns in time. One is analogous to the musical chord, a pattern of *simultaneous* events or stimuli. Musical chords, struck on a piano or played by a combination of instruments, express distinctive moods to the audience. We can easily feel the difference in mood produced by a major chord, a minor chord, augmented or diminished chords, and so forth. We can also distinguish between the effect of a single instrument and a combination of instruments, so that a given chord notation can convey a variety of expressive moods. Chords consist, however, of *simultaneous* events occurring in patterned relationships to each other.

The second kind of pattern with which we are concerned in describing role performances is the sequence of events, analogous to a musical melody, phrase, theme, or chord progression. This pattern expresses a mood or message through a sequence of events in a patterned relationship. We can easily distinguish between "Yankee Doodle" and the choral movement from Beethoven's "Ninth Symphony," whether they are conveyed by a toy flute or an orchestra.

Role performances consist of patterns. In this chapter we shall discuss four kinds of patterns which make up the total phenomenon of the individual role performance. These are:

1. Patterned *perceptions* and evaluations of the individual by others (what the "audience" sees and hears and how they feel about it);
2. Patterns of *behavior produced* by the individual (what he does);
3. Patterned *behavioral responses* to the individual by others (the "audience's" behavioral response) and
4. Patterns of motivation within the individual (what he is trying to do during the performance).

Each of these four systems of patterns has the two temporal aspects referred to above, simultaneous and sequential patterns of elements. This chapter will discuss these four patterns.

The integration of these four patterns in real-life relationships is what people know or want to know about each other in order to engage in predictable social relationships and to maintain their personal identities in the face of changing environmental conditions. Like our musical analogy, our description cannot do justice to the complexity and richness of the actual performance.   However, we shall present data and theory which may contribute to greater understanding and appreciation of some of the dimensions of competent role performances.

Although patterns of motivation, the fourth element in role performances, will be discussed in this chapter, the discussion will be more *descriptive* than explanatory.   Chapter Seven will be devoted to explanations of role performances, especially their motivational aspects. Chapter Eight, the final chapter in Part Two, will discuss the interpersonal dynamics of interacting role performances between two or more individuals.

## PERCEPTIONS AND ROLE PERFORMANCES

The perception by others of an individual's role performance in a situation is one result of the performer's appearance and behavior. The individual's appearance and behavior provide cues; other individuals perceive and interpret these as patterns.   In this section we shall discuss the schemes of organization by which others describe the individual's performance.   Three frames of reference are involved:

1. Social role expectations;
2. Personality traits; and
3. Group process requirements.

The perception of an individual's performance is not isolated from it.   It becomes part of the performance through determining how other individuals will respond, and thereby influences the performer's behavior.   First, we shall concentrate on the perception of the individual, reserving discussion of the effects on the performer of the perceptions and behavior of others for a later section.

## Social Role Expectations

One of the most common bases for defining an individual's roles in a group situation is the status and social role that that individual may be perceived to represent in the outside world.   These statuses and roles, and the behaviors expected of them, are learned through the individual's life experiences in the wider culture.

Imagine a new committee being formed, for example, in which the members are a middle-aged bank president, an older college professor, a young medical doctor, a female college student, and male engineering student. We can anticipate that, at least initially, the members will see and interpret each other's behavior in terms of the stereotyped expectations of the professional role each represents. The stereotypes would include expectations of how they will behave and of what their motivations and intentions will be. The individuals would be expected to promote and defend what they are supposed to represent, whether it be business, management, academic values, medical progress, the vitality of youth, the competence of women, the strength of men, the wisdom of age, or the importance of science.

These expectations, called social role-demands to distinguish them from the other aspects of role performances,[1] are derived from the social structure in which the individual plays a part. He carries the identity of that structure with him in terms of his various social status titles. For example, the bank president becomes identified with the banking aspect of the nation's socio-economic structure *and* with the position of president in the organizational structure of his bank. Other individuals' expectations for his behavior and attitudes are based on their perceptions of his position and their conceptions of how people in that position should behave. In this sense, the individual is seen as a *representative* of his various reference groups.

## Personality Traits

Another way that role performances may be described is in terms of personality traits, although in some cases these may be considered part of the social role expectation—for example, the stereotypes of the aggressive, back-slapping salesman and the absent-minded professor. Trait descriptions include such terms as aggressive or passive, warm and friendly or cold and distant, masculine or feminine, supportive or hostile, and decisive or vacillating.

Early forms of trait psychology were probably closer to the traditional religious-philosophical view of human behavior, and the layman's traditional form of explanation, than to the social-psychological points of view of this book. This explanation by traits would say that the individual behaved as he did because "he is that kind of person"— that is, aggressive, domineering, or friendly—and that the trait was "given" by God or nature. Traits may be a useful shortcut in predicting some behaviors, but they are explicable at a deeper level: traits are caused by the sequence of experiences over an individual's lifetime, operating within the limitations of his constitutional endow-

[1] See Daniel J. Levinson, "Role, Personality, and Social Structure in the Organizational Setting."

ments.[2] Aggressiveness, dominance, and friendliness are results of prior events in the individual's life.

Regardless of the real or theoretical chains of causality, individuals sometimes describe others in terms of traits and base their expectations of their behaviors on those traits. Public stereotypes combine traits with statuses in many instances; but in other instances trait and social role expectations may be considered independent of each other. For example, a person holding the *status* of professor may be expected to exhibit either aggressive, tough, and domineering traits in the classroom or patient, passive, permissive, and sympathetic traits, depending on the frame of mind of the audience, the individual who is the professor, and what he actually does.

Although traits may be considered attributes of individuals, it is clear that some traits, such as the ones listed above, refer to the individual's interactions with others. Friendliness, for example, cannot exist or be demonstrated in the absence of other people, although its accompanying motivational states may persist when the individual is alone.

Neither of these descriptive frameworks, traits or social role expectations, refer directly to the individual at work in a group. They encompass a larger portion of time and space than do a specific group's problem-solving activities. For example, the time duration within which the social role patterns of a "doctor" or "student" occur includes a sequence of activities both within and outside groups, with characteristic daily, weekly, and yearly activity phases. Similarly, character traits such as dominance or friendliness persist over relatively long periods of time, throughout a wide range of activities. In situational behaviors of shorter duration, role performances may be described in relation to the requirements of group processes. The relatively short time span and fixed spatial limits of the group meeting or series of task meetings, as discussed in the first part of this book, provide the frame of reference for this kind of description.

## Group Process Requirements

The descriptive system developed by Benne and Sheats, introduced briefly in Chapter Three, classifies the roles of group members on the basis of their relationship to task performance, group building and maintenance, and individual needs.[3] The *task* role categories were the

[2] See C. Kluckhohn, H. A. Murray, and D. M. Schneider, *Personality in Nature, Society, and Culture*, pp. 53–67.
[3] K. D. Benne and P. Sheats, "Functional Roles of Group Members."

following: the initiator-contributor, the information seeker, the opinion seeker, the information giver, the opinion giver, the elaborator, the co-ordinator, the orienter, the evaluator-critic, the energizer, the procedural technician, and the recorder. *Group building and maintenance* roles included: the encourager, the harmonizer, the compromiser, the gate-keeper and expediter, the standard setter or ego ideal, the group-observer and commentator, and the follower. And under *individual* roles, the following were listed: the aggressor, the blocker, the recognition-seeker, the self-confessor, the playboy, the dominator, the help-seeker, and the special interest pleader.

When we read over the categories of these lists, our earlier references to the importance of time and pattern in describing the role performances of an individual again seem relevant. We should hardly expect a group member to play only one of these roles during a group meeting. More likely, we should expect to find the individual playing one role at one time and other roles at other times. However, we should also expect to find that he played some of the roles more often than others, and that he would tend to avoid certain roles, even though engaged in only one role at a particular point in time.

Benne and Sheats' classification of task and group maintenance roles overlaps the scheme developed by Bales,[4] which was also discussed in Chapter Three. In either case, the description of the role performance of an individual would be in the form of a frequency distribution profile, showing the frequency with which he performed each kind of role or act over a given time period.

Benne and Sheats' major role classifications—task, group building and maintenance, and individual—presuppose theoretical sets of group problem-solving requisites and individual needs toward which the behavior of the individual in the group may contribute. Bales' scheme is based on sociological theory which differentiates between instrumental-adaptive behaviors, corresponding to task, and social-emotional-expressive behaviors, corresponding to group building and maintenance.[5] This theory describes the functional relationships between the two kinds of behaviors and between the corresponding roles in social organizations. The father and mother in the family are prototypes of this differentiation. Similar differentiation appears in formal organizations between line and staff positions and in occupational classifications such as workers and artists. The meaning of this differentiation in the structure of the small group was discussed in Chapter

[4] R. F. Bales, *Interaction Process Analysis,* and "The Equilibrium Problem in Small Groups."

[5] See T. Parsons, and R. F. Bales, *Family, Socialization, and Interaction Process.*

Three.  For the individual, these task and social needs of the group provide opportunities for playing either or both kinds of roles, as well as a variety of choices within each major type.  The group situation also provides opportunities for satisfaction of individual needs that may *not* be closely related to group requirements.  Behaviors of this nature are called *individual* roles by Benne and Sheats,[6] and *self-oriented* behavior by Fouriezos, Hutt, and Guetzkow.[7]

Other efforts toward describing role performances in relation to group work have been especially directed toward understanding leadership and managerial styles.  A series of such studies, undertaken by an Ohio State University research team, discovered through questionnaires and factor analysis two independent dimensions underlying subordinates' descriptions of their supervisor's behavior.[8]  One factor, called *consideration*, involved statements describing friendship, warmth, and trust on the part of the supervisor.  The other factor, *initiating structure*, involved statements referring to the supervisor's methods of clarifying job requirements and working procedures.  Their findings related to leadership will be discussed in a later chapter.  It is relevant to note, however, that according to their scheme, a supervisor could be either high or low on one or both factors, indicating four possible perceived role-performance patterns based on these two factors.

In connection with executive development work, Robert R. Blake developed "The Managerial Grid: A Self-Examination of Managerial Styles."[9]  This questionnaire asks the manager to rank five courses of managerial behavior according to how he would behave in certain situations.  The situations cover such areas as planning, execution, and follow-up and involve circumstances in which the mode of dealing with other people and task varies among the five statements.  The respondent's rankings are then scored on a two-dimensional grid which describes the manager's style preference in terms of two coordinate numbers, as shown on Diagram 6.1.  One dimension indicates concern with people, the other with task accomplishment.  Blake's training programs aim at the (9,9) pattern as the ideal, a score indicating high concern with *both* task and people.  The other styles represented by the statements are: (1,1)—the "bureaucrat" who is not

[6] Benne and Sheats, *op. cit.*

[7] N. T. Fouriezos, M. L. Hutt, and H. Guetzkow, "Measurement of Self-oriented Needs in Discussion Groups."

[8] See J. K. Hemphill, *Leader Behavior Description,* and E. A., Fleishman, E. F. Harris, and H. E. Burtt, *Leadership and Supervision in Industry.*

[9] R. R. Blake, J. S. Mouton, and A. C. Bidwell, "The Managerial Grid: A Comparison of Eight Theories of Management."

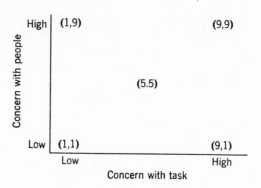

*Diagram 6.1   Blake's managerial grid.*

concerned with either dimension; (1,9)—the "country-club" manager who is high on people, low on task, (9,1)—the "task-master" who is high on task, low on people; and (5.5)—the "firm but fair" compromiser who fluctuates expediently.

In our discussion of perceptions of role performances, we have considered several methods of describing performances. One has to do with the social status of the individual and the external role-demands placed upon him by others as a result of their perceptions of his status. Another has to do with the unique personality characteristics of the individual, some of which are expressed in social situations. The third aspect has to do with what the situation requires in terms of task and social maintenance behaviors, so that work will be accomplished and the group conserved. The role performance of the individual, when viewed by someone other than himself, can be perceived and described in terms of:

1. A social role expectation (for example, "he is acting like a *boss*," "he talks just like a *professor*," "he acts like an immature *student*," "she is *mothering* the group");
2. Personality traits (for example, "he is loud and *pushy*," "he tries to *dominate* the discussion," "he just sits there *meekly* and keeps quiet"); and
3. Group process requirements (for example, "his ideas helped the group," "he encouraged them," "his sense of humor kept the group relaxed").

In discussing the role performance of the individual, our main interest at this point is in the aspects of his performance which are relevant to group processes. The most common research method for assessing perceptions of individuals' performances in groups is the Post Meeting Reaction questionnaire, discussed in Chapter Three. Participants are asked to rate each other on such factors as quality of ideas, contribution to group congeniality, procedural guidance, and general leadership. It is important to note that these are postmeeting perceptions of *performance* rather than the usual sociometric choice questions related to interpersonal *feelings*, such as choices of work partners or friends. Although the affective structure of the group is related to role performances, as discussed in Chapter Three, the performance questions are aimed at getting participants' perceptions of how they saw people behaving in the group, rather than their feelings toward those people; it is accepted, however, that group members usually perceive through their feelings.

Bales[10] and Slater[11] both found that within small experimental groups interpersonal perceptions, as well as actual behavior patterns, tended to center around task *or* social specialization. Men chosen for the quality of their ideas ("task specialists") tended to be *disliked;* well-liked members ("social specialists"), on the other hand, who were assumed to have performed integrative functions for their groups, were not chosen for their ideas or guidance. This finding is reminiscent of the school culture tradition of the "grind" versus the "playboy"—the idea that one can work hard *or* one can have friends. Other analyses of role perceptions have found that, under some conditions, individuals may be perceived as fusing the task and the social dimensions.[12]

Presently we shall elaborate the task and social dimensions of role performances in groups. But here our focus changes to the description of patterns of actual behavior, rather than perceptions and stereotypes. When we link perceptions with behavior, we assume that the manner by which the individual's role performance is perceived and evaluated by others is related to concrete behavioral acts of the individual. His behavior is a stimulus to which others respond and a source of rewards and punishments which reinforce their perceptions, evaluations, and behaviors.

## BEHAVIOR PATTERNS

In our discussion of behavior patterns, we refer to the individual's actions, rather than to his attitudes, feelings, and motives or to others'

[10] Bales, "The Equilibrium Problem in Small Groups."

[11] Philip E. Slater, "Role Differentiation in Small Groups."

[12] See E. F. Borgatta, A. S. Couch, and R. F. Bales, "Some Findings Relevant to the Great Man Theory of Leadership," and D. Moment and A. Zaleznik, *Role Development and Interpersonal Competence.*

perceptions of the individual as a person.   As a special kind of perception process, the systematic observation and description of actual behavior may proceed from many different points of view.   A major problem in describing and analyzing behavior involves determining an appropriate range or time limit for identifying behavioral acts.   At one extreme, we could study minute physical events such as eye-blinks, muscular movements, and the production of sounds.   At the other extreme we could talk about gross behavior patterns of longer duration, such as writing a report, getting married, or building a house.   Not only is a relatively uniform time span required, but so is a uniform frame of reference.

A clear understanding of the systematic observation process is necessary to differentiate between perceptions and actual patterns of behavior.   Members of groups often find it difficult, if not impossible, to observe while participating.   If they participate, their perceptions of the behavior of other individuals are necessarily filtered through their own emotional and evaluative reactions.   If they psychologically withdraw to observe "objectively," their presence as an observer causes the process to be different.   Hence, when we refer to descriptions of actual behavior patterns, we must bear in mind the trained perceptions and intellectual classification operations of the research observer.   He attempts to become invisible to the group, by gradually accepted or through the use of mechanical means such as the analysis of tape recordings or films, or by observation through a one-way mirror system.   By explicating his observation scheme and recording method, and by comparing his data with that obtained by other observers, he constantly checks his own reliability and objectivity.   We assume that his observations will be more accurate descriptions of the actual behavior than those of the untrained group member.

Bales' Interaction Process Analysis system[13] provides a model of an explicit behavioral-scientific observation method.   His basic unit of observation and analysis is the behavioral act, which he also calls the single interaction.   The unit is defined as "the smallest discriminable segment of verbal or nonverbal behavior to which the observer, using the present set of categories after appropriate training, can assign a classificiation under conditions of continuous serial scoring."[14]   His frame of reference was the theory behind his set of categories.   The theory involves categories of task and social consequences as referents for describing the units.

In our discussion we shall adopt a modification of Bales' definition

[13] Bales, *Interaction Process Analysis.*
[14] *Ibid.,* p. 37.

of behavioral acts. Each behavioral act produced by an individual in social situation can be identified by:

1. The *actor's* identity (who did it?);
2. The *object* upon which action is taken, including self, "the group," another specific individual, an abstract idea or symbol system, or a physical object (who or what is being acted upon?);
3. The nature of the action in terms of social or interpersonal intentions, *consequences*, or both (what is he trying to do to the other, or what did he actually do to the other?).*

Since we are interested in *patterns* of individual behavior, we should be aware of the quantity and sequence of the various interactions produced by the individual *over time*. We shall be concerned with two different time periods. One is represented by the duration of a group activity which results in some form of task completion or formal closure, such as a committee meeting or a series of committee meetings related to a common task.[15]    Another time period is related to the individual's life processes.    The importance of this time dimension is explained more fully in the chapter which follows, but we may anticipate later discussion somewhat by mentioning phases of human development as the reference points in the individual's lifetime.    For example, some behavior patterns are characteristic of adolescence while others are characteristic of a more mature phase of the individual's development.

To illustrate more clearly what is meant by the characteristic behavior patterns which go into a total role performance, let us draw upon a study by Moment and Zaleznik[16] which describes and analyzes the role performances of middle- and upper-level managers in experimental problem-solving groups.    Participants' post-meeting perceptions and evaluations of each other were measured and codified into a fourfold typology, based upon their relationships to task, social, and self-oriented needs.    Some individuals were perceived by co-participants as having good ideas but as not being congenial; these were called Technical Specialists.    Others, seen as being congenial but as not having particularly good ideas, were called Social Specialists.    Still

---

* Many researchers would *not* try to guess or impute the actor's intentions. This facet of social behavior becomes important when we are interested in the relationship of the individual's motives to his behavior.

[15] See discussion in Chapter Two of this volume regarding group identity and time.

[16] *Ibid.*

other participants were perceived and evaluated highly on *both* the quality of their ideas and their contribution of congeniality; these were called Stars. Finally, those members who did not stand out on either dimension and who received few, if any, sociometric choices were classified as Underchosen.

Patterns of actual behaviors were observed and described for the four role types.[17] The study utilized ten measures of the individual's behavior. Five of these were concerned with the group task and maintenance requirements of establishing social continuity, communicating sentiments, and managing tension; the other five measures were concerned with interpersonal activities and dealt with the management of aggression and the exchange of sentiments between individuals. Behaviors were scored by two different kinds of observations. One concerned the behavior itself, such as the aggressive connotation of the *act* of interruption; the other kind of observation dealt with *the intellectual content* of the words spoken, such as expressions of agreement or disagreement.

The Technical Specialists were relatively quiet and withdrawn, but tended to elaborate at length when they did speak up; they tended to *avoid* sociable behaviors but attempted to keep in touch with the others by joking. They were neither supportive toward others nor particularly aggressive or hostile. Their performance was characterized by the *extremity* of their behavioral tendencies; that is, they were in one of the extreme high or low positions on all five of the group process measures.

The Social Specialists were socially supportive and emotionally expressive. They tended to avoid criticizing or disagreeing. Their production of group maintenance behaviors was at the opposite extreme from the Technical Specialists; they tended to over-produce group maintenance behaviors.

The Stars' behavior patterns featured neither avoidances nor excesses in their task and social behaviors. They talked more than other participants and stood out from the other types in the degree to which they addressed the other individuals personally during the course of the discussions.

The Underchosen participants' behavior was the most aggressive, hostile, and otherwise self-oriented of the four types. They were relatively serious, engaging in little joking behavior.

The behavior patterns of the four role types seemed consistent with the perception patterns upon which the role typology was based. However, the behavioral analysis added some interesting information

[17] *Ibid.*, pp. 46 ff.

not revealed by the typology of perceptions. The Underchosen participants, for example, might merely have been quiet, relatively unnoticed members of their groups, judging solely from the numbers of choices they received. The behavior analysis demonstrated, however, that they participated more than either of the Specialist types, but less than the Stars. Apparently, it was what they did or did not do behaviorally that accounted for their relative lack of value to their groups as perceived by others, rather than "invisibility."

Another interesting finding in Moment and Zaleznik's behavioral analysis was the Technical Specialists' disproportionately high amount of joking. Most theories of group processes would lead us to expect that joking, as a form of tension release, was a group maintenance behavior to be expected of Social Specialists. However, the Technical Specialists' joking did not seem to contribute to their groups, since they received few choices for congeniality. The researchers' interpretation was that this joking was their only way of relating socially to their groups and that the jokes met their personal needs rather than the groups' need. Later in this chapter we shall mention data that contributed to this interpretation.

We have discussed various kinds of perceptions of role performances and the observation and description of the actual behavior patterns which produce the perceptions by others. The connection between perceptions and actual behavior takes place around the specific cues which the individual's behavior provides for others to interpret within their personal perceptual schemes. The other individuals not only perceive, evaluate, and react emotionally to the individual's performance; they also react behaviorally and thus contribute to the performance by co-determining the behaviors to which they react. Our next section will take up the influence that the reactions of others toward the individual have on his role performance.

## BEHAVIOR PATTERNS OF OTHERS TOWARD THE INDIVIDUAL

Social interaction involves two or more individuals. The individual's behavior to some extent causes the behavior of others, and their behavior patterns to some extent cause his.

In discussing the nature of the part others play in the individual's role performance, we shall employ the three factors used to describe perceptions: social role expectations, personality traits, and group process requirements. Behavior *toward* a representative of a particular social status will be called *social role reciprocation*. Behaviors evoked by particular personality traits in interaction will be called *interpersonal reflexes*. Behaviors stimulated by the group process roles played by others will be called *group role complementation*.

## Social Role Reciprocation

In our earliest discussion of role demands, we emphasized only one side of a social transaction. The individual in a recognized social position, such as a bank president or a medical doctor, was expected to behave in certain limited ways as a representative of his position. In some instances these expectations take the form of stereotypes. The emphasis has been upon the behaviors that others expect of the individual. To the extent that the individual has incorporated his social status and role into his personal identity, others' expectations will affect his own behavior. In settings where the person's professional status is relevant to the situation, he will, if he is a doctor, for example, behave as he thinks others expect a doctor to behave.

The other side of this transaction involves the patterned ways that other individuals actually behave *toward* the occupant of a social position. Extreme examples would include casual encounters of the public with priests, nuns, and policemen, all of whom wear uniforms which clearly identify their social positions. We would expect the general public to behave with deference, respect, and gentleness *toward* these positions. In military organizations, indoctrinees are taught to "salute the uniform, not the man."

Most conventional social situations do not involve persons in uniforms, but rather more subtle cues and staging effects. When the child's parents encounter his teacher at a P.T.A. meeting, for example, their behavior tends to follow a situationally defined pattern of interest, mutual concern, co-operation, and deference to the expertise of the teacher. This relationship may be strained if a parent is himself a professional educator or psychologist, but in most cases the interaction follows a predetermined pattern. Similar situations exist when a student sees a professor about his classwork, when a patient sees his doctor for a medical examination, when a citizen sees a policeman or judge about a traffic violation, or when a subordinate talks with his superior about his work.

The strength of the conventions which enforce these patterns becomes most evident in situations where they are misunderstood or violated, for instance, if the child's parents do *not* defer to the teacher's expertise because of their own professional concerns. These exceptions and violations are an abundant source of comedy scripts for television and films; policemen who do not act like policemen or are not regarded by the public as they should be are a case in point. Another theme involves on- and off-stage behaviors. Examples of this are found in the medical drama, where the line between the doctor's private life and his professional work is continually at issue. The plot often revolves around love interests with a nurse or patient and may also contain a task conflict between toughness and softness.

These comments refer to reciprocal role expectations which are based on social conventions and are independent of the unique personality attributes of the individuals in status positions. In the role relationships we have cited as examples—priest or nun and layman, police officer and citizen, military officer and enlisted man, teacher and parent, parent and child, teacher and student, doctor and patient, work superior and subordinate, and doctor and nurse—two consistent dimensions stand out. One is authority; all these relationships involve a power, age, or expertise differential. Another is sex roles: male-female. Parallel to both dimensions are underlying sentiment scales, ranging from tough, active, aggressive, and punitive on the one hand, to gentle, understanding, deferent, passive, and affectionate on the other hand.

These underlying emotional dimensions of reciprocal social role expectations engage with the personality predispositions of the role incumbents. As individuals learn the general imperatives of social role reciprocation through acculturation processes shared with others, they also learn the emotional preconditions and responses which accompany social role performances. These are learned through interpersonal relations with parents, peers, and teachers, and through the individual's experiences with community authority figures such as doctors, dentists, and law officers. The emotional content of a reciprocal social relationship becomes the core of the *interpersonal reflex*.[18]

## The Interpersonal Reflex

In discussing social role reciprocation, we have not been concerned with the interpersonal motivations of individuals in status positions, that is, what the individuals are trying to do to each other. These aspects of the role performance are usually described in terms of personality traits. In trying to separate the differences in conventional social behavior among statuses from the meanings of these behaviors to the personalities involved, we may assume that the purely social

[18] See T. Leary, *Interpersonal Diagnosis of Personality*, pp. 91 ff.

aspects of the behavior are primarily motivated by needs to maintain predictability and order in social relations. Stereotyped perceptions and behaviors result from these needs. The communications involved in such relationships usually emerge as formal messages between "representatives."

The interpersonal meaning of interaction involves a different level of analysis:

We determine the interpersonal meaning of any behavior by asking, "What is this person doing to the other? What kind of a relationship is he attempting to establish through this particular behavior?" The answers to these questions define the subject's interpersonal impact on the other one. For example, "He is boasting and attempting to establish superiority"; or, "He is rejecting and refusing to help."[19]

Leary arranged a scheme for classifying interpersonal behavior and reflexes along two dimensions—dominance-submission and hostility-affection. These were the underlying dimensions of the reciprocal social role expectations described earlier. These axes appear as follows:

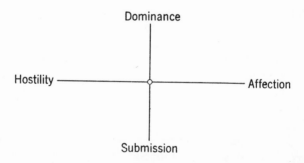

According to Leary's observation scheme, interpersonal acts produced by the individual are located around these axes. The central point represents an emotionally neutral event; the distance from the central point represents increasing intensity. Interpersonal events may lie between the axes. For example, a particular behavioral event may be both affectionate and dominating; "smotherly love" would fit this description. Leary developed sixteen categories of interpersonal behavior around these axes.[20]

For each kind of interpersonal act, there is a complementary act which is likely to be evoked. For example, dominating, bossing, and ordering tend to evoke obedience from the other person, while attack-

[19] *Ibid.*, p. 91.
[20] *Ibid.*, p. 65.

ing, unfriendly actions provoke hostility. Along the vertical axis, acts of one kind tend to evoke opposites—submissive behavior evokes domination, domination evokes obedience; along the horizontal axis, acts of one kind tend to evoke the same kind of act—seeking friendship evokes affection, acting hostile provokes hostility.

The concept of interpersonal reflex contains two important aspects relevant to describing and understanding the relationships between one person's behavior and another person's response. First, the term "reflex" indicates that the behavior and its interpersonal intentions are neither consciously thought out or planned, nor deliberately executed. They happen reflexively, as the eye blinks to avoid blowing dust, or as the body assumes a protective posture in times of physical danger.

The second important aspect is that one person's interpersonal mechanisms tend to "pull" a complementary reflex from the other. For example, an interpersonal challenge of an individual's competence or worth tends to pull a defensive response. Aggression will provoke counter-aggression from some persons, but passive submission from others. Referring back to our discussion of social role reciprocation, we can see that the other person's view of the authority involved in the social situation will determine his response. If a socially-defined and accepted superior is domineering, the subordinate will tend to submit. But if the situation is defined as one of peer-relationships, one person's aggressive, domineering behaviors may provoke competitively similar behaviors from the other. The other individual's definition of the social situation and his personality attributes will determine his response.

Similarly, warm and friendly behaviors will usually elicit like responses from an individual, but this tendency is often modified by his definition of the social situation and his unique orientations toward personal relations; some people become frightened at others' bids for friendly relations and react defensively. Some persons may reject bids for friendship from persons of different social status.

Although we are emphasizing the idea that the behaviors of two individuals mesh with each other systematically, we also have to emphasize that the particular form in which they do so varies according to:

1. The individual's personal definition of the social situation. The most important dimensions of his social definitions are: (a) perceived authority balance, (b) perceived sex-role relationships (male-female, male-male, female-male, female-female), and (c) perceived social distance.

2. The individual's unique personal predispositions toward interpersonal relations.

The individual's personal definition of the social situation results in part from social role expectations and social role reciprocation, both of which were discussed earlier. His acceptance of the conventional definition of the social situation is by no means a sure thing, even when the cues are clear, as would be the case when a police officer stops a speeding motorist. Some individuals might react violently to any potential display of authority, as symbolized by the police officer's uniform. Acceptance of conventional definitions of social situations varies from one person to another and with the same person on different occasions, even when the cues are clear. When the situation is ambiguous, as in most group discussions where people seldom wear their status symbols, the question of how the individual will define the situation is even more unsettled.

Authority, sex role, and social distance relationships are the most important dimensions of the individual's definition of the social situation. These dimensions apply to the most universal and visible status attributes within human cultures; the child learns to differentiate among other people according to age, sex, and inclusion in or exclusion from the family. Age and authority tend to go together, until the growing person discovers the difference, typically during adolescence. Learned sex-role relationships contain both negative and positive imperatives: incest and homosexuality taboos are the negative extreme, while the demonstration of gentleness toward women and the deference of women to the authority of men represent positive imperatives.

Social distance cuts across both the authority and sex-role dimensions as they are learned by the child and retained by the adult. Inclusion is measured along this dimension. The child differentiates between family members and all other individuals. Positive and negative imperatives hinge around this difference, as well as around age and sex differences. The incest taboo is an obvious example of a strong negative imperative; it differentiates along both sex and inclusion dimensions. Less dramatic, but equally as strong, are the imperatives of honoring parents and loyalty to brothers and sisters. A scale of social distance is eventually learned, running from immediate family, through relatives and friends, to various classes of outsiders.

With these dimensions as guides, and the family experience as the model for their application, the individual learns to define social situations in his own particular way. Under some conditions his definition may seem inappropriate to the others involved.   As a result of intrapsychic processes (which will be explained in the next chapter), he may reflexively apply the definition of an earlier, emotionally laden situation to a new situation on the basis of superficial cues.   For example, if a boss behaves in a way that reminds the individual of his father, he may react interpersonally toward the boss as if he actually were the absent father.

The second set of variables that determine the individual's response to another person is closely related to his definition of the situation; however, these are general responses to personalities, without regard for status differences.   Some people gravitate toward group relations regardless of the status differences involved, while others avoid them. Some reach out to be friendly, others tend to be cool and distant. Some exercise control over other people's behavior, others consistently let themselves be controlled.

The interpersonal reflex—the patterned response of one individual to the behavior of another individual—bears a close relationship to social role reciprocation.   Social role reciprocation is the patterned response of a person as a representative of one social status to the behavior of another person representing another social status.   These concepts are separable to the degree that individuals define their social relations as interpositional in some instances and interpersonal in others.   In ordinary group work situations both elements are present. But common expressions regarding human interaction attest the difference: "I don't feel that I know him *as a person*," "He can't stop treating me *like a child*," "He pulled his *rank* on me," "He won't let you forget *he's the boss*," and "He doesn't act *like a professor*."

## Group Role Complementation

Like their counterparts in our discussion of perceptions and behaviors, neither social role reciprocation nor the interpersonal reflex has direct relevance to the purposes of problem-solving groups at work, but both describe effects which are always present in groups. Within the requisites of group processes parallel phenomena exist: one person's behavior tends to draw complementary behaviors from others where complementariness is measured according to group needs rather than to external social roles or interpersonal processes.

This effect appears in some common public situations.   When a lost child cries on the street, an adult soon comes to his aid.   If someone starts a fight, someone else intervenes as peacemaker.   If someone is injured in an accident, one person administers first aid, another sends for help, another attempts to control the crowd, and someone offers emotional comfort to the injured person. In all these instances, the individual who intervenes acts upon the immediate demands of the situation with little regard for social status or personality differences.

Among military combat teams and highly effective work groups similar events take place. In spite of established work role definitions and status differentiations, emergencies are handled by whoever happens to be on the spot, and jobs are traded to suit situational demands. It is interesting to note that although such occurrences are logical and necessary for task accomplishment and group survival, they are sufficiently rare to evoke in participants and observers an unusual emotional feeling of cohesion and "rightness."

Similarly, in problem-solving groups some members are sensitive to "group needs"—both maintenance and building needs and task, directive needs—and behave toward the group according to their perceptions of its needs. In some instances this sensitivity is intuitive or "natural." At the same time, there are highly developed training programs directed toward teaching this sensitivity to group workers and leaders. These events are often accidental rather than intended; they can happen when an individual's self-oriented behavior happens to provide something that will help the group.

The problem of role differentiation in small groups was addressed in a study by Philip Slater.[21] Using measures of participation and voting choices regarding ideas, guidance, liking, and leadership, he found that:

> . . . role differentiation in the High [consensus*] groups seems to be bipartite, with an active "task specialist" and a Best-liked man. In the Low [consensus] groups it tends to be tripartite (as well as more extreme), with an active participator who is neither well-liked nor highly rated on task ability, a more passive task specialist who is not well-liked, and a popular individual who is neither active nor highly rated on task ability.[22]

Slater discovered that the Idea men initiated more problem-solving attempts, disagreed more, and showed more antagonism; the Best-liked men initiated more positive social reactions; asked more questions, and showed more tension. He summarized as follows: "The general

[21] Slater op. cit.

* Slater divided his groups into High consensus and Low consensus groups on the basis of the degree of agreement among the members of their voting choices. Members of High consensus groups tended to show more agreement in the way they ranked others than did the Low consensus group members.

[22] Ibid., p. 504.

picture is thus one of specialization and complementarity, with the Idea men concentrating on the task and playing a more aggressive role, while the Best-liked man concentrates more on social-emotional problems, giving rewards and playing a more passive role."[23]    He also found evidence that the Idea men and the Best-liked men tended to work together in a complementary team relationship.

The degree to which the role complementation in Slater's groups was accidental, rather than deliberate, was problematical.    But he did highlight a structural effect of group processes which suggested that the existence of one strong idea man in a group, for example, could force others to play other kinds of roles.

It is clear that under some conditions, the individual's role performance can influence others to perform complementary roles.    If one person pushes for task completion, for example, he may force others to divert their behaviors from task accomplishment toward social reconciliation.    Under other conditions we would expect to find competition for roles, rather than complementation.    Thus, an active idea man may provoke others to be even more active as idea men, under some conditions.

We have discussed three sorts of processes that determine the behavioral responses of others toward the behavior of a particular person: social role reciprocation, the interpersonal reflex, and group role complementation.    In any of these processes the individual's performance is affected by the others' responses.    He "trains" the others to accept him and to accord him reciprocal or complementary behaviors; but they also are training him through their implied interest or disinterest, approval or disapproval, and the presentation of their own behavioral demands to him.

In the Moment and Zaleznik study of role performances,[24] the behaviors of others toward each of the four role types followed four different patterns.    Technical Specialists, whose own behavior was relatively stiff and who avoided sociability except for joking, were interrupted more and yet received more personal recognition from others than did the other types.    The interruptions were forms of behavioral aggression, although the personal recognition may have represented bids to involve them socially.    Both these patterns provided access to the Technical Specialists and to their high quality ideas, in spite of their social distance.

On the other hand, the groups tended to respond to Social Specialists in kind.    Social Specialists behaved politely and respectfully toward

---

[23] *Ibid.*, p. 507.
[24] Moment and Zaleznik *op. cit.*

others, avoiding aggressive behaviors, and other individuals treated them similarly; they were perceived and treated as "nice guys." This pattern of behavior and response corresponded closely to the dynamics of Leary's interpersonal reflex scheme:[25] behaviors which seek friendship tend to pull friendship.

Stars also received responses in kind. Their own behaviors tended to be balanced in most respects, expressing aggression through criticism and warmth through support and personal recognition. From others they received similar responses and a balanced pattern of both aggression and support.

The Underchosen participants' response from others was one of complementation and neutralization. They were the most serious, critical, and aggressive of the four types. But rather than being engaged by others in argument, they received a pattern of polite, condescending behaviors. Interestingly enough, others agreed with them more often than with the other types, but private evaluation in the Post Meeting Reaction questionnaires indicated that their ideas were *not* considered good. Since their behavior pattern seemed to be the most self-oriented and the least group- and task-relevant of the four types, the behaviors of others toward them may have represented attempts to neutralize potential group destructiveness.

Moment and Zaleznik summarized and interpreted their findings regarding the produced and received behavior patterns of the four role types as follows:

The analysis of the behavioral patterns associated with the role types confirmed that the Stars tended to produce a pattern involving high activity and a broad variety of behaviors. The Social Specialists tended to give more behavioral attention to problems concerning the communication of sentiments and affective support of others, while the Technical Specialists tended to avoid these kinds of behaviors. The behavior pattern of the Underchosen suggested that they were relatively uncommitted to their groups, and that their behavior tended to be at the service of personal needs with low task and group relevance.

The behavioral findings may be restated in terms of ways in which the behavior patterns of the role types represented their handling of aggression and affection and their emotional relationship to the groups' processes. It seemed clear that the behavior patterns of the specialists represented avoidances; avoidance of aggression by the Social Specialists, and avoidance of interpersonal expressivity by the Technical Specialists. These patterns indicated differences in kinds of commitment to the group situation. The Social Specialists manifested commitment to the group as a group, while the Technical Specialists demonstrated commitment to the task (ideas)

[25] Leary, *op. cit.*

dimensions of the groups' processes.  The intellectual "armor" of the Technical Specialists may have tended to prevent the others from directly assaulting them intellectually and from directly "reaching out" to include them.  Instead, the Technical Specialists tended to receive *behavioral* aggression and recognition.  Hence, the Technical Specialists were involved in the exchange of aggression, but there is some evidence that they tended to prevent or deflect direct intellectual challenges.

The Social Specialists, on the other hand, could have defended themselves against aggression by avoiding aggressive behavior themselves.  They behaved like "nice guys" and were treated like "nice guys."  It seems likely that they maintained their social commitment to their groups by avoiding strong intellectual commitments to ideas that might prove to be disruptive or place themselves on one or the other side of an aggressive debate.

The Underchosen participants, although active in the production of aggressive behaviors, were not engaged with by the others; they tended to evoke condescension rather than aggression from the others.  Their behaviors were seen as being not particularly useful to the group; they received few choices on the PMR questionnaire.  This might imply that they brought relatively high levels of anxiety to the situations and had not been able to deal with the anxiety in ways which might engage them with either the social or task requisites of the group problem solving processes.

In terms of contemporary clinical theory, Rogers' concept of congruence seems to apply to the tendencies indicated in the Stars' behavior patterns.[26]  Their external behaviors tended to be congruent with their internal feelings, and they communicated honest involvement.  They let the others know where they stood, manifesting neither strong avoidances nor excesses in their behaviors.  They actively engaged themselves with the others, allowing the others to engage them and their ideas directly.  Their particular mode of aggressiveness did not prevent others from being directly aggressive toward them.  The implications are that they were not particularly anxious in the group situations, or that they could manage their anxieties through task and socially relevant behaviors.

These interpretations and speculations impute certain motivations to the role types, especially with respect to their handling of aggression and affection.  The next step in this analysis is to look at the internal conditions of the role types as assessed by certain measures of motivation and to find out the nature of the consistency between internal conditions and behavior patterns . . . .[27]

So far in our analysis of role performances we have discussed perceptions of role behaviors, actual behavior patterns, and the patterned responses of others toward particular kinds of behavior patterns.  We

[26] Carl R. Rogers, *On Becoming a Person,* pp. 282–283.
[27] Moment and Zaleznik, *op. cit.,* pp. 66–68.

have also described the relationship of perceptions to actual behaviors and the relationship of the individual's behavior patterns to the behavior he receives from others.    It is clear that the behavior received from others is directly related to perceptions.    Stars and Technical Specialists, in Moment and Zaleznik's study,[28] were perceived as producing outstandingly good ideas upon which the others could work; the behavioral accompaniment of the perception was aggression in the form of criticism and interruption.    Group members also responded to the perceived congeniality of the Stars and Social Specialists.    This was especially clear in the case of the Social Specialists.    The pattern of behavior received by the Stars was more complex: responses to ideas, as well as to congeniality, were involved in the pattern.

We have emphasized role specialization throughout our discussion, especially task as opposed to social activity patterns.    The tendency for individuals to specialize in their role performances is a prevalent empirical research finding.[29]    Role fusion can also occur under certain conditions.[30]    To complete our description of role performances and to probe deeper into their explanation, we need to examine the motivational conditions which accompany various kinds of role performances, be they specialized, fused, or primarily self-oriented.

## MOTIVATION AND PERFORMANCE

Patterns of motivation within the individual constitute a fourth aspect of his role performance in a group.    The other three elements, were: (1) perceptions and evaluations of the individual by others, (2) the actual behavior of the individual, and (3) the behavioral responses of others toward the individual.

Like the other elements of role performance, motivation may be described from several different points of view.    We shall discuss motivation in relation to three sets of dimensions:

1. Level of awareness, conscious or unconscious;
2. Internally located "pushes" or drives and externally located "pulls," goals, or objectives; and
3. The differences between motives involving other persons and motives involving impersonal objects or symbols.

We shall describe motivation more comprehensively in the following chapter, so the present discussion will be limited to ideas related to the other elements of role performance discussed earlier.

---

[28] *Ibid.*

[29] Bales, "Equilibrium Problem in Small Groups," Slater, *op. cit.*, and Moment, and Zaleznik, *op. cit.*

[30] Borgatta et al., *op. cit.*, and Moment and Zaleznik, *op. cit.*

From observations of the individual's behavior patterns, we can infer that he is conscious of some of his actions and unconscious of others. One of our guidelines for describing behavioral acts is the intention or the consequences of the act, or both. The consequences of most behavior in groups reach far beyond the individual performer's intentions, and may sometimes neutralize or reverse the intended result. On the other hand, unintended consequences may satisfy some unconscious need or motivation of the performer.

The elements of role performance that primarily involve unconscious motivation and unintended consequences are interpersonal reflex and group maintenance behaviors. Conventional social role behaviors and their reciprocations are fairly easy for a participant to understand and consciously accept, as are the task elements of group behavior processes. To accept and understand the motives behind the interpersonal reflex and group maintenance behaviors requires that we play the observer role; we must temporarily look inward and attempt to understand the psychological processes of others while avoiding the emotional reactions and evaluations characteristic of the participant role. We shall begin our explanation of the motivational aspects of role performances by examining the nature of the *objects* upon which the individual acts when he behaves in a group problem-solving situation, referring back to our earlier definition of the unit of behavior. We have specified three components to the behavioral act: the actor, the object, and the action itself described in terms of social or interpersonal intentions or consequences.

The objects of the individual's behaviors may be classified as physical things, symbols, persons, or combinations of these three forms. The most elementary form of human work consists of modifying the arrangements of physical objects in the environment. This involves the expenditure of energy by the person to modify aggressively an existing state in the process of creating a new one—the living tree is destroyed to make lumber; the piece of lumber is modified to build a house. Thus, the person's behavior modifies his physical environment when he performs physical work.

The analogy to physical work in the problem-solving group involves action by persons with *symbols*—words and behaviors are analogous to physical activities such as pushing, pulling, cutting, pounding, or lifting. The "objects" upon which action is taken are also systems of symbols, such as ideas, plans, or theories. In addition, important parts of the personality systems of other persons—their ideas, plans, theories, attitudes, goals, intentions, and emotions—become objects which are worked upon. The goal of individual intellectual work is the modification of the *individual's* own thoughts and the symbolic formulation of the modification in writing or in the memory. In discussion groups, the modification of *others'* ideas is the core of the work process.

The ordinary child or adult can consciously experience and describe work he does on things or with symbols. But he is usually only dimly aware, if at all, of "working on" other people or having others work on him. This is why Leary's interpersonal reflex[31] is described as a reflex rather than deliberate behavior. People work on one another explicitly at the intellectual level; ideas are exchanged and modified. This kind of work results in systems of formal logics, bodies of knowledge, and individual "knowing" in its conventional sense. For our purposes the most important, and least understood, aspect of interpersonal "work" involves expressions and modifications of emotions, sometimes explicit but more commonly implicit in their verbal behaviors.

The common element of emotional activity and conventional physical or symbolic work is the expenditure of energy. Although we cannot directly measure emotional energy, the evidence of its existence lies in its physical manifestations—for example, nervous behavior, physical tension, and chemical conditions within the body—and in the reality of an individual's subjective feelings.

The intentions and consequences by which we describe interpersonal behavior are located primarily in the emotional systems of the parties to the interaction. Therefore, when we examine the motivational conditions within the individual which accompany his role performance, we are primarily interested in his psychological view of things, symbols, and people, and its emotional concomitants. The motive of "wanting to succeed" tells us nothing about the individual's view of success; does he see "success" as the competent manipulation of things, as excellence in intellectual endeavour, as competent relationships with other persons, or as all these things? His concept of the *time* relationship between discrete events and personal success is also an important aspect of his motivation.

To be successful in making things involves a relatively short period of time and a continuous feedback of results. When a person builds a house, for example, he has day-by-day, if not minute-by-minute, evidence of his progress; he may feel his accomplishment at the end of each working day. When he is finished with a unit of work, he and the world knows it. Closure is clear and complete.

Evidence of success in symbolic activities is less concrete and visible; a longer time must pass before the results can be evaluated. Moreover, symbolic activity for the most part involves communica-

[31] Leary, *op. cit.*

tions with others; the individual must not only delay his gratifications, but he must also have a way of dealing with the *ideas*, if not the feelings of other persons. The completion of a unit of work is less obvious than when working with things. Symbolic closure may be attained, but the abstract processes symbolized have no beginning or end.

To experience success in the realm of interpersonal activities requires a more remote and ambiguous set of standards than those involved in working with things or ideas. Some interpersonal needs such as needs to aggress and needs for physical affection, may be gratified quickly. The goals of interpersonal competence include, however, the enhancement of lifetime development processes in one's self as well as others—one's children, work subordinates, and colleagues. The time scale for this kind of success is relatively long, and the standards are ambiguous. The process has its symbolic, ritualized milestones, such as births, graduations, weddings, job promotions, service anniversaries, and funerals, which symbolize status transitions and progress. But, by and large, success in helping people develop, in such roles as parent, teacher, supervisor, or administrator, requires emotional, intellectual, and behavioral attention to conversion processes which are more vague than is work with physical things or ideas.

Patterns of motivations as they apply to work and people may be organized into simplified clusters, including both conscious and unconscious elements, internal drives and external goals, and the potential differentiation between persons and things as objects toward which action is directed. One such organization was used by Moment and Zaleznik to measure motivation in their study[32] of role performances and is shown on Table 6.2.

*Table 6.2   Organization of Motivational Elements around Levels and Objects*[33]

| | Nature of Objects Other Persons | | Task and |
| *Levels of Awareness* | Affection | Other's Esteem | Self-Esteem |
| --- | --- | --- | --- |
| Conscious and related to current life goals | Belonging preference | Status preference | Job-intrinsic preference |
| Preconscious or Unconscious and related to persistent needs | need Affiliation | need Achievement ⟷ | need Achievement |

[32] Moment and Zaleznik, *op. cit.*, pp. 69 ff.   [33] *Ibid.*, p. 71.

The differences between the conscious and unconscious levels of
motivation involved in this organization scheme, as well as the differences among the kinds of motivating objects, may be explained by
describing the motivational elements to which each of the measurements listed in the table refer.  Belonging, status, and job-intrinsic
preferences refer to scores on a questionnaire which asks the person
to indicate his relative preferences among various kinds of rewarding
experiences.  Belonging experiences are those which bring people
together in primarily social relationships.  Status-rewarding experiences are those in which the person receives public recognition or a
visible symbol of an upward status transition; moving to a better
community or a better office and receiving a new job title are examples
of status rewards.  Job-intrinsic rewards are pleasant experiences relating to the content of a job.  Examples of this kind of experience
include beginning a job that is interesting and stimulating, completing
a project on time, doing a job well, and working alone on an interesting problem.  These preferences are expressed on the questionnaire
through the individual's conscious choice processes.  They refer to two
different sorts of relationships with people—being with them socially
and being recognized publicly—and a relationship with the intrinsic
content of work, distinctly separated from the membership and status
elements that also accompany work.

Unconscious, or preconscious, levels of motivation are tapped to
measure affiliation and achievement needs.  Affiliation refers to warm,
friendly, close relationships with people; the sort of object involved
makes the relationship similar to belonging preference.  The difference
lies in the method by which the preference, on the one hand, and the
need, on the other, are expressed and measured.  The preference is
expressed by conscious choice among items.  Need Affiliation is measured from the thematic content of imaginative stories written by the
individual in response to ambiguous pictures in the Thematic Apperception Test.[34]  The amount, kind, and intensity of Affiliation imagery
in his stories, as measured by a trained scorer, determine his need
Affiliation score.  Because of the differences in methodology between
the measurement of preferences and the measurement of these needs,
an individual may, for example, consciously reject Belonging rewards
and yet exhibit a strong unconscious need for Affiliation in his imaginative stories.  This may indicate a conflict between his conscious desires
and his unconscious needs.

Need Achievement is also scored from imaginative stories produced
in Thematic Apperception Tests.  Achievement imagery indicates the

[34] See J. W. Atkinson, *Motives in Fantasy, Action, and Society,* and Moment
and Zaleznik, *op. cit.,* pp. 272 ff.

pursuit of goals, competition with external standards of excellence, and the encountering of obstacles to some goal. It refers to a generalized need within the individual to be successful, but it is not specific as to means, recognition, or the roles of other persons in the process of achieving success. It can be related, therefore, to needs for esteem from others, needs for self-esteem, or both. Hence, it is included under both the other's esteem and task and self-esteem categories of the organization scheme in Table 6.2.

By measuring need Achievement independently of status and job-intrinsic preferences, several different combinations of these motives may be used to describe the individual's view of task achievement. Some people may consciously pursue status rewards but may not be concerned with achievement or job content; others may prefer experiences intrinsic to work, with or without the accompanying status rewards or achievement satisfactions.

Characteristic combinations of these motivational elements accompany particular kinds of role performances. For example, the Technical Specialists in Moment and Zaleznik's study were highly motivated toward achievement through concrete task work, but were relatively indifferent regarding people.[35] The Social Specialists exhibited weak needs for achievement, but were high in their preferences for belonging rewards and for the satisfactions intrinsic to concrete task work. However, there were indications that their preferences for task may have been more closely related to earning esteem from others than to attaining self-esteem. Underchosen participants' patterns of motivation featured conflict; they exhibited either high or low motivation to achieve, but whether high or low they saw achievement as taking place through concrete task completion. They tended psychologically to reject close relations with others, while exhibiting a conflicting need for affiliation. The Stars had a high achievement need, but in contrast to the Technical Specialists they did not value concrete task completion as the exclusive means. Rather, they expressed a preference for being with people, indicating an inclination toward the *process* of working with people.

The four patterns of role performances reported by Moment and Zaleznik represented combinations of attitudes toward the worlds of work and people, behaviors consistent with the attitudes, and behaviors and perceptions from others which reinforced the attitudes and behaviors. They summarized part of their findings by inferring how each of the role types might verbalize modes of experiencing work and people, based upon the combinations of motivation scores and the other components of the role performances:

[35] Moment and Zaleznik, *op. cit.*, pp. 76 ff.

The Stars' indicated mode of experiencing could be called a *process orientation*. Interest, involvement, and personal caring become invested into a total, ambiguous process of working and living with people. Interpersonal communication becomes the way that a person experiencing the process oriented mode would connect himself to the world around him. Process orientation is a *verbal* mode; it would be difficult for a person with under-developed verbal skills to experience this orientation.

This kind of experience is in sharp contrast to the *task-oriented* mode suggested by the Technical Specialists' orientations. They were relatively non-verbal . . . compared to the Stars. The description of their extreme orientation pattern suggested that work in their hands and ideas in their minds would provide their connections with the world around them. Either physically competent activities, such as involved in skilled arts and craftsmanship, and/or intellectual activity, rather than verbal activity, would characterize this mode. Other people would be experienced as audiences or as interferences to these activities.

The *social* mode of experiencing would exude a glow of affection onto the surrounding social situation. Peace, tranquility, interpersonal warmth, understanding, and acceptance would be the desired external conditions to a person experiencing this mode. He would inject affection to subdue any symptoms of disagreement, hostility, or conflict. He would feel upset if there were trouble out there which could not be controlled by his giving affectionate support. The feeling of disturbance would overpower his consideration of the logical aspects of the disturbing issues. He would rather not work than hurt people. He would rather see the group engaging in purely social, integrating activities than in work of a socially disruptive nature. He would attempt to steer work efforts away from potentially controversial issues.

The *uncommitted* mode of experiencing, suggested by the extremes of the Underchosen participants' orientation, would feature heightened awareness of self. External events would be interpreted in terms of their possible interpersonal meanings. Task work by others would be felt as bids, on the part of the others, for interpersonal dominance and group leadership. Support received from others would be overinterpreted as bids for affectionate pairing. Criticisms from others would be felt as punishment. While the *social* mode would feature sensitivity to external, social disturbances, the uncommittted mode would be sensitive to interpersonal dominance, affection, and hostility, as these effects impinged upon the self.

These various modes of experiencing represent conditions which could have occurred within *all* of the participants from time to time. They represent a synthesis of the internal motivational tendencies of the four role types which would be consistent with their behavioral tendencies and the perceptions and evaluations which others had toward them. They suggest that the Stars, for example, while probably experiencing all four modes before, during, and after the experimental situations, tended to fluctuate in their orientations and behaviors around the Process Oriented mode. Similarly, the Technical Specialists centered around the Task mode, the Social Specialists around the Social mode, and the Underchosen participants around the Uncommitted mode. This kind of explanation leaves open the possibility, and suggests the probability, that the Underchosen participants might have experienced and behaved according to different modes in different group situations. . . .[36]

The description of the motivational aspects of role performances rounds out our picture of the individual interacting with environmental objects—physical things, abstract symbol systems, and people—in his own unique way; his method of interacting may be compared with that of others along the several dimensions of role performances that we have analyzed. This complex totality of the person interacting with his environment has been described as if it were self-contained in time, with the motivational conditions, his behavior, and the others' responses all going on simultaneously, *here-and-now*.

The relationship of these events may be partially explained in terms of currently existing social forces and individual predispositions. We can measure motivational conditions using the kinds of instruments referred to in the Moment and Zaleznik study or any combination of similar devices for measuring here-and-now motivational conditions within the person. From these measurements we can predict how the person is likely to behave in certain clearly defined situations and what the responses of other persons are likely to be—assuming we have similar data for the other persons.

However, something is missing from this descriptive-explanatory package. If we organize our working lives exclusively around processes of selection that assume that attributes are static and if we base our anticipation of future events on our predictions from these static attributes, we may seriously miscalculate events. We may continually reinforce our own role performance and those of others and thus significantly reduce opportunities for further learning and development. And second, we may fail to recognize that, in spite of tendencies for role performances to be self-reinforcing, people do grow and change under certain conditions; hence, "static" attributes may change significantly over time.

Regardless of the practical difficulties implied in adopting the pure "here-and-now" point of view, the need still exists to know where the motivational conditions came from in the first place. Why does one person seek achievement through interaction with people, while another actively avoids interpersonal interaction in his pursuit of success? Why are some people less concerned with

[36] *Ibid.*, pp. 89–90.

achievement than others? Why are some people anxious in group problem-solving situations, while others engage comfortably in group work? What, if anything, can be done to make more effective our own and others' role performances? To pursue these kinds of questions we must assume that motivational conditions are results and look for their causes in the personal life histories of individuals. This approach has its practical aspects, since we are in the process of modifying our own and others' life histories as we work together.

These interests will be taken up in the next chapter when we examine the process of individual development. In our discussion of role performances, we have not examined in detail the individual's life cycle, one of the time referents mentioned earlier in the chapter. Role performances may fit the individual's life processes in two different ways, both of which are implied in the language and theories used in this chapter. Highly stylized role performances are normal expectations for certain stages of individual development. The role performances of different ten-year-old children, for example, are strikingly similar when compared with role performance styles of the adolescent, the young parent, the parent with older children and increased community responsibility, and the senior citizen. Each phase of individual development features similarities of individual needs and environmental opportunities for their satisfaction. In spite of differences among individuals at any one stage of development, there are more or less normal, phase-specific role performance styles, which will, under suitable conditions, change as the individual grows.

The second relationship of role performances to the life cycle concerns the individual who does not experience conditions which allow role transition. He becomes fixed in a style of role performance appropriate to an earlier stage of his life while his social-environment and biological constitution call for changes to more appropriate or "mature" role performances. Under these conditions, maintenance of the old patterns is a defensive mechanism for the individual. A role performance may contain inappropriately strong elements of defensive behavior as well as nonadaptive *intra*-personal defense mechanisms.

It is around these two themes—role performances as phase-specific stages of individual development and as aspects of the individual's system of defenses—that the next chapter will explain in more detail the motivational bases of role performances.[37]

[37] See also, Moment and Zaleznik, *op. cit.*, Ch. 7, "Developmental Trends," pp. 118–155.

# Chapter Seven

# Individual Development and Modes
# of Interpersonal Behavior

I<small>N</small> Chapter Six, we saw that role performances could be differentiated along four dimensions: (1) how others perceive an
individual's behavior, (2) the actual behavior, (3) the responding
behavior of others, and (4) the apparent motivation underlying all
this behavior.

Although role performances may range over the total spectrum of
behavior, the *style* of behavior represents the consistent way in which
an individual engages his environment and handles his relationships
with other persons. Observation of individual role performances
shows a remarkable variation in these styles. One individual is
active and participates; another is passive and remains withdrawn.
One individual presents himself to others as a humorous, easy-going
person; another presents himself as serious and hardworking. Each
type evokes a different mode of behavior, as we noted in Chapter Six.

In this chapter we shall examine the consistency within and the
variability among individuals in their modes of interpersonal behavior.
We shall try to account for the facts that a given person behaves with
a degree of consistency in performing along the behavioral spectrum
and that his pattern differs remarkably from that of other actors
in an interpersonal setting.

Our explanation shall follow the main hypotheses of psychoanalytic
theory. But before detailing a psychoanalytic explanation of modes
of interpersonal behavior or role performance, we must first examine
several of the basic assumptions underlying this theory.

## BASIC ASSUMPTIONS IN PSYCHOANALYTIC THEORY

Any theory of human behavior rests on certain basic assumptions or working hypotheses, and psychoanalytic theory is no exception. The basic assumptions are highly relevant, especially when the data to be explained—modes of interpersonal behavior—cannot easily be connected with the theory. Psychoanalytic theory, as an explanatory theory of human behavior, is built on four important working assumptions: (1) determinism; (2) unconscious motivation; (3) overdetermination; and (4) intrapsychic orientation.

### Determinism

Determinism assumes that all behavior is motivated and therefore can be explained. It may not be immediately apparent why an individual withdraws and becomes silent in a problem-solving situation, for example. But determinism assumes that if the forces at work are revealed and connected, they will provide explanations for the behavior, even though there may seem to be no obvious basis for explaining the events observed.

Sigmund Freud, who originated and developed psychoanalytic theory, followed the Western scientific tradition in his use of the deterministic orientation. The scientist pursues knowledge in the belief that explanations are possible; once achieved these explanations will serve as building blocks for continued exploration.[1] In the present context determinism means that human behavior is motivated by forces subject to clarification and statement.

In applying the principle of determinism, Freud showed, for example, how symptom formation in neurotic disturbances could be explained in the processes of illness by following his theory of mental functioning.[2] Similarly, he showed that common experiences such as forgetting or slips of the tongue were related to the dynamics of the mind.[3] Finally, in his classic study of dreams, Freud was able to relate the apparently bizarre and meaningless content of the dream to the psychic functioning of the individual.[4] Similarly, we shall examine the idea that the modes of interpersonal behavior of the individual are determined, in that his behavior results from his developmental history.

[1] A. N. Whitehead, *Science and the Modern World*, p. 4.
[2] Joseph Breur and Sigmund Freud, *Studies on Hysteria*.
[3] Sigmund Freud, *The Psychopathology of Everyday Life*.
[4] Sigmund Freud, *The Interpretation of Dreams*.

## Unconscious Motivation

Determinism in human behavior relies on the empirically demonstrated fact that much of human motivation resides in the unconscious region of the mind.   Such unconscious motivation serves as a working hypothesis in a theory of explanation of human behavior.

All individuals tend to be aware of themselves as participants in a situation.   They are capable of introspection so that they are to some extent aware of their actions.   They are conscious of perceiving events, of other persons, of experiencing feeling and thought reactions, and of intentions to act.   Despite this capacity for self-awareness, man's behavior springs, in large measure, from the unconscious functioning of his personality.

The unconscious represents the wishes, strivings, reactions, and functions of which the individual is not aware.   The processes of the unconscious absorb and utilize a considerable amount of energy even though the individual does not experience their workings directly. He does, however, experience the results of these processes in the form of feelings and ideas.   But again, it is not easy to infer the nature of unconscious processes from manifestations subject to awareness.

As a working hypothesis or assumption, the concept of the unconscious provides a direction for investigation and explanation since it assumes that much unexplained behavior is related to unconscious motivations.   In applying this hypothesis to the study of modes of interpersonal behavior, we seek to understand how the behavior relates to distributions of energy, to the inner conflicts of the individual and how he usually resolves them, and to the continuities in his developmental experience.   The line of investigation suggested by unconscious motivation is closely related to overdetermination, the third of the working hypotheses used in psychoanalytic theory.

## Overdetermination

The concept of overdetermination grows out of clinical experiences of psychoanalysis.   In examining the symptoms in a patient, Freud found no single explanation in the unconscious processes.   A symptom such as an animal phobia has several simultaneous causes. The phobia can bind anxiety or relate to unconscious hostile-aggressive wishes; it can serve as a means for maintaining earlier dependency relations with love objects or a device for punishing them, and as an aspect of many other unconscious processes.   The definition of overdetermination is that a single phenomenon such as a symptom is *simultaneously* related to a multitude of wishes and subject to a number of related interpretations.  A single act is motivated by a variety of forces and therefore has many meanings, both conscious and unconscious, to the actor.

Overdetermination is also related to how the mind works.  Behavior is motivated in that actions are directed toward achieving gratifications.  The individual is aware of only some of the needs he seeks to gratify through behavior.  Behavior tends, however, toward the greatest gratifications at the least expenditure of energy.  From this working assumption of overdetermination, we should expect to find a complex set of motivations underlying an individual's pattern of interpersonal behavior since any act has many meanings.

The fourth working hypothesis to be considered here is that the explanation of behavior resides in the intrapsychic process of the individual.

## Intrapsychic Processes

The focus on intrapsychic phenomena is a major distinguishing feature of the psychoanalytic approach to behavior and personality.  In assuming that intrapsychic processes determine behavior, the student must examine the internal development and dynamics of the mind in order to understand behavior.  This view stands in sharp contrast to that of behaviorists who maintain that the actions of men are determined by environment, which impels them to act through a conditioning process.[5]

Psychoanalytic and behavioristic theories of personality are sometimes differentiated as subjective and objective approaches to the study of behavior.  This distinction is misleading since it is possible to study the inner workings of the mind objectively, just as an individual's responses to environmental stimuli can be explained subjectively.

An investigator cannot study the inner workings of the mind directly; he can only make inferences from the data at hand.  In a psychoanalytic approach the existence of unconscious wishes and their part in internal conflict are inferred from data which are usually elicited through free association.  This process can be highly objective if the investigator is trained to observe carefully and to

[5] John B. Watson, *Behaviorism*. B. F. Skinner, *Science and Human Behavior*. Calvin S. Hall and Gardner Lindzey, *Theories of Personality*.

use his inferences to secure additional data that will confirm, alter, or elaborate the inferences.

Perhaps the most striking and simplest confirmation of the hypothesis of intrapsychic explanations is when an individual becomes aware of a wish and realizes that he has been fantasying its gratification. A person sitting in a crowded and warm meeting room may find himself fantasying the act of drinking a tall glass of cold water. Such fantasying is part of the intrapsychic functioning of the individual; it can be extended as a way of thinking about individual behavior in interpersonal settings.

As applied to interpersonal behavior, the intrapsychic approach examines the kinds of wishes evoked within the individual, the nature of the affects and ideas that derive from the wishes, and the mechanisms through which this basic energy is defined in a patterned mode of behavior. An intrapsychic approach does not examine how a situation evokes behavior, but rather how the inner workings of the mind determine the behavior produced in response to the situation.

The process of inferring an intrapsychic process in interpersonal settings is subtle, especially in view of the fact that such settings are typically far removed from the psychoanalytic setting and procedure. Yet by applying the theory derived from psychoanalysis and using its concepts to observe behavior in interpersonal settings, much can be learned about styles or modalities of interpersonal behavior and their *intrapersonal* correlates.

When discussing the basic working assumption of the psychoanalytic framework, we have not mentioned environmental influences. Psychoanalysis is concerned with the environment as it establishes the conditions under which attempts are made to control the instincts of the individual. These conditions vary from culture to culture, but whatever the specific environmental influences, they occur through the acts of parents or surrogate figures during the crucial developmental years. At some point, however, environmental influences become internalized; they become part of the intrapsychic processes and relatively autonomous from the environment.

The environment and its relation to the individual is important in another sense, one which brings us closer to the issue of explaining the modes of interpersonal behavior observable in work settings. The way the individual engages his environment at work, in the family, and in the community reflects his total developmental experience and the outcomes of the intrapsychic conflicts inherent in his development. We can say, therefore, that the environment imposes developmental conditions that become internalized and divorced from the environment. But the means by which an individual engages his environment—including persons, events, and settings—reflects the outcomes of the internalization process.

## MODES OF INTERPERSONAL BEHAVIOR AND PSYCHOANALYTIC EXPLANATIONS

In discussing the major working assumptions of psychoanalytic theory, we have indicated its distinctive orientation. The modes of interpersonal behavior are the individual's patterns of observable behavior in an encounter with another person or persons in a social setting. We can speak of behavioral acts as an interpersonal style since the acts are consistent and are gradually identified with the individual. When they describe a co-worker, individuals actually describe his pattern of behavior, that is, his behavioral traits or characteristics.

One of the central questions of psychoanalytic investigation and theory is how the total developmental experience of the individual results in the establishment of relatively consistent patterns of behavior. This is a question of ego psychology and, more specifically is a part of character structure as an aspect of ego functioning.

Ego psychology represents one of the more recent lines of investigation in psychoanalysis. It is concerned with that aspect of personality functioning that links the individual's internal reality with the external reality of the environment. The operation of this linking activity is basic to the study of ego psychology that applies the working assumptions outlined earlier.

The individual's character structure is his constellation of behavioral traits or the side of personality that he presents to his environment. Character is the individual's habitual and patterned mode of engaging with and responding to his environment; it belongs properly within the study of ego functioning. Ego psychology is a larger field of investigation than character structure. It includes perceiving, thinking, and problem-solving activities that are not necessarily observable or apparent in social interaction. Character, on the other hand, is the mode of interpersonal behavior presented to others in interactive settings.

Edward Glover says that "Character is a series of behavior reactions promoting a stable equilibrium between instinctual demands and gratification in reality." . . .[6] This is a functional definition of character which represents it as a process of balancing the instinc-

[6] Edward Glover, *On the Early Development of the Mind*, p. 248.

tual demands of the individual's internal reality with the necessity for obtaining gratifications in a form consistent with environmental conditions. This definition implies the conflict between internal and external realities in seeking gratifications. It is intrinsic to the understanding of human development and personality functioning.

Otto Fenichel develops this view of personality functioning and character in conflict resolution as follows:

Character, as the habitual mode of bringing into harmony the tasks presented by internal demands and by the external world is necessarily a function of the constant, organized and integrating part of the personality which is the ego; indeed, ego was defined as that part of the organism that handles the communications between the instinctual demands and the external world. The question of character would thus be the question of when and how the ego acquires the qualities by which it habitually adjusts itself to the demands of instinctual drives and of the external world, and later also of the superego. . . .

The term character stresses the habitual form of a given reaction, its relative constancy.[7]

This definition succinctly describes the path to be followed in developing a dynamic explanatory statement of the modes of interpersonal behavior as related to character development: (1) the relationship between instinctual processes and character, (2) the effects on character of the inner conflict produced by the developmental process, (3) the development of the ego and its relation to character, and (4) character structure as an aspect of the defensive functions of the ego.

## INSTINCTUAL PROCESSES AND CHARACTER

The psychoanalytic study of personality is based on the theory that instincts are the driving force or the energy source propelling the human organism. The source of psychic energy, its qualities, development, and elaboration, are of central concern in understanding total personality development and the character structure of the individual.

Freud proposed the view that there were, as a biological phenomenon, two main classes of instinctual energy: sex and aggression.[8] Energy of either type manifests itself as a state of tension or increased excitation whose aim is discharge. The cycle of excitation and dis-

[7] Otto Fenichel, *The Psychoanalytic Study of Neurosis*, p. 467.
[8] Sigmund Freud, *Beyond the Pleasure Principle*.

charge, or return to a relatively quiescent stage, is typical of the energy processes of men.

The mechanism of discharge of tension or energy operates according to the pleasure principle.[9] Tension is not pleasurable, although tension release or energy discharge is. The pleasure principle is adhered to through primitive thought processes that Freud called "primary process thinking."[10] Primary process thinking, in contrast to *secondary process thinking*, operates without rules of logic and demands immediate gratification of an instinctual urge or wish. It operates through condensation in that a fragmentary idea or fantasy is loaded with meanings and references. Condensation, and in fact, primary process thinking, is seen most clearly in dreams, where a fleeting image has rich associative meanings. Primary process thinking utilizes visual imagery and symbolization. Secondary process thinking utilizes verbal symbols and logical sequences of ideas for its elaboration. In the world of instinctual urges and primary process thinking, travel can represent death which is, in turn, indicative of aggressive wishes; money can represent feces and reflects sadistic-aggressive fantasies; body parts and body processes may be symbolized by imagery of terrain and earth features which reflect various sexual fantasies and wishes.

Instinctual processes are not experienced directly as are the derivatives of the instincts. Derivatives consist of ideation and affect or emotion. Both ideation and affect exist at conscious and unconscious levels of awareness. But they can be separated so that the wish or fantasy associated with an instinctual urge can become conscious, though perhaps somewhat disguised, and the attendant affect can be unconscious. Instinctual urges manifest themselves according to habitual modes of dealing with inner conflict; we shall discuss this presently. It is sufficient to note here that the direct discharge of instinctual drives following the mode of primary process thinking conflicts with other psychic processes and with reality. Secondary process thinking and the reality principle limit instinctual energy and ultimately serve the pleasure principle in ways that are consonant with environmental expectations and the internal precipitates of reality.

The energy of the instinctual drives may be regarded as a quantitative charge that has direction. The quantity of energy directed toward an object, or the mental representation of an object, is called a *cathexis*. Psychic energy, or the cathexes, is highly mobile

---

[9] Sigmund Freud, "Formulations Regarding the Two Principles in Mental Functioning."

[10] Sigmund Freud, *The Interpretation of Dreams*, pp. 588–609.

and subject to displacements from one object or representation to another. The cathexes may be directed toward objects outside oneself, such as persons and ideas, or they may be directed toward oneself. Freud used the legend of Narcissus to describe the fluidity of the psychic energy. Narcissus saw his image in a reflecting pool and fell in love with himself—or the image of himself. This legend represents the phenomenon of cathexis of the self in contrast to object cathexis. More specifically, the sexual energy attached to oneself is called narcissism, which is contrasted with object love. Aggressive energy directed toward oneself is called masochism, the opposite of sadism which is aggressive energy directed outward to objects.

This brief description enables us to connect instinctual processes with character and the mode of interpersonal behavior. In Chapter Six, we said that the relationship between role performances and modes of experiencing was a useful concept in describing the motivations of actors in interpersonal settings. The role performance types were Task Specialist, Social Specialist, Star, and Underchosen. The Task Specialist's primary mode of experiencing is through abstract tasks and the logics of problem solving in work; the object of his experience is inanimate, not human. The Task Specialist *cathects*, or invests, emotional energy with the abstract, or task-relevant area of work. The Social Specialist, on the other hand, experiences the time and space of interpersonal settings in terms of persons and interaction. His dominant cathectic pattern results in emotional investment in persons. The fusion type, or Star, cathects both human and inanimate objects in an interactive setting. He therefore experiences significant interpersonal relations as well as the logics of task and problem solving. Individuals who behave erratically, such as the Underchosen, seem to manifest shifting cathectic patterns; they fluctuate rapidly between investment in persons or ideas as objects and marked narcissistic positions which seem to indicate disinterest in the persons and ideas represented in interpersonal encounters.

Another way of looking at the cathectic patterns represented by the various types of role performance is to examine the blend of libidinal (sexual) and aggressive energies utilized or discharged through the behavior. Task Specialists utilize the derivatives of aggressive energy to a greater degree than Social Specialists. Stars seem to blend libidinal and aggressive derivatives in their capacity to be both expressive and instrumental in behavior.

Although we speak of cathectic patterns connected with interpersonal performance and the utilization of aggressive and libidinal energies, we should bear in mind that the performances represent the *derivatives* of the instinctual processes. In fact, the idea of energy discharge in ordinary work and human relationships is related to the concept of neutralized and sublimated energy. For energy to be utilized constructively it must be detached or freed from its primitive forms to become available for discharge in everyday activity. Energy that is not sublimated or neutralized is wasted in inner conflicts and not readily available for constructive activity.

Just how sublimation and neutralization occur is still problematical. Existing theories require an understanding of shifts or alterations in instinctual processes as a part of human development.

Psychoanalysis divides the developmental stages into four main divisions: (1) infancy, (2) latency, (3) adolescence, and (4) adulthood. The alterations in instinctual development within and between these stages are a major area for investigation in the psychoanalytic study of development. Such alterations are also important to our understanding of the modes of interpersonal performance during the adult years. *The behavior of the individual in any stage of the life cycle reflects the successive layering of experience and the crises in development of all previous stages.*[11]

1. INFANCY

Infancy is the period from birth through the fifth year. It is subdivided into three stages. But these should not be viewed as a rigid timetable. We must bear in mind that the theory of development is a complex subject; the exposition of any such complex theory necessarily simplifies reality.

In infancy, stages of development are marked by instinctual changes. Different body zones become central areas for instinctual excitation. Changes also take place in the infant's relations with parental objects. During earliest infancy, the mouth is the central body zone for instinctual gratification. As a result, the period is called the *oral* stage of development. The basic tension discharge process is closely related to feeding: gratification is achieved through sucking and intake of food from the breast or the bottle. The mother and the mental representation of mother become the center of the infant's world during this stage which roughly encompasses the first year and a half of life.

Although infants may seem removed from sexuality as most adults know it, they experience strong erotic urges in the oral stage, as well as in other stages of infancy. The erotization is involved in feeding

[11] Sigmund Freud, *Three Contributions to the Theory of Sex.* Erik Erikson, *Childhood and Society.*

and, associatively, in being cuddled, rocked, and kept warm. Body contact with the mother is the important source of gratification.

Besides the sexual instincts, aggressive drives become significant, particularly during the later oral stage when teething occurs. Aggression is expressed through the urge to bite and thereby to assimilate the object. This urge toward assimilation, or introjection, is significant for development; it represents the primitive way in which humans deal with basic frustrations. The wish to bite seems to coincide with the withdrawal of breast or bottle and weaning. This experience mobilizes and amplifies the aggression that first becomes manifest at delay in being fed. The wish to incorporate or introject the lost object becomes a patterned way of dealing with loss and frustration.

Sexual and aggressive instincts developed during the oral stage are later reflected in important personality characteristics. An infant who has experienced gratification during the oral stage develops what Erikson calls a sense of basic trust.[12] Basic trust reflects the successive experiencing of instinctual excitation or tension followed by gratification or reduction of tension as a result of being fed. It also reflects a well-established differentiation between the self and the object world so that later in life the individual will not attribute his own body sensations and feelings to the outside world. A sense of basic trust results in optimism, friendliness, and an attitude of openness in contrast to undue pessimism, hostility, and withdrawal of interests in other persons and ideas. Other personality traits clearly visible in interpersonal relations that are a legacy of frustrations during the oral stage of development include excessive dependency and greediness, the urge for succor, and the wish to be cared for by others. These reflections of oral frustrations are sometimes disguised, but they are apparent to the astute observer of interpersonal relations.

For example, a group of students met in a training group twice weekly as part of a human relations course. One student consistently asked the group to help him understand what was going on. In response to his pleas of "I don't understand," and "explain to me what is happening," group members would offer comments and observations, usually couched in gentle, understanding tones. Several group members began to bring coffee for one another to the meeting; this seemed to symbolize their membership in a subgroup in which the dependent member was not included. He usually eyed the coffee as it was brought in and glanced in the direction of the coffee drinkers as they sipped from their cups. One morning he noticed an unclaimed

---

[12] Erik Erikson, *Identity and the Life Cycle*, pp. 55–65.

cup of coffee—one of the regular subgroup members was absent. The dependent member asked in a plaintive voice if he could have the coffee. It was passed to him, and he sat with his feet bent close to his body up against the table, in a curled up position, sipping the coffee and sighing contentedly and audibly. The oral wishes in this illustration were initially disguised in pleas for help, knowledge, and understanding. The more obvious form followed in the sipping of coffee which unmistakably revealed the wish to be fed and nurtured by maternal figures.

However, oral deprivation is not manifested in interpersonal relations solely by dependency bids; quite the opposite behavior is also common. The individual who appears to be independent or withdrawn and uninterested in other persons and ideas may reflect a narcissistic quality that derives from oral deprivation. During the oral stage, frustrations lead to the transfer of cathexis from objects to the self or body parts. A clear-cut instance of such auto-erotic interests is thumbsucking, where the search for oral gratification is directed inward. In adults, derivatives of thumbsucking appear in the form of smoking, drinking, and lip chewing.

Orality and characteristic styles of verbal behavior are also closely related. The individual who "chews on his words" as though savoring them before reluctantly releasing them or the individual who spits out his words as if to assault his listeners reflects oral personality traits. Taking in, biting, chewing, and spitting out appear to be basic oral modalities in interpersonal relations; but the modalities are expressed through the verbal processes instead of with food.

The second stage of infancy, from about 1½ years to 3½ years, is called the anal stage of development. The anus becomes the center of erotic sensations. Object relations shift to the mother's attempts to toilet train the child. During this period, heightened aggressive and sadistic impulses are manifest. The relationship with the mother may seem to become a power struggle. The infant views body substances with a great deal of interest and delight. Feelings of shame, disgust, and loathing are acquired as a reaction formation at the penalty of losing the mother's love. Retention of the feces on the part of the infant stems from delight at, and overvaluing of, bodily products and the fear of self-destruction associated with giving up feces. Moreover, the retention of feces acts as a sexual stimulant and is experienced as pleasurable. Release of the body matter, on the other hand, is an act of compliance toward the loved object. These conflicts between the instinctual wishes and the demands of the loved object occur during a period of heightened aggressiveness. This heightened aggressiveness stems from increased muscular development and motor activity and enters into the conflict.

Successful resolution of anal conflicts results in interest being directed away from anal processes and in sublimation. Interests develop, for example, in modeling with clay, in painting, and in other constructive activities that resemble "smearing." The aggressiveness becomes channeled into motor activity, such as playing with building blocks. If the anal stage is dealt with successfully, the individual develops such personality traits as orderliness, neatness, persistance in work, methodical behavior, and perhaps thriftiness and interest in accumulating money and property. But any of these traits that become excessive or dominant in the individual's character reflect an excessive reaction formation and a channeling of energy to overcome still active anal wishes. The individual develops an obsessive-compulsive character pattern marked by orderliness, obstinacy, and parsimony. Orderliness and neatness are behaviors which oppose the wish to smear and be dirty; obstinancy reflects the stubborn refusal to give in to another person's will—in this case, the mother's; and parsimony reflects the urge to hoard valued property as a displacement from feces.

In severe forms of obsessive-compulsive neuroses, the extremes of behavior become marked restrictions on the ego and impoverish the individual. This illness may be manifest in acts of compulsive hard working, detached ideas that appear "out of the blue," and the need to perform rituals to undo harm implied in a thought or idea.

We observe the remnants of the anal stage in everyday behavior: interest in hoarding, stubbornness, and acts of orderliness. The highly task-oriented individual who constantly seeks to maintain order and logical flow in discussion reflects certain anal character traits. These traits can be very constructive in interpersonal relations, but when they become excessive or are adhered to rigidly they can prevent creative work. In group discussion, for example, it may be at times very constructive to encourage free-floating activity and to avoid over-logicized procedures as a way of stimulating ideas and thinking. Individuals with marked anal character traits frequently become uncomfortable during such unrestricted periods of interaction.

Body posture and motion are also frequent expressions of anal traits. Rigidity in posture and body movement, tightness around the lips and face, impassive facial expressions, and the relative absence of expression in the eyes indicate a "tight" or constipated person, to use everyday jargon. It is as though the individual is holding back or holding in because he is afraid to let go. What he is afraid to release is, of course, the aggression associated with the anal stage of development; the retention of feeling becomes associated with the destructive power of the feces.

Another feature of anality is the tendency to separate ideation from affect; affect may go underground or be repressed, while ideas and thoughts remain plentiful and conscious. This separation is valuable in logical thinking. But when it becomes a marked feature of the personality, the individual appears cold and lacking in feeling and is therefore subject to impoverishment in object relations. An individual who is unable to give free play to emotions may also lose intuitive qualities necessary in creative thought.

The oral and anal stages of development are usually set off from the third stage and called the pregenital stages of libidinal development. The third stage, the genital or more accurately the phallic stage, is the precursor of the mature achievement of adult sexuality.

Instinctual processes in the pregenital stages involve *component instincts* such as sucking, smelling, looking, and touching. Sexual and aggressive drive gratifications are achieved through the discharge of the component instincts. These instincts are the source of energy available for sublimation or the conversion of energy of partial instincts into socially desired activities. They are also incorporated within the personality of the individual as character traits which become the visible aspects of personality functioning in the interpersonal settings. A third manifestation is in acts of fore-pleasure, which are a part of mature sexuality.

The process of changing a child's instincts into sublimations or character traits is part of the child-parent educational relationship. Essentially, the educative process is built upon the frustration of the partial drives and the inhibition of their aim. Frustration of the drive and inhibition of aim involves conflict and conflict resolution, which will be discussed in the next section of this chapter. The important idea for consideration here is that the instinctual process places upon the organism, at each stage of infancy, certain developmental tasks; these tasks are the precursors of personality development.

The phallic stage roughly covers the period from 3½ to 5 or 6 years of age. During this period, the phallus becomes the organ or body zone that is the center of instinctual excitation. The shift from the oral to the anal and then to the phallic zone proceeds through the successive gratification, frustration, and inhibition of the aims inherent in the component instincts. The centering of instinctual pleasure in the phallic zone sets the stage for the mature functioning of the adult. Sexual functioning is central to the process of mature adult activity.

It is unlikely that any aspect of adult activity is independent of the capacity to achieve sexual gratification in a heterosexual relationship which is based on tenderness and caring.

Besides the shift of instinctual tensions to the phallus, the work of this third stage of infancy involves complex relationships with parents and siblings as objects of the instinctual drives. The child develops a strong attachment to the parent of the opposite sex. A boy child fantasys doing away with all rivals and having his mother as his exclusive possession. The main rival is the father, but siblings also appear to be rivals.

Freud used the Greek tragedy *Oedipus Rex* to conceptualize this intense struggle. In Sophocles' drama, Oedipus unknowingly killed his father and then married his mother and entered into an incestuous relationship with her. The punishment for his aggressive and sexual crime was to be blinded. The phallic stage of development involves the experiencing of the *oedipal conflict* and its resolution.

According to Freud, the wishes of the oedipus complex exist in the fantasy of the child. They may on occasion become directly evident when the child tells his mother that he will marry her when he grows up and send father away. But the manifestations are usually indirect. For example, during the oedipal period the child becomes very active and engages in aggressive play. He may become fearful when his parents leave, even for a short time. At times phobias develop, such as fear of animals or trains.[13]

The hyperactivity, along with the fears, reflects anxiety. Strong oedipal wishes are accompanied by the fear of retaliation: the male child fears that his hostile wishes will be discovered and that he will be castrated by his father. Castration anxiety is intensified when the child discovers the difference between the sexes. The boy may believe that the girl once had a penis but suffered the fate of castration as punishment. This primitive belief may feed the child's anxiety long after he discovers the true significance of this difference. Castration anxiety can easily become displaced in the form of fear of animals, as a substitute for the castrating father, or in the form of a depreciatory attitude toward women as "defective." Some forms of scapegoating, such as picking on the weak person or racial hatreds, are collective expressions of castration anxiety.

The oedipus complex will be discussed further in the next chapter when we consider authority relations as a central aspect of interpersonal dynamics. To continue with the discussion from the standpoint of the character structure of the individual, the oedipal period

---

[13] Sigmund Freud, "Analysis of a Phobia in a Five-Year-Old Boy."

affects character significantly.  The intense conflict it produces may
lead toward regression to the earlier anal-sadistic stage and the appearance of compulsive orderliness, obstinacy, and parsimony.  The individual may increase his tendency to separate emotions and ideas.

Oedipal conflicts may also lead to the development of marked
hysterical character traits.  "Hysterical" refers to the neurosis that
results from marked fixations and severe disturbances during the phallic
stage of development.  The term "hysterical character" parallels the
concept of "compulsive character," the traits associated with the anal-
sadistic stage of development and related to obsessive-compulsive
neuroses.

Hysterical character traits, following the description presented by
Wilhelm Reich,[14] include seductiveness (in the sexual sense) and
liveliness and expressiveness in mode of dress, manner of speech, and
posture.  The individual appears excitable and enthusiastic in a transitory way.  Hysterical traits include a high degree of obvious
emotionality.  In the compulsive character, for example, emotion is detached from ideas and goes underground.  In hysterical traits, emotion
seems to be on the surface but disconnected from the ideas to which
it was originally attached.  The ideas relate to oedipal wishes.
Relationships are easily sexualized, but without awareness on the part of
the individual.  Excitability as a hysterical characteristic is connected
with oedipal anxiety.  The individual appears to move toward the
source of instinctual danger, in a counterphobic sense, instead of
withdrawing.

Reich points out that the hysterical character may, on the other
hand, develop certain depressive features.  Depressive traits reflect
regression to earlier oral reactions—anger at the loss of love and the
nurturant figure.

A related set of character features attributable to instinctual processes
during the phallic stage is marked passivity, especially in males.  The
individual may appear soft-spoken and expressive and exhibit little
tendency to express aggression.  Such features are typically associated
with femininity in our culture.  The relation of instinctual processes
to the formation of passive character traits is essentially an unconscious reflection of aggressive wishes arising during the oedipal
conflict.  This rejection of aggression is accentuated when a sibling
is born during the child's phallic stage of development and he experiences displacement in his relationship with his mother.  If the
child acts on his wishes to destroy the interloper, even in small deeds,

[14] Wilhelm Reich, *Character Analysis*, pp. 189–193.

he is punished. The aggressive wishes then go underground or only appear in highly disguised forms of behavior.

The discussion of character traits associated with the phallic stage has emphasized the features related to the neurotic dispositions of individuals who have not succeeded in adequately resolving oedipal conflicts. But since instinctual conflicts at any stage in development are never completely resolved, we find that these traits are carried over into the interpersonal modalities of adults. We should emphasize again, however, that such traits should not be viewed as "good or bad." The test of the health or pathology of a set of traits is a complex one. Any set of traits that are adhered to rigidly and that become semi-automatic responses limit the individual's capacity to act and achieve gratifications through his behavior. But when such traits are appropriately manifested and utilized flexibly they become adaptive and useful to the individual and his society.

This last idea is best illustrated by Kubie. In discussing a scientific career, he points out how the characteristics of oral, anal, and phallic instinctual processes are indeed useful when applied in appropriate contexts. His views are worth quoting here.

. . . These can have comparable influence in research. During the exploratory phase, while crude data are being gathered, an investigator ought to be free from rigidity. He should be ready to abandon preconceived objectives and anticipated goals, so that any hints that come from unexpected findings can be pursued. He must be psychologically free to follow uncharted courses. Therefore, premature systematization of the data must be avoided. This requires that type of free and imaginative flexibility which is sometimes attributed to the so-called "hysterical" personality. Later, a more rigid process is required, one which has some of the features of the obsessional neurosis, or even some of the tendency of a paranoid patient to organize his delusions into logical systems. Scientific research thus seems to require that, as the work progresses, the investigator should be free to operate now with one type of personality and now with another. It would be profitable to compare analytically the personalities of those scientists who can change in this way and of those who cannot, especially in relation to their scientific productivity. This would seem to be a problem of basic importance for the optimal use of scientific personnel.[15]

This same idea can be applied to character traits as they relate to interpersonal modalities. Orality and verbal facility are useful in

[15] Lawrence S. Kubie, "Some Unsolved Problems of the Scientific Career," in Stein, Vidich, and White, *Identity and Anxiety*, p. 252.

general group discussion. The individual who is eloquent and verbally quick frequently helps generate useful discussion. But if the eloquence and verbal facility become a rigid mode of behavior, they lead to overdomination which may engender resistance and hostility in other group members.

Similarly, orderliness, obstinacy, and parsimony, the anal character traits, are useful if applied appropriately and without the compulsiveness associated with their severe manifestations. In the interpersonal structure of work settings the individual who can keep a group to the point and apply logic to its proceedings performs a highly valued function. Comparable views of hysterical character traits can be applied to interpersonal relations.

### 2. LATENCY

Many other features of the infancy stage of development require consideration to understand character and interpersonal modalities. These features will be discussed in succeeding sections of this chapter. For the present, we shall continue our brief outline of instinctual development and its relation to the formation of character.

The second main division of the life cycle in the psychoanalytic theory of instinctual development is called latency. It ranges from 6 years to the onset of puberty—about 12. Latency describes the period of relative quiescence in sexual development. The resolution of the oedipal conflicts is accompanied by a modification of the sexual instincts and an interest in learning, mastery, play, and the development of skills important to the individual's character. If the individual's interests do not change or instinctual conflict seems to continue unabated, the previous stages in instinctual development have not been successfully experienced. Common indications of developmental failures during latency are phobias, learning blocks, and regressive behavior, such as excessive dependency on maternal figures, enuresis (bed-wetting), and feeding problems.

Expected developmental gains during the latency period center around school and learning, the peer group and play, and the building of an ethical-moral base for later adult responsibility. Progress in learning and attitude toward education during this stage strongly influence career choice and occupational interests. The individual's constitutional endowment, his experience in a particular social class, and the subculture's support of his aims for formal education are all significant. Learning attitudes and experience are reflected in the individual's developing ego interests which become an important aspect of his personality.

The emphasis during latency of peer group relations and play are significant in a number of ways. The child learns more about the adult requirements of "give and take." His ability to share, already encountered in sibling relationships, is enhanced through learning to wait his turn in games and to follow the rules necessary to carry out increasingly sophisticated game activity. Sharing and co-operation are also related to the child's sense of morality and ethical behavior. In this connection, Piaget's experimental work on the latency child is worth consideration.

In his book, *The Moral Judgment of the Child*,[16] Piaget demonstrated how, in the course of play activity, the child learns the importance of rules in a setting *apart from* adult constraint. Games such as marbles are usually handed down from the older to the younger child with little or no direct influence from adult authority figures. The child soon learns that to achieve pleasure in games he must abide by the common rules of participants which are not subject to arbitrary manipulation. Such rules are significant because they are not imposed by powerful authority figures; they spring from a system of craftsmanship, competition, and fun enjoyed with contemporaries. The lessons of the world of games and play are invaluable in the adult world of work. If they are not solidified during the latency period, the boy-turned-man faces many difficult experiences in understanding the place of procedure and government by law instead of by the whims of man.

The sense of morality gained from the experiences of latency is also reflected in the transition from justice based on objective consequences to justice based on subjective intent. In experiments with children in the latency stage, Piaget found that older children sense that the intent of the actor is more significant in judging a crime than the consequences of the act. This idea is illustrated in his technique of asking the children to indicate which of two boys should be punished more severely: the one who accidentally broke 12 dishes or the one who broke 4 dishes while disobeying his mother. The younger latency children would mete out hypothetical punishment based on the damage—breaking 12 dishes deserves more punishment than breaking 4. The older latency children were all able to see that in one case an accident occurred while in the second the intent was to disobey.

Piaget's experiments and conclusions dramatize the importance of building the sense of justice necessary for the functioning of adults, in co-operative as well as competitive endeavors, during latency. The emphasis is on learning to co-operate *and* to compete with other persons. The absence of either capacity inhibits adult behavior.

[16] Jean Piaget, *The Moral Judgment of the Child*.

### 3. ADOLESCENCE

The adolescent period is marked by new intensities of the instinctual drives, especially the sexual drives. The biological as well as psychological changes are manifest.

Accompanying this instinctual reawakening is the re-experiencing of eariler conflicts, particularly the oedipal struggle. During the adolescent period the individual must secure his independence from the instinctual objects of prior periods and establish attachments to new and appropriate objects. The shifting of libidinal ties must be accompanied by the elimination of incestuous fantasies and the ambivalent feelings originally directed toward parents. The adolescent also must learn to use aggression to establish a successful career. The utilization of aggressive energies in school and work is directed toward learning increasingly complex skills and ideas.

The social learning during adolescence is often fraught with bizarre behavior. The adolescent, in collaboration with age-mates, experiments with roles in anticipation of the performance of these roles under conditions of responsibility. The absence of this responsibility during adolescence creates what Erikson has called a *psychosocial moratorium*.[17] This moratorium is produced by society which permits the adolescent to experiment, learn, and prepare himself for the complex role performances demanded of adults at work, in the family, and in the community.

The main outcome of adolescent development is the establishment of a basic identity.[18] Identity is knowledge of who one is in psychosocial space. It is built primarily on a well-established sense of one's sex role and the capacity to perform and experience pleasure without undue guilt. It includes an ability to accept and reject identities that society seeks to impose on the individual. Shakespeare's Polonius cautioned his son, "Neither a borrower nor a lender be." A sense of identity can be neither borrowed nor loaned without injuring the individual's secure knowledge of who he is, to himself and to his world. Polonius also advised, "This above all—to thine own self be true; and it must follow, as the night the day, thou canst not then be false to any man." The adolescent must recognize the wisdom implied in the idea.

To emphasize an idea presented before, the sense of identity rests on the foundation of mastery of the instinctual processes. The concept of identity may be misleading if it is interpreted as mere intellectual ruminations about the self and is separated from feelings and the grati-

[17] Erik Erikson, *Identity and the Life Cycle*, p. 111.
[18] *Ibid.*, pp. 110–111.

fication of instinctual wishes in ways that will enhance the individual and his society.

But the work of adolescence neither begins nor ends during the adolescent period. The foundation for the formation of a sense of identity is built upon the infancy and latency stages. The work of adolescence culminates in the successful performance of the many roles an individual assumes as an adult. Let us now turn to the developmental processes of the adult years and their meaning in interpersonal relations.

### 4. THE ADULT YEARS

Attempts to describe adult functioning and development from an instinctual point of view are based on the concept of "the genital character."[19] This concept refers to an ideal type of character and personality function. Adult behavior can represent only an approximation of this ideal type.

The genital character represents first and foremost the achievement of genital primacy. The genitalia become the center of libidinal excitation, and the pregenital-component instincts are subordinated to genital primacy or sublimated. As a result of genital primacy, instinctual pleasure is achieved and the individual functions within a cycle of excitation, or tension, and discharge, or pleasure.

This basic cyclical patterning becomes an aspect of character. The individual can work and rest, give conscious and sustained attention to matters of immediate concern, and permit his mind to reflect and wander. He can alternate activity with passivity, and work with play.

The ideal type described as the genital character experiences the full range of emotional reactions because ambivalences connected with early instinctual development are dissolved. Love and hate become identifiable reactions within the individual in response to situations and events.

The interpersonal correlate of the genital character is framed around the notion of flexibility in performance. Interpersonal "reflexes," to use Leary's term,[20] are not restricted so that varieties in performance are possible without waste of energy.

Object relations in interpersonal settings are relevant to here-and-now situations. The individual establishes the kind of relationships appropriate to his needs and to the realities of the situation. The individual encounters relatively few love objects—in the deepest meaning of the term—during his lifetime. The cathexes toward objects

---

[19] Karl Abraham, *Selected Papers on Psychoanalysis*, pp. 407–417. Wilhelm Reich, *Character Analysis*, pp. 158–179.

[20] Timothy Leary, *Interpersonal Diagnosis of Personality*, pp. 103–109.

are therefore appropriate to the kinds of gratifications likely to be achieved.

In discussing the developmental aspects of the adult years from the standpoint of instinctual processes, we are limited by the fact that adult functioning is based on complex personality organization. The position of the ego is crucial to this functioning. If we understand ego processes, we are better able to grasp the significance of instinctual gratification and how it is achieved in ways consonant with reality. The question of ego functioning will be discussed later in this chapter. For the present we shall proceed in the consideration of character and instinctual processes by turning to the subject of inner conflict and personality development.

## INNER CONFLICT AND CHARACTER

It is extremely important to discuss the relationship between the individual's instinctual processes and character development, keeping in mind the place of inner conflict in human development. In the preceding section we established the main steps in the instinctual time-table and their significance in the formation of character traits. How the precipitates of instinctual development result in the formation of character traits is related to conflict or conflict resolution as inner processes of personality development.

The significance of inner conflict in human development stems from the nature of instinctual processes.[21] Instincts are stimuli that emanate from within the organism and are to be differentiated from the outer stimuli. Outer stimuli can be dealt with through motor activity or flight, but this is not the case with instincts. Instincts create unpleasant tensions. Instincts and needs, their derivatives, demand discharge or satisfaction, which is pleasurable. Following the workings of the pleasure principle, the tensions of the inner needs seek *immediate* discharge. It is here that the basic condition of conflict arises. In order to develop, the organism must learn to delay discharge. The infant is completely helpless and must depend on objects outside itself for need gratification; instantaneous discharge of tension is not possible, therefore. This delay is the initial conflict between the biological condition of the organism and the environmental conditions of reality.

Tracing the developmental sequences in experiencing delay illuminates how character formation and the instincts are related. The initial step resulting from delay is the organism's attempt to achieve tension release through taking itself as object, that is, directing the

[21] Sigmund Freud, "Instincts and Their Vicissitudes."

energy inward rather than outward.   This process has been represented by Rapaport in the early infant-mother relationship as a two-step process: [22]

1. Restlessness → Appearance of breast and sucking →
   Subsidence of restlessness.
2. Drive → Absence of drive object: ⎫ → Hallucinatory image of the
            delay of discharge        ⎭      memory of gratification.

The initial gratification, according to this representation, establishes memory traces of the need-satisfying object and of activity within the organism.   When a delay occurs, the memory traces are cathected, making the initial delay possible.   This stage of delay leads to *primary narcissism;* self-object differentiation has not yet occurred.   Everything the infant experiences as pleasurable is part of the inner world, while everything unpleasurable is part of the outer world.

In adult experience the closest representation of this basic process of hallucinating the need-satisfying object is the dream.   A basic function of the dream is to permit the discharge of tension through visual imagery, making sleep possible.[23]

Later, in the oral stage of development, self-object differentiation occurs.   This is the beginning of the breakdown of the primitive thought mechanism which incorporates tension release or pleasure into the organism and externalizes or projects unpleasurable experiences into the environment.   As aspects of personality, oral character traits are then carried over into personality from this initial experience of delay.   Impatience, followed by withdrawal of interest from the outside world and depression, reflects the unresolved developmental conflicts of delay during this early stage; or more accurately, these developmental conflicts and the patterns for dealing with them during the oral stage become prototypes for later manifestations of tension and delay reactions.   Such conflicts and patterns of resolution appear in the narcissistic individual who betrays little interest in other persons as objects.   If conflicts from delay and gratification during the oral stage are severe, they are associated with psychoses and autistic thought patterns.   But they are also present, to some extent, in normal persons.

Another approach to the effects of delay on personality formation is representing the process as the attempt to resolve conflict over objects.   During the oral stage of development, object loss is equated

[22] David Rapaport, *The Conceptual Model of Psychoanalysis,* pp. 225 and 227.
[23] Sigmund Freud, *The Interpretation of Dreams.*

with the withdrawal of breast or bottle during weaning. When weaning occurs in a satisfactory mother-infant relationship based on actual gratification of needs, interest in the object is not abandoned to return to a narcissistic position. But the conflict arises over whether to give up the breast and move on to new developmental stages or to attempt to recoup the loss through introjecting the object and reverting to narcissism.

The second main instinctual conflict in the development of the individual occurs during the anal-sadistic stage. The term sadistic reflects the fact that during the anal stage the infant's aggressive instincts are strong. These drives are associated with the trend toward mastery during the anal stage: increased use of the muscles, heightened motor activity, and attempts at walking. The inner manifestations of the drive toward mastery are much more complex. During this stage in the development, the infant begins to think of himself as omnipotent. He seems to believe that his growing mastery will result in control of the world and that animate and inanimate objects will yield to his wishes. The loved object, the mother, asserts control upon the infant in the form of toilet training. The mother, in effect acting on behalf of society, seeks to regulate and control the infant whose slowly maturing thought processes are centered in his magical capacity to control the universe. The infant fears that he will lose his mother's love if he seeks to retain the feces—a significant danger to a fragile ego.

The meaning of the fecal matter to the infant is a significant feature of this instinctual conflict; it is regarded as pleasurable since it provides pleasurable anal sensations. Feces are also viewed as valuable possessions, prized products of the infant's own body and therefore not to be yielded readily. At times, the infant may not distinguish the loss of feces from the destruction of self; in other words, the fear of giving up feces may coincide with fears of self-obliteration. The generally high value placed on feces helps clarify why, in dreams and other symbolic aspects of life, feces and money are interchangeable.

Another meaning of feces is connected with the increased aggression of the anal-sadistic stage. The will to master, in a primitive sense, means the incorporation into the self of all objects that are pleasurable and the destruction of all objects that are not. The release of fecal matter can then symbolize the emission of explosive, destructive, and dangerous objects which if retained would destroy the self; but if they are released, they may destroy the "not-self," or the outer world. This conflict stems, therefore, from the fear of self-destruction on the one hand, and fear of destruction of the external world, including the mother as the loved object, on the other.

The tentative resolution of instinctual conflicts during the anal-sadistic stage rests on the desire to secure love and approval from the mother. The infant gives up feces and achieves control to secure her approval. He adopts her attitudes and by the process of *reaction formation*, the adoption of an opposite goal, gives up interest in the feces. Instead of viewing feces with pride, the infant views them with disgust and shame; instead of being valuable, they become worthless and are, therefore, easily given up. Reaction formation, under conditions of love in the mother-infant relationship, enables the energy tied to pleasure in anal processes to be *sublimated* or made available for socially acceptable ends. It is common to find a growing interest on the part of the infant in painting, coloring, and making products that will be genuinely admired by him and others.

Let us now re-examine the character traits associated with the anal-sadistic stage of development. We have said that obstinacy, orderliness, and parsimony are legacies of the anal stage. These traits are valuable carryovers of early experience if they are not rigid or excessive. Obstinacy can mean the ability to hold to ideas and not give in at the first indication of opposition. Failure to develop some such trait results in excessive uniformity and lack of independence in thinking and judgment. The ultraconformist in interpersonal work settings probably fears loss of love; the derivation of this fear is in the experiences of toilet training. On the other hand, excessive obstinacy, or unwillingness to submit or yield to another person's ideas, becomes disadvantageous to adult performance. It is sometimes reflected in the inability to complete a work project because it means forming and then giving up a valued internal product. Such stubbornness and refusal to yield the product are manifested as low productivity in work settings.

Similar statements can be made about orderliness and parsimony, traits which when applied appropriately and realistically are valuable aspects of character. But too much, or too little orderliness or parsimony will inhibit performance.

Let us briefly examine an idea which will be dealt with more fully in Chapter Eight. The expression of many character traits becomes highly significant in authority relationships, whether we consider these traits in their primitive formations or in their later expression in work situations. We can anticipate, therefore, that this discussion of character formation as an explanation of interpersonal modalities will illuminate the problem of interpersonal authority and relations in work settings. For the present, we shall continue consideration of instinctual conflict and character formation by turning to the significant conflicts of the phallic stage of development.

The theme of loss plays a central part in the instinctual conflicts of the phallic stage. In the oral stage, loss was connected with the process of weaning, the loss of the mother's breast. In the anal stage, the conflict centered around loss of body material and the danger of loss of love. In the phallic stage, the danger centers around the loss of the penis or castration anxiety.

The threat of loss arises out of the oedipal strivings of the infant. The instinctual wish of the male child is to displace the father and to have sole possession of the mother. Such wishes are connected with genital pleasure so that a primitive notion of sexual relations is attached to the idea of possessing the mother. This notion may arise from fantasies of sexual relations between the parents or from actual observation of sexual activity. These fantasies and observations contain strong aggressive features as though the active partner (the male) is assaulting or destroying the passive partner (the female).

Oedipal wishes therefore become dangerous. In the primitive thinking of the child, the wish and the deed are not yet separated, and fantasies which exist purely in the inner workings of the mind are the sources of danger. Another aspect of the danger exists in the idea of "an eye for an eye, and a tooth for a tooth." Aggressive wishes directed toward the father result in fear of retaliation in the form of castration. Another form of this same danger is the fear that the mother, who herself possesses no penis, will be envious and seek to take the possesion of this valued part.

The intense conflicts connected with oedipus complex may develop in several ways. The child may resolve the conflict by giving up the wishes and identifying with the parent of the same sex.[24] He may achieve *delay* of the wishes and resolve the conflict by deciding: "If I cannot replace father, I will be like him." This serves to retain the love of parents and to delay the wishes while the child enters a period of growth and learning. It is a major advance toward the development of the ideal genital character type discussed earlier.

On the other hand, the conflicts may remain largely unresolved so that the individual becomes fixated at the oedipal stage of development. Such a fixation is expressed in the form of hysterical character features: high anxiety, hyperactivity, and intense emotionality become major character traits.

Psychoanalytic studies have identified two other constellations of character traits connected with unresolved oedipal conflicts: (1)

[24] Sigmund Freud, "The Passing of the Oedipus Complex." Sigmund Freud, "Analysis of a Phobia in a Five-Year-Old Boy."

the masochistic character and (2) the phallic character.[25]    Masochism, or deriving pleasure from experiencing pain, is an intense form of neurotic suffering.    The actual seeking of physical punishment as a form of sexual gratification is a form of perversion.[26]    Masochistic character traits exist in varying degree in the everyday functioning of individuals and can readily be observed in interpersonal relations.

These traits take a variety of forms.    In terms of observable behavior, the individual may be self-deprecating.    He may act as though he hopes no one will notice him and appear awkward in physical gait and appearance.    He may complain and seek to give the impression that he is suffering.    The masochistic character often avoids success and has a low tolerance for praise.    He apparently seeks to avoid standing out in a group, he demonstrates little aggressive behavior.    Social Specialists appear to have masochistic features.    The desire to be expressive and nurturant to others is designed to elicit affection and caring in return.

In discussing masochism, Freud distinguished three types.[27]    The first, erotogenic masochism, is closely related to the perversion of experiencing pain at the hands of others for sexual gratification; it need not detain us in this discussion of character.    The second and third types, feminine and moral masochism, are more significant for our purposes.

Feminine masochism in the male is manifested in passivity, softness in features and expression, and a low level of aggressive activity.    Its development as an aspect of character results from attempts to resolve oedipal conflicts.    Instead of identifying with the father, the individual tends to identify with the mother, and to avoid castration anxiety he unconsciously incorporates the idea that he has already been castrated and therefore has lost his capacity of assertiveness.    Reluctance to exhibit ability and awkwardness and self-deprecation also reflect such attempts.

Moral masochism is based on a sense of guilt.    It is often reflected in a "do good" personality and identification with the underdog.    The crime to be expiated is oedipal in nature, and hypermorality is an attempt to obtain complete expiation.

In both feminine and moral masochism the instinctual energy connected with aggression, instead of being directed toward the outer

[25] Sigmund Freud, "The Economic Problems in Masochism." Wilhelm Reich, *Character Analysis*, pp. 205–247.

[26] Sigmund Freud, *Three Contributions to the Theory of Sex*, p. 158.

[27] Sigmund Freud, "The Economic Problems in Masochism."

world through work or sadism, is turned back on the self. Masochism is related to aggressive drives as narcissism is related to sexual drives. The instincts can be directed either toward objects or toward the self. When aggression is turned inward, masochistic character traits appear. Such aggression may have previously been directed toward the oedipal rival but is turned inward because of fear of retaliation. It results in the appearance of a need to suffer and to avoid achievement, success, and praise.

Masochistic character traits are related to the oedipus complex in still another way; the wish to suffer is connected with a regression to anality and acts as a reversal. Instead of expressing aggression toward the rival (father), aggression *from* the rival is sought. The individual psychologically assumes a passive, feminine position and seeks aggression at the hands of a masculine-assertive figure. In this way, the living out of the castration theme is maintained.

The phallic character is quite opposite in observable traits but related in origin to the masochistic character. The best description of phallic character traits is provided by Wilhelm Reich; we shall rely on his work to a considerable extent. Phallic character refers to traits of aggressiveness, assertiveness, sadistic behavior, and hypermasculinity. Both men and women exhibit these traits, but women tend toward especially strong exhibitionistic features. We shall, for the most part, confine our discussion to men.

Narcissistic traits are combined with assertiveness in the phallic character. The individual is exceptionally independent and acts as though he needs no one. Reich calls this character type phallic-narcissistic since both sets of traits are frequently manifest. Reich states that

the typical phallic-narcissistic character is self-confident, often arrogant, elastic, vigorous and often impressive. The more neurotic the inner mechanism, the more obtrusive are these modes of behavior. As to bodily type, they belong most frequently to Kretschmer's athletic type. The facial expression usually shows hard, sharp, masculine features but often also feminine, girl-like features in spite of athletic habits. Everyday behavior is never crawling as in passive-feminine characters, but usually haughty, either cold and reserved or derisively aggressive. . . . In the behavior toward the object, the love object included, the narcissistic element always dominates over the object-libidinal, and there is always an admixture of more or less disguised sadistic traits.

Such individuals usually anticipate any expected attack with attack on their part. Their aggression is very often expressed not so much in what they say or do as in the manner in which they say or do things. Particularly to people who do not have their own aggression at their disposal they appear as aggressive and provocative.   The outspoken types tend to achieve leading positions in life and resent subordination unless they can— as in the army or other hierarchic organizations—compensate for the necessity of subordination by executing domination over others who find themselves on lower rungs of the ladder.   If their vanity is hurt, they react . . . with cold reserve, deep depression or lively aggression.   In contrast to other characters, their narcissism expresses itself not in an infantile manner but in the exaggerated display of self confidence, dignity and superiority in spite of the fact that the basis of their character is no less infantile than that of others.[28]

Phallic character traits represent features of the oedipus conflict, as do masochistic character traits.   But where the masochistic character acts as though castrated and adopts a passive-feminine attitude, the phallic character behaves just the opposite, to counteract the castration fears.   Frequently in interpersonal relationships the phallic character assumes the role of castrator through assertiveness and aggression toward those who appear weak.   In fantasy, the object being castrated is the father.   Reich points out that it is not uncommon to find among these character types a weak or absent father and an aggressive mother.   When the individual takes over the aggression from the mother, he is faced with a conflict between imitating her and rejecting her.   Phallic assertive behavior appears as the resolution of this conflict.

The comparison of masochistic and phallic-sadistic characters reveals an important feature of character development.   Both character constellations are based upon oedipal conflicts experienced during the phallic stage of development.   Thus, opposing outward forms of behavior appear from somewhat similar roots.   This points out the dangers of oversimplifying character forms through strict correlations with stages in instinctual life.

Additional genetic factors exist in the development of character.   The ego and its development are significant in this respect, as implied in the previous discussion.   We shall now consider ego development and the formation of character traits which manifest themselves in modes of interpersonal behavior.

## THE DEVELOPMENT OF THE EGO AND ITS RELATION TO CHARACTER FORMATION

We can achieve an important but partial understanding of character development by examining the instinctual processes in the successive

[28] Wilhelm Reich, *Character Analysis*, p. 201.

stages of the life cycle. The development of the internal structure of the mind both determines and is a result of instinctual vicissitudes and their manifestation in character traits. In this section we shall review the theory of the psychic structure with particular emphasis on how the ego develops and its relation to character.

Among Freud's many contributions, his discussion of psychic structure in *The Ego and Id* and *Group Psychology and the Analysis of the Ego* are outstanding landmarks. These books are classics not only because of what they explain but also because of the new questions they pose.

Before *The Ego and the Id* was published, psychoanalytic theory equated all that was instinctual with the unconscious and all that related to the ego with conscious mental processes. From this assumption, it is difficult to understand how character traits function as aspects of the ego. The individual may not be aware of the particular constellation of traits inherent in his personality, much less their dynamic meaning. Traits are part of the unconscious mechanisms of the mind, but reasonably astute observers can describe the behavior of *other* individuals.

The first step necessary for further understanding is to establish that some of the ego processes, as well as all instinctual processes, belong in the realm of the unconscious. This was the aspect of personality structure that Freud established in *The Ego and the Id*.

Freud called the primitive, instinctual part of the mind, the basic source of energy that activates the personality, the *id*. The id is dominated by the pleasure principle; it seeks immediate discharge of psychic energy in the form of wish fulfillment. But common sense observation shows that, in the normal adult, behavior appears to be governed by rational processes of thinking, planning, and acting in accordance with notions of environmental conditions. This side of man's behavior is the work of the *ego*.

The ego is the executive apparatus of the mind. One of its functions is to stand between the id and the outer world. The healthy ego ultimately serves the pleasure principle or provides for instinctual gratification. But it functions in such a way as to avoid harm to the organism, on the one hand, and to the environment on the other. The healthy ego assumes control of the psychic energy, limits it, and uses it for constructive work and rewarding human relationships. Id gratifications are thus assured, along with constructive outcomes for society. The healthy ego attempts to formulate and carry out behavior that simultaneously fulfills a variety of needs with the minimum expenditure of energy. Robert Waelder has described this ego process as the principle of multiple function.[29]

There is much that is not understood about the development of the ego and its many functions. Psychoanalytic theory tends to postulate the idea that the organism exists in a totally undifferentiated state at birth; in other words, no ego exists. Later in development, an ego emerges and assumes the directing or executive functions of the mind. This, however, does not recognize innate or constitutional factors in ego development.[30] The ego, whatever its roots, maintains contact with both the id and the outer world. It mediates between the demands of these two influences which operate according to the opposing principles of pleasure, or instantaneous discharge of tensions, and reality, or the delay of immediate gratification for longer range and more durable gratification.

One significant aspect of ego development is the differentiation that takes place within the ego during the course of development. We have discussed the resolution of the oedipus complex through identification with the parent of the same sex. Such identification forms conscience and imperatives that prohibit certain wishes. Freud gave the name *superego* to this agency of the mind. The superego's prohibitive functions—"Thou shalt not"—are largely unconscious. It controls aggressive energy that has been turned inward and can act punitively to create a sense of guilt. In fact, the superego plays an important part in the compulsive character structure. The internalized prohibitions of the superego censure the wishes of the id and maintain the reaction formations of the ego. If the individual wishes to express aggression and hate toward rivals or substitute objects, the superego stands ready to punish and to influence the ego to convert the wish into its opposite: instead of hate, the individual may show tenderness. The ego may be impoverished by an overly harsh superego: so much energy may be bound up in dealing with prohibitions that the individual's character and personality become constricted. Thus he exhibits little expressivity and spontaneity because the actions are too closely related to prohibited instinctual wishes.

The effects of the superego on character become clearer when we contrast the compulsive character and the overly harsh superego with the impulsive character and the absence of superego controls.[31] The

---

[29] Robert Waelder, "The Principle of Multiple Function," *The Psychoanalytic Quarterly*, Vol. 5, 1936.

[30] Heinz Hartmann, *Ego Psychology and the Problem of Adaptation*, pp. 49–50.

[31] J. J. Michaels, "Character Structure and Character Disorders," *American Handbook of Psychiatry*, Vol. I, pp. 362–367.

individual who follows his impulses, or "acts out," generally has a malformed superego and feels few pangs of conscience about his behavior. In the extreme, the criminal falls into this class of character structure.

When the superego has been formed as a result of oedipal conflict, differentiated agencies that become more fully developed in succeeding stages of the life cycle exist in the mind. During latency, for example, the ego develops through experiences in formal education, and the superego develops through experiences with authority figures other than parents. Religion plays an important part in this development. Latency children exhibit interest in religion, ethics, and morality, that stems in part from the workings of the superego and the remnants of the earlier oedipal struggles.

We have indicated that the ego as the executive apparatus of the mind mediates between the id and the outer world. The concept of the superego provides additional considerations. The ego mediates among the id, the superego, and the outer world according to the principles of multiple functioning. The id is the source of the instinctual demands that may conflict with the restrictions of conscience and the outer world. The ego mediates and formulates behavior designed to secure id gratifications in forms appropriate to the imperatives of the superego and the realities of the environment.

The modes by which the ego functions become distinguishing features of personality that may be observed in their everyday interpersonal relations. These modes reflect basic abilities, interests, skills, thought processes, and inner conflicts. The development of the ego and its function reflect past experience in object relationships. Distinguishing features of an individual's ego result from relationships with early parental figures as well as later objects important in the individual's life. Relationships with parents are decisive in ego formation because they occur when the ego is weak and developing. Parental influences are maintained through the mechanism of *identification*.[32]

The mechanism of identification is the internalization of an object representation within the individual's ego. This process is largely unconscious, even though it is analogous to conscious imitation of an admired person (object).

As we have indicated, libidinal as well as aggressive drives can be displaced. The energy change, or cathexis, can be directed toward an object which is need satisfying; it can also be redirected toward the ego or shifted from an object cathexis to a cathexis of the ego. When the latter occurs, there is a shift toward narcissism. Identifica-

[32] Sigmund Freud, *Group Psychology and the Analysis of the Ego*, pp. 105–110.

tion as a psychological phenomenon occurs when the individual incorporates the representation of an object into his ego and directs emotional energy toward the ego. It arises out of the need for the object, but occurs in response to the object's actual or fantasied loss.

The work of identification is seen clearly in the process of mourning when an actual object loss has occurred. This similarity to the process of identification that occurs during the infancy stages of development is worth considering.[33]

At the death of a loved one, the bereaved faces significant psychological work before he can establish attachments to new objects. It is as though the individual has to settle accounts with the lost object before establishing new relationships. The psychological work proceeds in the following way: libidinal attachments to the lost object are broken upon death. The energy cannot remain free floating, so it must either attach itself to new objects or be incorporated into the individual's ego. The energy is withdrawn from the outer world and attached to the ego by the process of identifying with the lost object; the representation of the loved one is incorporated in the individual's ego, and interest in the outer world, relatively speaking, is withdrawn. The work of mourning then proceeds. This includes dealing with the ambivalences significant to most relationships with loved ones. The bereaved feels as though he has been abandoned; the hate or aggression generated by this feeling becomes focal for the hate that had already existed in the relationship. The aggression, however, cannot be readily directed outward; so it is turned inward and results in a form of depression that resembles melancholia. The representation of the object in the ego becomes the target for the reproaches meant for the lost object. Depression is amplified by the superego which directs aggression toward the ego as a form of punishment for its hostility toward the lost object. This process is evidenced in a sense of guilt during mourning. For example, the individual may feel he did not do enough for the loved one, or he was not loyal enough, or he was unworthy. This constitutes the process of grieving, or mourning the loss of a loved object. Eventually, a sense of reality and striving for gratifications in the real world takes over from the use of autistic devices. Reality is supported by the dissolution of the ambivalences that occur during mourning. New object ties then become possible.

The experience of object loss and the identifications that occur are inherent in development; they do not arise for the first time when a loved one dies during the individual's adult years. Early forms of

[33] Sigmund Freud, "Mourning and Melancholia."

coping with object loss become models for mourning behavior. They contribute lasting attributes of the ego and character structure, with identification as the important mechanism.

Object loss, or fear of loss, is a developmental process in each of the three stages of infancy. The first experience is in the oral stage, with loss of the breast during weaning. The ego is weak, and the primitive mechanism of introjection copes with the loss. Introjection binds aggression since it represents destruction of the frustrating object; but it also binds libidinal energy, since the object is retained within the self. In the anal-sadistic stage the child fears loss of love and its relation to loss of valuable body material. Again, the solution rests in identification: the child incorporates the attitudes of the loved object and conforms. This results in alteration of the ego and the first use of the mechanism of reaction formation; interest in feces is reversed to the feelings of disgust and shame needed to accomplish toilet training.

In the third stage, marked by the oedipal conflicts, the intense sexual longings toward the parent of the opposite sex must be relinquished. This loss is also made possible through identification and is accompanied by alteration of the ego and the character structure of the individual. The male child identifies with both parents; but for masculine development to become dominant, the strongest identification has to be with the father. The child must decide: "If I cannot take his place with mother, I will be like him." This formula is an essential step in the development of masculine attributes in personality and the ultimate capacity to take the masculine role in social and sexual relationships.

Freud pointed out, however, that during the oedipal stage of development the constitutional conditions of bisexuality were strengthened.[34] Individuals of both sexes have differing innate tendencies toward masculinity and femininity. These tendencies are amplified through the work of identification as a resolution of the oedipus complex.

The oedipus complex is experienced in two forms: negative and positive. In the negative form, the child identifies with the cathected object—the mother in the case of the male child—and the fantasy of taking her place with father as the loved object is established. If this negative resolution is dominant in the male child he will develop marked feminine character traits, depending, of course, on the mother's personality attributes. The presence of passive-maso-

[34] Sigmund Freud, *The Ego and the Id*, pp. 31–34.

chistic character traits is a result, in part, of the dominant place of the negative oedipal resolution in the male.

In the positive oedipus complex the loved object is the mother, for the male; the rival is the father. Instead of destroying the father in fantasy, the child identifies with him and he is incorporated within the ego. Thus, the male develops strong masculine character traits, depending on the attributes of the father.

The child experiences both negative and positive oedipal conflicts, resulting in identifications with both parents. A suitable combination of feminine and masculine identifications produces a rich, flexible adult personality and spontaneity in behavior. Such spontaneity and flexibility show up most clearly in the capacity of the individual to perform a wide variety of roles in interpersonal situations. The individual who can be not only assertive and aggressive but also expressive and caring has usually succeeded in incorporating both masculine and feminine character traits. The ego can perform in a conflict-free range of responses to the personal enrichment of himself and others. Less-well-integrated feminine and masculine identifications lead to anxiety, inhibited and rigid performance, and excessive use of energy for defense.

The concept of *defense* leads us to another area of character formation and modes of interpersonal behavior which we shall discuss in the next section of this chapter. As we shall see, defense is a function of the ego as a mediator in the psychic structure and as a mechanism for coping with the manifestations of instinctual drives.


## CHARACTER STRUCTURE AND THE DEFENSIVE
## FUNCTIONS OF THE EGO

We have examined the ego from two points of view: first, we described its function in the structure of the mind; and second, we described the course of its development, especially through the infantile stages of the life cycle. As we have indicated, the ego as the executive apparatus mediates among the id, the superego, and the external environment. Many of its mediating functions are conscious and utilize perception, thinking, and action to secure need gratifications and to manipulate the environment. But there is also an unconscious function of the ego that bears a significant relation to character and the modalities of interpersonal behavior observable in day-to-day interaction.

The unconscious work of the ego is largely *defensive;* that is, the ego tries to protect the organism against danger by destroying the danger or removing the organism. But apparent dangers to the organism come from *within* as well as from without. The ego mobilizes the unconscious process of defense to combat internal dangers.

In one of his later works, *The Problem of Anxiety,*[35] Freud specified the nature of danger arising from within the organism which comes from heightened instinctual tension. The helpless infant cannot discharge this tension without the aid of an external object. For instance, if the mother is not present when needs arise the infant will experience feelings of danger—that is, tensions resulting from the instinctual drives. The most primitive mechanism available for coping with this tension in the absence of the source of gratification (the mother) is the hallucination or the visual image of the object. A second primitive mechanism is taking oneself as the object of auto-erotic acts which include practices such as thumbsucking, biting one's fingernails, and masturbation. Hallucination of the object and auto-erotic acts are temporary—and in the end unsatisfactory—methods of discharge of instinctual tensions. Motor activity such as crying normally produces the object and results in need gratification. In the more mature person, the ego develops modes of action that result in need gratification that are appropriate to the environment.

The experience of object loss, or the fear of object loss, and the danger of unsatisfied needs determine how the organism will deal with internal danger in later experience. The ego learns to cope with internal danger through its experience with and reaction to *anxiety.* Anxiety is an unpleasant feeling experienced by the ego, a vague sense of unease, accompanied frequently by acceleration of the heart beat, perspiration, and shortness of breadth. There are, in other words, both psychic and physical manifestations of anxiety.

Anxiety alerts the ego to coming danger. As fear is experienced in response to danger in the environment, anxiety is a response to internal danger. Anxiety appears in forms specific to the stages of development. In the oral stage, it comes from fear of loss of the needed object and the pain of undischarged tension arising from the instinctual drives. In the anal stage, it arises from fear of loss of the object's love and loss of body products that are perceived as valuable. In the phallic stage, it is experienced in response to the instincts of negative and positive oedipal wishes and the resultant castration fears. During latency, when the superego is formed and

[35] Sigmund Freud, *The Problem of Anxiety.*

consolidated, anxiety is experienced as, in Freud's term, the "dread of conscience," or "social anxiety."[36]

Although the determinants of anxiety can be related to particular stages of development, they are also cumulative. Castration anxiety is made more real by the memory of loss of feces (separation from valued body parts) and the loss of the breast (separation from what was originally an undifferentiated part of the organism). Perhaps even more typical of anxiety as a response to real or threatened loss is birth and the trauma of physical separation from the mother.

In the adult, the affect of anxiety is not too different from that of earlier stages; but the ideation connected with it is either unconscious or disguised. Conscious preoccupation with or fear of death is a derivation of earlier dread of loss and separation; phobic reactions, such as fear of animals, are also derivatives.[37] In less extreme form, anxiety can develop from the idea of being excluded from a group or organization, that is, being an outcast. In the adult, all earlier experience of anxiety situations reverberate in the here-and-now of internal dangers.

In its attempts at synthesis, integration, and adaptation, the ego establishes various mechanisms for dealing with the instinctual danger from which anxiety emanates. These ego responses are called mechanisms of defense and form an important aspect of character. For our discussion of the mechanisms of defense we shall rely largely on the material presented by Anna Freud in *The Ego and the Mechanisms of Defense*[38] and on Freud's *The Problem of Anxiety*.

In *The Ego and the Mechanisms of Defense*, Anna Freud distinguishes among three types of anxiety that elicit defensive responses by the ego.[39] The first is *superego anxiety*: painful affects are experienced, stemming from the aggression directed by the superego toward the ego as a result of a forbidden instinctual wish. These pangs of conscience arise in response to a wish or fantasy, not in response to a deed. The existence of well-internalized parental representations is a legacy of the oedipus complex and provides the inner power to punish in anticipation of an act.

The second type of anxiety is called *objective anxiety;* it represents the painful affects associated with fear of punishment from the outside world, usually at the hands of parents. It occurs before the

---

[36] *Ibid.*, p. 128.

[37] Sigmund Freud, "Analysis of a Phobia in a Five-Year-Old Boy."

[38] Anna Freud, *The Ego and the Mechanisms of Defense*. Sigmund Freud, *The Problem of Anxiety*.

[39] Anna Freud, *The Ego and the Mechanisms of Defense*, pp. 58–70.

formation of the superego. The child's castration anxiety represents his response to the fear that father or mother will take away his valued penis. The experiencing of objective anxiety results in the use of ego defenses to reduce the pain and to ward off the danger.

The third type, *instinctual or id anxiety*, results from the excessive bombardment of the ego by instinctual impulses and the resulting painful affects and fear that the ego will be obliterated. To quote Anna Freud:

The effect of the anxiety experienced by the ego because of the strength of the instincts is the same as that produced by the superego anxiety or the objective anxiety which so far we have been studying. Defense mechanisms are brought into operation against the instincts, with all the familiar results in the formation of neuroses and neurotic characteristics.[40]

The various mechanisms of defense adopted by the ego include: projection, reaction formation, repression, regression, denial, isolation and undoing, turning toward the self, identification, and restriction of the ego.[41]

### 1. PROJECTION

Projection is avoiding an unacceptable wish within oneself by attributing it to an object. It is observed frequently in interpersonal settings when, for example, an individual says that another person is lazy, that he wants to get a job done quickly and to go off and relax. The individual himself probably wants to be done with the job and consequently experiences superego anxiety. In response to this unpleasant feeling, he attributes the wish to another person. The superego is, in effect, doing the talking; this may be reflected in tone of voice, body posture, and an inappropriate intensity of hostility directed toward the other person.

Projection is a primitive defense mechanism associated with the oral stage of development; the individual tends to incorporate or introject that which is pleasurable and to externalize or project that which is painful. If it becomes a notable feature of the individual's character, projection is then a trait of paranoid thought structure in which the external world is viewed as hostile and with suspicion.

### 2. REACTION FORMATION

Reaction formation consists of turning a feeling or wish into its opposite. If an individual feels extremely hostile toward another person, this hostility may reflect early feelings toward an object that resulted in either punishment from parents or a sense of shame.

[40] *Ibid.*, p. 64.
[41] Otto Fenichel, *The Psychoanalytic Theory of Neurosis,* pp. 141–167.

The feeling of hate may remain quite unconscious simply because it is unacceptable to the superego and therefore to the ego. To deal with the anxiety, the individual expresses opposite feelings—caring, concern, solicitude, and warmth. Reaction formation, as we have seen, is experienced during toilet training when interest in and pleasure with the feces are converted into loathing and disgust.

### 3. REGRESSION

Otto Fenichel describes regression very succinctly as follows:

Whenever a person meets a frustration, there is a tendency for him to long for earlier periods in his life when his experiences were more pleasant, and for earlier types of satisfaction that were more complete. The intensity of this tendency increases with two factors which are closely interrelated: the degree of hesitancy with which the individual accepts newer modes of satisfaction and the degree to which he is fixated to earlier types.[42]

The compulsive character develops the behavior traits of orderliness and parsimony as a result of regression from the phallic stage to the anal stage of development. The anal traits become deeply imbedded in his personality in an attempt to avoid the oedipal wishes and the attendent conflicts.

### 4. REPRESSION

Repression is one of the most basic and pervasive of the defense mechanisms. It usually operates in conjunction with other mechanisms of defense. It is the utilization of energy to bury an idea or feeling that is unacceptable to the ego and superego in the unconscious. Forgetting is the simplest example of repression and is evident in momentary lapses of memory as well as in childhood amnesias.[43]

Repression occurs first during the oedipal period. It accompanies the formation of hysterical or erotic character traits. When the instincts involved are not "safely" repressed, they may reappear in the form of hysterical symptoms such as loss of function of body parts. The instinct reappears, but in disguised form so that the anxiety is contained.

### 5. DENIAL

Denial is a primitive mechanism that distorts reality to ward off anxiety. It is evidenced, for example, in the individual who refuses to acknowledge a serious illness or infirmity. The denial is not conscious, but it results in a perceptual distortion. Another example

[42] *Ibid.*, pp. 160–161.
[43] Sigmund Freud, *The Psychopathology of Everyday Life.*

of denial is the older employee or executive who is unable to incorporate or accept forthcoming retirement. The wish in back of
denial is that the distortion of reality will remove the painful sensations. Of course, this wish is counter to reality, and if it persists
or dominates an individual's thought process, it is evidence of serious
psychic disturbance.

### 6. ISOLATION AND UNDOING

Isolation and undoing tend to occur together as parts of the thinking
structure of the compulsive character. Isolation is related to repression but in a special way. The derivatives of an instinctual wish are
feelings and ideas. Isolation consists of splitting the connections
between the two and repressing one of them. The compulsive character represses the feelings and allows the ideas to exist as cold
thoughts with which the individual is relatively uninvolved.

Undoing consists of more or less magical acts to ward off unacceptable ideas that appear in consciousness. One observes in latency
children, for example, the performance of rituals such as avoiding
stepping on cracks in the sidewalk for fear that harm will come
to a loved one. The ritual wards off the aggressive wishes within
the individual.

### 7. TURNING TOWARD THE SELF

This mechanism of defense consists of directing an instinctual wish
toward the self instead of toward an object which may retaliate or
arouse superego anxiety. It is an important mechanism in the functioning of the masochistic personality. Aggression or hostility is
turned inward instead of being directed toward objects; it may lead
to feelings of worthlessness and to self-punitiveness.

### 8. IDENTIFICATION

Identification as a defense mechanism seldom operates by itself
but is usually combined with other ego defense mechanisms. Anna
Freud discusses this defense in relation to a pattern called *identification
with the aggressor*.[44] This consists of warding off expected punishment from without by incorporating the attitudes and behavior of the
aggressor or would-be aggressor. The individual then projects the
wish onto an object and proceeds to act out the punishment as the
aggressor. He converts to activity the punishment that was once
passively endured.

This mechanism is extremely important in the personality make-up
of the so-called authoritarian personality.[45] Having passively endured

[44] Anna Freud, *The Ego and the Mechanisms of Defense*, pp. 117–131.
[45] T. W. Adorno et al., *Authoritarian Personality*.

aggression from authority figures, the individual identifies with the aggressor, projects his impulses, and acts instead of remaining passive.

## 9. RESTRICTION OF THE EGO

When an individual gives up an activity or pursuit that he once found enjoyable and productive, he imposes a restriction on his ego as a defense against anxiety. An activity arouses anxiety and activates defense when it becomes the locus for displaced sexual or aggressive wishes. If painting is eroticized with the component instincts of the anal stage of development, the ego may give up the activity by withdrawal of cathexes to avoid anxiety connected with it. Such anxiety arises when the unconscious connects the activity with another activity that is unacceptable.

Another example of restriction of the ego is withdrawal from competitive activity because the activity has been cathected with aggressive wishes of the oedipal period. The individual withdraws and prevents himself from completing work. He may also prevent himself from receiving rewards to which he is entitled because he fears his superego will punish him.

Defense mechanisms of the ego are usually employed together and rarely appear in pure form. They seem to be connected with the stages of development and therefore constitute a hierarchy. The nature and workings of this hierarchy are complex and need not detain us here.

All healthy egos employ defense mechanisms. The use of such mechanisms does not necessarily indicate personality disturbance. It is often difficult to distinguish the healthy from the more neurotic personality. The crucial issue is the extent to which energy is bound up in defending the ego. If too much energy is used, the result may be a general impoverishment of personality and a low level of productivity. The presence or absence of defense mechanisms is less important that the utilization of an appropriate amount of energy.

We have thus far established that the defense mechanisms of the ego (1) function in the unconscious; (2) operate in an interrelated way rather than singly; and (3) are deeply imbedded responses of the total personality of the individual. We shall return to the discussion of the broader concept of character and its relation to defense and adaptation. Wilhelm Reich in his book *Character Analysis* defines character and its function as follows:

By character we mean here not only the external manifestation of this element, but also the sum total of the modes of reactions which are specific of this or that personality, that is, a factor which is essentially functionally determined and expresses itself in the characteristic ways of walking, facial expression, posture, manner of speaking, etc. This character of the ego consists of various elements of the outer world, of prohibitions, instinct inhibitions and identifications of different kinds. The contents of the character *armor* [authors' italics], then, are of an external, social origin. Before entering upon the question as to what holds these contents together, what is the dynamic process which consolidates the armor, we must realize that while protection against the outer world was the main reason for the formation of the character, this does not constitute its chief function later on. Against the actual dangers of the outer world, civilized man has a wealth of means at his disposal, the social institutions in all their forms. Being a highly developed organism, he has at his disposal a muscular apparatus to flee or to fight with, and an intellect to enable him to forsee and avoid dangers. The protection mechanisms of the character typically come into action when a danger from the inside, from an instinctual impulse, is threatening.[46]

Reich used the concept "armor" to designate the defensive functions of character structure. It is the learned responses of the individual to instinctual conflict and anxiety, the ways in which the ego has become modified in the process of defense.

Character, as it appears in interpersonal relations, represents the total organization of the personality. In addition, it represents efforts to act and react in relation to the world of other persons in such a way as to secure, simultaneously, need gratifications and enhancement of the environment. The personality the individual presents to others in his interpersonal relations is determined by his developmental history: alterations in instinctual processes, internal experience with conflict, and patterns of energy utilization and defense.

The understanding of character within interpersonal settings is no easy matter; caution should be exercised, therefore, in attempting to describe and diagnose personality. On the other hand, depth of understanding of character, its manifestations in interpersonal relations, and its determinants provide a basis for intelligent observation and behavior in interpersonal settings.

## SUMMARY

This chapter has further explained, within a psychoanalytic framework, the modes of interpersonal behavior discussed and described in Chapter Six. We have discussed the major working assumptions of psychoanalytic theory and placed the modes of interpersonal behavior

[46] Wilhelm Reich, *Character Analysis*, p. 160.

within the general framework of ego psychology—more specifically, within the theory of character formation—in terms of instinctual processes, inner conflict and development, ego development, and the defensive functions of the ego.

A number of classic character types, such as hysterical, phallic-narcissistic, compulsive, and masochistic, have been discussed. Each type has many features readily observable in interpersonal relations. We have attempted not only to describe these character types, but also to show their roots in individual development, with emphasis on instinctual and ego processes.

The theory developed in this chapter not only relates to the explanation of role performances and modes of interpersonal behavior presented in Chapter Six, but it also serves as a valuable foundation for the problems that will be presented in Chapter Eight. In that chapter we shall return to the direct consideration of interpersonal processes, emphasizing the dynamics of interpersonal behavior when a situation involves two or more persons.

*Chapter Eight*

# Interpersonal Dynamics

I N *Group Psychology and the Analysis of the Ego,* Freud presented a basic working hypothesis on the source of group cohesion. This hypothesis will serve as a valuable point of departure for the discussion of interpersonal dynamics. It states that the cohesion found in interpersonal settings, that is, in groups of two or more persons, is based on the existence of a common object of identification—usually the leader. Group members incorporate within their ego a common ideal which is cathected or invested with libido. This attachment to the leader becomes the common characteristic of group members and serves to bind individuals to one another.

The working hypothesis suggests several leads for studying interpersonal dynamics. First, underlying interpersonal relations in groups are certain dynamic qualities that represent the unique responses of individuals to authority figures, as well as shared responses, based on the commonality of life tasks in personal histories. Thus in later interpersonal settings, their responses are recognizable to other individuals. But individual histories differ so that differences in responses may be expected. The simultaneous existence of shared and unique response provide the drama and richness in interpersonal relations.

The second lead suggested by the working hypothesis is that the individual's perspective in interpersonal dynamics, given the importance of authority relations, should shift depending on his view of the problem. For example, the authority figure's view of the interpersonal relations is different from that of a subordinate. Yet in any interpersonal setting, it is frequently difficult to distinquish between individuals who hold authority positions and those in subordinate positions. It would seem fruitful, therefore, to analyze *authority* and *subordinacy* as dynamic processes in interpersonal relations affecting every person in the interaction. To these we should add a third process suggested in *Group Psychology and the Analysis of the Ego*. The relations to authority establish the condition for member-to-member relationships and introduce *equality* as an aspect of interpersonal dynamics.

A third lead available to us from Freud's hypothesis is to examine historical prototypes of individual responses in interpersonal settings. Such responses result from individual histories, yet they are based in the culture, as evidenced by religion, myths, games, literature, and other expressive representations of the human condition. For example, the child's game of "follow the leader" presents in repetitive form the position of leader as both superior and bizarre. As a result, the position of follower is both inferior and bizarre—the follower can be neither better nor less ludicrous than the leader. The game therefore mocks the nature of human dependencies that begin in earliest infancy and that in reality never end.

Before we pursue these leads, let us identify somewhat more clearly the types of issues related to interpersonal dynamics. To assist in this connection we shall present a brief case study and examine the relevance of the themes discussed above.

## A CASE STUDY OF INTERPERSONAL BEHAVIOR IN THE SUPERIOR AND SUBORDINATE RELATIONSHIP

This case is an interchange between the director of a research laboratory and one of his subordinates. The director, whom we shall call Dr. Blackman, was a man in his late forties, with considerable stature as a researcher and research administrator. Many ambitious and able young researchers wanted to work in his laboratory. Dr. Dodds, his subordinate, was a promising young researcher who had recently been assigned to the laboratory as a staff scientist. He requested a meeting with Dr. Blackman at which the following interchange took place. (Dr. Dodds entered the office and showed his superior, Dr. Blackman, a letter. This letter was from Professor Wilkin of another research institution, offering Dr. Dodds a position; Dr. Blackman read the letter over.)

DODDS: What do you think of that?
BLACKMAN: I knew it was coming. He asked me if it would be all right if he sent it. I told him to go ahead, if he wanted to.
DODDS: I didn't expect it, particularly after what you said to me the last time. (*Pause.*) I'm really quite happy here. I don't want you to get the idea that I am thinking of leaving. But I thought I should go and

visit—I think he expects it—and I wanted to let you know that just because I was thinking of going down, that didn't mean I was thinking of leaving here, unless of course, he offers me something extraordinary.

BLACKMAN: Why are you telling me all this?

DODDS: Because I didn't want you hearing from somebody else that I was thinking of leaving here because I was going for a visit to another institution. I really have no intention of leaving here you know, unless he offers me something really extraordinary that I can't afford to turn down. I think I'll tell him that, that I am willing to look at his laboratory, but unless there is something unusual there for me, I have no intention of leaving here.

BLACKMAN: It's up to you.

DODDS: What do you think?

BLACKMAN: Well, what? About what? You've got to make up your mind.

DODDS: I don't consider too seriously this job. He is not offering anything really extraordinary. But I am interested in what he had to say, and I would like to look around his lab.

BLACKMAN: Sooner or later you are going to have to make up your mind where you want to work.

DODDS: [*Sharply.*] That depends on the offers, doesn't it?

BLACKMAN: No, not really; a good man always gets offers. You got a good offer and you move, and as soon as you have moved, you get other good offers. It would throw you into confusion to consider all the good offers you will receive. Isn't there a factor of how stable you want to be?

DODDS: But I'm not shopping around. I already told you that. He sent me this letter; I didn't ask him to. All I said was I think I should visit him, and to you that's shopping around!

BLACKMAN: Well, you may choose to set aside your commitment here if he offers you something better. All I am saying is that you will still be left with the question of you've got to stay some place, and where is that going to be?

DODDS: You really don't think that I could find a better job than the one you have offered me here?

BLACKMAN: I don't know. I'm not thinking about that.

DODDS: How would it look if I were to leave?

BLACKMAN: To me, if you wanted to go, I'd say fine, if that's what you want. But frankly I think there would be a few raised eyebrows if you were to leave now.

DODDS: But I'm not shopping around. I want you to understand that.

BLACKMAN: You've got the problem of all young men who are sought after. You've got to decide what you will accept and what you won't accept.

DODDS: Look, I came in here, and I want to be honest with you, but you go and make me feel all guilty, and I don't like that.

BLACKMAN: You are being honest as can be.

DODDS: I didn't come in here to fight. I don't want to disturb you.

BLACKMAN: I'm not disturbed. If you think it is best for you to go somewhere else, that's okay with me. We can get another plasma physicist any day, just as good as you. They are standing in line to get in here. What bothers me is how restless you want to appear to me and Wilkin. For one thing, you've got everything analyzed out in terms of what you want: tenure, appointment, and space. Things like that.

DODDS: That's obvious. I can't understand you. You really think that no one will ever be able to make me an offer that will make me want to leave this place.

BLACKMAN: All I am saying is that it looks funny. You asked me how it would look, and I'm telling you it would look funny so soon after you getting fixed up here.

DODDS: Well, I was just trying to be honest, and. . . .

BLACKMAN: [*Interrupting.*] All the jobs you get offered at this stage in your career are the same. They are all the same. One may give you a little more salary, but it will have a lousy lab. Another may offer you tenure and a higher title, but you would be dead in ten years if you went there. What you should be looking for is an opportunity to do work and to develop in an environment. Your colleagues, the really important ones, don't give a damn whether you are a Junior or Associate research worker. Don't get me wrong. I don't want to hold you back. If you feel it's best for you to go, I wouldn't want to hold you here under any circumstances. I just want to give you some advice.

DODDS: But I don't see what this has to do with me. All I said was I would consider his offer if it was so good I couldn't afford to turn it down. Do you think I should turn it down even if it is a better job?

BLACKMAN: All I'm saying is maybe it's too fast.

DODDS: What of it? Are you telling me that a young person coming up shouldn't take the best job offered to him?

BLACKMAN: What should they take?

DODDS: Young people should take the best jobs they can get, and go where they want.

BLACKMAN: Yes, but not too fast.

DODDS: How fast?

BLACKMAN: I don't know. Enough time to settle in and do a job of work.

DODDS: One, two, three years?

BLACKMAN: It depends.

DODDS: When should I be thinking of leaving this laboratory, then? When do you think would be the best time for me to go?

BLACKMAN: I can't answer that. It's up to you to decide.

DODDS: If I were to leave this year what would it look like?

BLACKMAN: I think it would look like Dodds had a lot of opportunism and self-interest. You know what I mean? Like he was restless. It would not look good.

DODDS: I don't understand you. I came in here to be honest with you, and you make me feel guilty. All I wanted was to show you this letter, and let you know what I was going to do. What should I have told you?

BLACKMAN: That you had read the letter, and felt that under the circumstances it was necessary for you to pay a visit to Wilkin, but that you were happy here, and wanted to stay at least until you had got a job of work done.

DODDS: I can't get over it. You think there isn't a place in the world I'd rather be than here in this lab. . . .

In our haste to delineate important features of interpersonal dynamics illustrated in this interchange we should not miss the innocent and poignant qualities of the talk between Dr. Dodds and Dr. Blackman. Each man was speaking for himself—a person with a unique history. Yet each was speaking universally. Dr. Dodds inadvertently represented every bright, young, and ambitious person who tastes daily both the sweet excitement of work and bitter anxiety for the future. The anxiety portrayed in the interview overcame the sense of aliveness available from the pleasures of work. Dr. Dodds presented, therefore, all his insecurities and doubts about himself as a professional worker and as a subordinate.

We could infer that Dr. Dodds was stimulating his environment to provide feedback important to his growing self-esteem. His innocent denial of any intent to seek reassurance, love, or status was contradicted by the assertion that he could leave the laboratory anytime he chose to, and that he was free of the enmeshing obligations intrinsic to work in organizations.

Dr. Dodds appeared to be acting out a denial of dependency and obligation while asserting a degree of independence and noncommitment not really his own. This denial probably echoed his past experience. How was the young researcher recreating a conflict externally and in reality that had long persisted internally and in fantasy? We are unable to answer this question from the case alone, but it remains a valid one. We can see that Dr. Dodds *evoked* the conflicts in such a way as to express simultaneously his strivings for independence and his uncertain sense of self-esteem.

The speculation on the continuity between a single event and a personal history raises for exploration two concepts important for understanding interpersonal dynamics. The first is the concept of *transference reactions;* the second is the *tendency to repeat.* Both processes enable the individual to connect the relationship between past and present in interpersonal relations.

Another affective quality apparent in the interview, one raised explicitly by Dr. Dodds, is the sense of guilt. "Look, I came in here, and I want to be honest with you, but you go and make me feel all guilty and I don't like that." Assuming that Dr. Dodds accurately represented the feeling as guilt, he did not indicate guilt over what. It is difficult to pursue this question without first establishing where the guilt resided and its origin. Dr. Dodds established the guilt as residing within himself, but he projected its genesis to something that his superior had done. He did not consider that it might have been generated from within himself and that *perhaps* it had existed before the conversation.

In Chapter Seven we discussed the mechanisms of defense. We said that projection, or the tendency to externalize feelings, ideas, and wishes, was one of the ego's methods of coping with anxiety. It is possible that the activation of the environment to produce guilt within one's self and the occasion for projection is a manifestation of an unconscious sense of guilt and attendant anxiety. But this is an interesting speculation not supported by the data at hand.

Other indications of defense appear in the form of denial. Dr. Dodds replied to the suggestion that he was receiving advice, "But I don't see what this has to do with me." The sequence of interaction following this statement connotes a shift into logicizing or intellectualizing the issue. Dr. Dodds assumed the position of questioner to assert the force of the rational issue of "Are you telling me that a young person coming up shouldn't take the best job offered to him?" It is with this interchange that we can conveniently shift our attention to the person in the superordinate position, Dr. Blackman.

The logical conundrum posed by Dr. Dodd's question "How fast?" an individual should move to a new job and a new setting illuminates some of the dilemmas facing the older person in a position of authority. The authority figure can respond to his own anger and mounting aggression when he feels himself being used or tested. Such anger and aggression are evident early in the interaction when Dr. Blackman, in response to the innocent question, "What do you think?," replied sharply, "Well, what? About what? You've got to make up your mind." Or, his response can establish the locus of responsibility in the subordinate by a comment such as: "It's up to you." He can respond as a kindly father would and offer advice: "You've got the problem of all young men who are sought after; you've got to decide what you will accept and what you won't accept." Or, he can speak with the organizational and professional responsibilities as his referent as illustrated by Dr. Blackman's comment, "I knew it (the letter) was coming. He asked me if it would be all right if he sent it. I told him to go ahead if he wanted to."

However, to maintain that the authority figure can choose a response does not do justice to the individual. The choice the superior has is in fact constrained by his own personal history, and more immediately by how much affect is aroused, by the nature of his own authority problems (transference reactions), and by the structure of his defenses. Yet the issue of choice is a real one, despite the constraints of history, since each of the response possibilities creates new consequences. The subordinate who cannot tolerate being "fathered" because his dependency doubts are too real to be acknowledged will react angrily to such attempts, no matter how well intended they are. Perhaps every possible response will be to no avail, at least temporarily, because of the latent historical implications of events. Stated more clearly, the subordinate may present such live intrapersonal issues, for instance, dependency and doubt, as to render the authority figure almost helpless. The possibility of helplessness in a superior-subordinate relationship has to be reckoned with and may in the end be the most singular of all the dilemmas of exercising authority. Issues and situations exist in which all that can be done is to avoid making matters worse. This experience is common in parent-child relationships during adolescence; remnants of such relationship appear in the interview. The balance between dependence and independence is precarious during adolescence and does not become secure until long afterward. It is related to the stabilization of identity discussed by Erikson[1] and White.[2] The interpersonal setting in organizations is one area in which this battle is fought.

During the interview helplessness was apparent when Dr. Blackman offered the most frank answer at his command in response to Dr. Dodds' question, "What should I have told you?". Dr. Blackman replied, "That you had read the letter, and felt that under the circumstances it was necessary for you to pay a visit to Wilkin, but that you were happy here, and wanted to stay at least until you had got a job of work done." This statement represents what Dr. Blackman *wished* to hear. In a real sense, he could say little beyond this suppressed wish. Dr. Dodds' next comment indicated that he had not heard Dr. Blackman: "I can't get over it. You think there isn't a place in the world I'd rather be than here in this lab. . . ."

[1] Erik Erikson, *Problem of Ego Identity*, p. 101.
[2] R. W. White, *Lives in Progress*, pp. 333–339.

The response toward the inductions of helplessness, "the point of no return" in interpersonal relations, is yet a matter of choice, subject to all the constraints alluded to above. Helplessness often produces rage; frequently a subordinate unconsciously seeks to produce a sense of helplessness in a superior, at least at the latent level. Sometimes individuals in subordinate positions, faced with their own ambiguous identities and tenuous senses of self-esteem, are on the brink of helplessness themselves; they are overcome, if only momentarily, with the gaping knowledge that their dependency wishes run counter to the demands of responsibility and cannot in reality be gratified, even if disguised. This taste of helplessness seems to dissolve only when a similar sense of helplessness can be evoked in the authority figure.

The discussion of helplessness leads indirectly to the consideration of the two latent issues in interpersonal relations referred to above: *transference reactions* and *the tendency to repeat*. These bind the historical with the here-and-now of interpersonal relations. We shall use them as the basis for our exploration of authority, subordinacy, and equality.

## LATENT ISSUES IN INTERPERSONAL RELATIONS

The distinctive quality of human beings is their existence within a matrix of history. Nations, societies, groups, and individuals have relevant histories that provide the continuities of experience and set conditions for the unfolding of events in the future. History is nowhere more poignantly seen than in the life of the individual as he works and builds relationships with others. The sense of history, or the experience of the past in the present, enters into interpersonal relations most vividly in acting out *transference reactions* and in the *tendency to repeat*.

### Transference Reactions

Psychoanalysis, besides contributing a theory of human behavior based on clinical evidence, provided a method of investigation. This method of investigation became the instrument for therapeutic change within the individual and thereby represented a joining in methodology of a means for scientific study and for cure.

The psychoanalytic method is a two-person relationship in which the patient, or analysand, seeks to follow the basic rule of *free association*. Through free association the derivatives of the unconscious are brought to light, examined, and interpreted. But the application of the basic rule is only partial because of *resistances* that are built up within the patient.  There are many sources and impelling motives for these resistances.  One of the major sources, and the only one to concern us, is in the reactions that can be typified as transference reactions since they replicate attitudes, wishes, and fantasies experienced consciously or unconsciously in some earlier human relationship of deep significance to the individual.  The analyst may stand in a surrogate position as father, mother, and siblings, quite apart from age, sex, physical appearances, and other external similarities to past objects.

The re-experiencing of past relationships in the present with full affective force is called a transference reaction.  Transference reactions are not restricted to the psychoanalytic setting but occur in interpersonal relations in everyday life.  The main difference, however, is that in the psychoanalytic setting the transferences are analyzed and brought within the understanding and control of the ego.  In ordinary life, the transferences are experienced emotionally and acted upon but the actor usually gains little insight.  The basic therapeutic effect occurs in psychoanalysis when the transference reactions become intensified and crystallized into a transference neurosis.  A transference neurosis consists of the full replication of the state in back of the infantile conflicts that led ultimately to the neurosis.

To illustrate the manifestations of transference reactions, let us turn to a second case, one concerning a woman in her late thirties. The data for this illustration are taken from a series of interviews in a factory where the woman, Mary, was employed in assembly work. She was a well-dressed, attractive woman who was unmarried.  During the course of the interviews, she talked about her background and attitudes toward a wide range of subjects.  Her comments are presented below as taken from the verbatim interview notes.[3]  (Mary briefly described her background.  She was born and raised in a crowded section of a large city.  Her parents were immigrants.)

My father was a wonderful person.  Gosh, I don't know what to say to describe him.  There just aren't words.  He was so alive; he had such a wonderful personality.  He was a real go-getter, and he pushed himself. Even though he was uneducated, he could talk real well.  We were something precious—china.  He could give you more self-confidence.  He had a tremendous personality.

[3] For a description of the interview procedure from which this excerpt is presented, see Zaleznik, Christensen, and Roethlisberger, *A Prediction Study,* pp. 13–14 and 21–22.

At one time, when I was born, he was a wealthy man. He owned three stores and an apartment building. I can still remember it. Then something happened and he lost it all. I remember we moved to the North End, a real dismal place. It was real tough. His health wasn't right, and he became nervous.

During the war, my brothers went into the service. He took it real hard and couldn't stand the thought of losing them. I remember when we got letters, he used to break down and cry. He wouldn't control himself. He had a heart attack and when he was 59, he had a shock and went real fast. I remember the funeral. People sent flowers from all over. I didn't know half the people who sent flowers. When we lost him, we really lost something. It was a hard adjustment to make.

My mother is a different person altogether. She's real strict and straight-laced. She'll do things for you, but she won't show affection. Not anything like my father. He was a bubbling personality.

Italian people are very strict. I could never bring a fellow to the house. I always had to meet my dates on the corner. Even today, my mother will question me if I bring a man to the house. She'll say: "Are you serious about him?" And I'll say no. Then she'll say: "Why do you fool around with him?"

(Mary continued the interview by describing the educational backgrounds and work accomplishments of her brothers. Her family consisted of four brothers and one sister. All the brothers, with one exception, were away from home and married. The sister lived at home with Mary and their mother. Mary seemed to compare her background and accomplishments unfavorably with her brothers. "My brothers managed to educate themselves and they're doing all right.")

When I was seven years old, I had a series of operations on my leg. It took three years out of my schooling. It was an ordeal—two major operations and it didn't seem to do any good. I had to wear braces for two years when I was nine. As far as my childhood is concerned, I was not let out. My mother kept me tied down because of my leg. It makes a girl self-conscious. It affected my confidence and it still does affect me, although I think I've adjusted to it.

When I went into the first grade, I only stayed there a couple of months. I started when I was seven because of the operations. But I was real smart and they skipped me.

(Mary then described her work experience, including five months away from home working. She said: "I was having fun, but my mother wanted me back." She then continued, describing her outside interests.)

I like to go out and relax. I'm not much for sports. I did join the bowling league but I got self-conscious. I got palpitations and went to a doctor. He told me to stop bowling.

I think twice about dancing because I'm self-conscious. It depends on who I'm with.

I like to have a highball and relax and listen to music. I like to talk to people. If I go out with girls and men try to buy me a drink, I don't go for it—unless the man fascinates me (*laughs*). After all, I'm human too.

I've had my share of dates. When I was between 17 and 26, I could have been married at least six times. I got engaged when I was 23; it didn't work out because his mother broke it up. He still keeps after me even though he's married, but I don't want to get involved with him. He just doesn't interest me. He broke up with his wife and wanted to go out with me.

I'm always becoming interested in a man who I shouldn't be interested in. I like a man who is popular with women. If a man tries to get wise with me, I know how to handle him. I really don't know what I want in a man. Some men just seem to attract me. One fellow I liked happened to be Jewish. He wanted to marry me, but because of religious differences I couldn't tell my folks. I may have been wrong in letting him go because he really loved me. He set a date to elope two or three times, but I backed down. I was afraid my parents wouldn't like it. When you're young, you don't have nerve. I think I broke his heart.

I was wrong to start in this work. I'm not satisfied. I make a week's pay and hate to make a break. My lack of education is a hindrance. When I first came here, I thought I would eventually get married, but it didn't work out that way. I'm at the point now where—well, I know what I want. I'm thinking of going back to school.

I've been working here and getting along—I used to have a lot of social life, but I don't go out as much as I used to. I'm not getting the same pleasure out of life anymore. You change as you get older. In a way, I think marriage would answer it, but then maybe not. I'm afraid of marriage—of being poor and having a rough time. Marriage is very, very serious. I could have been married at least six times, but I back away from it. I probably didn't like the fellow enough. I wouldn't chance it unless I could go all out for him. It has to be genuine, otherwise, I'd rather stay single.

At times, I get positively discouraged and disgusted, but then I think of people who are less fortunate and then I get happy.

I've had my share of boyfriends, but I couldn't feel comfortable. I just fight it off—never feel sorry for myself. Sometimes I just talk to myself. I get in front of a mirror and talk to myself. It builds up my confidence.

I could have gotten married a couple of times. I got pretty close to it and maybe I will still because I like men, but I don't see myself getting attracted to anyone. Maybe I'm getting too old or too fussy. I used to have one romance after another. Now I can't seem to be interested. I'd rather stay home and watch TV. It's difficult to get attracted to someone. I suppose if the right man came along, but I don't know.

There are times when I wonder what will become of me, but I feel there is something in the future for me. Not being married doesn't bother me as much as it should. I had chances, lots of chances, but maybe it's because I've always feared poverty that I didn't want to get married. I didn't live a life of luxury, but maybe it's because we had hard times that makes me worry about it. Today if I want something new I know I can go out and get it, I don't have to worry about it. And I don't think I'd get married if I had to worry. They say a woman could work while she's married, but I don't believe in that. If a woman has to work the marriage just won't work out. The woman becomes too independent and that's not good for marriage and eventually it shows its mark. If I was married and working, I would feel very independent—why should I do this or that, if I'm working I would say; but if you stay home, you can look up to your husband. I like to feel that I want to look up to a man. If I can't respect him I can't love him, and if I won't respect a man I won't go out with him. I want to feel he knows more than I do and the answer I get from him is *the* answer. If I get a man who can't give answers, I have to take matters into my own hands. That's the way I feel about men, bless their hearts, I guess I really do like them and I got tangled up with a few of them so I know. If a man doesn't like me, and I liked him, it used to bother me why he didn't like me more. As far as men go, though, it has to be someone I've got to look up to. Once you know what you want, it's hard to take a substitute. The last time I went steady was three years ago. Since then I haven't gone steady. I meet a man and I go out with him a few times and then I always find an excuse to stop going with him, but if I do meet the right man I'll love him and I'll be true to him, but it has to be someone I can go overboard for. I met a man last year and went out with him a few times and then he asked me to get married. Well, I just stopped going out with him. I told him to forget about me, that there was nothing to it.

The significant features of these excerpts center around Mary's relationships with men. She was openly concerned about being unmarried and revealed quite indirectly a partial explanation in the following statements: "I like to feel I want to look up to a man . . . . I want to feel he knows more than I do and the answer I get from him is *the* answer."

These comments and similar ones suggest a tendency to over-idealize men. If a man fell short of these standards the relationship was broken, if indeed the tendency to evaluate had permitted its establishment.

The overidealization of the men in her life strikes as reminiscent of her attitude toward her father who manifestly established and met her ideals. With this continuing strong attachment to her dead father, new and more mature relationships with men were difficult to establish and maintain. At a somewhat deeper level, the fact that relationships with men contained elements of *transference reactions—*

attaching attitudes from past to present relationships—was a source of anxiety.

Marriage and sexual relations, as long as they remained colored by early, overidealized attitudes toward her father, were taboo. They had unconsciously taken on incestuous qualities and aroused considerable anxiety. Yet the forbidden object, the father, was attractive, as evidenced by her more serious relationships with married men and her comment: "I'm always becoming interested in a man who I shouldn't be interested in."

In this interview, positive transference reactions are primarily evident as love attractions to forbidden objects and in the maintenance of the ideal image of the father-lover. Only dimly apparent are the opposite feelings or the negative transference reactions where the individual experiences hatred toward a person in the present because of a past relationship. The source of negative transference reactions, in the form of hostility, is the failure of the love object to gratify wishes. An individual who loves, particularly in its infantile form, cannot get enough—the desire for gratification is unlimited. These wishes are typically frustrated and become the motive power in back of hatred in human relationships. To be sure, negative reactions are subject to repression and may appear only in disguised form. In Mary's case, the only clear-cut expression of hostility and aggression was reflecting to an individual his failure to meet her standards and expectations. An individual who in his human relationships communicates the idea, "You are not good enough," may also frequently mean "You, too, will not give enough and become to me a disappointment."

Another form in which transference reactions appear is in expressions of ambivalence, the simultaneous experience of love and hate reactions. The individual who in these instances idealizes a boss—"He can do no wrong—and immediately finds chinks in the armor"—"He can do no right"—is living out ambivalences whose roots are to be found in infantile relationships.

Still another form in which the past permeates the present is in the tendency to split transference reactions. Individuals in work groups may, for example, attach positive feelings to one supervisor and negative to another. Or as is frequently found, the immediate boss becomes the object of hostile reactions, while the company or the president, the more distant authority figures in the individual's experience become the objects for positive feelings. Distance permits a continued idealization. In Mary's case, the splitting of affect in her experience occurred in her parental relations. Her father was all positive, while her mother was negative, at least on the surface. Below the surface, we would expect to find, at deeper levels of experience, the opposite feelings: mother was once the loved object, and father was hated for not giving enough.

## The Tendency to Repeat

The discussion of transference reactions brings us close to a second latent issue in interpersonal relationships—the tendency to repeat or the repetition compulsion. The best introduction we can provide to the place of the repetition compulsion in interpersonal relations is to quote from Freud, who discussed the concept in *Beyond the Pleasure Principle*.

What psychoanalysis reveals in the transference phenomena of neurotics can also be observed in the lives of some normal people. The impression they give is of being pursued by a malignant fate or possessed by some "daemonic" power; but psychoanalysis has always taken the view that their fate is for the most part arranged by themselves and determined by early infantile influences. The compulsion which is here in evidence differs in no way from the compulsion to repeat which we have found in neurotics, even though the people we are now considering have never shown any signs of dealing with a neurotic conflict by producing symptoms. Thus we have come across people all of whose human relationships have the same outcome: such as the benefactor who is abandoned in anger after a time by each of his *protégés*, however much they may otherwise differ from one another, and who thus seems doomed to taste all the bitterness of ingratitude; or the man whose friendships all end in betrayal by his friend; or the man who time after time in the course of his life raises someone else into a position of great private or public authority and then, after a certain interval, himself upsets that authority and replaces him by a new one; or, again, the lover each of whose love affairs with a woman passes through the same phases and reaches the same conclusion. This "perpetual recurrence of the same thing" causes us no astonishment when it relates to *active* behaviour on the part of the person concerned and when we can discern in him an essential character-trait which always remains the same and which is compelled to find expression in a repetition of the same experiences. We are much more impressed by cases where the subject appears to have a *passive* experience, over which he has no influence, but in which he meets with a repetition of the same fatality. There is the case, for instance, of the woman who married three successive husbands each of whom fell ill soon afterwards and had to be nursed by her on their death beds. The most moving poetic picture of a fate such as this is given by Tasso in his romantic epic *Gerusalemme Liberata*. Its hero, Tancred, unwittingly kills his beloved Clorinda in a duel while she is

disguised in the armour of an enemy knight.  After her burial he makes
his way into a strange magic forest which strikes the Crusaders' army
with terror.  He slashes with his sword at a tall tree; but blood streams
from the cut and the voice of Clorinda, whose soul is imprisoned in the
tree, is heard complaining that he has wounded his beloved once again.

The repetition compulsion is strongest around those experiences
that have been the most painful for the individual.  The tendency
to repeat is the attempt to master and solve the original painful
experience, but usually without success.  The interview between
Dr. Dodds and Dr. Blackman suggests repetition in that the subordinate *created the reality* of a new job possibility as though to suggest
that he accepted and rejected *actively* in contrast to being accepted
or rejected *passively*.  The repetition compulsion frequently occurs
around expressing actively the painful experiences one endured
passively.

The tendency to repeat, as a psychological phenomenon, has deep
implications for interpersonal relations.  The choice of persons with
whom to interact, the modes of behavior, the experienced emotion
during interpersonal encounters would have some relationship to the
dilemmas of the past which the individual sought to solve through
repetition.

## PERSISTENT THEMES IN INTERPERSONAL RELATIONS: AUTHORITY, SUBORDINACY, AND EQUALITY

The case material presented for illustrative purposes in this chapter
and the concepts developed in their presentation demonstrate the
value of exploring interpersonal dynamics through selected themes.
Authority, subordinacy, and equality are central to the dilemmas
of human relationships.  Perhaps the most crucial fact about these
dilemmas lies in the simultaneous and interlocking portrayal of authority, subordinacy, and equality issues for any given individual at any
specific point in time.  Thus, it becomes artificial to separate the
themes for discussion.  The individual in his interpersonal relations
can be likened to a symphony in which three themes are inter-
woven, with one theme dominant at one point and another at another
point.  A classic and perhaps more direct illustration of this idea
is in the relationship between superior and subordinate when it becomes evident that the superior is living out his own dependency
wishes (a facet of subordinacy) while providing gratification (an
act of authority).  This simultaneous experiencing of giving and

[4] S. Freud, *Beyond the Pleasure Principle*, pp. 21–22.

getting occurs through narcissistic identification. The individual in authority is both subject and object in the interaction because he sees himself reflected in the subordinate. Something like this may occur in parent-child relationships and, if carried to extremes, may cause difficulties.

In discussing authority, subordinacy, and equality in interpersonal relations, we shall emphasize the critical developmental issues as these become manifested in interaction. In addition, we shall present role patterns that are typically encountered in interaction and that reflect the attempt, through character formation, to resolve these developmental issues.

## Authority

An individual in an interpersonal setting who occupies a position of authority is faced with the problem of how to utilize the power and influence available to him. Power, or the capacity to influence and control the behavior of others, derives from several sources, including the position one occupies, the expertise at one's command, and emotional ties established in the relationship. (The sources of authority will be discussed more fully in Chapter Twelve.) Our main concern for the present is to understand the dynamic issues affecting the behavior of the authority figure.

The individual learns to behave in an authority position through his experience in past relationships; the infantile stages of development are crucial in this regard. The individual portrays a style of behavior reflecting the authority figures, especially the parents, with whom he has identified. Let us show the importance of the infancy stages of development and how these stages affect the individual's capacity to use authority.

The exercise of authority frequently involves a renewal of oedipal conflicts. An individual who experiences anxiety as an authority figure probably has carried over unresolved legacies of the oedipal struggle. We find, for example, the superior who is unwilling to delegate responsibility to subordinates and who is jealous of their capacity to act competently. The anxiety underlying such behavior reflects the belief, albeit unconscious, that the subordinates seek to overthrow him and assume his position. Such an unconscious belief results from the individual's oedipal strivings which he projects onto subordinates.

An authority figure's unresolved oedipal strivings may become evident in a variety of ways. He may, for example, choose subordinates who are weak and ineffectual. These subordinates unconsciously reflect to him the image of "castrated males" who, as "defectives," are not in a position to compete and overthrow him. Or, an authority figure may seek anonymity through various devices, such as isolating himself from others or completely submerging his authority by the attempt to transfer it to others. Such methods of structuring the superior-subordinate relationship stem from castration anxieties; the individual unconsciously seeks to avoid displaying his power for fear that it will arouse the envy of others who will destroy his strength. The success with which the individual has resolved oedipal conflicts will determine how effectively he behaves in the authority setting. The anxiety underlying these conflicts becomes contagious and affects the responses of subordinates.

One expression of the evolution of the oedipal conflicts is in the capacity of individuals in authority positions to behave freely: to act aggressively as well as passively, to delegate as well as to supervise, to reward as well as to punish. Another expression of resolved conflicts is in the capacity of the authority person to identify with subordinates and to establish appropriate empathic relationships with them. This form of identification is to be contrasted with the projection referred to earlier where the individual's fantasies and wishes are imparted to others. Empathic identification is best understood by an example.

A group of children in a religious school were studying the portion of the Old Testament in which Abraham engages God in a dialogue concerning the fate of Sodom, an evil city. God is portrayed as being wrathful and as seeking to destroy this abomination. Abraham is portrayed as being compassionate and as seeking to save the righteous. Abraham then asks God if He would be willing to save the city if He could be shown 50 righteous men. God agrees, whereupon Abraham forces Him to accept the dilemma that the existence of one righteous man is as crucial as 50 in tempering one's indignation. Upon hearing this portion read, one student became concerned and asked the teacher how it was possible for God, who is omnipotent, to be outwitted by Abraham, who after all was only mortal. How was it, the student inquired, that God did not become so angry that He destroyed Abraham. The teacher suggested that the real meaning of the dialogue was in understanding that a powerful, omnipotent object could reflect in pride over the accomplishments of one less powerful, particularly if the authority figure felt he had some hand in training the subordinate.

We suggested earlier that there exist certain behavior patterns of authority figures that serve as useful examples in understanding the dynamics of authority. There are four such prototypes of patterns of authority: (1) paternal-assertive; (2) maternal-expressive, (3) fraternal-permissive, and (4) rational-procedural.

*Paternal-Assertive.* The paternal-assertive authority pattern represents a characterological resolution of authority dilemmas whereby the individual builds his role around the following behavioral traits: aggressiveness, dominance, and initiation of interaction. He avoids tender feelings, but concerns himself with the advancement and reward of subordinates, particularly those who accept his form of authority. He tends to be visible and also may appear quite independent, as though he needs no one but himself.

*Maternal-Expressive.* The maternal-expressive pattern is based on a strong feminine identification in which passivity and nurture are the main dynamic features. Here there is avoidance of initiation and aggressiveness. The behavioral mode is based on creating affectionate ties, and control is exercised through withdrawal of affection and the underlying fear of rejection. In relationships with the paternal-aggressive type of individual, subordinates may experience fear; in relationships with the maternal-expressive type, they may experience anger at not getting enough attention from the authority figure. In a sense, these affective reactions are reminiscent of responses to oral transactions, where giving and getting imply the acts of nurturing and being nurtured.

*Fraternal-Permissive.* The fraternal-permissive type of individual establishes the kind of relationship in which status differentiation is consciously avoided in favor of equality. Authority is invested in external objects, such as the task or a set of ideals. Frequently, a relationship of authority built along the lines of the fraternal-permissive prototype utilizes a totem, symbolic of a father image, that binds the permissive leader and his subordinates. The permissive aspects of behavior consist of sharing responsibility and encouraging subordinates. The needs of the subordinates appear dominant in the relationship.

*Rational-Procedural.* The fourth prototype of the authority role is the rational-procedural individual who keeps the affective ties to a minimum. Whereas fear is the characteristic response to the paternal-assertive prototype, love to the maternal-expressive, and friendship to the fraternal-permissive, the rational-procedural is typically devoid of affect and in this sense is probably an ideal of bureaucratic work structures. The investment is in objectives, laws, and regulations. This type of authority figure seeks to invoke the constraints of impersonal authority. Feelings therefore tend to be suppressed. The authority figure attempts to establish his behavior as a model and to create involvement in the rationality of purpose and procedure that are traditional and therefore widely accepted.

These four authority types represent the extremes of behavior; they do not typify the behavior pattern of any particular authority figure. Such "idealizations" are useful in describing the affective qualities and dynamics of authority relationships. However, an actual relationship may reflect a synthesis of the four ideal types.

For purposes of convenience and for further reflection, we present a summary of the four prototypes in the following figure.

| Authority Prototypes | Behavioral Mode | Affective Quality | Source of Control | Problematic Subordinate Response |
|---|---|---|---|---|
| 1. Paternal-Assertive | Dominant; active | Distance; fear | Reward-punishment | Castration anxiety |
| 2. Maternal-Expressive | Quiescent; passive | Closeness; affection | Loss of love; rejection | Anger-depression |
| 3. Fraternal-Permissive | Moderate; "give and take" | Warmth; friendship | Totemistic; ideals | "Groupiness" and low motivation to work |
| 4. Rational-Procedural | Moderate; controlled | Regulated; neutral | Logic and law | Lack of involvement |

The summary figure is mainly self-explanatory in that it draws together the preceding descriptions. We should comment, however, on the column, "Problematic Subordinate Response." In this column, we attempt to characterize the type of response elicited from the subordinate by the behavior of the prototype.

The paternal-assertive prototype may elicit anxiety in the subordinate about the latter's own power and capacity to act assertively. This response is symbolically equivalent to castration anxiety of the earlier oedipal conflicts.

Anger and depression, the problematic subordinate response characteristic of the maternal-expressive prototype, reflects a response to interaction in which nurturance and affection are dominant. This response is related to the oral stage of development and dependency.

The fraternal-permissive prototype may evoke responses that are inimical to work. The stress on "groupiness" reflects itself in a low motivation to work, since work implies differentiation and evaluations.

Finally, the lack of involvement, as a response to the rational-procedural prototype, stems from the failure to reach individuals at levels in their emotional experience that produce creative activity. "Man lives not by bread alone" can be taken in this context to mean that he seeks to inspire and be inspired in his interpersonal relations.

## Subordinacy

Subordinacy is presented at the outset as a descriptive concept. We shall seek to establish the various dynamic issues impinging upon individuals who experience a lesser degree of authority than other relevant persons in an interpersonal setting. The several dimensions of authority in relation to which individuals are hierarchically arranged need not detain us. All individuals experience subordinacy in some respects and in relation to some persons, no matter how much authority they command by virtue of position or knowledge. What are the significant psychological conflicts in subordinacy? What identifiable role prototypes appear as attempts at resolution of these conflicts?

There appear to be three significant areas of psychological conflict in subordinacy: (1) the rivalry for power; (2) the struggle for autonomy and control; and (3) the establishment of patterns of gratification without excessive dependency. Each of these potential experiences of conflict stems from the impingement of the individual's past upon the "here-and-now" interpersonal structure in which he is in the subordinate position. Most of the individual's relationships throughout the early stages of the life cycle develop under conditions where he is subject to the control of objects with considerably more power than he. Initially, the mother and father are the relevant power figures, followed by teachers, and later supervisors in work settings. The issues of power, control, and gratification occur early and never cease to act as significant internal issues that must be resolved for development of a satisfying subordinacy pattern in the appropriate interpersonal structure. Let us examine each of these issues in subordinacy.

*The Rivalry for Power.* Rivalry in the realm of subordinacy refers to the feelings of jealousy and envy experienced as part of subordinacy and directed toward those objects who are perceived as more powerful. Rivalry with authority figures relates to the earlier oedipal strivings in relation to the father. The individual in the subordinate position develops transference reactions toward authority figures reminiscent of earlier oedipal feelings. The rivalry can take at least two forms, following the main trends of the oepidal situation. If the individual continues to experience actively the negative oedipal conflict, then his transference reactions result in a perceived maternal object against whom the jealousy and hostility become activated. A perceived paternal object activates warmth and affection. The reverse situation exists if positive oedipal strivings are latent. The perceived maternal figure is the desired object and the perceived paternal figure is the rival. In either case, the existence or creation of triadic relations appear as the significant interpersonal structure for the acting out of concerns over rivalry.

For a vivid portrayal of the issue of rivalry as an aspect of subordinacy, we can refer to Shakespeare's *Hamlet*. Hamlet was obsessed with the idea of revenge. His mother and uncle had killed the king, his father. They had married, and the uncle became king. To have proceeded to direct revenge would have meant a clear-cut determination of the crime, the guilty ones, and the retribution. Hamlet's obsessional doubting could only have meant that unconsciously he shared the crime, the guilt, and the need for punishment, because he had in fantasy experienced the rivalry and jealousy that must have led the uncle to commit his crime.

*The Struggle for Autonomy and Control.* Most interpersonal settings at work involve a structure in which the individual's work goals and activities are determined in some measure by superordinate figures. Under such conditions individuals at times feel as though they are being *acted upon* more than they are *acting* to secure the intrinsic satisfaction they feel is their rightful due. In the extreme, they may come to feel that their productivity is somehow locked into a struggle with power figures who initiate and direct activity and who control the output of work.

Subordinacy requires being open and responsive to the influence of authority figures. The unconscious exaggeration of the individual's own need for autonomy and control leads to a stubborn and often passive resistance to the influence attempts of others. This resistance and the entire struggle for autonomy then becomes an issue of "either-or"; the individual comes to believe that he is *either* in complete control and has full autonomy over his activities *or* he has no control and is responding passively to the desires of the authority figures. This "either-or" thinking is a false dichotomy and is suggestive of compulsive character traits and obsessive thinking.

The "either-or" dichotomy, reflected, for example, in the Blackman-Dodds case illustration, is a carry-over from infantile experiences with autonomy and control. During the anal-sadistic stage of development, the battle of wills and the struggle for control take place in the relationship with mother as she attempts to toilet train. The struggle in the primitive thinking of the child is over a valuable product seen as a part of the self. If this struggle was excessive and was not fully resolved, it is reflected in preoccupation with control in the later superior-subordinate relationships of the individual.

*Establishing Patterns of Gratification Without Excessive Dependency.* A third issue of deep psychological significance in subordinacy is securing adequate gratifications without the lingering suspicion that one is getting either too much or too little. Getting, in interpersonal relationships, occurs around the ordinary rewards of everyday behavior such as attention, respect, approval, and warmth, as well as the more visible rewards of position. These rewards can be symbolically related to the primitive "getting" in the mother-child relationship.

In the subordinacy of the interpersonal work setting, "getting" may become a repeated issue in the experience of the individual. If his early experiences in securing gratifications have been satisfactory, the individual can continue to secure gratifications without either making excessive demands or refusing the rewards offered to him.

The individual who is constantly demanding of his boss, who is excessively conscious of how his rewards compare with others, and who appears constantly to authority figures as a "needful" person reflects the carry-over of oral problems from the past to the present. The individual who, to take a different pattern, refuses the nurture which others are glad to provide and who develops almost an ascetic and spartan-like approach to life experiences subordinacy as a continuing resistance to gratification. It is as though the individual will not accept the rewards of interpersonal relations lest the taste of the gratifications create a yearning of intolerable proportions. In this connection, it is interesting to note the findings of studies of individuals with stomach ulcers. Franz Alexander reports that the underlying psychological problem for the ulcer case is repressed dependency needs.[5] The individual experiences an underlying sense of anger and

[5] R. W. White, *Abnormal Personality*, pp. 430–433. This reference is a summary of the concept of repressed dependency needs and its relation to stomach ulcers. The original formulations were made by Franz Alexander, "The Influence of Psychological Factors upon Gastro-Intestinal Disturbances," *Psychoanalytic Quarterly*, III (1934), pp. 501–539.

emptiness because he feels deprived. These feelings are related to an excessive flow of stomach acid and the development of the ulcer condition.

The precipitates of the various psychological issues of subordinacy are to be found in certain prototypical behavior patterns. The prototypes selected for attention here are: (1) the rebel, (2) the slave, and (3) the responsible individual.

*The Rebel.* As a prototype of subordinacy, the rebel seeks to deny dependency needs and the achievement of gratification through the defiance of authority. In modern times, the rebel appears as the angry young man or, in the extreme, as "the beatnik" who cares little for the conventions of society. In a positive sense, the rebel is highly constructive when the conflicts are sublimated into the search for new knowledge or solutions to long-standing problems. The rebel may also be instrumental in instituting changes, activities that are highly valued in segments of organizations and society.

The theme of the angry young man, suggestive of the prototypical rebel, is much alive today in literature, the theatre, the cinema, and the arts in general. One common plot is the aggressive, highly masculine male who rages within a love relationship with an older woman as in the British films, "This Sporting Life" and "Saturday Night and Sunday Morning." Love and hate are almost indistinguishable because the demand for love is excessive; it is like an unquenchable fire and can only lead to severe disappointment and anger. The juxtaposition of the themes of masculinity and oral needfulness reveals the contradictive and ambivalent characteristics of the rebel.

The same theme appears in the interpersonal relations in everyday work settings, although with less severity and clarity than is revealed by the modern writer and artist.

*The Slave.* The slave as a prototype in the subordinacy relationship exhibits an excessively acquiescent pattern of behavior. The singular direction of behavior seems to be to serve a master, preferably in a pairing relationship. An example from the modern novel is Meyer Levin's *Compulsion*, a fictionalized account of the Leopold-Loeb relationship. Leopold is portrayed as a slave to Loeb, the sadistic and intellectually brilliant psychotic who plots a murder and dominates Leopold to the point where he joins in the crime as a test of his submission and loss of will.

Another example may be found in the pattern portrayed by Adolph Eichmann. The master to which Eichmann was slave was the bureaucratic system dominated by the dictator. Slavish adherence to the commands of others resulted in a complete absence of choice, moral responsibility, and consequently, humanity.

Again, the appearance of this prototype in organizations is usually not as extreme as the examples above indicate. But the slave prototype is a revealing indicator of one pattern of subordinacy.

*The Responsible Individual.* The third prototype of subordinacy is the portrayal of the responsible individual. The subordinate assumes the role of the agent of the authority figure and authority system and attempts to support it as much as possible. In a sense this role is an extension of the father-surrogate position opted by the eldest son.[6]

Although the rebel and the slave are defined primarily in the relationship toward authority, the responsible individual, the father-surrogate, is meaningful in both the relationship toward authority and toward other subordinate figures. Extending the analogy of the eldest son, the responsible individual serves as a representative or agent of authority in relation to other subordinates who stand symbolically as siblings. He may attempt to control the rebels who defy authority and translate the desires of authority figures to subordinates. In turn, he may become the object of displaced hostility toward authority. The success of the responsible role depends on securing an alliance with the authority figure.

In formal organizations, the position of the responsible individual is coveted by subordinates and may be the focus of vying and competitive behavior. On the one hand, the individual who secures the position of the eldest son, or the father-surrogate, establishes a uniquely close relationship to the authority figure; on the other hand, he exercises control over other subordinates, a position that appears rewarding.

The discussion of the responsible individual as a prototypical subordinate relationship brings us close to the third theme in interpersonal relations, that of equality. The previous discussion dealt with authority and subordinacy as dynamic issues in interpersonal behavior. To complete the discussion of the underlying psychological dynamics of interpersonal relations requires exploration of peer relations and the issue of equality.

## Equality

The theme of equality concerns the emotional and behavioral experience in the relations among two or more persons who are perceived as peers by the actors in the interpersonal setting.

---

[6] D. Moment and A. Zaleznik, *Role Development and Interpersonal Competence,* Chapter 7.

The initial experience of peer relations occurs in the family among siblings. The fact that the siblings have the same love and identification objects in the form of their parents creates strong emotional bonds among them. The earliest of these bonds is one of hate and rivalry. In the eyes of the child, the parents control only a finite amount of love and attention so that the rewards secured by one sibling seem to deprive another. The arrival of a newborn baby in the family constellation does, in fact, divert attention from other children, especially in the behavior of the mother who must devote her care to the infant, the most helpless and dependent of the siblings. The hatred generated by this displacement is the basic condition in the experience among the siblings. The love and devotion of siblings for one another is a later attitude adopted through identification with the parents.

One of the most significant threats to the interpersonal relationships among peers in later life and outside of the family is the potential rivalry that is closely akin, dynamically speaking, to the early forms of sibling rivalry. The movement toward equality, where all peers seek and receive equal rewards, is a method of coping with the latent sibling rivalry. No form of behavior is apt to arouse stronger feelings than the activity of a peer figure who asserts individuality, seeks more reward and recognition from authority, or attempts to secure the leadership of a group of peers. The story of sibling rivalry is told and retold in the Bible and in literature. The biblical story of Joseph and his brothers develops this theme. When Joseph received a coat of many colors as a gift from his father the brothers were angered and cast Joseph into a pit as punishment. He was saved and later became an advisor to the king. Instead of seeking revenge against his brothers, he helped them during a famine when they were in need. There are many social and moral inferences to be drawn from this story which thematically, at least, represent the type of norms governing peer relations. One is the risk of receiving visible reward and individual attention among a group of peers. The moral is that individuality is to be achieved at some risk; the individual must bear the consequences without becoming bitter and hostile. Another inference or norm derived from the story is the suggestion that among a group of peers the one who achieves individuality and power should use these ego gains to help his peers. We shall return to the theme of helping as one of the prototypical solutions in peer relations.

In discussing the striving for equality and its genesis in the sibling relations, Freud summarized as follows:

Something like it first grows up in a nursery containing many children, out of the children's relation to their parents, and it does so as a reaction to the initial envy with which the elder child receives the younger one.  The elder child would certainly like to put his successor jealously aside, to keep it away from the parents, and to rob it of all its privileges; but in the face of the fact that this younger child (like all that come later) is loved by the parents as much as he himself is, and in consequence of the impossibility of maintaining his hostile attitude without damaging himself, he is forced into identifying himself with the other children.  So there grows up in the troop of children a communal or group feeling, which is then further developed at school.  The first demand made by this reaction-formation is for justice, for equal treatment for all.  We all know how loudly and implacably this claim is put forward at school.  It one cannot be the favourite oneself, at all events nobody else shall be the favourite.  This transformation—the replacing of jealously by a group feeling in the nursery and classroom—might be considered improbable, if the same process could not later on be observed again in other circumstances.  We have only to think of the troop of women and girls, all of them in love in an enthusiastically sentimental way, who crowd round a singer or pianist after his performance.  It would certainly be easy for each of them to be jealous of the rest; but, in the face of their numbers and the consequent impossibility of their reaching the aim of their love, they renounce it, and, instead of pulling out one another's hair, they act as a united group, do homage to the hero of the occasion with their common actions, and would probably be glad to have a share of *his* flowing locks.  Originally rivals, they have succeeded in identifying themselves with one another by means of a similar love for the same object. . . .

What appears later on in society in the shape of *Gemeingeist, esprit de corps,* "group spirit," etc., does not belie its derivation from what was originally envy.  No one must want to put himself forward, every one must be the same and have the same.  Social justice means that we deny ourselves many things so that others may have to do without them as well, or, what is the same thing, may not be able to ask for them.  This demand for equality is the root of social conscience and the sense of duty.[7]

The resolution of sibling rivalry through establishing rigid norms of equality represents one pattern in peer relations.  The difficulty with this pattern is that it does not free individuals to be themselves and to establish their unique identities.  It also fails to recognize the differences among individuals and the fact that age peers are not necessarily equal in ability and capacity to work and contribute.  Thus, in addition to the egalitarian group, there are several other prototypes in interpersonal behavior: (1) the scapegoat, (2) the clown, (3) the helper and (4) the hero.

*The Scapegoat.*  It is common to find in peer relations an individual who becomes the object toward whom members direct aggres-

[7] S. Freud, *Group Psychology and the Analysis of the Ego,* pp. 119–121.

sion and hostility. The aggression may stem from two motivational conditions. First, if the hostility and frustration experienced among peers in relation to an authoritarian or autocratic leader has no direct outlet in aggressive acts directed toward the leader, the members may vent their aggression against a seemingly helpless or defective peer— one who is least capable of retaliating.[8]   The existence of a scapegoat *binds* the aggression within a group and prevents open rebellion against the power figure or complete abandonment to the helplessness generated by hostile feelings.

Observations of the scapegoat frequently reveal the unconscious acquiescence in this role on the part of one or more persons in the peer group.   In terms of individual dynamics, the scapegoat may be driven by a sense of guilt and a need for punishment, making himself available as an object against whom others can vent their pent-up hostility.

The scapegoat as a prototype in the theme of acquiescence of subordinates toward a seemingly omnipotent figure is reflected in biblical references.   In the Old Testament, Abraham showed his act of submission to an omnipotent God in his willingness to sacrifice his son. Upon seeing this willing submission, God took as a substitute a goat, which symbolically represents the complete dominance of an omnipotent authority figure.

The theme of the scapegoat as a prototypical peer role should remind us that relations among equals do not exist in a vacuum but must be understood as a part of authority and subordinacy.

*The Clown.*   Following the theme of peer relations as a fact of authority and subordinacy, we turn to a second prototype, the clown. In this case, a peer assumes a role in a group in which he generates joking, teasing, and other playful behavior. Others participate or act as audience but vicariously become a party of a performance in which hostility toward authority is a dominant theme.   Freud noted in *Wit and Its Relation to the Unconscious* how frequently humor is directed with aggressive intent toward authority figures.   The clown expresses such humor through word and deed and serves as an object who permits the discharge of aggression.   The most subtle and least subject to retaliation is the clown who expresses the hostility toward authority in ways that block retaliation.   The effective clown portrays himself, therefore, as a tragic-comic figure against whom retaliation is unlikely to be directed.   The most striking example of the clown as prototype

[8] Ronald Lippitt and Ralph White, "Leader Behavior and Member Reaction in Three 'Social Climates,' " *Group Dynamics: Research and Theory*, Chapter 40.

is to be found in the circus.  The delight in the clown and its appearance in so many different cultures suggests its underlying significance in human experience.

*The Helper.*  The helper as prototype in relationships of equality is a highly socialized form of expressing differentiation among peers without destroying the norms of equality.  The individual who assumes the role of the helper has skills and qualities that are deemed valuable among his peers.  By offering these skills in a helping relationship, the individual utilizes his talents in ways that do not amplify his position of expertise vis-à-vis his peers.  The helper is rewarded by the liking and warmth of his peers; but he pays a price in the form of low recognition from external authority figures.  Psycho-dynamically, the helper avoids differentiation to maintain his support within a comfortable peer group culture and avoids the risk of individuality and loneliness.

A good example of the helper in a peer relationship has been presented by Zaleznik in his study of an informal leader in a work group of machinists in a factory.  Ron was the key figure in helping co-workers.  We present here an excerpt from the description and interpretation of his role.

Ron was a Negro, forty-one years old, married, with one child.  His parents were well-educated professional people; his father was an agricultural specialist, and his mother a teacher.  He had spent most of his life in a large metropolitan area in the northeastern states where he had received his education.  Ron had completed one year of college but had dropped out because he lacked funds to continue.

He was a tall, well-built individual, quiet in manner and speech.  Observing Ron's gentle manner, one could scarcely believe that he had been a professional boxer.  Ron was athletically inclined, and had participated in college track, and later amateur boxing.  He turned "pro" and started what appeared to be a promising career as a heavyweight.  In fact, we were told that he had won a decision in a three-round match with Rocky Marciano and several men in the shop called him "our uncrowned heavyweight champion of the world."  His boxing career was cut short, however, by an injury which had also kept him out of the service.

After leaving college Ron went to a technical school where he learned the fundamentals of his trade.  He worked in several shops and gained diversified experience.  During the war he worked in the same Navy Yard as Clyde, his foreman, but they had never met there.

Ron had shown some ability and inclination toward leadership in his previous jobs.  He had voluntarily helped out new workers in the Navy Yard.  One of these workers had just arrived from Texas, and despite racial barriers Ron's skill was such that he was able to help this man. He further showed his inclination toward leadership by bringing four of the machine shop group into the present company. Two of these men were white and had worked with him in another shop.

Ron had many mixed feelings about himself and his position in life. It seemed as though all his major experiences had been less than complete. In his early life he had been separated from his father. He described how one time he and his mother were all packed to join his father. He had said goodbye to his friends with anticipation of the future. At the last minute the plans were changed. The feelings of disappointment and frustration associated with this experience had not left him even in adulthood.

He had much to live up to in meeting his family's expectations of his educational achievements. His parents had had professional educations, something unusual for Negroes in their day. Yet he had dropped out of college after one year. He explained that he had to drop out because he had no money, and in the next breath he would berate himself for "not having gumption to see it through." He would say, "If I had wanted it bad enough, I could have made it somehow."

His position in the shop as informal leader, while rewarding to him, also carried its frustrations. His role, like virtue, was its own reward; it received no formal recognition in the organization, either in pay or in formal status. At one time he had been promised a promotion to group leader in the machine shop, but this promise was not fulfilled. As a consequence, Ron tended to withdraw. Sometimes he felt like quitting. Other times, the security had to be considered. Ron had been offered a job with a company for which he had formerly worked. His mixed feelings about his position had something concrete around which he could weigh the "pros and cons" of his immediate life situation. But his debates always came out to a draw and never reached a conclusion. Ron sometimes concluded that in life he was destined to be like the girl who was "always the bridesmaid, but never the bride."

His role of informal leader was full of ambiguity. The satisfaction in helping men was important, but the position itself was insecure because it depended solely on his performing a group function rather than on formal standing. And this function did not depend solely on himself. The possibility always loomed that another machinist might be sought for help and might take over his function. On the one hand, Ron would say, "I think I'd be better off just doing my work and minding my own business." On the other hand, the satisfaction of being sought out for help was important.

In stressing both the rewards and costs of the helper, we point to the inherently conflicting nature of this attempt at resolving the need for individuality on the one hand, and the press of equality in peer relations on the other. The final prototype we shall present deals with this same conflict, but with the resolution leaning in the direction of individuality.

*The Hero.* In discussing equality as one of three central themes in interpersonal relations we stressed the significance of sibling rivalry and reactions to powerful authority figures. The scapegoat and the clown as interpersonal prototypes tend to be relevant psychologically in the reactions of the less powerful peers to the more powerful authority figures. The helper prototype protects the peers against authority and uses himself to enhance the peers without asserting direct authority or control.

The hero, the fourth prototype evident in the relations among peers, acts as an object of both envy and identification for the peers. He simultaneously achieves liberation from the rigid egalitarian control of the peer group and the dominance of the authority figures.

We select the term hero to denote this prototype following a suggestion by Freud in his *Group Psychology and the Analysis of the Ego.*[9] Freud was concerned with the relation between individual and group psychology—how the individual emerged from the restrictive and coercive bonds of group formations built upon identification with a common authority figure and hence mutual identifications among members. Freud suggested that within the myth of the primitive group ruled by a despotic figure lay the illusion that the despot was overthrown by a hero who succeeded in liberating himself from the rule of the despot while the other group members formed a fraternal social system with a totem as a symbol of authority.[10]   Unlike brothers, or equals, the hero is permitted instinctual gratifications, denoting of course, the achievement of maturity and autonomy.

This legend of the primal horde and the emergence of the hero illuminates the psychology of peer relations. The structure and ritual of adolescent peer groups such as fraternities and other secret societies attest to its relevance. Other evidence is available in behavior in various types of leaderless groups. The struggle for authority and the false resolution in the establishment of an egalitarian system reflect the deep ambivalence toward authority among individuals and the strength of the wish for equality.

The emergence of the hero who establishes his individuality suggests

[9] S. Freud, *Group Psychology and the Analysis of the Ego,* pp. 122–128 and 135–137.

[10] For a discussion for the psychological meaning of myths dealing with the hero, see Otto Rank, *The Myth of the Birth of the Hero.*

another resolution to the dilemma of equality as an attempt to resolve the conflicts inherent in authority and subordinacy. The individual who achieves the autonomy implicit in the conception of the hero is free to be a leader, a member, or a solitary worker in answer to his own needs and the judgments regarding relevant behavior. In this sense, the hero is both admired and envied.

## SUMMARY

We have discussed the dynamics of interpersonal relations in light of the psychoanalytic framework presented in Chapter Seven. Two main features of interpersonal relations are the existence of transference reactions and the tendency to repeat. These reflect a basic tendency in human relationships to merge the past and the present. Interpersonal relations are indeed freer when the transference reactions and the tendency to repeat are at a minimum. But without these concepts, we are able to secure less of an understanding of what actually takes place dynamically in interpersonal interactions.

Transference reactions and the tendency to repeat occur around three pervasive themes in interpersonal relations: (1) authority, or the relations experienced by a figure who has power in an interpersonal structure; (2) subordinacy, or the relations experienced by those whose behavior is subject to control and influence from authority figures; and (3) equality, or the relations experienced by those in peer structures. In discussing themes of authority, subordinacy, and equality we have developed the relevant psychological conflicts and presented typical roles which appear as classic attempts at conflict resolution.

We should stress at this point the idea that authority, subordinacy, and equality are not isolated or easily separable experiences. Any individual in the development of his relationships with others and in the elaboration of his role performances is experiencing simultaneously the relevant tensions imbedded in a matrix of authority, subordinacy, and equality. Sometimes one of these three themes appears dominant in an interaction, and the others appear as background. Yet if interaction persists, the astute observer will see the relevance of all three issues in the unfolding of interpersonal relations.

# *Part Three*

# *Organizational* *Aspects* *of* *Group* *Behavior*

$H$AVING examined the processes in motion within groups, between individuals, and within individuals, we shift attention to the processes occurring between the work group and its environment. For the purposes of this book the environment includes both the formal organization within which small groups operate and the broader culture in which their members live. The organization imposes clear demands on the group. These demands pertain to the resources it controls, such as materials, machines, and manpower, and to its outputs, the goods and services produced for others both within and outside the organization. In addition, the social and cultural backgrounds of group members make social and interpersonal demands, and provide the yardsticks for measuring how well these demands are met. Yet this is not a one-way street; the groups and their members reciprocate with demands on the organization, which evolve from their needs as individuals. These demands have to be satisfied in some fashion if the group relationship is to endure.

The chapters in this section dwell on these mutual demands and interests, and the processes for their realization. Chapter Nine, Environmental Constraints, considers the organizational setting as a collection of standards, an assortment of spatial, temporal, and functional limitations, and a series of activities—all affected by the values of the wider culture. Within these confines, group development and interpersonal relationships occur. Chapter Ten, Productivity, covers the economic measure of group output and the factors determining it. Chapter Eleven, Satisfaction, concerns what individuals expect from the organization, the rewards available within it, and the balance between expectations and rewards.

*Chapter Nine*

# Environmental Constraints

GROUPS are identified by the *position* they occupy in a formal organization. The names they are given connote various scales, relationships, and frames of reference. These locate the place of the group in relation to other groups within the organization, in relation to the organization as a whole, and in relation to other groups in the wider culture. For example, in many organizations the names Division, Department, and Section represent concrete relationships, size, and authority. One of these contains the other, is larger than the other, and controls the other. The names also are clues to the communication process—who reports to whom, who gets what kind of information, and who is excluded from certain data. Identification becomes more specific when functional, geographic, and other types of titles apply. Thus, Sales, Advertising, Engineering, Machining, Assembly, and Inspection all describe functions common to a group and imply a set of links among the several group activities within an organization. These have cultural counterparts—white collar, blue collar, professional, occupational, and trade. Geographic identifications indicate where the group's work is to be carried out—field, office, factory, nation, state, city.

How an organization defines and identifies its work groups sets the standards and the limitations for actual group development. A second set of standards and limitations derives from the surrounding culture and subcultures. Together these express the meanings of work. The organizational standards and limitations state them in economic terms; the cultural standards and limitations convey them as social values, religious values, and the value of the individual as well. The former result from the logic of work, the latter are brought into the organization by its members from their own worlds. Within the confines of the two occur the natural processes of group development and inter-personal dynamics described in previous chapters.

## THE FORMAL ORGANIZATION

In viewing the formal organization, three of its aspects are upper-most. The structure of authority, the structure of communications, and technology each have important social and psychological con-sequences for the development of group and interpersonal relation-ships. These consequences stand out when the organization is viewed as a system of social symbols.

### The Authority Structure

An authority structure is a set of formally designated relationships between positions. It prescribes the "flow" of authority, or "chain of command," and locates the position of people whose orders a member of an organization must obey and the positions of those who must obey him. Blau and Scott name two criteria which distinguish *authority* from other forms of control, such as power, persuasion, and personal influence. These are "voluntary compliance with legiti-mate commands and suspension of judgment in advance of com-mand."[1] The authority structure is represented graphically by an organizational chart, traditionally scaled so that the amount of author-ity increases toward the top of the chart.

The standard authority structure, derived from the church and the military, prescribes a pyramid. This hierarchical structure assumes a limited span and a fixed, unilateral direction of control. One position, at the top of the pyramid, controls a certain number of subordinates. Each of these subordinate positions in turn controls a similar number of subordinates. These divisions extend downward through the ranks as far as necessary to reach the positions at the bottom.

If positions at any one level remain constant while those of one or more higher levels are removed, the pyramidal structure flattens. Then the positions immediately above the level of those removed either acquire a larger span of unilateral control or relinquish some control to the subordinates. Since the time, attention, and emotional energy available to occupants of the higher positions are relatively fixed, the flattening of the pyramid tends to increase the autonomy of subordinates.

[1] Blau and Scott, *Formal Organizations,* pp. 27–32.

The structural differences between a pyramidal hierarchy and a flat organization stem from a distinct vertical distribution of power, influence, or control among the positions. Barnes compared the effects of these two kinds of authority structure on the development of two groups of technical workers.[2] In the flatter structure he found greater autonomy among subordinates, a greater degree of mutual influence between levels, and more opportunities for inter-action by subordinates. Here the level of task performance was higher and satisfaction was greater. There was a closer relationship between social subgroups and the requirements of the task, and a lesser relationship between subgroups and status outside the group.

Barnes, Dalton, and Zaleznik introduced another aspect of authority structure, differentiating between two possible *sources* of authority.[3] The *authority of position* underlies hierarchical relations in traditional organizational structures. Hierarchical power is rooted in cultural history as well as in the genetic history of growing individuals. The imagery of God, the father, the powerful, is taught as an idea and, even more important, is reinforced by the fact that adults really have physical coercive power over their children. Fears of coercion, punishment, and deprivation persist into later life when the power distinction is no longer what it was in childhood. Moreover, the cultural traditions of power and authority are learned by successive generations. As a result, the individual brings his awareness of positional authority into the organizational settings which further dramatizes the concept through a unique set of authority symbols.

The second source of authority, *professional authority*, is based on knowledge, ability, and reason. In modern society, even those in the highest *positions* of authority defer to professional authority on specialized matters. For example, medical doctors tell us what to do on medical problems; even a young intern has more of this kind of authority than a corporation president. Modern organizations and modern society, confronted with complex technical problems, have attached an increased importance to professional authority in rela-tion to positional authority for the obvious reason that positional power cannot solve technical problems.

Although Barnes, Dalton, and Zaleznik dealt with only two sources of authority, position and professional competence, there is a third which is of considerable importance in the study of individuals, groups, and organizations. Weber and others call this *charismatic authority*.[4]

[2] Barnes, *Organizational Systems and Engineering Groups.*

[3] Barnes, Dalton, and Zaleznik, "The Authority Structure as a Change Variable."

[4] Weber, *The Theory of Social and Economic Organization,* pp. 324 ff.

According to some formulations it is derived from imputed divine or supernatural powers. Charismatic authority involves processes of individual identification and feelings of dependency. In contrast to positional and professional authority, which are bound to culture systems, this type of authority resides in the nature of relatively primitive individual and interpersonal emotional processes.

Barnes, Dalton, and Zaleznik described a planned change in organizational structure. This change tended toward "flatness" of authority structure and a realignment of positions which gave more importance to professional authority. In studying groups of scientists, engineers, and managers, they observed that for some people the change involved an increase in influence consistent with their roles. Some scientists experienced an increase in professional authority while some managers increased their positional authority. In both cases, the individuals sensed increased autonomy, greater personal involvement, higher productivity, and more satisfaction. The changes affected patterns of interaction as well as authority relationships. New groups developed around subordinate and superordinate tasks, providing new identifications around which individual and group identities could form.

The authors stated the following conclusions as hypotheses:

I. Every complex organization includes several competing authority systems which make up the organization's over-all influence network. Influence based upon any of these authority systems can be transferred to other authority systems within the organization.

II. Among these several competing authority systems are two whose influence is derived respectively from: a) hierarchial position, and b) technical expertise.

III. In any organization, one of the authority systems tends to be dominant. Individuals whose authority stems from the dominant system will have more influence than others. Individuals entitled to use more than one source of authority at different times tend to maximize their influence by the dominant source of authority most of the time.

IV. A shift in the authority balance can be achieved either by successful open rebellion or by sponsorship and protection from the dominant authority system. Under these two conditions, the secondary authority systems will increase in influence.

V. Sponsorship and protection of secondary authority systems by those whose occupational role identifies them with the dominant authority system leads to ambivalence and internal role conflict on their part.

VI. Sponsorship and protection of secondary authority systems can be accomplished a) by establishing formal procedures which force conformity to the operating norms of the secondary system, or b) by role occupants identified with the dominant system establishing relationships which re-enforce the secondary system's operating norms. The two alternatives are not mutually exclusive or incompatible.[5]

Authority structure influences group development through the various ways that an organization's culture attaches meanings to symbols, objects, and behavior. Authority structures can differ from each other in at least two important respects: first, the relationship between the number of levels and the number of positions at each level describes a pattern ranging from hierarchical to flat; and second, the relative importance attached to positional or professional authority, and the ways in which this balance varies between levels and among tasks, describe the sources of authority characterizing the structure. The type of structure depends on the distribution and direction of influence. Unilaterally *downward* influence signifies an hierarchical form; a greater degree of *mutual* influence—upward as well as downward—denotes the flatter form. Barnes, Dalton, and Zaleznik implied that effective problem solving required a redistribution of positional and professional sources of authority. Increased autonomy, influence, and personal involvement resulting from such a shift produced greater productivity and satisfaction.

Thus, authority structure can affect patterns of interaction, activity, and influence, and the sentiments of individuals who belong to groups. These are some of the elements of group development. Besides noting the impact of the authority structure on these elements, researchers have observed over-all patterns of group culture, including the group's unique system of goals, norms, beliefs, and values, as reactions to an authority structure. Sayles, for example, has set up a study of types of industrial work groups which is based on the nature of group relations to management authority, ". . . on the level of acceptance of and co-operations with management decisions, or, contrariwise, on the frequency and nature of the challenge issued by the group to management."[6]

Sayles' study included apathetic groups, erratic groups, strategic groups, and conservative groups.[7] The apathetic groups were least likely to exert concerted pressure on management. They manifested low cohesiveness and widely distributed leadership. The erratic groups behaved inconsistently toward management. "There seems to be no relation between the seriousness of their grievances (from the point of view of the employees themselves) and the intensity of their protests . . . . The groups may be exhibiting a type of 'fixation.'

[5] Barnes, Dalton, and Zaleznik, *op. cit.*, pp. 11–12.
[6] Sayles, *Behavior of Industrial Work Groups*, p. 7.
[7] *Ibid.*, pp. 8–40.

The kinds of activities they indulge in are not contrived to solve their problems. Emotional reaction to some deep frustration has blinded them to their failure to adjust their reactions to circumstances."[7a] These groups tended to feature clear-cut, autocratic leadership.

The strategic groups

. . . seemed to be shrewdly calculating pressure groups which never tired of objecting to unfavorable management decisions, seeking loopholes in existing policies and contract clauses that would redound to their benefit, and comparing their benefits with those of other departments in the plant. They demanded constant attention for their problems and had the ability to reinforce their demands by group action. The departments so classified seemed highly cohesive. The leadership consisted of a small core of highly active and influential group members, each of whom specialized in such functions as dealing with management, dealing with the union, maintaining internal unity, or taking the lead in voicing dissatisfaction."[7b]

The conservative groups were the relatively secure, powerful elite, who were relatively independent of union activities. Their jobs involved critical, relatively scarce skills. "They are self-consciously assured, successful, and relatively stable in their external relations with management as well as in their internal affairs."[7c] Their group development often had a history of cyclical moods:

Passivity—gradual rise in the feeling of being left out.
Activity—success in improving relative position.
Satisfaction with new relative position.
Passivity—and so on around the cycle.[7d]

Sayles explained the differences in these types of work groups by describing the nature of the organizational authority structure and other kinds of environmental constraints which will be taken up later in this chapter. He listed the following factors as most influential on the over-all behavior of the groups toward management:

1. Relative position on the promotion "ladders" of the plant.
2. Relative size and importance of the group.
3. Similarity of jobs within the group.
4. The degree to which their work is indispensable in the functioning of the plant or department.
5. The precision with which management can measure work load and pace for the group.[8]

[7a] *Ibid.*, p. 13.    [7b] *Ibid.*, p. 19.    [7c] *Ibid.*, p. 35.    [7d] *Ibid.*, p. 38.
[8] *Ibid.*, p. 69.

## The Communication Structure

Two aspects of the authority structure have direct relevance to communication; these are *influence* and *interaction*. The organization may be thought of as a network through which messages flow. Messages become interactions insofar as the originator's message leads to a change in the behavior of the recipient. They are influence-laden insofar as the recipient's behavior is controlled by the originator's intentions through his message. We measure interaction by observation of behavior and assessment of consequences. We impute *influence* when we compare the *intentions* to the consequences. Common experience tells us that the behavioral outcome of a message is contingent upon knowing who sent it as well as its content. In real organizations the authority structure cannot be separated from the communication structure; they become one when informal authority and communications are included in the analysis.

Experimental research on pure communications systems has yielded some interesting findings with regard to the effects of communication structure on influence patterns, productivity, and satisfaction. In experiments described by Harold J. Leavitt twenty groups of five men were assigned a uniform task.[9] The members of each group were required to communicate with each other according to one of four communications patterns; Circle, Chain, Y, or Wheel, as diagrammed in Figure 9.1.

The points on the diagrams indicate the positions occupied by the men, and the lines between positions indicate the communication channels open to them. For example, the person in the *A* position in the Circle could communicate only with persons *B* and *E*. In the Chain, *A* could communicate only with *B*. In the Wheel, *C* could communicate with all of the others, who could not communicate with each other. Communications consisted of written

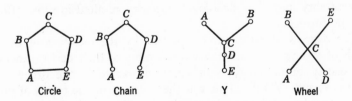

Circle        Chain        Y        Wheel

*Figure 9.1  Communication patterns.*

[9] Leavitt, "Some Effects of Certain Communication Patterns on Group Performance."

messages in the experimental groups. The groups were all assigned the same task. No authority structure was externally imposed.

The results of the experiments were analyzed in two ways. Some differences in group results could be attributed to the communication patterns. Some differences in outcomes for the individuals could be attributed to their positions within the structures. Group productivity was measured by the time taken to complete the task and by the number of errors. Although variability between groups of each type was greater than between types of groups, there were indications that the Wheel and Y groups tended to work faster than the Chain and Circle groups, and to have fewer errors. However, the Circle groups were more likely than the others to correct their errors. Ranking the groups on the number of messages required to complete the tasks, from maximum to minimum, yielded the ordering Circle, Chain, Y, and Wheel.

The members' perceptions of the existence and clarity of an authority structure (their answers to the questions, "Did your group have a leader? If so, who?") *increased* in the order Circle, Chain, Y, and Wheel. Members of the Wheel groups were more likely to perceive some organization in their groups than were members of the other kinds of groups. In answer to another question, members of Circle groups tended to emphasize a need for their groups to "get organized" and work out a "system."

One characteristic of the communication patterns is the degree to which they feature a clear, unambiguous, central position. In the Circle there is no clear central position. In the Chain, position $C$, and to a lesser extent $B$ and $D$, provide potential communication centers, while positions $A$ and $E$ are clearly peripheral. Position $C$ is clearly central in the Y and the Wheel.

Clear centrality indicated clearly perceived authority; the existence of a communications center made it likely that the position would also become a *decision* center. Thus, authority in decision making would come to be located in the central position. This combination of centrality and clear decisional authority resulted in more effective task performance.

The degrees of satisfaction expressed by the members of the four kinds of groups were in *inverse* relationship to their performances and the clarity of authority; satisfaction *decreased* in the order Circle, Chain, Y, and Wheel. This was the ordering of the types, of course, on the number of messages transmitted. That is, satisfaction stemmed from amount of communication generated.

The average enjoyment of the job expressed by each position in

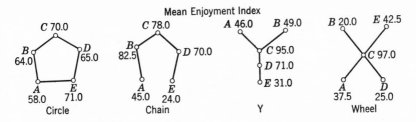

*Figure 9.2  Enjoyment of the job, by positions in communication structures.*

each of the communication structures is shown in Figure 9.2.   The index ranges from 0 for low enjoyment to 100 for high enjoyment.

Although the enjoyment of work was higher, on the average, for members of Circle groups, the enjoyment of persons in *central positions* in the other groups was higher than for *any* position in the Circle groups.   Furthermore, the more central the position was in its structure, the greater the enjoyment: *C* was more central in the Wheel than in the Y, more central in the Y than in the Chain, and more central in the Chain than in the Circle.   Persons in peripheral positions in the Chain (*A* and *E*), the Y (*A*, *B*, and *E*), and the Wheel (*A*, *B*, *D*, and *E*) expressed less enjoyment with their jobs than persons in any position in the Circle groups.   Leavitt summarized, ". . . it is our feeling that centrality determines behavior by limiting independence of action, thus producing differences in activity, accuracy, satisfaction, leadership, recognition of pattern, and other behavioral characteristics."[10]

The research studies on authority structure dealt with some of the same factors involved in communications research.   Opportunity for interaction and mutual influence concerns communications as readily as authority.   Autonomy is related to centrality in communications networks; that is, peripheral positions are in dependent relationships to the other positions, and thus are characterized by a lesser degree of autonomy.   When pure communications networks are free of any imposed authority structure, there are strong tendencies for the relationships between positions to determine the authority structure, and, along with it, ranges of probable performances and sentiments toward the work.   However, this kind of "natural" positional authority is not to be confused with arbitrarily imposed positional authority.   In the latter, the social meaning of the position is meant to carry authority with it, regardless of its place in the communication network.

[10] *Ibid.*, 562.

Examples of the distinction between natural positional authority and arbitrarily imposed authority are found in the Grayson Company and the Denver Transportation Company case studies.[11] In both, the technology required a central message center. The telephone service and installation work in the Grayson case revolved around a test group, which handled telephone messages to and from field workmen. This central group had more frequent interaction and more influence on the field workmen's activities than their formal foreman, who rarely saw the field workmen. In the Denver Transportation case, the taxi and bus dispatchers, who processed communications from customers to drivers, were in the central position of the communication network. In the formal organization, these dispatchers reported to supervisors. There was some ambiguity among drivers, dispatchers, and supervisors as to the relative statuses of the dispatchers' and supervisors' positions.

With this distinction between "natural" and "arbitrary" authority in mind, it becomes clear that one important aspect in the study of organizations and groups is the degree to which arbitrary authority positions coincide with the natural authority in the formal communication structure. When discrepancies exist, *informal* authority and communications systems are likely to develop to bring both kinds of authority into closer correspondence if the group is to operate effectively. A similar prediction can be made with respect to informal remedies for imbalances between formally prescribed sources of authority. Existing authority and communications systems within an organization provide sets of constraints and unique problems for the groups working in it. They establish lines around which many of the groups' social elaborations, norms, and rituals form; and in some cases they provide irritants which the groups' processes would tend to contain, neutralize, or modify. The technology of the groups' task provides still another set of influences which constrain and direct group development.

## Technology

The term "technology" refers to the specific ways in which work operations perform a task, including how tools, work methods, time, and space constrain, enable, and direct social interaction. The discussion will be divided into two parts: (1) physical arrangements of

[11] Lawrence et al., *Organizational Behavior and Administration*, pp. 528 ff., 808 ff.

time and space, and (2) functional interdependence between work operations. The first part implies that face-to-face interaction is the basic element of social processes and that the individuals must be together at the same time in the same place for face-to-face interaction to occur. The second implies that work methods, tools, and technical procedures tend to require certain forms of social interaction as well as interdependence among workers.

*Physical Arrangements: Time and Space.* Feelings of identity tend to be strongly rooted in spatial arrangements. The family becomes identified with its physical home. Members of the family become identified with the particular rooms within the home. Even the lower animals stake out their personal and group space limits.[12] Possession and privacy often have dimensions of time as well as space. Bedrooms become more private at night, more public during the day. The family's living space expands out of the house during the summer, retracts inward during the winter. Daily, weekly, and seasonal rhythms determine how particular areas become invested with particular social meanings at particular times. Thus, one of the effects of spatial and temporal arrangements is to provide or prevent a basis for psychological identification, both for individuals and for groups.

A second effect of the physical arrangements has to do with constraining or enabling interaction, as well as physically channeling communication processes. It is easier for people to talk to each other when they are close to each other in space than when they are separated. Walls and other physical barriers tend to prevent interaction. Noise makes it difficult to talk in a normal tone of voice. People will have a greater tendency to talk to others located near them than to others located at a distance. The location of a work position in relation to aisles and doorways will affect the opportunity of its occupant to interact with people walking through the area or coming into the area.

The degree to which people are visible to each other tends to determine feelings of inclusion or exclusion and privacy or publicity. Sound barriers tend to have similar effects. The direction that a worker faces, if uniform, usually defines a "front" and a "rear" for the area. Children in school rooms, as well as their parents, become conscious of the possible social meanings of the "front of the room" and the "rear of the room." If work positions face toward a central location, being "in the center of things" spatially may have social

---

[12] Hall, *The Silent Language*, pp. 146–164.

implications as we noted in the communications experiments. School children used to be punished by standing in a corner of the schoolroom, facing away from the class, visibly excluded.

Some of the effects of time on social development are obvious, others are more subtle. Not only do people have to be near each other in order to interact, they also must be there at the same time. Shift workers do not have the opportunity to interact with workers on other shifts, even though they may work at the same work places. When groups at several levels in an organization are compared, significant differences may be found in the amount of time they spend together. For example, a factory work group would normally be together over the entire 40-hour working week, while certain management groups (committees and task groups) would be together only one or two hours during each working week. More subtly, conflict over roles arises out of membership in many groups. This dilemma is expressed by the frequency with which the individual meets with each of the groups to which he belongs, the different amounts of time he spends with each, and the sequence in which he encounters them. Similarly, the relationship between particular members and a group may be expressed by their seniority in the group. And the life of the group itself can be measured and compared in terms of time, depending on whether its tasks have fixed beginnings and ends, or run continuously.

Some selected research findings on the effects of spatial and temporal arrangements on group development will help illuminate the foregoing points. An early study of an M.I.T. housing development by Festinger, Schachter, and Back examined the relationship between the location of couples' apartments in standard buildings in Westgate West and the friendship choices of the couples.[13] There were five apartments in a row on each of the two floors of the buildings. Each apartment was entered from a common front porch or balcony. The second floor apartments were reached by two stairways running from near the front doors of the end apartments on the first floor up to the second-floor balcony. Three sets of findings are of interest:

1. Couples were more likely to choose as friends others who lived in apartments adjacent to their own; the closer they lived to each other, the more likely that they would become friends.

[13] Festinger, Schachter, and Back, *Social Pressures in Informal Groups*, pp. 33–59. Also discussed in Homans, *Social Behavior: Its Elementary Forms*, pp. 208–214.

2. Couples who lived in the apartments which were in the center of each floor were more likely to be chosen as friends than couples in the other positions; centrality (lowest average distance to all other apartments on the same floor) was found to be associated with receiving friendship choices.

3. First floor couples living at the ends, near the stairways going up to the second floor, tended to make more friendship choices of second floor couples than did the occupants of the three middle positions on the first floor, and were more likely to receive choices from second floor couples than were the occupants of the middle positions; the greater the likelihood that "paths would cross," the greater the likelihood of friendship choices.

These findings establish a tie between spatial relationships and sentiments of liking among people. The binding factor is the opportunities for interaction as determined by the spatial arrangements. In contrast to the communication experiments, in which communication was required in order for the groups to perform the assigned task, the housing development study involved voluntary activities, interactions, and sentiments; no external authority required the residents to share activities, interact, or like one another. These patterns were the results of predispositions to social activity brought into the housing development by the couples from their wider cultural and personal experiences, constrained and activated by the spatial arrangements of the buildings in which they lived.

Two studies of work groups point out the significance of work place layout and the application of social values to it. In the Bank Wiring Observation Room of the Western Electric studies, there was a clear social differentiation between the *front* of the room and the *back* of the room.[14] The fixtures holding the work on the work benches were tilted upward so that the natural work position involved facing in one direction.[15] Since work benches paralleled each other in rows, and all fixtures faced the same direction, the men faced the same direction as they worked. Two distinct subgroups developed in the room: " 'The group in front' and 'the group in back' were common terms of designation among the workers themselves."[16] The group in front was considered to be a "better," "superior," or higher-status group than the one in back. In Zaleznik's study of a machine shop, high-status machinists were located at benches at the front of the room, while lower-status operators occupied the rear.[17]

[14] Roethlisberger and Dickson, *Management and the Worker,* pp. 392 ff.
[15] *Ibid.*
[16] *Ibid.,* p. 508.
[17] Zaleznik, *Worker Satisfaction and Development,* pp. 14 ff.

Thus, physical distance and barriers are not the only socially relevant aspects of spatial arrangements; the direction people face or where they are positioned in relation to each other and to significant physical objects also determine interaction opportunities, social evaluation, and the social definition of the interpersonal situation.

A study of social relations and satisfactions on an assembly line points to the relative instability of the specific spatial arrangements for group development:

. . . . The particular assembly line we have in mind consisted of thirty-five workers stationed at a moving belt doing simple wiring and soldering operations.

From one point of view, workers on this mechanized assembly line were interdependent to a very high degree. Any one operator failing to work within the allowed time cycle could "gum up" the entire line. Division of labor as a work organization concept had been carried out to almost an ultimate, since each operator on the line added to the component just a little more than the worker preceding her. Yet, the job required absolutely no interaction between workers. On the assumption of perfect work flow, each unit moved from one operator's position to the next. Each operation, while vital to the whole product, was self-contained. In addition, assuming perfection, there was no need for interaction with the group leader since ten-minute rest periods were allowed in the morning and afternoon, besides a half-hour lunch period, which, according to plan, appeared adequate for personal needs.

Besides the job requiring no interaction, work organization also limited interaction quite rigidly. An operator could talk easily only with workers on her immediate right and left. From the point of view of any one worker, her only possible spontaneous group during working hours consisted of two workers and herself, or a group of three. A threesome, however, tends to make a very unstable group because of the likelihood of pairing. It is easy, therefore, for some operators at least to find themselves socially isolated. A simple diagram will clarify the grouping arrangements feasible with limited interaction on the assembly line.

Looking at operators A to H on an assembly line such as we have described, possible groupings of three are indicated by the circles with the dotted lines. Thus, ABC, BCD, CDE, DEF, and so on could form into a group. Focusing on operator E as an example, E is involved in three clusters of three individuals, CDE, DEF, and EFG. In none of these clusters is it convenient for a threesome to engage in cross conversation. In cluster DEF, E can easily talk with D or F, but D and F can converse directly only by talking "around" E. If two operators develop an affinity for each other, they are likely to be adjacent to each other so that pairing off would take place as indicated by our solid line circles around AB, CD, and FC. E is therefore isolated, as may happen to any of the operators.

Groupings on an Assembly Line

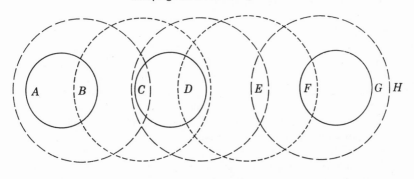

(Straight line: mechanized conveyor)

The above analysis of a limited interaction pattern on an assembly line assumed conditions of perfect technical operation. Once something goes wrong, there is considerable interaction, but under conditions of extreme tension and anxiety. On this particular assembly line, some operators were unable to keep pace with the conveyor. The need for shutting down the conveyor became the major content of increased interaction among workers and their supervisor. As the problem persisted, tensions mounted and, in one case, an operator broke down and had to leave the belt.[18] Under conditions fraught with negative feelings and hostility, interaction was actually harmful and contributed further to feelings of anxiety.[19]

Where technological organization of work acts as a constraint on a group because of severe limitations on interaction, the burden for developing an effective group falls heavily upon supervisors. They become the centers of communication and must exercise a high degree of skill to relate workers to each other where in other technical settings workers can develop their relationships on their own.

Another study of mass production workers [by Walker and Guest], in an automobile assembly plant, supports the importance of technology as it affects social organization of work groups.[20] A sample group of 180 workers holding various jobs in the plant were interviewed to determine the sources of satisfaction and dissatisfaction with the job. The authors concluded through examination of qualitative comments in the interviews that social interaction was important to the men. The authors summarize their conclusions from interview data as follows:[21]

(1) Slightly less than half of the workers had frequent social interaction with others near them. Slightly more than half had infrequent social interaction.

[18] Zaleznik, *Foreman Training in a Growing Enterprise*, Ch. VIII. [19] Whyte, Leadership and Group Participation. [20] Walker and Guest, *The Man on the Assembly Line.* [21] *Ibid.*, pp. 79–80.

(2) Factors such as noise, pace, and character of the work often restricted men from talking as freely as they might otherwise have done. These limitations were consciously recognized by the workers as a source of frustration.

(3) The nature of the assembly line process determined the functional relationships of workers and thus had a crucial bearing on their social groupings. The largest number of men, including most of those on the main conveyor line, were related to each other through proximity and not through interdependent function. *Each man had a slightly different group from that of the man next to him. Few were conscious of being members of any identifiable social group.*[22]

(4) In a few cases men worked in almost complete isolation. Such workers gave social isolation as an important reason for not liking the job.

(5) In some areas, usually not on a moving line, men worked in teams. Geographically they were apart from other operations. Each man was functionally dependent upon his partner or his teammates and social interaction was virtually constant. Jobs were usually rotated within the group. According to the qualitative comments, most of the men were favorably aware of the fact that they constituted a work team.

(6) In certain instances, even on the moving conveyor, a group consciousness was found among those workers who were able to move into different operations in their section from time to time. This was true of utility men, some repairmen, and some workers whose foremen allowed them to rotate their jobs throughout a given section. Such workers named these features as desirable characteristics of their jobs.

(7) The ultimate value and importance of the more satisfying kinds of social relationships were demonstrated by the qualitative comments. In discussing the amount of talking they did, the isolates were the most vehemently negative. The largest group, those working side by side but independently, were more likely to refer to their social relations in the negative terms of how they would feel were they not able to talk and of the effects of interaction in counteracting other job tensions. In marked contrast, those who were members of true teams spoke of their group interaction in positive and cheerful terms.[23]

*Functional Interdependence.* Certain patterns of social interaction, specializations of role, and patterns of dependency are essential to the performance of particular tasks. These conditions have to be met if the task is to be completed. In addition, job content is subject to social evaluation. Jobs become invested with value derived from the organizational system and the wider culture. For example, some groups identify particular jobs as "clean" work or "dirty" work, and

---

[22] Italics added by Zaleznik.
[23] Zaleznik, *Worker Satisfaction and Development*, pp. 120–123.

tend to identify holders of these jobs as "clean" or "dirty" persons; the expression "white-collar job" carries the connation of "clean" work. The potentials for identifying a job with the product or service, and the ultimate user or client, become additional bases for social evaluation. These evaluations, derived from both organizational and cultural standards, in turn feed back on task-required interaction, specialization, and dependency to dilute technical considerations with social.

Because of the relative clarity and simplicity of the jobs and the physical arrangements of the Bank Wiring Observation Room, the bank wiring task at the heart of the room's social structure illustrates very well how the conditions intrinsic to the task bear on group development.

## RELATIONS BETWEEN NONSUPERVISORY OCCUPATIONAL GROUPS

The first question the investigators asked was this: There are four occupational groups in the department: wiremen, soldermen, inspectors, and trucker. From a purely technical standpoint the members of these groups are all "operators,"[24] that is, they are of nonsupervisory rank. Are they differentiated only from the standpoint of the jobs they perform; or have these technical divisions of labor become the basis of a social stratification? Do workmen in one group look upon themselves as superior or inferior to workmen in another group and, if so, how is this social distinction manifested? In order to answer this question, similarities in the behavior of different people in each occupational group, which could be said to be independent of the personalities involved, were noted. Wiremen as a group were considered in relation to soldermen as a group, and so on.

## CONNECTOR WIREMEN IN RELATION TO SELECTOR WIREMEN

The wiremen in the department worked upon two types of equipment, one type called "connectors," the other "selectors." The technique of wiring was exactly the same for both types. The only differences, apart from the names, were (1) that a connector equipment might be and usually was eleven banks along, whereas a selector equipment was never more than ten, and (2) that a connector fixture weighed only about half as much as a selector fixture. In the observation room $W_7$, $W_8$, and $W_9$ ordinarily worked on selectors, and the other operators worked on connectors.

Some of the wiremen interviewed in the regular department expressed a preference for connector wiring. The reasons given usually related to the

[23a] From Roethlisberger and Dickson, op. cit., pp. 495–500.
[24] This word was commonly used at Hawthorne to designate employees of nonsupervisory status. [Ibid., pp. 11–12.]

lightness of the fixture. In reality, however, the weight of the fixture was inconsequential. The fixtures were easily lifted, and only two of them had to be carried during an average day. The effort required was scarcely great enough to be felt by healthy young men who frequently engaged in strenuous sports after work. This explanation, therefore, could hardly be taken as the reason for their preference. Further study revealed the real significance of the preference for connector wiring. In the department the connector wiremen were all placed together toward the front of the room, the direction the men faced while working, and the selector wiremen were located back of them. They were, therefore, spatially arranged in such a way as to suggest that the connector wiremen, since they were in front, were somewhat superior to those to whom their backs were turned. From talking to the supervisors and some of the wiremen the investigators learned that the newer members of the wiring group and some of the slower ones were located "in back." As these men "in back" acquired proficiency and new men were added, they were moved forward. Inasmuch as increases in efficiency were usually rewarded by increases in hourly rates, this meant that the people who were moving forward spatially were also moving upward socially. An individual's location roughly reflected his relative standing in efficiency, earnings, and the esteem of his supervisors. The connector wiremen represented the elite. Indeed, some of the wiremen looked upon "going on connectors" as a promotion even if their hourly rates were not changed. Conversely, some of the connector wiremen felt injured if they were "put back on selectors" and regarded such a change as a demotion even though their hourly rates were not changed. Here, then, a minor technical distinction had become so elaborated that it provided a basis upon which the wiremen were in some measure socially differentiated.

## WIREMEN IN RELATION TO SOLDERMEN

The position of wireman was regarded in the department as somewhat superior to that of solderman. Beginners were usually started as soldermen, and from soldering they passed on to wiring. The change in job usually accompanied by an increase in hourly rate. This, together with the fact that the wireman's job required more specialized abilities than that of the solderman, gave the wiremen a slightly higher status in the department, which was expressed in numerous ways, some of which will be described below.

One of the most frequent ways in which the wiremen demonstrated their superior standing was in job trading. Theoretically, there was supposed to be no job trading. Wiremen were supposed to wire and soldermen were supposed to solder. The purpose of this rule was, of course, to promote efficiency through specialization. In spite of the rule, however, the men did trade jobs. The important point here is that in practically every case the request for trading originated with a wireman and the soldermen almost always traded without protest. Sometimes the wiremen presented their requests to trade to the group chief but more frequently they did not. Though occasionally the soldermen protested over trading, they usually gave in. In other words, the wiremen ordered and the soldermen obeyed.

In the task of getting lunches for the group the difference of status between wiremen and soldermen was apparent. It was common practice in the department for one of the men to go out to one of the near-by lunch counters and get lunches for those in the department who wanted them. This practice prevented congestion at the lunch counters, and it saved the people in the department a great deal of trouble. The person who got the lunches was called the "lunch boy," even though he was a grown man and was not assigned the duties of an office boy. When the men were moved to the observation room, they continued with this practice until the regular "lunch boy" was transferred. The group chief, after announcing the transfer, asked if anyone in the group wanted to take over the job. After some discussion $S_1$ said that he would. On the first day the group chief went with $S_1$ to assist him. On the second day, however, the group chief refused to go, saying that there was no use in wasting two men's time. As long as the group chief lent his prestige to the task the group said nothing, but as soon as the solderman had to go alone they started "kidding" him. $S_1$ kept on getting the lunches for about a week, and then $S_4$ started getting them as a regular part of his job. Toward the end of the study, when $S_4$ was moved out to the department, the job reverted to $S_1$. He kept the job until the group chief himself took it over. The group chief, however, was careful to explain to the observer that he was not actually getting the lunches but merely taking the orders and giving them to a man in the department. He apparently felt that the job was a bit below his dignity. In the observer's record there was no instance of a wireman's getting the lunches. One day $W_1$ went around and took the orders for lunches and collected the money, but when he had done so he turned the orders over to $S_1$. As soon as $W_1$ started taking the orders, $I_1$ shouted, "Look who's getting the lunches today," which may be taken as an indication that it was an unusual thing for a wireman to do. $W_1$ continued taking the orders for some time, but $S_1$ always bought the food and brought it back to the room.

The following illustration also serves to show that the wiremen felt themselves a little superior.

The section chief came in and found $S_1$ soldering without goggles. He told $S_1$ to stop until he put them on. $S_1$ had mislaid them and spent about five minutes looking for them. He grumbled about having to wear goggles as he looked for them.

$S_1$: I don't know where the hell those glasses are. I suppose one of you guys hid them. There ain't no sense to wearing them anyway. I soldered for four years before they ever thought of glasses. Now you've gotta keep them on. There ain't no solder gonna splash in a fellow's eye. That's just the damn fool notion somebody's got. I've gotta go around here all day in a fog just because some damn fool wants us to wear goggles.

sc: Never mind why you've got to wear them, just get them and put them on.

w₂: I worked on a job for three years where I had to wear goggles and it didn't kill me.

s₁: Yes,, and I suppose you wore them all the time.

w₂: Well maybe I didn't, but it didn't hurt me to wear them when I had to. There's one thing you have to remember, S₁. Do you hear? Don't do as I do—do as I say. Get that?

s₁: Why don't you guys wear glasses when you fix repairs?

w₃: We don't have to put them on for that little bit of soldering, but you're a solderman. You've got to wear them.

s₁: Aw, you guys are all a bunch of damn fools.

## WIREMEN AND SOLDERMEN IN RELATION TO THE TRUCKER

The trucker's job was to keep the group supplied with piece parts and to remove completed equipments from the room. Before loading the completed units on his truck, which was pushed by hand, he stamped each one with an identification number, the purpose of which was to enable the Inspection Branch to trace the work back to the inspector who had passed upon it.

During the first few weeks nothing happened to indicate the relation the trucker had with the group. However, when the men felt more at ease in the presence of the observer, certain events began to occur which seemed to reflect the trucker-operator relation. For example, the group started referring to the trucker as a gigolo and as "Goofy." They annoyed him in numerous small ways: by spitting on the place where the identification number was supposed to be stamped, by jogging his arm just as he was about to affix the stamp, by holding the truck when he tried to push it out of the room, or by tickling him in the ribs while he was lifting an equipment onto the truck. That these incidents reflected a relation between occupational groups and not special personal relations is attested to by the fact that most of the wiremen and soldermen behaved in the same way toward the trucker, and by the fact that they displayed the same attitude toward a second trucker who replaced the first one about the middle of the study. Their general attitude was independent of the personalities involved.

## WIREMEN AND SOLDERMEN IN RELATION TO THE INSPECTORS

The inspectors belonged to an outside organization, the Inspection Branch. They reported to a different set of supervisors, were paid on an hourly basis, and on the whole had more education than the men whose work they inspected. Their function as inspectors gave them a superordinate position to the operators. This was manifested in many ways. For example, when the wiremen and soldermen came to be interviewed they invariably appeared in their shirt sleeves, or, if it were chilly, in sweaters. The inspectors, however, always came dressed in coats and vests. The significance of this cannot be understood without knowing something about the subtle distinctions in dress in the Operating Branch. The foreman and his assistant usually wore ordinary business suits with coats and vests, the vest being optional. The section chiefs and group chiefs usually wore vests but not coats. Their shirts were usually white, and they wore neckties. Operators as a rule wore neither coats nor vests. They might wear white shirts and a necktie, but ordinarily left their shirts open at the throat, or if they wore a tie, the knot was not pulled up tightly around the neck and the collar button was usually left unfastened. This was the general pattern. There were many exceptions and deviations from it, but the fact remains that dress did have some social significance. Thus, the fact that the inspectors wore coats and vests when they came to be interviewed might be taken as a reflection of their social status in the company.

The inspectors were considered outsiders, and this was indicated in many ways other than by the fact that they did not report to the Operating Branch supervisors. That they did not trade jobs or go for lunches was evidence of this relation between the operators and the inspectors, but perhaps the best demonstration of it was in the matter of control over the windows. The wiremen who were situated on the side of the room facing the court took a proprietary interest in the windows opposite their workbenches. If $W_6$, for example, wanted the window open, he opened it even though other people protested. The people who were farthest removed from the windows protested a great deal, because the draft was thrown on their side of the room. Endless controversy resulted. The point to be brought out here is that an inspector entered into one of these controversies only on one occasion, and it was this one occasion which demonstrated clearly the relation between operators and inspectors. The inspector involved was a man who was substituting for $I_3$. He complained that the room was cold. Someone had turned the heat off and one of the windows was open. Since his complaint was unheeded, he walked over to close the window. As he was about to release the chain which held it open, $W_9$ ordered him to leave it open and seized the chain. The inspector then tried to turn on the heat, but $W_9$ scuffled with him and finally took the handle off the valve. During all this the other men lent $W_9$ their verbal support. Finally, after the operators had convinced the inspector that he had no jurisdiction over the window and he had given up, one of the soldermen walked over and closed the window. The inspector thanked him, and the controversy ended. Wiremen and soldermen might fix the windows if they pleased, but the inspectors could not do so without getting into trouble. The other inspectors probably sensed the situation and never attempted to overstep.

## SOCIAL STRATIFICATION IN THE OBSERVATION GROUP

The foregoing analysis of the relations among the occupational groups in the observation room shows that social significance did attach to the occupations the several groups performed. An ordering process had taken place in the organization of the human element in the department, and social significance had become attached to the various tasks. From an informal standpoint, then, the observation group was differentiated into five gradations, ranging from highest to lowest in the following order: inspectors, connector wiremen, selector wiremen, soldermen, and trucker.[25]

*Identification with Technical Occupations, Products, and Users.* The degree to which the group's product is visible, concrete, and clearly identifiable provides another aspect of technology as it relates to group development. In an unpublished study of an engineering department, one of the most interesting differentiating factors among the engineers was the kind of objects which they held in their hands and talked about during the course of their daily work. The department contained three subdepartments consisting of mechanical, electrical, and control systems engineers whose tasks were identified by these specialities. All three kinds of engineers repeatedly handled blueprints, slide rules, pencils, and reference books, common badges of the engineering trade. However, the subdepartments' "products" differed substantially in concreteness and visibility as well as physical size and dollar value. The mechanical engineers, who could pick up, handle, and manipulate what they produced, were commonly seen carrying these devices in their hands. In contrast, the electrical engineers could not carry or see their product, electrical circuits in the abstract; it was carried in one's head. *Technicians* handled wires and electrical components, and although electrical engineers occasionally got their fingers into the wires and boxes, the "hardware" was visible mainly in the technicians' work areas. For the control systems engineers, photographs of the control centers they installed were the symbols of their "product." Hence physical size, dollar value, and relative concreteness or abstractness of the product became bases for social differentiation. In addition, the relative timeliness or fashionability of the function mattered; mechanical engineer-

[25] *Ibid.*, pp. 495–500.

ing skills were almost "obsolete," electrical and electronic engineering were currently in fashion but giving way to solid-state physics, and systems engineering was ascending. One old-timer among the mechanical engineers referred to himself as a "plumber" in relation to the other specialized engineering functions in vogue. Much of the banter and kidding among engineering groups had to do with relative rankings. Mechanical engineering was clearly the lowest at the time, but there was still some uncertainty about the comparison between systems and electrical engineering.

Among the differences which distinguished these groups was the degree to which the members interacted with outsiders and how far away the outsiders were located. The mechanical engineers interacted with some outsiders, mainly from other departments in the company. The electrical engineers interacted with more outsiders from other company departments and, in addition, with some people from outside the plant. The control systems engineers interacted with even more in-company outsiders and were especially involved in relations with people outside the plant. In addition to evaluating "how far" outside the department an individual was located, the social system apparently differentiated among kinds of outsiders: company salesmen, suppliers' salesmen, suppliers' insiders, customers' buyers, customers' insiders, and professional colleagues. Personal identification with the user of the group's product was important; one symbol of this identification was a visit by an engineer to a customer's plant.

Excerpts from the researcher's notes highlight some of the engineers' identifications related to their occupation, their work, their products, and contacts with outsiders.

In their talk together, Bob described to the researcher how the Control Systems Engineering department operated; what kind of work the group did and how it was organized. Bob was a special assistant to the department supervisor, Sam. Bob was talking about the engineers' contacts with customers, their trips into the field to follow-up problems on new systems installations, when the researcher asked:

RESEARCHER: Have you done much traveling yourself?

BOB: Oh, yes, quite a bit. Right now I'm involved in technical society activities. This is taking about 10 per cent of my time now, and I expect more later. I'm on the technical committee of the AIEE,[26] and a committee on standards with the ISA.[27] I make about six field trips per year on this work.

[26] AIEE: American Institute of Electrical Engineers.
[27] ISA: Instrument Society of America.

RESEARCHER: This is for the company?

BOB: Oh, yes. I'm a member representative of [the company]. The company assigns people to committees. For example, the AIEE has committees on recording, control, instrumentation, and so forth. Now, for example, I'm on this committee with ISA that's working on standardizing wiring specifications for instrument installations in hazardous areas. You see, we're working on this in conjunction with revisions in the National Electric Code. . . .

RESEARCHER: I take it this—being appointed to technical society committees by the company—is sort of an honor?

BOB: Yes, it is. You've got to show some ability and potential. . . .

Peter worked in Sam's department, Control Systems Engineering. Sam had his department organized into project groups. The heads of these groups were called project engineers, the 4 to 6 men under each of them were called job engineers. Peter worked under George, a project engineer.

RESEARCHER: Are all of the men working in [your department] engineers?[28]

PETER: Well, I'm not—I'm not a graduate engineer—there are about four of us who aren't graduate engineers. So I really don't know, I don't know what we are.

You know, when I fill out an application, like to start a charge account or something like that, I don't know what to answer when they ask "occupation." They don't really let us know what we are. I have asked Pat and Tom,[29] but I didn't get any satisfaction. Tom said, "Well, you're doing engineering work, aren't you?" But if I put "engineer" down as my occupation on an application, and it got back to the company, I don't know if they'd back me up or maybe say that I'm not really an engineer. I want to be honest when I tell people what I do.

You know, a couple months ago all of us filled out applications for registering as professional engineers.[30] That cost $15, and as far as I know, it was probably a waste for me. But on the application they required that I have some registered engineers say that I was doing engineering work, and I saw several of our registered professional engineers and they all said that I was. They didn't even hesitate. But I don't know. I doubt whether I'll be accepted. Now I just have to wait.

RESEARCHER: How long does it take?

[28] The researcher knew that some engineering departments in the company had a job category of technician, as well as engineer.

[29] Tom was administrative assistant to Pat, who was superintendent over all three engineering departments. He kept salary and promotion records on the engineers in Pat's departments.

[30] This referred to the state's procedures for registering professional engineers and surveyors. Registered engineers could use official seals on their engineering documents. This was required on engineering work involving public safety and certain kinds of contracts.

PETER: That's the thing. It can take a long time. So you're not really sure. You just wait. And if you're not accepted, the $15 is just wasted.

RESEARCHER: Well, Peter, I hope you're accepted. . . .

PETER: Boy, I hope so—it sure would make a big difference. . . .

At about 11:55 one morning, just before the engineers were to go to lunch, Peter was standing at his desk handling a stack of fresh green money. He was surrounded by two "co-ops"[31] and a few of the girls who worked in the department. They were kidding Peter about the money. He laughed back and explained that the money was for airline tickets for a trip he was taking that afternoon.

At about 12:55, just before the "back-to-work" whistle was to sound, Peter was at his desk dressed in a suit and tie, in contrast to the slacks and sport shirt he wore that morning. Most engineers and some of the supervisors regularly wore sport shirts on the job. A group again formed around him, and kidding banter was exchanged. Peter was going to the airport directly from the company early in the afternoon.

About a week later, the researcher saw Peter at his desk and stopped by. He said, "Hello," and asked, "Say, how was your trip down South? Hot down there?"

PETER: Oh, it wasn't bad.

RESEARCHER: How long were you down there?

PETER: Oh, let's see—we left Wednesday and got back here Friday.

RESEARCHER: Where was that, again?

PETER: [Industrial City], North Carolina.

RESEARCHER: Do you get out like that often?

PETER: Oh no: Actually, once in a dog's age. Last time was a long time ago, down to New Jersey. There I had to do work. We installed a. . . .

RESEARCHER: *(Interrupting—laughs.)* Do *work?* You mean you usually. . . .

PETER: *(Interrupting—laughs.)* Oh, I mean I had to actually install a new instrument on a control board and change the diagram. They had two instruments at a certain place on the control board and wanted three. I had to move the two over to make room for the third. We made a subpanel for the three here and I took it down there with me. I had to cut out the panel around the two instruments and put back the subpanel with all three instruments. Then I had to erase and change the diagram— you know, it's painted on plastic. . . . But we rarely get to go out on trips. . . .

RESEARCHER: What did you do on the North Carolina job?

PETER: No work, just engineering.

At this point, the researcher and Peter joked about his distinction between engineering and work.

[31] "Co-ops" were students of engineering in a cooperative program with a university. They alternated periods of about 10 weeks each between working in industry and studying at the university.

RESEARCHER: Was this engineering on something before entering an order?

PETER: No, we already had the order. This is it here (points to a blueprint on his desk.) There were just some questions before I could go ahead with the job.

RESEARCHER: Do some people get to go out more than others?

PETER: No, except George.[32] He's a project engineer and has a lot of that kind of thing. Of course, we're getting more and more of it.

RESEARCHER: I imagine it feels pretty good to get out of here once in a while.

PETER: Oh, yes! You see, the relation of it is—well, it shows they deem you able to do something, you're of some importance—you really get a boost out of it after plugging along—not being given credit . . . after all, unless you drive your own car, it costs the company money. . . .

RESEARCHER: Does anything else happen in your day-to-day work that gives you a boost like that?

PETER: Oh, yes—but sometimes the other way, too. But like the other day (points to a stack of papers and blueprints), some engineers from this customer came in. I was called over to talk with them.[33] At least they recognize that you are good enough to do something. Yes, that makes you feel good. . . .

These data indicate some of the social values attached to various activities required by the technology of the engineering jobs and to the relative rankings of the different kinds of engineering groups and their activities. In Bob's case, trips away from the plant were identified with important professional society activities. These were clearly differentiated from trips which involved calling on a customer. Peter pointed out that outside contacts with customers could involve "work" —mechanical operations with the hands—or "engineering," which consisted of manipulating symbols and interpersonal communication, in contrast to working with things. Peter was especially sensitive to occupational identity, since he had not attended engineering school and lacked the status of "real" engineer, even though much of the work he did was the same as that done by "real" engineers. He clearly differentiated between "engineering," which was what engineers did, and "work," which was the job of technicians.

The data also referred to symbols important for social differentiation in the department. Registered professional engineers had official seals which they embossed on the corners of blueprints for projects

[32] George was the head of Peter's project group.

[33] The researcher had seen the two men, dressed in business suits, carrying brief cases, come into the department and talk to Sam. Sam took them over to Peter and introduced them to him. Then Sam left the three and returned to his own desk.

involving governmental agencies or governmental regulations. The clothing Peter wore the afternoon of his trip clearly identified that he was going outside the company on business. Similarly, the clothing worn, and the brief cases carried, by the outsiders introduced to Peter by his boss, Sam, showed every one in the department that Peter was transacting important business with outsiders. This stood out boldly in the department because the engineers, including Peter, worked at desks in an open area where the engineers, co-op students, secretaries, clerical workers, and supervisors could all see each other. It is also interesting that the people who clustered around Peter to joke with him about the money in the first episode, and about his clothing in the second episode, were of lower status than he was, and he was in a position of ambiguous status himself because of his problem of occupational identity, which was a well-known issue among the engineers and technicians in the company. His status relationship to the co-op students was especially incongruent; he was doing the kind of work to which they aspired, but they were getting the formal engineering education which he lacked. In this atmosphere of status ambiguity and incongruity, the organization's formal rewards served as the basis for individual and group identities.

To Bob, the professional identification was sponsored by the company, and represented a highly selective distinction within the organization. To Peter, the actual money he held in his hand for the airline tickets represented a reward in that he was recognized and sponsored by the company as its representative to the customer. Yet, when in the supervisors' view, the actual money identified Peter as lower status within the organization because higher level people who traveled quite often would have expense accounts and would use checks or else charge the airline tickets. Once more we see the pattern whereby concrete objects (mechanical things, actual money, "work") were identified with lower-status activities, while abstract symbols (circuits, blueprints, credit cards, expense accounts, checks, "engineering") were identified with higher-status activities. These identifications became quite personal. They told individuals who they were and where they stood, in terms of the values of the wider culture, the profession, the organization, and the unique social systems of the engineering departments.

## The Organization as a System of Social Symbols

The organization may be viewed as a "hall of mirrors," reflecting to the individual various cues as to his own personal identity. These cues are transmitted through the symbolic meanings of the objects and events he encounters during his organizational life. As he shares symbolic meanings with others, his personal identity becomes bound up in the process of group identification. These cues originate in the authority system, the communication system, and the technology, and the ways in which these are organized into complex systems of symbols. They tell the individual who he is historically, how he is expected to behave, and the values to which he can and should aspire in the future.

Authority and status are symbolized in dress—military uniforms are the most explicit form of this symbolization—and also in spatial arrangements and physical objects. The size and location of an office and the quality of its physical appointments symbolize the position of its occupant in the organizational hierarchy. Similarly, communications objects (telephones, secretaries, intercommunication system transmitters and receivers, letters and reports) and communication patterns (the numbers and kinds of people with whom the person interacts, when and where the interactions take place, who initiates the interactions, and the content of the interactions) symbolize a place in the authority structure.

The solderman's goggles in the Bank Wiring Room study are a clear instance of social symbolism superimposed on the technical meaning of an object. The technical purpose of the goggles is to protect the solderman's eyes from spattering bits of solder and flux. There is no technical reasons for wiremen to wear them since their work does not involve hazards to the eyes. The goggles become a symbol of the status differentiation between wiremen and soldermen. They remind the wearer who he is: a relative newcomer and not as skilled, competent, or socially valuable as a wireman. They also remind him how to behave; the wearer of goggles will trade jobs with the wireman if he is asked by a wireman, but will not initiate the request. They further remind him of the group value system; by aspiring to become a wireman, and behaving as he should in the meantime, he may hope one day not to be socially required to wear goggles. This pattern is similar to that of the freshman "beanie" and the progression through short pants, knickers, and long pants which marked the status transitions of an American boy in the nineteen twenties. The symbol, whether it be goggles, beanies, or short pants, carries with it the identification of the social newcomer, the inferior position, and the aspiration for a more socially desirable status in the group that shares its symbolic meaning.

In Zaleznik's machine shop study, tool boxes and shop coats had special symbolic meanings:

Job title and pay rates, however, were not the only symbols of difference in job status among the men. In the machinist trade, despite tendencies toward job standardization, the tradition for expressing job status differences is through the kind of tool box the machinist owns and even the work clothes he wears. These other symbols of skill and experience were important means for differentiation in the machine shop. Axel, Ron, Steve, George, Jim, Charlie, Vito, and Marc, all being machinists, each owned a tool box filled with various hand tools and instruments and located conveniently near their most frequent work position.

There were even differences among the tool boxes owned by these eight men, differences which carried with them elements of prestige. Axel's tool box was made of wood, old and battered, and filled to capacity with about every tool imaginable to the untrained. This old tool box was fitting for Axel; it was a symbol of his many years of experience in the machinist's trade. On the other hand, Vito, who was only 25 years old, had a spanking new tool box made of metal with a fine, gray finish. Needless to say, Vito's tool box was not so well filled, nor did it contain the assortment of tools found in Axel's box.

On many occasions the men explained the significance of the tool box to this writer, particularly in how they used it to size up a new man coming into the shop. Say, for example, a new machinist is hired. He reports on Monday morning carrying his tool box. The men glance at it. If it is a large box and old looking, the presumption is that he is a person to be reckoned with in determining his position in the shop. This would be noted especially by the older and more highly skilled machinists. If the new worker, on the other hand, carries a small and obviously new tool box, the men are not likely to think that he will vie for "top dog" in the shop. The men admitted, however, that sometimes they were fooled. Ron described an incident where a newly engaged machinist had arrived at work carrying not one but two wooden tool boxes. Ron said that the foreman was very much impressed and thought they had hired a very experienced and skilled machinist. It turned out, according to Ron, that the new man was a "screw-ball" and could not do his work despite the impressive tool boxes.

Similar in nature, but not in degree, to the tool box as a symbol of a machinist's prestige was the machinist's coat—a long-sleeved, button-down, knee-length garment. A number of the men stated that it made little difference what a person wore in the shop; it was a matter of his own choosing. Those who said this, if they wore aprons, pointed out that it cost 10 cents to get a fresh apron, the standard shop apparel, from the laundry man who called every Wednesday noon, while it cost 25 cents for a coat; and if any one wanted to spend the extra 15 cents for a coat, that was his business.   To a large exent, the men stated it was up to each man to determine what he wore.   Significantly enough, however, only four men wore coats.   These men were Axel, Ron, Steve, and George.   In other words, all the machinists in the top two pay grades with one exception, Jim, differentiated themselves from the other workers by wearing a coat instead of an apron.

One day Vito got a coat in place of his usual apron.   He wore the coat for one week, but then went back to an apron.   The men still felt it was a matter of individual choice, yet, individual choice seemed to be a function of group codes and an individual's desire to conform to these codes.   While no one said as much, Vito's behavior in switching to a coat did not seem quite appropriate, given his job status in the shop.

The folklore associated with the machinists trade is important, not only to the machinists who can use it to gain in prestige, but also to the unskilled workers.   Although these codes serve initially to accentuate status differences in a shop, they provide on the other hand a goal to which low status members may aspire.   An ambitious worker like Luke had available concrete ways in which to indicate his desire to get ahead.   Luke bought a tool box and placed it on a bench.   The job did not require that he own a tool box; in fact, he and Bruce were the only two operators who owned one.   In addition, Luke rarely used the few tools in his box.   Nevertheless, the mere fact that he had acquired one was evidence of his desire to move up the ladder.   Bruce's situation was somewhat different from Luke's. Bruce had had a good deal of machine shop experience, but he was hired as an operator and had remained at that level.   His already elaborate tool box, to which he continually added new tools, served to reassure him and possibly to remind others that although he was not classified formally as a machinist and did not get a machinist's pay, he was of machinist quality.[34]

In the Bank Wiring Room study, shirt sleeves, sweaters, vests, coats, neckties, and the way in which neckties were worn (shirt collar unbuttoned and open, tie knot slipped down, as against the normal "buttoned-up" and "tie knot up" configuration), served to differentiate statuses within the plant.   In the engineering group study, shirts with ties and suit coats identified outsiders, company salesmen, and group members who were going out of the plant on business.

In addition to hierarchical and occupational symbols, symbols of masculinity and femininity are found to be socially important in some organizational settings.   In one work group, machine work was considered to be masculine and assembly work was considered to be feminine.   "Big" work pieces were masculine, "little" work pieces were feminine:

[34] Zaleznik, *Worker Satisfaction and Development,* pp. 20–22.

MARGARET MAHONEY: I love my work. It's a funny thing, it's a messy job but I'm not happy when I'm not doing it. A carpenter came to my house to fix my kitchen cabinets. He got a big kick out of it when I told him I was a finisher on an assembly job. Imagine a woman finisher! I guess he thought I worked on big assemblies, but they're only little ones . . . .

RICHARD CARLETON: . . . There is work around here that women shouldn't do. Now take Betty (a fellow worker). She's working on cams. That's the work I do. She shouldn't be doing that. You have to tighten up the vise and it takes a lot of pressure, but I've got to hand it to her, she doesn't squawk, but it certainly is man's work. All the jobs in the department except the light machine work is men's work.[35] . . .

The wider culture attributes masculinity or femininity to certain occupations and work activities on the basis of the kinds of people, male or female, who do the work as well as the active or passive content of the activities. Anne Roe reported correlations between interests in certain occupations and masculinity-femininity scores as measured by psychological tests.[36] For example, among males, high interest in the occupations of production manager, aviator, farmer, and forestry was positively correlated with masculinity, while interest in art, advertising, writing, law, teaching, the ministry, and sales tended to be negatively correlated with masculinity. Although the particular findings must be interpreted with caution, they do highlight the existence of social psychological relationships between sex roles and work activities. The cultural desire for correspondence between sex role and occupation is expressed by children through the terms "sissy" or "tomboy" which apply to incongruities between prescribed sex roles and activities.

Before the individual experiences male-female distinctions of role among his peers, in school, and on the job, he encounters them in his family. His mother and father engage in different kinds of activities with him, and there is a further distinction according to whether the child is a boy or a girl. Thus, from childhood the individual learns to associate masculinity and femininity with certain patterns of activities and relationships. Later, as he enters an organization, he finds activity and interaction patterns which are similar, in many cases, to those he had learned to identify as predominantly masculine or feminine. Production work in heavy industries tends to be identified as mas-

[35] *Margaret Mahoney*, HP 521, and *Richard Carleton*, HP 522, are Harvard Business School case material which were taken from the data collected for the *Prediction Study* (Zaleznik, et al., *op. cit.*, 1958).
[36] Roe, *The Psychology of Occupation*, p. 89.

culine; the workers often take pride in the hardships of their working conditions. In these settings, manners of dress become matters of pride: men dressed in suits, white shirts, and ties are seen as relatively effeminate when compared to the coarse, informal, masculine, and often dirty-looking attire of the worker. Similarly, other kinds of objects and processes may become invested with masculine or feminine meanings within the unique culture of an organization and within the particular subculture of a specific work group.

. . .

The authority structure, the communication structure, and the technology of an organization provide a set of activities, interactions, and physical objects to which symbolic social meanings become attached. The formal rules, procedures, organization charts, and organization manuals prescribe the meanings that are expected to result in organized, purposeful activities, interactions, and sentiments. For example, eight o'clock in the morning may mean "start working." Work itself is defined in terms of responses to symbols. The symbol may be the combinations of clothing, title, and physical location which identify a supervisor as an authority figure; it may be a blueprint or written instructions, or it may be defined in terms of symbolic operations (thinking, writing, talking, figuring) in response to other individuals' symbolic communications.

In addition to the meanings attached to the symbols by the formal organization, the same symbols and objects have other meanings that have no direct relevance to organizational purposes or practices. For example, the social meaning of the tool boxes described in Zaleznik's machine shop study was not part of the organizational design. In terms of the organization's purposes, procedures, and rules, tool boxes were technical objects with no particular meanings for status. To the workers the condition and contents of the boxes symbolized the experience and probable competence of their owners. Similarly, the solderman's goggles in the Bank Wiring Room were technical objects for the protection of the eyes of the wearers from the point of view of the formal organization's logics, but served to differentiate the status of solderman from that of wiremen within the informal social organization of the work group. In some cases, the organization may assign one set of meanings to a particular pattern of symbols, while the work group may assign a different, and even contradictory, meaning to them. Standards for operating procedures and formal performance describe how people should behave from the point of view of the formal organization, but to the informal social organization these standards may symbolize managerial ignorance, confusion, arbitrariness, and distrust, and thus lead to behaviors and sentiments very much unlike those intended by the people who formulate the official standards.

The wider culture is the source of the meaning of symbols, both the meanings upon which the formal organization is constructed and those around which the informal social organization of the work group evolves. The next section of this chapter explores some of the important ways in which the wider culture provides standards and constraints which, along with the authority, communications, and technology patterns unique to the organization, determine how the work group can develop.

## CULTURAL INFLUENCES

As we have seen, groups can be identified by their positions and functions in formal organization. They may also be identified through standards and values which derive from the wider culture. Three aspects of individual identity pervaded the discussion of the organization as a system of social symbols: the past, the present, and the future. They are reflected in the questions: (1) Where have I been? What have I accomplished? (2) How am I expected to behave in this particular situation? (3) What may I hope to become? Partial answers to these questions come from the meanings of the symbols in the individual's environment. To understand more fully the cultural sources of these meanings, we might examine how the individual learns the social meanings of symbols.

### Learning the Social Meanings of Symbols

In its broadest sense, the "social contract" implies that certain behaviors by a person in a particular social position will be followed by predictable responses by other people in particular positions within an expected period of time. This process corresponds to the sequence of events which composes behavioral reinforcement, especially since the predicted behaviors of others constitute rewards or punishments for the individual who initiates the action. For the learner, predictability means "trusting" the environment.

The learning of the social contract may be observed in the rudimentary communications of infants and children. Crying, laughing, and smiling behaviors come to be followed by certain responses from others. Asking, giving, taking away, approving, and punishing take place around certain communication symbols, both verbal and nonverbal. The earliest words learned by children may actually be learned for their social and interactional meanings rather than as the things or abstract processes to which the dictionary refers. For example, the sounds "mommy" and "daddy" have social meanings for the particular situations in which they are used by the child. These meanings go far beyond the simple identification of the mother or father as objects. The spoken word and its context may signify "help me," "give me attention," "give me love," "I need you," or a variety of meanings which bind the child and its parents together in a relationship in which behavioral responses become predictible to all concerned.

Part of this process of learning symbols includes learning to differentiate among kinds of people by categories that ultimately denote social positions. The symbolic meaning of father's behavior becomes distinct from the symbolic meaning of mother's behavior. Similarly, brothers versus sisters, family "insiders" as against "outsiders," older people as contrasted with younger people, all become distinguished by the appropriate symbols. The child learns these distinctions when, for example, he finds that his crying leads to different responses from different kinds of people.

The development of the individual can be measured by a sequence of entrances into new groups. In each of these, there are different meanings attached to certain common symbols as well as new symbols to be assimilated. From the family group the child enters groups of playmates, the nursery school group, elementary school groups, special activity groups, and so on, each demanding from him that he learn the appropriate symbols. Using inappropriate symbols results in feelings of embarrassment and being ridiculed by others.

By the time the individual enters work groups, he has already experienced ridicule and embarrassment many times, and as a newcomer may be especially sensitive to the problem of learning the appropriate symbol system. He may receive formal indoctrination into the meaning of formal organization symbols through learning rules, regulations, standard procedures, and the organization chart. At the same time, he is exposed to the informal group's indoctrination processes. Here friendship, approval, and help become the rewards, and hostility, isolation, and ridicule become the punishments as he undergoes socialization into the new group.

Excerpts from an interview with a line supervisor of an assembly group illustrates the nature of this process of learning symbols. Al, the supervisor, was talking about the entry of a new man into his supervisory group. The new man had also just joined the company.

Both men had attended Harvard Business School. Al had been in his job a few years.

AL: Can you imagine: The first time he came into the plant I went down to meet him at the door. He was carrying an *attaché case* and an *umbrella!* As we walked by the personnel office, I just grabbed them (the attache case and the umbrella) and said, "Let's just leave these here." My gosh, if he had carried them into the department, the workers would have seen them and he wouldn't have had a chance! Later, he asked me if there was anything he could do to help me on the job. I took him aside and told him it would be better if he didn't bring his attaché case and umbrella into the department.

The newcomer's expectations of what the job would be like were apparently conditioned by his contacts with "downtown office" people, both during his graduate school education and his early job contacts. The company he was joining was geographically *not* downtown, and was engaged in manufacturing rather than "office work." Al had learned the meanings of certain symbols within the culture of his manufacturing plant, and protected both his work group and the new man from the disturbance and embarrassment which could have resulted from the presence of inappropriate symbols.

Although the situation of the newcomer entering an established group highlights the problem of learning a symbol system and its nature, it does not explain how symbolic meanings originate in the group. The simplest explanation is that they are brought in from other groups by the various members and modified through continuing group processes into a unique group code. To trace the origins of symbol systems, and especially the values and feelings they represent, requires tracing the history and current activities of the individual in terms of his membership in a multiplicity of groups, and the particular values, feelings, and behavior codes which characterize these groups.

## Multiple Group Membership

Group membership, as it is experienced by the individual, involves both a sequence of memberships over a period of time and simultaneous memberships at any one time. In both types, it is possible to find situations where membership in one group (for example, the teenage gang) involves psychological or behavioral repudiation of another group (for example, the original family), or both. There are also situations where membership in one group is a requisite for membership in another. For example, to become a member of a community leaders' group it may be necessary to hold membership in a family, a church, a work organization, or a profession, as well as other groups which symbolize responsibility.

Another quality of membership pertinent to work groups is the degree to which membership in the group involves actual interaction with the other members, or either purely psychological identification or membership at a distance. The first situation has been called the *primary* group, the interacting group, or the face-to-face group. The second has been called the *reference* group. In either case, the affiliation is part of the individual's psychological identity, and the values, norms, feelings, and behavior codes appropriate to the group influence his behavior. But it is only in the first type of group that interpersonal rewards, punishments, and emotions are exchanged, and social control in its raw form is brought to bear. One feels embarrassment and ridicule in the here-and-now presence of other people; one's reference groups communicate from a distance, involving symbols which may evoke feelings, ideas, and behaviors. The latter groups lack the effects of immediate feedback and response which mark the effectiveness of face-to-face interpersonal situations for communications and control.

The particular kinds of outside historical and current group memberships which have proved useful for understanding the behavior of work groups and their members are numerous. They include the family into which an individual is born, its ethnic and religious environment, and its background—socio-economic, rural or urban, and regional characteristics. They also include educational activities as group experiences, occupational or professional reference group affiliation, the age group as well as the sex group, and the present family and its socio-economic, ethno-religious, and geographical ties. Finally, they include current ties with historical groups, such as the family of birth and the "old school." All these affiliations supply the individual with sets of standards for evaluating behavior and persons in specific situations.

## Cultural Influences Within Work Groups

One of the most pervasive cultural influences in the wider culture is that of the socio-economic class within which the individual is reared and to which he aspires.[37] Membership in, or aspiration to,

[37] See, for example, Warner and Lunt, *The Social Life of a Modern Community*.

a particular socio-economic class is manifested in styles of behavior. The Bank Wiring Room and the engineering groups mentioned previously exemplify this pattern.

The men in the Bank Wiring Room engaged in certain types of behavior which the researchers identified as "games":

. . . For the most part, these were games of chance which included the following: matching coins, lagging coins, shooting craps, card games, bets on combinations of digits in the serial numbers of their weekly pay checks, pools on horse racing, baseball, and quality records, chipping in to purchase candy, and "binging."[38]

These activities were not only manifestations of the "working class," they also provided means for differentiating the statuses of the two cliques within the room. Clique A engaged in games of chance, whereas clique B engaged more often in 'binging.'[39] Both groups purchased candy from the Club store, but purchases were made separately and neither clique shared with the other. Clique A bought chocolate candy in small quantities, whereas clique B bought a less expensive kind in such large quantities that $W_9$ one time became ill from eating too much. Clique A argued more and indulged in less noise and horseplay than clique B. The members of clique A felt that their conversations were on a higher plane than those that went on in clique B; as $W_4$ said, "We talk about things of some importance."[40]

Although the bank-wiring group was set within the American culture of the late 1920's and the study of the three engineering groups took place in the late 1950's, there were some behaviors of the engineers which, in contrast to the bank-wiring workers, indicated a more "middle-class" style of life. The engineers talked about golf and fishing. During lunch periods they could be seen reading the financial pages of newspapers and paper-bound books. Their major form of interpersonal "gamesmanship" consisted of trying to catch each other's engineering errors.

Another cultural influence brought into work groups is the ethno-religious subculture within which the members were reared and are currently living. In the Zaleznik, Christensen, and Roethlisberger *Prediction Study*, "Irishness" was found to be the "in-group" value

[38] Roethlisberger and Dickson, *op. cit.*, pp. 500–501.
[39] "Binging" was a ritualized physical punishment, wherein the victim was struck sharply on the side of his upper arm by the knuckles of the punisher's fist.
[40] *Ibid.*, p. 510.

that was a major determinant of membership and rank in the informal social organization of the work group.[41]   The researchers found a striking similarity between the values, norms, and interpersonal behavior patterns of the group and the culture described in Arensberg's *Irish Countryman*,[42] especially in the reproduction of traditional familial roles.

A similar bond may be seen in the Slade Company case where apparent Italianness and real familial affiliation became a condition for group membership as well as a source of many values, much interpersonal behavior, and patterns of sentiment.[43]   In the Superior Slate Quarry case Welsh, Irish, and Yankee ethnic groupings were reflected in strict technological separation in the quarry and its mill: the Welsh were skilled quarrymen, the Irish worked in the mill, and the Yankees were in managerial positions.[44]

In all three situations, the standards and values learned by the individuals within their ethnic subcultures shaped the norms of the work groups.   A second influence of ethnic subcultures is that they provide attributes that are socially evaluated in relation to behaviors. The ethnic affiliation indicates "what one is" historically, "where he came from," and thus provides one element of identification and evaluation of individuals and groups.

Urban and rural distinctions perform similarly, but are strongly correlated with ethnic and occupational identifications.   William F. Whyte reported a factory situation where rural values, as they embodied the Protestant ethic, differentiated high-producing individuals and subgroups from those sharing urban values, which correspond with Catholic minority group ethnic identities.[45]   The urban-rural distinction was also found to be relevant in a study of two power plants by Mann and Hoffman.[46]   One of the plants studied was located in an urban industrial setting.   The other was located in a rural setting.   The workers' residences also tended to be urban and rural, respectively.   Confirming the cultural values normally associated with the urban-rural difference, the workers in the rural plant leaned toward Republican political sentiments, while the urban workers were largely Democrats.   The "rural-Republicans" expressed a stronger preference for a mobile, growing company than the "urban-Democrats" who tended to prefer a more stable company.   The

[41] Zaleznik, Christensen, and Roethlisberger, *The Motivation, Productivity, and Satisfaction of Workers*, pp. 209 ff.

[42] See *Bibliography*.   [43] Lawrence, et al., *op. cit.*, pp. 62–74.   [44] *Ibid.*, pp. 98–106.

[45] Whyte, *Money and Motivation*, pp. 45–46.

[46] Mann and Hoffman, *Automation and the Worker*, pp. 38–43.

"rural-Republican-mobile" workers had rejected attempts to unionize their plant, while the other plant was unionized. The rural workers essentially felt more influential in the company and satisfied than the urban workers. Thus, active as against passive behaviors and modes of sentiment also generally corresponded to the rural-urban difference in values.

In the engineering groups whose patterns were reported earlier in the chapter, the urban-rural differentiation was involved with professional and institutional identifications, and became especially important because of changes in the company's technology in the direction of more professional and scientific skills. The plant was located in a rural, small-town setting, and the company had built up a paternalistic relationship with its employees and the community. Many of the old-timers were local, rural people who learned engineering through practice. However, the newer technologies were being derived from the big city and its many institutions of higher scientific learning and research. Geographically, the city was an hour's drive away; historically it had been farther away in commuting time. Thus, the relative newcomers, upon whom the company's future would depend, were more "professional" compared with "institutionalized" old-timers. The old-timers thought of themselves primarily as company men and secondarily as engineers in the professional sense. The newcomers were more urban, or cosmopolitan, in values if not in actual residence. To complicate the matter further, age-group values appeared; the newcomers were younger men. Thus, conservatism of age augmented conservatism of rural and institutional outlooks, as both came under pressure in changing company policy, changing membership patterns within groups, and changing relationships among groups.

Age groupings as reference groups contain at least two different factors which differentiate values. Older people in any era tend to reflect different values from those of younger people because of the greater quantity and quality of life experiences they have encountered. Second, age differences also reflect the fact that the individuals have experienced different historical eras. This was not very important in the past when the child's world was not substantially different from that which his parents encountered as children. But to grow up with horses and buggies is a qualitatively different experience than growing up with automobiles, airplanes, radio, television, and higher social mobility. Similarly, to grow up during a period of economic depressions is a different experience emotionally from growing up during a period of relatively prosperous economic conditions.

Because of biological realities, and the qualities of personal experience they determine, age and sex are timeless and placeless factors of social differentiation which tend to have important consequences for the development of groups in any culture. In primitive societies, authority patterns, communication patterns, and patterns of technology remained relatively stable over time. Here age and sex differences could be viewed as independent and relatively stable influences upon individual and group growth and development. However, amid current cultural conditions of rapid change in communications and technology, as well as social mobility, the older certainty of expectations with respect to age and sex differences has yielded to ambiguity and incongruity. Younger, more highly educated men, with sophisticated decision-making and problem-solving methods at their disposal, have more influence upon the group, the organization, and the society than is traditionally "proper" for their age. Merely having lived for 50, 60, or 70 years no longer has the intrinsic value it once had. Along with the ambiguities and incongruities around the differences in age, the actual roles of women have changed drastically from their traditional roles in relation to men. Although ambiguous compared to the past, age and sex are still factors that differentiate authority and role in the primary family group. Individuals still bring their childhood lessons about these roles and authority to their work organizations. But the requirements for group and organizational problem solving call for vastly different roles and authority. Given the fundamental need of individuals and groups for relative certainty, predictability, and comfort in social relations, much of what goes on in groups and organizations may be understood as processes which seek to give life a more stable, clear, and predictable identity in the face of changes that foster conflict and ambiguity.

## SUMMARY

In this chapter we have indicated how various aspects of formal organization and the surrounding culture bear on the development of groups and individuals within organizational settings. The major theme underlying the discussion was that of individual and group identity. Organizational and cultural processes may be viewed as the frames of reference which provide external standards and symbols whereby the individual and the group may define themselves historically, in terms of current behavioral expectations, and in terms of aspirations for the future.

We have observed some of the environmental constraints within which group development takes place. Among other things, we have noted how particular tasks, tools, times, places, and procedures take on social meanings beyond those that are the primary requisites for getting work done.  We have seen how these social meanings become parts of individuals' or groups' continuing efforts to discover and maintain their identities.  We now have some understanding of why any technical change may have social consequences which go far beyond technical purposes; in some cases the social consequences can cancel out the technical purposes or even result in a lesser achievement of technical purposes than existed before the change.  We also have some understanding of the multiplicity of human motives in work group situations, especially in contrast to the relatively limited rewards which external agents, such as managers, can use in their efforts to control group behavior.  At the same time, we have seen that external agents can and do control the environmental conditions within which group development and individual pursuits take place.  This analysis has suggested that control of environmental conditions is an important, if not the most important, function of external agents who are concerned with the development of groups.

Recent theoretical and research work has sought to bring together these various ideas into a single scheme from which predictions about future group developments can be made and tested.  For those concerned with sociological and psychological analysis, the results of these studies may be of interest as they pertain directly to the concepts developed in this chapter and in the two succeeding ones.  The details of this material are presented in the accompanying technical reference note.

### TECHNICAL REFERENCE NOTE

Three interrelated theories, all working with the same measurements but each interpreting their meaning somewhat differently, provide a convenient form in which some of the ideas in this chapter may be summarized.  The theories are called *social certitude, distributive justice,* and *external and internal rewards.*  All three theories include the idea of social behavior as an exchange process.  The dynamics of this exchange process will be carried into the chapters which follow, where productivity and satisfaction become measures of two important results of the social exchange process.  The three theories will provide some of the connecting strands among these three chapters.  In addition to the theoretical connection, we shall provide some empirical continuity by repeated reference to a particular study throughout the balance of this chapter as well as in the two that follow.[47]

[47] Zaleznik, et al., *op. cit.*

*The Theories of Social Certitude and Distributive Justice.* *Social certitude* refers to the feelings of comfort and predictability or discomfort and anxiety which an individual may experience in the company of others. The behaviors both direct toward each other are related to these feelings. Uncertainty over personal identity and interpersonal relationships in social situations is associated with anxiety. Processes then take place which, among other things, try to reduce anxiety by increasing certainty; for example, social ranking increases the degree to which the sentiments and behaviors of group members are predictible to each other. The mechanisms of social certitude are directed toward the need for some degree of order and predictibility in the individual's social future.

*Distributive justice* concerns the feelings of rightness or wrongness in the balance between environmental rewards and social investments. For example, according to values which consider age to be a social investment, older people should earn more money and have higher-status jobs than younger people. Similarly, educational achievements, according to some value systems, also measure a social investment; the more education a person has, the higher should be his economic and status rewards.

Distributive justice has an historical basis; the individual's current rewards should bear some continuous relationship to who he is historically and what he has done in the past. Ideally, in a just world, man gets what he deserves; "as he sows, so shall he reap." When a man feels that he is not getting what he deserves, he complains. When he feels that he is getting more than he deserves, he feels guilty and will compensate by trying to increase his "investment," typically by trying to behave more responsibly and thus re-establish the condition of justice. This becomes a social process when the individual compares others' returns on their social investments with his own "rate of return." His behavior toward them reflects his assessment of the degree of distributive justice which obtains between them.

Investments are a combination of historical attributes and current behaviors. A common example of this formula is the situation in which a new man is brought in from outside to take over an existing group. Group members often feel this to be unfair, especially if the newcomer is "too young" and receives "too much" salary. He and the group will address the discrepancy in their behaviors in order to restore a just balance. One possibility is that he will attempt to "earn" his status by being oversolicitous and extremely helpful to the group, thus increasing his social investment through his behavior. Another possibility is that the group will behave *less* responsibly, thus decreasing their investment in the social situation. Either way, sentiments and behaviors will be used to re-establish a condition of distributive justice.

Both of these feelings—certitude and justice—take place around those aspects of what people "are," what people "do," and what people "get," which are socially evaluated in the culture or subculture. The degree to which these factors are in- or out-of-line with each other is indicated by operational indices called Status Congruence and the Reward-Investment Index.

*Status Congruence.* When we talk about status congruence, we are no longer talking about how people really feel and behave. We are talking about a pattern of social attributes other than feelings and behaviors. If our understanding of multiple group membership, values, and the reduction of anxiety is correct, this pattern will enable us to predict the actual feelings and behaviors in a specific social situation.[48]

The elements entering into the construction of the Status and Status Congruence Indices are called status factors. These factors are thought to be socially evaluated and of considerable importance to the multiple cultures and reference groups affecting the members of a work group. The factors used in the *Prediction Study* were pay, age, seniority, education, ethnic background, and sex. The selection of these particular factors as likely to be relevant to a specific work situation was based on the findings of previous research efforts. Status congruence was defined as follows:

> The more a member's status position on one status factor occupies the same position on other status factors, the more congruent his status is. According to this definition, for example: Give status factors A, B, C, . . . N and positions 1, 2, 3, . . . *n*, a member whose position is 1, 2, 3, or *n* on all status factors from A to N would be 100% status congruent; on the other hand, a member whose position is 1 on A, 2 on B, 3 on C, and *n* on N, would be 0% status congruent.[49]

It is important to understand that status congruence is a relative measure. The numerical value of the index indicates a relationship between the status factor scores for one person and the scores for the other members of the particular group. Scores, or the word "positions" in the definition, refer to relative rankings in the group, or to scoring values that award points for the amount of the factor to be ascribed to the individual. About 50 subjects were involved in the *Prediction Study*. Rather than work with the complication of about 50 rank positions on some factors (age and seniority) and only two on others (male or female), the authors used a system of assigning points (5, 10, 15, or 20) to each individual on each status factor.

To clarify the construction of the Status Congruence Index while avoiding the complexity of the system used in the *Prediction Study*, we can go through the operations with a simplified sample and procedure, using eight people, four factors, and simple rank positions instead of point

[48] The Zaleznik, Christensen, and Roethlisberger *Prediction Study* provided a model in which the authors, along with George Homans, tested empirically the theories of Social Certitude, Distributive Justice, and External and Internal Rewards.

[49] *Ibid.,* pp. 48–49.

*Table 9.3    Group X Status Factors\**

| Name | Age | Seniority | Education | Family Residence in U.S. |
|------|-----|-----------|-----------|--------------------------|
| John | 57 | 12 | 18 | 170 |
| Carl | 52 | 9 | 10 | 20 |
| Pat | 49 | 5 | 15 | 50 |
| Abe | 45 | 3 | 13 | 40 |
| Joe | 39 | 1 | 11 | 5 |
| Tom | 35 | 4 | 9 | 35 |
| Bill | 31 | 10 | 16 | 75 |
| Jeff | 26 | 6 | 8 | 100 |

\* All figures are years.

scores.  In this "group X," we shall assume that the members prize age, seniority, education, and "being American." In interviews with them, and hearing them talking among themselves, it seemed that the older one was, the longer one had been in the work department, the more education one had, and the longer one's family and ancestors had been in the United States, the better.  None of these factors refer to actual behavior. The first step in the status congruence (and status) analysis is to arrange the relevant information about each person in tabular form (Table 9.3).

The next step is to assign the rank-order number to each person's position on each status factor and to compute status and status congruence scores from these numbers.

Reading across Table 9.4, we see that John ranks first in the group on all four factors. Carl ranks second in age, third in seniority, sixth in

*Table 9.4    Group X Rankings on Status Factors*

| Name* | Age* | Seniority* | Education* | Family* | Status† | Status Congruence† |
|-------|------|------------|------------|---------|---------|--------------------|
| John | 1 | 1 | 1 | 1 | 4 | 0 |
| Carl | 2 | 3 | 6 | 7 | 18 | 18 |
| Pat | 3 | 5 | 3 | 4 | 15 | 7 |
| Abe | 4 | 7 | 4 | 5 | 20 | 10 |
| Joe | 5 | 8 | 5 | 8 | 26 | 12 |
| Tom | 6 | 6 | 7 | 6 | 25 | 3 |
| Bill | 7 | 2 | 2 | 3 | 14 | 16 |
| Jeff | 8 | 4 | 8 | 2 | 22 | 22 |

\* Figures are rank order positions.

† Figures are indices, computed as described below.

education, and seventh in length of time that his family and ancestors had been residing in the United States. The rankings are all relative to the group. If any given member of this group were moved to another group, his Status and Status Congruence Indices relative to the new group would be different from those in the old group.

In computing the values of the indices, the researcher starts out with the assumption that the four factors are of approximately equal value. If he finds in his preliminary investigation that they do not seem to be of equal value, he can use a technique for weighting the factors differentially in computing the indices. The Status index is computed by simply summing up the rank numbers assigned for each factor. This yields an inverted scale in the example: the lower the resulting number, the higher the status.

Status congruence, which is also an inverted scale in this example[50] (the lower the number, the higher the congruence), is computed by adding the differences between the rank number on each factor and the rank number on each other factor. For John, there were no differences, so that his Status Congruence Index is zero, indicating perfect congruence. For Carl, the computation of status congruence was made as follows:

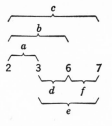

From the table of rank orders: Carl

Computation of differences:

(a) The difference between 2 and 3 is 1
(b) The difference between 2 and 6 is 4
(c) The difference between 2 and 7 is 5
(d) The difference between 3 and 6 is 3
(e) The difference between 3 and 7 is 4
(f) The difference between 6 and 7 is 1

The sum of the differences is    18, which becomes Carl's Status Congruence Index.

Going one step further with the example, the eight men can now be ranked in relation to each other on their Status and Status Congruence Index numbers (see Table 9.5).

[50] The definition of status congruence given in the *Prediction Study* indicated that the highest possible status congruence would be assigned the value 100%, while the lowest possible would be 0%. This was accomplished in that study by substracting the sum of the differences in assigned scores from 100, and calling the remainder the Status Congruence Index. In this manner the index scale was turned "right side up" so that a high index number meant high congruence.

*Table 9.5    Group X Rankings on Status and Status Congruence Indices*

| Name | Status | | Status Congruence | |
|------|--------|------|-------|------|
|      | Index  | Rank | Index | Rank |
| John | 4  | 1 | 0  | 1 |
| Bill | 14 | 2 | 16 | 6 |
| Pat  | 15 | 3 | 7  | 3 |
| Carl | 18 | 4 | 18 | 7 |
| Abe  | 20 | 5 | 10 | 4 |
| Jeff | 22 | 6 | 22 | 8 |
| Tom  | 25 | 7 | 3  | 2 |
| Joe  | 26 | 8 | 12 | 5 |

The measurement methods and assumptions are known to be rough approximations, at best, of the group's consensus about its values, which in reality could be quite ambiguous. Further simplification will help summarize the data, compensate for some of the error, and provide for easier analysis at later stages. This is accomplished by assigning the top four ranks to the category "high" and the bottom four ranks to the category "low," on both status and status Congruence. This division in two areas will yield a fourfold classification scheme.

|        |      | Status Congruence | |
|--------|------|-------------------|------|
|        |      | Low  | High |
| Status | High | Bill<br>Carl | John<br>Pat |
|        | Low  | Jeff<br>Joe  | Abe<br>Tom  |

An important idea contained in this analysis is that status level and congruence are theoretically independent of each other. Persons high in status, when status is conceived of as an aggregate of several factors, can be either high or low in congruence. Similarly, a low-status person could be high in congruence.

Some kinds of status factors are not really independent of each other, so that in real group situations status and congruence would tend to vary together. Dependence upon the passage of time is a characteristic of age, seniority, education, and pay. The longer a person lives, the higher he will (or can) go on all of these scales. Of the six factors used in the *Prediction Study*, sex was the only one that was really independent of the passage of time. When specific nationalities are arranged on a value scale, it becomes evident that the passage of time enters into the evaluation of ethnic background; "better" nationalities are those that have been in the United States the longest time. The most recent immigrant group tends to start at the bottom of the social ladder in the established culture; the Puerto Ricans in New York City are an example of this. In any case, the selection of status factors for analyzing a group situation is at best a rough approximation and is debatable. But this is true of the reality of social values also; the degree to which a particular group agrees on the relevant evaluation system is in itself an important characteristic of the group. One test of the method is in its empirical results; the findings of the *Prediction Study* confirmed the strength of its theories for the particular group studied, in spite of the methodological problems.

*Rewards and Investments.* Testing the Theory of Distributive Justice required an operational method by which rewards could be compared with social investments for each individual in the group. Job status was taken as the relevant organizational reward in the *Prediction Study*. Pay was taken to be the single measure of job status. The attributed aspects of social investment was measured by a Social Status Index, constructed in the same manner as the Status Index in the previous example described here, except that five factors were used; age, seniority, education, ethnic background, and sex. By weighting pay five times the weight assigned to each of the social status factors, it was possible to compare the reward (job status) with the attributed social investment (social status) to determine the degree to which each individual's rewards and investments were in- or out-of-line with each other, and to compare individuals to each other in this respect. The resulting number was called the Reward-Investment Index and allowed comparison regardless of the social status of the individual; even a relatively low-paid person could be experiencing a rewarding condition if his job status were higher than his attributed social status.

*The Theory of External and Internal Rewards.* The theories of social certitude and distributive justice are designed to explain and predict how individuals will feel and behave within the group. The theory of *external and internal rewards* is intended to explain and predict how those feelings and behaviors will relate to the behavior demanded of the group by its organizational environment. The group is the source of internal rewards, the formal organization is the source of external rewards. The most important external demand on the group, in the case of an industrial work group, is productivity. Job status is the reward that the organization—company management—confers for productivity. The group, however, rewards the individual with membership, which hinges on his social attributes and his behavior in the group. The acid test is how well he conforms to group norms. Because the norms of work groups tend to include control over the level of production, and the level in many cases may be lower than members' potential capabilities, the individual may be caught in a conflict. External rewards are won by high productivity which may be anathema to the group which withholds internal rewards for producing above group norms.

In the *Prediction Study*, individuals' feelings and behaviors were predicted from the various factors considered in this chapter. The particular aspect of behavior and sentiment which emerged from group development was called membership rank and included the categories of informal leader, regular, isolate, and deviant. Membership rank was the group's reward to the individual. Regular membership, including informal leadership, was a higher reward than isolation or the membership in a deviant subgroup. External reward was measured by the individual's Reward-Investment Index. Productivity and satisfaction were predicted from the individuals' conditions of external and internal rewards, four such conditions being possible:

| Condition | External Rewards | Internal Rewards |
|-----------|------------------|------------------|
| 1 | High | High |
| 2 | Low | High |
| 3 | High | Low |
| 4 | Low | Low |

In terms of the ideas presented in this chapter, the source of external rewards is a reference group, while the source of internal rewards is the primary group. Although this summary will be brought together around the findings of the *Prediction Study*, one other piece of research is especially notable because it centered in the potential conflict between the aspirations of reference groups and face-to-face group membership. It is also relevant to the contents of our next chapter, on productivity, and anticipates some of its ideas and findings. In a study of a group of furniture salesmen, C. J. French found that the high producers, who violated the group's norms (about protecting each other) in order to achieve higher sales, tended to be the least-liked men in the group.[51] When all the men were asked to name outside friends and their occupations, it was found that the high producers tended to name people of higher occupational status than themselves; they were psychologically oriented away from the face-to-face group, toward the outside reference group of people in higher-status occupations. In this case, psychological membership in a reference group allowed violation of the work group's norms, and made the violators inaccessible to group control.

This summary has discussed three theories related to the influences of environmental constraints on individuals' sentiments and behavior and

[51] C. J. French, "Correlates of Success in Retail Selling."

on group development. Special attention was given to explaining how these theories could be made operational, and how their variables could be translated into concrete measurements and mathematical processes. We shall conclude with some specific propositions, hypotheses, and predictions related to group development, which can be derived from the theory of social certitude, as well as from the theories implied by some of the earlier parts of this chapter. These will be discussed in relation to the findings of the *Prediction Study*.

*The PREDICTION STUDY: Hypotheses and Findings.* The authors of the *Prediction Study* worked out an elaborate set of hypotheses from the theories with which they were working. They translated these hypotheses into specific predictions of what they would find in the particular work group under investigation. They tested their predictions by field research including systematic observation and interviewing. To demonstrate the relationship between the various kinds of environmental constraints discussed in this chapter and certain aspects of group development, we shall list some of these hypotheses and related findings, and indicate their relevance to the ideas discussed here. In some instances the hypotheses used language and concepts somewhat different from those in this chapter. In these cases, the differences will be explained. In other hypotheses, the language and concepts were so close to the ideas discussed here that no further elaboration will be necessary.

HYPOTHESIS 1: The closer the functional proximity of individuals or subgroups, the more frequent the interaction between them.[52]

The *Prediction Study* used the expression "functional proximity" to mean the same as we meant by "functional interdependence." This refers to the degree to which their imposed task required the workers to co-operate. It is not the same as spatial proximity. Frequency of interaction is a measure of group development; it refers to social, in contrast to individual, activities where two or more people influence each others' behaviors by some form of communication. The hypothesis was confirmed for all four of the functional subsystems within the departmental group, and indicated that there were interesting differences among the subsystems which suggested different conditions of development within each.

HYPOTHESIS 2: The higher the status of an individual or subgroup, the higher the frequency of interaction.[53]

The frames of reference provided by the organization and the wider culture supplied value scales against which the status of individuals and subgroups could be measured. The organizational scale was pay. The cultural scales included age, seniority, education, ethnic background, and sex. Frequency of interaction was a behavioral measure of group develop-

[52] Zaleznik, et al., *op. cit.*, 171.
[53] *Ibid.*, p. 173.

ment. It was found that there was more interaction in the higher-status subsystems than in the lower-status subsystems.

HYPOTHESIS 3: The higher the total status and the more well established the social status ranking of individuals or subgroups, the more nearly their internal system activities (work and nonwork) will realize the norms and values of the group.[54]

In this hypothesis, "established" status ranking refers to what the Status Congruence Index was intended to measure, the in- or out-of-lineness of the individual's status attributes. Thus, the organizational and cultural value scales were expected to influence group behavior patterns in the two different ways: (1) the aggregated effect of status positions on several scales, and (2) the degree of clarity or ambiguity reflected by the differences between the positions on the several scales. The "internal system of activities" means actual behavior in the group situations, and includes those aspects of actual behavior which represent externally imposed requirements and those aspects of actual behavior which the group elaborates above and beyond the external demands. The "norms and values of the group" refers to the particular code of behavior and sentiments which controls the behavior of the members; this code is unique to the particular face-to-face group, and is relatively specific as to what the members should and should not do and what they should and should not believe, value, and feel. Hence, internal systems activities and norms and values represent measures of group development, and the correspondence between the activities and the norms was predicted to be influenced by external status and status congruence. The hypothesis was confirmed with respect to "extended nonwork activities," but was not confirmed with respect to "limited nonwork activities." The actual patterns of limited nonwork activities were explained in terms of combinations of variables not taken into account by the hypothesis.

HYPOTHESIS 4: Rank or social position in the internal system varies directly with status in the external system.[55]

"Rank or social position in the internal system" refers to the actual patterns of sentiments which exist within a group, in contrast to the prescribed patterns of evaluation which may be attributed to the external organizational and cultural value scales. The hypothesis is one way of saying that external evaluation systems are expected to be effective inside the group. Although this is in some ways an obvious statement, it does indicate a need for understanding the multiple sources of external values as determinants of internal rank; many managers and formal leaders, especially new and young ones, sometimes are surprised to learn that their organizational status is one, and only one, of many determinants of their relationship to the group. The hypothesis was confirmed.

[54] *Ibid.*, p. 176.
[55] *Ibid.*, p. 183.

HYPOTHESIS 5: The more frequently individuals or subgroups interact with one another, the stronger the sentiments of friendship.[56]

This hypothesis is different from the others in that it predicts from one aspect of group development (actual interaction) to another (sentiments of liking), rather than predicting from an external organizational or cultural constraint to an actual internal condition. However, since other hypotheses had predicted from the external attributes to actual interaction, this one may be seen as a link between external attributes and sentiments as shown in Table 9.6.

*Table 9.6    Casual Relationships among Variables*

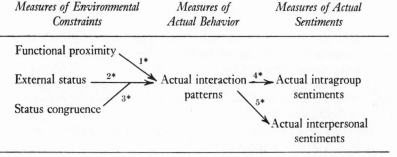

| Measures of Environmental Constraints | Measures of Actual Behavior | Measures of Actual Sentiments |

\* Numbers refer to Hypotheses.

The hypothesis was confirmed, but detailed analysis of expressed disliking as well as liking, and the location of the object person as within or outside of the particular subsystem, indicated a more complex set of relationships than the simplified hypothesis took into account.

The next set of hypotheses dealt with qualities of group membership which an individual may be observed to exhibit in his behavior toward others and in their behaviors toward him. The categories of membership used in the *Prediction Study* were membership in a regular subgroup, membership in a deviant subgroup, and isolate. Informal leadership was a special case of regular membership. Regular members were the "in-group" who abided by the group's norms and enforced them. Isolates were behaviorally and sentimentally "out" of the group, though related to them through spatial and functional proximity. Deviant members were in subgroups or cliques which violated the in-group norms and values with respect to what a person should be (his external social attributes), or how he should actually behave, or both. Informal leaders were those who were in central positions of influence in the group.

HYPOTHESIS 6: The more socially congruent the individual is (the higher his status congruence), the more likely he will become a member of the group.[57]

[56] *Ibid.*, p. 189.
[57] *Ibid.*, p. 199.

The finding is shown in Table 9.7.

*Table 9.7    Status Congruence and Number of Regulars, Deviants, and Isolates*[58]

| Status Congruence | "Members" | | | |
|---|---|---|---|---|
| | Regulars | Deviants | *Isolates* | *Total* |
| High | 13 | 7 | 4 | 24 |
| Low | 7 | 6 | 10 | 23 |
| Total | 20 | 13 | 14 | 47 |

The likelihood that a person with high-status congruence would be a regular member was 13/24; the likelihood that a person with low-status congruence would be a regular member was 7/23.  The likelihood that a highly congruent person would be a member of a regular or deviant subgroup was 20/24; the likelihood that a person with low congruence would be a member of a subgroup was 13/23.

HYPOTHESIS 7: The higher the external status of an individual, the more likely he will become a group member.[59]

The findings are shown in Table 9.8.

*Table 9.8    Total Status and Number of Regulars, Deviants, and Isolates*[60]

| Total Status | "Members" | | | |
|---|---|---|---|---|
| | Regulars | Deviants | *Isolates* | *Total* |
| High | 15 | 1 | 8 | 24 |
| Low | 5 | 12 | 6 | 23 |
| Total | 20 | 13 | 14 | 47 |

It is most interesting to notice that although the hypothesis was verified with respect to the difference between regulars and deviants, it was not between isolates and members of regular or deviant subgroups. The interesting phenomenon of the high-status isolate was yet to be explained.

HYPOTHESIS 8: The higher the total status and the higher the status congruence, the more likely an individual will be a group member; the lower the total status and the lower the status congruence, the more likely an individual will be an isolate.

[58] *Ibid.*, p. 202.
[59] *Ibid.*
[60] *Ibid.*, p. 204.

This hypothesis took into account only the two extremes out of four possible combinations of status and congruence. It did not say anything about the effects of high status along with low congruence or low status along with high congruence. As it turned out, the hypothesis was not confirmed. But an examination of the two conditions which were omitted yielded some interesting indications, especially when compared to the *three* membership categories (Table 9.9).

*Table 9.9   Regular, Deviants, and Isolates by Total Status and Status Congruence*[61]

|  | "Members" | | | |
|---|---|---|---|---|
|  | Regulars | Deviants | *Isolates* | *Total* |
| 1. High status, high-status congruence | 13 | 1 | 2 | 16 |
| 2. High status, low-status congruence | 2 | 0 | 6 | 8 |
| 3. Low status, high-status congruence | 0 | 6 | 2 | 8 |
| 4. Low status, low-status congruence | 5 | 6 | 4 | 15 |
| Total | 20 | 13 | 14 | 47 |

This analysis yielded clear indications that high-status persons who were highly congruent tended to be regular group members, high-status persons with low congruence tended to be isolates, and low-status persons who were congruent tended to be members of deviant subgroups. The results of low status along with low congruence were less clear, although there were weak indications that these people tended not to be members of regular groups. In the authors' pursuit of further explanation, they examined the single variable, ethnic origin and its effects on group membership.

The researchers found that the major ethnic differentiation in the department was between Irish and non-Irish workers. About half the workers were Irish. Out of the 20 regulars, 16 were Irish. Out of 23 Irish workers, 16 were regulars. From this the authors concluded that "Irishness" was a dominant value in the group. They also found that all five of the low-status, low-congruence workers who were members of regular subgroups were Irish. However, four low-status, low congruence Irish workers were *not* regulars. Thus, Irishness appeared to be a necessary, but not sufficient, condition for regular membership among the low-status, low-congruence workers.

The final hypothesis related to group development was concerned with leadership:

HYPOTHESIS 9: Individuals with high status and high-status congruence who are members of work groups with high status and high-status congruence will tend to become leaders.

[61] *Ibid.*, p. 207.

There were actually five people in the larger group (which consisted of four functional subgroups, called "subsystems" in the study) who were identified as leaders. Four of these five met the conditions specified in the hypothesis.

These nine hypotheses establish relationships between organizational and cultural constraints and certain aspects of group development, namely, interaction patterns, membership, and interpersonal sentiments. The *Prediction Study* went on to present additional hypotheses relating aspects of group development to productivity and satisfaction. These will be discussed along with other ideas in the two chapters of this book which follow. The theories of *distributive justice* and *external and internal rewards*, while relatable to the aspects of group development discussed in this present chapter, were formulated for the special purposes of understanding and predicting satisfaction and productivity.

# Chapter Ten

# Productivity

T HE more concrete a group's task is, the easier it is for its members, as well as outsiders, to see, measure, and understand the relationship between actual behavior and productivity. For example, a machine operator can see and count the number of parts produced by his behavior. His unit of production is defined and his output can be measured objectively. The more abstract the task is, the more difficult it is to describe, measure, and understand productivity. For instance, the productivity of a management group might ultimately depend on the behavior of *other* groups. In any case, productivity is an outcome of behavior.

In discussing productivity, we shall analyze how it fits into a scheme of causal relationships. Among the determinants of productivity, one that is especially relevant to group development is the productivity norm set by the group. This norm constitutes the group's control over production and tempers the influence of the formal work organization, including the rewards and technological arrangements, which also effect productivity. The discussion will conclude with an examination of the relationships between productivity norms and organizational rewards.

The second part of this chapter will be devoted to a presentation of some selected research findings relating group productivity to other factors. These other factors include group cohesiveness, organizational rewards, group membership, competitiveness, and leadership behavior. We shall discuss some of the findings of the *Prediction Study*[1] referring to the Theory of External and Internal Rewards presented in the technical reference note to the previous chapter. We shall then consider some ideas about the more general relationships between productivity and group leadership, membership, and individual development.

[1] Zaleznik, et al., *The Motivation, Productivity, and Satisfaction of Workers.*

## THEORETICAL ASPECTS OF PRODUCTIVITY

### Productivity as an Element in Behavioral Analysis

The isolation of productivity in a set of causal relationships is crucial to the understanding of organizational effectiveness. The historical development of industrial psychology and industrial sociology may be traced in terms of the ways that productivity has been treated by organizational theorists, managers, and behavioral scientists. One of their earliest models was that of "economic man," which Elton Mayo called "the rabble hypothesis."[2] This view sees a direct, one-to-one relationship between economic rewards and the amount a man will produce. It sees groups only as collections of individuals, each pursuing his own economic goals. From the point of view of this book, the most important aspect of the "economic man" model is that it does not allow for, or account for, social relationships between men, other than the elementary economic contract between worker and employer. The residue of this mode of thought is the practice of individual piecework compensation, where individual workers are paid according to the amount they produce. Managers and researchers, however, have been forced to extend and complicate this economic model. They have found that other than economic rewards seem to be involved in a more complex set of causal relationships; social relationships, as well as economic rewards, seem to influence the productivity level of workers.

A social-psychological point of view, as represented by the Hawthorne studies of the Western Electric Company, sees the social processes of the small work group as a factor modifying organizational rewards and practices and the characteristics of individuals in significant ways to influence productivity levels.[3] Thus, productivity becomes a social outcome rather than an outcome of purely individualistic behavior. Informal social contracts among workers interact with the formal economic contract between managers and workers to determine productivity. Individual and group productivity become symbolic expressions of attitudes toward external authorities, as well as expressions of intragroup solidarity and structure. Individual motivations contain social as well as economic needs, so that motivation to produce for an external authority becomes bound up in a complex relationship with desires for membership and esteem in a social group.

[2] Mayo, *The Social Problems of an Industrial Civilization.*
[3] Roethlisberger and Dickson, *op. cit.*

Our analysis of productivity as one link in a causal chain sees three different kinds of factors involved: (1) environmental constraints, (2) group properties and performances, and (3) outcomes. This classification corresponds roughly to what others have called inputs (or imports), conversion processes, and outputs (or exports). It also resembles George Homans' external system, internal system, and consequences.[4] Still others might think of determinants of behavior (forces, needs, constraints, and so forth), actual behavior, and the consequences of the actual behavior. We see the causal chain as follows:

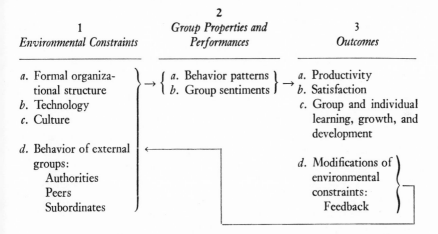

Environmental constraints include, as we saw in the previous chapter, the authority structure, communication structure, and technology of formal organizations, as well as cultural influences. If we take the broadest connotations of the concept of culture, all these elements, organizational and technological, are cultural phenomena. However, since our major interest in this book concerns groups in organizations, we are treating them more in the way that they appear to the formal leader of a group, to the organizational planner, and to the administrator. We have separated technology from formal organization at this stage to indicate that it can, and should, be treated as a primary element in planning and administration; ideally, formal organizational structures would be designed to fit particular technologies. The constraint that we call culture really refers to aspects of the cultural environment other than organizational and technological.

We have added here the behavior of external groups as a class of environmental constraint. This allows us to distinguish *plans* for how

[4] G. Homans, *The Human Group*, pp. 81 ff.

people should behave from the *actual* behaviors of outsiders important to the group, whether or not those actual behaviors conform to the organizational, technological, and cultural plans.   Thus, we can deal with the actual behavior of other individuals and groups as influences on the development of the primary work group.   These others include outsiders in various authority relationships to the group, from customers and suppliers to supervisors, managers, staffs, peers, and subordinates.

From these environmental constraints, group performances, and also from outcomes, we obtain a framework within which to analyze productivity as a dependent variable.   It also provides a frame of reference for studying satisfaction in the next chaper.   Later chapters build upon this same scheme of relationships for examining the problems of modification in individuals, groups, and organizations and for analyzing the role of leadership behavior as a determinant of productivity, satisfaction, and change.

## The Measurement of Productivity

The major measurement problem, as we see it, centers around the technological differences between different kinds of work.   Of special interest are the differences in the levels of abstraction necessary for defining work and the status of the particular level used for measurement.   The productivity data measured most easily come from groups operating at the lower levels.   These data cover the output of production workers—visible, discrete, and relatively easy to count.   On the other hand, the output of service and management groups is highly abstract—neither visible, except in the symbolic forms of numbers and written documents, nor often identifiable.   It cannot be counted directly.

The more abstract the task, the more ambiguous the measurement and evaluation of productivity becomes.   The abstractness increases the higher the status is in the formal organization.   One paradoxical fact of organizational life is that although the higher levels of management publicly value "results," they also value certain performances, independent of the results.   This is best understood by considering management as a group which has norms governing members' behavior.   In one study, for example, a supervisor whose behavior led to the best results for the organization lost out on a promotion to a rival whose results were less effective but whose behavior was more in line with the norms of the management group.[5]

[5] Spear, *Feelings, Skill, and Leadership.*

Numerous studies of groups of workers have described behavior patterns of individuals, which were of great importance for the productivity, satisfaction, and development of the group, but which went unrecognized, unconfirmed, and unrewarded by the formal organization.[6] Yet these same performances are highly valued in managers and are recognized and rewarded as abilities to cooperate and to elicit co-operation from others and among others. Insofar as organizations reward both performances and results, the environment of the organization is much more favorable for those in higher-status levels than for those in lower-status levels. Those at lower-status levels are rewarded mainly for results. However, the basis for favorable results is the performance, for which no visible organizational reward is provided.

Three aspects of the problem of measuring productivity, then, stand out: (1) the more abstract the task, the more difficult it is to measure and evaluate productivity, performance, or both; (2) abstractness of the task varies directly with the status level in the organizational hierarchy; and (3) managements tend to reward outcomes *and* performances at higher levels, but to reward only outcomes at lower levels. These factors generally alienate low-level groups from higher-level groups, workers from managers. From the point of view of a worker group, the difference in the way managerial, as opposed to worker, behavior is evaluated is arbitrary and based on social class rather than the real value of contributions.

For example, it is quite acceptable for managerial groups to take two-hour lunch periods, including cocktails at fine restaurants, and to charge these to an expense account, but parallel practices among workers are seen as "goofing off," "drinking on the job," "talking too much," and so forth. It is part of a manager's job to spend quite a bit of time talking with people, but talking is seen as distracting from productivity when it occurs in groups of workers.

There are, of course, real differences in the technical requisites for task accomplishment at the various levels. There are also real differences in the proportion of discretionary behaviors included in job requirements at the various levels. However, it is difficult to see the line between discretionary behaviors based on task requirements and those based purely on status and social-class differences. Where this problem occurs *within* an interacting group, some communication channels exist or are possible for increasing the mutual understanding of real differences in task requisites, as well as the amount and kind of

[6] See Zaleznik, *op. cit.*, Zaleznik et al., *op. cit.*, and Lawrence et al., pp. 334–343, "The Livingston Company" case.

social differentiation required for group maintenance. Where this problem occurs *between* socially isolated groups, such as managers and workers, the tendency is to resort to institutionalized means for resolving intergroup conflict in lieu of primary systems of communication. Unions, contractual job definitions, negotiation through representatives, and the use of raw power characterize some of these means.

The social distance between groups, and its accompanying conditions of poor communications and mutual misunderstanding of motives, complicates problems of change. This becomes especially severe when change is imposed upon status differences which contain mutual hostility, distrust, and stereotyping. It is therefore of utmost importance to understand the differences between performances and results, and to understand the cultural settings in which their measurement and evaluation is imbedded.

## Productivity as a Norm of Behavior

Norms are a special kind of shared sentiment within the group. They can be seen as implicit, and in some cases explicit, conditions for group membership. They state what a person should *be* (that is, his "cultural properties"), what he should *do* (his performances), and what should be the consequences of his behavior (the outcomes). Guided by norms, the group can then bestow upon the individual particular types of membership such as informal leader, member of a regular subgroup, member of a deviant subgroup, or isolate.

The salient features of norms which were discussed in the earlier chapter on Social Control included the following:

1. Norms are ideas in the minds of men with respect to the question, how should a member of this particular group behave? The emphasis is upon *should:* how people should behave under certain circumstances.

2. In a given group, there tends to be greater consistency as to the idea than there is in actual performances that measure up to this standard. There is more agreement on the idea than there is in actual behaviors.

3. The maintenance of a particular person's or subgroup's behavior pattern at an existing level of conformity is based upon the capacity of the group to reward conformance and punish deviation.

*a.* A certain level of conformity will be associated with a certain quality of membership.

*b.* Reward and punishment by the group maintains the existing levels of conformity. For example, "regulars" may be rewarded for some behaviors for which "deviants" would be punished, and the reverse. The emphasis in this point is on the maintenance of an *existing* structure of membership categories and relationships.

*c.* The conformance of individuals in the absence of actual punishments and rewards for actual behaviors is accomplished through the individuals' capacity to imagine the outcomes of altering their behavior. The individual may say to himself, for example, "If I become more friendly with Joe he will probably reject my bid and the group will ridicule me, and I would feel humiliated and embarrassed. I should wait until I have been around longer and Joe takes it upon himself to become more friendly with me."

In lower-level groups in an organization, there is little gap between observable behavior and measurable productivity; the members can see each other work and how much they produce. Their productivity is visibly measured and evaluated by outsiders. The results appear in supervisors' comments and written records. Because correspondence between performance and results is close, productivity itself becomes an appropriate target of group norms. The significance of productivity as part of an exchange between the group and pertinent outsiders makes it a suitable device for the expression of intergroup feelings. Widespread occurrence of "group restriction of output" in industry, as well as in educational settings and other organizational contexts, indicates a uniformity of social control over production. Output is not always restricted; in some groups the norm pegs production at a relatively high rate. The important factor is social control, whether it is manifested in restrictive norms or in high-productivity norms.

Although it is difficult to analyze group productivity norms without considering their relationship to other norms, to the structure of a specific group, and to the environmental conditions surrounding the group, certain regularities among groups permit generalizations, within limits, about the utility of productivity norms to the group. Two sets of relationships affect the analysis. One is the group's external relations to its environment, in which the productivity norm represents the group's control over its exchange with the world. The other is the internal system of relationships among group members; here the productivity norm maintains some degree of predictability and stability concerning members' social relationships.

A restrictive productivity norm serves to protect a group from external threats. The economic threat is the most obvious one. It forms the basis for much folklore whether or not the threat really exists at a particular time. The logic is simple. If the group increases its output, one or both of two bad outcomes are feared. Production standards may be changed so that group members will have to work harder for the same amount of money. Another possibility is that some group members will be laid off, leaving fewer workers to produce the same or a higher amount. Thus, the norm serves to protect the group against a loss of jobs for individuals and from working harder without an increase in pay. The interesting thing about the economic basis for the norm is that the norm exists even in situations where there is no real economic threat. It exists during periods of economic expansion as well as during periods of recession or depression. Thus, we must search for additional explanations of the norm.

Another economic aspect of the productivity norm is its function as a means of negotiating "a fair day's work for a fair day's pay." With the advent of the methods of scientific management, including job design, job evaluation, time-and-motion study, production standards, and logically derived piece rates and hourly base rates, the worker and his supervisors were overwhelmed by "scientism." Instead of invoking the authority of power, or in addition to this kind of authority, the management group was invoking the authority of science and rationality. As is the case whenever any form of absolute authority is invoked, whether it be God, Motherhood, the American Way of Life, or Science, the subordinate finds it difficult, if at all possible, to raise questions. Yet there was something disturbing about this new authority. Perhaps it was the fact that it appeared to change a negotiation process, which involved mutual influence, into a unilateral power play. Within the scientific method of setting standards a provision remained for certain fatigue and other kinds of allowances, known to the trade as "fudge factors." By skillful use of these allowances, industrial engineers could informally maintain the process of negotiation and address the workers' sense of justice. Even so, the process of having one's standards of behavior determined by an outsider was uncomfortable, partly because of considerations discussed earlier in relation to the measurement of productivity. The truth is that wages and production standards are negotiated through conceptions of power and justice. Group productivity norms maintain a balance in negotiations when inaccessible absolute authorities are invoked which cannot be questioned logically.

Alienation between workers and management, as we have seen, can be explained by differences in status and social class. It also is evident in the fact that lower-status groups consider the difference between the evaluations of worker and managerial behavior to be arbitrary and unrelated to real contributions.  Furthermore, the work group regards certain management behaviors as arbitrary and unpredictable. It sees fluctuations in demand, layoffs and hirings, technological changes, or changes in formal organizational structure as unilateral influences from outsiders, which cannot be controlled directly or predicted by the group.  Any such change threatens to break up established social relationships.  Old friends are moved away, strangers are moved in.  Old skills, upon which social respect is based, become obsolete.  New skills brought in by young outsiders, are the criteria of a changing system of rewards.  The productivity norm, under these circumstances, gives the group something it can and does control, which can provide predictability about internal group relationships, if not external relationships.  It also allows the group to assert counter-dependency against an external authority whose behavior emphasizes and reinforces dependency on it for the group's future.  Through the norm the group demonstrates some ability to exercise autonomous control over its own destiny.

Another external function of the productivity norm is to protect the group's internal relationships from interference by outsiders.  The logic of this function is expressed in this way: If individual differences among members were expressed by different rates of productivity, external authorities could look inside the group to see why some people could do more than others.  The outsiders' inquiry would put members in competition with each other, unsettling the established social relationships.  This threat is met by enforcing as much uniformity as possible in the level of output among group members, to mask any potential differences in ability among them.

The degree to which co-operation and mutual support are important to members of the same group, in contrast to competition and individual prominence, tends to relate to cultural considerations.  Identifications of social class and the values of individuals have much to do with a person's attitudes toward his work group and his job.  The findings of several research studies, as noted in Chapter Nine, highlighted the presence and meaning of distinctions between urban and rural values.  Groups dominated by urban values, for example, are relatively passive in their alienation to authority.  They feel relatively powerless in relation to external events.  Things "just happen" to them.  Under these conditions, strong norms are likely to develop which emphasize "sticking together" rather than "pulling apart" in a competitive rivalry.

The internal functions of productivity norms maintain the integrity, stability, and predictability of interpersonal relations, which are important sources for satisfying individual needs.  The productivity norm contributes to the solidification of the group by providing a means, as do other norms, for the individual to express his desire to be liked by others, to like them, and to be psychologically included.  It allows the more proficient to protect the less proficient workers and earn liking and respect for doing so.  It enables the newcomer, as his proficiency increases, to demonstrate his pledge of mutual support by leveling off at the group rate rather than "showing off" by exceeding it.  It permits members to compensate for each other's day-to-day fluctuations in mood or health, giving them a tangible commodity of social exchange; one member will overproduce to help another in a time of need.  In groups where no social interaction is required by the jobs, it gives members something tangible around which they may interact.

Productivity norms also provide a basis for the expression of individuality within the group.  Differentiation of membership roles and rankings is an important aspect of group development, as has been observed.  Group structure is by no means monolithic.  The membership includes persons who vary in the degree to which they conform to group norms.  The behavior of regular members, for example, tend to conform closely to the norms.  In the case of productivity norms, regular members tend to produce "on the line."[7]  Deviant members and isolated members may express their unique individualities and their hostility to the group's regular members by producing at either higher or lower levels than the norm.  Similarly, a newcomer to a group will usually face the expectation of older members that he initially produce at a rate lower than the norm, regardless of his individual capability.  However, some group situations allow consistently high production by a member who has earned, through other behaviors, such as helping and support, the right to deviate in productivity while retaining regular membership.[8]

In this section we have indicated some of the reasons for the pervasiveness of productivity norms in work groups.  Let us now explore how the formal organization's reward systems relate to the group's informal social controls and rewards as influences on productivity.

## Productivity and Rewards

When external demands for productivity are compared with the group's demands for conformity to its norm, we can visualize a

---

[7] Zaleznik et al., pp. 220 ff.

[8] See, for example, Alice in the "Marshall Company (MR3)" case in Glover and Hower, *The Administrator,* pp. 389–404.

potential conflict situation.   These demands are accompanied by two different sets of rewards.   On the one hand, there are the external rewards of pay, job status, job security, opportunity for advancement, interesting work, and recognition from management available from the formal organization.   On the other hand, there are the internal rewards of friendship, liking, respect, support, and the opportunity to fill a socially needed role available from the work group itself.   To some individuals at some stages of their lives this potential conflict becomes real; they then feel that they must choose to pursue one set of rewards at the cost of renouncing the other set.

Many studies of work groups in traditional organizations show these two reward systems to be working against each other; a high producer is forced to violate group norms while a regular group member is forced to constrain his potential contribution to the organization. However, the analysis which illustrates the importance to the individual, and to the group, of these different reward systems suggests that other conditions may be possible.   For example, group norms could develop which include organizational values.   Conversely, organizational reward systems could be developed which included group values, as in fact they do with regard to higher-level groups in the organization.   To the degree that the organization is in close communication with its members, both directions of movement can take place simultaneously.

When the individual becomes the center, it is by no means clear that the potential conflict between organizational and group rewards always materializes.   The cultural values and attitudes, as well as the other personality characteristics brought to the situation by the individual, can so strongly predispose him to one reward system or the other that he is never confronted with a need to choose between them.   Or he may have other reward systems so strongly influencing his life that his patterns of group and organizational behavior are more affected by factors outside the situation than by organizational or group rewards.   These conditions might arise when, for example, a newly arrived immigrant takes his first job after having experienced extreme economic deprivation, or when an individual is facing severe personal or family problems outside work.   In these instances membership in the work group is of little or no importance to the individual.   His indifference to membership rewards and punishments places him beyond the control of the group, and he feels no conflict between group rewards and organizational rewards.

These possibilities suggest a third source for change in addition to changes in organizational reward systems or group norms.   This would be the processes of individual development as governed by institutions outside the organizational context—formal education, community groups, and therapeutic institutions. Finally, there is the assumption that some unexplored aspects of individual, group, and organizational development may ultimately provide the basis for more creative resolutions of the potential conflicts of individual versus group, individual versus organization, and group versus organization than is possible with existing cultural definitions. From this point of view, the findings of empirical research may be interpreted in two ways: they indicate what is going on, including description of the conflicts derived from the culture, and they indicate some possible directions for future efforts in organizational action and research. Interpretations may sometimes tend to confuse "what exists" with "what is possible"; however, both require working from empirical data.

## SELECTED RESEARCH FINDINGS

Each of the research studies which will be discussed here deals with more than two research variables. This is a characteristic of most research on small groups. In our introductory paragraphs on productivity as an element in behavioral analysis, we emphasized the importance of taking complex sets of relationships into account, rather than looking for simple one-to-one relationships. When studying productivity, it is especially important to keep the complexity of the systems in mind, because it is on this very point that oversimplifications have prevented the achievement of optimum results for individuals as well as for groups and organizations. The manager has asked, "How can I get more work out of my subordinates?" The teacher has asked, "How can I get my students to improve their performance?" The parent has asked, "How can I get my child to do better in school?" Paradoxically, some research findings indicate that authorities who act as indicated by these questions—a behavior pattern sometimes called "production-oriented" or "procedures-oriented"—tend not to get as good results as authorities whose behavior indicates other approaches.[9]

### *Seashore: Group Cohesiveness in the Industrial Work Group*[10]

Three major variables were analyzed in this study: group cohesiveness, productivity, and perceived supportiveness by the company. Cohesiveness is a property of the work groups, describing a pattern of sentiments. Productivity represents a result of group behavioral

---

[9] See Likert, *New Patterns of Management*, pp. 5 ff.
[10] See Bibliography.

processes. Perceived supportiveness by the company points to a specific environmental condition. Perceived or not, supportiveness describes management's relationship to the work group.

Group cohesiveness refers to the attractiveness of the group to its members, their willingness to participate in its activities, and the extent to which they see themselves being rewarded potentially by their experiences in the group. To many individuals, the word "group" denotes cohesiveness; when they say "this is not a real group" they mean that people feel little attraction to each other. However, when groups are defined independently of cohesiveness, this property provides one important way in which groups differ. Our definition of a group is based only on proximity and interdependence.

As we have seen, membership in a group must be valued by an individual for him to be controlled by its norms. Conferring and withholding membership are the rewards and punishments that make norms effective; if an individual does not care about membership, these rewards and punishments mean nothing to him. Isolates are beyond the control of the group. Thus, the cohesiveness of a group, its value to individuals, has to be associated with the effectiveness of its norms.

Several indices of productivity apply when groups serve as units of analysis. One is the average productivity level of the group, which can be compared to the average productivity levels of other groups. Another is the variance within the group, the degree to which productivity levels differ among the individuals in the group. The lowest possible within-group variance occurs when every person in the group produces at the same level. The more they differ, the higher the within-group variance. The final productivity index used in Seashore's study is variance between groups. This refers to the degree to which the average productivity of all groups is identical.

The third consideration in Seashore's study, perceived supportiveness by the company, refers to the workers' views of the company and its representatives, its foremen. High perceived supportiveness is characterized by workers' feelings that their foreman is trying to help them and that the company is a good place to work.

In the study, productivity indices were based on actual records available in the organization. Cohesiveness and perceived supportiveness were measured by worker responses to questionnaire items related to feelings about the immediate work group, the foreman, and the company. The study included 228 groups, with a total of 5871 members, taken from a single large company.

The first finding of interest was that *the higher the cohesiveness of the group, the lower the within-group variance in productivity.* This is represented by Diagram 10.1.[11]

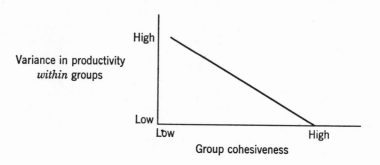

*Diagram 10.1    Variance in productivity within groups and group cohesiveness.*

This finding confirmed the proposition that the effectiveness of group norms depended upon the attractiveness of the group to its members. The stronger the effects of the norm, the less variance there was among the productivity levels of individual members. The finding also showed that productivity norms were of importance in the groups studied; control over productivity was an activity that affected cohesion. It is conceivable that highly cohesive groups could have a number of kinds of norms other than productivity norms, and that social control over productivity would not be a necessary part of the code of the group. However, the data indicated that control over productivity was of some importance to the groups studied.

This finding did not answer the question: At what level do highly cohesive groups tend to stabilize productivity? The norm could operate at low levels of productivity or at high levels. Among less cohesive groups, with less effective norms, we should not expect to find much difference between group productivity levels. In the absence of social control, productivity rates among groups would be expected to fit a normal distribution curve, individual distinctions being attributed to differences in learning and ability. In this case, the average of one such group lacking norms would be expected to be close to the average of another normless group, assuming a random distribution of experience and ability among groups. On the other hand, the distribution of productivity rates among members of groups with strong norms would be expected, and was found, to be tighter, or closer together, than it would be by chance. Further, since one characteristic of group norms is their uniqueness to the specific group, we should expect to find greater differences in productivity among

[11] Seashore, *op. cit.,* p. 67.

highly cohesive groups than among less cohesive groups. We should expect to find the productivity of highly cohesive groups higher or lower than the average productivity for all groups, with the productivity of less cohesive groups clustering closer together somewhere between those of the highly cohesive groups. When group cohesion was examined in relation to between-group variance, it was found *that the higher the cohesiveness, the greater the between-group variance.* This finding is illustrated in Diagram 10.2.[12]

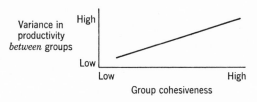

*Diagram 10.2   Variance in productivity between groups and group cohesiveness.*

In attempting to account for the differences between the actual productivity levels of highly cohesive and less cohesive groups, the study introduced the factor, "perceived supportiveness by the company." When the groups were divided into "High Support" and "Low Support," based on their indices of perceived supportiveness by the company, and the relationship between productivity and cohesiveness for each of the two kinds of groups was plotted, the pattern shown on Diagram 10.3[13] resulted.

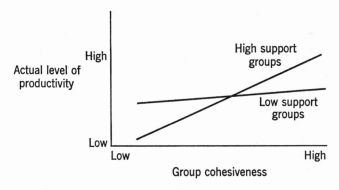

*Diagram 10.3   Actual levels of productivity and group cohesiveness for high and low support groups.*

Although the differences were of relatively low statistical significance, the same pattern appeared in other tests of the indicated relationships. The findings demonstrated a tendency for highly cohesive,

[12] *Ibid.,* p. 71.
[13] *Ibid.,* p. 76.

high producing groups to feel more positive toward the company than highly cohesive groups which produced at lower levels. In terms of the theory of external and internal rewards, this would indicate that *under conditions where external authority is not viewed as punitive and where there is less alienation between the group and external authorities, there would be a greater degree of correspondence between group norms and the goals of the external authority figures.*

A second meaning of these findings can be inferred from holding the degree of perceived support constant and observing the effects of cohesion. High support groups with less cohesion tend to produce *lower* than low support groups with less cohesion. Moreover, in the absence of cohesion, perceived supportiveness reverses the predicted direction, assuming that external rewards are directly related to productivity. This indicates that socially isolated individuals (those in groups featuring low cohesiveness) who view external authorities as supportive tend to produce less than isolated individuals who view external authorities as less supportive.

Some other findings of the Seashore study are of interest for the more general problem of group development.

Members of high cohesive groups exhibited less anxiety than members of low cohesive groups. . . .

The prediction regarding degree of group cohesiveness and similarity among members was *not* confirmed, using as measures, similarity in age and similarity in education level.

Group cohesiveness was positively related to the degree of prestige attributed by the group members to their own jobs.

Group cohesiveness was positively related to opportunity for interaction as measured by (a) size of group, and (b) duration of shared membership on the job. . . .[14]

The finding about anxiety would be consistent with the view that the primary work group can be an important source of emotional support and satisfaction of needs for the individual. Similarities among members of age and education level were not found to affect cohesiveness, but prestige attached to jobs, size of the group, and duration of group membership did influence it. These considerations highlight the differences in relative importance of the various kinds of constraints on group development; similarity in age and education level—the cultural inputs—was not as important a constraint for the development of group cohesion as those in time, space, and technology which characterize the organization of work.

[14] *Ibid.,* pp. 98–99.

## Zaleznik, Christensen, and Roethlisberger: The Motivation, Productivity, and Satisfaction of Workers: A Prediction Study[15]

The theories developed in this study, which we refer to as the *Prediction Study*, were discussed in the Technical Reference Note to the previous chapter. Therefore, we shall not present an elaboration of these theories here, but shall concentrate on the findings related to productivity and rewards.

The elements employed in the productivity analysis in this study were (1) internal rewards, (2) external rewards, and (3) productivity. Internal reward was the membership rank accorded to an individual by his work group. For the analysis of productivity, only two conditions of internal reward were used in the study; regular group members were rewarded by the group, while nonregulars were not rewarded by the group.

The measurement of external rewards entails use of the Reward-Investment (R-I) Index.[16] In the *Prediction Study*, pay was considered as the single measure of reward from management, since it measured status and recognition as well as economic reward. However, the study also assumed that the individual's feelings of being rewarded by external authority would be based on the balance between pay and his social investments, including age, seniority, ethnic background, education, and sex. Holding pay constant, the lower the individual's social investment, the greater would be his relative reward by management. Holding social investment constant, the greater the pay was, the greater the feeling of being rewarded. Reward-Investment indices were computed for each group member. When the indices were listed in order of rank, those in the top half were classified as considering their conditions for reward as favorable, whereas those in the bottom half were classified as considering them unfavorable.

Combining external and internal reward conditions yielded a fourfold classification:

### Reward Conditions

| External | Internal |
|---|---|
| 1. Favorable | Rewarded |
| 2. Unfavorable | Rewarded |
| 3. Favorable | Not rewarded |
| 4. Unfavorable | Not rewarded |

[15] See Bibliography.
[16] See Technical Reference Note, Chapter 9.

Data regarding productivity were obtained from company records, which were used to classify individuals into three types: (1) those whose productivity records were close to the group norm—the "on-the-line" producers; (2) high producers, who exceeded the group norm; and (3) low producers, who fell below the group norm. The group norm, expressed in actual productivity, became the basis for comparison. The original hypothesis related reward conditions to productivity conditions. The theory stated that external reward would tend to raise an individual's productivity, while internal reward would be a force constraining individual productivity toward the group norm. The actual form of the hypothesis was as follows:

HYPOTHESIS 12: Individual productivity varies as the rewards received from management and the group.

(a) Where an individual is rewarded both by management and by the group, he will produce close to the norms of the group, i.e., on-the-line.

(b) Where an individual is not rewarded by management, but is rewarded by the group, he will produce close to or slightly lower than the norms of the group.

(c) Where an individual is rewarded by management but not by the group, he will be a "rate-buster," i.e., high producer.

(d) Where an individual is neither rewarded by management nor by the group, he will produce below the norms of the group, i.e., low producer.[17]

The findings are indicated on Table 10.4. They strongly confirm the predicted effects of group rewards, but they indicate that external

Table 10.4    Productivity and Conditions of Reward: Number of Cases
in Each Cross-Classification

| Reward Conditions* | | Productivity Class | | | |
|---|---|---|---|---|---|
| Mgt. | Group | Low | On-Line | High | Total Cases |
| 1. + | + | 1 | 8 | 2 | 11 |
| 2. − | + | 1 | 6 | 2 | 9 |
| 3. + | − | 6 | 3 | 1 | 10 |
| 4. − | − | 3 | 3 | 9 | 15 |
| Total | | 11 | 20 | 14 | 45 |

* + means favorable or rewarded, − means unfavorable or not rewarded.[18]

[17] Zaleznik, Christensen, and Roethlisberger, op. cit., p. 237.

[18] Ibid., p. 238.

rewards, as measured by the R-I Index, tend to counter the direction proposed in the theory; the effects of the relationship between the two kinds of rewards were more complex than the hypothesis suggested.

The data showed that management rewards had no effect on individuals who were rewarded by the group. For individuals who were not rewarded by the group, they illustrated that management rewards had an opposite effect to the normal intentions of managers. In further analysis of productivity, the data indicated that regular group members tended to be on-the-line producers, deviants tended to be high producers, and isolates tended to be low producers. The low productivity of the isolates, regardless of external rewards, takes us back to Seashore's finding that groups of relatively low cohesion tend to have lower productivity than groups of higher cohesion. Furthermore, in groups of low cohesiveness perceived support by the company tends to counter the expected effect; those low cohesiveness groups who perceive the company as supportive tend to be lower producers than similar groups who perceive the company as less supportive. The connection between the two sets of findings lies in the theoretical assumption that the social isolation that characterizes the *Prediction Study's* isolates applies also to a large proportion of the members of groups of low cohesion.

The authors of the *Prediction Study*, searching for an explanation of the ineffectiveness of management rewards as motivations toward high productivity, analyzed the data of their interviews. They found the individual's emotional attitude toward the group, including his particular mode of moralizing, as a key determinant of high and low productivity among nonregulars.

In comparing the motivation of low producing, low status nonregulars with that of the high producing low status nonregulars, the difference in level of output seemed to be a function of the individual's identification with the group. Where the individual identified positively with the regulars, but was not an accepted member, he tended to produce low in line with his membership rank. This low output expressed behavioristically the individual's low membership rank in a group of which he wanted to be a member or with which he identified.

When the individual did not identify positively with the group, as in the case of the high producing nonregulars, the high productivity expressed simultaneously the negative attitude toward the group, conformity with task or work-oriented beliefs which were diametrically opposite to the beliefs of the regulars, and the failure of the mechanisms of social control of the regulars.[19]

[19] *Ibid.*, pp. 345–346.

These conclusions followed the authors' examination and rejection of the more obvious possibility that individuals who were relatively deprived of management rewards would work harder, and produce more, in order to increase their receipt of such rewards. The rejection of this possibility was based on the fact that the interview data contained no such implications. Instead, the interviews contained expressions of sentiments relating to work in general, to authority, and to group membership.[20]

The author's use of the psychological concept of identification, along with their description of behaviors as *expressing* the particular emotional processes of both psychological and group identification, marks an important qualification to theories of social behavior as exchange. Such theories are based on economic theory; the individual is seen as producing behaviors in exchange for rewards.[21] The utility of these theories has been amply demonstrated; the relatively successful confirmation of the *Prediction Study's* hypotheses is a case in point. But from the point of view of the study of individual behavior, the social exchange theories deal with the coping, or instrumental-adaptive, aspects of behavior to the neglect of the expressive functions of behavior. Thus, it is difficult to understand high productivity as an expression of hostility or of personal righteousness, independent of reward, unless we believe that social behavior serves to convey feelings as well as functions as a medium of social exchange. This means that simple notions of reward and punishment are insufficient to explain individual and group behaviors, including productivity. The earlier chapters of this volume, especially Chapters Five through Eight, describe and explain some of the characteristics of expressive behaviors which are necessary, in addition to purely sociological ideas, for a more complete understanding of the behaviors of individuals and groups.

### Blau: The Dynamics of Bureaucracy[22]

Blau's book described two different studies; in this section we shall discuss only the first of the two, the state employment agency. The people involved were in white-collar, semiprofessional jobs. Many of them had college educations related to their work. The agency's activities were twofold. It processed prospective employers' requests for qualified people to fill available jobs and processed people

[20] *Ibid.*, pp. 329–330.
[21] Homans, *Social Behavior: Its Elementary Forms.*
[22] See Bibliography.

who were looking for jobs. The purpose was to place qualified
people in appropriate jobs. Related to this was the fact that job
placements took people off unemployment compensation. This made
rapid placement of individuals desirable. Sheer quantity of placements per given time period could be a misleading index of performance because it would not indicate the quality of the placements.
Quality of placements would reflect the satisfaction of both employer's requirements and applicant's needs, and would contribute
toward reducing the amount of unemployment compensation funds
paid through another department of the state public employment
agency.

The part of Blau's study which particularly interests us is his comparison of productivity records between two sections in the agency.
In addition to productivity, two more elements figured in the analysis.
One was competitive behavior, a group performance for which Blau
developed an ingenious measurement index. The other was the
difference in the structural properties of the two sections. These
properties were directly related to differences between the environmental constraints acting upon the two sections.

During the course of Blau's study, the management introduced
detailed statistical productivity records as part of the measurement
and evaluation of individual interviewers' performances. This emphasized only one aspect of the entire range of performances required
to achieve the agency's over-all goals, the number of placements made
by the individual interviewer. It de-emphasized, and actually ran
counter to, the goal of successfully matching employers' needs with
the needs of the applicants.

Blau gave the name *competitiveness* to the behavior designed to
maximize an interviewer's own rate of making placements, and constructed the following competitive index. Adams, a member of
Section A, received 34 notices of job openings from employers during
the first half of April. There were six other interviewers in the section. If there were no hoarding, and job opening information were
equally available to all seven members of the section, Adams would be
expected to refer applicants to about one-seventh of the openings
which he received personally; six-sevenths of his openings would be
filled by other interviewers. Thus, Adams' expected referrals to his
own openings would be thirty-four-sevenths, 4.85. Adams actually
referred 19 applicants to openings he received; 19/4.85, or 3.9 times
as many as there would be in the absence of competitive practices.
This figure, 3.9, was Adams' index of competitiveness. The index
was also constructed for the six other members of Section A and for

the five members of Section B.[23]    An index of 1.00 would indicate perfect co-operation.    The higher the index for an individual or a group, the more competitive was the behavior of the individual or group.

A productivity index was constructed for each individual by comparing the number of placements made by the individual to the number of openings available in the section per interviewer.    By similar analysis, section productivity indices were computed.    Section A's index of competitiveness was 3.0.    Section B's index of competitiveness was 1.8.    Section A's productivity index was .59, while Section B's productivity index was .67; the less competitive section was the most productive.[24]

Individual competitiveness was compared to individual productivity for the two sections.    In Section A, the more competitive and less productive section, there was a high correlation $(+ .92)$ between the two; the more competitive the interviewer, the more productive he was.    However, in Section B, the less competitive but more productive section, individual competitiveness and productivity were negatively correlated $(- .20)$; here the more competitive individual was less productive.    Adding this to the finding that there was more variance among individual indices of competitiveness in Section A than in Section B, leads to the idea of enforced norms against competitiveness in Section B.    In other words, the members of Section B could punish a competitor among them by jointly withholding openings from him and thus decrease his productivity while increasing their own relative to his.    Hence group sanctions operated both to facilitate sharing and to discourage hoarding.

Further analysis and interpretation of the two sections led to the description of some interesting differences in the quality of group development in each.    Section B was found to be more cohesive, as we might expect.    The paradox was that in Section A the more competitive and more productive individuals engaged in more "running around" and social discourse than the less competitive and less productive members of the section.    To keep their productivity up, they had to negotiate socially with others to get access to the others' available openings.    In other words, the anxieties and interpersonal competition characteristic of Section A forced members to devote time and energy to repairing interpersonal relations in order to be productive, while this extra effort was unnecessary in Section B. In both sections, co-operation was a requisite for productivity, but

[23] Blau, *op. cit.*, pp. 52–53.
[24] *Ibid.*, pp. 53–55.

in Section A special effort was required to overcome reluctance to co-operate, while this effort could be devoted to the primary productive task in Section B because of the co-operative attitude prevailing.

The competitiveness and productivity findings were explained by the developmental conditions of the section groups. Section B was more cohesive and had a strong co-operation norm, while Section A was less cohesive and more competitive, beset by more individual and interpersonal anxiety. These differences in internal development could be related, in turn, to important differences in the environmental constraints which impinged upon the two sections. There were major differences in supervisory behavior, the professional orientations of the members, and employment security between the two sections.

These findings highlight the differences between rewarding performances and rewarding results. It appeared in the study that emphasizing productivity (the result) led to poorer actual results than an emphasis on co-operation (a performance). We can understand how this pattern was built into job technology and the evaluation of performance.

## Barnes: Organizational Systems and Engineering Groups[25]

So far, we have looked at some of the determinants of productivity in three studies, two of which focused on "blue-collar" worker groups, and one of which involved "white-collar" professional and semi-professional groups. Barnes' study centered upon groups of engineers in two industrial organizations. Although Blau's subjects were involved in relatively highly skilled, professionalized work, their individual jobs were characterized by the wholeness of their task; one interviewer could process the employer's request, then interview and place the applicant entirely by himself. The need for co-operation was limited to sharing information on availabilities, although there was most likely some need for interaction between interviewers as a training means and as a means of keeping professional skills up to date. In Barnes' engineering groups, however, there was a strong need for co-operation built into the groups' tasks. Each man's work was technologically interdependent with the work of other engineers, even though he could work on his own particular part of a larger task by himself. Hence, Barnes' groups are characterized by a greater degree of task-required interdependence and a more complex task than was the case with Blau's employment agency groups.

[25] See Bibliography.

Implicit in much of our discussion of organizational constraints was the idea that their patterns might vary in the degree to which they were consistent with task requisites. A spatial layout which prevents interaction in a system where interaction is required would be an example of a constraint running counter to task requisites. Similarly, the combination of a supervisor's behavior (which encourages competition) with an evaluation system (which measures individual output) provides a set of constraints which work against co-operation.

Barnes' study sets up organizational systems, or what we call patterns of organizational constraints, as an independent variable, with group and individual development, performance, and satisfaction as dependent variables. After studying one group in a particular organizational system, he found in a strikingly different kind of organizational system a second group whose task was similar enough for valid comparisons. He characterized the two systems as relatively "closed" and "open" in relation to the kinds and degrees of constraints acting on the groups in the different settings.

Barnes used three parameters to indicate the relative closedness or openness of the organizational systems. They were (1) the balance of influence between superiors and subordinates, (2) the degree of autonomy which individuals enjoyed on their jobs, and (3) opportunities for interaction beyond those narrowly required by the job.[26] The two systems, Company A and Company B, differed in a consistent manner on all three of these characteristics, as they impinged on the particular departments studied. The influence pattern in Company A tended to be unilateral, from superior to subordinate, while it tended more toward mutuality in Company B. The engineers in Department B (in Company B) had more autonomy in the selection of work assignments, and in determining the way in which work was to be carried out, than did the engineers in Department A. Finally, the supervisory pattern, everyday work procedures, and physical layout of Department B provided more opportunities for interaction both within and outside of the group, than did the corresponding constraints on Department A. Thus, Barnes characterized Company A as a relatively closed system and Company B as a relatively open system, compared with each other.

One of Barnes' contributions in this study was to bring together reference group theory and small group theory in field studies of group behavior. He made operational the distinction between reference group membership, and its attention to external values, and face-to-face group membership, with its attention to internal social controls.  His study highlighted the dilemma of professionalization as it affects group problem-solving efforts.  On the one hand, the engineering profession, along with other professions, is supposed to provide external standards, methodologies, and knowledge suitable for resolving certain kinds of problems.  On the other hand, the professional identification of an individual provides him with an external status and personal identity which may not bear directly on group problem-solving efforts.  Actually, the invocation of external status to determine behavior in a problem-solving situation can work against the application of suitable competences.  Under this condition, external status, as measured against values brought in from outside the group, determines who should engage in what kind of activity.  In an ideal group problem-solving situation, the distribution of competences determines this.

One theoretical assumption underlying Barnes' study was that the closed system tended to force individuals to fall back on somewhat arbitrary reference group values as determinants of behavior, whereas the open system allowed individuals and the group to develop in a manner more closely related to performance of the immediate task. The closed system, through reliance on arbitrary statuses and procedures as the source of authority, tended to force the individual and the group to rely on equally arbitrary external reference group values as sources of authority.  Thus, group development took place around these external standards which were not necessarily relevant to the task.

In addition to the three system parameters mentioned above, Barnes used as "input" variables individual values as measured by the Allport-Vernon Study of Values: social status as measured by age, seniority, education, and sex; and job status as measured by job title (engineer or technician) and salary levels.  For him the differential effects of the two kinds of systems were reflected by differences in the ways that values and social status related to job status, group membership, performance, and satisfaction in the two groups.  In the relatively open system, external values and social status were expected to be less closely associated with these various factors than in the relatively closed system.  This expectation was confirmed by his findings, some of which follow:

In the relatively closed system, members tended to polarize their identifications around the values of science *or* the values of management and business.  This polarization was not found in the relatively open system.

In Department A (surrounded by the relatively closed system), there was a strong association between values and group membership.  "Regulars" tended to be High on Economic values, while "nonregulars" tended to be low. In Department B (surrounded by the relatively open system), there was little association between values and membership.

The supervisor's evaluations of engineers' performances were more closely associated with the engineers' values in Department A than in Department B.

Informal subgroups in Department A tended to contain members of single status levels, while the subgroups in Department B tended to cut across status levels.

In Department A, high job status individuals tended to be "nonregulars" while low job status people tended to be "regulars." In Department B there was no such clear-cut relationship between status and membership.

In Department B there was greater agreement between the supervisor's evaluation of individuals' performance and their job status, than was the case in Department A.

Social status was found to be closely associated with the supervisor's evaluation of performance in Department A, but education was the only one of the social status factors found to be associated with performance in Department B. Department B was less status congruent than Department A; its older, high seniority engineers tended to have less education than its younger, lower seniority men.

Similarly, job status was more closely associated with social status in Department A than in Department B.

Department B's members tended to be more satisfied with their jobs than members in Department A.

"Nonregulars" in Department A tended to rank higher in performance than did "regulars." In Department B, where there were proportionally fewer nonregulars, there was no apparent opposition between membership in a social subgroup and high performance.

The over-all performance of Department A, as measured by management evaluations, customer complaints, and intergroup complaints, was lower than the over-all performance of Department B.[27]

Barnes' study stressed once more the importance of understanding productivity and performance as parts of a complex system of elements arising from group development. The closed system's constraints influenced a form of development in Department A which was less adaptive to task demands than was the case with Department B. Performance was not the only aspect of group development constrained by the organizational system; individual satisfaction and individual development were also affected. However, the relative openness of Company B, and the relatively more effective results in Department B,

[27] *Ibid.*

are not to be taken as defining an ideal set of environmental conditions which will promote optimum results for all groups, for all kinds of individual members, or for all kinds of tasks. The particular engineering tasks in which the two departments were engaged *required* certain patterns of interactions, activities, and sentiments. The particular conditions in the surrounding culture, especially the worlds of science and technology, reinforced these requirements as bases for optimum individual performance, satisfaction, and development. Many kinds of group tasks, involving other kinds of individuals, would require different sets of conditions for the optimum performance of group work.

## SUMMARY

Productivity is determined by complex relationships emerging from processes of group development. There are undoubtedly many kinds of work and cultural situations in which group development might play a less central role in influencing productivity. But one fact of the changing cultures of this century is the relative decline of the extended family unit as the stable source of membership, support, and affection for the individual.[28] This is reflected in increased geographical mobility of individuals, as well as in strong aspirations for higher status among some social classes. Uprooted individuals will therefore be more susceptible to finding personal social meanings in their relatively transient relationships with others. Thus, even those work activities which appear to be independent, such as individual work which requires no social interaction for its completion, can form a basis for the development of social groups by virtue of bringing individuals together in time, space, and general purpose. Consequently, whether or not group activity is required for completion of a task, productivity will, in most cases, result from group processes. For managers, group leaders, and other agents of change, this means that changes in productivity will require taking action on and within group processes. The traditional external controls of personnel selection, wage and salary administration, job design, legislated rules and procedures, policing, judging, and punishing individuals provide important constraints to group development and hence productivity, but they do not directly bring about results. Knowledge about group development and competence in influencing its direction, both outside and within the group, are necessary to increase predictability and control results.

[28] Homans, *The Human Group*, pp. 276–280.

This analysis of group development, which the manager, group leader, and group member must learn to make for himself in his specific situation, will ultimately lead to an examination of organizational and personal objectives. The Blau study pointed to the difference in outcomes attributable to the two different productivity objectives, individual productivity versus group productivity. Organizational constraints, including leadership behavior, can attain one at the expense of the other. If group productivity is more important to organizational goals than individual productivity, then the organizational system of constraints, including rewards, should be designed to contribute toward that end. On the other hand, if individual productivity is the main concern, the system of constraints and rewards should be designed to reward individual accomplishment.

The cultural problem of the relationships between individuals, groups, and authority figures is implicit in any discussion of productivity. The individual's life problems of working through conditions of dependency, counter-dependency, independence, and interdependence in his relationships with potential authority figures takes place in social situations which confront the individual with conflicting internal (to the individual) and external demands. The work group, in which the individual's work, occupation, career, or professional identity may become crystallized, is an especially salient situation for him with regard to resolution of the authority problem. Thus, when we center attention on individual development and personal productiveness, we are confronted with the strategic nature of the group situation for influencing personal development. The work group becomes a testing laboratory for the individual's motives and competences.

The measurement and evaluation of productivity is borne upon cultural conflicts between social classes and status levels. The cultural side of the individual's authority problem is manifested in intergroup, interclass, and interstatus conflict. The measurement and evaluation of productivity is a directional process; its formal organizational aspects involve the higher-status person or group unilaterally measuring and evaluating the lower-status person or group on the higher party's own terms. On the other hand, dependency tends to flow in the opposite direction; the lower-status person is more dependent on the higher-status person. Where adequate communications exist between status levels and the problems of measurement, evaluation, and dependency can be approached face-to-face, reality can confront the obsessive fantasies each has about the other. Under these circumstances, emotions can be addressed as such, and ultimately individual and group energies can be applied to problem solving rather than be expressed in hostility, withdrawal, and conflict.

There is a strong need in organizations for a broader concept of productivity. This broadened concept would include performances as well as results. In Barnes' study of the engineering group, it had to be "performance" rather than "productivity" which was evaluated by supervisors and higher management. Similarly, the more effective supervisor in Blau's study evaluated "total personal performances." We know from our study of the determinants of productivity that many unique performances are required within work groups for the effective accomplishment of a group's tasks. These include social maintenance, training, informal but task-relevant communications, and interpersonal co-operation. At higher levels in organizations these performances get rewarded. In some instances these performances may be too heavily rewarded, since their overemphasis can result in a conservative, ingrown perpetuation of the status quo. There is some need for recognizing and rewarding these performances at the lower levels of the organization, where they are no less necessary for performance of the task by the work group. The predominant lack of recognition and reward for these performances at lower levels has reinforced the interstatus conflict. The individuals who engage in these important performances do get rewarded by their group, by union organizations, or by social activities. But the fact that the reward comes in forms which may diverge from organizational goals perpetuates the potential conflict of interests, and in turn makes interstatus communication more difficult.

In the next chapter we shall look at individual satisfaction, another product of group development. Again, we shall find that the group intervenes between the formal organizational reward system and the satisfaction attainable by the individual from his working life. We shall give special attention to what the individual brings with him from the surrounding culture in the way of expectations. We shall continue to work with the same theoretical scheme introduced in this chapter, which differentiates among environmental constraints, group properties and performances, and results.

*Chapter Eleven*

# Satisfaction

THERE have been times and places when it was thought that worker satisfaction caused productivity. This assumption may underlie what has been called "paternalistic management." Its slogan may be paraphrased, "A happy worker is a high producer." Managers operating under this theory direct a major amount of their energy to making workers happy in a conventional sense. For example, they provide liberal fringe benefits in the hope that increased worker satisfaction will lead to increased production.

Let us look at some findings on the relationship between satisfaction and productivity. These are shown in Table 11.1.

*Table 11.1   Patterns of Deviant Productivity and Satisfaction: Number of Individuals in Each Condition*[1]

|  | Productivity | | |
| --- | --- | --- | --- |
| *Satisfaction* | High | Low | *Total* |
| High | 5 | 8 | 13 |
| Low | 9 | 3 | 12 |
| Total | 14 | 11 | 25 |

The apparently negative correlation between satisfaction and productivity is neither an isolated nor an unusual finding. Two other studies came up with similar results, as shown in Table 11.2.

The results of other investigations cover the full range of possibilities: in some situations satisfaction correlates positively with productivity,

[1] Zaleznik et al., *The Motivation, Productivity, and Satisfaction of Workers*, p. 278.

*Table 11.2    Job Satisfaction and Productivity*[2]

| | Percentage of Workers Reporting Their Intrinsic Job Satisfaction as: | | | |
|---|---|---|---|---|
| Routine clerical work[2a] | High | Medium | Low | Total |
| High-producing sections | 26% | 32% | 42% | 100% |
| Low-producing sections | 37% | 25% | 38% | 100% |
| Maintenance-of-way crews[2b] on railroad | | | | |
| High-producing sections | 13% | 65% | 22% | 100% |
| Low-producing sections | 25% | 50% | 25% | 100% |

in some there is no correlation, and in others as in those from which the foregoing tables were taken, a negative correlation obtains. We may thus conclude that there is no necessary direct relationship between satisfaction and productivity applying to all work situations.

There are important relationships among satisfaction, productivity, and other outcomes which are of primary concern to the organization, but they are not as simple as the paternalistic slogan would have them. Putting it briefly, we see *motivation* as a key variable, and productivity, satisfaction, and individual and group development as dependent variables.

Persons primarily concerned with goals other than organizational effectiveness also have reason to understand the sources of satisfaction. Their interest pertains to individuals' effectiveness in life, in and out of formal, businesslike organizations. Feelings of satisfaction relate to motivation, development, personal effectiveness, and over-all mental and emotional health.

This chapter is organized around three major sections and a summary. We shall first address the theoretical problems arising from defining, identifying, and measuring satisfaction. Thus far, the meaning of satisfaction has deliberately been left ambiguous; perhaps we could have used the word "morale" interchangeably with satisfaction. The second section of the chapter will address the sources of satisfaction. The results of certain investigations will be presented and discussed. The third section will discuss the Theory of Distributive Justice and the expression of complaints by organization members. When complaints arise, within ourselves or from others, we become

[2] Likert, *New Patterns of Management*, p. 15.
[2a] Katz et al., *Productivity, Supervision, and Morale in an Office Situation.*
[2b] Katz et al., *Productivity, Supervision and Morale among Railroad Workers.*

aware of and attentive to problems of satisfaction. In the summary we shall explore some of the implications of our analysis for organizations, administrators, and responsible members of society.

## THEORETICAL CONSIDERATIONS

The term "satisfaction" refers to the state of mind of a person, to some processes going on within him. It relates to an individual, not to a group. The distribution of satisfaction among members of a group may be described statistically in terms of an average and the spread of individual satisfaction scores around the average. As observed in Chapter 9, the "Mean Enjoyment Index" (see Figure 9.2) of the various kinds of communication structures masked the important differences among the ways that *individual* enjoyment was associated with the centrality of one's position. At the extremes, the mean enjoyment was greatest for the "Circle" pattern, least for the "Wheel." But the enjoyment of the individuals in the central position in the Wheel was far greater than the highest enjoyment in any position in the Circle. That is to say, any average satisfaction index for a group can result from a variety of patterns of individual satisfaction.

Satisfaction emerges from an individual's feelings and thoughts, which may be related to the rewards he is receiving from his environment. Since our analysis concerns the individual in a group within an organization, we shall dwell on the rewards that come to him from his organizational environment. His response to his reward condition will result not only from the rewards themselves, but also from his wants and his perceptions of what other persons are receiving from the same sources.

We should expect to find some relationship between a person's behavior and his internal state of satisfaction. But feelings and behavior are not the same thing. Motivation in terms of needs, desires, wants, preferences, or expectations, explains behavior. Satisfaction does not.

Satisfaction may be viewed as an individual's emotional measure of the balance he is experiencing between what he wants and what he is receiving from his environment. He wants certain rewards and not others in specific situations. The more he gets of what he wants, the more satisfied he will be, but this says nothing about his behavior. His behavior, we assume, is directed by his wants.

The term "wants" refers to inner motivational conditions. Krech, Crutchfield, and Ballachey define wants as follows:

*wants.* The initiating and sustaining forces of behavior. Wants may be either positive or negative. A positive want (e.g., a desire) is an assumed force which impels a person toward the achievement of a goal. A negative want (e.g., anxiety) is a force which repels a person from certain objects or conditions. Common synonyms for positive wants are *drives, needs;* for negative wants, *fears, aversions.*[3]

As to relationships between productivity and satisfaction, if a person wants the rewards that he can get by turning out production, the more he produces the more he gets, and the more satisfied he will be. On the other hand, if he wants other kinds of rewards, his satisfaction will stem from his receipt of those rewards, not from his productivity rate. Under this condition a high producer can be satisfied, not with his returns for production, but with the other rewards he receives. Similarly, a high producer can be dissatisfied with his rewards.

Negative wants, or avoidances, also play an important part in understanding the relationships between satisfaction and other variables. In the last chapter, we cited some results of the Zaleznik (et al.) study which indicated that high productivity was part of an expression of hostility by some workers to the regualr members of the group.[4] The behaviors that generated high productivity were a form of indirect "detour" by which individuals could express *dissatisfaction* with an "object or condition" (the regular group members), rather than a means of attaining high productivity as a goal in itself.

Another simple explanation of the negative correlations between satisfaction and productivity holds that productive work is perceived by some people in some situations as a form of *punishment.* It is undertaken to avoid more severe punishments. An extreme example would be the slave crews of ancient Mediterranean galleys. They would work hard to avoid the lash of the master, but would hardly be expected to be satisfied with their lot. Not working hard would result in severe punishment—painful wounds, disability, or death. These were usually even less desirable than painful physical labor.

The next step is to consider the kinds of rewards that people might be seeking in the organizational environment, and the kinds of rewards that the environment can deliver, as well as some of the objects of negative wants which may be present. In Chapter Ten we distinguished between external and internal rewards; the rewards that come from the formal organization and those that derive from group membership.

External rewards include those related to economic security: pay, job security, and economic fringe benefits. Another kind of external

[3] Krech et al., *Individual in Society*, p. 102.
[4] Zaleznik et al., *op. cit.*, pp. 345–346.

reward are those rewards intrinsic to the person's job: interest, variety, and the opportunity to develop mastery over intricate problems. Status rewards are still another kind of reward conferred by an organization. These include all of those symbols that publicly communicate the importance of the person. They cover such symbols as the amount of pay received above economic survival requisites; the form in which one is paid (monthly salary as against hourly wages); one's title, workplace location, size, and furnishings; one's use of privileged facilities such as certain wash rooms, entrances, and eating accommodations; and one's working hours. The promise of future advancement, which involves both specific job content and status connotations, is also an external reward. For example, a management trainee doing temporary clerical work is rewarded by a promise for the future which is lacking in the case of the permanently assigned clerical worker.

Internal rewards, in contrast, are those that are distributed among members of the work group through interpersonal relationships. These include liking and friendship, esteem and respect, support and help, and the opportunity to perform socially important and personally gratifying roles. Previous chapters have pointed out that in many work groups, the internal and the external reward systems are at odds with each other. In these instances, the individual is forced to choose one type of reward at the expense of the other.

The organizational situation can provide these various kinds of rewards for the individual. Conversely, individuals bring a variety of wants with them into the organizational setting. Individuals differ in their wants. Any one individual's wants may vary from time to time as his organizational and nonorganizational roles change over his lifetime. Some wants may become so fully satiated that they no longer motivate; the "rabbit" may become so full of "carrots" that he will fail to respond to more carrots as rewards. The individual may have a difficult task in trying to understand his own wants at a particular time, and in trying to discover his own particular order of preference. He has an even more difficult task trying to understand the changes in his motivations. And yet it is all too common for this same individual to impute his own wants to others, and to try to influence their behaviors by rewards and punishments that might be important to himself, but bear little relationship to their actual wants. This means that without an understanding of individual motivation, the administration of rewards and punishments to others will yield unpredictable and unexpected results.

Analysis of individual motivation involves two major problems.

The first is that of conceptualization and measurement. The second concerns the limits to the pursuit of causes.

A variety of conceptualizations have been developed by various theoreticians and researchers. These include the ideas of instincts, drives, needs, motives, wants, values, interests, goals, objectives, and others.[5] One important distinction among these ideas is made between conscious and unconscious motives. Conscious motives are those wants that are known to the individual. They become part of his conscious reasoning scheme, his personal basis for rational, goal-directed behavior. He can explain why he does certain things by his conscious wants. But he cannot explain all of his relatively persistent behaviors in the same way. He and others may "explain" some of his behaviors as basic character traits or as part of his unique version of "human nature." For example, he may consistently engage in nervous behaviors, such as chain-smoking and finger-nail biting, but will explain them by saying that he is a nervous person. This, of course, explains nothing. It merely describes the behavior pattern.

The explanation of these recurring behavior patterns, whether they involve purely private expressions or interpersonal communications, lies in unconscious motivation. Freud is credited with the discovery and elaboration of this concept. The causes of these behaviors lie in intrapsychic processes which take place within the person even though he may be unaware of them. The boundary line between the unconscious and the conscious is guarded by mechanisms of defense, which themselves become important motivating elements, as was explained in earlier chapters. One strong negative want is the anxiety related to uncovering the unconscious. Hence, unconscious motives affect behavior in two ways; they push the individual toward or away from external objects and through the mechanisms of defense protect him by generating defensive behaviors.

Some ideas concerning motivation refer to internal states, or sources of internal energy or "push." Other ideas refer to external objects or goals. These goals tend to "pull" the person or "repel" him, from outside. Yet some uniformities stand out when comparing empirical analyses of motivation. One is the multiplicity of motives—the idea that the individual is motivated by *many* internal and external sources at the same time. Another is that some kinds of motives remain relatively constant as an individual moves from one situation to another. Other kinds of motives, aroused by the situation, may vary within an individual as he moves from situation to situation. Still

[5] McClelland, *Personality*, pp. 383 ff. See also Chapter 7 of this volume.

other kinds of motivation change within the individual over longer periods of time as he moves through his life cycle.

The second major problem in understanding motivation involves the limits acceptable in pursuing causes. One such limit, acceptable for some purposes, sees motivation as a "given," independent variable. For other purposes, motivation is regarded as a dependent variable, whose sources we seek. In the first instance, we seek only to determine the relationship between motivation and behavior. In the second instance, we seek to determine the relationships between personal histories and current motivational states. Instead of taking motivation as given, we now ask *why* the person has the particular motives that determine his behavior in specific situations. In this kind of investigation, we look at the individual's personal history for the causes of his current motivational state.

In several earlier chapters we indicated some of the ways in which events occurring at one stage of an individual's life tend to determine how he will respond to later situations. The literature on personality development abounds with descriptions and explanations of these processes.[6] Yet a few major processes which are important for understanding the research findings to be discussed presently may be worth reviewing here.

If we consider the individual's life through his sequence of wants, some biologically based, others derived from cultural experiences, we can trace patterns of reward and deprivation emanating from his environment. We can analyze these rewards and deprivations as learning experiences, from the point of view of behavioral reinforcement. That is, any behavior followed by a reward which satisfies an active want is "learned" as an appropriate way in which to satisfy the want henceforth.[7] Similarly, behaviors that are followed by deprivation of wants will tend to be avoided. Furthermore, under some conditions, rewards may lead to satiation of certain wants; in such cases the satisfied want no longer motivates the individual's behavior. Under other conditions, success feeds on itself. The individual continues to pursue easily available rewards. In addition, the individual's internal states of wanting, feeling, and thinking become modified by reward and deprivation. Not only is behavior learned by reinforcement, but so are the internal conditions which accompany the behavior patterns as parts of the total personality.

Put another way, the individual learns to have attitudes and feelings. He learns to expect certain rewards from the environment in return

---

[6] See, for example, White, *Lives in Progress.*

[7] See Skinner, *Science and Human Behavior,* and Homans, *Social Behavior: Its Elementary Forms.*

for certain behaviors.   He acquires levels of aspiration in relation to certain kinds of rewards.   He may learn, for example, that it does not pay to pursue friendship or trust people too much because he has been disappointed in the past when he sought friendship, trusted people, or both.   On the other hand, he may have learned that trust pays off. Similarly, he may have learned that it does not pay to want too much to achieve success, because through past failures at task mastery he may have learned that shame and disappointment were not worth risking.   Another possibility is that along with reinforcement of attitudes toward particular rewards, the individual acquires a differential order of preference for various kinds of rewards.   For example, he may have learned that it is better for him to go after career success than after friendship, love, and warm human relationships.   On the other hand, he may have learned that it is preferable to pursue friendly relationships rather than to seek success.

From his past history of environmental rewards and deprivations, the individual enters the work situation wanting some kinds of rewards from it and not being concerned about other rewards.   The situation provides opportunities for satisfying some of his wants but not others. It may provide opportunities for satisfying many of his wants, but the constraints may force him to choose to pursue one kind of reward at the expense of another kind.   This scheme is represented by Diagram 11.3.

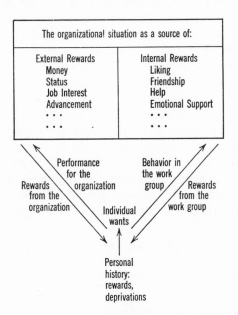

*Diagram 11.3   Sources of satisfaction in work groups.*

The individual's level of satisfaction is a function of his *receipts* of rewards from the situation and the *wants* which he brings to it.[8] Holding wants constant, the more he receives, the more satisfied he becomes. Holding receipts constant, the more he wants, the less satisfied he becomes. In mathematical form, Satisfaction $= f\left(\dfrac{\text{Rewards}}{\text{Wants}}\right)$. What the individual wants from the situation is determined by his personal history of rewards and deprivations, in a manner too complex to attempt to formulate in a simple equation. What he receives from the situation is a function of his behavior and the behavior of the other persons in his environment, as constrained by the organizational and cultural systems. Once involved in the situation, the individual's wants become modified further in the process of being rewarded and deprived; experiences in the organizational setting become part of the individual's personal history.

The differentiation between external and internal rewards is shown in the diagram. Depending on the nature of the organizational constraints and the state of work group development, the presence of alternative sources of rewards may put the individual in a position of conflict, forcing him to choose one kind of reward at the expense of the other. We would suggest that the greater the degree of conflict, the more the individual is forced to compartmentalize his experiences; for example, he might be forced to feel that he likes the job but not the people, or likes the people but not the company, or likes his boss but not his work associates, and so on. Since this condition is not uncommon in organizations, researchers have attempted to measure satisfaction along the specific, compartmentalized scales. For example, a satisfaction questionnaire might ask the person how he liked his specific job, his immediate superiors, the company in general, his work associates, and his pay, as well as how satisfied he was "in general" with his work situation. Since individual wants are many and varied, both in kind and in intensity, and the opportunities for rewards make up a complex pattern, the theoretical question of what is meant by "satisfaction" and how "it" is determined can be approached in only the most general of terms. However, empirical research can help to understand certain limited aspects of the problems.

## SOURCES OF SATISFACTION

The foregoing section suggested four sets of variables as relevant to the analysis of satisfaction. The first of these was satisfaction

[8] See Morse, *Satisfactions in the White Collar Job,* pp. 27–39.

itself. It may be measured through contentment with various kinds of rewards such as economic remuneration, status, job interest, group membership, or through a general response to a situation, or both. The second kind of variable is the actual receipt of rewards. These would be pay, job title or hierarchical position, the nature of the job content—its variety, complexity, and so forth—and the actual liking and esteem which the person's associates confer on him. The third variable is motivation, which we have called "wants." This refers to the kinds of rewards that are of concern to the individual and their relative values. The final variable we have called personal history; in relation to it we may measure, or count, the absence or presence of rewards and deprivations.

## Wants and Rewards

One simple example of the relationship among these variables is seen in a study of business executives conducted by Zaleznik.[9] From a questionnaire developed to measure individual preferences for the various kinds of rewards available in organizational situations, the executives were compared as to expressed partiality for economic rewards. This comparison showed 48 men as relatively high in their preference for economic rewards and the remaining 50 as relatively low.

The second variable was the actual dollar amount of economic reward—annual salary plus bonus—which was obtained from a separate questionnaire. The third variable was expressed satisfaction with economic rewards; their answers to the question, "To what extent do you feel that the money you make from your job measures up to your responsibilities and position?" were indicated on a scale running from little to great satisfaction. The men's responses were compared with each other and were classified as relatively high or low. The first step in the analysis compares actual reward with expressed preference for it, as shown in Table 11.4.

The table shows that men in the $20,000 to $30,000 range indicated a relatively stronger preference (62% high) for economic rewards than men at the extremes, whose proportions of high and low were identical —41% high and 59% low. Use of the salary range as an indicator of some facts about individual personal histories as well as of their economic rewards yields some plausible explanations of the finding. All of these executives were participants in an advanced management

[9] See Moment and Zaleznik, *Role Development and Interpersonal Competence*, pp. 285–287.

*Table 11.4  Preference for Economic Rewards and Actual Economic Rewards: Number of Cases and Percentage in Salary Class*

Annual Salary Plus Bonus

|  |  | Under $20,000 | | $20,000 to $30,000 | | Over $30,000 | | Total N | Total % |
|---|---|---|---|---|---|---|---|---|---|
|  |  | N | % | N | % | N | % |  |  |
| Preference for Economic Rewards | High | 16 | 41% | 23 | 62% | 9 | 41% | 48 | 49% |
|  | Low | 23 | 59% | 14 | 38% | 13 | 59% | 50 | 51% |
| Total |  | 39 | 100% | 37 | 100% | 22 | 100% | 98 | 100% |

training program, where the average age was about 45 years.  The men in the middle salary range were "on the way up," the men at the top had "arrived" or had *almost* arrived, while the men on the bottom were either just starting or had experienced relative "failure," compared to the others.  The basis for these views was economic success, as valued in the management culture.  Thus, we may account for the difference in the strength of economic motivation by referring to the stages in the success path of an ideal career.

Of the men at the bottom, the beginners had not yet tasted the rewards; economic rewards are relatively remote compared with the immediacy of the problems of new membership in the managerial group.  The beginners had learned to devalue a goal which they had not yet been successful in attaining.

The men at or approaching the top had been rewarded historically.  They might have become relatively satiated with economic success while relatively more concerned with other measures of personal achievement.  For example, the children of the older, economically successful men were leaving home, getting married, and starting their own families.  Similarly, these men were experiencing increased consciousness of advancing age.  Concern over both developments, plus relative satiation and other possible concerns, tended to decrease the relative importance of economic rewards to them.

The men "on the way up" had received some economic rewards and were relatively close to attaining more of them.  They were being reinforced but were not yet near satiation.  In addition, the turns in their personal lives were very likely expanding their standards of living, including the need to provide for children of college age. Hence, not only were simple reinforcement processes at work, but there were also current environmental demands upon them for money; they needed it for more than psychological satisfaction.

So far we have said nothing about satisfaction. We have looked only at economic rewards received and expressed preferences for them. Table 11.5 expands the same data, adding as a third variable expressed satisfaction with monetary rewards.[10]

*Table 11.5   Preference, Rewards, and Satisfaction: Numbers of Cases and Percentages High in Satisfaction*

*Annual Salary Plus Bonus*

| | | Under $20,000 | | $20,000 to $30,000 | | Over $30,000 | | |
|---|---|---|---|---|---|---|---|---|
| | | Satisfaction: | | Satisfaction: | | Satisfaction: | | |
| | | High | Low | High | Low | High | Low | Total |
| | | N | % | | N | % | | N | % | | |

| | | | | | | | | | |
|---|---|---|---|---|---|---|---|---|
| Preference for Economic Rewards | High | 4 | 25%* | 12 | 10 | 43% | 13 | 5 | 56% | 4 | 48 |
| | Low | 7 | 30% | 16 | 7 | 50% | 7 | 9 | 69% | 4 | 50 |

\* These percentages are based on the total number of cases in each Preference–Reward class. For example, of the 16 cases whose earnings were under $20,000 *and* who expressed High preference for economic rewards, 25% were also High in expressed satisfaction with their earnings.

Table 11.5 is broken down into six Preference-Reward classes, and the percentage of cases in each class which were also high in expressed satisfaction is indicated. Extracting these percentages yields the following matrix:

$$25\% \qquad 43\% \qquad 56\%$$
$$30\% \qquad 50\% \qquad 69\%$$

As we read toward the right on both lines, we find that satisfaction increases as the actual economic rewards increase. The more money each executive received, the more satisfied he was with his monetary

[10] *Ibid.*

rewards. This finding held for high preference for economic rewards, the top row of figures, *and* for low preference, the bottom row
of figures.

When we shift the comparison of figures from the horizontal rows
to the vertical columns, we find another uniformity. Regardless of
the actual monetary rewards, the higher the want (preference), the
*lower* the satisfaction. Conversely, the lower the want (bottom
figures) the higher the satisfaction. Putting these two uniformities
together confirms the theoretical proposition presented earlier:

$$\text{Satisfaction} = (f) \ \frac{\text{Receipts of actual rewards}}{\text{Wants}}$$

## Conflicts Among Sources of Rewards

This example referred to only one individual want—economic
rewards—and the corresponding return from the organizational environment. Economic wants and rewards are much more easily expressed in numbers than other kinds of human wants and rewards.
Monetary rewards are easily converted into other kinds of rewards,
ranging from food, clothing, and shelter at the subsistence level,
through entertainment and education, to symbols of power and
prestige. "Economic" satisfaction, therefore, represents the satisfaction of many different wants. In the case of Zaleznik's executives,
and the culture in which they work, the pursuit of economic rewards
does not, by and large, conflict with the pursuit of nonmonetary *group*
values, although it may clash with other personal wants such as spending time with one's family. Yet in worker groups the pursuit of
economic rewards may evoke conflict for the reasons mentioned under
"Productivity Norms" in the last chapter.

In discussing productivity, we presented data from the *Prediction
Study* on sources of reward—external and internal—and productivity
in a group of workers.[11]  The results as they relate to the sources of
reward and over-all satisfaction are shown in Table 11.6.

These findings highlight the importance of the work group as the
source of rewards. Management rewards tend to have no effect on
satisfaction, but the group's rewards are inclined to be associated with
it. Actually, the most satisfying condition appears to be that in
which the individual is favorably rewarded by the group but *unfavorably* rewarded by management; eight out of nine such cases express
high satisfaction.

[11] Zaleznik et al., *op. cit.*

*Table 11.6   Satisfaction and Reward by Management and the Group:
Numbers of Cases[12]*

| Reward | | Satisfaction | | |
|---|---|---|---|---|
| From Management | From the Group | High | Low | *Total* |
| Favorable | Favorable | 7 | 4 | 11 |
| Unfavorable | Favorable | 8 | 1 | 9 |
| Favorable | Unfavorable | 5 | 7 | 12 |
| Unfavorable | Unfavorable | 5 | 10 | 15 |
| Total | | 25 | 22 | 47 |

## Ethnic Background, Group Membership, and Satisfaction

Another aspect of the *Prediction Study* that throws additional light
on the problem of individual satisfaction, has to do with the in-group
value system.[13]  The study found that among the 50 workers in the
department, Irishness represented an extremely important in-group
value.  In small groups, the lines along which membership rewards
are distributed are defined by the group itself.  The people who
receive these rewards score highly against the predominant in-group
value system.  In the *Prediction Study's* work group, a reward system
based on the Irish background of the most influential workers rewarded
behavior and personal backgrounds that conformed to the norms
and values of "Irishness."

Ethnic background influences group development in two different
ways.  One form of such influence relates to the values brought into
the group by its members, which derive in part from their ethnic
origins.  The other form of influence concerns the connotations for
status of ethnic identifications in the wider culture surrounding the
group.

The values shared by group members are the basis of social exchange.
An exchange of favors implies social obligations because the favors are
of value to both parties.  The process of social behavior as exchange
is explained in detail by Homans.[14]  For our present analysis, it is only
important to understand that the human wants described in the previous sections are strongly influenced by the individual's cultural background.  His family and ethnic traditions set the values by which

[12] *Ibid.*, p. 271.
[13] *Ibid.*, pp. 209–212.
[14] Homans, *op. cit.*

his more basic wants may be expressed. This may be seen in the distinctions between urban and rural values. The values of rural workers, in their extreme form, embody the Protestant Ethic of individual responsibility and achievement, hard work, competition, and upward mobility for the individual and his family. The values of urban workers, in their extreme form, attribute responsibility and blame, over which the individual is seen to have no influence, to external authorities and hold that the individual's best interest is served by group loyalty and group action.[15]

In the American culture, these values tend to become identified with the length of time that the individual's ethnic group has been in the country. Old-timers become identified with conservative individualism, partly as a group defense against the newcomers, who are forced to band together as minority groups, even though they emigrated to acquire the values prized by the old-timers. Thus, the second effect of ethnic factors on group development attributes status to the individual on the basis of his ethnic background.

(1) . . . Values are assigned implicitly in the American society which differentiate various ethnic groups, and (2) . . . the rankings of ethnic backgrounds correspond roughly to the waves of immigration. The more nearly identified an individual is with the American culture, the higher his status; or stated another way, an individual's status diminishes the more easily he is identified with a particular ethnic group whose immigration history is in the twentieth century. It is true that associating status with ethnicity runs counter to another American value that a person's family background should make no difference in the kind of job he gets, his social position, and so forth. The history of FEPC legislation attests to the existence of conflicting values regarding ethnicity. On the one hand, the fact that legislation is necessary indicates the existence of differentiation along ethnic lines. On the other hand, the creation and enforcement of this legislation portray the constant striving of our society to achieve the ideal of equality.[16]

In the *Prediction Study*, the authors constructed status indices based on the two assumptions stated at the outset of the foregoing quotation.[17] Group members of Irish-Catholic background were rated as of lower social status than Yankee-Protestants. In the greater culture, the Yankee-Protestants are the "regulars," whereas the Irish-Catholics are lower-status "deviants." However, among the 50 workers studied in the group, the reverse statuses obtained. Irishness was a character-

[15] See Mann and Hoffman, *Automation and the Worker*, pp. 37–43.
[16] Zaleznik et al., *op. cit.*, p. 209.
[17] *Ibid.*

istic of regular group membership, so that non-Irish workers tended to be deviants or isolates. The importance of group membership as a source of satisfaction to these workers is reflected in the finding shown in Table 11.7. This relates satisfaction to ethnic background, which, among these particular workers, was a major source of values upon which to base regular group membership. The Irish members tended to be more satisfied than the non-Irish workers.

*Table 11.7   Satisfaction and Ethnic Background*[18]

|  | Satisfaction | | |
|---|---|---|---|
| *Ethnic Background* | High | Low | *Total* |
| Irish | 17 | 6 | 23 |
| Non-Irish | 8 | 16 | 24 |
| Total | 25 | 22 | 47 |

$$p < .01.$$

## Level of Aspiration

When researchers seek to measure different aspects of satisfaction they find tendencies for some individuals to feel that everything about their work situation is satisfactory or that everything is unsatisfactory. These different aspects might be pay, the nature of the job itself, supervision, work associates, and general working conditions. This general well-being or dissatisfaction which covers all aspects of the situation is called the "halo effect" by some behavioral scientists. Furthermore, different individuals receiving similar rewards from work may have quite opposite feelings about them. For one person, everything might be wholly satisfactory, while for another, everything might be quite unsatisfactory. Drawing on the theoretical ideas explored in this chapter, we may interpret this kind of response as indicating important differences in the strength as well as the objectives of individual patterns of motivation. The same rewards which would satisfy individuals who expected little from a situation could very well dissatisfy others with higher expectations.

Table 11.8 shows the results by sex for *over-all* satisfaction with the work situations among the workers interviewed in the *Prediction*

[18] *Ibid.,* p. 273.

*Table 11.8    Over-all Satisfaction by Sex: Numbers of Cases*[19]

*Satisfaction*

| Sex | High | Low | Total |
|---|---|---|---|
| Female | 12 | 6 | 18 |
| Male | 11 | 18 | 29 |
| Total | 23 | 24 | 47 |

$p < .10.$

*Study.* In this case wants were not measured directly but were inferred from interview data and cultural uniformities regarding differences in the sexes; men wanted more from their work situation than did women.

The findings in Table 11.8 indicate that men were generally less satisfied than women with their over-all work situation. The work situation was the same for both sexes; they were doing the same kind of work in the same department. Although the women tended to earn less than the men, their increased satisfaction could be attributed to their lower expectations. "On the whole, women expect and are expected to achieve less from their work situation than men, stemming from traditional roles in society.[20]

Behind these data lie the facts that the rewards of group membership and informal social activities were important sources of satisfaction to most of the workers, and that social satisfactions were even more important to the women than to the men. The women expected little more from their jobs than social satisfactions, while the men had to face up to the cultural expectations for the male role. Men, according to cultural prescriptions and the way they are brought up as children, are expected to be more active, aggressive, and successful *in work* than women.

This notion of how much of various kinds of rewards the individual feels he should try to achieve, and the degree of difficulty he will persist in overcoming, is called his level of aspiration. Not only is this feeling related to sex roles, it is also related to ethnic background, patterns of child raising, and the position of the child in the family. These influences produce general motivational conditions within the individual as he moves through life. Research has found that standards of the groups to which a person belongs or aspires to

[19] *Ibid.,* p. 260.
[20] *Ibid.*

belong influence his level of aspiration at a particular time and in a particular social setting. This is also found to be true of the individual's actual experiences of success and failure in attaining rewards, of the recency of these successes or failures, of his development of competences, and of the performance of the others in the social situation.[21]

Our interest in level of aspiration centers on its effects on the satisfaction of individuals in organizational settings over relatively long periods. Experimental work on the subject has been concerned mainly with situations of short duration, such as dart-throwing games and other activities involving immediate measurement and receipt of results. McClelland's "need Achievement," which purports to measure the individual's motivation to be successful in relation to external standards, is one measure of the relative long-range aspects of levels of aspiration. His theoretical and empirical work with the achievement motive ranges from individual behavior through the economic development of societies and nations.[22]

Need Achievement, is a global, rather than a specific concept, implying a need to succeed irrespective of particular means. Thus, scientists, authors, and artists could be just as strong in their needs to achieve as would the most extreme case of the stereotype of the rising executive. The concept transcends particular occupations or professions, although there is no doubt that particular cultures and groups would tend to channel the need into relatively limited means. A person with high need Achievement would normally follow culturally prescribed roads to success. In Western cultures this would tend to rule out such occupations as the ministry, education, or social work for people who really wanted to be "successful."

The same group of executives from which the data for the analysis of economic preferences, rewards, and satisfaction were drawn (see Table 11.5) were given the Thematic Apperception Test (TAT) to measure the strength of the achievement and affiliation imagery they would produce in imaginative stories. The test was given to them as a test of imagination. They were asked to write imaginative stories in response to ambiguous pictures. Their stories were analyzed for content by a trained scorer who indicated for each subject the amount of achievement and affiliation imagery present in his stories. These measures were called *need Achievement* (nAch) and *need Affiliation* (nAff). We are concerned with need Achievement scores as a

[21] See Deutsch, "Field Theory in Social Psychology," pp. 208–209, and Lewin et al., "Level of Aspiration."
[23] See McClelland, *The Achieving Society*.

measure of general levels of aspiration. These scores measured something different from the reward preferences referred to earlier. Reward preference scores resulted from the exercise of conscious choice among limited possibilities. Need Achievement scores measured responses to ambiguous stimuli, which were limited only by the requirement that the stories be put into writing. The stories could include any kinds of themes which happened to arise within them in response to the pictures.[23]

The differences which individual *nAch* made in satisfaction, in the cases of the 99 advanced management executives, are shown in the five tables, Table 11.9 through 11.13. These tables relate need Achievement scores to responses to five different questions concerned with aspects of satisfaction.[24]

On four of the five of the questions leading to the findings in Table 11.9 through 11.13, persons in the lowest quartile in *nAch* scores tended to express the highest satisfaction, while persons in the highest quartile tended to express lower satisfaction. The persons in the middle quartiles tended to express satisfaction to a degree somewhere between the two extremes in most cases, although the relationship did not appear to be perfectly linear. The questions covered: (1) satisfaction with career, compared with others; (2) satisfaction with career, compared to own early expectations; (3) satisfaction with job, expressed in terms of willingness to leave company (assuming that the more willing a person is to change companies, the less satisfied he is with his present job); (4) satisfaction with immediate superior; and (5) satisfaction with the opportunity for advancement offered by the present job.

The consistency of the tendencies in these findings stress the effect of the individual's over-all level of aspiration, as measured by need Achievement, on his assessment of the adequacy of his environmental returns.

As we have noted, at a given level of rewards, the more the person wants, the less satisfied he is with his rewards. The scheme illustrated in Diagram 11.3 sees the individual's personal developmental history as the source of his current level of aspiration. McClelland's research and writing has illuminated some of the specific conditions which tend to "train" the individual to have a high need for achievement.[25] These

---

[23] See McClelland et al., *The Achievement Motive,* and Atkinson, *Motives in Fantasy, Action, and Society.*

[24] Other results of this study appeared in McClelland, *The Achieving Society,* and in Moment and Zaleznik, *op. cit.*

[25] McClelland et al., *op. cit.,* Chapter 9.

Table 11.9   Need Achievement and Satisfaction with Career:
Responses to the Question,
"When you compare yourself with others, how satisfied do you feel
with your own career?"

| nAch Score, by Quartiles | Very Satisfied | Less Satisfied | Total |
|---|---|---|---|
| Low | 48% | 52% | 100% |
| Middle Low | 32 | 68 | 100% |
| Middle High | 36 | 64 | 100% |
| High | 31 | 69 | 100% |
| Total | 36 | 64 | 100% |

Table 11.10   Need Achievement and Success:
Responses to the Question,
"Compared with [your early expectations], how well would you
say you have done?"

| nAch Score, by Quartiles | Much Better | Somewhat Better | Equal or Lower Than Expected | Total |
|---|---|---|---|---|
| Low | 53% | 17% | 30% | 100% |
| Middle Low | 24 | 44 | 32 | 100% |
| Middle High | 32 | 28 | 40 | 100% |
| High | 35 | 23 | 42 | 100% |
| Total | 35 | 28 | 37 | 100% |

Table 11.11   Need Achievement and Willingness to Change Jobs:
Responses to the Question,
". . . How seriously would you consider changing companies?"

| nAch Score, by Quartiles | Not at All | Interested | Total |
|---|---|---|---|
| Low | 61% | 39% | 100% |
| Low Middle | 60 | 40 | 100% |
| High Middle | 64 | 36 | 100% |
| High | 46 | 54 | 100% |
| Total | 57 | 43 | 100% |

*Table 11.12  Need Achievement and Satisfaction with Superior:*
*Responses to the Question,*
". . . *How satisfied are you with the man to whom you report in*
*your own company?"*

| nAch Score, by Quartiles | Very Satisfied | Somewhat Satisfied | Mildly Dissatisfied | Total |
|---|---|---|---|---|
| Low | 70% | 22% | 8% | 100% |
| Low Middle | 51 | 36 | 13 | 100% |
| High Middle | 52 | 28 | 20 | 100% |
| High | 50 | 23 | 27 | 100% |
| Total | 56 | 28 | 16 | 100% |

*Table 11.13  Need Achievement and Perceived Opportunities for*
*Advancement: Responses to the Question,*
". . . *Do you feel that your present position . . . offers you as much*
*opportunity for advancement as you would like?"*

| nAch Score, by Quartiles | As Much as I Would Like | Not as Much as I Would Like | Total |
|---|---|---|---|
| Low | 78% | 22% | 100% |
| Low Middle | 59 | 41 | 100% |
| High Middle | 64 | 36 | 100% |
| High | 46 | 54 | 100% |
| Total | 61 | 39 | 100% |

conditions involve the behaviors of the mother and father toward the child—their encouragement, challenge, rewards, emotional support, and independence training.

In Zaleznik's work with the executives, the men were asked how close to their families they felt while growing up. The results of comparing their responses to this question with their need Achievement scores are shown in Table 11.14.

The executives who indicated that they felt very close or close to their families tended to score lower on *nAch* than the executives who felt "not so close" to their earlier families. At least two different explanations may account for the association between closeness and relatively low need Achievement. One explanation is that close family ties may have been attained at the expense of independence. Individuals who still feel somewhat dependent on close family ties would

*Table 11.14   Feelings of "Closeness" to Early Family and Scores on Need Achievement: Per Cent of Cases in Each Scoring Class*

Checked Response to "Closeness" Question

| Relative Scores on nAch | Very Close | Close | Not So Close |
|---|---|---|---|
| High | 43% | 41% | 63% |
| Low | 57% | 59% | 37% |
| Total | 100% | 100% | 100% |

be reluctant to take the risk of breaking them in the pursuit of external achievement.   Another explanation is that experience of failure could have devalued achievement and increased dependency on close familial ties; the recollection of closeness could have been distorted toward more warmth than was originally there by the deprivations of later events, evoking a kind of longing for the security of the family.

Barnes' study of engineering groups included an indication that current career values, which had some continuity with the level of education attained by the men, were associated with levels of aspirations.[26] He found that professionally oriented engineers, who had slightly more formal education than persons more oriented toward the organization, were usually less satisfied than the "Organizationals," while also tending toward higher performance.   This was explained by the higher level of aspiration expressed by the professionals in interviews with them. They conveyed greater concern with professional growth and development than did the "Organizationals."[27]   Their wants could not receive immediate gratification from their work, since their expectations covered a relatively long time period.   In contrast, the persons oriented toward more immediately attainable goals such as organizational rewards, that is, the "Organizationals," tended to express relatively higher satisfaction than the professionals.

The concept of levels of aspiration includes an implicit time scale; some wants, such as career success, require a relatively long period of time for their satisfaction.   The relatively low satisfaction expressed by the high *nAch* persons in Zaleznik's study and the professionals in Barnes' study may reflect the problem of having to renounce immediate gratification of some wants as part of the commitment to longer-range goals.

[26] Barnes, *Organizational Systems and Engineering Groups.*
[27] *Ibid.*, pp. 70–73.

One more set of data from Zaleznik's work with the executives suggested the association of career choice with levels of aspiration. When Zaleznik correlated the executives' job functions with their *nAch* scores, he found the differences shown in Table 11.15.

*Table 11.15    Job Function and Need Achievement: Per Cent of Cases in Each Class*[28]

|  | Production and Engineering | Control and Finance | Marketing | Total |
|---|---|---|---|---|
| Number of Cases | 25 | 29 | 24 | 78 |
| Relative Scores on nAch | | | | |
| High | 36% | 41% | 75% | 50% |
| Low | 64% | 59% | 25% | 50% |
| Total | 100% | 100% | 100% | 100% |

In interpreting Table 11.15, we start with the assumption that the executives' particular job functions *and* their levels of aspiration were *both* determined by personal histories.   We find that men in marketing tended to have higher levels of aspiration than men in control and finance.   These men, in turn, tended to have stronger motivation to achieve than men in production and engineering.   Through examining the meanings of these *job* functions in the organizational setting, we may infer that their implied social-psychological mobility increased in the same manner as the motivation to achieve among the *men* in these functions.   Comparing the functions, production and engineering work was relatively rooted "inside" the organization, control and finance activities required some interaction with the company's external environment, while the marketing function was on the "outer edge" of the company's relationship to its environment, identifying more with entrepreneurial behavior than did the other functions.[29] Similarly, the concreteness and immediacy of accomplishment decrease as one moves in this outward direction.   The completion of a task is measured over a longer period of time in marketing than in control and finance, which, in turn, have longer time scales than the measurement of success in production and engineering, where tasks tend to be completed more quickly.

Thus, we see that satisfaction is a function of rewards *and* aspirations.   Both elements of the equation have global, over-all bases such

[28] See also, McClelland, *The Achieving Society*, p. 267.
[29] McClelland, *op. cit.*

as general "success" and a broad need to achieve.   In addition, there are specific kinds of rewards and specific kinds of wants, such as economic security, status, job interest, and membership in a group. Up to this point, we have examined how the individual assesses the degree of balance or imbalance he is experiencing between what he wants and what he receives and have seen that feelings of satisfaction may emerge from assessment of the balance.   However, we have not examined the social context of this process, whereby the person evaluates his rewards in relation to those received by others, as well as in relation to his own wants.   We observe in children, for example, unhappiness and dissatisfaction when *other* children receive rewards. We also observe in history that underdeveloped societies may become dissatisfied when they learn what they are missing; they feel deprived *relative to others*, rather than relative to their own wants.   "Keeping up with the Joneses" is a particular kind of want which becomes activated only when we know and can see the rewards that the Joneses are receiving.   We shall investigate this important influence on individual satisfaction, which is called relative deprivation by some writers,[30] by analyzing the sources of common complaints in group and organizational situations.

## JUSTICE AND COMPLAINTS

The individual's wants or aspirations, the denominator in the equation for satisfaction $\left( \text{satisfaction} = (f) \dfrac{\text{rewards}}{\text{wants}} \right)$, are determined, as we have observed, by the personal history he brings to the situation. Some of these wants have their basis in fundamental physiological needs such as food, water, warmth, elimination, and sex.   These primary needs are so elaborated, modified, and augmented by cultural processes that the goals pursued by the adult bear little relation, on the surface, to primary biological sources.   Yet these learned wants motivate the human no less strongly than instincts motivate the lower animals.   In terms of practical human affairs, it does not matter how important the satisfaction of a particular want is for the *physical* survival of the person; his behavior is determined by what he thinks or feels that he wants.

Part of the socialization process by which the values of a culture are passed down from generation to generation includes a concept of social justice.   The particular elements in the set of justice equations

[30] See, for example, Merton, *Social Theory and Social Structure*, pp. 225–280.

may vary from culture to culture. For example, in some cultures increasing age "deserves" increasing respect, while in other cultures the relationship between age and respect might be inverse (that is, infants would deserve the most respect) or curvilinear (for example, adolescents might deserve the most respect.) The components of the equation constitute an investment and a reward, age being the investment and respect being the reward.

For understanding complaints in their social context the most important aspect of these cultural equations for social justice is the formula for *proportional distribution* of rewards among persons. One man's rewards should hold the same proportional relationship to another man's rewards as their respective social investments. In a culture where age and respect are supposed to hold a linear relationship with one another, an older man should receive more respect than a younger man regardless of their absolute ages. In a group in which the members' ages vary, the respect should be distributed in proportion to the ages. When this does not happen, when one person does not get as much respect as he deserves, he feels that "it isn't fair." This is a condition of felt *injustice*, and the individual will find some way to express his dissatisfaction in a form of complaint. On the other hand, a person who feels overrewarded will also sense injustice, but will tend to feel guilty about it and attempt to re-establish a just balance by increasing his investment in other areas. If he is "too young" he can do nothing to make himself older relative to the others, but he can try to behave more responsibly and thus increase his behavioral investment.

The ideas discussed above are called the Theory of Distributive Justice, which was discussed briefly in the note to Chapter Nine.[31] One of the most interesting examples of the actual patterns of behavior and sentiment to which the theory refers appears in William F. Whyte's *Street Corner Society*.[32] Whyte's description of the Norton Street Gang's bowling activities was analyzed from the point of view of Distributive Justice by Homans in *The Human Group*.[33] The gang had developed a culture in which the social position of each member became well established, and in which the values and norms against which position was measured were clear. When the gang took up bowling, social pressures were applied to make sure that individual bowling scores were proportional to social positions, with a few allowable and explicitly stated exceptions.

[31] See, also, Homans, *Social Behavior: Its Elementary Forms*, pp. 232–264, and Zaleznik et al., *op. cit.*, pp. 50–56.
[32] See Bibliography.    [33] Homans, *The Human Group*, pp. 156–189.

Another illustration, this one in the setting of work groups in an organization, is contained in Homans' *Status Among Clerical Workers*.[34] In this case there were two kinds of jobs, cash posters and ledger clerks. The ledger clerks' job was considered by the workers and the management to be a "better" job; it involved more variety and mental activity. Workers, who were women, were normally "promoted" from cash poster to ledger clerk. This was a clear status promotion, but there was no increase in pay. The reason for this was that management thought the cash poster job was so unpleasant that they had to offer high pay to get women to take it. Thus, the cash posters were relatively overpaid compared to the ledger clerks. The ledger clerks liked their jobs and were satisfied with the amount of their pay but complained that the cash posters received the same pay, that they, the ledger clerks, were "put down to work on posting" from time to time, and that their supervisor did nothing to correct these glaring injustices.[35]

Part of the Hawthorne study conducted in the late 1920's was a systematic analysis of the worker and supervisor complaints which were gathered in a widespread program of individual interviews.[36] The "facts" in the complaints did not make "objective" sense, but the *sentiments* behind the "facts" almost invariably referred to conditions of injustice felt within the informal social structure of the plant. Some of the complaints involved relative earnings in comparison with job content, seniority, male versus female, married versus single, education, or ability.[37] When the researchers understood the ways that social differentiation was expressed in the informal organization, they saw the complaints as symbols of conditions violating what we now call Distributive Justice. The problem for the worker and for the interviewers in the early stages of the study was that there was no direct way in which one could legitimately state his feelings of injustice directly. The worker had to rationalize the feelings around semifactual ideas and values. The injustices they felt existed partly because management's rewards of job title, pay, and working hours did not agree with the many bases for evaluation built into the social structure. But even when a management does try to keep its rewards more closely related to the workers' values, there will still be some injustice felt because of the *differences* in value systems held by various individuals, who grow up in different subcultures, and by face-

---

[34] Homans, *Status Among Clerical Workers*, p. 396.
[35] See Homans, *Social Behavior . . .*, pp. 237–240, for his later analysis of the study.
[36] Roethlisberger and Dickson, *op. cit.*, pp. 255–269, 358–376.
[37] *Ibid.*, pp. 262–263.

to-face groups, who develop their own systems of social evaluation.

The effects of Distributive Justice go considerably beyond the limits of face-to-face groups and single organizations. They apply also to relations among reference groups, such as ethnic minorities, occupational classes, social classes, age groupings, and sex groupings. Reference group theory has pointed to individual and group feelings of relative deprivation.[38] Outstanding examples of these feelings were brought out in Stouffer's studies of *The American Soldier*.[39] For example, married draftees were more dissatisfied with their situation than unmarried draftees.[40] Members of the Military Police, where the actual promotion rate was about the lowest anywhere in the Army, were *more* satisfied with their opportunities for promotion than were men in the Air Corps, where objective promotion rates were the highest. "The *less* the promotion opportunity afforded by a branch or combination of branches, the *more favorable* the opinion tends to be toward promotion opportunity."[41]

The married draftees could have felt that military service was more of a deprivation for them than it was for single men because they were forced to leave their families. According to the Theory of Distributive Justice this condition would be called felt injustice as it would apply to "classes" of people rather than to members of a primary group. In the case of the Military Police, the actual infrequency of promotions would provide fewer incidents where men would be able to compare their own progress with others; *everyone* had to wait a long time to be promoted. On the other hand, promotions in the Air Force were relatively rapid and frequent. Air Force men would not only *expect* rapid advancement; they would also see others promoted frequently and be in a position to compare the "rewards" of these others with their relative "investments." The simple fact of increased opportunities for felt injustice to occur could account for the greater expression of complaints and dissatisfaction.

These examples of the workings of Distributive Justice barely scratch the surface of reference group theory. For example, to which reference group does the individual apply himself as a measure of deserved reward in what kinds of situations? What happens when the individual's multiple reference group affiliations impose conflicting standards upon him? What constitutes deprivation in its reference group sense? These and other questions are pursued by Merton.[42] For the purposes of this chapter, these few superficially interpreted

[38] Merton, *op. cit.*  [39] See Bibliography.  [40] Stouffer, *op. cit.*, p. 125.  [41] *Ibid.*, p. 256.
[42] Merton, *op. cit.*

instances indicate the pervasiveness of the process of social comparison at all levels of social organization, not just within the confines of the face-to-face group. The relevance of the Theory of Distributive Justice to international relations, race and ethnic relations, and social class relations is clear. It is also clear that remedial attempts, such as racial integration in the United States, the breakdown of caste barriers in India, and the emergence of the African nations to full status in the world, all involve deep-seated personal and group standards in the attempt to expand the dimensions of social justice at a "supercultural" level.

## SUMMARY

Our study of the individual in the group, especially in the work group in the formal organization, has dealt with satisfaction as a result of the encounter between the individual and his work environment. We see satisfaction as a function of the rewards received from a situation in comparison with the wants brought to it.

In studies of work groups in industry, it was found helpful to analyze two different major sources of reward. External rewards come from outside the face-to-face work group; the management of the organization is the rewarding agent. These rewards include pay, status, intrinsic job interest, and opportunities for advancement. Internal rewards are distributed by the face-to-face group; to a large extent they are beyond the direct control of managers or organizational planners. These rewards include membership, affection, respect, emotional support, task and personal help, and the opportunity to fill a specialized role in the informal organization. These two sources of reward conflict with each other in many, if not most, work situations. The individual is often forced to choose to pursue one and not the other kind of reward. Because of the complexity of the reward systems as well as the individual's wants, the relationships among productivity, satisfaction, and individual development are indirect and do not allow simple cause and effect analysis.

The more the individual gets, given his wants, the more satisfied he will be. On the other hand, the more he wants, given the rewards he receives, the less satisfied he will be. Different people bring different wants to the work group, based on their unique personal histories of rewards and deprivations. The same individual will experience different strengths and kinds of wants over his lifetime; what is a reward to him at one time and place will not be a reward to him at another time and place.

Along with individual differences in the strengths and kinds of wants, we may also observe an over-all level of aspiration which tends to spill over onto all individual wants. One such pattern of generalized motivation has been measured by McClelland's "need Achievement." By use of this kind of measure, as well as inference from individual reports, we have been able to identify some individuals as "undermotivated" or "overmotivated." In these cases, the individual's entire pattern of wants is dominated by an over-all avoidance of competition and risk, on the one hand, or a strong need to compete and be successful in every venture, on the other hand. Rewards of any kind will tend to be more satisfying to persons with low motivation rather than strong motivation to succeed. The findings presented, as executives' need Achievement scores were compared with their satisfactions, tended to emphasize this over-all impact of the level of aspiration on the way the individual reacted to the rewards he was receiving.

Having examined how individual satisfaction was a result of the rewards received from a situation and the wants brought to it, we inspected the effects of social comparison on individual satisfaction. The Theory of Distributive Justice holds that group cultures, as well as the cultures of larger social units, develop codes of social justice. These codes prescribe how social rewards, such as rank and respect, should be distributed among members of the group according to each one's social investments—such as, age, ethnic origin, education, and seniority. The basic form of the code specifies that individual rewards, when compared with the rewards received by other group members, should be proportional to social investment. When rewards and investments are out-of-line, underrewarded individuals experience a feeling of injustice—"it just isn't fair." They tend to be dissatisfied, to complain, to feel irresponsible. Overrewarded individuals tend to feel guilty and overresponsible. Persons whose rewards are in line with their investments tend to feel satisfied.

Prescriptions for the distribution of rewards and deprivations among larger social units, such as age groups, marital status categories, and social classes, are also found to apply to the culture beyond the work group. The individual reacts to his rewards and deprivations in terms of social comparison not only within his face-to-face group but also with reference groups. Thus, in addition to, or in place of, feelings of satisfaction or dissatisfaction with the distribution of rewards within a face-to-face group, the individual may experience similar feelings compared to others in the same reference group or in other reference group categories. For example, the oldest member of a particular work group may be satisfied with his respect, salary, and status within his group, but may feel dissatisfied compared to others of his age group in other situations.

In order to understand the over-all feelings of satisfaction or dissatisfaction of an individual in a particular situation, we need to know several things. We need to know his demands of the situation, his receipts from it, his social investments in it, the distribution of social rewards among members of his face-to-face group, his reference group affiliations, and the comparison of his rewards with those received by others in the reference groups. Even under conditions of relative social stability and relative stability in his wants the individual will have the continuing problem of trying to maintain a balance between his wants and rewards in the many situations in which he is involved. He will also have the problem of finding a just distribution of rewards in relation to his numerous reference groups. Under conditions of rapid social change and ambiguity in individual wants, these problems become more severe, both for the individual and for the social systems within which he works and lives.

The changing nature of human wants and the rewards available in organized work situations, as well as the increase in individual mobility in the wider culture, produce certain clearly identifiable problems. These are some of them.

One common area of dissatisfaction in organizations is within the middle management ranks. Whereas these "white-collar" jobs have provided in the past a range of status, salary, and job interest possibilities for the individual, the increasing importance of automation, the use of computers, and the centralization and depersonalization of decision making are eliminating or drastically changing the kind of rewards available to him. Increased numbers of subordinates were formerly measures of success; now automated production methods and data-processing methods tend to decrease the significance of traditional supervision and personal control. The staff specialist, who understands, programs, and manages the newer technical systems, is ascending in importance and salary compared to the line supervisor. Increased opportunities to make increasingly significant decisions were once indicators of success for an individual in the organization, but the newer decision technology takes some of this type of reward away from the individual in middle management levels. New forms of organizational hierarchies are emerging with respect to status, salary, and influence. Individuals whose wants are gauged to traditional reward systems find it more difficult to comprehend the evolving systems and organize their own wants to fit clear career goals. This kind of uncertainty, which is intrinsic to periods of social change, becomes itself a source of dissatisfaction.

Along with these changes within organizations, parallel changes are taking place in career development and training. Although organizations are using larger numbers of professionally trained and oriented personnel, even larger numbers of professionals are being turned out by the educational system. Physical scientists, engineers, mathematicians, and behavioral scientists acquire their professional competence in the academic environment. The relatively high importance of these skills to the organization, their relative scarcity, the difference between managing routinely productive and "creative" task groups, and the influence of the academic environment have led certain parts of the business world to attempt to adopt the climate of the university. This climate, with its different control and reward system, and its different personal motivations, is placed within or adjacent to the more traditional business organization's control and reward systems. Along with new sets of values regarding the distribution of rewards, this atmosphere creates a situation in which justice becomes increasingly difficult to maintain.

The changing needs of individuals, the differing needs of particular ones, and the modifications in organizational climate and structures demand performances of multiple roles by individuals if they are to serve their tasks and their wants effectively. For example, the technician has to perform as an administrator under some conditions, while the administrator has to behave as a technician at times. Since more flexibility of individual performance is demanded, it seems that the organization must broaden its reward systems to accommodate and reinforce this development.

A continuing problem which is intensified by the foregoing changes is the traditional conflict between seniority and performance as bases of reward. The just distribution of rewards in our culture prescribes that seniority, age, and loyal service be rewarded *and* that competent individual performance also be rewarded. The problem is one of relative weighting; how can seniority be rewarded without simultaneously creating dissatisfaction and disappointment among younger persons whose competences need to be developed and reinforced? A reward to one class of persons may create a relative deprivation for another class. At the same time, individuals change classes over their lives; if the senior members are not valued and rewarded, the younger man, who will become senior in time, may not see much future for himself in staying with the organization. Thus, maintaining equity in the distribution of rewards becomes an increasingly important part of organizational management.   Under conditions where individual wants as well as organizational rewards are both changing, the bases for the distribution of rewards will also have to change, and will most likely continue to change.

The potential conflict between the values of seniority and competence is heightened by current developments in science, technology, and training.   Increased bodies of transferable knowledge and skills, along with their increased rate of obsolescence, mean that experience, as represented by age and job seniority, is no longer related to competence in a linear fashion.   On the contrary, years of experience within a particular work setting may serve to isolate some persons from the developments outside their fields of competence.   One result is a market place filled with young scientists and engineers, where "piracy" on the part of employers and opportunism on the part of the scientists and engineers create problems for the career development of the individual as well as for the development of stable work organizations. The sense of social justice among employers and workers becomes strained and unclear.

These considerations point to a need for a flexible, continually changing system of organizational rewards.   At the same time they point to a need for individuals who can engage in performances of multiple roles while they tolerate the uncertainty and ambiguity of the changing reward systems.   These demands on the individual break sharply with a former condition wherein he had only to learn the performances that were needed and rewarded in a relatively stable social organization.   He could count on the presence of a certain kind of hierarchy.   All he had to do was discover it and work within its structure.   Now he cannot even count on a stable structure even if he did try to find it.

A final problem stems from the increasing demands on the individual for flexibility in roles, uncertainty over status, and tolerance for continuing ambiguity.   He will need help.   This means that the organization must lend its support to community mental and emotional health resources and somehow aid individuals who experience problems in adapting to these demands.   Not only must help for the individual be made available, it should also be made as legitimate as help in borrowing money for the purchase of a home.   Seeking help on emotional problems somehow gets stigmatized in even the most progressive organizations and communities.   In the business world it often gets identified as a sign of personal weakness.   But the overmotivated, "strong," compulsively overresponsible, hard worker can be experiencing just as severe problems under the demand for role flexibility as the undermotivated, relatively apathetic person. Hence, if the flexibility required by organizational systems is to be effective, in spite of individual needs for certainty, the organization must provide some means for individual and groups to find the help they need in adapting to change.

In the next two chapters, we shall deal with some of the problems encountered as individuals, groups, and organizations change to meet current developments. Leadership and the process of change itself are the topics with which the text will conclude.

# Part Four

# Leadership and Change

T HE study of individual and group behavior in organizations has been motivated historically by a strong interest in the practical problems of managing human groups and organizations. These problems were originally voiced by managers. Schools of business administration and industrial management, as well as members of the established disciplines of psychology, sociology, and social psychology, responded to the plea for solutions.

The manager and group leader expressed their problems in forms consistent with their interests. How can we get more work out of our people? How can we get people to co-operate with us and with each other? How can we better select good workers and managers? How can we train and develop individuals and groups for more effective performance? The manager asked for techniques, devices, and procedures which he could use to obtain closer conformity between individual and group behavior and the purposes of his organization.

Some behavioral scientists responded by investigating the processes that the manager was talking about and telling him that he was asking the wrong kinds of questions; they would not accept his "definition of the situation." The manager's behavior, including the questions he asked, was seen as part of the problems he experienced. Thus the degree to which the man of practical affairs will accept the behavioral scientists' definition of his situation is still open to question, since such definitions require that he examine himself as part of the situation.

As knowledge about the determinants of individual and group behavior in organizations was being accumulated, the importance of the supervisors' and managers' behaviors in determining the outcomes was noted. They became the focus of specific studies of leadership behavior. The fateful Relay Assembly Test Room at the Hawthorne Works of the Western Electric Company provided, during the late 1920's, the origin of the so-called "Hawthorne Effect."[1] It was found that morale and productivity in the experimental work group continued to increase even after improved physical working conditions were returned to their original level. The key variable accounting for these results seemed to be that the group's external authorities behaved much differently in the experimental situations. For example, the supervisor did not act like the usual supervisor. He was permissive, interested in the employees, and influenced by them. Furthermore, important outsiders accorded the group greater attention and respect. The strange aspects of the case, from the point of view of conventional managerial theory, is that although the supervisor exercised *less control* over the workers, in the traditional managerial sense, their productivity was higher than it had been under former conditions of *greater* supervisory control.

Since the Hawthorne studies, there have been many different research efforts into the dimensions of effective supervision, as well as attempts to improve supervisory practices through various kinds of training programs. One result has been that the relatively primitive behavioral-scientific efforts of the early researchers have been grasped with cult-like zeal; many well-intended individuals and groups have interpreted the research results through their own humanistic leanings. This process has been accelerated by the strong need and hope for practical improvements on the part of progressive management people. A variety of "Human Relations" schools of thought, research, and training have resulted. The components of this mixture included religious hope and fervor, the ideals of humanism and democracy, the practical demand for improved effectiveness, and last of all—and in some cases least of all—a scientific way of looking at and understanding human behavior.

In this, the final part of our book, we shall examine processes of leadership and of change. Having described and explained individual and group behavior in organizations, we shall now, cautiously and

[1] See Roethlisberger and Dickson, *Management and the Worker*, pp. 3–186.

perhaps pessimistically, shift to the action questions.  Our intent is to separate what is known and what is unknown about human behavior from what is hoped for and wished.  We are not attempting to deny the need of managers and leaders for moral principles and objectives. The existence of these aspects of any individual are real and important. Rather, we are strongly urging that people in such positions learn the difference between their own motivations, hopes, ideals, and potentials —one form of reality—and the individual, group, and organizational processes going on outside of themselves—the second form of reality. The significance of this difference involves the issues of self-control and influencing others, on the one hand, and the deterministic point of view necessary for investigation, explanation, and learning, on the other.

Our analysis of leadership in Chapter Twelve and our analysis of change in Chapter Thirteen will differentiate between natural and planned processes.  When looking at the natural processes of leadership, we shall view the leader as only one of the social positions constituting the social structure of the group.  We shall assume that the leader's behavior is determined by natural causes and that the relationships between his behavior and the behaviors of others are mutually determined by natural processes.  We shall then shift from the deterministic point of view to examine alternative leadership behaviors. In this respect, we shall be talking about *planned* leadership behavior, as if rational understanding of behavior process can allow the individual leader some choice of what to do.  This will lead us directly into problems of change, since the shift from playing a highly determined social role in a group to that of thoughtful examination of other possibilities and their possible outcomes, constitutes a major change in the structures of individual personalities, groups, and organizations.

Initially, we shall discuss the natural process by which changes in individuals, groups, and organizations are unconsciously resisted or facilitated.  From this understanding, we shall proceed into the problems of planned change; that is, where some particular individual wants to see some specific changes take place in himself, in other individuals, in the groups of which he is a member, in other groups, or in a total social organization. Problems of consciously designed leadership and change lead to considerations outside the realm of behavioral scientific thought; we unavoidably have to deal with issues involving the philosophic and religious bases upon which our cultures are built.  Although we can attempt to define responsible leadership and administration in behavioral-scientific terms, the ultimate meanings of the ideas lie outside the field of purely scientific thought.

*Chapter Twelve*

# Leadership

I N the first section of this chapter we shall briefly examine the interpersonal, historical, and cultural backgrounds of leadership. This
will be followed by a discussion of the systematic study of leadership:
theories, research findings, and some important unsettled issues. The
research and theory of leadership is concerned with descriptions of the
leader's behavior, others' perceptions of him, the consequences of his
behavior in group performance, and attempted changes in leadership
behavior through training programs. The internal psychological conditions associated with the leader's role will occupy our third section.
And finally, we shall summarize the social demands, individual needs,
and organizational task requirements facing individuals in responsible
leadership positions.

## INTERPERSONAL, HISTORICAL, AND CULTURAL BACKGROUNDS

Between societies' demands and organizations' requirements for
effective leadership, on the one hand, and the strong desire on the
part of many individuals to become leaders, on the other hand, lies
a gulf of confusion. The meeting of social demands and organizational
requirements are by no means intrinsic to the individual's motivation
to lead in its earliest manifestations. The paradox arises around the
fact that individuals must want to lead to become leaders. But the
form their motivations take may, in many instances, prevent them from
effectively carrying out leadership functions.

### Interpersonal-Emotional Bases[1]

When we look at early leadership bids on the part of children, some
of the motivations of leadership are easily apparent. Prominence, at-

[1] See also Chapters Six through Eight.

tention, and power seem to be the goals of the child's activity when he wants to lead his peers in games.  At later stages of development, the individual's desires may assume a more socially acceptable form, such as wanting to create order from chaos or wanting to see a job done.  One of the basic components of motivation toward leadership is a desire to dominate others.

In interpersonal dynamics, the leader is the one who controls others. The parent-child relationship is the prototype, especially the relationship between the dominant parent, the father in most cultures, and the child.  The relationship is emotionally colored by arbitrary dominance and compliance, distant affection or respect, and unilateral dependency. Along with the interpersonal emotions experienced by the child in his first encounter with leadership behavior, he learns of parallel situations in his culture's history.  For example, children in the United States learn of the dependent colonists' revolt against the parent, England, and the establishment of an autonomous group of peer-like states.  The individual's own emotional orientation toward authority, as discussed in Chapter Seven, provides the basis for his interpretation of leadership in historical events.

The emotional dynamics underlying the descriptions of historical events closely parallel the child's emotional experience in the family, among his playmates, and in the school situation.  Colorful hero-leaders in stories provide objects with whom the child may identify. The primary impact of hero-leaders upon growing children is not necessarily in what they do or did, but more in the fact that they have been prominent and noticed, have had power to influence others, and are remembered with respect and affection.  Fame is valued by children and adults who are themselves engaged in rivalry for attention in their everyday lives.  Hence, ideas about leadership get confused with ideas about notoriety or fame.

In our cultural histories, the leadership spotlight falls upon two contrasting kinds of persons.  One is the member of an elite group, the representative of the highest social class, whose elevated status carries with it power, influence, socially bred knowledge, wisdom, and responsibility.  The contrasting hero arises from social anonymity through mystical inspiration.  Hence, among the emotional connotations of the idea of leadership bred by our cultural tradition, these two threads dominate: status elevation, with its accompanying power, prominence, and respect, and "divine" charismatic inspiration.  Both threads lead to the implications that "leaders are born, not made."

None of these emotional connotations of leadership have anything to say about what the leader does, except perhaps that he acts aristocratically and as if he were possessed of omniscience.  They are primarily status denotations, rather than concrete behavioral prescriptions.  Thus, we find that many individuals who are strongly motivated to be leaders view their goal as occupancy of a position, with all its attendant privileges, rather than as the performance of certain specific activities and interactions.

## Manipulation

In *The Prince*, Machiavelli[2] gave what amounted to the first behavioral-descriptive attention to the tactics and strategy of leadership. The study was an amoral, how-to-do-it manual for prospective successful princes.  The term "Machiavellian" has come to mean manipulative, in the most cunning, devious, and immoral sense of the word. Current attempts to apply the behavioral sciences are sometimes so labeled, perhaps because the acquisition and use of knowledge about humans is considered "unnatural" in our culture.  The difference between "manipulative" and "good" leadership may lie in the intentions of the leader: if his intentions are good, he is a "good guy," but if his intentions are bad, he is a "manipulator."  Or, the term manipulator may be applied when deception is practiced, when the leader outwardly communicates one set of intentions but actually pursues another.  However, current knowledge of the existence and universality of unconscious motivation, sketchy and speculative as it may seem, makes deceptiveness meaningless as a criteria.

One thing that Machiavelli, current behavioral scientists, and many effective leaders—both "good guys" and "bad guys"—have in common is the explicitness with which they examine their own motives, their behaviors, and the possible consequences of other behaviors.  Deliberateness of thought, an accompanying spirit of investigation into human personality and behavior and the formulation of explicit plans consistently underlie the accused manipulator's behavior.  It seems that to many sectors of our culture, and to many particular individuals, spontaneous, unplanned, thoughtless behavior is "natural."  Attempts to understand, explain, predict, and plan with respect to human and social relations are "manipulative."  This view supports the aristocratic and charismatic theories of leadership that demand arbitrary acceptance of authority and the avoidance of investigation and explanation.

Accusations of manipulation that come to the surface under certain conditions are one more cultural fact adding to the confusion of the

[2] See Bibliography.

leadership problem.   Not only are the variety of ideas associated with leadership emotionally laden to the individual and to the culture, but the activity of studying leadership in order to explicate its processes is also an object of emotional significance, especially to many of those already in recognized positions and to those who aspire to lead.

## Traditional Organization and Leadership[3]

The church and the military provide the historical prototypes for complex organizational structures.[4]   The military organization provides the dominant model for leadership in the traditional organization.   Several aspects of leadership according to the military model interest us at this juncture as we move closer to the description of actual leadership behavior.

The military organization features a clear and explicit set of hierarchical status relationships and appropriate symbols.   Although officers engage in planning and decision making, either in solitude or in peer-group settings, their primary *social* leadership activity is popularly seen as issuing or passing orders to subordinates and ensuring compliance to those orders through training and policing activities.   The social control of behavior involved in this *legal* system of leadership consists of the following elements:

1. A source of authority is internalized into the emotional system of the individual members.   This source may be God, the State, or an abstract superordinate goal, such as the protection of society or the production of goods and services.   Members do not participate in setting goals or deciding upon the source of authority; it is "given" and unquestionable.

2. A code of behavior, in the form of rules, regulations, and procedures, is created by the top members of the hierarchy or inherited historically by them.   These formal codes are modifiable by the leaders; one function of legal leadership is to legislate codes of behavior within pre-established limits.

3. The members of the organization are informed and trained in the meaning of the formal code of behavior and the hierarchical status system.

4. The officers issue and pass on orders; they tell persons of subordinate status what they should do.

[3] See, also, Chapter Nine.
[4] See Freud, *Group Psychology and the Analysis of the Ego*, p. 93 ff.

5. The officers act as policemen; they note and act on violations of the behavior code and the specific orders issued.

6. The officers also act as investigators and judges; each behavioral event which violates orders, the code, or the theoretically expected results of the orders, is investigated to determine who is responsible, the seriousness of the violation, the punishment that fits the violation, or revisions of the code or training procedures to remedy the situation.

7. The officers reward obedience over time. According to the strictest interpretation of this legal system, obedient incompetence is of greater value than disobedient competence to the organization.

The above statements are, of course, extreme. The organization could not possibly accomplish any goals other than maintaining authority relations by strict adherence to these practices. Consequently, although it never appears in the formal procedures, members are required to learn the *informal* codes of behavior necessary for the accomplishment of task. These informal codes are crucial to the leader's success, yet they appear nowhere in explicit written form, except perhaps in the writings of social investigators.[5]

The legal model of leadership is important, not because it is an accurate description of what actually happens in organizations or of how leaders actually behave, but because it is part of the cultural tradition within which individual leaders and members must work. It is a source of beliefs, ideals, attitudes, and language, if not a primary determinant of individual and group behavior. Unity of command, chain of command, individual responsibility, saluting the position and not the person, and a variety of similar expressions and ideas derive from this model and are active influences in leader-group relationships, regardless of the actual behavior and influence patterns involved.

The development of the large, complex organization amidst increasing social mobility has required the introduction of the concept of leadership training into our culture. The existence and importance of training activities modify an earlier cultural derivative: "Leaders are born, not made." It becomes instead "whether or not leaders are born, they must be trained." As soon as leadership training becomes an explicit organizational activity, the goals and content of the training must be addressed. These, in turn, require some explicit definition of the requisites of leadership character and behavior. In addition, conscious planning of training activities carries with it the necessity of selecting those who are to be trained on some basis of predicted trainability and future performance.

[5] See Roethlisberger and Dickson, *op. cit.,* pp. 525 ff., and Homans, *The Human Group,* p. 281 ff.

The interpersonal, historical, and cultural backgrounds of leadership have resulted in strong emotions being attached to leadership. As with the study of religion, leadership may invoke deep-seated emotional attitudes toward authority, toward nature, and toward the act of investigation itself. The gulf of confusion separating individuals' desires to lead, social demands, and organizational task requirements for effective leadership remains confused, largely as a result of the emotional underpinnings of individual motives. The leader is a satisfier of others' needs, as well as his own. The very ambiguity and complexity of individual and social needs determine the degree of confusion and conflict which are inherent in the processes of leadership.

## THE SYSTEMATIC STUDY OF LEADERSHIP

In this section, we shall present some theoretical approaches to the study of leadership, the findings of some research investigations into leadership, and our interpretations of these theories and findings in terms of current issues in leadership selection and training.

### Theoretical Considerations

The confusion centering around the question of leadership is reflected in the variety of definitions of leadership held not only by the general public, but also by researchers and theorists. We have referred earlier to formal leaders and informal leaders, task leaders and social leaders; in our discussion of cultural backgrounds we mentioned "hero-leaders." Gibb[6] lists and explains several definitions of the leader:

The leader as an individual in a given office.
The leader as focus for the behavior of group members.
. . . the leader in terms of sociometric choice.
The leader as one who exercises influence over others.
The [leader as one whose] authority is spontaneously accorded him by his fellow group members, the followers.
[Headship as a condition in which] the authority of the head derives from some extra-group power which he has over the members of the group, who cannot meaningfully be called his followers. They accept his domination, on pain of punishment, rather than follow.
The leader defined in terms of influence upon [group progress].
Leadership . . . as a group quality, as a set of functions which must be carried out by the group.[7]

[6] Gibb, "Leadership."
[7] *Ibid.*, pp. 880–884.

A most important aspect of Gibb's discussion of leadership is that the leader cannot be studied meaningfully apart from his group. Leadership is a *relational* attribute, including the behavior of the leading person *and* the behavior of the followers. This is in sharp contrast to thinking about leadership as an attribute of an individual, standing alone. Using one of our earlier formulations, leadership can be defined in terms of a total role performance, involving the person's behavior and internal conditions, as well as the internal and behavioral responses of the others (see Chapter Six). From this point of view, we would define a leadership event as *an interaction in which the conscious intentions of one person are communicated in his behavior, verbal and otherwise, with the consequence that the other person wants to and does behave in accordance with the first person's intentions.* This description includes *consequences* of the person's intentions and behaviors. In the headship situation described by Gibb, where compliance is not willingly submitted, the consequences of alienation and hostility within the subordinate and the likelihood of the appearance of related behaviors at a later date add up to a total of consequences that do *not* match the originator's conscious intentions.

Identifying leadership as a particular kind of interaction event, rather than as a particular set of characteristics of a person, conforms to the temporal, sequential, and patterned aspects of the role performance. The individual who engages in leadership events becomes a sometimes leader. Thus, the group leader would be the person or persons who engaged in more leadership events than others. We would use the term *influence* as synonomous with leadership only when the term *intended* preceded it. Behavioral analysis describes the ways in which all members of an interacting group influence one another; we identify as leadership only those interaction events in which *intended* influences are consummated.

If we observe the interaction sequences—and their consequences— in which a series of individuals are involved over their lifetimes, the conclusion will be that some individuals are predominantly leaders in their social relations, while others perform different roles. If we study these leaders as individuals, we are searching for leadership traits in accordance with relatively simple views of human nature; a substantial amount of research has been done in this fashion. The over-all result has been that particular traits, such as height, weight, health, appearance, self-confidence, social skills, and dominance appear to be important correlates of leadership only when the social situation demands that they be. Among the range of social interaction situations in our culture, there is enough similarity of demands that some personal traits are more likely to be found in leaders than others. "But, in every instance, the relation of a trait to the leadership role is more meaningful if consideration is given to the detailed nature of the role. A person does not become a leader by virtue of his possession of any one particular pattern of personality traits, but the pattern of personal characteristics of the leader must bear some relevant relationship to the present characteristics, activities, and goals of the group of which he is a leader."[8] These ideas represent the views of the "situationalists" in regard to leadership, rather than those of the "trait theorists."

We cannot easily overlook the phenomenon of charismatic leadership, which may appear to be a clear confirmation of a trait theory. "Charisma" is a mystical quality that some people seem to possess in their social relations. The charismatic leader is inspirational, spellbinding; he evokes blind loyalty and emotional enthusiasm. He possesses his followers in the same sense that he seems to them to be possessed by divine inspiration. This kind of interaction is almost purely emotional. It is more a mass phenomenon than an event within a group problem-solving situation which outwardly, at least, has rationalizable goals and methodologies. The bases for the charismatic event lies purely within the emotional systems of the leader and the followers. However, "rational" leaders can and do use charisma; they either practice it themselves or use social prophets as instruments.[8a]

It is difficult to include charismatic effects in our description of what we call leadership, since conscious intentions and total consequences are parts of our description. Charismatic leaders are unquestionably influential; but it is difficult to judge whether or not they know what they are doing and whether or not they consciously intend to bring about the consequences that follow. Charismatic events are laden with the reinforcement of dependency, the psychodynamic of transference and counter-transference, orgiastic acting-out, and catharsis of emotions. The total dynamics of the process reinforce individual and mass defensive systems, rather than contribute to adaptability or competence. As ritualistic interludes within life patterns that include other modes of social relationships, emotional performances may contribute indirectly toward group and individual identification and survival. Such is the case with religious rituals, military ceremonies, academic ceremonies, dramatic theatrical performances, and individual encounters with moving works of literature and music. Similarly, the charismatic role performance on the part of an individual in a group

[8] Gibb, *op. cit.*, p. 889.
[8a] See "The Central Person and Group Emotions" in Chapter Five of this present volume.

may be of adaptive value to the group to the degree that it meets existing emotional-expressive needs. But the selection of prospective leaders on the basis of charisma, and the attempt to train prospective leaders in the techniques of emotional suasion exclusively, represent gross misevaluations of the leadership process as it relates to the accomplishment of work, to group development, and to individual growth.

In sharp contrast to our comments on charismatic processes, George Homans has situationally analyzed leadership behavior in terms of social structure and processes of social control.[9] He characterizes the leader as moving the group from one social state to another while maintaining its equilibrium; we shall discuss change and equilibrium further in the following chapter. According to Homans, "What a leader needs to have is not a set of rules but a good method of analyzing the social situation in which he must act."[10] The conceptual scheme and theories developed by Homans provide one analytical method for this purpose. His "rules of leadership" are a very different sort of generalization from the leadership principles offered in traditional organizational texts; they relate the leaders' behavior to the characteristics of his group's social structure and its unique forms of social control.[11]

*Rule 1.* "The leader will maintain his own position." Position refers to the individual's place in the group's social structure, rather than his externally conferred status. A new formally designated leader brought in from outside initially has no position in the group; his first task is to earn his position by meeting the group's conditions for membership and leadership.

*Rule 2.* "The leader will live up to the norms of the group." This describes the manner in which the leader becomes established and maintains his position.

*Rule 3.* "The leader will lead." Maintaining his position requires that he initiate interaction in the group and that he make decisions.

*Rule 4.* "The leader will not give orders that will not be obeyed." Here is where the leader's ability at analyzing the social situation in his group is crucial. It also raises the question, who is ultimately controlling whose behavior? If the leader must anticipate how group members will react, it would seem that they have a good deal of indirect control over his behavior. Thus, the prospective manipulator

[9] George Homans, "The Job of the Leader," *The Human Group* . . . *pp.* 415–440. See Bibliography.

[10] *Ibid.*, p. 424.

[11] *Ibid.*, pp. 425 ff.

must learn that the physical law of conservation of energy also applies in social affairs; to influence others he must in some ways be subject to their influence. Influence is consummated through an exchange process.

*Rule 5.* "In giving orders, the leader will use established channels." This is the traditional organizational imperative, "follow the chain of command." The important difference is that Homans is referring to channels within the established social structure of the group which may or may not conform to externally designated status titles.

*Rule 6.* "The leader will not thrust himself upon his followers on social occasions." He must maintain the social distance implicit in his rank within the group. This implies that in order to maintain his position in the social structure, he must comply to its interaction patterns: he interacts with his lieutenants and his lieutenants interact with members of lesser rank.

*Rule 7.* "The leader will neither blame nor, in general, praise a member of his group before other members." This would affect the social rank of the member; the rule allows the group to maintain its proportionate share of control over the ranking process. It also enables the leader to avoid the risk that his judgment will not match that of the group.

*Rule 8.* "The leader will take into consideration the total situation." He will understand and base his actions on his understanding of the group's processes.

*Rule 9.* "In maintaining discipline, the leader will be less concerned with inflicting punishment than with creating the conditions in which the group will discipline itself . . . the leader will treat the group as a group and not as a set of individuals." Here Homans is referring to the self-policing found in some groups under conditions similar to those that would be created by his leadership rules.

*Rule 10.* "The leader will listen." He needs to know conditions within his group in order to behave according to the previous rules. "He may be the most active member of the group, and yet he must often keep silent."

These rules resulted from Homans' analysis of empirical studies of several work groups.[12] Some of them seem to resemble traditional leadership principles, attesting to the intuitive wisdom of some of the early formulators of organizational principles. At the same time, however, this resemblance stresses the importance of understanding the phenomena to which they refer, the behavioral processes of real groups. Even Homans' rules are meaningless to a prospective leader

[12] Homans, *op. cit.*, pp. 425–440.

unless he clearly understands the reasons behind them and the nature of the elementary social processes to which they refer in his specific group situation.

This and most other behavioral views of the leader as a "situationalist" are in marked contrast to the trait theory, exemplified in extreme form by charismatic leadership. It is disappointing and disturbing to the young, naive individual who is strongly motivated to lead that the leader must operate within a highly *interdependent* set of social relationships, rather than as a strong-willed, independent world-beater who will be followed, regardless of his behavior, by virtue of his title and character. Perhaps the discrepancy between idealized types and reality is a good thing; if people clearly saw what leadership demanded and required of them, fewer would be motivated to take the risks of assuming leadership roles.

The most reliable research undertaken in the quest for leadership traits has invariably led to a situational interpretation. Hence, we shall limit our brief discussion of leadership research to situational analyses, although the trait issue is never completely divorced from it. This is especially evident when researchers study leadership patterns situationally and then attempt to apply their findings to general training programs; they unavoidably get involved with the character, if not "traits," of the trainees. We shall discuss this problem of application and in so doing shall deal with problems of change.

### Research on Leadership

The research we shall describe assumes that leadership behavior is an independent variable and compares differences in leadership behavior with the dependent variables of group productivity and satisfaction. Group properties and performances thus become intervening variables, according to the schema introduced in Chapter Ten.

The major problem in leadership research has been the choice of dimensions along which to compare leaders' behaviors. Popular conceptions of leadership are often unidimensional, "tough" and "nice" or "high pressure" and "low pressure" being the extreme points on the scale. During the past few years, the sporting pages of the popular press have commented from time to time on the managerial styles of baseball team managers; "nice guys don't win ball games" was one such slogan, referring mainly to the success of Casey Stengel and the New York Yankees. However, Al Lopez was characterized as a "nice guy," and he was the only manager to beat out the Yankees for the American League pennant during the preceding ten years.

When it comes to observing the actual behaviors of "tough guys" and "nice guys," we often find that the tough guy is not really as tough within his group as he talks when interviewed by outsiders; and the nice guy sometimes disciplines members and presses for performance. Ultimately we conclude that there is a vast difference between global characterizations and actual behavior patterns.

In an experimental study of adult leadership in boys' groups, Lewin, Lippitt, and White set up three different styles of leadership behavior: authoritarian, democratic, and *laissez-faire*.[13] The researchers planned the specific ways in which the leaders adopting each of the three styles should behave and analyzed actual behaviors to determine the accuracy of the designed patterns. They also included controls to differentiate between behavioral styles and the basic personalities of the leaders. The same and different groups, selected and controlled for consistency along all other dimensions, were exposed to various leadership styles. The effects of the leadership styles were then compared.

The individuals selected to perform each of the three leadership roles exhibited all kinds of behaviors while leading their groups; but each style featured emphasis on particular kinds of behavior. The authoritarians gave orders, issued disruptive commands, engaged in nonconstructive criticism, and issued praise and approval. The democratic leaders gave guiding suggestions, stimulated self-guidance, were more jovial and confident, and were more "matter-of-fact." The *laissez-faire* leaders, who were intended to be passive, permissive, and friendly, actually gave more information than did the others, but otherwise resembled the democratic leaders more than the authoritarians. The main difference between democratic and *laissez-faire* leaders was that the democratic type took the initiative in attempting to promote individual and group freedom and ability, while the *laissez-faire* leaders were passive, giving out information only when it was sought.

The predominant reactions to authoritarians were dependence and apathy, but in one instance, the group responded with aggressive rebelliousness. Both kinds of autocratic groups responded with more leader-dependent actions and demands for attention than did the democratic or *laissez-faire* groups. The aggressive autocracy group expressed more critical discontent than other groups. The democratic and *laissez-faire* groups responded with more friendly confidence to the leader and offered more group-minded suggestions. The *laissez-faire* groups asked for more information. The apathetic autocracy and the democratic groups featured work-minded conversation. There was more irritability and aggressiveness among members in

---

[13] Lippitt and White, "An Experimental Study, of Leadership and Group Life."

the autocratic and *laissez-faire* groups than in the democratic groups. The members depended on one another in the democratic and *laissez-faire* groups. The authoritarian groups were almost as cohesive as the others, but their cohesion centered around rebelliousness or shared apathy, instead of their work. The members of the democratic groups initiated more group activities and policies than the others. Group achievement was lower in the *laissez-faire* groups than in any of the others.

The experiments clearly demonstrated the differences that leadership styles could make on group atmosphere and performance. The democratic atmosphere was a healthier one for individual development and growth. Democratic leaders who deliberately arrived late found that their groups had taken the initiative to start work; this was not true in the autocratic groups. *Laissez-faire* groups were active but not productive. The democratic groups were self-policing in the absence of their leaders, while working time dropped drastically when the authoritarian leaders left their groups. In the *laissez-faire* groups, productivity tended to increase when the leader left the room—group members took over leadership in the *laissez-faire* leaders' absence. Expressions of individuality were highest in the democratic groups, while some tendency toward uniformity existed in the *laissez-faire* groups; the authoritarian groups had a much narrower range of individual differences in behavior.

Although group "health," in general, was highest in the democratic groups, there was no conclusive indication that democratic leadership was best if productivity were the only goal. Many other researches have maintained that greater group and individual health seem to go along with democratic leadership, but there is a lack of conclusive data on the effects of democratic leadership on productivity levels. This brings us back to an important part of our discussion in the chapter on satisfaction—happy groups are not necessarily high producers. Nor are happy groups necessarily the healthiest. Hence, it is important to note that the particulars of the democratic style in the Lewin, Lippitt, and White study were not directed toward making the members happy, but rather toward promoting autonomy and self- and group-development. The *laissez-faire* type was the nearest to the permissive, "happiness-factory" model, but the results in productivity and health were not outstanding.

Leadership studies tend to be much more normative than the other kinds of research we have discussed in this book. The researchers, the writers, and presumably, their readers are looking for the best method.    As a result, the leadership dimensions used as variables in the studies may come to have evaluative, rather than purely descriptive, connotations.    The authoritarian, *laissez-faire*, and democratic styles in the Lewin, Lippitt, and White experiments are obvious examples of such labels.

Likert has compared some of the various dimensions used in other research studies and their results.[14] The following chart lists the leadership dimensions, or styles, and the findings of some of these studies in abbreviated form:

| *Leadership Dimensions* | *Results* |
| --- | --- |
| Employee-centered versus Job-centered | Higher production under employee-centered leadership |
| Low-pressure versus high-pressure | Higher productivity under low-pressure condition |
| General versus close supervision | Higher production under general supervision |
| Nonpunitive versus punitive | Higher production under nonpunitive foremen |
| Workers' felt freedom to set own work pace | Higher productivity where men felt most free. |

When we list the various names given the more effective styles, we come up with the ideal "human relations" type that has become a training objective in many leadership development programs.    According to the over-simplified stereotype, the good leader is democratic, employee-centered, low-pressure, nonpunitive, and permissive.    Such human relations, or social skill, dimensions of leadership behavior represent a reaction to earlier over-emphasis of principles of scientific management in supervisor training, such as methods, procedures, and various forms of control.    Behavioral research efforts have been directed toward uncovering attitudinal and social behavioral correlates to effective supervision.    Understandably, they have not attended, in detail, to the importance of differences in technical competence.    The unfortunate image produced by the research findings— and the directions taken by many training programs—has tended to be that social skills alone made the difference, that effective leadership could be developed through "charm school" training.    In addition, many of the earlier research efforts did not take into account the effects on the leader of being a member of a group other than

[14] Likert, *New Patterns of Management*, pp. 5–25.

the one he supervised, that is, how he would interact with management people and peers, as well as his subordinates.[15] He is not "alone" with his work group.

A three-phase Ohio State leadership study tested the applicability of a leadership idea; the results of this attempt at application tell us more about the nature and problems of leadership behavior than do many original searches for the ideal type. The Fleishman, Harris, and Burtt study,[16] part of a series of leadership and management studies, started out to find the dimensions of leadership behavior relevant to group performance in an industrial work setting. The researchers had the results of similar surveys in other settings. Using questionnaires to get descriptions of supervisory behavior, they scored individual supervisors on factors they called *Consideration* and *Initiating Structure*, which had been uncovered through extensive mathematical analysis of previous leadership questionnaires. Consideration included such elements as warmth, friendship, and trust between superior and subordinate, the so-called "human relations" elements. Initiating Structure pertained to prescribing communications channels and work methods, the "scientific management" elements. Both factors were considered important components of effective supervisory behavior. But which of these factors was more important, the conditions under which each was important, and what happened when you attempted to train leaders with the factors in mind provided the lead to some interesting and unexpected results.

The study grew out of the International Harvester Company's interest in the content and effectiveness of supervisory training programs, especially with respect to human relations or social skills. Along with many other companies, it had been carried along with the trend toward training foremen and supervisors to deal more effectively with people on the job. In the terminology of the Ohio State group, the intention of these programs was to increase the foremen's or supervisors' scores along the Consideration dimension.

The foremen, who were the main subjects at the early stages of the study, were given the questionnaire before and after their two-week training program. Their Initiating Structure attitudes went down, while their Consideration attitudes went up. This much was consistent with the program's intentions.

The next question was, what happened to the foremen after the training program? Comparing foremen who had been through the program

[15] Zaleznik, *Foreman Training in a Growing Enterprise*, was an early study which brought out these problems as they pertained to foreman training.
[16] See Bibliography.

with a control group who had not, the study found that gradually the foremen who *had* been trained came to have scores *higher* in Initiating Structure and *lower* in Consideration than foremen who had *not* been trained. These results were opposite to the intentions of the training program.

To explain these results, we must point out a significant difference between the situation at International Harvester, or for that matter, the situation in any complex organization, and the situation in which the Lewin, Lippitt, and White work was carried out.[17] The leaders of the Lewin, Lippitt, and White's groups were themselves organizationally autonomous, regardless of their assumed style. They did not report to bosses, nor was their work with the experimental groups directly related to their personal success over their lives. Foremen in the complex organizations are by no means independent agents; they must please their bosses to survive and progress. The foreman is a man-in-the-middle;[18] the leaders of the other groups did not experience comparable pressures from above.

When the foremen were "sent to school" by the International Harvester, the implied message was, "Management wants us to talk as if we are more Considerate." They learned the language and compiled, but back on the job their own bosses talked a different language. Paradoxically, the training program was management's form of Initiating Structure upon the foreman. This led the Ohio State group to study the leadership climate within which the foremen worked.

The researchers asked the foremen to describe their bosses' behavior, and asked the bosses to indicate their own attitudes. Foremen whose bosses scored high on Consideration scored high on this factor themselves. Similar results were obtained with respect to Initiating Structure. This meant that regardless of what they were taught in the training program, each foreman's behavior was more strongly influenced by the behavior of his superiors than by the content of the training program.[19]

The next stage of the study was an investigation into the value of the Consideration and Initiating Structure factors in the plant; perhaps Consideration was not such a "good thing" after all in this company's climate. It was found that workers liked working for foremen who were high on Consideration and disliked working for foremen who were high in Initiating Structure. Although it was impossible to

[17] Lewin, Lippitt, and White, *op. cit.*
[18] Roethlisberger, "The Foreman: Master and Victim of Double Talk."
[19] See, also, Zaleznik, *op. cit.*

measure productivity directly, superiors' proficiency ratings of the foremen were compared with the foremen's behavior scores. In production groups, foremen who were high on Initiating Structure had higher proficiency ratings. However, in the nonproduction, service groups, higher proficiency ratings were given foremen who were high in Consideration. Using other criteria, it was found that groups with considerate foremen had lower absenteeism, but there was no relationship between either factor and turnover or accident rates. Workers expressed more grievances under high structure foremen than under considerate foremen.

Although democratic leadership, as defined in the Lewin, Lippitt, and White study, or Consideration, as defined in the Ohio State studies, may provide ideals that under certain conditions lead to more effective group performance, the Ohio State study emphasizes the fact that the leader himself is a member of groups which place social demands upon him. The way he behaves is not really an "independent variable" in organizational situations.

The importance of the supervisor's total role performances in the organization, not merely his behavior toward subordinates, was also emphasized in studies by Pelz[20] and Shepard.[21] The degree to which the supervisor was influential with his own boss was found to be as important as his style of behavior toward subordinates. If the supervisor's behavior pattern was *inconsistent* with that of his boss, whether an autocratic-democratic or democratic-autocratic pattern, group productivity and satisfaction were poorer.

One of the major subjects of early human relations research and training was the value of "participation." By and large, research on leadership behavior found that situations in which the subordinate was allowed to participate in decisions affecting himself were healthier and more productive. Findings regarding the supervisor's relationships with his boss indicated that a participative climate should permeate the organization and not merely be an isolated characteristic of the leader's relationships with his subordinates. Hence, organizational consultants and trainers attempted to revise the entire organizational climate.[22] New problems were confronted in this effort: although research findings and theories of individual and social health indicated that participation should be good for everyone, some people did not

[20] Pelz, "Influence: A Key to Effective Leadership in the First Line Supervisor."
[21] Shepard, "Some Social Attributes of Industrial Research and Development Groups."
[22] See, for example, Argyris, *Interpersonal Competence and Organizational Effectiveness* and Jaques, *The Changing Culture of a Factory.*

want to participate. Vroom[23] found that some individuals did not benefit from the opportunity to participate, either in their productivity or their personal development. These people were the "authoritarian personalities"; their personality structures were rigid and dependent upon unilateral sources of external authority and their needs for independence were weak. Thus, supervisory behavior and organizational climate are not the only determining factors; the individual's personality, as it reflects his historical experiences outside the organization, is an important element on the total leadership situation.

Other environmental influences have important effects on the relationships between the supervisor and his boss and between the supervisor and his subordinates, as well as on the outcome of these relationships in productivity, satisfaction, and individual and group development (see Chapter Nine). In a comparative study of two engineering groups, Barnes[24] isolated the factors of mutual influence, opportunities for interaction, and autonomy as key elements in boss-supervisor and supervisor-group relationships (see Chapter Nine). The supervisor of one of two departments, Department B, and Supervisor B's boss were found to have an "open" relationship. This was reflected in Supervisor B's relationships with his subordinates and, ultimately, in a higher level of performance among the men in his department than in the other.

In a later unpublished field study of Supervisor B's boss, whom we will call Chief B, and the three supervisors under him, B, B2, and B3, Moment found that Chief B's relationship to B2 and B3 was strikingly different from his relationship to B, as reported in Barnes' study.[25] Chief B supervised B2 much more closely than he did B and B3 and supervised B3 more closely than B. This can be explained by several aspects of the situation:

1. Chief B was, by background, training, and experience, a Mechanical Engineer, while Supervisor B was an electrical engineer. Chief B was unfamiliar with the *technical* content of the work of Supervisor B's group. Hence, Chief B was forced to rely upon Supervisor B and could not be too directive with him, even if he wanted to be.

This unequal distribution of the necessary technical knowledge also existed between Supervisor B and his group, as described by Barnes. Supervisor B had valuable technical experience, but some of his subordinates had more specialized technical education than he, forcing him to be technically dependent upon them.

[23] Vroom, *Some Personality Determinants of the Effects of Participation.*
[24] Barnes, *Organizational Systems and Engineering Groups.*
[25] *Ibid.*

2. In contrast, Supervisor B2 was a mechanical engineer, as was Chief B. Hence, Chief B was familiar with the technical details of B2's work. Not only did Chief B spend more time with B2 than with B3 or B, but he personally talked with B2's subordinates, also mechanical engineers, more than he talked with the other supervisors' subordinates. In plant language, "he put his fingers into the work" with which he was familiar, but stayed away from projects with which he was unfamiliar.

3. Department B3 was the newest group of the three, and its work featured both mechanical and electrical engineering skills. It was becoming more prominent within the company, and its work involved more contact with outside people than did that of either department B or B2. Chief B gave a good deal of personal interest to Department B3's work and because of its increasing importance, interacted more with Supervisor B3 and his men than with B and his men. However, he supervised B3 somewhat less closely than B2.

4. The physical layout of offices and departments reinforced the tendencies noted above. Chief B's office was physically located between groups B2 and B3, on the same floor of a multistory building. Supervisor B and his department were located in a far corner of a lower floor. By merely stepping out of his office door, Chief B was in Department B2; by taking about 10 steps, he was in Department B3. But to reach Department B he had to walk about 50 yards, including going down a flight of stairs. Further reinforcing his proximity to Supervisor B2 and his department, when entering and leaving his office in the building, Chief B had to walk through Department B2 and directly past Supervisor B2's cubicle.

Physical arrangements other than location also reinforced the pattern. B3 and B2 worked at desks located in open cubicles, walled in by shoulder-high partitions; Supervisor B had a completely walled and glassed-in office space. Thus, physical access to interaction with B2 and B3 was easier than with B, whose office configuration forced the visitor to feel that he was stepping into a more private situation.

From these various research studies of leadership and supervisory behavior we may reach several conclusions. What the leader lets his subordinates do themselves makes a significant difference. Some subordinates tend to feel more satisfied with relative autonomy, to learn and develop to a greater extent, and to be more productive. However, this does not imply that the leader should do nothing. His interventions can help the subordinate and the group when they need help in defining or solving problems and when they need the emotional support necessary to maintain and develop their relatively autonomous skills. In general, some leadership behavior styles do lead to more effective results than other styles. *But this does not imply that the leader is free to choose a style as he chooses a new pair of shoes.* He is subject to the social demands of groups other than his subordinates. His peers and superiors, as well as his family and community groups, demand that his behavior be relevant to their needs. Thus, his total role performance includes more than his behavior in his work group.

The distribution of necessary technical competences among the leader, his subordinates, and his superiors has much to do with the leader's behavior. In some matters the nature of the task requires that he follow, that he allow himself to be influenced instead of initiating activities himself. Some empirical research confirms the idea that both technical and social skills are required for effective leadership.[26]

The final question asked of leadership research is how to train competent leaders. Conventional training formats attempt to put the trainee in the role of learner. But the realities of his continuing membership in groups that demand conformity to their own standards tend to be stronger forces than the individual's needs to learn. We shall elaborate the problems of role choice and leadership training in our discussion of current, unresolved issues raised by leadership research.

## ISSUES IN LEADERSHIP

The findings of leadership research, and the various attempts to apply them, raise several fundamental issues. One has to do with the definition of the leadership problem. Should leadership be taught as a skill, like mathematical analysis or music, or is the process different from the more usual conflict-free areas of competence? The second set of issues has to do with views of authority. We shall briefly re-examine the ideal of egalitarianism in light of this issue. The third set of issues revolves about the content of permissiveness: What is it about participative decision-making, or permissive leadership behavior, that yields encouraging results in the research? The discussion of this issue will lead us into an examination of reality-testing for individuals and groups, and will lay the groundwork for a section about the internal psychological and emotional conditions associated with the leadership role.

## The Leadership Problem Redefined

The individual who is concerned about his own behavior in relation to others, and who therefore studies leadership, is apparently confronted with a series of choices. In a cultural setting where leaders are born, not made, the individual is not called upon to make

---

[26] See, for example, Moment and Zaleznik, *Role Development and Interpersonal Competence,* and the discussion in Chapter Six of this present book.

choices regarding his behavior; what he is, in terms of social status, he is.  In our culture, where social mobility is an ideal, where any individual's aspirations to leadership are approved, where scientific modes of inquiry, description, and explanation are encouraged, and where application is demanded, the individual is continually confronted with behavioral choices.

A parallel situation exists in the area of child raising.  Parents are confronted with a variety of "how to raise children" methods just as managers and managerial aspirants face a barrage of advice on "how to be a leader" and "how to be successful in business."  Even the advice itself is parallel: discipline or permissiveness in the parents' case, "initiating structure" or "consideration" in the supervisor's.  In both instances, an already puzzling situation is made more puzzling by the need for choice implied by the new knowledge derived from research and its implications.

In response to this super-sensitive self-consciousness, which can in itself become a source of anxiety and reduced effectiveness, the individual, parent, or supervisor is told to "be yourself"; intrapersonal and interpersonal honesty ultimately pay off in human relations.  But in order for the individual to be himself he must know himself.  And the very set of developments that raise this demand make it more difficult for the individual to know himself.  Identity diffusion and ambiguity are the major problems of the individual in the twentieth-century world, partly because knowledge has shaken traditional foundations of belief, and partly because social mobility and technological change have tended to destroy the stability of two of the individual's primary sources of identity, the family and the place he once called his home.[26a]

The person who sets out to learn how to be a better parent or how to be a better leader ultimately has to learn how to be himself in order to improve his performances in any role.  This direction of inquiry does not eliminate the need for choice; it only makes the choices more fundamental.  Rather than choosing between being tough or nice, for example, the individual has to choose what he wants to become.  Thus, the leadership problem, as it affects individuals' behavioral choices, comes down to a more fundamental problem of identity.  Any individual, regardless of occupation, profession, or social role, has to deal with the problem in order to enhance his personal competence.

This deflection from the question of how a person can become a better leader, does not imply that a clearer understanding of

[26a] Wheelis, *The Quest for Identity*.

leadership dimensions, styles, and behavioral elements is unimportant. It means that they must be understood within the context of individual development, rather than merely within the framework of management techniques and procedures. The processes of leadership are of a different sort than other managerial concerns, such as accounting techniques and procedures or economic decision making, which involve the development of skills independent of emotional conflict. The need to view leadership from outside the management culture may be concluded from the repeated evidence that, in human groups and organizations, the greater the exercise of traditional managerial controls, the poorer the individual and group performances tend to be.

This shift in emphasis from "how to do it" to "who are you?" is reflected in the gradual change in the training focus of the National Training Laboratories in Human Relations, an offshoot of the original work of Lewin, Lippitt, and White.[27]   Initially, the organization was called the National Training Laboratories in Group Development. In its earliest training programs, it used "skill exercises" as part of a design to train individuals to be better group leaders; its intellectual focus was upon the workings of the dynamic processes of groups. It emphasis gradually moved toward fostering individual development, with less direct attention to group and leadership problems. Early emphasis was on democratic leadership and the egalitarian ideal; later efforts moved more and more in the direction of recognizing the uniqueness of the individual, his needs, and his competences.

## The Egalitarian-Authoritarian Dilemma

John W. Gardner's book, *Excellence,*[28] is subtitled, "Can we be equal and excellent too?" According to Gardner, there are three principles at work in determining who shall fill leadership positions in our society: hereditary privilege, egalitarianism, and competitive performance.[29]   Gardner deplores the misinterpretation and misuse of the egalitarian imperative in the democratic ideal, as he deplores hereditary privilege and unbridled, irresponsible competition. To grant each person equal *opportunity* to fulfill his potential is not the same as assuming that all persons are equally competent in all respects. Yet this confusion complicates the problem of selecting potential leaders and constrains the behavior of individuals in leadership posi-

---

[27] Lewin, Lippitt, and White, *op. cit.*
[28] See Bibliography.
[29] Gardner, *op. cit.,* pp. 21 ff.

tions. Gardner points out that a misplaced egalitarian emphasis constrains an individual, a group, an organization, or an entire nation, to compromise on standards, resulting ultimately in mediocrity and collapse under the pressure of external forces. He states his ideal in the question, "How can we provide opportunities and rewards for individuals of every degree of ability so that individuals at every level will realize their full potentialities, perform at their best and harbor no resentment toward any other level?"[30]  Resentment, and its consequences, is the major problem to be overcome, largely because of the misinterpreted egalitarian principle.

This dilemma and its consequences have been evident in United States military history, where the issue has been survival against external forces.  In the American Revolution, rebellion against authority created the emotional tone of the colonies; this was evident in the attitudes and behaviors of officers and soldiers at the time of Washington's appointment as commander-in-chief.[31]  Local aristocratic tradition acted in alliance with the egalitarian ideal against developing competence and unity of command.  During the War Between the States in the 1860's, volunteer militiamen elected their officers at the same time that politicians were appointed generals.[32]  In both conflicts, the slow processes of overcoming resentment towards violations of the egalitarian ideal, neutralizing the aristocratic principle, finding competent leadership, and allowing competent persons to lead extolled a heavy price in time and loss of life.

Small work groups, committees, and task groups spend a tremendous amount of time and emotional energy in airing resentments, in allowing members opportunities for self-expression, and in setting up task-relevant authority structures.  The paradox is that this aspect of the democratic process yields an outcome identical in form to the emotionally resented autocracy: differential expertise and power is

---

[30] *Ibid.*, p. 115.

[31] See, for example, "Holding the Army Together," pp. 157–164, in Commager and Morris, *The Spirit of 'Seventy-Six*. This is a series of writings by participants, describing the chaotic state of military organization in the early days of the American Revolution.

[32] See "The Problem of Discipline," Chapter XIV in Commager, *The Blue and the Gray*, pp. 481 ff. An excerpt entitled "Thomas Wentworth Higginson Explains the Value of Trained Officers," pp. 482–487, is especially relevant to the egalitarianism *versus* competence issue, as it was raised in 1864 by a Unitarian clergyman who became a volunteer officer in the United States Army. His paper expresses his strong feelings about the incompatibility between democratic principles and competence in war, supported by his observations of leadership problems at the time. "No mortal skill can make military power effective on democratic principles (*Ibid.*, p. 483)."

accepted on faith and trust. The major difference is that in the autocratic process the resentment smolders rather than being openly expressed, and the democratic process seems less arbitrary in some instances. Yet, some democratic procedures can be as arbitrary as those which are autocratic. Majority rule or the acceptance of an expert's authority by people who have no criteria for evaluating his competence are examples of arbitrary "democratic" processes. In some groups, the tyranny of egalitarianism is no less arbitrary and oppressive than the tyranny of other forms of power in other groups.

The optimum solution of group problems calls for the expression of competences by individual members; inevitably, some members will be more competent than others in certain areas. Hence, heirarchical authority structures will be created on various kinds of group issues. The difference between this and the traditional autocratic model is that the autocratic leader is supposed to be the best at everything; he makes all of the group's decisions. On the other hand, a truly democratic model, unencumbered by misplaced egalitarianism, allows expertise to be practiced by those who have it. Different members may lead at different times because of the different competences required. This is not to be confused with such egalitarian rituals as rotating chairmanships alphabetically or the individual avoiding leadership activity to maintain equality.

In spite of the existence and clarity of the authority structure in effective problem-solving groups, research evidence strongly suggests that a group must experiment with democratic, participative, consultative, group-discussion or leader-permissive processes in order to arrive at a suitable authority structure and to work within the structure without resentment of differences. The best or optimum structure cannot be imposed externally with the expectation that it will work. It apparently must arise through the social processes that take place within the group. One leadership function is to help provide the group with means for continually readjusting its authority structures in the face of changing individual competences and changing external demands. The importance of this process to leadership behavior draws our attention to participative or permissive leadership practices.

## What Does Permissiveness Permit?

Numerous research studies and nondocumented common experiences have indicated that, under certain conditions, participative, relatively permissive leadership has been accompanied by marked improvement in group productiveness, morale, and the emotional involvement of individual members of the group. These experiences also indicate that members' attitudes toward authority figures change; they become less resentful.

Over the years, there has been much disagreement about the important elements of these processes. One theory, which might be called catharsis, sees the important element as the individual's "ventilation" of his hostile feelings in the presence of sympathetic listeners. Somehow, expressing the feelings relieves the individual, and he no longer feels the need to resist authority and change. However, the validity of this view is doubtful because some disturbed people incessantly ventilate their feelings, seem to enjoy it, and do not change.

Another view sees personal involvement as the crucial element. If the individual has participated in making decisions affecting himself, he feels he has more at stake in the group and its work. In a study by Edith B. Bennett, where several elements in group decision making were controlled experimentally, it was found that group discussion and individual public commitment did *not* make a difference in the subsequent behavior of group members. However, the fact that a decision was actually made with the existence of a high degree of group consensus did make it more likely that action would be taken.[33] In order for the individual's involvement to lead to results, particular kinds of group processes had to transpire, as evidenced by a decision and by consensus; mere discussion and public professions did not lead to action.

As with catharsis, mere emotional involvement does not lead to positive outcomes for the individuals or for the group. Many a well-meaning leader, who has allowed his workers to go through the motions of expressing their feelings and who has even encouraged them to suggest action, has ended up with highly involved workers. But the involvement ultimately featured increased frustration and hostility, since neither he nor the group had found a way to channel it into positive action. The satisfactory group experiences, which may have included some catharsis and involvement effects, definitely included the element of *reality testing*, which provided a focus for the leaders' and members' activities. The group processes involved testing the validity and relevance of attitudes and ideas. Reality-testing theory assumes that this process is essentially interpersonal; reality is validated through achieving consensus in relation to an audience. Even the

[33] Bennett, "Discussion, Decision, Commitment, and Consensus in 'Group Decision.'"

stereotyped lonely scientist engages in this kind of reality testing; his audience is the scientific community.

If maintaining continuing reality-testing processes is one of the requisites for effective leadership, as we tend to believe, then the question of optimum leadership style begins to take on a different form. Is permissive, considerate, participative leadership a necessary condition for reality orientation? Or does the reality orientation grow out of a combination of conditions under which leadership styles vary from the warm and permissive to the stern and demanding?

One aspect of the leadership issues we have been discussing is that they involve processes of change. Even a fairly stable group must gradually change to meet the demands of changes going on in its environment. Reality testing and reality orientation, which appear to be the most important aspects of the leadership process, are also basic processes when change becomes our focus. We shall discuss these processes further in the concluding chapter of the book.

To summarize briefly, in our comments on issues in leadership, we redefined the leadership problem as a question of individual development, rather than as a matter of skill training in its conventional sense. We then brought up the egalitarian-authoritarian dilemma and the misconception that equality of opportunity means equal competence and authority. This distortion, we concluded, unduly constrains individuals, groups, and organizations and leads to mediocrity. We examined the components of permissive and participative leadership, catharsis, involvement, and reality testing, and decided that the concept of reality orientation might, in fact, cut across leadership styles.

Within these issues, as well as within leadership issues which we have not discussed here, a multitude of pressures act upon the person in a position of leadership. How should he, as an individual and leader, behave? Under what conditions should he act as an equal? Under what circumstances should he stand upon his unique competences? To what extent should he attempt to be patient, warm, and permissive? What should he do about his feelings of impatience and anger, and his desire to have others comply with his wishes? He constantly faces social demands from his subordinate group, from his colleagues, and from his superiors. Moreover, he has individual needs to meet, as well as the needs of persons who are important to him. On top of these emotion-laden social demands and individual needs, he must get the job done. Task requirements, which he deals with through technical competences, cut across and sometimes conflict with these demands and needs.

We shall now turn our attention to some of the problems the leader faces as a result of his psychological and emotional response to these conflicting demands, needs, and requirements, and the behavioral consequences of his intrapsychic processes.

## THE LEADER'S RESPONSE TO PRESSURES

Historically and culturally, the motivation of persons in leadership positions has tended to remain unstudied, except by their political opponents and critics. Loyal supporters and followers are trained to believe that leaders are selfless embodiments of organizational purpose. However, recent biographical studies and research on the characteristics of successful executives has cut through some of the mystique of the leader. They have described him as an individual who is possessed of needs, motives, conflicts, unique competences, and particular combinations of early experiences closely related to his motives and life path.[34]

Achievement motivation tends to be relatively strong in rapidly developing societies and in individuals who rise to leadership positions within such societies.[35] But as we pointed out in our discussion of individual role performances in groups, a strong desire to achieve may be satisfied in a variety of ways, involving different styles of using things, symbols, and other persons. Furthermore, achievement motivation can be associated with a fundamental need for externally recognized status, for esteem and affection from others, and for security in a social system, as well as with the individual's self-esteem and purely internal standards.[36]

The social demands of the leader's role tap his personal needs for external recognition and interpersonal affection. The task requirements of his role measure his technical competence and self-esteem against internal standards of excellence.

Since the leader, or the individual in any social role, contains within himself a variety of not entirely consistent needs and motives, and the environment in which he works provides a parallel variety of sources of satisfactions, it would seem that the ways in which the individual resolves these potential internal conflicts, manages his personal defenses against anxiety, and orients himself emotionally toward work and people, at least partially determine the effectiveness of his behavior patterns.

[34] See, for example, Warner and Abegglen, *Big Business Leaders in America*, and McClelland, *The Achieving Society*.

[35] McClelland, *op. cit.*

[36] Moment and Zaleznik, *op. cit.*, p. 69 ff.

Moment and Zaleznik's study of role performance in groups included an analysis of imaginative stories written in response to ambiguous pictures on the Thematic Apperception Test.[37]   Individuals were categorized into four role types according to differences in their role performances in experimental problem-solving groups.   One type, the Stars, performed both task and social roles in their groups and were perceived by the others as outstanding leaders.   Technical Specialists tended to concentrate on the groups' task and to avoid social behaviors; they ranked second in the number of choices received on the leadership question.   Underchosen participants, who characteristically performed  in response to their own needs rather than group needs, and Social Specialists, who performed group maintenance roles, were chosen least often as leaders.

The thematic content of the stories written by four role types led to the following analysis of differences among them:

*Stars* [The predominant leaders]

These men were more likely than any other type to express conflict between family and business success and correspondingly were less likely to present happy endings to their stories.   Their stories tended to be concerned with imperatives, providing for family, and giving family love, care and concern.   They tended to express more consciousness of failure, in terms of work and in dealing with people.   At the same time, they were less likely to decribe work as intrinsically gratifying and they did not express concern with growth through work.   On the whole, their stories tended to be more insightful, less guarded and more candid about psychological pressures than the stories written by the other types.

*Technical Specialists* [Second choice on leadership]

The stories these men wrote tended to stress the idea that if one shows competence and works hard, he will achieve a highly valued success, but they tended to minimize an underlying concern about achievement and expressed a feeling that the system was vaguely hostile.   They did not express concern with interpersonal relations, which may explain their lack of concern about impersonal systems.   They expressed little conflict between family and business success, assuming that the family will be provided for and satisfied vicariously through the central person's business success.   If the family did appear to make conflicting demands, their tendency was to reject its demands on them.   They did express a conflict between personal task satisfaction and external requirements, indicating that their heroes sought primary fulfillment through work.   They appeared

[37] Moment and Zaleznik, *op. cit.*, pp. 318 ff.  See also Chapter Six of this present volume.

to express confidence in their heroes' ability to cope with the business world. It would appear that Technical Specialists guarded their heroes against themselves and others, and that a need to achieve was balanced against basic doubts and fears about other people, which was expressed in a diffuse anxiety.

## Social Specialists [Few choices on leadership]

Social Specialists tended to describe the world as pleasant, happy, and favorable to the individual. They tended to describe the business system as hostile to the individual, but this hostile perception did not seem to include the idea that people within the system are cold and uncaring. While they expressed dependency on personal relationships, they did not seem worried about interpersonal failure, for they described individual people as helpful and pleasant. However, when the individual shaded into the large "they" it disturbed their general equanimity. The impersonal system might have thwarted their heroes' efforts to relate warmly to others. While they expressed anxiety, personal responsibility and guilt, they were less likely than Stars or Technical Specialists to emphasize it, and they may have projected it onto the impersonal system which was impervious to close identification. They described little conflict between success and family, and like the Technical Specialists, they identified their heroes' satisfactions with those of the family, but they differed from the Technical Specialists in that this identification tended to arise out of a close relationship rather than rejection and distance.

## Underchosen [Few choices on leadership]

These stories were relatively conflict free and generally ended happily. They expressed a positive concern for the family and perceived its members as sources of gratification and happiness. They expressed more dependence on families than any other type, referring to them as supports, anchors, and possible retreats from an impersonal system. At the same time, the Underchosen showed a tendency to reject and repudiate the family. They discussed obligation, but they tended to express less personal guilt and responsibility than any other group, choosing instead to project incapacities and inabilities on the machinations of the impersonal systems. The Underchosen tended to be less insightful, more guarded, more insecure, more vacillating, and more distant from and rejecting of work and family than the other types in the content of their stories.[38]

The researchers' analysis of the modes of managing anxiety and resolving conflict characteristic of the two extreme types, the Stars and the Underchosen, is especially relevant to our discussion at this point:

The Star's [the predominant leaders] stories tended to be more conflict-laden, and the Underchosen participants' [nonleaders] stories tended to be

[38] *Ibid.*, pp. 331–333.

free of conflict, compared to the stories of the Specialists and compared to each other. A comparison of these findings with the results of the . . . analysis of anxiety themes will help interpret both sets of findings as well as the theoretical relationship between conflict and anxiety.

The themes scored as anxiety-laden had to do with expressed or implicit feelings of failure; concern with chaos, confusion, and conflict; focused and unfocused fears; concern with death, loss, and embarrassment; concern with values, worth, and worthlessness; and general inconclusiveness, tentativeness, uneven terseness, and lack of imagination. These themes did not center around choosing or alternatives; they referred to emotional states independent of action or behavioral alternatives. . . .

The Underchosen tended to score high in anxiety while expressing relatively conflict-free stories. For the other types, anxiety and conflict themes apparently tended to occur together. This could mean that in the Underchosen members' stories, felt anxiety tended not to be associated with action alternatives while in the other types' stories anxiety and action alternatives did tend to occur together. When this interpretation is coupled with the previous indications from the Underchosen participants' stories—lower emotional involvement with work, perception of the work system as impersonal, dependence upon the family as a support and anchor, and a tendency to repudiate the family—a characteristically different manner of dealing with anxiety is suggested. Instead of coupling the anxiety with a search for alternative ways of reducing the anxiety through action, as would be involved in the conflict themes, *this mode would attempt to place the causes of the trouble in events and entities outside of the person, rather than internalizing the concern in the form of guilt and feelings of personal responsibility,* as tended to be the case in the Stars' stories. *The extreme alternative to internalization would be projection; the person would feel irresponsibly dependent upon external objects and forces, such as the work system and the family, and would feel incapable of influencing the course of external events.* He would not feel guilty because he could not see himself as causing events outside himself. His behavior would be expected to be primarily expressive of his anxieties rather than adaptive or coping, which would imply searching for and testing action alternatives.[39]

Moment and Zaleznik's study confirmed other researchers' findings that one consequence of the leadership role, when carried out effectively, is the internalization of conflict and guilt, the inner manifestations of responsible behavior by the leader. To his family and friends the leader may seem to be overresponsible toward other people; even this concern is internalized in the form of additional guilt, or remorse, about "neglecting" his family.[40]

[39] Moment and Zaleznik, *op. cit.,* pp. 329–331, italics added in this present volume.
[40] *Ibid.,* p. 325.

In *The Human Dilemmas of Leadership*, Zaleznik discusses internal conditions characteristic of leaders as they pursue success.

1. *Status anxiety*. This refers to those dilemmas frequently experienced by individuals at or near the top in their organizational world.

2. *Competition anxiety*. This refers to the feelings generated while climbing to the top.

These two prevalent types of anxiety, while resembling each other in a number of respects, are worth keeping separate for purposes of furthering understanding.

## STATUS ANXIETY

When an individual begins to achieve some success and recognition in his work, he may suddenly realize that a change has occurred within himself and in his relations with associates. From a position of being the bright young man who receives much encouragement and support he, almost overnight, finds himself viewed as a contender by those who formerly acted as mentors. A similar change takes place in his relations with persons who were his peers. They appear cautious with him, somewhat distant, and constrained in their approach, where once he may have enjoyed the easy give-and-take of their friendship. The individual in question is then ripe for status anxiety. He becomes torn between the responsibilities of a newly acquired authority and the strong need to be liked.

There is a well-established maxim in the study of human behavior that describes this situation tersely and even poetically; namely, that "love flees authority." Where one individual has the capacity to control and affect the actions of another, either by virtue of differences in their positions, knowledge, or experience, then the feeling governing the relationship tends to be one of distance and (hopefully) respect, but not one ultimately of warmth and friendliness.

I do not believe that this basic dichotomy between respect or esteem and liking is easily changed. The executive who confuses the two is bound to get into trouble. Yet in our culture today we see all too much evidence of people seeking to obscure the difference. Much of the current ethos of success equates popularity and being liked with competence and achievement. In Arthur Miller's *Death of a Salesman*, Willie Loman in effect was speaking for our culture when he measured a person's achievement in the gradations of being liked, well liked, or very well liked.

### Reaction and Recognition

In what ways do executives react when they are caught in the conflict between exercising authority and being liked?

Sometimes they seek to play down their authority and play up their likability by acting out the role of the "nice guy." This is sometimes called status stripping, where the individual tries in a variety of ways to discard all the symbols of his status and authority. This ranges from proclaiming the open-door policy, where everyone is free to visit the executive any time he wants, to the more subtle and less ritualistic means such as democratizing work by proclaiming equality of knowledge, experience, and position. And yet these attempts at status stripping fail sooner or later. The executive may discover that his subordinates join in gleefully by stripping his status and authority to the point where he becomes immobilized; is prevented from making decisions; is faced with the prospect of every issue from the most trivial to the most significant being dealt with in the same serious vein. In short, problem solving and work become terrorized in the acting out of status stripping.

The executive soon becomes aware of another aspect of his dilemma. Much to his horror, he finds that attempts to remove social distance in the interests of likability have not only reduced work effectiveness, but have resulted in an abortion of the intent to which his behavior has been addressed. He discovers that his subordinates gradually come to harbor deep and unspoken feelings of contempt toward him, because he inadvertently has provided them with a negative picture of what rewards await them for achievement—a picture unpleasant to behold. In effect, the process of status stripping helps to destroy the incentives for achievement and in the extreme can produce feelings of helplessness and rage.

There is yet another side to the dilemma of status anxiety which is well worth examining. This side has to do with the hidden desire to "touch the peak." Executives frequently want to be near the source of power and to be accepted and understood by their bosses. Such motivations lead to excessive and inappropriate dependency bids, and to feelings of lack of autonomy on the part of the subordinate and of being leaned on too hard on the part of the superior. Under such conditions, communication between superior and subordinate tends to break down.

So far I have discussed the problem of status anxiety as an aspect of seeking friendship, warmth, and approval from subordinates and bosses. Status anxiety is also frequently generated by the fear of aggression and retaliation on the part of persons who hold positions of authority. Executives sometimes report feeling lonely and detached in their position. A closer look at the sense of loneliness reveals a feeling that one is a target for the aggression of others. This feeling occurs because the executive is called upon to take a position on a controversial issue and to support the stand he assumes. He must be able to take aggression with a reasonably detached view, or the anxiety can become intolerable. . . .

. . . Sometimes this [status anxiety] will appear in the form of hyperactivity—the case of the executive who flits from problem to problem or from work project to work project without really seeing an activity through to completion. In this case, the executive is utilizing the tactic of providing a shifting target so that other persons have difficulty in taking aim at him.

## Constructive Approach

Now, in referring to aggression and the avoidance of aggression as aspects of status anxiety, I do not mean to imply hostile aggression. I mean to suggest instead that all work involves the release of aggressive energy. Solving problems and reaching decisions demand a kind of give-and-take where positions are at stake and where it is impossible for everyone concerned to be equally right all the time. But having to give way or to alter a position in the face of compelling argument is no loss. The executive who can develop a position, believe in it, support it to its fullest, and then back down, is a strong person.

It is just this type of person who does not suffer from status anxiety. He may love to provide a target because he knows this may be a very effective catalyst for first-class work accomplishment. He is secure enough to know that he has nothing to lose in reality, but much to gain in the verve and excitement of interesting work. This type of executive is able to take aggression, and in fact encourage it, because he probably has abandoned the magical thinking that seems to equate his position of authority with omnipotence. No one has the power to make everyone else conform to his wishes, so it is no loss to learn that one has been wrong in the face of the arguments aggressively put forth by others. In fact, such ability to retract a stand results in heightened respect from others.

I am suggesting, in other words, that we should not be misled into equating the virtue of humility with executive behavior that appears modest, uncertain of a stand, and acquiescent toward others—behavior which frequently is feigned modesty to avoid becoming a target. True humility, in my opinion, is marked by the person who thinks his way through problems, is willing to be assertive, is realistic enough to encourage assertiveness from others, and is willing to acknowledge the superiority of ideas presented by others.

## COMPETITION ANXIETY

The second main pattern of inner conflict that badly needs attention is what I have termed competition anxiety, a close kin of status anxiety. It goes without saying that the world of work is essentially a competitive one. Competition exists in the give-and-take of solving problems and making decisions. It also exits in the desire to advance into the more select and fewer positions at the top of a hierachy. An executive who has difficulty in coming to terms with a competitive environment will be relatively ineffective.

From my observations of executives—and would-be executives—I have found two distinct patterns of competition anxiety: (1) the fear of failure and (2) the fear of success. Let us examine each in turn.

### Fear of Failure

You have perhaps seen the fear of failure operate in the activities of the child, where this type of problem generally originates:

The child may seem to become quite passive and unwilling to undertake work in school or to engage in sports with children his age. No amount of prodding by parents or teachers seems to activate his interests; in fact, prodding seems to aggravate the situation and induce even greater reluctance to become engaged in an activity. When this child progresses in school, he may be found to have considerable native talent, and sooner or later becomes tabbed as an "underachiever." He gets as far as he does thanks in large measure to the high quality of his native intelligence, but he does not live up to the promise which others observe in him.

When this child grows up and enters a career, we may see the continuation of underachievement, marked by relative passivity and undistinguished performance. Where he may cast his lot is in the relative obscurity of group activity. Here he can bring his talents to bear in anonymous work. As soon as he becomes differentiated, he feels anxious and may seek to become immersed once again in group activity.

An important aspect of this pattern of response is the ingrained feeling that whatever the person undertakes is bound to fail. He does not feel quite whole and lacks a strong sense of identity. He is short on self-esteem and tends to quit before he starts in order to avoid confrontation with the fear that he might fail. Instead of risking failure he is willing to assume anonymity, hence, the sense of resignation and sometimes fatigue which he communicates to those near to him.

A closer study of the dilemma surrounding the fear of failure indicates that the person has not resolved the concerns he has with competing. It may be that he has adopted or "internalized" unrealistic standards of performance or that he is competing internally with unreachable objects. Therefore he resolves to avoid the game because it is lost before it starts.

If you recall James Thurber's characterization of Walter Mitty, you may get a clearer indication of the problem I am describing. Walter was a meek, shy man who seemed to have difficulty in mobilizing himself for even the simplest tasks. Yet in his inner world of fantasy, as Thurber portrays so humorously and touchingly, Walter Mitty is the grand captain of his destiny and the destiny of those who depend on him. He populates his inner world with images of himself as the pilot of an eight-engine bomber or the cool, skillful, nerveless surgeon who holds the life of his patient in his hands. Who could ever work in the world of mortals under standards that one had best leave to the gods!

You can observe from this description that fear of failure can be resolved only when the person is able to examine his inner competitive world, to judge its basis in reality, and to modify this structure in accordance with sensible standards.

## Fear of Success

The fear of failure can be matched with its opposite, the fear of success. This latter pattern might be called the "Macbeth complex," since we have a ready illustration available in Shakespeare's *Macbeth*. The play can be viewed symbolically for our purposes:

Macbeth was an ambitious man. It is interesting to note that the demon ambition is projected out in the form of the three witches and Macbeth's wife, who, Macbeth would lead us to believe, put the idea into his head to become king. But we do not believe for a minute that the ambition to become number one existed anywhere but within Macbeth himself. You remember that to become king, Macbeth killed Duncan, a nice old man who had nothing but feelings of admiration and gratitude for Macbeth.

As the story unfolds, we find the crown resting uneasily on a tormented head. Macbeth is wracked with feelings of guilt for the misdeed he has committed and then with uneasy suspicion. The guilt is easy enough for us to understand, but the suspicion is a bit more subtle. Macbeth presents himself to us as a character who committed a foul deed to attain an ambition and is then suspicious that others are envious of him and seek to displace him in the number one position. So, there are few lieutenants to trust. And, paradoxically, the strongest subordinates become the ones least trusted and most threatening.

The play portrays in action the morbid cycle of the hostile-aggressive act followed by guilt and retribution. In addition, if we view the play symbolically, we can say that the individual, like Macbeth, may experience in fantasy the idea that one achieves position only through displacing someone else. Success, therefore, brings with it feelings of guilt and the urge to undo or to reverse the behavior that led to the success. If such concerns are strong enough—and they exist in all of us to some degree—then we may see implemented the fear of success.

The form of this implementation will vary. One prominent pattern it takes is in striving hard to achieve a goal, but just when the goal is in sight or within reach, the person sabotages himself. The self-sabotage can be viewed as a process of undoing—to avoid the success that may generate guilt. This process of self-sabotage is sometimes called snatching defeat out of the jaws of victory. . . .

## MANAGING INNER CONFLICTS

To summarize the discussion thus far, I have called attention to the not easily accepted notion that conflicts of interest can and do exist within individuals and are not restricted to the relations among men in the ordinary conduct of affairs. I have said that the inner conflicts rooted in the emotional development of the individual are at the core of the leadership dilemma. It is misleading, in other words, to seek for causes of conflict exclusively in external forces.

Then, touching on a few of the inner conflicts of executives, I grouped them into two main types: (1) status anxiety and (2) competition anxiety. Both of these forms of inner conflict are rooted in the very process of human development in the strivings of individuals for some measure of autonomy and control over their environment. The forms happen to be especially crucial in the executive's world simply because he acts in the center of a network of authority and influence that at any point in time is subject to alteration. In fact, one can think of decision making and action in organizations as a continuing flow of influence interchanges where the sources of the power to influence are many. But whatever the external source through which any one person achieves power to influence, its final manifestations will reflect the inner emotional condition of the man.[41]

These comments regarding the inner demands of the leadership role, and some possible resolutions, refer to the first issue of leadership discussed earlier in the chapter: the difference in emphasis between concentration on leadership styles and skills on the one hand, and the alternative focus upon the leader as an individual in the process of development. The latter view sees the leader's most important problem as the building of a stable self-identity.[42] Although this problem is faced by any individual in the pursuit of competence in his career, the particular personal issues to be resolved by the leader of task groups in purposeful organizational settings are unique to his chosen role.

## SUMMARY

Initially, we described the future leader as a child whose raw, unsocialized attempts to get attention and aggressively dominate others become a core around which he learns to internalize socially acceptable purposes. Through the effects of his interpersonal relations in the family and the emotional coloring such relations lend to his cultural heritage, he learns to aspire to the *position* of leader, with little understanding of the requirements of the job. He has little idea of who he will lead or toward what goals. The specification and internalization of these demands await the slow, deliberate development of his self-identification, the deepening of his interests, the freeing of his personal relations from their early bases in the family, and the clarification of his personal values.[43]

These personal resolutions take place against a background of cultural tradition; the tradition confuses the individual with regard to interpersonal authority relations and social class attitudes, distant heroes as role models, conventional assumptions about the authority hierarchy, and conventional principles of leadership. Research into the characteristics of effective leadership, and parenthood, confront him with additional choices. Trying on various social roles and personality facades is an inherent characteristic of the adolescent's

[41] Zaleznik, *The Human Dilemmas of Leadership*, pp. 51–54.
[42] See also White, *Lives in Progress*, pp. 327–366.
[43] *Ibid.*

identity crisis. Thus, the imposed self-consciousness exemplified in the behavioral-scientific study of leadership behavior inadvertently prolongs adolescent identity diffusion.[44] Awareness that other behaviors are possible—"leaders are made, not born"—heightens the sense of conflict with the demand for choice.

Studies of leadership tend to polarize the underlying dimensions into human and technical aspects. This is not a new dichotomy. Freud is reputed to have summarized the demands of the good life as "to love and to work." Family life revolves about the distinction between work and play. Prototypical roles in most, if not all, societies polarize around the social-emotional, expressive style exemplified in the mother's role in Western culture and the instrumental-adaptive mode of the father's role.[45] The individual in modern society not only has to choose the kind of specialization he will pursue in education and work, he also has to face the possibility of fusing specialities into situationally demanded role performances. He faces transitions from one characteristic role performance to another and the assimilation of sometimes divergent role performances into some form of personality integration.

The leadership process involves the meeting of social demands from the variety of groups and groupings of which the individual leader is a "member." It involves engaging interpersonally with the needs of other specific individuals. In addition, the leader's technical knowledge prescribes the ways in which work should be done. And his personal needs and motives must be met. Encompassing all of these demands, needs, and requirements is his over-all emotional orientation toward the human processes of getting work done while living in rewarding interpersonal relationships with others.[46]

A most important part of the leader's orientation toward his role is his feeling toward change—that is, the way he thinks about it and the manner in which his own behavior impedes or facilitates it. He is concerned with the maintenance of a dynamic equilibrium within his group and with his group's relationships to its environment, as well as with needs for change within himself and others as they develop. The general problem of behavior and attitude change mentioned in this chapter will be the major focus of the concluding chapter of the book.

---

[44] See Erikson, "Identity and the Life Cycle," for a description of identity crises and identity diffusion.

[45] See Parsons and Bales, *Family, Socialization and Interaction Process.*

[46] See also Roethlisberger et al., *Training for Human Relations,* "The Multi-dimensional Milieu of the Practitioner," pp. 124 ff.

*Chapter Thirteen*

# Change

W^E have organized our study of interpersonal relations in organizations according to: (1) group processes, (2) the individual and interpersonal dynamics, (3) organizational aspects, and (4) leadership and change. The first three sections each analyzed particular processes and their interrelationships. The final section, beginning with the preceding chapter on leadership, has thus far discussed the personality of the individual as leader in relation to the social processes of the group and within the constraints of the organizational and environmental systems. Our analysis of change will start with the nature of organic processes in general, drawing upon some of the concepts and problems represented in general systems theory. We shall then discuss problems of planned changes in individual, group, and organizational behavior and attitudes, citing some research findings on these processes. A laboratory learning model for change will precede the conclusion of our study.

We are concerned with changes in human behavior and attitudes. Other classes of change, such as technological change and economic development, ultimately involve problems of behavior and attitude change in individuals, groups, and organizations. Although the substance of particular technical and economic plans are of utmost importance, we shall not deal with them directly. Some of the social implications of technology and economic reward systems were discussed earlier but our major focus is on the dynamics of change in individuals, groups, and organizations.

## THE GENERAL THEORY OF CHANGE

Organic processes take place in the relationships among living units. The units are arranged into systems of increasing complexity, starting with the individual cell. Combinations of particular kinds of cells make up organs such as the liver, the heart, or the lungs. Such organs exist in functional relationships to other organs and to the next larger unit. They are connected by such systems as the nervous system, the circulatory system, and the respiratory system, to make up the total individual organism, the living plant or animal. However, even the total individual cannot exist without other individuals; each unit is engaged in exchange processes with other individuals and with groups. The individual human is dependent on animal and vegetable systems, weather systems, and in modern life, social groups and larger social organizations.

The major attribute of organic processes—as opposed to mechanical processes such as an internal combustion engine—which must lie at the base of any theory of individual and social change, is the inherent regenerative potential of the life processes and the eventual death of the individual unit. Organic systems reproduce and maintain themselves, even though each individual member is destined to eventually perish. Such processes maintain temporal continuity in the identity of the individual, the group, the complex organization, the total society, and the civilization in spite of the transient existence of the individuals comprizing the larger entity at any one time.

## Basic Forces toward Conservation and Change

The processes by which continuity is maintained provide the media in which both resistance to change and the consummation of change takes place. The development of the individual over his life provides a model for the workings of processes of continuity and discontinuity within the individual, the group, and the organization over time.

At age 40, John Jones is the same individual as he was at birth in certain important respects. But his is strikingly different in other respects. The maintenance of the continuity of his identity is crucial for both his personality and the groups of which he is a part. If today and tomorrow he does not feel and behave as the same John Jones he was yesterday, he is suffering severe emotional or mental illness and cannot function coherently. On the other hand, if the groups with which he interacts do not accept him today as the same person he was yesterday and will be tomorrow, severe social pathology exists, and he and the groups cannot function co-operatively.

This required continuity of individual and social identity is the basis of forces toward conservation and the maintenance of the *status quo*. It implies that, in some respects, conditions must *not* change in order for the individual and the group to continue to function effectively. John Jones and his social world would collapse if he felt and acted like a responsible, adult person at work one day, a "beatnik" the next, and an infant the following day. Hence, the time-binding sameness of identity along with social trust in its predictability become tremendously strong forces toward conservation and resistance to change in individuals, groups, and organizations.

With all his sameness of identity, John Jones, age 40, is clearly not the infant John Jones in many important respects. Most obviously, his physical appearance and capabilities are different. The social world behaves differently toward him as an adult than it did when he was an infant. And it expects and counts on different behaviors from him. The inherent biological growth of the individual and the social expectation that he will grow up constitute forces toward change in the individual and his social relationships. Hence, along with inherent forces toward conservation, the life processes contain inherent forces toward change. Paradoxically, the socially expected sequence of changes may become a form of extreme conservation; for example, the expectation that the son would follow in his father's footsteps. Thus, natural processes of change may become institutionalized into sets of conservative forces.

One characteristic inherent in organic processes is the polarity between forces toward conservation and maintenance of identity, on the one hand, and forces toward change, adaptation, growth, and development on the other. Both sets of forces fight a losing battle for the individual; he will not live forever no matter how effectively he maintains himself. The processes of growth and development can only be culminated in an eventual return to nonexistence. Thus, the amazing thing about life processes is how they strive against the inevitable; life *is* hope in this respect. The institutionalization of this hope, this tremendous output of energy directed toward fighting a losing battle, becomes the basis for the continuity of identity of the larger unit, which persists in spite of the loss of identity of its individual members. Superordinate goals, systems of philosophical and religious belief and transcendental causes, become the outside sources of identity continuity to the individual. The institutionalization of hope into external causes defends the individual and the group against the most immobilizing form of anxiety, the awareness of the condition of nonexistence or the fear of death.

Our discussion has pointed to the tremendously strong bases on which forces resisting and facilitating change rest; these bases distinguish life processes, especially those involving humans, from mechan-

448 LEADERSHIP AND CHANGE

ical processes. The piston in an internal combustion engine is not aware of the fact that it is being used up; it doesn't fight against the process. Humans and their groups do care. They devote considerable energy to expressing their concern.

The workings of the processes of conservation and change have been described from the point of view of the individual, the group, the complex organization, and an entire culture. Since the problems of behavioral and attitudinal change cut across all of these levels of analysis, we shall briefly discuss some of the theories relevant to each.

## Culture Change

One of the causes which has captured the imagination of, and has become an object of identification for, many Americans since the Second World War has been helping the economically underdeveloped nations of the world. The exotic flavor of this cause is important because the same, well-meaning Americans who enthusiastically contribute time and effort to helping Africans and Asians do not seem to devote as much attention to the less exotic, but physically closer, needs for development within their own families, work relationships, neighborhoods, communities, geographic regions, and nation. Somehow, remoteness in space, time, and experience is a stronger motivation toward understanding and help than the familiarity of problems such as slums, delinquency, unequal opportunities, and intergroup conflict.

The distinctness of cross-cultural differences not only captures the imagination and interest, it also makes the job of understanding, in both its intellectual and emotional senses, appear to be easier. People can more easily accept that the Greeks have different work, eating, and child-raising practices than they can accept a similar observation about their neighbors. However, the earliest attempts at offering cross-cultural help were often accompanied by serious misunderstanding on the part of the well-meaning helpers; the ingratitude of those being "helped" was attributed to ignorance and stubbornness rather than to the existence of strong cultural patterns which change tended to disrupt.[1] Offering help was not a simple matter of two members of the same group in interaction; the intent was to change the recipient culture.

Cross-cultural helpers may become exasperated when a particular technical improvement or health measure is accepted readily in one

[1] See, for example, Mead, *Cultural Patterns and Technical Change.*

culture but rejected by another, or when one culture accepts one kind of change and rejects another.   At first glance, the patterns of acceptance and rejection seem to be arbitrary.   Uniformities of rejection lie at deeper levels; the social-emotional meaning of a particular technical object or activity pattern may vary from culture to culture, and the significance attached to objects and activities may vary within a culture in ways which bear little relationship to the meaning of the object or activity to the outsider.   Moreover, the social-emotional interpretation of helping and receiving help vary from culture to culture.

Edward T. Hall[2] discusses three distinct levels of culture discovered and described by anthropologists: formal, informal, and technical. Each of these levels transfers the learning of sentiments and practices in a different manner, and each of them features a different strength of emotional resistance to change.   Formal traditions are unquestioned imperatives, things that are *done* or *not done* in a particular culture. To our culture, wearing clothing in public is a formal tradition.   The child is taught that this is done; no other explanation is offered or even thought of.   Formal traditions are learned by precept or admonition.

Informal traditions, on the other hand, are learned by imitating models.   These involve doing as certain other people do.   Again, the tradition is not explained or deliberately thought out.   But, unlike formal traditions, informal traditions may change as models change. General styles of clothing would fit this level; men wear trousers and women wear skirts; the child is taught to dress and act like a little man or a little lady.

The technical level of culture is fully explained by teacher to student; it includes practices which are consciously describable.   The child is taught how to tie shoelaces, how to tie a cravat, and when to wear particular kinds of clothing.   The questions of whether or not to wear shoes, a formal matter, and whether to wear boys' shoes or girls' shoes, an informal matter, are not involved.   Hall points out that all cultural behavior patterns contain all three levels.[3]

According to Hall's analysis, in matters of externally introduced changes, the level of the culture involved and the nature of the emotional aspects of the change are important matters.   The degree and kind of affect involved in the three levels of culture differs markedly.   Violations  of the formal level are perceived with shock and considered "unnatural" events; an adult walking down a city street naked would meet with such a reaction.   The violation of an informal

[2] Hall, *The Silent Language.*
[3] *Ibid.,* pp. 63 ff.

tradition, on the other hand, would cause discomfort and invoke conventional social controls, such as giggling, kidding, or embarrassed nervousness. But social processes are not traumatically interrupted by informal violations, as they tend to be with violations of formal traditions.

In contrast, technical levels of cultural practices are relatively free of affect; the "right way" can be logically explained. However, the fastidious technician will get emotionally disturbed if the technical rules of the game are violated. In Hall's words, ". . . the formal is supported by technical props. It is the technical that people often resort to when all else fails."[4] Thus, technical devices, such as explicit laws, rules, and regulations, may be invoked when a formal tradition is violated, or the devices may become formalized.

The problem in efforts toward cross-cultural change is that the levels and emotional significances attached to the same practice may differ drastically between two cultures. Hall and Mead[5] give many examples of misunderstandings that arise as a result of these differences. Some of them involve agriculture, dietary practices, and community sanitation, which to the American advisor, are primarily technical problems. In many cultures, however, these activities involve formal, religious traditions, as well as informal traditions, and attempted changes meet with strong resistance. Even in the United States, where health and medical practices are, by and large, treated technically, attempts to fluoridate town water supplies have met strong opposition. Groups felt that their formal traditions were being threatened by having nature, as they defined it, violated and by having something done to them against their will.

The idea of several levels of culture carries with it two important elements which tend to apply to other processes. One is that of differential awareness or consciousness on the part of individual members as to the existence of underlying rules of behavior. Few people give any thought to the formal tradition of wearing clothing in public and would be ill at ease to think of the practice as anything but natural; alternatives are normally not conceivable.

In addition to differing levels of awareness, the idea of levels of culture also describes a hierarchy of emotional involvement and a directly proportional set of forces which tend to resist changes and to maintain the predictable *status quo*. The purely technical can be changed easily; the purely formal is the most persistently unchangeable. But the several levels are all contained in any one practice, so that some continuity of tradition will be maintained at one or more

[4] *Ibid.*, p. 77.   [5] Hall, *op. cit.*, Mead, *op. cit.*

levels, even when another level is apparently changed. The form may change while the function persists, as in the case of the substitution of animals for human sacrifices in some cultures. On the other hand, the form may persist while the function changes, as with buttons on men's coat sleeves which are reputed to have been used originally to discourage men from wiping their noses on their coat sleeves.

The process of culture change includes another element which will arise later in our discussion of planned change. This is the fact that change processes involve the raising to awareness and explicit examination of processes that have been taken for granted. Conscious examination of the otherwise unconscious emotional attachment to traditions is a major focal point in the process of change in cultural settings.

## Organizational Change

Roethlisberger and Dickson's description of the industrial organization closely parallels the three levels of culture described by Hall.[6] The same three terms are used, that is, formal, informal, and technical, but in different ways. We have abbreviated Roethlisberger and Dickson's scheme as follows:

Technical Organization
Human Organization
Individual
Social Organization
Formal Organization
Informal Organization[7]

Technical organization refers to the requirements of the productive processes, such as tools, materials, conversion processes, and products. Above the level of the individual, the human organization features two important levels: the formal and informal organizations. This is where Roethlisberger and Dickson's definitions differ from Hall's. The formal organization corresponds to Hall's technical level of culture; in industry it consists of the explicit sets of rule and regulations which prescribe the authority hierarchy and the relationships between the technical organization, that is, the logics of work, and the social organization. In other words, who is supposed to do what with whom and for whom.

The informal organization, as described by Roethlisberger and Dick-

[6] Roethlisberger and Dickson, *Management and the Worker*, pp. 565 ff.
[7] *Ibid.*

son, consists of actual behavior patterns and sentiments, regardless of the formal prescriptions. Since the actual behaviors and sentiments of work groups are based on largely unrecognized social norms, values, and traditions, they correspond to Hall's formal and informal levels of culture.

The concept of equilibrium is central to Roethlisberger and Dickson's description of the total organization. It is implicit in Hall's description of levels of culture. Briefly stated here, the concept refers to a state of balance that exists among parts of a system. Thus, any change in one part is accompanied by changes in the other parts. Any change in external pressures on the total system will result in tendencies within the system to maintain, or return to, its original condition. Any particular activity pattern within the total organization contains elements of the technical, formal, and informal systems. An attempted change in a technical procedure, for example, will affect other technical procedures, formal activities, and especially the informal organization of interactions, activities, and sentiments.

Countless field studies of change in organizational systems attest the resistances of the informal organization to changes at the technical or formal levels.[8] These resistances represent the conservative forces operating within the organization of face-to-face relationships among individuals. Such relationships tend to have the most real and immediate impact on individual members.

Attempted changes in organizational behavior patterns are usually introduced in terms of specific and explicit modifications of technical or formal requirements. They do not, however, normally address the informal patterns of behavior and sentiments. One reason is that the leaders who attempt to initiate change, as well as the members of the groups themselves, are not too aware of the existence of such patterns. A second reason is that even if the change agent is aware of the informal, implicit organization, he has no socially legitimate way of addressing it without overstepping the boundaries of his formal and technical role. As a result, organizational changes which are consummated successfully inevitably involve *informal* behavior patterns. The formal boss, for example, will step out of his boss role and address members of the work group as individuals, even though his formal job definition may exclude, or even prohibit, this kind of behavior.

Analysis of culture change has highlighted the existence of several levels of culture, the different kinds and degrees of emotional attachment at each level, and the need for making the implicit explicit in

---

[8] See, for example, Zaleznik, *Foreman Training in a Growing Enterprise,* and the Lightner series of cases which are included in Zaleznik and Moment, *Cases on Interpersonal Behavior in Organizations.*

order to consummate culture change. Organizational analysis adds the importance of the concept of equilibrium. Change takes place through existing internal behavior patterns, even when imposed from without by purely external agents. The study of changes in group behavior confirms these generalizations and principles.

## Group Change

Since the small group has a characteristic culture and social organization, the observations regarding processes of change in larger cultures and in formal organizations are applicable. The major difference is the relative ease with which an entire small group can be observed, its attributes measured, and experiments performed. Consequently, the dynamics of the change process may be described in more specific detail in the case of the small group.

The identity and continuity of the group are closely related to its social structure and norms. One function of its norms is to maintain the stability and predictability of its social relationships. Externally imposed changes in its task requirements and formal relationships to outsiders will invariably change the group's social structure and violate or invalidate some of its norms. Thus, the equilibrium of the group can be maintained only through the existence of resisting or compensating forces.

A major aspect of the change problem in groups is the group attitude toward external authority. Obviously, when alienation and hostility exist toward the authorities which impose change, strong group reaction may be predicted. A common pattern under this condition is one of surface compliance and informal sabotage. Such sabotage can take the form of the group's insistence on following all formal rules and procedures, to the detriment of task performance and to the embarrassment of the authorities.

Research on leadership behavior has highlighted the importance of the leader's behavior to the group's performance, satisfaction, and ability to change. Leadership behaviors which allow and actively encourage the group to address its problems explicitly tend to be more effective. In studies of leadership, the part *group* processes play in the outcomes is of utmost importance. Research findings related to group processes, leadership behavior, and group change will be discussed later in this chapter.

The small group is the major source of emotional support for the individual, as well as the major source of pressures to conform socially. Asch demonstrated that group pressure can change the unsupported individual's perceptions of physical stimuli and that the individual's ability to resist social pressure is tremendously increased if he is supported by even one other person.[9]

Our general comments on group change have added one more important observation to our discussion of change in larger social systems. Prospective changes affect cultural and organizational systems at several levels of awareness and emotional strength. But they are invariably brought to bear in systems of small, face-to-face, group interactions. The small group is a strategic focus for practical, applied change programs as well as for research because it transforms social abstractions, such as culture, values, and tradition, into concrete, observable, and to some degree controllable interpersonal events.[10]  The small group setting is where reality testing, on the one hand, and emotional contagion, on the other, actually take place.  At the same time, the small group is the primary unit with which authority figures, including agents of change, must deal in practical affairs.  The group's attitude toward authority, its conservative forces which resist change, and its potential for adaptation and development all affect the strategic interaction between the authority figure and the group.

The object of change, in planned change programs and in the study of change processes, is the behavior and attitudes of *the individual*. The analysis and understanding of cultural, organizational, and group processes are indispensable for understanding problems of change in the individual. But the basic dynamic forces of all these other systems, in conservation and in adaptation and development, lie rooted in the dynamics of the individual's personality.  The emotions attached to the various levels of cultural traditions are the emotions of individuals.  The logics of technical organization, sets of formal organizational rules and procedures, and the norms of the informal group all exist as ideas and sentiments within individuals.  The workings of social processes of behavior control, resistance to change, and reality testing for change take place as intrapersonal and interpersonal processes, in their most fundamental forms.  We shall conclude our discussion of the general theory of change with a brief examination of its meaning to the individual's personality.

## Individual Change

The concept of individual identity, as developed by Erikson,[11] is a convenient point at which to begin our examination of change in in-

---

[9] Asch, "Effects of Group Pressure upon the Modification and Distortion of Judgments."   See also Schein, *Coercive Persuasion*, p. 242.

[10] See Schein, *op. cit.*

[11] Erikson, "Identity and the Life Cycle."

dividual behavior and attitudes. When we demand that a person change his behavior and attitudes, we are, in effect, asking him to become someone else. Since he may not have a very well-developed sense of identity to begin with, the demand for change may cause an identity crisis. This has been one consequence of the leadership training programs described in our discussion of the leader.

The individual's identity problem and its relationship to the consistency of his behavior and attitudes involves several levels of his personality. Unconscious and conscious processes, the self he presents to his various publics, and his private self are all related to such dimensions as level of awareness, overt behavior and internal processes, and personal role differentiation. The equilibrium problem is clearly evident in this complex set of subsystems contained within the individual's personality. A change in any one of these levels or processes is accompanied by balancing changes in other levels or processes. In addition to the interrelationships among these systems, the total personality and its parts all respond homeostatically to external disturbances; they exhibit a tendency to return to their initial state of equilibrium.

Freud and others have discussed the tendency of the person to long to "return to the womb," the most comfortable, initial human condition.[12] This is accompanied by an opposing tendency to be active: to experience a variety of human events, to attain competence in interacting with the environment, and to continue to develop into something more than the animal that the individual is biologically.[13]

Ego processes and the mechanisms of defense are the work centers and work procedures by which the individual's relationships to the environment and to his internal responses are governed. Some ego processes are relatively conflict free, such as mathematical ability and physical skill in playing games or working. Other ego processes are potentially laden with conflict; one of these, interpersonal relations, is especially relevant to the problems of the leader and group member. Rapaport has described the ego as vacillating between *autonomy*, where conflict-free competences may be exercised freely in relation to external realities, and *dependence* upon unconscious, emotional-laden, over-determined internal sources of energy and direction.[14]

The problems of individual change with which we are concerned

[12] For example, see Schachtel, *Metamorphosis*, pp. 8–9.
[13] See, for example, White, "Motivation Reconsidered: The Concept of Competence."
[14] Rapaport, "The Autonomy of the Ego," and "The Theory of Ego Autonomy: A Generalization."

invariably involve the individual's relationship to external authority. To change behavior and attitudes in response to *impersonal* external demands is a relatively simple problem for the individual. His application of relatively conflict-free competence to solving external problems may sometimes be thwarted by feelings of frustration and anger, but by and large he can go on trying, limited only by fatigue and lack of ability. On the other hand, to change in response to the demands of other *persons* is an entirely different matter; it involves an emotional response to who the other person is and what he is doing to the individual interpersonally. To be told or advised what to do or think by another person is quite different from discovering or learning what to do or think by one's self. Feelings of counter-dependence, rebelliousness, hostility, and anger are not the only interpersonal emotions involved in external demands for individual change; the opposite feelings of comfortable dependency, affection, wanting to be close and friendly, wanting to please, and wanting to comply can also emotionally color such responses. Although many leaders and agents of change would favor the latter emotional response, it represents no more autonomy, development, or learning to deal with reality than does the more aggressive and hostile one, even though it may appear to facilitate change. There is an important difference between *conformity*, which represents no change on the part of the individual, and individual change at deeper levels in the direction of autonomy and enhanced reality orientation.

Growth, learning, self-actualization, the development of competence, ego-autonomy, improved potential for adaptation, and similar concepts point to the ideal of individual development aimed for by responsible agents of change. In the case of the individual, these ideals are usually pursued through therapy in which the counselor, psychiatrist, or psychoanalyst are the agents of change. Current trends in leadership training attempt to prescribe these same goals for the administrator, group leader, and community leader; the change agent is considered the helper and facilitator of individual, group, and organizational change toward the ideal.

In some early forms of individual therapy, the agent was often defined out of the situation. The individual was the object of change and the therapist was the external expert who intervened; but he was not part of the change process, which was considered to be entirely internal to the individual subject. Hypnosis and shock treatment are examples of this situation. In another view, the therapy situation was primarily a special kind of human relationship; the change agent and the subject were involved together in a process of changing their relationship to each other, as well as changing their internal conditions through "therapeutic interaction."[15]

The problem of individual change necessarily involves changes in object relationships for the individual.   It also involves changes in the way the individual thinks about himself, about other people, and about his relationship to his work.   In addition, his emotional responses and intellectual processes will be modified, and his motivations will be open to personal questioning.   Such changes normally take place within individuals as they develop from infants to mature adults over their lifetime.   However, the same processes which result in stable self-identification and the ability to function effectively with others at work tend to solidify the mechanisms of defense and prevent further learning and development along some lines.   The process of individual change must be examined, therefore, as a form of therapy, even though the subjects are in all significant respects "normal."   Since the modern environment for the individual is *not* stable and normal, special attention must be given to the problem of helping stable individuals continue to learn in the midst of rapid, continuing change in their social and technical environments.

Individual change is an *interpersonal* process, as well as a process in which *intrapersonal* aspects of the individual are altered.   This points up the problem of distinguishing between conformity and significant change.   Many change programs, such as executive development programs, supervisor training, and human relations training groups, contain pure socialization elements as well as self-education elements.   For example, the newly-promoted executive learns how to behave as a member of his new status group; much of his training for the new role is purely social in nature.   Similarly, members of human relations training groups often learn to conform to a new and different set of norms: medical students learn to act like doctors and officer candidates learn to act like officers.   This kind of learning has to do with entry into a new group, rather than improved personal competence of a more significant nature.

Pure social conformity is manifested in the apparent changes in behavior and attitudes which accompany the individual's transition from membership in one group to membership in another.   Since the individual usually learns and changes over his lifetime as a result of his experiences, social and otherwise, it is difficult to separate pure socialization processes from more basic changes in personality structure. This means that the agent of change, if he is concerned with significant

[15] Harry Stack Sullivan emphasized the *interpersonal* nature of the disturbance and of the treatment.   See Bibliography,

learning rather than conformity, has to make a special effort to distinguish between the socialization processes to which he and the client are subjected, and more basic and permanent personality change.

From the point of view of external agents of change, an important set of characteristics are the individual's motivation to self-examination and change, his intellectual and emotional readiness to change, and the resistances to change which are inherent in his particular personality structure at the time. The fine and delicate edge between forces toward change and conservation is where the change agent must focus his attention. In the development of the personality system of the individual, the timing of environmental demands in relation to his biological and psychological readiness is a crucial factor. Such demands occur according to implicit social plan or accident in some instances and according to explicit plan in others. The age at which the child enters school is determined by social plan and is characterized by close limits and tight control. On the other hand, the age of marriage, though generally prescribed by a broader social plan, often occurs by accident. In either case, the experience is not consummated satisfactorily unless the timing is right in relation to the physical and psychological readiness of the individual.

Even though subjects have the physical appearance of mature adults, their readiness for change cannot be taken for granted by agents of planned change. Concepts and findings of developmental theory suggest that it is important to examine the positions in the cycle of development where learning is rapid and where useful analogs may be sought for the implementation of change. Two learning phases in the life cycle contain some interesting parallels. One occurs during the so-called latency period of development and the second during adolescence.[16]

The latency period is the phase of development marked by rapid learning of basic cognitive skills and content. The capacity to learn during this phase depends on the recession of certain instinctive processes that were dominant in earlier development phases. Where the instinctive processes of fantasy and activity stay in the forefront, however disguised, there tends to be a failure in learning. In essence, the learning process of the latency period is predicated upon the existence of a *moratorium* in instinctual development.[17] When the moratorium is well established internally, the learning process for the individual tends to be rapid and productive.

[16] These ideas are also presented in Moment and Zaleznik, *Role Development and Interpersonal Competence*, pp. 164 ff.

[17] Erikson, *op. cit.*, p. 111.

The second period which serves as a useful analog to the problem under consideration is that of adolescence. This period is marked by rapid change of another kind. The greatest changes are biological and social. The individual matures sexually and experiences an increase in the magnitude of instinctual drives. Accompanying this change is a period of social experimentation characterized mainly by: emphasis on peer relations and withdrawal from parental control; role experimentation in highly ritualized forms; and highly unstable patterns of behavior, with rapid fluctuation in mood and action.

The behavior of the adolescent is understood best in the light of the social tasks facing him in anticipation of later life tasks. At the conclusion of the period of adolescence, the individual must make a series of significant decisions. He must choose a career and select the mate with whom he will share his work, family, and community life. The learning problem of the adolescent period is the establishment of a sense of identity in which occupational and sex roles assume paramount importance.[18] The experimental behavior of the adolescent in formulating his identity is sanctioned by society and made possible by the establishment of a second moratorium in development. The role responsibilities of the growing person are suspended in anticipation of his later full acceptance of the diverse and complex roles of adulthood.

It is significant to note the correlation between the existence of these two moratoria and the rapidity of experimentation and learning. It is also significant to note that the moratorium of the adolescent period is the last fully sanctioned period of experimentation in the individual's life. Beyond adolescence any dramatic developmental experience will depend upon an individual's self-declared moratorium.

During adult phases of development, the main type of socially recognized moratorium occurs when the individual presents himself for psychotherapeutic help. Within this highly specialized relationship, rapid learning and experimentation can take place. But this type of learning is available mainly to persons who have experienced severe alienation from their social environment or for whom the maintenance of relationships causes severe pain and anxiety.

It is difficult to establish moratoria for adults who are fully engaged in working and family life. Such individuals do not define themselves as sick or in need of significant personal change. But for some, the changing demands of their work and social environments seem to call for a significant learning experience supported by their society.

[18] *Ibid.*, p. 110.

In our brief overview of changes in cultures, organizations, groups, and individuals, several uniformities stand out which must be taken into account by any general theory of change in groups and individuals:

1. Change processes involve at least two, and possibly three or more, levels of meaning. These levels are described by such terms as overt and covert, manifest and latent, conscious and unconscious, formal and informal, form and function. For the unit undergoing change, continuity will always be maintained at some level while changes take place at other levels; forced discontinuities must be supported by reinforced continuity of identity or complete disintegration will result.

2. During processes of change, the implicit or latent meanings of behavior and attitude patterns are raised to awareness for conscious examination; new patterns are substituted for old in such a way as to maintain the continuity and identity of the system. Some old patterns may be retained, but conscious examination may change their meanings.

3. Face-to-face interaction settings are strategic in the change process; the counseling relationship and the small group process provide testing-out and acting-out opportunities for the individual. Interaction by itself is not sufficient to ensure change; individual and group behavior and attitudes are reinforced, as well as tested, in social processes. Although individual change takes place through social interaction, socialization, as reflected in conformity, also takes place.

4. For the individual, significant changes normally take place during the specific periods of his life when social demands are relaxed and when he is physically and psychologically ready for change.

We have introduced the term "change agent" to refer to the person who consciously attempts to initiate change in a system; the term focuses attention on problems of planned change. However, it may be misleading when applied descriptively to natural process of change.

Throughout history there have been many people who were change agents and leaders by intent. But the complexity of human processes has made it difficult to assess the degree to which the consequences of their behaviors matched their intentions and the degree to which their roles in the changes were merely incidental to other influences. The teacher teaches, but the degree to which his behavior causes the student to learn is another question. Thus, our attempts to understand processes of change and the change agent's role must be tempered with the critical awareness that "contributing to" or "influencing" change processes is quite different from "causing" change, or "making change happen." Some of the most significant agents of change could not have been aware of the extent of their influence, for example, Darwin, Einstein, and Freud. Conversely, overly self-conscious efforts at change, such as various moral reform movements, often have less influence on human events than they intend.

## PLANNED CHANGE

We shall begin our discussion of planned change by introducing two pervasive facets of the change problem: resistance and authority. We shall then discuss the orientation of the change agent in these terms and examine research findings concerning planned change.

### Resistance and Authority

The major common element in problems of change in cultures, organizations, groups, and individuals is the resistance which is experienced by the initiators of change. From universal changes—for example, the communist master plan for social reform—down to such two-person interaction as the counseling interview, the change agent is confronted with resistances to change, as well as some form of resistance to himself. In earliest attempts at large-scale social and individual change, the change agent, an authority figure, countered resistance with physical force. The resistance of the pathological personality was neutralized by treating him as a criminal, administering punishment, and isolating him from society. Even today, armies' deal with the resistances of outsiders, while special police deal with internal resistances.

Several influences have led to different approaches to overcoming resistance to change. Humanitarian ideals and moral reform have been one influence toward a more gentle treatment of resistance. Another influence has been that practitioners and sociological and psychological investigators have discovered that physical coercion drives the resistance underground instead of eliminating it. In the practical administration of human groups, it is more difficult to deal with hidden resistance than with open resistance.

Another influence that has shifted attention to means other than physical coercion has been the rationality of the resistance to some changes. Someone usually stands to lose something when a change takes place. In groups and organizations, changes in the distribution of power and autonomy inevitably deprive somebody. In such instances, resistance to change is quite rational. Hence, the initiators of change are forced to bargain with those whom they wish to change. The exchanges taking place involve realities within their social and personal contexts.

The reality of power is an important factor in the change problem.

Although hierarchical authority presumably flows downward, the influence process inescapably involves an exchange. The "manipulator" is significantly affected by the "manipulated." An extreme version of this reality is the leadership principle practiced by many politicians: find out where the followers are going or want to go, and try to run in front of them. In current affairs, this form of leadership is evidenced in the widespread use of the public opinion poll as a guide to top-level decision making.

Many well-meaning members of the helping professions—teachers, consultants, social workers, ministers, doctors of medicine, and mental and emotional health experts—do not like to admit to wielding power and influence. But no study of change is complete if it overlooks the important reality that the change agent possesses power, influence, and authority. Perhaps this tendency to overlook or underrate the importance of power is a consequence of the egalitarian distortion of the democratic ideal.

In the development of psychoanalytic practice and theory, the attention devoted to resistance as a primary manifestation of pathology and to the emotional relationship of the patient and analyst led to the discovery and understanding of some underlying intrapsychic and interpersonal processes in the patient, the analyst, and in their relationship. When the practice of consulting with an organization on its problems was developed, the consultant's authority relationship to the system and the reasons for hiring him became focal points for investigations.[19] Similarly, in group therapy and human relations training, much attention and energy are expended by the trainer and the group in examining their relationship; such relationships are inseparable from members' resistances and motivations toward learning.[20]

The pervasiveness of resistance and authority problems, and the importance of change agents' attitudes toward their roles in relation to client systems, point to the necessity of examining the role of change agent in more detail. As we concluded in our discussion of leadership, the prospective leader, or change agent, benefits more from learning to examine who he is and what he is trying to do, than from devoting his attention exclusively to how-to-do-it techniques.

## The Orientation of the Change Agent

If the person in the position of initiating change in another individual, a group, or an organization, learns to define himself as a

---

[19] See Jaques, *The Changing Culture of a Factory.*

[20] See Seashore and Van Egmond, "The Consultant-Trainer Role in Working Directly with a Total Staff."

change agent, he has taken a major step toward understanding and facilitating the changes he desires.    To illustrate the importance of this role definition problem, let us cite two extreme examples.    One might be called a traditional, legalistic approach to change; the other involves the approach of the knowledgeable, responsible agent of change.

The legalistic approach to change is exemplified in the Dashman Company case.[21]    A newly appointed vice president, brought in from outside the company, attempted to initiate change by edict.    After being duly introduced to the company through its formal channels, he decided to centralize the company's purchasing procedures.    He sent an official letter to the several purchasing agents, who were not located in the central office.    He cited his source of authority—the board of directors—and requested a change in the procedures for reporting purchases above a certain dollar value.    According to the legal model, the purchasing agents should have complied.    The request came from a person of higher status who had explicit, formally granted authority for issuing the order.    Most of the purchasing agents wrote back official statements of their intent to comply.    However, the new vice president received no actual evidence of compliance during the period allotted to institute new procedures.    In other words, there was no apparent change in the behavior of the purchasing agents in spite of the fact that the change procedure followed the official, legal form prescribed by the formal organization of the company and by general cultural definitions of legal authority.

Further evidence of the vice president's legalistic view of his role was provided when he turned down the suggestion of his assistant, an old-timer with the company, that he personally visit and get to know the purchasing agents.    Because of his lack of knowledge of the informal processes of the organization, he ultimately had no way of understanding the response to his request nor did he have a way of responding to the latent message.

This is a clear example of an ineffective attempt to initiate change in an organization through purely legalistic procedures.    The experience of legal prohibition of alcoholic beverages in the United States during the 1920's provided an even more dramatic example. Not only did it demonstrate the ineffectiveness of the legislation and enforcement, it also clearly showed the overriding importance of the unintended consequences—racketeering and crime in this instance. These examples are not meant to imply that legal systems and legal procedures are valueless, or even dysfunctional, for implementing change.    They do imply, however, that explicit legal codes should relate realistically to human behavior and attitudes, and perhaps, that

[21] Lawrence et al., *Organizational Behavior and Administration*, pp. 4–5.

effective formal codification often *follows* informal measures of social control, instead of preceding them.

It is difficult to illustrate effective programs of planned change and effective initiating without appearing to idealize one type.  However, as evident in the example we shall cite, the behaviors of others in the change process are at least as important as the behaviors of the initiators; there are vast differences between an effective change process and the procedures followed in the Dashman case, and an understanding of organizational, group, and individual processes is crucial.

Eight girls spray-painted toys in the group where changes were impending.[22]  The first change was similar in implementation to that of the Dashman Company.  Engineers, authority figures external to the group, designed and installed a conveyor system for the girls' work and established production standards which prescribed how many toys the girls should paint per day and the rate they would be paid.  The girls' response was to produce at a level lower than planned and to complain about the speed of the conveyor and the rates to their foreman.  Some girls quit.  The engineers felt that the group was resisting change.

A consultant was brought in to work with the foreman.  They talked together about the problems in the group, and the foreman set up a general discussion with the girls about their complaints.  He then discussed their complaints with the engineers and plant superintendent, who thought the complaints were groundless.  At the next meeting, the girls proposed that fans be brought in to improve ventilation.  Some time was spent trying out various locations for the fans, and the relationship between the girls and the foreman improved.  The group discussions were continued.

Ultimately it was found that the real complaint about the conveyor was its constant rate throughout the day.  It was not that the girls could not keep up with it, they just could not work at the same pace all day long.  Against the wishes of the engineers, and with some hesitation himself, the foreman had a variable speed control installed and allowed the girls to regulate the speed themselves.

Deciding upon the speed settings throughout the day was a group problem which the girls discussed at lunch.  Within three weeks their production rate had increased 30 to 50 per cent above the original standard set by the engineers.  Satisfaction was higher, and the girls reported that their work was easier.  Since the production standards

[22] Example taken from Whyte et al., *Money and Motivation*, Ch. 10, also reported in Lawrence et al., *op. cit.*, pp. 802 ff., in the "Hovey and Beard Company" case.

were associated with a group piece-rate bonus plan, the girls' earnings began to exceed those of many skilled workers in other parts of the plant.

As result of the inequity in pay between the girls and people in other parts of the plant, relations among the foreman, the superintendent, and the engineers became strained. The superintendent finally changed the pay base and returned the conveyor line to its original constant pace. Production dropped, and soon after that six of the eight girls and the foreman quit their jobs.

Several points stand out in this experience. The ultimate outcome of the situation is reminiscent of the problem of group interrelationships brought out in the Ohio State leadership training research (see Chapter Twelve). Foremen's relationships with their bosses had much to do with their behavior with their groups; behavior toward the groups was reflected in performance and satisfaction.

In the toy company case, the girls' opportunity to participate and to test the reality of their feelings and the technical requirements was clearly related to their improved performance, satisfaction, and interest. But the engineers and superintendent had relinquished *their* former participation in the girls' work without going through the same process which the girls and their foreman experienced. Thus, their customary behavior patterns and attitudes were upset by what went on in the painting group. When the pay inequity was exposed, the system of work and pay standards of the *entire* company seemed invalid; this threatened the identity of the managers and engineers as competent authorities. The sequence and location of resistances in the case vividly illustrates system and intersystem equilibrium in action. When authority was imposed from outside the group, the group resisted. When power was transferred from the formal authorities to the girls, the formal authorities resisted. Ultimately, the entire company system became upset and returned to its former state, at tragic expense.

If we concentrate on the dynamics of the change process, we note several kinds of change going on at once. Something about the consultant's behavior with the foreman led the foreman to try something different; his behavior changed. In the girl's discussions, many feelings were expressed and their validity tested. The girls took concrete action—requesting the fans—as their foreman had done in calling the meetings. The foreman accepted influence from them and transmitted it upward. Eventually they cut through their own confused complaints to discover a technical reality which made a difference—the effects of a constant work pace as against a varying work pace.

Again they exercised influence on external authorities through their foreman. When their efforts were finally cancelled out by reversion to the older system, six of them and the foreman again took action; they quit.

If we look upon the consultant in the case as a change agent, we see that his "client system" was primarily the foreman. The consultant took no action on or with the group; the foreman did. Presumably, the consultant-foreman conversations were a supportive testing ground for the foreman's feelings and ideas. Viewing the foreman as the change agent, we see that his basic activity was sponsoring group discussion, thereby establishing a procedural change and relinquishing his customary form of supervisory influence. In the original report of the case[23] he was described as having mixed feelings about what he was doing and taking action with some reluctance. In addition to sponsoring the discussions, he responded to them by acting as a representative, presenting the group's feelings and ideas to the engineers and superintendent, and experiencing some awkward feelings while doing so.

The group, on the other hand, engaged in a different sort of behavior in response to their foreman's changes in behavior. The girls went considerably beyond the "gripe-session" stage into reality-testing and problem-solving activity. They began to exercise influence upon their environment, felt good about it, and became more interested and responsible in their attitudes toward their work. The final outcome was a somewhat dramatic test of the realities in the group's external environment. In this company, and among the particular engineers and managers involved, the maintenance of customary status relationships and the accompanying influence pattern and power balance was apparently more important than the increase in satisfaction and productivity of the one particular work group. Hopefully, the higher-status groups may have learned the consequences of allowing the avoidance of embarrassment to be a motivating force behind their customary behavior patterns and attitudes.

The consultant's role in the events was severely proscribed by the boundaries of the systems with which he worked; he was limited to working with the foreman. Clearly, the problem involved not only the foreman in relation to his group, but also the foreman in relation to the engineers and to management, and the relationships among management personnel. A similar dilemma is faced by other professional helpers. The school teacher, for example, is limited to working with individual children and groups of children within the temporal

[23] *Ibid.*

and spatial limits of the school environment.   The children's relationships with their parents and peers outside of the classroom, which are largely inaccessible to the teacher, are as important as determinants of what goes on in the classroom as the teacher's behavior.

One aspect of the foreman's "new" behavior pattern in the toy painting group case leads to the next step in this analyzis, the examination of some research on change and change agent behavior. Among the many ways of describing the foreman's behavior, it is possible to identify certain aspects of his role as research activity.   The foreman became an inquirer during the change process.   He gathered data from the girls, the engineers, and the superintendent and, to some extent, interpreted its meanings while transmitting information up and down the line.   Although this data gathering and processing activity was not strictly scientific, in the usual sense of the word, it was sufficiently different from the activities implied by the legalistic model to be noteworthy as an aspect of the change agent's role.   It is not coincidence that the theory and practice of planned change, as we describe it, has resulted from the activities of men and women whose basic professional training was in behavioral research.[24]

There is an extremely close relationship between formal behavioral research and the practical application of programs of planned change. Formal research activities are also closely related to formal educational processes and institutions.   As we continue to submit data and theoretical ideas about change, the elements of practice, research, and education will emerge as dominant in the process of planned change and will form the bases of a laboratory learning model for change.

## Research on Change

To illustrate the connections among education, research, and practical action, we shall describe one of the earliest studies of change in an industrial setting.   This study of the mule-spinning department of a textile mill located near Philadelphia was undertaken in 1923 and 1924 by a research team for the University of Pennsylvania.   Along with other studies and their implications, it has been reported in Elton Mayo's *The Social Problems of an Industrial Civilization*[25] and in earlier articles in professional journals.

The problem was an extremely high labor turnover on the mule-spinning job—250 per cent per year, compared to 5 or 6 per cent in

[21] See, for example, Bennis, Benne, and Chin, *The Planning of Change.*
[25] Pp. 59–67.  See Bibliography.

other jobs in the mill. The initial management response was *not* to inquire, "why does this condition exist?," but to take action in the conventional managerial sense, by bringing in efficiency engineers who introduced financial incentive schemes as the remedy. The engineers, of course, assumed that it was a problem of economic motivation. Their efforts were fruitless. As a last resort, possibly still in pursuit of action rather than information, management consulted the University of Pennsylvania team.

The team introduced changes as part of their research. They put a nurse into the plant to deal with the worker's physical complaints. This provided the researchers with first-hand data on how the mule-spinners were reacting to their job; the men talked quite freely to the nurse and the researchers. It is important to point out that the very act of collecting data directly from the workers constituted a major change in the workers' environment; the efficiency engineers had not bothered to consult the workers before instituting their incentive plans.

The researchers learned that the men complained of foot trouble and aches and pains in their limbs; the job required standing and walking while tending machines during the working day. In addition, the men presented a uniformly pessimistic, melancholy outlook in their obsessive preoccupations with their work and personal condition. The researchers discovered that the men worked *alone;* the job did not require interaction nor did it provide the opportunity to talk among themselves. The men reported that they did not engage in social activities after hours because they were too tired. Some of them suffered emotional outbreaks at work, leaving their jobs in anger.

The men expressed strong loyalty to the company president and "the company" in general, but their pessimism about themselves alternated with outbursts of angry hostility against their immediate supervisors. The men were out of touch with reality on their jobs. Their minds and emotions floated in moody detachment from the relatively dull, monotonous, physically fatiguing job. They held their distant, war-hero president, "the Colonel," and his company in highly affectionate esteem, but their actual contacts with lower-level management representatives were colored by hostile emotional conditions.

The management agreed to let the researchers allow an experimental group 10-minute rest periods on the job. This procedure directly addressed the manifest level of the workers' complaints—fatigue; the men were told they could sleep on sacks on the floor during the 10-minute periods. But the workers' response indicated that something else was involved. The experimental group expressed pleasure and interest, their melancholy pre-occupations diminished considerably, labor turnover dropped, morale improved, and productivity was maintained.  The surprising thing was that the same results were experienced with the men who were *not* given the rest periods, but who had talked about the experiment with their co-workers during their lunch periods.  The practice was extended to cover all the men in the mule-spinning department, and productivity increased significantly.

The supervisors were upset to see the men lying down during working hours.  But when the practice was revoked production fell, so it was reinstituted at the order of the president who demonstrated sincere interest and concern for the workers.  At one stage, staggered rest periods were introduced which required the men to decide on the actual details.  Productivity increased even further.

It is interesting to note the various meanings that can be attached to the rest period practice.  Superficially, this practice would appear to allow rest, and thus address the fatigue problem.  It would seem to allow free time, in effect shortening working hours and thus giving the workers an "economic" fringe benefit.  But Mayo's conclusions were much more complex and far-reaching:

At the time when we completed our part in this work, we were sure that we had not wholly discovered the causes of the high labor turnover. We could not even attribute the change to the mere introduction of rest periods; inevitably many other changes had been simultaneously introduced. For example, we had listened carefully and with full attention to anything a worker wished to say, whatever the character of his comment. In addition to this, we—supported by the president—had demonstrated an interest in what was said by the introduction of experimental changes, by instruction in the best methods of relaxation. The Colonel also had demonstrated unmistakably a sincere interest in his workers' welfare; he had lived up to his Army reputation. The supervisor who instituted the earning of rest periods was swept aside by the president and the company —thereby "placing" the company's attitude in the minds of its workers.

But, in addition to this—and we did not see this clearly at the time—the president had effected another important change. *He had helped to transform a horde of "solitaries" into a social group.* In May, 1924, *he placed the control of rest periods squarely in the hands of the workers* in an alley with no one to say them nay. *This led to consultation,* not only between individuals, but between alleys throughout the group—and to a feeling of responsibility directly to the president. And the general social changes effected were astonishing—even in relationships outside the factory. One worker told us with great surprise that he had begun taking his wife to "movies" in the evenings, a thing he had not done for years. Another, equally to his surprise, gave up a habit of spending alcoholic week ends on bootleg liquor.  In general the change was complex, and the difficulty of assigning the part played in it by various aspects of the experiment impossible to resolve.  We should have liked to experiment further, but this desire—probably wisely in the circumstances—was disallowed.  Thus the inquiry left us with many questions unanswered, but it pointed a direction for further studies, the results of which later proved helpful in reinterpreting the data of this first investigation.

But we had moved onwards.  The efficiency experts had not consulted the workers; they regarded workers' statements as exaggerated or due to misconception of the facts and therefore to be ignored.  Yet to ignore an important symptom—whatever its character—on supposedly moral grounds is preposterous.  The "expert" assumptions of rabble hypothesis and individual self-interest as a basis for diagnosis led nowhere.  On the other hand, careful and pedestrian consideration of the workers' situation taken as part of a clinical diagnosis led us to results so surprising that we could at the time only partly explain them.[26]

The important question raised by the mule-spinning study, from our point of view, is "what really happens when people talk together?"  Is social interaction merely a nice privilege to give people, a source of pleasure to them which is granted in exchange for more work and loyalty?  This tends to be the view of many managers and group leaders operating under a theory of economic exchange and of some moralistic human relations experts; if you are nice to people they will be nice to you.  We do not think that exchange, either of economics or purely social niceties, really explains the worker's response to *all* of the concomitants of the rest period experiment.  Merely allowing groups to be formed addressed the problem of the social isolation and the accompanying morbid preoccupations of the individual; but under some conditions the particular nature of the group's development might have worked against the individual members', as well as the organizations' interests.[27]  Groups and individuals can become preoccupied with fantasy, morbid and otherwise, unless their development provides some means for continued reality testing.

The interpersonal communication process meets individuals' needs to belong and feel wanted by others and to participate in purely social-emotional-expressive rituals.  Moreover, it is the only way the individual can keep in touch with reality, which is at best a vague conception to anyone.  Not all communication involves testing reality,

[26] Mayo, *op. cit.*, pp. 66, 67; italics added.
[27] See, for example, Zaleznik, et al., *The Motivation, Productivity, and Satisfaction of Workers.*

CHANGE 471

but testing reality in social-technical systems does require some form of confrontation. Psychological experiments in sensory deprivation, where the individual is isolated from all forms of external stimuli, both physical (no sounds, absolute darkness, no objects to touch and feel) and social, have found that under these conditions the individual provides his own internally derived sources of stimulation, in the form of imaginative, detached fantasy. He withdraws into, rather than goes "out of," his mind and emotions.[28] This corresponds closely to the internal states experienced by the mule-spinners in Mayo's study in their condition of social isolation.[29]

Mayo was also involved in the Hawthorne studies which confirmed and elaborated the general findings and implications of the textile mill study.[30] In the case of the Relay Assembly Test Room, more rigorous experimental controls were attempted by the researchers. But as with the textile mill study, several aspects of the social environment were changed simultaneously so that it was difficult to isolate which of several changes was the most important cause of the dramatically increased morale, interest, and productivity of the girls in the small work group. The importance of allowing the individual to express himself freely in the permissive personal interview situation was highlighted even more. However, the most significant change in the Relay Assembly Text Room was in supervisory behavior, which became relatively permissive, accommodative, and supportive, compared to the girl's normal supervisory situation. For example, there was an increase in talking among the girls on the job which normal supervisory practices would have discouraged or prohibited.

In the textile mill and Hawthorne studies the researchers introduced a spirit of inquiry into the situation. A "learning" atmosphere accompanied the planning, data collection, experimentation, and evaluation of results. Such attributes also characterize effective supervision and change administration by nonscientific practitioners. Leaders and change agents need to know what is going on in their groups; permissiveness and listening allow social-emotional events to take place openly. They can then be observed, heard, and addressed, not only by the researchers, leaders, and change agents, but by the group members themselves. Taking positive action through experimentation and investigation provides the change agent with a way of testing and learning.

[28] See Bexton, et al., "Effects of Decreased Variation in the Sensory Environment."
[29] *Ibid.*
[30] Roethlisberger and Dickson, op. cit.

Experimentation with the implementation of planned change on a total organizational scale is exemplified in the work of the Tavistock Institute of Human Relations in London, England. One of its projects involved broad cultural, technological, and organizational changes in a textile weaving mill in Ahmedabad, India.[31]

The Tavistock project, reported by Rice, took place over a period of three years, 1953 through part of 1956; but the change process introduced and facilitated by the consultants presumably continued after the three-year period. The change problem originally arose as a result of the economic necessity for introducing modern equipment. Three major phases were involved. The first was the reorganization of the social system of work around recently introduced automatic equipment. The second addressed technical and social changes around the use of older, more traditional nonautomatic looms. And the third phase involved changes in management organization.

Our interest is in the sequence of activities involved in implementing the change, rather than the technical content or specific problems encountered. The change agents brought into the situation some ideas about relationships between the technical and social organization of work which they had learned from previous research experiences.[32] These ideas allowed for the possibility that a variety of social arrangements could meet the technical requisites of work, instead of the traditional industrial engineers' approach of the one best way. In addition, they allowed for a balance among technical requisites, economic realities, and human individual and social needs.

The consultants started with an idea of a desirable end-state toward which the changes would be directed. This was based on several realities—technical, economic, and human—rather than limited to the relatively narrow logics of theoretical technical efficiency. They had developed an explicit set of propositions about the optimum equilibrium conditions in a socio-technical system.[33] The initial phase of the field work involved an analysis of the existing systems, the object of their change efforts. They knew where they wanted to go but had to understand where they were beginning. From the idea of the end-state and the reality of the existing condition, they drew up plans for a work organization they thought would fit. Their plan

[31] Rice, *Productivity and Social Organization: The Ahmedabad Experiment.* See also Jaques, *op. cit.,* for another example of Tavistock's work.

[32] Some of these ideas were discussed in our Chapter Nine, "Environmental Constraints," under the sections on authority, communications, and technology.

[33] Rice, *op. cit.,* pp. 31–47.

for the automatic mill centered around the idea of a group of workers for a group of looms, rather than an individual worker for each loom.

Extensive discussion and consultation among the managers, the consultants, and the workers accompanied the planning and initiation of the changes in all phases of the project. New problems were uncovered at each step, including unanticipated technical problems and resistances by elements of the social systems involved. But the initial plans featured enough "goodness of fit" among the various subsystems' needs to encourage spontaneous acceptance of the spirit, if not all the details, of the change program. The ultimate results were satisfactory, although many new problems were inevitably raised as old ones were resolved.

Although Rice carefully described the properties of ideal work organization, he did not detail the process of change beyond describing plans and discussions. The impression given by his reports was that the effectiveness of planned change depended only on the quality of the plans. In Tavistock's case, this was an important element in their work; they were "technically" competent planners. But the Tavistock people were also competent in their action relationships with the client systems; they provided models of the inquiring, experimenting, mode of leadership and change management which had built-in provisions for continually gathering and processing feedback data from the systems undergoing change, as well as modifying plans in the face of newly-discovered, unanticipated problems. Hence, their clients benefited not only from the immediate consequences of their practices, but from learning to behave as the consultants did by using them as models.

The Tavistock conceptualization of the change process encompasses the management of continuing differentiations and integrations, corresponding to the discontinuities and continuities we discussed earlier. The consultants point up the need to define and protect the various client systems during the change process in which the number and rapidity of new differentiations and integrations are high.[34] In effect, the client system is isolated in some important ways from its environment; if the appropriate isolation did not occur, the environment would continue to reinforce the attitudes and behaviors the change program is attempting to modify. In Rice's view, the degree of protection decreases over the course of the change, until the change system is completely reintegrated into its environment. The duration of the protection period varies directly with the degree of change involved.

[34] Rice, *op. cit.*, pp. 248 ff.

This idea parallels the observable differences in parental protection of the young of various species, depending upon the degree of change from simplicity to complexity in the development of the particular species. The human child is protected and isolated from the demands of the human environment for a considerably longer period than other animals, since he must undergo more change to reach an adult state.

The three research studies discussed so far—the Philadelphia textile plant, the Hawthorne studies, and the Ahmedabad experiments—all took place in the setting of organizations at work. All of them involved many changes, rather than the institution of one, single, experimentally controlled change at a time. It is difficult, therefore, to analyze the relative importance of each of the elements in the change process. All of these experiences of satisfactory change, as well as others not reported here, involved several common elements.

1. A redefinition of the situation into one of inquiry and experimentation, in which the managers, workers, and researchers knew that something special was going on. Individuals and groups received more attention, understanding, and acceptance than was the case in their usual situations. The atmosphere moved toward one of interest, inquiry, and some degree of excitement.

2. Information was gathered from individuals and groups through listening, interviews, observation, and discussion. People were encouraged to express their feelings and ideas.

3. The researchers—if not the others—made deliberate efforts to conceptualize, theorize, and explain what was going on. Resistance was dealt with as something which needed to be understood by both parties, rather than with moral indignation or anger. Authority problems were similarly confronted and addressed directly.

4. Power and influence were redistributed along the organizational hierarchy. In general, lower levels acquired influence, while upper levels lost influence. In the many instances where management personnel revoked experimental conditions, such as in the toy factory, they had not benefited from the same attention and opportunity to participate as had the lower levels.

5. The redistributions of influence broadened the relevant systems from the single group to include all those groups with which the single group interacted. No one system can experience change without having effects upon other systems.

6. The systems were visibly and actively protected and isolated from their customary environmental influences.

7. Although the climate became emotionally supportive and accepting, it also featured heightened awareness of and confrontation with reality.

The groups were allowed and encouraged to participate actively in solving their own problems.

An experiment reported by Coch and French[35] compared the results of changes in a pajama factory in which three different methods of programming the change were experimentally introduced: (1) no participation, (2) participation through representation, and (3) total participation. The changes were most successfully effected through total participation and were least successful with no participation.

In a later study by Bennett[36] an attempt was made to examine separately the effects of four different elements that were found in activities generally called "group participation" (see Chapter Twelve). These elements were: (1) participation in a group discussion, (2) reaching a decision regarding future action, (3) indicating public commitment to act, and (4) the degree of group consensus regarding intention to act. As a criteria for effectiveness, the experiments noted whether or not the group members took action after the group discussions. The discussions were organized to induce students to volunteer for behavioral experiments; whether or not they did so was easily determined. This measured the effectiveness of the particular elements for influencing the individual's behavior. It was found that decision and consensus made a difference but that mere discussion and public commitment did not influence the individual's behavior after the discussions.

In our discussion of leadership, we ultimately concluded that the crucial element in effective leadership behavior was reality testing. Although permissiveness and acceptance may facilitate the reality testing processes, such considerate behaviors were not sufficient to assure leadership effectiveness or effective change in behavior and attitudes. We shall now attempt to summarize our discussion of planned change with a description of the change agent's job, specifying what is required of him by the dynamics of change processes in individuals, groups, and organizations.

## The Job of the Change Agent

The differences between "task" and "social" activities in groups have been a recurring theme throughout our discussion of group processes, the individual, the organization, leadership, and change. In regard to familiar role performances they were called instrumental-

[35] Coch and French, "Overcoming Resistance to Change."
[36] Bennett, *op. cit.*

adaptive and social-emotional-expressive behaviors. In leadership behavior, they were known as "initiating structure" and "consideration." They were differentiation and integration in the discussion of individual learning and growth, and discontinuity and continuity of identity in processes of individual and group change. This same division provides a framework for describing change agent's activities.

One kind of activity involved in change is *confrontation*. The system encounters problems which demand resolution if it is to survive and improve its adaptive abilities. This is the reality of the external problem. That the reality will always "get through" to the system, be it a person, a group, or an organization, can by no means be guaranteed. Intrapsychic and social mechanisms of defense have many ways of resolving dissonances between external realities and existing conditions other than by direct engagement in problem-solving activities. For example, a demand may be rejected as unreal because it does not fit, it may be ignored because of perceptual distortions, or the system may disintegrate in panic.

One function of the change agent is to confront his client system—and himself—with external realities demanding change. Confrontation is the most common aspect of change agent behavior; technical specialists throughout history have performed this function. No more drastic confrontation has been experienced by an entire civilization than has been the case with the invention of the nuclear bomb, based upon a purely scientific, technical, amoral, and asocial product of technical sophistication in modifying and dealing with the physical environment. Yet, because of the existence of individual, group, and mass defenses, this event has not been experienced universally as a confrontation. This is a real problem which calls for social problem-solving efforts. Hence, just because the technician or change agent says he is presenting a problem does not mean that the confrontation actually takes place.

The need to deal with the second kind of reality, the conservative resistance to change embodied in individual and social mechanisms of defense, calls for different behavior from the change agent. He must contribute *emotional support* to the object system, whether he, another individual, or a group is the object of change. He must contribute toward the maintenance of the continuity and integration of the client system. This is where our traditional technicians have fallen down, and where our overenthusiastic human relations experts have gone overboard. Although support is necessary, it is not enough to facilitate change. The fact that needs for social maintenance have been largely ignored by our rapid technological development justifies a counteremphasis to restore balance.  But if the need for emotional support is not tempered by the need for confrontation, oversupporting and overaccepting the social-emotional realities can result in just as tragic an imbalance.  Hence, we picture the change agent's job as requiring two different modes of activity toward the client system: confrontation and support.

If we adopt a view of personal integration in which the individual wants to be everything to everyone, including himself, at one point in time, the job is impossible.  This image of "simultaneous integration" just does not hold water.  The reality of integration of human personality and behavior lies in the *sequencing* of activity modes over time.  This means that the change agent "confronts" when required and "supports" when required; he does not try to do both simultaneously.  Nor does he have to do both personally; but he has to be sure that someone in the system is attending to each kind of problem when necessary.  In many instances, he must sit and wait patiently for nature to work; in others he intervenes actively as part of the process of change.

Having established confrontation and support as the major elements of the change agent's job, we shall describe their utilization in the process of behavior and attitude change.  Edgar Schein's elaboration of the Lewin model of change will provide our frame of reference.[36]

## Social-Psychological Influence

The initial condition of the individual or the group is referred to as "frozen" if the parts of the system are so balanced that they resist external efforts at change.  Such an individual or group has attained relatively stable identity which helps to maintain integration from day to day, from situation to situation, and in the face of continuous external demands and influences which, if not withstood, lead to chaotic disintegration.

The stages of the change process are *unfreezing, changing, and refreezing*.  When an external event impinges upon the system in such a manner that its normal defenses are inadequate, the state of equilibrium is disturbed.  The dissonance between internal beliefs, attitudes, and motivations and the external reality cannot be neutralized or reconciled by the normal processes of the person or the group. The system is aware that it has a problem and that it cannot immediately cope with the problem.  If the disturbance is serious enough, the system may actively seek help.

[36] Schein, *op. cit.*, pp. 117 ff., and Lewin, "Frontiers in Group Dynamics: Concept, Method, and Reality in Social Science."

In its unfrozen state, the system is susceptible to influences which will help it "pull together," reintegrate itself, and re-establish some form of identity stability. It is important to note that this change is not necessarily for the better, with respect to individual or group competence. *Any* kind of influence which will help restore stability may be effective, whether it moves toward increased health and competence or toward regression and pathology. To a man without identity, even the identity of criminal is "better" than none at all. In this very disturbing unfrozen state, the system grasps for causes, beliefs, logical answers, and behaviors which will restore its stability. External influences, in the form of a deliberate change agent in some instances, provide the answer; the system experiences "insight" as its manifestation of reintegration and becomes refrozen in the new condition.

This refreezing process requires social reinforcement. Rewards and social support must be forthcoming and continuing. If this does not happen, as with individuals who undergo permissive leadership training and return to an environment which does not reward or support the change, the system will search for and return to a state that is rewarded and socially supported.

This social-psychological model for change fits the ordinary, as well as the extraordinary, socialization situations faced by growing persons. It happens to some extent when the child leaves the family and starts school. It happens when the young person arrives at college. It is ritualized in the fraternity initiation. It happens in settings for professional training, such as business schools, medical schools, law schools, and military academies. It happens in religious institutions in the training of nuns and priests.[37]

Common forms of socialization attempt to change the individual to conform to a common set of attitudes and behaviors. The individual is initially separated from the sources of social support to which he has become accustomed and which have reinforced the behaviors, attitudes, and over-all identity with which he entered the change situation. He is isolated and protected from these influences through strict rules, sanctions, and physical barriers governing his use of time and restricting his spatial mobility.

Although isolated from his *former* social influences, he is not socially isolated in the new situation. On the contrary, the presence of companions undergoing the same process is an important element. As Schein points out,[38] solitary confinement, as practiced in some institutions, is a poor form of influence, since the social sources of

[37] Schein, *op. cit.*, pp. 269 ff.
[38] *Ibid.*

reinforcing new behaviors is absent.  The indoctrinee group, whether
they are freshmen, pledges, plebes, or apprentices, share the experience
of losing their prior status and having their former identity denied.
Their sameness is emphasized by the institutional agents.  They are
punished socially for trying to maintain their former accomplishments
or social status.

The presence of recent converts, such as upperclassmen or old-
timers who exercise influence and reward conformity, is an important
part of this process.  They become the primary, face-to-face agents
of the change institution.  Such converts have been rewarded for
learning the new behaviors and attitudes, and their rewards increase
as they influence the newcomers.

In such institutions, stages of the change process are visibly ritualized
in initiation, transitions from freshman to sophomore to junior to
senior, and graduation.  Continuing social reinforcement is institutionalized in alumni bulletins, alumni contacts, and professional
society affairs; it is informally maintained through social contacts with
members of the appropriate reference groups.  The shared training
experience, which constitutes a shared deprivation experience, actually
increases in psychological value over time.  It becomes a form of
resolution of the dissonance between tolerating deprivation and having
a feeling of self-worth, even though the "good old days" were not
so good while they were being experienced.[39]  These are ordinary
events which occur within the lifetime of normal individuals as they
move through the series of statuses and experiences prescribed as the
path to maturity.

The extraordinary events of the Chinese Communist practice of
thought reform on civilian political prisoners, and the Korean "brainwashing" incidents led Schein and others to investigate what took place
in order to learn more about processes of influence and change.
Even though the general pattern of these processes, as practiced in
deliberately designed change programs or informal socialization procedures, seems to fit a large number of cases, the exceptions stand out.
The character structure of some individuals provides them with
defenses that are strong enough, or rigid enough, to resist some change
efforts; they can resist being unfrozen.  This was proposed by some
post-Korean war critics as a good thing, for which American soldiers
should be deliberately indoctrinated (notice this paradox!).  But a
defensively rigid character structure can be disastrous.  Individuals
trained to know what is going on and to play the game as they would
exercise any other form of competence are ultimately more useful

[39] See Festinger, "Cognitive Dissonance."

to society and to themselves than are dead or pathological heroes. The price is that the individual will also learn to play the game with the institutions that are trying to train him to play the game. At worst, "knowing what is going on" can lead to embittered cynicism. At best, it can lead to increased competence and understanding in human affairs.

## Role Transition and the Enhancement of Competence

The change processes we have described are forms of external, social influences on the individual. When they are successful, the individual behaves and thinks like a member of the new reference group and seeks his rewards through the means prescribed by that group. He has learned and accepted their conditions for membership and, in turn, imposes them upon younger prospective members. These aspects of the over-all development of the individual are important components of his pursuit of increased competence; but they are not the only components. A purely "other-directed" comformist who has learned the game of social mobility can follow the social path easily, while learning little in the process. There is an important difference between socialization processes and individual development processes, even though the two occur together in life experiences.

This difference poses a dilemma for the change agent. While confronting, supporting, and influencing to bring about change, he provides a model for his clients to imitate. Although his goal may be to foster individual and group autonomy and increased competence, the socialization processes and role imitation involved in his work can easily result in the opposite—conformity and dependence. If he sees the client system only as an organization, his efforts may increase conformity to and dependency on the organization's authorities. On the other hand, if he sees his client systems as being comprised of all the individuals and groups within the organization, thus including the authorities in the system undergoing change, he can proceed toward the goal of individual autonomy and competence without becoming an instrument for the enhancement of one group's power at the expense of another group.

When confronted with this need to define his client systems and to explicate his goals, the change agent is forced to face his own needs. Where economic and status rewards are concerned, acting as a socializing agent usually provides a higher payoff than acting as an agent for autonomy and competence goals. A power group, such as a management or a political organization, can afford to pay well for help in increasing its influence, whereas only the most foresighted and understanding authority figures can easily grasp the longer run payoff of enhanced individual, group, and organizational competence. Hence, the change agent's knowledge of himself is of primary importance in the effectiveness of his actions, regardless of the particular causes and techniques which capture his interest.   In psychoanalysis, this need has been institutionalized so that the professional candidate must undergo psychoanalysis himself before he can be qualified to help others.   Although the intention of this requirement makes sense, it may be misunderstood as a demand for conformity to the authority of a social tradition, even though the tradition is based on the authority of empirical realities.

The only solution for the change agent is to accept his own confrontation with the authority problem.  He must grapple with the authoritarian-egalitarian dilemma in his relations with others in his client systems.  He has to face and accept their resistances and work with them to understand their problems.  At the same time, he must work out these same problems within himself.  Although we cannot prescribe the answer for the individual, whether he is the change agent, leader, or group member, some general ideas stemming from the educational, research, and practical roots of the study of change can suggest a general methodology for resolving these kinds of problems.

## THE LABORATORY LEARNING MODEL FOR PLANNED CHANGE

The learning laboratory is an attempt to define a unique social learning situation as a counterpart to the physical science laboratory. The learning laboratory as a device for dealing with the kinds of problems discussed in this book, is a product of the National Training Laboratories, an affiliate of the National Education Association.[40]   It represents an ideal; but its activities are carried out by change agents whose personal attitudes affect their individual efforts.   As with any group value or norm, there are wide variations in the actual behaviors of the proponents.

The scientific laboratory is an accepted institution in current culture.  Since exploration and experimentation in human behavior is held by some to be "unnatural," the use of the term laboratory may lend the process a more legitimate naturalness.  Hence, the concept learning laboratory.

[40] See Bradford, *Explorations in Human Relations Training.*

There are several essential ingredients to the laboratory ideal. One is isolation and protection; the learning laboratory is a setting devoted to the search for truth and unencumbered by the practical demands of the surrounding world. A second ingredient is the spirit of inquiry. In the learning laboratory, conventional limits to investigation may be overstepped and conventional explanations questioned. Understanding and learning are accepted as goals in themselves. The demand for immediate applicability is, in some respects, laid aside, while in other respects it provides the immediate test of what is learned. For example, the participant in the learning laboratory often asks: "How will this help me be a better leader back on the job?" His social environment responds by confronting him with what he is doing *in the lab* in relation to leadership problems.

Laboratory conditions provide a new set of norms and rules for learning, which the individual is conditioned to accept as in any other socialization process. One ingredient of the laboratory ideal, too often not realized, is the examination of the individual's response to these rules and norms, transcending socialization and reaching the development of the individual. Emotional supportiveness and a relaxation of interpersonal defensive behaviors are part of the climate. The individual's identity and competence problems are heavily laden with mechanisms for avoiding loneliness and achieving membership. It follows all too often that groupiness, belonging, and interpersonal affection become ends in themselves in the laboratory setting. An almost mystical emotional acceptance can spill over into the egalitarian fantasy. When this happens, the importance of technical competences, the relationship between technical and social competences, and inherent individual differences in kind and degree of competence are lost from view.

However, the laboratory ideal assumes that the individual will pass through this group dependency, as well as earlier conditions of counterdependency or rebellion against group influences, to understand the logical bases for the rules of learning. He may "learn to learn" rather than learn to get along in groups. The ideal presupposes the availability of adequate time, as well as spatial isolation. The time dimension is treated rather casually in some laboratory planning; one-week laboratories are expected to undo the individuals' total life experiences, as if by magic. Quite a bit of socialization can take place in one week, but how much individual learning can take place in such a short time?

The learning model followed by the change agents in the laboratory situation involves addressing the emotional, motivational, and intellectual aspects of individual and group competence. Conventional organizational behavior patterns tend to intellectualize emotional and motivational problems, disposing of them by naming them. The learning model, on the other hand, leans quite heavily in the opposite direction of addressing emotions and motivations directly and stripping away their intellectual covers. Although individual emotions and motives are accepted as real and valid, this kind of reality is confronted with their equally real consequences in interpersonal behavior and task performance.

The handling of individual and group emotionality in the laboratory setting is an important variable. It is quite possible for the learning laboratory ideal to become subverted to a religious-emotional revival experience. Heightened experiencing of emotions is an important aspect of the laboratory, in that it emphasizes learning through experience. However, if the emotional experience becomes dominant and is not examined as a human phenomenon, the laboratory results may be similar to those obtained in other settings without the use of the change-agent's reality-testing resources. For example, religious retreats and artistically expressive orgies can attain the same results.

Some change agents do not want to see their educational, scientific definition of the laboratory setting distorted into a purely emotional experience. This experience can happen in the laboratory, but it can also happen elsewhere. The laboratory's major resources are its staff's competences: controlled inquiry, conceptualization, experimental testing, and the evaluation of outcomes. These allow a much broader scope of possibilities than emotional experience alone.

We have indicated so far that the laboratory learning ideal includes the definition of the situation as one for learning through experience and experimentation, observation, analysis, and evaluation of results. This definition implies isolation and protection from external influences. It redefines "practicality" in here-and-now terms and attempts to teach procedures for continued learning. It provides the emotional support and confrontation necessary for these purposes. It examines the authority issues of independence, dependence, counterdependence, and interdependence as they occur within the real interactions in the laboratory. It accepts and examines the emotional and motivational bases of behavior as they occur in the laboratory setting. It attempts to help the individual organize his learning in cognitive terms and encourages him to experience less communicable, but equally important, personal insights. It uses time within the lives of the individuals.

These ideal conditions have been lumped together under the "cultural island" concept. This concept indicates the required spatial, but not the temporal, isolation. It highlights the process of constructing the different culture inherent in the laboratory ideal. Organizational consultants have experimented with trying to implement the laboratory ideal within the time and space of the organizational setting, as in Rice's Ahmedebad experiments. The problem lies in isolation and system boundaries. In Ahmedebad, the entire scope of organizational life was defined as "experimental." In most organizations, however, the press of "normal operations" makes such redefinition extremely difficult; it would affect outsiders—such as suppliers and customers—as well as organizational members, and management is often reluctant to involve them in internal problems. The Tavistock Institute, which handled the Ahmedebad problem, has included relations with outsiders as part of some of their consulting-research efforts; thus, the possibility of defining an entire organization as being in the laboratory condition is possible.

An important condition for the learning laboratory is the participant's readiness for the particular kinds of complex learning experiences involved. The relevancy of the individual's current phase of development and motivations toward change were mentioned in our discussion of individual change. Many organizations select individuals to attend executive development and human relations training programs. In some cases, being selected is itself a reward and a precursor to promotion. The individual must define the laboratory period as a learning period for himself, rather than a requirement for job and status transitions. This is by no means an easy step for the individual to take, especially since it is difficult to understand the implications of the experience before becoming involved in it. This means that in spite of the change agent's ideal definition of the laboratory situation, the individual participants bring to it a variety of expectations and definitions, many of which may deter the desired learning. The way the individual includes laboratory time within his current life time is crucial.

The conservative forces within individuals and groups emerge as continuing reinforcement of existing behaviors and attitudes. Mere survival in the hectic jungle of social and interpersonal relations constitutes "success" to the individual. Recognition and status promotion are even more strongly reinforcing rewards. When a successful person is put into a laboratory situation which tells him, in effect, to re-examine himself and the world, he is being asked to deny the basis for his success. Changing from a known and reliable pattern of attitudes and behaviors to a new and untested one involves a high degree of risk. Although status stripping tends to become ritualized in learning laboratories, and in other socialization processes, it would perhaps be more appropriate in some instances to provide supportive affirmation of identity as an initial preparation for change.

The less successful person provides a different problem in terms of readiness for laboratory learning. Since his status and confidence are lower, and since his relative lack of success will be accompanied by identity problems, the status-stripping ritual and the egalitarian ideal will be quite appealing to him. In addition, since his feelings of competence which compensate for the loneliness of adult life are not as strong, he will be extremely susceptible to the appeal of membership and affectionate emotions in the group aspects of the laboratory experience. The problem with the less successful person is over-enthusiasm and overconformity to pure socialization. The more successful person is more likely to resist or reject the experience.

These considerations suggest that more careful selection and pre-laboratory individual orientation and counseling might enhance the effectiveness of the laboratory experience and economize in the utilization of relatively scarce change agent skills. They also suggest that laboratory training might *not* be a good thing for all people at all stages of their lives. To some people, at some times in their lives, purely cognitive learning experiences might be more suitable than the complex focus on emotional and motivational, as well as cognitive, aspects of learning in the laboratory setting.

Although we are talking mainly about the change agent's problems in planning the laboratory, we are also implying that prospective participants have other choices available. If the individual feels that he can learn and change in these ways, and wants to do so, the learning laboratory is only one course. Another course is that he can follow the cognitive route and learn more about the study of human behavior and personality through reading and conventional course work. He can initiate investigation in his everyday human relationships. Or he can seek counseling from a variety of professional helpers, including the church, the psychologist, or the psychoanalyst. He can enroll in laboratory-like courses, or can attend a "cultural island" type of laboratory, such as offered by the National Training Laboratories and the Western Training Laboratories.

Choosing to attend a learning laboratory, rather than being sent, is a preferable condition for both the individual and the prospective helping agency. The very act of seeking help is one of the most important facilitators of individual development and competence, provided that the individual is psychologically prepared for the implications of being influenced, of more than superficial self-examination, and of establishing new and different kinds of interpersonal relations. One of the distinguishing features of help in solving human and social problems, in contrast to technical help, is that it must be sought, rather than sold, in order for effective and lasting change to take place.

## STRUCTURAL MODELS FOR PLANNED CHANGE

The major theme of this book has been interpersonal processes. In viewing change, we have tended to limit our discussion to *interpersonal* methods of implementing change. Interpersonal processes are the object of change as well as the method. However, interpersonal processes are not the only method by which changes in interpersonal relations may be effected. As indicated in our discussion of environmental constraints, organizational structure, communications patterns, and job design—including temporal and spatial work arrangments—are important influences on the quality of group and interpersonal processes within the organization. For example, the interpersonal behavior pattern between two individuals can be drastically modified by separating them. Where organizational and group effectiveness, rather than individual learning and development, are primary goals, structural changes can, under certain conditions, be more direct and economical ways of initiating changes in interpersonal processes.

Structural changes can lead to desirable changes in interpersonal behavior patterns if the technical design and the interaction processes by which the plan is implemented are of high quality. If the organization of work and technical job design are problem areas, no amount of laboratory experience or "good human relations" can compensate for poor or unclear structural and technical designs.

We have introduced the concept of structural change at this point merely to indicate that the laboratory learning model for planned change is severely limited in scope and intention. It can help in the formulation of good organizational and technical plans, but it does not in any way substitute for that kind of activity. We shall not discuss the theories of structural change here, since several excellent books on the subject are available.[41]

## CONCLUSIONS

The question asked in the opening pages of this book was why should the individual be concerned about understanding human be-

[41] See, for example, Chapple and Sayles, *The Measure of Management;* Jaques, *Equitable Payment;* Miller, "Technology, Territory, and Time;" and Rice, *The Enterprise and its Environment.*

havior in groups and organizations?  The topics covered describe the most important aspect of the individual's environment: the complex of social and interpersonal relations among people in pursuit of competence in work and human relationships.  If we can understand the nature of individual, group, and organizational processes more fully instead of disposing of human problems by moral judgment or by attributing them to uncontrollable human nature, we shall have taken a large step in the direction of more effective problem solving at all levels of human endeavor.

Our mode of investigation and expression has been primarily scientific, rather than literary or aesthetic.  The scientific ideal forces us to be explicit in our communications, and it emphasizes sharing insights.  But we are also unscientifically normative, since we do not conceal the fact that we think the scientific mode of investigation, explanation, experimentation, and evaluation is a good thing for some human problem solvers.  We want to be imitated, not from any desire to set social fashions, but because we are confident that this path of investigation may lead some individuals to ultimate autonomy and competence.  Through inquiry, the individual can learn to accept his authority figures, whether they be bosses, teachers, or personal heroes, for what they are rather than for what he wishes them to be.  Similarly, the path of investigation leads to discovery of the self for what it is, separating the reality of wishes, hopes, and fantasies from the reality of conflict-free competences, so that the individual can develop in both areas.

By our emphasis upon the interpersonal areas of learning and action, we do not intend to ignore another important aspect of human activity, the application of power in political action.  We do not agree with the position of cultural relativists who say that because a human practice exists, it must be functional, and hence a good thing.  We hope that increased understanding will not decrease the individual's capacity for anger and indignation at the unfortunate states of social life in our neighborhoods, communities, groups, organizations, our nation, and the world.  Our society fortunately provides channels through which the individual can constructively utilize his energy toward improvement through political action.  To confuse the dynamics of interpersonal problem solving with the dynamics of concerted power stultifies both kinds of activity.  Political competence has to be learned, as does interpersonal competence.

One of the touchiest choices the active, responsible individual has to make is between the interpersonal and the political arenas.  He must choose when and under what conditions each should be engaged.

To most of us, the deciding line is the limit to our patience. We will accept and attempt to understand the other person or group for just so long. Greater understanding of human and social problems can extend this limit, but not indefinitely. That infinite understanding can ultimately resolve all of the world's problems is a noble hope. But most of us cannot wait that long, even though we share the hope.

Planned change and the ideal of the laboratory for learning constitute extensions of the usual limits of interpersonal action in everyday life. Although we did not discuss conflict directly, it was implicit in our discussion of resistance and authority. The laboratory model, and the principles of mutual influence, consultation, and reality testing upon which it is based, represents a way of dealing with conflict through extending direct contact and interaction. The more usual response to conflict is the political mode. This involves withdrawal, separation, the cessation of interaction, and the show of power. In one sense, this is an extreme form of reality confrontation.

From the study of behavior and change, we ultimately learn that there are courses of action of which we are not always aware. Much social interaction involves the proposal and examination of the choices available; this is how reality gets tested. But broadening the range of choices, and comparing the choices, are only parts of the problem-solving process, whether it involves individual decision making or interpersonal behavior. In the end, the individual must choose.

# Bibliography

Abraham, Karl. *Selected Papers on Psychoanalysis*. London: Hogarth, 1927.

Adorno, T. W., et al. *The Authoritarian Personality*. New York: Harper, 1950.

Arensberg, Conrad M. *The Irish Countryman*. New York: Macmillan, 1937.

Argyris, Chris. *Interpersonal Competence and Organizational Effectiveness*. Homewood, Ill.: Irwin-Dorsey, 1962.

Asch, S. E. "Effect of Group Pressure Upon the Modification and Distortion of Judgments," *Groups, Leadership, and Men*, Harold Guetzkow, Ed. Pittsburgh: Carnegie Press, 1951.

Asch, S. E. *Social Psychology*. New York: Prentice-Hall, 1952.

Atkinson, John W. *Motives in Fantasy, Action and Society*. Princeton: Van Nostrand, 1958.


Bales, Robert F. *Interaction Process Analysis*. Cambridge: Addison-Wesley, 1951.

Bales, Robert F. "The Equilibrium Problem in Small Groups," *Working Papers in the Theory of Action*, by T. Parsons, R. Bales, and E. A. Shils. Glencoe, Ill.: Free Press, 1953. Pp. 111–161. Abridged in *Small Groups*, A. P. Hare, E. F. Borgatta, and R. F. Bales, Eds. New York: Knopf, 1955. Pp. 424–456.

Barnes, L. B. *Organizational Systems and Engineering Groups*. Boston: Division of Research, Harvard Business School, 1960.

Barnes, L. B., Dalton, G. W., and Zaleznik, A. "The Authority Structure As A Change Variable," a paper presented at the 57th annual meeting of the American Sociological Association, August 1962, in Washington, D.C.

Benedict, Ruth. *Patterns of Culture*. New York: Mentor Book, New American Library of World Literature, 1949.

Benne, K. D., and Sheats, P. "Functional Roles of Group Members," *J. soc. Issues*, Spring 1948; Vol. IV, No. 2.

Bennett, Edith B. "Discussion, Decision, Commitment, and Consensus in 'Group Decision'," *Human Relations*, Vol. VIII, No. 3, 1955.

Bennis, Warren G., Benne, Kenneth D., and Chin, Robert, Eds. *The Planning of Change*. New York: Holt, Rinehart and Winston, 1961.

Bennis, Warren G., and Shepard, Herbert A. "Group Observation," abridged in *The Planning of Change*, W. Bennis, K. Benne, and R. Chin. Eds. New York: Holt, Rinehart and Winston, 1961.

Bennis, Warren G., and Shepard, Herbert A. "A Theory of Group Development," *Human Relations,* Vol. IX, No. 4, 1956.

Bexton, W. H., Heron, W., and Scott, T. H. "Effects of Decreased Variation in the Sensory Environment," *Canad. J. Psychol.* No. 8, 1954.

Bion, W. R. "Experiences in Groups: I–IV," *Human Relations,* Vol. I, Nos. 3 and 4, 1948; Vol. II, Nos. 1 and 4, 1949; Vol. III, Nos. 1 and 4, 1950.

Blake, R. R. and Mouton, J. S. "The Developing Revolution in Management Practices," *ASTD Journal,* July 1962.

Blake, R. R., Mouton, J. S., and Bidwell, A. C. "The Managerial Grid: A Comparison of Eight Theories of Management," *Advanced Management— Office Executive,* 1962.

Blau, Peter M. *The Dynamics of Bureaucracy.* Chicago: University of Chicago Press, 1955.

Blau, Peter M. and Scott, W. Richard. *Formal Organization.* San Francisco: Chandler, 1962.

Borgatta, E. F., Couch, A. S., and Bales, R. F. "Some Findings Relevant to the Great Man Theory of Leadership," *Small Groups,* Hare, Borgatta, and Bales, Eds. New York: Knopf, 1955.

Bradford, Leland P. "The Case of the Hidden Agenda," *Adult Leadership,* September 1952.

Bradford, Leland P., et al. *Explorations in Human Relations Training.* Washington: National Training Laboratory in Group Development, 1953.

Breuer, Joseph, and Freud, Sigmund. *Studies on Hysteria. The Standard Edition of the Complete Psychological Works of Sigmund Freud,* Vol. II. James Strachey, Ed. London: Hogarth, 1955.

Cartwright, Dorwin, and Zander, Alvin. *Group Dynamics.* New York: Row, Peterson, 1956 (Second Printing).

Cattell, Raymond B. *Personality and Motivation Structure and Measurement.* New York: World Book, 1957.

Caudill, William. *The Psychiatric Hospital as a Small Society.* Cambridge: Harvard University Press, 1958.

Chapple, Eliot, D., and Arensberg, Conrad M. *Measuring Human Relations: An Introduction to the Study of the Interactions of Individuals.* Provincetown: The Journal Press, 1940.

Chapple, Eliot D., and Sayles, L. R. *The Measure of Management.* New York: Macmillan, 1961.

Chase, Mary C. *Harvey: A Play.* New York: Oxford University Press, 1953.

Coch, Lester, and French, J. R. P., Jr. "Overcoming Resistance to Change," *Human Relations,* Vol. 1, 1948. Also appear in *Group Dynamics,* D. Cartwright and A. Zander, Eds. Evanston, Ill.: Row, Peterson, 1956.

Commager, Henry Steele, Ed. *The Blue and the Gray.* New York: Bobbs-Merrill, 1950.

Commager, Henry Steele, and Morris, Richard B., Eds. *The Spirit of 'Seventy-Six.* New York: Bobbs-Merrill, 1958.

Conant, James B. *On Understanding Science.* New York: Mentor Book, New American Library of World Literature, 1951.

Cooley, C. H. *Social Organization.* Glencoe, Ill.: Free Press, 1956.

Dahl, Robert A., Hare, Mason, and Lazarsfeld, Paul F. *Social Science Research on Business: Product and Potential.* New York: Columbia University Press, 1959.

Deutsch, Morton. "Field Theory in Social Psychology," *Handbook of Social Psychology*, Vol. I. G. Lindzey, Ed. Cambridge: Addison-Wesley, 1954.

Durkheim, Emile. *Elementary Forms of the Religious Life*. London: Allen & Unwin, 1926.

Durkheim, Emile. *Le Suicide*. Paris: Alcan, 1930.

Erikson, Erik H. *Childhood and Society*. New York: Norton, 1950.

Erikson, Erik H. "Identity and the Life Cycle," *Psychological Issues*, Vol. I, No. 1, 1959.

Erikson, Erik H. "The Problem of Ego Identity," *Identity and Anxiety*, Stein, Vidich, and Manning, Eds. Glencoe, Ill.: Free Press, 1960.

Fenichal, Otto. *The Psychoanalytic Theory of Neurosis*. New York: Norton, 1945.

Festinger, Leon. "Cognitive Dissonance," *Scientific American*, Vol. 207, No. 4, October 1962.

Festinger, Leon. "Group Attraction and Membership," *Group Dynamics*, D. Cartwright and A. Zander, Eds. New York: Row, Peterson, 1956.

Festinger, Leon. "Informal Social Communication," *Group Dynamics*, D. Cartwright and A. Zander, Eds. New York: Row, Peterson, 1956.

Festinger, Leon. *Theory of Cognitive Dissonance*. Evanston, Ill.: Row, Peterson, 1957.

Festinger, Leon. "A Theory of Social Comparison Processes," in *Small Groups*, Hare, Borgatta, and Bales, Eds. New York: Knopf, 1955.

Festinger, Leon, Reichen, Henry W., and Schachter, Stanley. "When Prophecy Fails," in *Readings in Social Psychology*, Macoby, Newcomb, and Hartley, Eds. New York: Holt, 3rd edition, 1958.

Festinger, Leon, Schachter, Stanley, and Back, Kurt. "Matrix Analysis of Group Structures," *The Language of Social Research*, P. Lazarsfeld and M. Rosenberg, Eds. Glencoe, Ill.: Free Press, 1955.

Festinger, Leon, Schachter, Stanley, and Back, Kurt. "The Operation of Group Standards," *Group Dynamics*, D. Cartwright and A. Zander, Eds. New York: Row, Peterson, 1956.

Festinger, Leon, Schachter, Stanley, and Back, Kurt. *Social Pressures in Informal Groups*. New York: Harper, 1950.

Fleishman, E. A., Harris, E. F., and Burtt, H. E. *Leadership and Supervision in Industry*. Columbus: Personnel Research Board, Ohio State University, 1955.

Foulkes, S. H., and Anthony, E. J. *Group Psychotherapy: The Psychoanalytical Approach*. Baltimore, Md.: Penguin Books, 1957.

Fouriezos, N. T., Hutt, M. L., and Guetzkow, H. "Measurement of Self-Oriented Needs in Discussion Groups," *J. abnorm. Soc. Psychol.* No. 45, 1950. Condensed in *Group Dynamics*, D. Cartwright and A. Zander, Eds. Evanston, Ill.: Row, Peterson, 1956.

French, C. J. "Correlates of Success in Retail Selling," *Amer. J. Sociol.*, Vol. LXVI, No. 2, 1960.

Freud, Anna. *The Ego and the Mechanisms of Defense*. London: Hogarth, 1937, 1954.

Freud, Sigmund. "Analysis of a Phobia in a Five-Year-Old Boy," *The Standard Edition of the Complete Psychological Works of Sigmund Freud*, Vol. X. James Strachey, Ed. London: Hogarth, 1955.

Freud, Sigmund. *Beyond the Pleasure Principle. The Standard Edition*, Vol. XVIII. James Strachey, Ed. London: Hogarth, 1955.

Freud, Sigmund. "The Dissolution of the Oedipus Complex," *The Standard Edition*, Vol. XIX, 1961.

Freud, Sigmund. "The Economic Problems in Masochism," *The Standard Edition*, Vol. XIX, 1961.

Freud, Sigmund. *The Ego and the Id. The Standard Edition*, Vol. XIX, 1961.

Freud, Sigmund. "Formulations Regarding the Two Principles in Mental Functioning," *The Standard Edition*, Vol. XII, 1958.

Freud, Sigmund. *Group Psychology and the Analysis of the Ego. The Standard Edition*, Vol. XVIII, 1955.

Freud, Sigmund. *Inhibitions, Symptoms and Anxiety. The Standard Edition*, Vol. XX, 1959.

Freud, Sigmund. "Instincts and Their Vicissitudes," *The Standard Edition*, Vol. XIV, 1957.

Freud, Sigmund. *The Interpretation of Dreams. The Standard Edition*, Vol. IV and Vol. V, 1953.

Freud, Sigmund. "Mourning and Melancholia," *The Standard Edition*, Vol. XIV, 1957.

Freud, Sigmund. *The Psychopathology of Everyday Life. The Standard Edition*, Vol. VI, 1960.

Freud, Sigmund. *Three Essays on the Theory of Sexuality. The Standard Edition*, Vol. VII, 1953.

[Several of Freud's works appear in paperbound volumes.]


Gardner, John W. *Excellence.* New York: Harper, 1961.

Gibb, Cecil A. "Leadership," *Handbook of Social Psychology*, Vol. II, Special Fields and Applications. Cambridge: Addison-Wesley, 1954.

Glover, Edward. *On the Early Development of the Mind.* New York: International Universities Press, 1956.

Glover, J. D., and Hower, R. H. *The Administrator.* Homewood, Ill.: Richard D. Irwin, 3rd edition, 1957.

Goffman, Erving. *The Presentation of Self in Everyday Life.* New York: Doubleday, 1959.


Hall, Calvin S., and Lindzey, Gardner. *Theories of Personality.* New York: Wiley, 1957.

Hall, Edward T. *The Silent Language.* New York: Doubleday, 1959.

Hare, A. Paul, Borgatta, Edgar F., and Bales, Robert F. *Small Groups.* New York: Knopf, 1955.

Hartmann, Heinz. *Ego Psychology and the Problem of Adaptation.* New York: International Universities Press, 1958.

Heider, Fritz. *The Psychology of Interpersonal Relations.* New York: Wiley, 1958.

Hemphill, J. K. *Leader Behavior Description.* Columbus: Ohio State University, 1950.

Henderson, L. J. *Introductory Lectures* (unpublished) to his course, "Concrete Sociology," at Harvard University.

Homans, George C. "The Cash Posters: A Study of a Group of Working Girls," *Amer. sociol. Rev.*, Vol. 19, No. 6, December 1954.

Homans, George C.  *The Human Group.*  New York: Harcourt, Brace, 1950.
Homans, George C.  *Social Behavior: Its Elementary Forms.*  New York: Harcourt, Brace, 1961.
Homans, George C.  "Status Among Clerical Workers," *Human Organization,* Vol. 12, 1953.

Jaques, Elliott.  *The Changing Culture of a Factory.*  London: Tavistock, 1951.
Jaques, Elliott.  *Equitable Payment.*  London: Heinemann, 1961.
Jaques, Elliott.  *Measurement of Responsibility.*  London: Tavistock, 1956.
Jennings, Helen H.  *Leadership and Isolation: A Study of Personality in Inter-personal Relations.*  New York: Longman, Green, 1950.
Jones, Maxwell, et al.  *The Therapeutic Community: A New Treatment Method in Psychiatry.*  New York: Basic Books, 1953.

Katz, D., Maccoby, N., and Morse, Nancy.  *Productivity, Supervision and Morale in an Office Situation.*  Ann Arbor, Mich.: Institute for Social Research, 1950.
Katz, D., Maccoby, N., Gurin, G., and Floor, L. G.  *Productivity, Supervision and Morale Among Railroad Workers.*  Ann Arbor, Mich.: Institute for Social Research, 1951.
Katz, Elihu, and Lazarsfeld, Paul F.  *Personal Influence.*  Glencoe, Ill.: Free Press, 1955.
Kemeny, John G., Snell, J. Laurie, and Thompson, Gerald L.  *Introduction to Finite Mathematics.*  Englewood Cliffs, N.J.: Prentice-Hall, 1957.
Kluckhohn, Clyde.  *Mirror for Man.*  Greenwich, Conn.: Fawcett, 1957.
Kluckhohn, Clyde, Murray, H. A., and Schneider, D. M., Eds.  *Personality in Nature, Society, and Culture.*  New York: Knopf, 1956.
Kluckhohn, Florence.  "Dominant and Variant Role Orientations," *Personality in Nature, Society, and Culture,* Kluckhohn, Murray, and Schneider, Eds. New York: Knopf, 1956.
Krech, David, Crutchfield, Richard S., and Ballachey, Egerton L.  *Individual in Society.*  New York: McGraw-Hill, 1962.
Kubie, Lawrence S.  "Some Unsolved Problems of the Scientific Career," *Identity and Anxiety,* Stein, Vidich, and White, Eds. Glencoe, Ill.: Free Press, 1960.

Lawrence, Paul R.  *The Changing of Organizational Behavior Patterns.*  Boston: Division of Research, Harvard Business School, 1958.
Lawrence, Paul R., Bailey, Joseph C., Katz, R. L., Seiler, John A., Orth, Charles D., III, Clark, J. V., Barnes, Louis B., and Turner, Arthur N. *Organizational Behavior and Administration.*  Homewood, Ill.: Irwin-Dorsey, 1961.
Lazarsfeld, Paul F.  "Problems in Methodology," *Sociology Today,* Merton, Broom, and Cottrell, Eds.  New York: Basic Books, 1959.
Leary, Timothy.  *Interpersonal Diagnosis of Personality.*  New York: Ronald Press, 1957.
Leavitt, Harold J.  "Some Effects of Certain Communication Patterns of Group Performance," *J. abnorm. soc. Psychol.,* Vol. XLVI, 1951. Also appears in *Readings in Social Psychology,* Maccoby, Newcomb, and Hartley, Eds. New York: Holt, 1958.

Levinson, Daniel J. "Role, Personality, and Social Structure in the Organizational Setting," *J. abnorm. Soc. Psychol.*, Vol. 58, No. 2, March 1959.

Lewin, Kurt. "Frontiers in Group Dynamics: Concept, Method, and Reality in Social Science," *Human Relations*, Vol. I, 1947.

Lewin, Kurt. *Resolving Social Conflicts*. New York: Harper, 1948.

Lewin, Kurt. "Studies in Group Decision," *Group Dynamics*, Cartwright and Zander, Eds. Evanston, Ill.: Row, Peterson, 1953.

Lewin, Kurt, Dembo, Tamara, Festinger, Leon, and Sears, Pauline. "Level of Aspiration," *Personality and the Behavior Disorders*, J. McV. Hunt, Ed. New York: Ronald Press, 1944.

Likert, Rensis. *New Patterns of Management*. New York: McGraw-Hill, 1961.

Linton, Ralph. *The Study of Man: An Introduction*. New York: Appleton-Century, 1936.

Lippitt, Ronald, and White, Ralph K. "An Experimental Study of Leadership and Group Life," *Readings in Social Psychology*, Maccoby, Newcomb, and Hartley, Eds. New York: Holt, 1958.

Lippitt, Ronald, and White, Ralph K. "Leader Behavior and Member Reaction in Three 'Social Climates'," *Group Dynamics*, Cartwright and Zander, Eds. Evanston, Ill.: Row, Peterson, 1953.

Lombard, George F. F. *Behavior in a Selling Group*. Boston: Division of Research, Harvard Business School, 1955.

Loomis, Charles P. *Social Systems: Essays on Their Persistence and Change*. Princeton: Van Nostrand, 1960.


McClelland, David C. *The Achieving Society*. Princeton: Van Nostrand, 1961.

McClelland, David C. *Personality*. New York: Holt, Rinehart and Winston, 1951.

McClelland, David C., Atkinson, John W., Clark, Russell A., and Lowell, Edgar L. *The Achievement Motive*. New York: Appleton-Century-Crofts, 1953.

Machiavelli, Niccoló. *The Prince*. New York: Mentor Classic, New American Library of World Literature, 1952. (Originally published in 1537.)

Malinowski, Bronislaw. *Magic, Science and Religion*. Garden City, N.Y.: Anchor Book, Doubleday, 1954.

Mann, Floyd C., and Hoffman, L. Richard. *Automation and the Worker*. New York: Holt, 1960.

March, James G. and Simon, Herbert A. *Organizations*. New York: Wiley, 1958.

Mayo, Elton. *The Human Problems of an Industrial Civilization*. Boston: Division of Research, Harvard Business School, 1946.

Mayo, Elton. *The Social Problems of an Industrial Civilization*. Boston: Division of Research, Harvard Business School, 1945.

Mead, Margaret. *The Coming of Age in Samoa*. New York: Mentor Book, New American Library of World Literature, 1961.

Mead, Margaret, Ed. (UNESCO) *Cultural Patterns and Technical Change*. New York: New American Library of World Literature, 1955.

Mead, Margaret. *Male and Female*. New York: Mentor Book, New American Library of World Literature, 1960.

Merton, Robert K. *Social Theory and Social Structure*. Glencoe, Ill.: Free Press, 1957.

Michaels, J. J. "Character Structure and Character Disorders," *American Handbook of Psychiatry*, S. Arieti, Ed. Vol. I., New York: Basic Books, 1959.

Miller, Eric J. "Technology, Territory, and Time," *Human Relations*, Vol. XII, No. 3, 1959.

Mills, Theodore M. "Power Relations in Three-Person Groups," *Group Dynamics*, Cartwright and Zander, Eds. Evanston, Ill.: Row, Peterson, 1956.

Moment, David. *Motivation, Role Behavior, and Development: A Study of Middle and Upper Management Individuals in Four Experimental Group Settings*. (Unpublished doctoral dissertation submitted at the Harvard Business School, 1961.)

Moment, David, and Zaleznik, Abraham. *Role Development and Interpersonal Competence*. Boston: Division of Research, Harvard Business School, 1963.

Moreno, Jacob L. *Who Shall Survive?: Foundations of Sociometry, Group Psychotherapy and Sociodrama*. New York: Beacon House, 1953.

Morse, Nancy. *Satisfactions in the White-Collar Job*. Ann Arbor, Mich.: Institute for Social Research, 1953.

Newcomb, Theodore M. "An Approach to the Study of Communicative Acts," *Small Groups: Studies in Social Interaction*, Hare, Borgatta, and Bales, Eds. New York: Knopf, 1955.

Newcomb, Theodore M. "Attitude Development as a Function of Reference Groups," *Readings in Social Psychology*, Maccoby, Newcomb, and Hartley, Eds. New York: Holt, 1958.

Parsons, Talcott. "Age and Sex in the Social Structure of the United States," *Amer. Social. Rev.*, October 1942.

Parsons, Talcott, and Bales, Robert F. *Family, Socialization and Interaction Process*. Glencoe, Ill.: Free Press, 1955.

Pelz, D. C. "Influence: A Key to Effective Leadership in the First Line Supervisor," *Personnel*, Vol. 29, 1952.

Piaget, Jean. *The Moral Judgment of the Child*. New York: Harcourt, Brace, 1932.

Radcliffe-Brown, A. R. *The Andaman Islanders*. Glencoe, Ill.: Free Press, 1948.

Radcliffe-Brown, A. R. *Structure and Function in Primitive Society*. Glencoe, Ill.: Free Press, 1952.

Rank, Otto. *The Myth of the Birth of the Hero*. New York: Vintage Books, 1959.

Rapaport, David. "The Autonomy of the Ego," *Bulletin of the Menninger Clinic*, Vol. 15, No. 4, July 1951.

Rapaport, David. "The Conceptual Model of Psychoanalysis," Psychoanalytic Psychiatry and Psychology, Vol. 1, Robert P. Knight, Ed. New York: International Universities Press, 1954.

Rapaport, David. "The Theory of Ego Autonomy: A Generalization," *Bulletin of the Menninger Clinic*. Vol. 22, No. 1, January 1958.

Reich, Wilhelm. *Character Analysis*. New York: Noonday Press: a subsidiary of Farrar, Straus, and Cudahy, 1949.

Rice, A. K. *The Enterprise and its Environment*. London: Tavistock, 1963.

Rice, A. K. *Productivity and Social Organization: The Ahmedabad Experiment*. London: Tavistock, 1958.

496    BIBLIOGRAPHY

Riecken, Henry W., and Homans, George C. "Psychological Aspects of Social Structure," *Handbook of Social Psychology*, Vol. 2, Special Fields and Applications. Cambridge: Addison-Wesley, 1954.

Riesman, David, et al. *The Lonely Crowd: A Study of the Changing American Society.* Garden City. N.Y.: Anchor Book, Doubleday, 1953.

Roe, Anne. *The Psychology of Occupations.* New York: Wiley, 1956.

Roethlisberger, Fritz J. "The Foreman: Master and Victim of Double Talk," *Harvard Business Review*, Spring 1945.

Roethlisberger, Fritz J. *Training for Human Relations.* Boston: Division of Research, Harvard Business School, 1954.

Roethlisberger, Fritz J., and Dickson, William J. *Management and the Worker.* Cambridge: Harvard University Press, 1943.

Rogers, Carl R. *On Becoming a Person.* Boston: Houghton Mifflin, 1961.

Samuels, Gertrude. "Rescue for the Wayward Girls," *The New York Times Magazine*, July 23, 1961.

Sayles, Leonard. *Behavior of Industrial Work Groups.* New York: Wiley, 1958.

Schachtel, Ernest G. *Metamorphosis.* New York: Basic Books, 1959.

Schachter, Stanley. "Deviation, Rejection and Communication," *Group Dynamics*, Cartwright and Zander, Eds. New York: Row, Peterson, 1956.

Schachter, Stanley, et al. "An Experimental Study of Cohesiveness and Productivity," *Group Dynamics*, Cartwright and Zander, Eds. New York: Row, Peterson, 1956.

Schein, Edgar H. "The Chinese Indoctrination Program for Prisoners of War: A Study of Attempted Brainwashing," *Readings in Social Psychology*, Maccoby, Newcomb, and Hartley, Eds. New York: Holt, 1958.

Schein, Edgar H., Schneier, Inge, and Barker, Curtis H. *Coercive Persuasion.* New York: Norton, 1961.

Schutz, W. C. *FIRO: A Three-Dimensional Theory of Interpersonal Behavior.* New York: Rinehart, 1958.

Schutz, W. C. "The Interpersonal Underworld," *Harvard Business Review*, Vol. 36, No. 4, July-August 1958.

Seashore, Charles, and Van Egmond, Elmer. "The Consultant-Trainer Role in Working Directly with a Total Staff," *J. soc. Issues*, Vol. 15, No. 2, 1959.

Seashore, Stanley E. *Group Cohesiveness in the Industrial Work Group.* Ann Arbor, Mich.: Institute for Social Research, 1954.

Shepard, Herbert A. "Some Social Attributes of Industrial Research and Development Groups," unpublished article. Cambridge: School of Industrial Management, Massachusetts Institute of Technology, 1954.

Shepard, Herbert A., and Bennis, Warren G. "A Theory of Training by Group Methods," *Human Relations*, Vol. 9, No. 4, 1956.

Sherif, Muzafer. "Group Influences Upon the Formation of Norms and Attitudes," *Readings in Social Psychology*, Maccoby, Newcomb, and Hartley, Eds. New York: Holt. 1956.

Sherif, Muzafer. *The Psychology of Social Norms.* New York: Harper & Brothers, 1936.

Sherif, Muzafer. "A Study of Some Social Factors in Perception," *Archives of Psychology*, No. 137, 1935.

Skinner, B. F. *Science and Human Behavior.* New York: Macmillan, 1960.

Slater, Philip E. "Role Differentiations in Small Groups," *Small Groups*, Hare,

Borgatta, and Bales, Eds.   New York: Knopf, 1955.

Spear, Harold S. *Feelings, Skill, and Leadership: An Observation-Interview Study of Four Factory Work-Group Supervisors.* Unpublished doctoral dissertation submitted at the Harvard Business School in August 1961.

Stouffer, S. A., Suchman, E. A., DeVinney, L. C., Star, S. A., and Williams, R. M. *The American Soldier: Volume I: Adjustment During Army Life.* Princeton: Princeton University Press, 1949.

Strauss, Anselm L. *Mirrors and Masks: The Search for Identity.* Glencoe, Ill.: Free Press, 1959.

Strauss, Anselm L. *The Social Psychology of George Herbert Mead.* Chicago: Phoenix Books, University of Chicago Press, 1956.

Sullivan, Harry Stack. *The Interpersonal Theory of Psychiatry.* New York: Norton, 1953.

Thomas, William I., and Znaniecki, Florian. *The Polish Peasant in Europe and America.* 2 vols. New York: Dover, 1958.

Vroom, V. H. *Some Personality Determinants of the Effects of Participation.* Englewood Heights, N.J.: Prentice-Hall, 1960.

Waelder, Robert. "The Principle of Multiple Function," *The Psychoanalytic Quarterly*, Vol. 5, 1936.

Walker, Charles R., and Guest, Robert H. *The Man on the Assembly Line.* Cambridge: Harvard University Press, 1952.

Warner, W. Lloyd, and Abegglen, James. *Big Business Leaders in America.* New York: Harper, 1955.

Warner, W. Lloyd, and Lunt, Paul S. *The Social Life of a Modern Community.* New Haven: Yale University Press, 1941.

Watson, John B. *Behaviorism.* Chicago: University of Chicago Press, Phoenix Books, 1961.

Weber, Max. *The Theory of Social and Economic Organization*, translated by A. M. Henderson and Talcott Parsons, and edited by Talcott Parsons. Glencoe, Ill.: Free Press and Falcon's Wing Press, 1947.

Weiner, Norbert. *The Human Use of Human Beings.* (Second edition) Boston: Houghton-Mifflin, 1954.

Wheelis, Allen. *The Quest for Identity.* New York: Norton, 1958.

White, Robert W. *The Abnormal Personality.* New York: Ronald Press, 1948.

White, Robert W. *Lives in Progress.* New York: Dryden Press, 1952.

White, Robert W. "Motivation Reconsidered: The Concept of Competence," *Psychol. Rev.* Vol. 66, No. 5, September 1959.

Whitehead, Alfred North. *Science and the Modern World.* New York: Mentor Book MD 162, New American Library of World Literature, 1948.

Whitehead, T. M. *The Industrial Worker.* Cambridge: Harvard University Press, 1938.

Whyte, William F. *Leadership and Group Participation.* Ithaca: New York State School of Industrial and Labor Relations, Bulletin 24, May 1953.

Whyte, William Foote. *Money and Motivation.* New York: Harper, 1955.

Whyte, William Foote. *Street Corner Society.* Chicago: University of Chicago Press, 1943.

Zaleznik, A. *Foreman Training in a Growing Enterprise.* Boston: Division of Research, Harvard Business School, 1951.

Zaleznik, A. "The Human Dilemmas of Leadership," *Harvard Business Review*, Vol. 41, No. 4, July–August 1963.

Zaleznik, A. "Science vs. 'Common Sense' in Human Relations," *Harvard Business School Bulletin*, December 1960.

Zaleznik, A. *Worker Satisfaction and Development*. Boston: Division of Research, Harvard Business School, 1956.

Zaleznik, A., Christensen, C. R., and Roethlisberger, F. J. *The Motivation, Productivity, and Satisfaction of Workers: A Prediction Study*. Boston: Division of Research, Harvard Business School, 1958.

# Author Index

Abegglen, J., 434
Abraham, K., 233
Adorno, T. W., 36, 252
Alexander, F., 277
Anthony, E. J., 13
Arensberg, C. M., 69, 326
Argyris, C., 424
Asch, S., 134–135, 454
Atkinson, J. W., 208, 390

Back, K., 94, 110, 300–301
Bales, R. F., 21, 65, 73, 75–77, 79–84, 86, 154–157, 186, 189, 190, 204, 444
Ballachey, E. L., 374–375
Barnes, L. B., 291, 293, 365–369, 393, 425
Benedict, R., 8
Benne, K. D., 21, 79–80, 148, 185
Bennett, E. B., 432, 475
Bennis, W. G., 37, 81
Bexton, W. H., 471
Bidwell, A. C., 187–188
Bion, W. R., 13, 161, 175
Blake, R. R., 187–188
Blau, P. M., 86, 99–102, 110–111, 113–114, 118, 290, 362–365
Borgatta, E. F., 86, 189, 204
Bradford, L., 13, 37, 481
Broom, L., 17
Burtt, H. E., 187, 422–424

Caudill, W. A., 10, 150, 158
Chapple, E. D., 69, 71, 486
Chase, M. C., 34
Christensen, C. R., 22, 30, 31, 73, 78, 106–108, 139, 264, 325–326, 329–342, 359–362
Coch, L., 475
Commander, H. S., 430
Conant, J. B., 18
Cooley, C. H., 14

Cottrell, L., 17
Couch, A. S., 86, 189
Crutchfield, R. S., 374–375

Dahl, R. A., 9
Dalton, G. W., 291, 293
Deutsch, M., 389
Dewey, J., 152
Dickson, W. J., 9, 95, 103, 114, 134, 301, 305–310, 325, 344, 397, 406, 412, 451–452, 471
Durkheim, E., 139

Erikson, E. H., 36, 129, 223, 232, 262, 444, 454, 458–459

Fenichel, O., 219, 250–251
Festinger, L., 29–30, 32–33, 94, 108–110, 300–301, 479
Fleishman, E. A., 187, 422–424
Foulkes, S. H., 13
Fouriezos, N. T., 187
French, C. J., 336
French, J. R. P., Jr., 475
Freud, A., 249, 252
Freud, S., 18, 63, 158, 214, 215, 219–222, 227, 234–235, 238–239, 242, 244–246, 248–249, 251, 256–257, 269–270, 280–282, 285, 377, 411, 455

Gardner, J. W., 429–430
Gibb, C. A., 413–415
Glover, E., 218–219
Glover, J. D., 352
Goffman, E., 29, 40
Guest, R. H., 139, 303–304
Guetzkow, H., 187

Hall, C. S., 18, 216
Hall, E. T., 299, 449–452

# Subject Index

# Research Index*

* Page numbers refer to references in this book.

RESEARCH SUMMARIES AND THEORIES

Bales, R. F. *Interaction Process Analysis.* A classification system for inter-personal behavior. 73, 75–77, 79–84, 86, 154–157, 189, 190.

Barnes, L. B., Dalton, G. W., and Zaleznik, A. "The Authority Structure as a Change Variable." Sources, kinds, and structures of authority. 291–293.

Benne, K. D., and Sheats, P. "Functional Roles of Group Members." 185–186.

Blake, R. R., Mouton, J. S., and Bidwell, A. C. "The Managerial Grid." Classification of managerial behavior styles. 187–188.

Hemphill, J. K. *Leader Behavior Description.* Fleishman, E. A., Harris, E. F., and Burtt, H. E. *Leadership and Supervision in Industry.* Results of Ohio State University leadership studies. 187, 422–424, 465.

Homans, G. C. *The Human Group.* Five field studies of groups drawn upon to form general propositions. 4, 5, 34, 44–45, 85, 98–99, 102, 104, 109, 117, 128, 345, 369, 396, 412, 416–418.

Kluckhohn, F. "Dominant and Variant Value Orientations." A conceptual scheme for cultural values. 60–61.

Leary, T. *Interpersonal Diagnosis of Personality.* A scheme for classifying interpersonal behavior. 195–197.

McClelland, D. C. *The Achieving Society.* Studies of achievement motivation. 389–390.

Sayles, L. *Behavior of Industrial Work Groups.* Classification of types of industrial work groups. 295–298.

Schein, E. H. "The Chinese Indoctrination System for Prisoners of War." Studies of Chinese Communist prison camp practices. 97.

Stouffer, S. A., et al. *The American Soldier.* Studies of satisfaction of military personnel. 398.

SURVEY RESEARCH

Seashore, S. E. *Group Cohesiveness in the Industrial Work Group.* Study of cohesiveness, productivity, and perceived supportiveness by the company. 109, 354–358.

Zaleznik, A. A study of executives' monetary wants, rewards, and satisfaction reported in Moment, D., and Zaleznik, A., *Role Development and Inter-personal Competence.* 381–384, 389–393.